THE
CIVIL WAR
IN
NEW MEXICO

THE CIVIL WAR IN NEW MEXICO

by
F. Stanley

New Foreword
by
Marc Simmons

SANTA FE

New Material © 2011 by Sunstone Press. All Rights Reserved.

No part of this book may be reproduced in any form or by any electronic or mechanical means including information storage and retrieval systems without permission in writing from the publisher, except by a reviewer
who may quote brief passages in a review.

Sunstone books may be purchased for educational, business, or sales promotional use. For information please write:
Special Markets Department, Sunstone Press,
P.O. Box 2321, Santa Fe, New Mexico 87504-2321.

Library of Congress Cataloging-in-Publication Data

Stanley, F. (Francis), 1908-
The Civil War in New Mexico / by F. Stanley, new foreword by Marc Simmons.
   p. cm. -- (Southwest heritage series)
Includes bibliographical references.
Originally published: Denver : World Press, 1960.
ISBN 978-0-86534-815-8 (softcover : alk. paper)
 1. New Mexico--History--Civil War, 1861-1865. 2. United States--History--Civil War, 1861-1865. 3. Confederate States of America--History, Military. I. Title.
E571.S73 2011
978.9'04--dc23
                          2011028169

WWW.SUNSTONEPRESS.COM
SUNSTONE PRESS / POST OFFICE BOX 2321 / SANTA FE, NM 87504-2321 /USA
(505) 988-4418 / ORDERS ONLY (800) 243-5644 / FAX (505) 988-1025

CONTENTS

THE SOUTHWEST HERITAGE SERIES / I

FOREWORD TO THIS EDITION / II
The Controversial F. Stanley
by
Marc Simmons

A MAN'S REACH / III
from
The F. Stanley Story
by
Mary Jo Walker

TRIBUTE TO F. STANLEY / IV
by
Jack D. Rittenhouse

1960 EDITION / V

I

THE SOUTHWEST HERITAGE SERIES

The history of the United States is written in hundreds of regional histories and literary works. Those letters, essays, memoirs, biographies and even collections of fiction are often first-hand accounts by people who wanted to memorialize an event, a person or simply record for posterity the concerns and issues of the times. Many of these accounts have been lost, destroyed or overlooked. Some are in private or public collections but deemed to be in too fragile condition to permit handling by contemporary readers and researchers.

However, now with the application of twenty-first century technology, nineteenth and twentieth century material can be reprinted and made accessible to the general public. These early writings are the DNA of our history and culture and are essential to understanding the present in terms of the past.

The Southwest Heritage Series is a form of literary preservation. Heritage by definition implies legacy and these early works are our legacy from those who have gone before us. To properly present and preserve that legacy, no changes in style or contents have been made. The material reprinted stands on its own as it first appeared. The point of view is that of the author and the era in which he or she lived. We would not expect photographs of people from the past to be re-imaged with modern clothes, hair styles and backgrounds. We should not, therefore, expect their ideas and personal philosophies to reflect our modern concepts.

Remember, reading their words and sharing their thoughts is a passport back into understanding how the past was shaped and how it influenced today's world.

Our hope is that new access to these older books will provide readers with a challenging and exciting experience.

II

FOREWORD TO THIS EDITION

The Controversial F. Stanley
by
Marc Simmons

As a professional historian, I've often been asked my opinion of the author who wrote under the pen name, F. Stanley. According to his 1996 obituary, he published 190 books and booklets on New Mexico history, quite a record by any standard. The problem is, F. Stanley has been almost universally condemned for the innumerable flaws that litter his writings. However, behind the man and the work lurks a curious story.

He was born Louis Crocchiola in New York's Greenwich Village on October 31, 1908 to Italian immigrant parents. After receiving a Bachelor's degree in English at Catholic University in Washington, DC, Louis entered the priesthood in 1938. On that occasion, as was allowed, he formally added the new names Stanley and Francis to his birth name, Louis Crocchiola. Thereafter, he was called simply Father Stanley.

Shortly after his ordination, the young priest was diagnosed with the beginnings of tuberculosis. Following medical advice of the day, the Church sent Father Stanley to Hereford, Texas in the Panhandle, hoping the arid climate might cure him. It did! Something else occurred at the same time. Father Stanley fell under the spell of the Southwest, leading him to become one of the most prolific historical writers of his day.

In 1940 he applied for pastoral work in New Mexico, since he was fluent in Spanish and thought he could be most useful there. The Archbishop of Santa Fe accepted him, assigning Father Stanley first to the Guadalupe church in Taos and then to the San Miguel church at Socorro.

During the 1940s, he served six or so different parishes in northern or eastern New Mexico, thereby becoming familiar with rural and small town life. It was while stationed at Taos, though, that Father Stanley caught the writing bug through mingling with local authors. But later as he was transferred by the Archbishop from one parish to another, he would begin looking into the history of his temporary residence and compiling a file of notes.

His first book, *Raton Chronicle*, appeared in 1948. Then in rapid succession F. Stanley published full-length histories on Cimarron, Socorro, Las Vegas, and the Maxwell land grant. Soon to his line of books, F. Stanley added an on-going series dedicated to a single small town or fort that other writers had ignored. These little booklets remain easily recognizable with their canary yellow covers and crimson red lettering, plus the New Mexico state emblem, the Zia sun symbol. Eventually, these small works alone numbered 123 titles.

One of the earliest treatments of the historic and controversial Maxwell Land Grant was published by F. Stanley in 1952, titled *The Grant That Maxwell Bought*. Although other books on the subject have appeared since, serious readers still need to go back and examine what Father Stanley had to say. Otherwise, small nuggets buried in his pages, and nowhere else, may be missed.

Remarkably, F. Stanley personally financed all of his publications, often going deeply into debt. The several printers he used were generally tolerant of the delay in paying his bills.

Even more stressful for Father Stanley was the harsh criticism his writings received from historians and book reviewers. They unmercifully picked apart his unedited and untidy prose, pointed out frequent mistakes, and condemned the neglect of standards in the composition or format of his books.

For one example, a serious slip occurred in the naming of F. Stanley's longest work, a history of the New Mexico state capital in three volumes, titled *Ciudad Santa Fe*. Under the old Spanish system, Santa Fe in reality never achieved the rank of a *ciudad* (chartered city), but retained the status of a town (*villa*). The author had missed that pivotal fact and thus launched his three volume set with a conspicuous error on the covers.

In 1985 Mary Jo Walker, a librarian at Eastern New Mexico University, Portales, published a sympathetic biography, *The F. Stanley Story*. The book contains quotes from interviews given by Father Stanley in which he defends himself and his methods.

His main plea was: "Pardon the mistakes, but say a kind word for my effort." Painfully aware of his failings, he claimed that his intent was merely to assemble fugitive information from obscure courthouse records, old newspaper files, and archives so that others more able could pick up the thread where he left off and carry on.

After publication of Walker's biography, some historians, myself included, began to look more charitably toward Father Stanley Crocchiola. The fact is, despite his deficiencies, he managed to make in his own quirky way a not insignificant contribution to our regional history.

Today, F. Stanley books and booklets are worth collecting. I'm always happy when I can add another one of his to my personal library. I just wish he was still around so that I could tell him that.

Sunstone Press in choosing to include F. Stanley books in its honored Southwest Heritage Series is wisely making this book available again to the reading public.

III

A MAN'S REACH
"Take him for what he is worth"
from
The F. Stanley Story
by
Mary Jo Walker

It is difficult to say to what extent negative criticism and neglect may have personally affected Father Stanley. Some of his works in the 1970s showed considerable care in preparation, but no more so than his major efforts in earlier decades. He knew his own limitations as well as any of his critics did, but he believed quite sincerely that the flaws in his work were largely literary in nature and therefore of little overall significance; or alternatively that they represented realities over which he had little control, such as his limited time or the cost of typesetting footnotes. His first reactions may be surmised from comments in the foreword to *Dave Rudabaugh*.

> *I used to apologize for my mistakes. Come to think of it, why should I? I tried; that's more than my critics did. I investigated to the best of my ability, often going sleepless and hungry in order to attain the facts. No patron has come along the way. I had to rough it alone.... The book may not be literary, but it is factual. In the long run, truth survives.*

Two years later, in *The Duke City*, he confessed from a somewhat different perspective:

> *I am grateful for all criticism—constructive or otherwise.*

And in *Satanta and the Kiowas*, 1968, he pled:

> *Let my mistakes be my Calvary, and let my readers be my confessors from whom we hope to obtain pardon and forgiveness.*

Simply and with a kind of humble determination, he persevered for many years, his principal resources being his formidable drive and his eagerness to help preserve the history of the region he loved so well. No doubt he attempted too much; probably, as with so many of us, his reach exceeded his grasp. His hope, which he stated over and over again, was that his books would provide guidance for others and "prove a...contribution to Western Americana." That purpose and his dedication to it do not serve to be lightly dismissed.

Taken as a whole, with all its human flaws, F. Stanley's work stands as a unique contribution, as much a part of the written record "as Coronado's visit." Even Ramon Adams acknowledged that "he deserves a full measure of credit for supplying hitherto unpublished information," for putting something into print about obscure places and people, for adding to the body of recorded knowledge about the Southwest. Whatever the final evaluation may be, however, it is certain that F. Stanley has earned a place in southwestern history in his own right.

F. Stanley

IV

TRIBUTE TO F. STANLEY
by
Jack D. Rittenhouse
from
The F. Stanley Story
by
Mary Jo Walker
Albuquerque, New Mexico / March, 1984

Some historians write because they hope their writing will bring them money or promotion or tenure. Some write to espouse a cause. A few write because they must, because it is the only way they can quench an inner thirst or scratch an itch of curiosity. The last class is the happiest, and F. Stanley is in this group.

The term historian has many shadings. Among academic people, a historian is a certified scholar whose commission of rank is a degree of Doctor of Philosophy in history, and whose income results from full-time teaching or writing history. Some of these go on to glory and excellence in their work; some gain renown as researchers or as teachers, become a historian's historian, but find writing a difficult task. Many bank their inner fire when they don their doctoral robes and are content to plod along as routine teachers, living as comfortably as a toad in a puddle of buttermilk, looking upon their diploma as a union card.

The grass roots historian is another type, curious about people and places around them. Their writings are their only certification. Some become antiquarians, with a dilettante interest in ancient things and more curious about precision in minutiae than in the social significance of their subject. The term antiquarian has a different meaning among historians than among bookmen.

Still another type of historian is the buff, an individual who is an enthusiast or devotee of a specific subject. When it comes to sheer bulk of knowledge about a subject, or even to accuracy on a point of information, I have seen many buffs who outclassed Ph.D's. I personally know only three individuals who have their own microfilm readers at home, and all three are buffs. They travel great distances to look at a gravestone or a courthouse record, which is not to say that professional historians and grassroots historians also do not do this, of course.

We owe much to the grassroots historian and the buff. They are the prospectors who discover new lodes. They are curious about people and places and customs, combining the interests of the folklorist and the historian, and if they are good at what they do, they find their work accepted and even honored.

F. Stanley is one whose curiosity and inner fire has drawn him to the study of people and places and events that had gone unnoticed until he saw them. He advanced knowledge in many directions, lit many candles to dispel darkness.

His works are only beginnings, and he knows this. In a sense, history writes itself merely by occurring, and thus there is the axiom that history is not written but rewritten. Another New Mexico local historian, Fray Angélico Chávez, once spoke to El Corral de Santa Fe Westerners and said that history is not a static, pure thing that can be discovered once, written down, and preserved intact forever. Instead, he said, history is a living, growing body that must be nurtured...and which occasionally requires surgery.

F. Stanley has wandered across the Southwest like a Johnny Appleseed of history, planting seedlings in the form of booklets and leaving their later nurturing to others. Later historians will convert these seedlings into trees, by pruning, fertilizing and grafting. The work will require more research, more verification, correction and amplification. But F. Stanley planted the first seed.

The historian who uses only *one* source for his work is a fool, but the historian who refuses to review any source is an idiot. Any source may have errors caused by lack of information, or poor proofreading, or hasty writing. But some questionable bit of old-timer's lore may raise the possibility of truth; it is then up to the later historian to prove or disprove the fact. Once, when I was gathering information about the New Mexico ghost town of Cabezón, I read an old-timer's memoir that mentioned a stage line running through the town. Nowhere else did I find any mention of this, and I sought to verify the story. A usually reliable professional historian scoffed at the notion that the town had ever been on a commercial stage line. Then a museum curator found a printed timetable of the Star Stage Line, listing the route and showing Cabezón as a stop. Although many dissertations do not list F. Stanley works as sources, the padre's booklets have nonetheless been studied for similar possible clues. Given the time and resources, F. Stanley himself would have gone farther; he leaves that to others.

His severest critics often have been people who never wrote a recognized book, or whose books themselves are not without the flaws of typesetters and human errors, or whose dyspeptic nature made them discard a sculpture because of a chip.

The body of work produced by F. Stanley will become part of the vast lore about the Southwest. It will remain as long as libraries stand and will be consulted and used by generations as part of the grassroots literature. Future writers will correct its errors, just as their mistakes will be corrected by still later scholars. But someone had to start it, and F. Stanley was the man.

V

1960 EDITION

THE CIVIL WAR
IN
NEW MEXICO

by

F. STANLEY

COPYRIGHT 1960
BY
F. STANLEY

No part of this book may be reproduced without the express permission of the author except for quotes in book reviews and lectures.

Printed in the United States of America

DEDICATED
TO
THE NEW MEXICO VOLUNTEERS
WHO DESERVE
A BIGGER MONUMENT
THAN I CAN BUILD

CONTENTS

Foreword / ix

Section One

    1—Washington, D. C. / 1

    2—The Texas Claim / 53

    3—The New Mexico Scene / 91

    4—Baylor's Babies / 123

    5—The California Column / 159

        Part One-Arizona

        Then Western New Mexico

    6—The Colorado Volunteers / 187

    7—Confederates in New Mexico and Arizona / 211

    8—Valverde / 231

    9—The California Column / 253

        Part Two-In New Mexico To The Year Ending 1862

    10—The Campaigns of 1863 / 271

    11—1864 / 307

    12—1865 / 345

Section Two

    1—General Carleton / 367

    2—The New Mexico Volunteers / 387

    3—Official List of New Mexico Volunteers / 401

Bibliography / 503

FOREWORD

The doors of the Civil War in New Mexico are not closed by the mere mention of the battle of Valverde. This engagement was but a spoke in the wheel of events that made New Mexico conscious of the conflict and tested her loyalty. The motive behind this deference for the Union was Statehood. Had the politically ambitious realized how long would be the wait perhaps this story would not have unfolded as here chronicled. As always, there are two schools of thought regarding the attitude toward Statehood. Naturally, those appointed by the President of the United States, hardly relished the idea of another star on the flag. The true New Mexican hungered for the days when he would cease calling the land a Territory and proudly point to it as a State. 1912 was still many decades away.

The writer has been to the Valverde battlefield twenty-eight times; the Glorieta battlefield over a hundred times, as well as various other places covered in this book. Truth and authenticity are hard to come by in this age of microfilm readers, photostatic copies, planes, research students—for a price. These latter save one a trip. Usually they live near the place that has the records you want. For a dollar an hour they look up the material. Cozy, isn't it? If you can afford it all. Fortunately, I have lived in New Mexico a number of years and was thus able to acquaint myself with places, people and events. Archives, field reports, official reports, letters, diaries, newspapers, courthouse records, libraries, not only in New Mexico but Colorado, Arizona, Texas, New York, Kansas, California and other States were more than a necessity—they became an obsession. The investigation began on November 29, 1940, and ceased on November 29, 1959. Nineteen years of it. The F. B. I. might have been more efficient, but I doubt if they could be more thorough. The going was not always a joy ride. More often it proved to be a crucifixion. Much more could be included in the story than is here told. But the line must be drawn somewhere and we hope to get this book to the press before prevented by the infirmities of old age or the unrelenting hand of death. The book was written three times. Once in long hand; twice by the hunt and peck system, even though many good friends offered to type. An author has to do his own typing, if only for last-minute changes.

It is only fair to include the total list of the New Mexico Volunteers even if the only excuse offered for doing so is that every State in the Union—North or South—has such a list except New Mexico. I trust that now one may say: "Including New Mexico." The Sunshine State, sad to relate, is notoriously delinquent in honoring its heroes. Stress is placed on the beauties of the State rather than the momentous events that took place there from Coronado to the Bataan marchers. The markers at Valverde and Glorieta are gifts from Texas. New Mexico is content to let her heroes lie in their graves. Commemorative days in the Land of Enchantment are few and far between. Business establishments maintain the "open door" policy on days that neighboring States keep theirs very closed indeed. In Texas, you know, Alamo Day, San Jacinto Day, R. E. Lee Day, and so many others. In New Mexico one knows Christmas, Easter, New Year's Day. So does the rest of the nation. Kearny Day, Coronado Day, DeVargas Day are dreams for the future. Perhaps.

Until I began this study, I followed the common opinion that the New Mexico Volunteers fled the field of Valverde out of fear. A re-evaluation of the facts convinced me otherwise. All the documents seem to deal with the California Column and the Colorado Volunteers. It stands to reason. The officers spoke and wrote English. Most of the officers of the New Mexico Volunteers wrote only Spanish. Many others like Kit Carson were able to write their names. No more. Officers of the Regular Army or from the California Column wrote out their reports. Yet, throughout the war there were more native New Mexicans serving their country than the Missouri, California and Colorado contingents combined. One finds very little mention of the Missouri companies that served side by side with the Californians and New Mexicans. The Coloradans went home after Glorieta. New Mexico had numerous independent companies in uniform before Carleton marched from California to become the military might of New Mexico until 1866. The New Mexico Volunteers were not concerned with numerous reports. They were content to obey orders. Nor were they in quest of gold. The lure of gold did more to keep Carleton's men in New Mexico than the Confederate threat from Texas. The adjutant's office was adept at keeping alive the reports from the California Column. The reports in Spanish were aimed at the waste basket. After all, who would expect anyone in Washington to understand such jibberish? Besides, this was America. Let them learn English. Such righteousness! As if the New Mexican wasn't aware that he was an American! Wearing the American uniform! Receiving government pay! Fighting the war as Americans! Even Donaciano Vigil, beloved as he was by all, could not raise such an army. The rush to the colors was spontaneous. New Mexicans wore the Blue because they chose to do so. This same loyalty would return when a plea went forth for the famous Rough Riders; a call came to save Democracy and New Mexico boys marched to the bloody altars of Bataan and Guadalcanal. From Onate to Okinawa the soldiers of New Mexico have proved themselves. Their centuries of warfare against the Utes, Comanches, Navajos, Kiowas, Apaches and Pueblos have made them anything but cowards, despite Canby, Carleton and others. The trouble with Canby and others is that they never forgot the Mexican War. They had their minds made up—war propaganda always dies a slow death—nor did the fact that New Mexicans were not concerned with the Mexican War change the horrible way of thinking. Consequently, to this day, the New Mexican is forever apologizing for the hordes who refuse to recognize his part in moulding America. He was tilling the land before our Pilgrim Fathers landed on you know what rock. He was fighting Indians before Washington met Braddock. He was content with his economics and modus vivendi before economics became a science. His was indeed a heritage.

The lists of the Confederates, the California Column, the Colorado Volunteers, are omitted rather from the lack of space than from rudeness. Besides, these are readily found. This is the first time the New Mexico Volunteer list appears in print. Some California Volunteers remained to make New Mexico history—Captain Fritz, Zimmerly, Gilbert, Miller, Brady and others who came to New Mexico without benefit to the column from California are herein noted. New Mexico Volunteers were active from 1861 to 1867. They fought Indians, guarded caravans across the country, helped build military posts, built roads, cut hay, timber, rock, made adobes, fences, corrals. They garrisoned the various posts they helped to build and suffered privately as an adjunct of war. They knew how to fight Indians. They had been doing it for almost three centuries. The Regulars learnt a thing or two from them just as the New Mexican taught the cowboy how to brand, lasso, trail, corral, herd cattle. Not that the cowboy will admit it. The very names are Spanish.

A work of this nature is never the fruits of individualistic achievement. It can never be completed without the co-operation and aid of others. Librarians, scholars, archivists, teachers, antiquarians, collectors, members of the various Westerner groups who "think for themselves" are of more importance than the know how. The State Historical Societies with their invaluable collections have been a source of inspiration as well as confidence. They are the Samsons of Truth, the bulwarks of Fact upon which a work such as this must necessarily rest. The wildfire spread of Westerners clubs in all the major cities of our country are ample proof that searchers after truth are not as dead as TV would have us believe. After all, one would hardly expect a script writer to conform to the exact truth. It has to be embellished a bit in the field of entertainment. Oddly enough, far too many viewers accept such blandishments as gospel truth. One hardly expects a throng to thumb through these pages of solid facts. We trust that students of the Civil War period, research scholars, antiquarians, collectors of Southwestern Americana will be rewarded for their confidence and the work comes up to their expectations.

Nominated for "oscars" because of the aid they rendered are Alice B. Good, of the library and archives department of the State of Arizona; Gertrude Hill, of the Museum Library in Santa Fe; Ruth Rambo, of the staff of the American School of Research Library at Santa Fe; the efficient and capable staff working under the direction of Miss Hill; Dallas Irvine, Chief Archivist, War Records Branch, General Services Administration of the National Archives Building at Washington, D. C.; F. R. Blackburn and his associates, members of the Kansas Historical Society who staff the Freeman Memorial Library at Topeka, Kansas; Leslie Bliss and his associates who take care of the Huntington Library in San Marino, California; Albert Ely and his helpers at the Palace of the Governors in Santa Fe; Mr. Blackburn and Mrs. Stephenson of the Library at West Texas State Teachers College, Canyon, Texas; William Kelleher of Albuquerque, New Mexico; the Librarian and staff protecting the Bush Collection at Amarillo, Texas; Bishop L. FitzSimon and Bishop John Mokovsky of Amarillo, Texas; Very Rev. J. Lopez, Rector of the Montezuma Seminary; the Librarian at the

University of Texas Library; Fred Rosenstock of Denver; Paul Galleher of Glendale, California; J. J. Lipsey of Colorado Springs; the Librarian of the Barker Barker Library, Austin, Texas; the library staff at Texas Tech, Lubbock, Texas; the staff at the Plains Museum, Canyon, Texas; Alys Freeze of the Western History Department of the Public Library of Denver, Colorado; the librarian of the Public Library at Las Vegas, New Mexico; the librarian at the Public Library of Albuquerque; Otis Kelley, librarian at the University of New Mexico; John Littleton of the U. S. Park Service; Ed Bartholomew of Ruidoso, New Mexico; the Custodian of the Rare Book Department of the New York Public Library; librarian of the Public Library at Socorro, New Mexico; librarian of the Public Library at Raton, New Mexico; Mable E. Willoughby and the staff of the Hardin-Simons Library at Abilene, Texas, always willing to help with the loan of a microfilm reader; the Valdez family of Springer, New Mexico; Viola Webster, of Albuquerque, New Mexico, related to L. B. Maxwell, Clouthier and other great families of New Mexico; Evelyn Shuler of Raton, New Mexico; Mrs. Troy Smith, related to M. M. Chase, Frank and Charles Springer; Mrs. Long; James Barber; Frank Pfeiffer of the *Raton Range*, newspaper; Mrs. Harris and the staff of the Public Library at Santa Fe; the county clerks of the various cities in New Mexico who placed the county records at my disposal; Mrs. Halcomb of Albuquerque, and so many others who helped make this book possible. No doubt there will be the hawkeyes who will hunt for the mistakes. Do not blame these good people for them. I will shoulder the blame. But to all who helped in any way, even if only with a word of encouragement (as scarce as hen's teeth) my sincere and hearty thanks.

F. STANLEY.

White Deer, Texas
December 31, 1959

SECTION ONE

CHAPTER ONE

WASHINGTON, D. C.

Off in the distance, sitting like a crown atop the trees, was the dome of the building, underneath which his voice so often boomed and thundered in oratory. To his right, but a short distance away, was the more recently founded Soldiers Home. Even now the sound of hammers told of a new building. Neither the builders nor the lone listener imagined that this would be the home of one Abraham Lincoln during the conflict known as the Civil War. Directly in front of him, patterned after the famed home of Thomas Jefferson, was the mansion of his friend. Very Georgian and very domed. There was a very slight breeze that rustled through the large copper-beech tree underneath which Daniel Webster was practicing the speech that would indicate his stand on the Wilmot Proviso. Somehow his words sounded hollow as they echoed through the branches of the widespread tree. What actually did he really want to say? He was a New Englander. His stand was clear. But there were others in Congress who were not New Englanders. There was the rub. No matter what the approach the path always steered to the ticklish question of slavery. Right now on the Senate floor a Territory was under fire. Some place called New Mexico. He had never been there but he had heard stories, none of them very comforting nor consoling. It was a barren wasteland not fit for Indians, much less for a white man. So he was told. And he believed it. Give it back to Mexico. But there was too much opposition. Wilmot came along with his bombshell and the whole country was in an uproar. Why did people like Wilmot get elected to Congress anyway? This would be the oration to end all orations. It had to be good—the fate of a nation depended on it.

New Mexico. The home of coyotes, snakes, droughts, dust storms, Apaches, Pueblos, and some thousands that were a heritage of the Mexican War. Bah. And to think that a group of Southerners were willing and ready to throw careers to the wind just to live in this desert. That was their privilege. They were more than anxious to introduce slavery into this newly acquired terrain. This, as a true Abolitionist, he would fight. It might be the habitat of coyotes but it was still a possession of the United States. As such it must be devoid of slaves and slavery. The Chamber was a beehive stirred up by the rotund, five-by-five Wilmot. At last the speech met his approval. He entered his carriage; took up the reins and headed beyond the Harewood residence through the trees to the capitol. Coming events were already forecasting shadows—ominous, dark, deep, black. A nation divided by rivers of blood. This was the beginning. The Wilmot Proviso sired Valverde, Glorieta, Peralta in New Mexico as well as Manassas, Murfreesboro and other well known battlefields in the South. The first shot may have been fired at Fort Sumter but the Proviso primed the gun.

The year General Kearny marched his troops over the angular New Mexican Alps known as the Raton Range was that of Manifest Destiny. A speech was made from a housetop in Las Vegas; a flag was unfurled in Santa Fe and the scramble was on. Washington concerned itself over the problem as to whether this vast territory should be Slave or Free. The general kept his powder dry and kicked up a trail to San Pasqual in California. No one bothered to thank him for New Mexico. The Free Soil Party was very much in favor of the Wilmot Proviso and letters were sent to Calhoun, Cass, Van Buren, Buchanan, Francis P. Blair of the *Washington Globe*, and Thomas Ritchie of the *Washington Union*.

Thomas Hart Benton was not amenable to excitement over the new acquisition. It was of no earthly use to the United States and he was anxious to return it to Mexico. His resentment against President Polk knew no bounds because he was convinced that this thing left a bad taste in everybody's mouth. He felt that the President provoked the war with Mexico by annexing Texas without the positive consent of the nation south of the border. If Benton was the realist; Polk was the visionary. A coast-to-coast America would command the respect of England and France. To achieve this, Texas, New Mexico (which also included present Arizona), and California would have to be subjugated. It aroused the enmity of Santa Anna and brought on the war. The results merited the risk. Polk always insisted that the Oregon Trail was widowed without the courtship of the Santa Fe Trail. Opposition was strong, as well it could be under the leadership of Benton, Webster, Silas Wright, Van Buren and several other political giants. Polk, being sui generis, weathered the storm.

Daniel Webster insisted that we annex nothing. Calhoun maintained that we draw a line from the Gulf of Mexico to the city of El Paso (Franklin) and there stop. Bancroft suggested we take all of Mexico by right of conquest. Calhoun prevailed. He worked out the Gadsden Purchase which gave us, for a price, a little more of New Mexico than General Kearny had in mind. The war proved costly to President Santa Anna and the money came in handy to replenish his resources. As the nation rejoiced David Wilmot pulled a rabbit out of the hat by bringing to light the long lost Ordinance of 1787. It was too well timed for inspiration. If he hadn't done so a dozen Northern senators stood ready to introduce the bill. August 8, 1846, the very day Kearny's troops conquered the arduous Raton Pass, Wilmot stood up and spoke his piece. So certain was he of victory that he spoke of New Mexico as an American possession before Kearny reached Apache Canyon where he expected enemy resistance. It was a long shot but Wilmot took it. While New Mexicans were learning how happy they should be because now they were Americans, the Senate was debating whether or not New Mexico should be considered part of the Free Soil plan or the Slave State plan.

Born in Bethany, Pennsylvania, January 20, 1814, Wilmot was twenty years of age when he posted his barrister's shingle at Towanda in his native State. Eleven years later he was elected to Congress by the Democrats who liked his direct approach. He attacked slavery with the zeal of an Abolitionist. He rejoiced at the breach between Benton and Polk as fitting into his own ambitious plan. He was deeply hurt when Benton rejected the offer of commander-in-chief of all the volunteer troops infiltrating into Mexico. Wilmot argued that Thomas Jefferson established that the lands to the northwest of the Ohio were to be slave free. This meant that all lands coming into the jurisdiction of the United States whether by force of arms, trade, purchase or election fall into this category as delineated by Jefferson. Texas he declared the exception because that State

3

settled the issue as a Republic prior to seeking admission into the Union. He entertained no doubts concerning New Mexico and California. They had no priority rights. They belonged to the United States by right of conquest. The government would legislate for them. Wilmot was sucessful only because Kearny made Santa Fe without mishap. Had Armijo been more of a patriot and disputed passage, Kearny would have had a difficult time indeed. There was never any doubt about the final outcome. It merely would have been delayed. And Wilmot would have sweated, if not beating a hasty retreat.

Wilmot took the floor again that Saturday night at 8:20, and spoke for ten minutes. He was respected by his fellow senators as a courageous fighter despite his shortness of stature. He had stamina and was fettered to his convictions. He fought for the rights of labor, and was regarded by the opposition as an upstart reformer. He is forever enshrined in the hearts of the common people as burying the system that imprisoned a person for debt. The senators listened as to a lonesome drum. Ten minutes that culminated in the Civil War. A bill was introduced placing the sum of $2,000,000 at the disposal of President Polk for the purpose of negotiating peace with Mexico. Wilmot asked for an amendment to that bill:

"Provided, that, as an express and fundamental condition to the acquisition of any territory from the Republic of Mexico by the United States, by virtue of any treaty which may be negotiated between them, and to the use by the executive of the moneys therein appropriated, neither slavery nor involuntary servitude shall ever exist in any part of said territory, except for crime, whereof the party shall first be duly convicted . . ."

The House was very pleased with Wilmot and the bill passed. The Senate was divided. Clever debaters, eyeing the clock, talked on to the hour fixed for dismissal, thus hoping to defeat the bill. Wilmot was not easily discouraged. An opportunist, he again produced the bill on February 8, 1847, after everyone believed it consigned to the tomb. Newspapers in New York, Vermont, Massachusetts, Michigan and New Mexico sang Wilmot's praises. Virginia, North Carolina, South Carolina and Mississippi denounced him. The North and South were already aligned. Alabama and other Southern States termed it as grossly unfair and charmingly insulting to the thinking people of the South. They argued the preponderance of a Northerner to dictate the prospects concerning slavery in New Mexico and California. The Proviso was unfair to the South for several reasons, the main one being that soldiers from the South as well as the North spilt their blood in the Mexican War. The spoils of war were not essentially for the North. Many held that if Southerners moved to New Mexico or California there shouldn't be any more argument over their bringing slaves with them to their new homes as there would be in retaining them in Texas or Virginia or the Carolinas.

President Polk, when approached for his stand, maintained that the Southerners were unduly agitated and confusing the issue. The Proviso said nothing of slavery but dealt with whether or not New Mexico should be considered a slave Territory. Nor was the question as to whether or not New Mexico would permit them to bring in slaves under discussion. The issue was whether or not the South considered New Mexico slave or Free Soil. Senator William Butler of South Carolina called for Wilmot's impeachment, declaring him to be a traitor and guilty of treason to the Constitution. Calhoun ventured the opinion that the South would secede from the Union rather than submit to the Wilmot Proviso. Polk assured Wilmot that the clamor would die a natural death since the reports he received concerning New Mexico indicated no need for slaves. The country was arid rather than fertile. Plantations had little hope of survival. There was no more hope for cotton as there was for any other stable commodity raised in the South. Some decades later New Mexico farmers were to prove that cotton could be raised in the disputed area. On July 6, 1849, the President addressed Congress:

"The War with Mexico having terminated, the power of the Executive to establish or continue temporary civil governments over these territories, which existed under the laws of nations whilst they were guarded as conquered provinces in our military occupation, has ceased. By their cession to the United States Mexico has no longer any power over them, and until Congress shall act the inhabitants will be without any organized government. Should they be left in this condition, confusion and anarchy will be likely to prevail."

On July 12th, a committee consisting of four Whigs and four Democrats representing both North and South, was appointed to settle the question of governments for Oregon, California and New Mexico. All were agreed that New Mexico should organize a Territorial Legislature. By tacit consent all conspired to take no action pro or con over the slavery issue in New Mexico. This policy involving a constitutional issue was relegated to the Territorial Court from which appeal could be made to the Federal Supreme Court. Senator Clayton, Chairman of the Committee, placed great confidence in the powers of the Supreme Court and hoped that by falling into the laps of the judges it would be out of the hands of the Senate. The dodge proved unsuccessful. The Supreme Court refused the nibble and the last state became worse than the first. Senator Clayton effected nothing more than to guarantee the ascendancy of the Free Soil Party. They moved now to outmaneuver Chief Justice Taney, whom they suspected of pro-slavery proclivities. The South took up the challenge and answered that the Supreme Court could not possibly make a decision without involving itself in a sectional controversy. Cass, Calhoun and Jefferson Davis voted for the Clayton Compromise and it passed the Senate. The House snubbed it completely. Worried and addled, the President made another attempt on July 24th:

"New Mexico and Upper California were among the territories conquered by our forces, and temporary governments were established over them (i.e., the Military Government). They were established by the officers of our Army and Navy in command, in pursuance to the orders and instructions accompanying my message to the House of Representatives of December 22, 1846. In the routine of duty some of the officers of the Army and Navy who first established temporary governments in California and New Mexico have been succeeded in command by other officers upon whom light duties devolved; and the agents employed or designated by them to conduct the temporary governments have also, in some instances been superceded by others. Such appointments for temporary civil duty during our military occupation were made by the officers in command in the conquered territories respectively."

Benton, Clay and Webster were convinced that the issue was far from being settled and agreed that the mere presence of troops and the authority of officers over the territories in question did little or nothing toward solving the question of slavery in these parts. Nor would they agree that a decision by the Supreme Court would establish harmony. Webster, champion of the Free Soilers, took the floor of the Senate and hurled thunderbolt after thunderbolt, legal and historical, in his stand that Congress maintained the constitutional right to keep California, Oregon and New Mexico free of slaves and slavers. He argued that a slave holder was free to take his slaves to New Mexico but he could not constitutionally take with him the local law—the law of any Southern State which made a man a slave. Senator Corwin stood up and shouted that Free Soilers were attempting to interpret the Constitution of the United States by geography. He further remarked:

"It is a sad commentary upon the perfection of human reason that with very few exceptions, gentlemen coming from a slave state have . . . argued that you have no right to prohibit the introduction of slavery into . . . New Mexico, while on the other hand, there is not a man, with few exceptions, and some highly respectable, in the free states but believes in his conscience that you have a right to prohibit slavery. . . ."

Meantime, a tall, emaciated, ascetic-faced member of Congress (1847-49) from the Middle West listened attentively to every word as he evaluated the line of thought presented by Calhoun, Webster, Wilmot, Cass, Davis, Benton and others. The Emancipation Proclamation was conceived during these fiery days of the Wilmot Proviso debates. Birth was still a few years off. The Free Soil Party was aware of his potentialities and merged with the Republican Party in proposing him for the highest office in the nation. The direct abolitionists known as the Liberty Party approached the Conscience Whigs of Massachusetts, who were the main protagonists supporting the Wilmot Proviso and won their agreement that slavery was out of the question in any part of New Mexico. Next they approached the Barnburners, as the Van Buren clique of New York Democrats were called, and asked them to join hands in uniting for a No Slavery for New Mexico fight. Van Buren contended that none of the territory acquired from Mexico was to be the property of slave holders. He also agreed with the Liberty Party that the Polk administration deserved a good spanking. It would be good for Polk to start a thorough house cleaning, beginning with members of the Cabinet. Van Buren was bitterly opposed to the annexation of Texas, thus closing the door of opportunity for the presidency in 1844. The Liberty Party, Conscience Whigs and Barnburners settled their differences and joined hands as the Free Soil Party during the Democratic Convention of

1848. The meeting was held in Buffalo, New York. Banners told of four freedoms: Free Soil, Free Speech, Free Labor and Free Men. Slavery in the States was beyond the control of Congress, and since Congress could not make slaves it was bound to refuse admission of slavery within the confines of California, Oregon and New Mexico.

Ten thousand men gathered under the folds of a huge tent in Buffalo's city park for the first Free Soil Convention. Only 465 of this number were actual voters. William Cullen Bryant, as active in politics as he was in journalism, spoke effectively, wrapped up as he was and buttered in the idealism of the Transcendentalists and abolitionists as were Giddings, King, Chase, Butler and others, who, weak politically were strong in singleness of purpose. In this they stood united: no more slave territory; no more compromises with slavery anywhere. The delegated voted a platform calling for cheaper postage rates, river and harbor improvements, free lands to actual settlers and the dissolution of unnecessary governmental offices and salaries. Van Buren was chosen as candidate for the presidency.

If Bryant's *Evening Post* sponsored Van Buren, Bennett's *New York Herald* went all out for the hero of the late war. Sizing up the two candidates Webster was of the opinion that neither one of them was capable of settling the slave question. Horace Greeley, ever the enemy of the Free Soilers, nevertheless advised his readers to support General Taylor, although he personally favored Van Buren not because he liked the gentleman but because the Free Soil Party should be given an opportunity to see if their land reforms were practicable or mere pipe dreams. No man could be a success any more than a failure unless he put his experiment to work. Greeley always admired a fighter whether he agreed with him or not.

Webster laughed off the Free Soilers' stand as of no practical importance. Slavery would not thrive in Oregon any more than California, he remarked to Hiram Ketchum (July 21, 1848); and if New Mexico had any part of it where slavery might prove practical as some maintained then that section should be turned over to Texas. On election day the old general outran Cass by one hundred and forty thousand votes. Van Buren had no electors on his side despite his three hundred thousand votes and only too late did the Free Soilers realize what Bryant, Webster and others already knew—he was not the old political firebrand of former years: One lasting result of the election was that it left regional animosities distended and thin-skinned. A small group of Northerners vowed with solemn promise that slavery would never be part of the make-up of New Mexico or California. Free Soilers took nine seats in Congress. Southerners came up with equal resolve: New Mexico and California would have slaves if only to prove that they (the Southerners) knew how to fight for their rights. Unexpectedly, a prospector in California lowered the boom. Of all the idiotic things to do at this particular time—Gold.

Marshall, the mechanic building a mill-race channel for Johann Sutter, discovered gold in the Sacramento Valley and turned the course of history. Who wanted free soil when there was gold for the digging? Men would doff their hats at the mere mention of California. Polk asked the people to remain calm. He pleaded with Congress to retain California as a territory. It was not ready for Statehood. New Mexicans demanded equal rights. It wanted Statehood. Polk insisted that granting Statehood to either New Mexico or California at this time was tantamount to a criminal act. Before he bowed out of office he left three thoughts with Congress: (a) Carry the Missouri Compromise line to the Pacific; (b) Let the people of the territories involved decide the slavery question when they applied for admission into the Union—not to be readily given; (c) Let the Supreme Court make the ultimate decision. Neither the Free Soilers nor the Southerners would agree to any of these proposals.

Texas selected this time to put a scare into the Free Soilers by demanding that her boundaries be extended to the source of the Rio Grande. This is a time when the Free Soilers were devising a plan whereby the area of Texas would be cut into two States; one for slave holders; the other for Free Soilers. Some belligerent Texans foresaw war as the only solution and started recruiting men to capture Santa Fe as well as to police the disputed area and separating Arizona from New Mexico as a slave State. There was no doubt that a war would break out. They wanted to be on the winning side. The Arizona they cut off New Mexico would include the present towns of El Paso (then Franklin), Hart's Mill, Magoffinsville, Paraje, Las Cruces, Santo Tomas and other villages of lesser note. Another try was made during the war.

Next Webster came up with the idea that since New Mexico

was taken from Mexico the Mexican anti-slavery laws should be allowed to remain in force pro-tem. Calhoun suggested that since New Mexico was now a possession of the United States, Webster had better read the Constitution of his own country rather than that of a foreign power. He stoutly maintained that the Constitution ex proprio vigore carried slavery wherever the flag floated. Webster's retort was that a territory was not to be considered a part of the United States unless its governing body was a certainty, an idea favored by the newspapers of New Mexico and Arizona and preached throughout New Mexico by Donaciano Vigil. Nothing angered the former governor of New Mexico so much as to hear someone say: "I am going to the States." It made him feel unclean. As if he had no country, no allegiance, no flag—a man without a country. He was largely responsible for Kearney's success, and succeeded Bent as governor. The military government that followed was not to his liking. Websted had a good idea. New Mexico needed civil rather than military government. Many people unsuccessful in their quest for gold left California to settle in New Mexico. It had something to offer despite Webster's belief that it was a desert.

March 4th. Inaugural Day. The wind was fierce; the cold raw, weather wet. The sky hung like a funeral pall over the city. Polk complained that he was suffering from a chronic diarrhea ailment aggravated by the stormy weather. His enemies said he had to place the blame somewhere but his suffering was actually the result of his defeat by Congress which favored the introduction of a bill making New Mexico a State. They were wrong. Polk was to be many years in the grave before New Mexico won its fight for Statehood. Polk greeted his successor. Together they marched to the carriage that would bring them to the place of speech making and hail and farewell. Taylor was bubbling over with enthusiasm. California and New Mexico would become States. He would see to that. Polk groaned. It was like hitting a man when he was down. This man above all others should know better. He had spent some time in Mexico and observed conditions there. New Mexico was no better. Polk wanted to crawl into a hole somewhere and die. He felt defeated, lost, sick. This man sitting next to him would destroy all he had worked for. Not so fast. Please, not so fast. Territories might be won in a day but States were not made in a day. Who would bear the burden of taxes? Now that California had gold there might be hope for her. But New Mexico? What right had New Mexico to Statehood? The carriage halted and Polk walked the path to oblivion.

For a time California and New Mexico were mentioned in the same breath. Gradually the talk concentrated on California. Gold helped. Taylor realized what was happening and addressed Congress recommending that it receive New Mexico into the Union upon application. He intimated that California was decidedly against slavery and New Mexico was free soil by heritage since the Mexican government outlawed slavery prior to the occupation. He asked Congress to respect this law even though promulgated by a foreign power. Taylor was not concerned with California nor New Mexico at the moment but the attitude of Texas over the northwestern claim. He was opposed to slicing any part of New Mexico for the benefit of the Lone Star State, feeling that Texas should have taken care of all this during her days of independence or at least at the time she was admitted into the Union. The claim was too tardy to satisfy him that it was a just one. He steered Congress around the dispute by pointing to Utah. Difficulties there called for drastic measures. When cornered again about slavery in California and New Mexico he answered that the Mexican laws would remain in force until superceded by governmental regulations. Asked whether Utah would be slave or Free Soil, Representative Root answered that it would become another State known as either Deseret or Utah only if the Wilmot Proviso be attached to its constitution. The same held for New Mexico. Benton stood up and introduced a bill calling for another state to be carved out of Texas, which would take in all the land east of the Brazos. This was also to be a slave state to balance the Free Soil states of California, Utah and New Mexico. He wanted fair representation for slavery in the Southwest. Another Senator argued that all the talk of Statehood for either Utah or New Mexico was ridiculous since neither place had sufficient population to make one fair sized city. The discussion finally ended when Taylor promised to regard New Mexico at least, and possibly Utah, in status quo until such time as a graph would show a definite rise in population. Politicians had taken over New Mexico. Statehood would only kill the goose that laid the golden egg. Donaciano Vigil and those who followed his line of thinking would have to be put to pasture. Taylor was fed political tranquilizers. Every picture emanating from New Mexico was solid black. The by-word was "Give it back to the Indians." Politicians in Washington, however, must make certain that the President ignore these sibilations and keep the issue of Statehood dangling. Between them they disproved New Mexico as a barren wasteland. The more politicians in New Mexico, appointees of the Federal Government, vituperated the Land of Enchantment, the more politicians in Washington built up the possibilities. Many retired wealthy as a result.

Clay proposed that New Mexico be given a Territorial type of government without delay. Sick, disillusioned, weak, he faltered as he made his appeal: "I firmly believe that our country can rid itself of its main differences by the easy method of recognizing facts. The first great fact is the Wilmot Proviso as absolutely unnecessary. Nature and man have already decreed that California and New Mexico must be free soil." In his hand he held a piece of wood cut from Washington's coffin. Raising it aloft that all might see he addressed it and in pleading tones asked that the spirit of a man so noble be generous with the nation and ward off the inevitable conflict. Far better for the nation to divide into Free Soil and slave than bloodshed. Far better for America to enjoy non slavery in the North and New Mexico, California, Oregon, District of Columbia, than hazard a war by restricting the rights of the Southern States. He agreed that it would be ruinous and dishonorable for the South to drop out of the Union and he offered a compromise very much in accord with the plan outlined by Daniel Webster. Clay and Webster held an all night conference. Webster promised to accept whatever solution Clay had to offer. When Free Soilers heard that Webster gave in to Clay they branded him a traitor, and an abolitionist poet of note in New England immortalized the incident in a poem:

> So fallen! So lost! The light withdrawn
>   Which once he wore!
> The glory from his gray hairs gone
>   Forevermore!
> Let not the land once proud of him
>   Insult him now,

>   Nor brand with deeper shame his dim
>   Dishonored brow.
>   All else is gone; from those great eyes
>   The soul has fled;
>   When faith is lost, when honor dies,
>   The man is dead.
>
>   (*From* ICHABOD, *by John G. Whittier*,
>   1807-1892)

Webster agreed with Clay that if New Mexico were left to herself, without any outside interference, she would never tolerate slavery, not because of class distinctions or from a sense of human dignity but because of the internal situations evolving around land around land grants, peons, ricos, heritage and custom. It was ridiculous to raise an issue over slavery in a place where it did not and could not exist. Why should Congress wrangle over New Mexico when by its very nature it could be nothing other than Free Soil?

A man of Webster's caliber was not to be intimidated by New England abolitionists any more than feel the ridicule of poetry. Webster felt that the literary people of Massachusetts produced tracts pointing in many and all directions leading nowhere. The reader always came to a dead end and was more confused than when he started. None of the ills of the nation were solved by tracts or poems. Free Soilers were sincerely concerned over the fate of Utah and New Mexico. Webster felt they missed the point. If they really felt for these politically torn areas they should knuckle down and study internal problems rather than the possibility of the penetration and infiltration of slavery. Greeley's *New York Tribune* and Bryant's *Evening Post* painted Webster as a strut-jacket. He was asked by many to defend his position. To take one side of the fence or the other, not to straddle the fence. Was he for slavery in New Mexico or was he a Free Soiler? All eyes focused on him as he walked to the platform:

"Mr. President—I wish to speak today not as a Massachusetts man, not as a Northern man, but as an American . . ." Because the preservation of the Union now seemed the all-important issue, he turned to the Southern block with the words: "Hear my cause." They listened for three solid hours.

". . . All the land taken from Mexico is free by the immutable decrees of nature which makes slavery impracticable and unprofitable. This region needs no Wilmot Proviso. Why re-enact the will of God? Why wound the pride of Southerners by a wanton denial of equal privileges derogatory to their character and their rights. . . . Secession! Peaceful secession! Sirs, your eyes and mine are never destined to see that miracle. The dismemberment of this vast country without convulsion! The breaking up of the fountains of the great deep without ruffling the surface! Who is so foolish as to expect any such thing? He who sees these States now revolving in harmony around a common center and expects to see them quit their places and fly off without convulsion may look the next moment to see the heavenly bodies rush from their spheres and jostle against each other in the realms of space without causing the wreck of the universe! There can be no such thing as a peacable secession. . . ."

New England was aghast. Was this all he had to say for all those trips to the spreading copper-beech tree on Harewood Road? Edmund Quincy, Whittier, Longfellow, spoke their minds in no uncertain terms. Nothing complimentary. Bryant brushed aside his poetry to pen: "Mr. Webster stands before the public as a man who has deserted the cause which he lately defended; deserted it under circumstances which force upon him the imputation of a sordid motive. . . . It is but little more than two years since he declared himself the firmest of friends of the Wilmot Proviso, professing himself its original and incurable champion, and claiming its principles as Whig doctrine . . ." Greeley would not be outdone by Bryant. Among other things his March 9th editorial noted: "We look to no compromise that perils or looks toward periling freedom in New Mexico . . ." Seward gave a speech in the Senate in which he stated that not a single foot of land acquired from Mexico would belong to anyone in favor of slavery. Douglas and McClernand (this latter Chairman of the Territorial Committee) pressed for California's admission into the Union which others in the House agreed to vote upon provided New Mexico and Utah were first promised no congressional exclusion from slavery, and if the residents of these two territories were expressly empowered to legislate for the admission of slaves as well as to frame their own constitutions with respect to slavery as they saw fit.

Clay was appointed chairman of a committee of thirteen to

settle the issue once and for all as to whether or not New Mexico should be admitted into the Union as a State. As a result of this meeting which took place on May 8th, the committee voted on seven proposals:

    a. Whenever any new State or States formed from Texas asked for admission into the Union, Congress was to redeem its compact with Texas and grant the request;

    b. California, boundaries unchanged, was to be made a State;

    c. Territorial governments were to be established for New Mexico and Utah without any stipulation for or against slavery;

    d. The provisions respecting California, Utah and New Mexico, as constituting the territory obtained from Mexico were to be bound up in the same bill;

    e. Texas was to be paid for surrendering her jurisdiction over the lands she claimed within the old boundaries of New Mexico and her northern and western boundaries were to be fixed by the Rio Grande and up that river to the point commonly called El Paso, and running thence up that river twenty miles, measured thereon by a straight line, and then eastwardly to a point where the one hundredth degree of west longtitude crosses the Red river;

    f. A fugitive slave law was to be passed;

    g. Slave trade was to be abolished within the District of Columbia.

President Taylor bided his time. First things first. He called upon Congress to vote California into the Union. He failed to establish any civil government for New Mexico and Utah despite the fact that the Treaty as well as constitutional rights called for them. He failed to fix boundaries for New Mexico east of the Rio Grande, and left the settlers of that area open to threats of Texas invasion. (See: Nevins—ORDEAL OF THE UNION, Vol. 1, page 319). Actually his scheme was to see just how far Texas would go. He was hoping for war if only to alleviate the pressure over the slavery question and the Wilmot Proviso. If Texas carried out her threat and marched into New Mexico then he would retain not only the disputed area for New Mexico but slice off the western part and give it to New

Mexico and crown the deal by Statehood. Many politicos in Santa Fe sighed with relief when death put an end to the plan. None of these sighers was a native New Mexican.

Native New Mexicans were a cause of grief to Taylor. They were not anxious to bide their time any more than California. They wanted Statehood not merely because the gold happy land along the Pacific coast was assured it but because they wished to settle down to the life of practical American citizens with all the privileges accruing to their status. They scoffed at the claim of Texas to any land that was theirs time out of mind. The success of the Santa Fe Trail excited the cupidity of Texans. Several attempts to conquer New Mexico failed. They wanted to know by what authority Texans claimed Albuquerque, Santa Fe, Las Vegas. True, Texas had her beginnings through Spain. So did California, but the region to the west was not making claims on New Mexico for that reason. Actually the Spaniards settled New Mexico before California, Arizona, Texas. The Lone Star State was exorbitant not only over land but included the commerce of the prairies. New Mexicans urged Texas to look elsewhere for money. In Washington whenever Taylor mentioned the possibility of Statehood for New Mexico his opponents countered that it was a fit habitation for wild Indians and Mexicans. No self-respecting American would live there. Whereupon his blood pressure mounted and he would storm into his office to write another letter to his cronies in Santa Fe urging them to kick up a rumpus for Statehood and not to cease until obtained. He could not understand how so many merchants continued to do business along the Santa Fe Trail if the land was as destitute as claimed. He suspected that someone was pulling his leg or that Shakespeare was not the only one to suspect something rotten in Denmark. Books had been written about the commerce of the prairies. The public was aware of the overland trade. Many of Donniphan's and Kearny's men found New Mexico much to their liking and returned after the war. Trappers, mountain men, lawyers, merchants, soldiers were impressed. All this and more Taylor hurled back at those whom he suspected of ulterior motive for throttling New Mexico's Statehood. He told a few friends in secret that he would like to take a few of these oponents out in the street and publicly horsewhip them, or otherwise pound some sense into them. He sent letters repeatedly to Santa Fe urging them to form a Constitution. He hoped that Donaciano Vigil would indoctrinate the people and saturate them with the need for Statehood and constitutional rights. No president before or since was so sincere in his efforts for the rise and betterment of Sunshine Land. Nor was New Mexico ever to have another Donaciano Vigil. Taylor's cabinet warned time and again that New Mexico had no population justifying his stand. "Population be hanged," he would fire back, "aren't the native New Mexicans people? Count the Indians, then, if population is all you want." He would slam the door and sit and brood over the foibles of men that waved flags one day and shook their fists at you the next. He would show them. Perhaps he might have. Death is no respector of persons.

Colonel John Munroe, commandant at Fort Marcy and in charge of all the U. S. troops in New Mexico, called in Donaciano Vigil, Gallegos, Padre Martinez and other influential New Mexicans and asked them to set a day for a convention. Ten days (May 15-25, 1850) guided by the direction of these men the delegates sat in session and drew up a Constitution. Much to the horror of Southerners it made no reference to slavery.

President Taylor was pleased with the Constitution. Donaciano Vigil made a "whistle stop" tour of the mountain villages and explained it to the natives. Within a month most New Mexicans were aware of their new status. The next stop was Statehood. This Taylor wanted immediately, if only to dump the New Mexico-Texas boundary dispute into the lap of the Supreme Court, where he felt certain of a decision favoring New Mexico. Meantime the area desired by Texas was to remain in the hands of New Mexico. Instead of alleviating the situation, he aggravated Texas, already annoyed with him, for the cold reception he gave the Rangers in the Mexican War. The proposal that New Mexico keep the land until the Supreme Court reached a decision stirred Southern radicals into an outcry against what they considered a grave injustice against the Lone Star State. They sent a delegation of three Southern Whig members of Congress to expostulate, and bring the President to reason, if possible. If Taylor persisted in his errors they were to force his hand with the trump card of secession.

Taylor glared at them. He had faced cannon and bayonets. These three were put harmless puppets dancing to the tune of the slave owners. He banged his fist on the desk to emphasize his stand. Threats would not move. At least not theirs. Secession would be dealt with when the time came. Meantime California would be admitted into the Union as a Free Soil State; New Mexico would follow just as soon as the newly drawn up Constitution arrived. He scorned as preposterous the Texas claim to the upper Rio Grande. He made threats of his own. If Texas persisted in the silly notion and made any attempt to take the land in question he would call out the troops and defend the New Mexico border if he had to spill the blood of every soldier in the American Army. Civil War both North and South expected but not on the New Mexico-Texas border. Had Taylor lived the whole story of the war would have been differently written. The major battle would have been fought in the Southwest rather than Virginia, Maryland, Tennessee, Pennsylvania and the South. Even now he was preparing his July 5th message which called for troops to defend the New Mexico border. The trio realized he was deadly serious. They would not enjoy the Fourth. Why all the fuss over desert wasteland that was as yet an unknown quantity to the nation? What did New Mexico have that was worth the risk of plunging the nation into war? Was there any other way of settling the question? These were questions they would have to sleep on. After the holiday they hoped to come up with some answers.

When they left he picked up the unfinished speech but found he was too tired to think clearly. His hand was shaking. He hadn't realized how much they had unruffled and disturbed him. Perhaps he was too hard on them. After a whole lifetime of barking out commands it was hard to swallow arguments. He would finish the paper early on the morning of the 5th. One must draw the curtain on what might have happened had that speech been completed. In a broad sense one might say that Taylor was killed by long-winded speakers celebrating the Fourth. They took the floor for hours and really said nothing. As President, and as an American, he felt duty bound to accept an invitation to the ceremony dedicating the base of the Washington Monument.

Only residents of Washington, D. C., can appreciate what Taylor went through. The terrific humidity and the baking sun make the city a rather undesirable place to be in July. The day of casual wear was yet to be. Bareheaded, President Taylor remained at attention during the Kosciusko dust ceremony. An hour passed. He felt like a baked potato. Sweat poured down his face, saturated his garments and his underclothing. Time dragged on. He was unmovable as a statue. He could stand it more than others because of his military training. But he was not as young as he used to be. It was an ordeal. Speaker after speaker whiled away the time paying tribute to Kosciusko, whom they had never seen, much less really cared about. They loved the sound of their own voices droning in the July heat. The excuse was that this ceremony would cement North-South relations; would unite America; cause Texas to drop her claim to a good portion of New Mexico. If this would have the desired effect Taylor was willing to stand in the uncomfortable heat all day. He knew human nature. Patriotism and flag waving on the Fourth; fist waving and secession on the 5th. It seemed a sham as is the case with so many public ceremonies. Taylor heard nothing. He was too involved in his own thoughts to note the way the speakers were sounding off. The fact that not one word of any of the speeches is found in any textbook today is proof enough of how words rather than thoughts were pumped out. Some of these very men praising America to the skies had but yesterday threatened to impeach its President. Why? What was so horrible about New Mexico that the South would be willing to sacrifice its blood rather than see it become a State? And if it were such a barren wasteland, why did Texas want it?

They spoke about everything and anything—the Galphin Scandal, the situation in New Mexico; the danger from Texas; the ambitions of Toombs, Stephens and others. Suddenly, he felt old, disillusioned, tired, so very tired. There was a throbbing about the temples that wasn't there when he came to the celebration. When he sought out his own carriage it seemed to be a mechanical action. Back in the White House he gulped down glass after glass of ice water. None satiated his thirst. He tried ice cold milk. He tried some cherries; picked up the *Washington Union* and read the editorial calling for his impeachment. By the time he was ready for bed he was a sick man. The doctor called it cholera morbus. Later on during the night he woke up with typhoid fever. He lingered a few days, then died.

He deserved a better fate.

Millard Fillmore, his successor, announced the death to the Senate and House: "I have to perform the melancholy duty of announcing to you that it has pleased Almighty God (and many of Taylor's enemies—this anno. by the author) to remove from this life Zachary Taylor, late President of the United States. He deceased last evening at the hour of half-past ten o'clock, in the midst of his family and surrounded by affectionate friends, calmly and in full possession of all his faculties. Among his last words were these, which he uttered with emphatic distinctness: 'I have always done my duty. I am ready to die. My only regret is for the friends I leave behind me.' Having announced to you, fellow citizens, this most afflicting bereavement, and assuring you that it has penetrated no heart with deeper grief than mine, it remains for me to say that I propose this day at 12 o'clock in the Hall of the House of Representatives, in the presence of both Houses of Congress, to take the oath prescribed by the Constitution, to enable me to enter on the execution of the office which this event has devolved on me."

Margaret S. Taylor pondered these words in her heart.

But the skies cleared quickly enough. Funeral black was laid away against the death of the next notable personage; the flag was pulled up full mast and politicians rolled up their sleeves over the same old problems of Statehood and the Wilmot Proviso. How Fillmore handled the Texas claim will be seen in the next chapter. Of more interest to us at the moment is Buchanan.

President Buchanan was interested in appeasement. He believed in a restricted central government which should do as little and spend as little as possible without causing a stir. He sought to table all Free Soil administration because he wanted to be fair to the South. When Marcy, Cass and Houston sent delegations to Buchanan for his support in their case for his office not a hair on his head was ruffled. He received each delegation, made nice pep talks and hoped that the best man would win. He also told them very calmly that he enjoyed being President. He rather relished the idea of many candidates, which weakened each one's chances. Balloting began on June 3rd. There were two hundred and eighty-eight delegates present at the Baltimore convention. Cass was the favorite from the very first ballot. Marcy still entertained hopes that eventual victory would be his. His friends said he was fighting a lost cause and should swing his votes to Buchanan. He refused. Cass and Buchanan were bucking and butting like two goats. If they locked horns and died of sheer exhaustion he would emerge triumphant. Also, he feared that if he gave his votes to Buchanan most delegates would swing to Douglas. Pierce, the dark horse, abided his time. On the 49th ballot, North Carolina, tired of factionism, cast for Pierce. Other states followed. Final count: Pierce 282; Cass 2; Douglas 2; Houston 1.

Free Soilers, realizing this doomed them as a party, united with the Democrats. The Whigs concentrated on Webster and Clay. Clay, on his death bed in the National Hotel, hoped for the satisfaction of knowing that he was nominated before he passed away. Webster said that there would be no question of his (Webster's) nomination if Fillmore would give ground. There was less talk now of secession as the country focused its attention on the Kossuth and European revolutions. The Whigs abandoned Buchanan and Webster as unreliable and concentrated on General Scott, who was well liked by the South.

The Whig convention opened in Baltimore on June 16. There were three hundred and ninety-six delegates present. On the first ballot Webster received 29 votes; Scott 131; Fillmore 133. Webster never went over 32 at any one time. Fifty-three ballots later Pennsylvania broke the deadlok and cast for Scott. Other states fell in line and Scott won the Whig nomination. In the national election the South voted for Pierce as more willing to protect the rights of slave owners. The North voted for Pierce because it felt he could keep the South in line. Webster did not live long after his final humiliation and followed Taylor, Calhoun and Clay to the grave.

The first thing on the agenda was the Compromise Bill. Pierce maintained that it constituted an irrevocable settlement of the slavery question. But gay Washington was too infected at the moment with teas, parties, art exhibits, dinners, high society and the theatre to cock its ear. Pierce was given a nice pat on the back and told to sign the Gadsden Purchase which affected that "barren wasteland" known as New Mexico. *Uncle Tom's Cabin* and the Douglas Bill created more of a stir than Pierce.

The Wyandotte Indians had long noted with interest the number of covered wagons passing through their land on the way to Oregon and California. On July 24, 1853, these Indians met in the council house and organized the Kansas-Nebraska Provincial Territory, electing a delegate to the Thirty-third Congress. No one seemed particularly bothered by all of this until Senator Douglas of Illinois made it a hornet's nest. He, and his committee, he argued, looked to the Compromise of 1850 under which men fixed their own domestic institutions instead of having them determined by an arbitrary geographical line. The government had long fought to separate slavery and freedom by a geographical line. He made another reference to the Ordinance of 1787, as Wilmot before him, claiming that it marked the Mason-Dixon line. He also made mention of the Missouri Compromise. He argued that the principles laid down by the Ordinance and the Missouri Compromise required the extension of the general line to all new territories acquired. He had devoted many years of his life to the study of this problem and always came up with the same answer. Let the South keep its slaves but none must enter New Mexico, California, Utah, Kansas, Nebraska. He claimed that the Free Soil Party was always interfering with the good he could do in maintaining the Mason-Dixon line.

Douglas was a belligerent stick of dynamite. What he lacked in height he made up for in his loud, raging voice that roared through the Senate chamber like the sound of the whirlwind. He told Chase and Sumner that the very men now proposing the Compromise as a solemn pact were repudiating it and he suspected they were responsible for the Compromise measures of 1850 which superseded the Missouri pact.

When the Free Soilers and Abolitionists refused to believe that the new Compromise actually constituted a subrogation, Douglas cynically remarked that they had overlooked the obvious—it buried completely the old principle of Congressional non-intervention and popular self-determination. This rule, he told them, applied not only to New Mexico and Utah but to any or such lands within the jurisdiction of the United States. A section of New Mexico projected north of the 36° 30′ line, nevertheless the rule of popular government was just as valid under the Compromise of 1850 above the line as below it. This did not hold for New Mexico since it was acquired from Mexico, not bought from France at the time of the Louisiana Purchase. Douglas mistakenly convinced himself that the Missouri Compromise had established a geographical principle which it failed to do in the case of a State north of the line. No one said that the special rule applied to New Mexico and Utah should later be used in speaking of the Platte country.

J. H. Stringfellow moved into Kansas solely for the purpose of developing the slave trade. It seemed to be a common practice of so many Missourians living near the Kansas border. A Congressional committee (34th Cong. 1st Sess. Report No. 200, page 925 ff.) called him in to testify: "At the time of the passage of that bill," he said, "I never heard any man in my section of Missouri express a doubt about the nature of the institutions which would be established here provided the Missouri restriction was removed. The conviction was general that it would be a slave state."

Three weeks after the Douglas Bill was introduced the Washington scene changed. For a brief moment it seemed that all the wounds were bound and well on the way to healing. Douglas refused to let well enough alone and the sting of the viper began to fester. He intended to mollify the sectional conflict for the unification of the party but succeeded only in exposing the wounds. Far from uniting the Democratic Party he tomahawked it, down to the very roots. He did succeed in destroying the Whigs who were casting about for a potential to replace Webster and Clay. Unwittingly, Douglas set the groundwork for a new party that would eventually eat up all the others. Many refused to blame Douglas, placing the blame on the times and the moments. For the first time in many years politicians in Washington felt helpless. The first convention of the new party was held at Worcester. Composed of fusionist groups opposed to Douglas and the Kansas-Nebraska Bill, it called itself the Republican Party. It asked that Nebraska be classified with New Mexico and Utah as Free Soil; Kansas would be slave. The New England Emigrant Society pounced on the resolution and nipped it in the bud. This Aid Company was the brainchild of Eli Thayer of Massachusetts, who hoped to send twenty thousand Free Soilers to Kansas each year to counteract the rapid rise of slavery there. Nor was the opposition dormant. Southern sympathizers retaliated with societies of their own known as Sons of the South, Blue Lodge, and many others. All eyes were on Kansas.

Andrew H. Reeder of Pennsylvania was named the first Territorial Governor, June 29, 1854. During his administration the pro-slavery group had the upper hand. At the election of the Territorial Legislature on March 30, 1855, almost five thousand armed men from Missouri, inspired by the pro-slavery pronouncements of David R. Atchison and General B. F. Stringfellow, appeared at the polls to harass Free Soilers and disturb the peace of Kansas. In April, 1855, Dr. Robinson, agent for the New England Emigrant Aid Society, sent an order to Eli Thayer requesting one hundred Sharps rifles, which some wag immediately dubbed "Beecher's Bibles." Two months later another shipment of rifles and a small brass cannon arrived. Kansas armed for the Wakarusa War.

On May 21, 1856, the pro-slavery party raided Lawrence with all the fury of the Romans at Jerusalem. Not a stone left upon a stone nor one left to tell the tale. Almost. One of the worst massacres in the annals of American history. Three days later John Brown reciprocated with the Potawatomi Massacre. Then followed in rapid succession the battles of Black Jack, Franklin, Fort Titus; the plunder of Palmyra and Prairie City; the sacking of Osawatomie.

Meantime Douglas returned to Illinois. Thousands of visitors were in Springfield to witness the State Fair. The politically ambitious Douglas could not let this opportunity slip without an address to the crowds. He told them of the House Divided at Washington. How the peace of the nation depended on Free Soil or slave. One of the audience was opposed to the remarks and the next day addressed the visitors in rebuttal. Lincoln argued that the Utah-New Mexico Acts applied solely to those two territories; no other. He aired his views on slavery, Nebraska, Kansas, the Universal Principle, the Missouri Compromise, Washington and Free Soilers. He not only amused the crowds with his home-spun manner, he captivated them by his sincerity. The Lincoln-Douglas Debates became part of the fair. Reporters took notice. Lincoln suddenly became copy and all over the country people were reading: ". . . nearly eighty years ago we began by declaring that all men were created equal, but now from that beginning we have run down to the other declaration that for some men to enslave others is a 'sacred right of self-government' . . . These principles cannot stand together . . ." Northerners licked their chops; Southerns raised their eyebrows. This lanky lad from Illinois was certainly adding fuel to the fire.

The Know-Nothing Party refused to be outdone by Abolitionists, Free Soilers and debators. To the rancor against pro-slavers they added racial and religious prejudices. They emulated the Lawrence raiders in the shedding of innocent blood. All of this failed to move Pierce. His State of the Union message touched on the situation in Central America, the Fugitive Slave Act as menaces to the American way of life and threats to American peace. These theories of government were abstract rather than concrete. He touched lightly the situation in Kansas as a bird in flight. The senatorial audience listened with wholehearted disgust. Members of the Cabinet whispered words in secret chamber and on February 11th the President issued a proclamation calling on both sides to desist from violence. Partisans in Congress took up the cry and Washington again buzzed as swarming bees in the early fall.

"At this day Kansas is becoming more distinctly than ever before, the scene of a conflict of irreconsilable opinions to be determined by brute force. No immigrant goes there unarmed; no citizen dwells there in safety unarmed; armed masses of men are proceeding into the Territory from various parts of the United States to complete the work of invasion and tyranny which he has thus begun, under circumstances of fraud and perfidy unworthy of the character of a ruler of a free people. . . . Whether, under the circumstances, it (the conflict in Kansas) can be circumscribed within the limits of the Territory, must be determined by statesmen, from their knowledge of the courses of civil commotions which have involved questions of moral right and conscientious duty, as well as balances of political power." (Steward—CONGRESSIONAL GLOBE, 34th Cong. 1st Sess. App. 399 ff.)

"The admission of Kansas into the Union as a slave state," wrote Representative Preston S. Brooks of South Carolina, in a letter addressed to the Atchison *Squatter Sovereign*, March 25, 1856, "is now a point of honor with the South. . . . It is my deliberate conviction that the fate of the South is to be decided with the Kansas issue. If Kansas becomes a hireling state, slave property will decline to half its present value in Missouri as soon as the fact is determined. . . ."

Butler and Douglas were the objects of Sumner's scorn in an address before the Senate. Representative P. Brooks resented the tirade against his aged uncle, a gentleman of the old school, and decided to come to his defense. He waited until the Senate chambers were emptied. Most of the Representatives had voted for adjournment, following the news of the death of one of the members, the Representative from Missouri, leaving Sumner very much alone. The Senator decided to address some mail he wanted in the next post. The avenging angel descended upon him with all the fury of a cyclone on a rampage. The *New York Herald* printed the story on May 23, 1856:

"About half-past one, after the Senate adjourned, Col. Preston S. Brooks, M.C., of South Carolina, approached Senator Sumner, who was sitting in his seat, and said to him: 'Mr. Sumner, I have read your speech against South Carolina, and have read it carefully, deliberately and dispassionately, in which you have libeled my State and slandered my white-haired old relative, Senator Butler, who is absent, and I have come to punish you for it.'

"Col. Brooks then struck Senator Sumner with his cane some dozen blows over the head. Mr. Sumner at first showed fight, but was overpowered. Senator Crittenden and others interfered and separated them. Mr. Keith of South Carolina did not interfere, only to keep persons off. Senator Toombs declared that it was the proper place to have chastised Mr. Sumner. The affair is regretted by all. The stick used was a gutta-percha, about an inch in diameter, and hollow, which was broken up like a pipe stem. About a dozen Senators and many strangers happened to be in the chamber at the moment of the fight. Sumner, I learn, is badly whipped. The city is considerably excited, and crowds everywhere are discussing the last item. Sumner cried: 'I'm most dead—Oh, I'm most dead!' After Sumner fell between the desks, his own having been overturned, he lay bleeding, and cried out: 'I'm most dead . . . almost dead'."

So badly had he been beaten and so keenly did he feel the humiliation that he was unable to face the Senate again until December, 1859. In discussing the affair with some cronies about a week later Keith remarked that if any of the Northern men had stood up in Sumner's defense, the streets of Washington would be drenched with their blood. "The fact of the matter, gentlemen, is that partisan feeling is wild and fierce. The Kansas fight has just occurred and the times are stirring. Everybody here feels as if we are upon a volcano."

In 1856, the Republicans cast their ballot for John C. Fremont. William L. Dayton was their choice for his running mate. Democrats favored Buchanan. Both sides expected war. "I hope and pray that Fremont may be elected. I think that with his energy and force of will he would straighten things out at once, and lick the South into good behavior . . . if they rebel, our people are ready for any sort of fight. There never has been anything like it. I think we should send an army from New Hampshire that would whip South Carolina, and set all her niggers free. New Hampshire will go for Fremont two to one, I should think by the present signs . . ." (H. F. French to B. B. French, Exter, N. H., July 20, 1856.)

Thomas Hart Benton ridiculed the idea that the election of his son-in-law, Fremont, was the solution for peace. Past experience with the mountain explorer taught him what to expect, and what his daughter's husband could dish out. He threw his hat in the ring for Buchanan even though they had not spoken to each other for six years because of differences of opinion from the Senate floor. Throughout the North the slogan for all editorials was: Free Speech, Free Soil, Free Men, Free Press, Fremont—and Victory. When the votes were counted Buchanan carried nineteen States and accounted for one hundred and seventy-four electoral votes Fremont won the support of eleven States and received one hundred and fourteen electoral. Fillmore also ran on the loyalty of one State and eight electoral votes. Had he dropped out of the race Fremont would have picked up his nine hundred thousand votes. Benton was rather happy. Whatever the attributes of his son-in-law, being President wasn't one of them. Arizona did more for Fremont than Thomas Hart Benton.

James Buchanan was not a newcomer to the back-biting, tongue-lashing, viper-striking game known as politics. He moved in seneschal circles for forty-three years, as quiet as a backwoodsman on the track of a deer. He enjoyed shadows rather than light, quietly stepping from office to office without dramatics. He was not addicted to fiery speeches.

No wife or family enjoyed his successes. Once he had given his love, with all the zeal and ardor of youth, but a lovers' quarrel made him turn his back. Suddenly, he received word that she died. Her parents blocked his efforts to view the remains and kept him from the funeral. He locked his love in the grave with her and threw away the key. He was a man of many friends but no intimates. He never trusted himself, much less others. His climb to the highest office in the nation was merely a sublimation for the descent into the earth he so often made in his lonely hours. Very few men are capable of that sort of love—less women merit it. The South baked in his reticence. He had been scrutinized and studied and not found wanting.

Nevertheless, of his very nature he was too apprehensive to stand firm polemicly. He made no pretense as a crusader, nor was he outspoken for any given cause. Aggressiveness was not his outstanding virtue. Southerners sized him up as malleable and vacillating. If they presented strong arguments against the Union, he would agree—too flaccid, yielding, limp and bending to strike tap roots. His method of appeasement was to their liking for while they couldn't entirely badger him neither could the North completely brow-beat him. He was a self-seeking character utterly devoid of imagination or inspiration, perhaps he willed it so, but there were instances in his career that proved he could rise to the occasion and he could use tact and adroitness when expedient. He was the ideal Foreign Minister, which fails to make him the ideal President. At least that was the opinion of many Southerners. He gave four of seven places in his cabinet to Southerners in an effort to ease tensions. The first major problem confronting him was the Dred Scott decision. (At least the press made it out to be a major problem.) Any student of the Civil War knows the background. But for the sake of those who have forgotten as well as for those who have slighted its importance as a factor in the Great Conflict, the account as given by the AMERICAN ENCYCLOPEDIA (1907 ed.) is followed.

Dred Scott was born in Missouri in 1809. Dr. Emerson, an army surgeon, took him to Rock Island in 1834. Two years later master and slave were at Fort Snelling, Wisconsin Territory (present Minnesota). There Scott married a woman called Harriet, also a slave in Dr. Emerson's possession. Slavery was illegal in both places—Illinois by its Constitution; Wisconsin (the northern extreme of the Louisiana Purchase) by the Missouri Compromise. In 1838, Scott, Harriet and their two children were taken back to St. Louis, Missouri, the home also of one Francis P. Blair, Jr., a good lawyer and a zealous Free Soiler. In 1848 he found out about Scott's peregrinations with his master, and, wishing to put to the test the right of slavery to reclaim persons once free—or the lack of this right—he induced Scott, who has been flogged by the doctor, to hail him to court on an assault and battery charge. He insisted that the case be tried in the State Circuit Court, County of St. Louis. Blair and his Free Soil friends furnished ample funds and legal assistance. The suit was sustainable only if Scott was a free citizen charging another citizen with violence. The court upheld that since Scott lived on Free Soil he was free and no legal power could re-enslave him. Appeal was taken to the Supreme Court of Missouri, which reversed the decision of the lower court. The two associates who voted against the chief justice maintained that the doctor had made domicile—not residence—and even this domicile was temporary from the beginning due to army life—since he moved on orders from the Federal Government. Had he not been an army man he would not have selected those places as his abode at any time. His property was held in accordance with the laws of permanent residence; Scott's servile character was merely in abeyance and fully resumed upon return to his master's proper home, Missouri. Just when the doctor thought his case was won, the Supreme Court waived the consideration that the Illinois Constitution was relevant and sent the case back to the lower court.

Dr. Emerson, either thoroughly disgusted, or because his many duties hindered his lingering about courtrooms, sold Scott to John A. Sandford of New York, who was charged with assault and battery in carrying off Scott. This time the case was tried in the Federal Circuit Court of Missouri on the constitutional ground that Scott was a citizen of a different State than Sandford. The new owner denied that the court had any right to try the case since the person in question is not a citizen but a "negro of African descent," the progeny of negro slaves. Scott's legal advisor admitted these facts but denied their sufficiency, holding that even though Scott was a negro it still did not prevent his being a citizen. The court sustained him. Sandford denied charges of assault and battery, asserting his rights as owner. Furthermore, as treatment of slaves went, he had been quite lenient with Scott. The court instructed the jury that it was not trying Sandford's light hand or heavy hand—merely seeking justice for a citizen who had been harshly dealt with by another citizen. Eventually the court admitted that a slave owner had the right to punish a recalcitrant subject. It was the law. Scott's counsel took exception and the case was brought before the United States Supreme Court. Slavery was a mighty ticklish question in Washington, especially after the national election. It was decided to let Chief Justice Taney study the case first and write a full and careful review of the whole law on the subject of slavery in the hopes that the Free Soil Party would allay agitation and propaganda. Taney and six assistant judges ruled against Scott; Curtis and McLean decided in his favor. Two days after Buchanan assumed office the decision was made public. It held that Scott, as a negro, was not a citizen of the United States within the intent of the Constitution; therefore, the circuit court had no jurisdiction, the suit should be dismissed. This decision remained law until the Fourteenth Amendment.

Had it rested here the whole case would have died a natural death. But neither the court nor the counsel for the defense closeted their triumph or defeat. It was taken to the press, pulpit, public forum, man on the street. Three points were argued, pro and con: (a) African negroes had never been by American law as persons; (b) Congress had no power to legislate regulations for territories acquired after the Constitution was adopted, except under the Constitution which recognized slaves as property; (c) The Missouri Compromise, already repealed by the Kansas-Nebraska Bill, had never been constitutional.

Scott's counsel failed to recognize that the circuit court ruled that negro blood was no bar to citizenship. The Supreme Court brought it in merely as a basis for overruling the decision. One lawyer involved in the case went so far as to say that negroes were regarded as so inferior as devoid of all rights which a white man was bound to respect. (Have we really come very far in the past one hundred years?) The court held that they were regarded in the Constitution as only chattel property, and not included in the terms people or citizens. Curtis and McLean maintained that there was a difference between the terms citizen and suffrage; that the Constitution repeatedly referred to negroes as persons, and the fact that free negroes were actually voters in five of the States in 1787 would make civil rights of free negroes the same at least as those of women and minors.

As to the Territories (and this included New Mexico), it was agreed that since the Constitution admitted slaves to be property, and, by the Fifth Amendment, Congress had no right to take away any citizen's property without compensation, nor did it have the right to make laws barring slave property from the Territories more than any other, its rules and regulations must be in conformity with the Constitution. Curtis and McLean also held that both by common law and the Constitution slavery was purely a State institution, sustained only by State law and State police power of quelling resistance. State law could not, should not, follow Scott around the territorial possessions of the United States. The decision that the Missouri Compromise was unconstitutional; that it interfered with the natural right of the slave owner to take his property wheresoever he pleased; that it was contrary to the constitutional equality of the citizens of various and different States, followed from the court's decision on the second point. The pair of justices crossing swords with Taney held that the Compromise was a rightful exercise of the constitutional power of Congress to legislate for the Territories, and had never before been questioned since the day George Washington took office as first President. It did not violate the equality of citizens simply because only those States permitting slavery and enforcing it regarded them as property.

For the years from the Kearny Entrada to the actual outbreak of the war, the two factors (both bearing on New Mexico) to date were the Wilmot Proviso and the Scott Decision. The Texas Claim was only indirectly concerned with slavery although in itself it was sufficient to bring on the conflict prevented only by the untimely death of Taylor. The third factor was the depression that struck on August 24, 1857. The president of the New York branch announced to its Gotham clientele that the Ohio Life Insurance and Trust Company had suspended payment. The cashier and their deposits proved bosom friends. (That hasn't changed in a hundred years either.) The resulting panic was responsible for low tide at the stock market. Crash went the stocks; crash went industry. Northerners sang their woes while cotton pickers in the South sang their spirituals. Crops have a nasty way of taking a fall when the bottom is out of everything else. Word from the Middle West was disheartening. Crop yield thumbed its nose at the farmers and encircled the gloom of a puzzled North. The only recourse left to real estate agents was to sell western lands as quickly as possible, sinking land values lower than the sin laden stock. Deflation, sister of Panic, let loose a flood of tears and the howls were heard all over the land. The South did not escape. Tennessee and Kentucky stacked up towers of tobacco and courted buyers, but they refused the honor. Agents were sent forth to the highways and byways to compel them to look at the nice piles but they all had excuses for putting off the visits. Tobacco growers went to the banks but the doors were closed as tight as the gates of heaven against Satan. Meekly, they looked to the North. The promise of only half the value was neither edifying nor gratifying. The North wanted food, not tobacco. That winter over eighty per cent of the Virginia manufacturers of tobacco ceased operations because the banks refused to recognize their drafts. It was pointed out to them that cigars and chewing tobacco hit an all-time low. When the tobacco factories closed down, hired slaves were returned to their masters who were now confronted with the problem of feeding them at a time when both income and food were as scarce as sugar in the Salt Lake. Many plantation owners cursed themselves for planting tobacco where formerly vast cotton fields heard the constant chatter of dark skinned workers. He was not a little envious of the neighbor who maintained his faith in cotton. Despite the crash and the depression, cotton still commanded a market, not as high as in normal years, but an income, nevertheless.

But the cotton farmer had his problems also. Although not as preceptable as tobacco, there was a steady decline in prices. In September the market price was sixteen cents a pound; at Christmas time it went down to nine. The irony of it all was the fact that it was the year of the greatest harvest yield before or since. It was white and fluffy and soft and velvety, like the soft fur of a well-fed kitten. No plague of any sort molested it that season. Only the plague of depression. Not in the South. Where else? All the troubles of the South seemed to stem from that "where else." The North said that the Southerners blaming them were no knights in shining armor either.

The depression bothered New Englanders. Acutely aware of the suffering about them their pinch-penny economy abetted the desolation instead of helping. Puritanical consciences sought the reason for this visitation on the nation. Transcendentalists and Universalists preached repentance for the crime of luxurious living, the sin of waste in the endless miles of railroad tracks, wanton spending in stocks and commodities. Also, the nation was being chastised for the sins of the South. Human bondage was not part of the Divine plan. Southerners ridiculed the idea that slavery had anything to do with the depression.

Poets in New England and writers in the South were not the only pen-pushers fermenting revolt and agitation. Crusaders disseminated anti-slavery propaganda from Maine to Oregon with tracts such as "The Impending Crisis of the South—How to Meet it," written by Hinton Rowan Helper; "Southern Wealth and Northern Profits," by Thomas Prentice Kettell, and others of lesser note. In Santa Fe the editor of the *Gazette* echoed the sentiments of the *Tribune* and Henry Carey's book, "The Harmony of Interests," "Agricultural, Manufacturing and Commercial" was as forceful in its day as "Uncle Tom's Cabin."

On a winding, dusty road leading out of Lawrence, Kansas, beyond the ruins of old Fort Titus, remembered now as a landmark of a bloody, stormy past, the little village of Lecompton basks in the sun of its former glory. The rolling hills, flow from the Kansas river, mists and quiet are all the realistic present that witnessed the third factor that brought on the war. Even today the population does not exceed much over three hundred. It was founded in 1854 and named for Samuel D. Lecompte, the first Chief Justice of the Kansas Territory. When the legislature at the Shawnee Mission voted to change the seat of government to Lecompton, a thirteen-acre tract on the east side of the year-old village was set aside and Congress was induced to make generous appropriations for the construction of a large stone building to house the legislature. It was a miniature Washington. Pro-slavers, Free Soilers, made it a battle ground. Governor Walker was decidedly against the Lecompton Constitution. In Washington, Buchanan and his cabinet favored it. Kendall, no lover of New Mexico, due to mistreatment at the hands of Salazer during the days of the Texas-Santa Fe Expedition, was the Washington correspondent for the New Orleans *Times-Picayune*. The April 29, 1863, issue of his paper carried this article.

"The President was informed in November, 1857, that the States of Alabama, Mississippi and South Carolina, and perhaps others, would hold conventions and secede from the Union if the Lecompton Constitution, which established slavery, should not be accepted by Congress. The reason was that these States, supposing that the South had been cheated out of Kansas, were, whether right or wrong, determined to revolt. Senator Hunter, to my knowledge, believed it (Hunter was from Virginia).

Many other prominent men did, and perhaps not without reason. The President determined, in November, four or five months after his famous letter to Governor Walker, to submit the Lecompton Constitution to Congress and recommend its acceptance . . . I was myself at the time disposed to go with Governor Walker, Mr. Douglas and others, but became convinced, from facts presented to me, that the course of the President was expedient, and I supported him in it. It was not worth while, as I thought, to provoke a quarrel with the South, or any part of it, upon a matter of opinion, which was of little practical importance. Everybody knew that the danger in Kansas itself had passed over. It remained to concede an abstract question to the South. . . ."

The Lecompton Constitution stemmed from a form of territorial government for Kansas adopted by a convention held at Lecompton in 1857. In June of that year, the territorial legislature, composed of pro-slavery sympathizers, chosen at an election in which Free Soilers would have no part since they insisted that the proceedings were illegal, met at Lecompton and among other acts, passed one providing for the election of a special committee to frame a State constitution for Kansas. At the same time Congress passed a bill declaring void all the enactments of the Kansas legislature, pointing out that they were appressive. The meeting for the purpose of electing delegates to the constitutional convention took place on June 15th. The Free Soilers were indeed conspicuous by their absence. Only two thousand votes were cast. Eight thousand voters chose to remain at home. The convention met at Lecompton in November and adopted a constitution which devoted four sections to slavery. It declared that the rights of the owners of slaves were inviolable. It prohibited the Kansas State Legislature from passing acts of emancipation. This provision alone was to be submitted to the people an an election scheduled to take place in December. It actually boiled itself down to this: A constitution with or without slavery. A provision was inserted preventing any amendment to the constitution until the year 1864. Buchanan favored a constitution in which the people, not the legislators, ironed out for themselves the advantages or disadvantages of slavery.

On December 21, all the counties along the Missouri border went to the polls, casting over three thousand votes where the total number of voters did not number over a thousand. Even in other sections the move was pro-slavery. When all the votes were in (6,000) it was found that only 569 opposed slavery for Kansas. Free Soilers stayed at home. The next step was the election of officers. The legislature met in special session and determined that the Lecompton Constitution be turned over to the citizens for their approval by vote. Since the election was held on the same day as the State election, over ten thousand votes were cast against it. Congress, following a long, bitter discussion, again brought the issue before the public, asking for another election to be held on August 3, 1858. Again, ten thousand voters spurned it. Again, Congress called for another election. It never took place. The July, 1859, Convention, however, outlawed slavery in Kansas. On July 29, 1861, Kansas became a State, much to the horror of New Mexico, which felt it had been slighted. The blow did not shake its loyalty to the Union. It was not the native New Mexican who destroyed these opportunities, it was political appointees from out of the Territory influential enough to hold the ears of Congress. Eyes? These were the blind days when Washington could see no farther than the Wilmot Proviso, Free Soilers, slavery, gold in California, desolation wrought by a depression, rising hatreds through partisan editorials, fear preached from pulpits, propaganda in books, and sentiment oozing from the pages of "Uncle Tom's Cabin."

The Lincoln-Douglas debates were another factor in bringing on the war. The tall, gracile congressman from Illinois, once told by an eleven-year-old admirer that a beard would lend dignity to his lantern-jawed appearance, was opposed to the Nebraska bill, the Scott decision, the Lecompton Constitution. His "House Divided" speech won the approval of editors all over the North. The Republican Party considered him presidential timber.

"We are now in the fifth year (he could never erase the Wilmot Proviso disturbance from his mind) since a policy was initiated with the avowed object and confident promise of putting an end to the slavery agitation. Under the operation of that policy that agitation not only has ceased but has constantly augmented. In my opinion it will not cease until a crisis shall have been reached and passed. 'A house divided against itself cannot stand.' I believe this government cannot endure permanently half slave and half free. I do not expect the Union to be dissolved. I do not expect the house to fall; but I do expect it will cease to be divided. It will become all one thing, or all the other. Either the opponents of slavery will arrest the further spread of it, and place it where the public mind shall rest in the belief that it is in the course of ultimate extinction, or its advocates will push it forward until it shall become alike lawful in all the States, old as well as new, North as well as South. . . ."

Douglas sought to boycott Lincoln's "House Divided" doctrine and further proscribed him for his stand on the Scott case. Suddenly, the whole nation found itself interested in the debates. Newspapers took readers to Ottawa, Freeport, Jonesboro, Charleston, Galesbury, Quincy and Alton—all in Illinois—as they enacted the scenes on paper. Lincoln did not condemn Southerners for possessing slaves but he did think that Congress had the right to ostracise slavery anywhere in the Union as well as exclude it from New Mexico, Utah, California, Kansas, Nebraska and the newer territories. It was during the debate at Galesburg that the lanky politician mentioned the negro as equal to the white man in his right to life, liberty and the pursuit of happiness; which, of course, was not the way of thinking of the majority of Southerners. The debates became history when Douglas was elected over Lincoln for a seat in the legislature. No sooner had the South breathed easier now that the lid was placed on the coffin of the debates than John Brown of Ossawatomie came to life.

How much of a link John Brown was in the chain that forged the Civil War is even now debatable. It would have been fought without the part he played. Cutting a scene from a play doesn't necessarily kill it. Brown traveled through New England and parts of Canada, his doctrine ever the same. No slavery. He was a successful rabble rouser, the kind that likes to lead a mob for a lynching. How much of it was sincerity, how much vainglory only John Brown knew. Zealots are a breed all their own. They win disciples. In Kansas, John Brown won James Montgomery to his cause and together they renewed guerila warfare with a raid on Fort Scott where a prisoner of the State was detained. Almost seven thousand dollars worth of loot was seized by the marauders, and a storekeeper was killed. On December 20th, Brown led a night raid against Missouri border towns, dividing his men into two groups, one under his command, the other in charge of Aaron D. Stevens. This latter is a well known figure to students of New Mexico history for his exploits at Fernando de Taos especially when he downed too much Taos lightning. Brown raided without a killing; Stevens killed the owner of the house he raided. President Buchanan offered a reward for Brown.

About eighty miles west of Baltimore by rail, and less than sixty from Washington by turnpike, on the banks of the Potomac in Virginia, the little village awaited John Brown and destiny. Perhaps no one outside of Harper's Ferry would have ever known its history if Brown had by-passed it. The quiet spot housed an armory maintained by the government for the manufacture of arms and an arsenal for military stores and rifle works. This arsenal suddenly became the pivot, the focal spot, the Jerusalem, Rome, Mecca that would over-ride slavery. The crusader was hopeful. There was indication that the townspeople and the slaves in the surrounding areas would rise and follow his standard. However, this was not their fight. Not yet. The agitator succeeded only in bringing about his own destruction. President Buchanan ordered three companies of artillery from Old Point Comfort to Harper's Ferry. What was Brevet-Colonel Robert E. Lee thinking as he marched the men to surround Brown? Within thirty-six hours Brown's attempt collapsed. The day for arming the slaves had not arrived. Ten of his followers had been killed or seriously wounded; five were held for further questioning. Brown was taken to the Charleston jail.

The next link in the chain was forged on election day, November 6, 1860. The South supported Bell and Breckinridge. The North was in favor of Lincoln and Douglas. The Democrats of the North were a "house divided" against Douglas, thus costing him the presidency. The returns showed:

Candidate	Electoral Vote	Popular Vote
Lincoln	180	1,866,452
Douglas	12	1,376,957
Breckinridge	72	849,781
Bell	39	588,879

That did it. The scramble for secession began on the night of November 7th. Would the war have been averted had any one of the other three been elected? Who can say. Douglas, in a speech at Chicago, May 1, 1861, made mention of it:

"The present secession movement is the result of an enormous conspiracy which matured a year ago. The conspiracy was formed by the leaders of the secession movement twelve months ago, and they have used every means to urge it on. They have caused a man to be elected by a sectional vote, to demonstrate that the Union was divided; and when the history of the country from the time of the Lecompton Constitution to the date of Lincoln's election is written, it will appear that a scheme was maturing in the meantime which was for no end except to break up the Union. They desired to break it up, and they used the slavery question as a means. They desired to create a purely sectional vote, to demonstrate that the two sections could not live together. The disunion card dictated that the South was to carry its own elections, and that the North was to elect Lincoln. Then a united South was to assail a divided North, and gain an easy victory. This scheme was defeated by the overthrow of the disunion candidates in Kentucky, Tennessee, and Virginia. Still the grand conspiracy existed and the disunion movement was the result of it. . . ."

On March 4, 1861, in his Inaugural Address, Lincoln said: "I therefore consider that, in view of the Constitution and the laws, the Union is unbroken, and, to the extent of my ability, I shall take care, as the Constitution itself expressly enjoins upon me, that the laws of the Union be faithfully executed in all the States. . . . In doing this there need be no bloodshed or violence; and there shall be none, unless it be forced upon the national authority. The power confided to me will be used to hold, occupy and possess the property and places belonging to the government, and to collect the duties and imports; but beyond what may be necessary for these objects, there will be no invasion; no using of force against or among the people anywhere. . . ."

Friday, April 12, 1861, a mortar shell screeched over Fort Sumter.

✺ ✺ ✺

NOTES AND COMMENTS

Numbers are unnecessary since the notes parallel the text. This facilitates reading and serves as a running commentary for the research student, the scholar sincerely interested in broadening his knowledge of New Mexico. The arm-chair general we leave to the Mercy of God.

The Robinson property lay between Brookland and Soldiers Home in Washington, D. C. The enormous tree under which Webster practised his oratory stood to the left of the red brick mansion. Close by, during the Civil War, soldiers dug trenches in preparation for the defense of the city. The tree was still standing in 1940. The Robinson estate was known as the Vineyard because of the grapes grown there. It was purchased by the Friars of the Atonement in 1923 and the old mansion was converted into a seminary.

Daniel Webster—Born in Salisbury, New Hampshire, January 18, 1782. Died at Marshfield, Massachusetts, October 24, 1852. Graduated from Dartmouth in 1801. Admitted to the bar in Boston 1805. Elected to the House of Representatives as a Federalist in 1812. President Fillmore appointed him Secretary of State in 1850. Some historians contend that his death was hastened by the shock of learning that General Scott was nominated over him for the Presidency.

David Wilmot—Born in Bethany, Pa., January 20, 1814. By the time he was twenty he was practicing law at Towanda. He is best known for his opposition to the extension of slavery into the lands conquered by the United States during the Mexican War. In June, 1862 the Wilmot Proviso was embodied in the act prohibiting slavery in all existing and acquired territory. He died at Towanda, Pa., March 16, 1868.

Abolitionist—An uncompromising opponent of slavery in the United States. As a minority group, Abolitionists date from 1831, the year William Lloyd Garrison began his "Liberator" series to the year of the Emancipation Proclamation. In 1856 they nominated Gerrit Smith for President; Frederick Douglass for Vice-President.

General Stephen Watts Kearny—Born in Newark, New Jersey, August 30, 1794. Entered the Army as Lieutenant, March 12, 1812. Remained with army after the war with England.

He commanded the Army of the West that gave California and New Mexico to the United States. Served as military governor of California for three months in 1847. He wrote: "Manual for the Exercise and Maneuvering of the United States Dragoons"; "Organic Law"; "Laws for the Government of New Mexico" (also known as the "Kearny Code").

Thomas Hart Benton—Born near Hillsboro, North Carolina, March 14, 1782. Attended the University of North Carolina for a short time before moving to Tennessee, where he was admitted to the bar. Served in the War of 1812. After the war published a paper in St. Louis, Mo. Elected Senator in 1820. Called "Old Bullion" because he sponsored a gold and silver currency. Favored admission of Texas into the Union. Popular in politics for many years. Author of "Thirty Years' View." Died in Washington, D. C., in April, 1858.

John Caldwell Calhoun—Born in South Carolina, March 18, 1782. Graduated from Yale College in 1804. Opened law office at Abbeville, South Carolina. Elected to South Carolina Legislature in 1807. On June 3, 1812, as Chairman of the Committee on Foreign Affairs, he recommended war with England. 1817, Secretary of State under Monroe. 1824, one of the several candidates for the Presidency. Became Vice-President of the United States. Active in politics to the end of his life. Was recognized as spokesman for the South. Died in Washington, D. C., March 21, 1850. His last words were reported to have been: "The South, the poor South."

James Knox Polk—Born in Mecklenburg County, North Carolina, November 2, 1795. Parents moved to Tennessee in 1806. Graduated from North Carolina University in 1818. Admitted to the bar in 1820. Attracted to politics, his oratory won him the title of Napoleon of the Stump. 1823, elected to the State Legislature of Tennessee. 1824, married Sarah Childress. 1825, elected to Congress. Supported the Jackson Administration. Became Governor of Tennessee. Inaugurated President of the United States, March 4, 1845. He offered to buy New Mexico and California from Mexico because of his belief in a coast-to-coast America. These territories were eventually acquired by conquest. He died in Tennessee June 15, 1849.

Manuel Armijo—Much of what we know concerning him comes from his enemies. They are not expected to present unbiased opinions. The story of his stealing sheep and re-selling them back to his patron is legend. Actually, the Armjio family was well off; there was not need to resort to stealing. The name is still heard around Albuquerque. Manuel was already in politics by 1827. There is no doubt he schemed to become Governor of New Mexico. It is said that Magoffin paid Armijo a large sum to abandon New Mexico to Kearny. A more intense search reveals that it was Donaciano Vigil rather than Armijo who influenced the bloodless conquest. Armijo eventually returned to Chihuahua, settled for a time in Albuquerque, then Limitar, where he died. He is buried in the San Miguel Mission at Socorro.

Henry Clay—Born in Hanover County, Virginia, April 12, 1777. Studied law, opening up his first practice in Lexington, Kentucky, 1797. Served in the Kentucky Legislature from 1803 to 1806, when he went to the U. S. Senate to fill an unexpired term. Continued in politics to the end of his life. He sponsored the Compromise of 1850 in the hopes of avoiding the Civil War. He was known as The Great Compromiser. He died on June 29, 1852.

Lewis Cass—Native of New Hampshire, where he studied law for a time before moving to Ohio. Elected to the State Legislature. When thirty-one years of age he was appointed Governor of Michigan Territory. In 1838, he was named minister to France. He was U. S. Senator from 1845 to 1848. He was violently opposed to the Wilmot Proviso. He resigned as Secretary of State because President Buchanan refused to strengthen the garrison at Fort Sumter. He was sixty-four years of age when he died in 1866.

Abraham Lincoln—(1809-1865). The name speaks for itself.

Free Soil Party (1848-1855) was in reality the old Liberty Party. It advocated Free Soil, Free Labor, Free Speech, Free Men. It espoused the cause of the Wilmot Proviso, sought the abolition of slavery, fought for the repeal of the Fugitive Slave Law. Insisted that every American had the right to farm in New Mexico, California, Kansas.

Martin Van Buren—Born in Kinderhook, New York, December 5, 1782. Commenced reading law at the age of fourteen. Admitted to the bar seven years later. Married Hannah Hoes in 1807. Elected to the New York Legislature in 1812. Became a U. S. Senator in 1821. Resigned as Secretary of State in 1831 to become Minister to England. One year later became United States Vice-President. Became President in 1836. Was nominated again in 1840 but lost to William Henry Harrison. Made four other unsuccessful tries. Died at Kinderhook July 24, 1862.

William Cullen Bryant—Born at Cummington, Mass., November 3, 1794. At 10 he was translating the Latin poets; at 16 he was a sophomore in Williams College; at 18 he gave the world "Thanatopsis." Practised law for a few years in Massachusetts. Moved to New York City in 1826, to join the staff of the *Evening Post.* Three years later he became editor and part owner. He died in New York City on June 12, 1878.

James W. Marshall—When he brought samples of his find to Sacramento he was laughed out of town. Nevertheless, he staked claims and went to San Francisco where he appealed to publisher Sam Brannan to tell the world of his wonderful discovery. Prospectors jumped his claims and employed armed guards to keep him off. He lost his friends, was denied by his lawyers, laughed at by the courts. For ten years he was the butt of jokes, often beaten, spied on, swindled, threatened. It was impossible for him to make a living. He turned to the lecture platform but California beckoned and he returned twenty years later. Public opinion forced the California legislature to render financial assistance. He died in poverty August 10, 1885.

Francis Preston Blair (1791-1876)—Journalist, politician, he edited the *Washington Globe* from 1830 to 1845. His anti-slavery sentiments were responsible for his becoming one of the founders of the Republican Party. Later on in life he became a Democrat. Thomas Ritchie, editor of the *Washington Union,* supplanted Blair as administration mouthpiece. He supported Clay's Compromise, opposed slavery, resented Southern Senators. Financial reverses forced him to look for a new editor for his paper in 1851.

John Augustus Sutter- -Born in Germany, February 15, 1803. Came to American in 1834, locating in St. Louis. Crossed the Rockies in 1838 to see California. Sailed to Hawaii and Alaska. Stranded at the site of San Francisco in July, 1839. The colonizing venture at Fort Ross proving a failure, the Russians sold the place to Sutter. He founded New Helvetia (Sacramento) and was made governor of the frontier country. Shortly afterwards the territory was conquered by America. The discovery of gold on his land ruined him. In time the State Legislature voted him a pension. He settled in Pennsylvania in 1873. He died in Washington, D. C., June 17, 1880.

Donaciano Vigil—One of the unsung heroes of New Mexico. Born in Santa Fe September 6, 1802. First schooling at home, then at the parroquia under Padre Rascon. Enlisted in the army to fight Navajos. Spoke and wrote French and English as well as Spanish. Married at Santa Fe. Fathered ten children. Served in the Garrison at San Miguel del Bado and at Taos. Took part in the expedition against Texas intrusion and was promoted for his activities in the so-called Texas-Santa Fe Expedition. Fought in the Revolution of 1837, was taken prisoner, but released to serve as secretary to the new governor. He continued in political life almost to his dying day. He is mainly responsible (Magoffin to the contrary, notwithstanding) for the bloodless conquest of New Mexico by Kearny's troops; he saved the land grants for the Pueblo Indians, became Territorial governor, fought for Statehood, protected the peon against the ricos, gave New Mexico a code of laws, invited colonization, advanced commerce, fostered education, expelled land grabbers, re-settled Pecos, founded Gusano, Las Ruedas and El Macho, testified in behalf of many who retained their homes and land because of him, founded the University of New Mexico (first started in Santa Fe, years later moving to Albuquerque), and did more for New Mexico than any man before or since. Twitchell said of him: "The story of Donaciano Vigil, the firm friend of liberty and humanity, belongs to the people of New Mexico. His is a record of which people may be proud; a record which all lovers of free government will the more delight to honor as time elapses and his distinguished merits are best understood. . . ." He died in Santa Fe on August 11, 1877.

Horace Greeley—Born in Amherst, New Hampshire, on February 3, 1811. When ten years of age the family moved to Vermont. At fourteen he became a printer's apprentice. At eighteen he was a journeyman, moved to Pennsylvania and came to New York in 1831. At twenty-one he started a printing office. On April 10, 1841, he issued the first issue of the *New York Tribune*. He married Mary Young Cheney, also a writer. His influence for the Union cause was powerful. He was the Democratic Party choice for President in 1872. He died at Pleasantville, New York, November 29, 1872. Greeley Square in New York City is named for him.

Stephen Arnold Douglas—Born at Brandon, Vermont, April 23, 1813. His father died three months after his birth. At fifteen he became a cabinet-maker's apprentice. Attended Brandon Academy. Studied law. Taught school for a time at Winchester, Illinois. Admitted to the bar in 1834. He was dubbed Little Giant because his mental powers were tremendous compared to his delicate health and smallness of body. Moved to Springfield, where he became acquainted with Abraham Lincoln. Elected to State Legislature. In 1841 appointed Judge of the State Supreme Court. 1843, elected to Congress. He introduced the Kansas-Nebraska Bill, which excluded slavery from the Louisiana Purchase north of the 36° 30' line, which won him friends in the North but lost him possible election as President because of the defection of the South. He tried again in 1960 and would have won had his opponent been any other than Abraham Lincoln. He died in Chicago June 11, 1861.

John Alexander McClernand—Born in Breckinridge County, Kentucky, May 30, 1812. Admitted to the bar in 1832. Was a volunteer in the Black Hawk War. Remained in Illinois and was elected to the Legislature. Later served two terms in Congress. He supported the Compromise Bill, voted in favor of the Texas-New Mexico boundary but not in favor of New Mexico, neither as a State nor as a Territory. In the Civil War he led the command against Forty Henry, took part in the battle of Fort Donelson, led a division at Shiloh, and might have achieved even greater heights if he had not resented promotions of those he considered subordinates. In 1870 he was circuit judge for the

Sangamon, Illinois, district. Died in Springfield, Illinois, September 20, 1900.

Zachary Taylor—Born in Orange County, Virginia, November 24, 1784. His father was a Colonel in the Revolutionary War. After the war the family settled in Kentucky. In 1808, Zachary was appointed a lieutenant in the Seventh Infantry. That same year he married Margaret Smith of Maryland. Was occupied with the Black Hawk and other campaigns until transferred to Florida for service in the Seminole War. In 1838 he was appointed chief of command in Florida. In 1845 he was ordered to the defense of Texas. He is best known for his work during the Mexican War. He was inaugurated as President on March 5, 1849. In his first Annual Message to Congress he said: "The people of New Mexico will also, it is believed, at no very distant period, present themselves for admission into the Union. Preparatory to the admission of California and New Mexico the people of each will have instituted for themselves a republican form of government, 'laying its foundation in such principles and organizing its powers in such form as to them shall seem most likely to effect their safety and happiness.' By awaiting their action all causes of uneasiness may be avoided and confidence and kind feeling preserved. With a view of maintaining the harmony and tranquillity so dear to all, we should abstain from the introduction of those exciting topics of a sectional character which have hitherto produced painful apprehension in the public mind; and I repeat the solemn warning of the first and most illustrious of my predecessors against furnishing 'any ground for characterizing parties by geographical discriminations' . . ." He died in Washington, July 9, 1850. He is buried in Louisville, Kentucky.

Colonel John Munroe—Born in Scotland c. 1890. Family came to the United States soon after. Entered West Point, graduating fourth in the Class of 1812. Took part in the war against England. Served under Taylor in the Seminole War and Mexican War. Was military commander in New Mexico to organize it for a possible war with Texas. Died in New York, April 28, 1861.

Millard Fillmore—Born in Cayuga county, New York, February 7, 1800. Married Abigail Powers in 1826. Admitted to the bar in 1827. Elected to the State Legislature in 1828. Elected to Congress in 1832. Elected Vice-President, he succeeded to the office of President upon the death of Taylor. After his wife died he married Caroline C. McIntosh. When asked by Congress whether he would admit New Mexico into the Union he said he would first have to clear the Texas Claim. He also said: "No government can be established for New Mexico, either State or Territorial, until it shall be first ascertained what New Mexico is, and what are her limits and boundaries. These cannot be fixed or known till the line of division between her and Texas shall be ascertained and established; and numerous and weighty reasons conspire, in my judgment, to show that this divisional line should be established by Congress with the assent of the government of Texas. In the first place, this seems by far the most prompt mode of proceeding by which the end can be accomplished. If judicial proceedings were resorted to, such proceedings would necessarily be slow, and years would pass by, in all probability, before the controversy could be ended. So great a delay in this case is to be avoided if possible. Such delay would be every way inconvenient, and might be the occasion of disturbances and collisions. For the same reason I would, with the utmost deference to the wisdom of Congress, express a doubt of the expediency of the appointment of commissioners, and of an examination, estimate, and an award of indemnity to be made by them. This would be but a species of arbitration, which might last as long as a suit at law . . ." Fillmore died in Buffalo, New York, March 8, 1874.

James Buchanan—Born in Pennsylvania April 23, 1791. Graduated Dickinson College, Pennsylvania, 1809. Practiced law in Lancaster, 1812. Enlisted in the war against England for the defense of Baltimore against British troops. Elected to Pennsylvania legislature in 1814. Elected to Congress in 1820. Inaugurated as President of the United States on March 4, 1857. He was of the opinion that both New Mexico and Arizona would do better if split: "I recomment to Congress the establishment of a Territorial government over Arizona, incorporating with it such portions of New Mexico as they may deem expedient. I need scarcely adduce arguments in support of this recommendation. We are bound to protect the lives and the property of our citizens inhabiting Arizona, and these are now without any efficient protection... Besides, the proposed Territory is believed to be rich in mineral and agricultural resources . . ." He had little use for New Mexico; devoting most of his time to Nebraska, Kansas, Utah and Arizona. He died in Pennsylvania on June 1, 1868.

Franklin Pierce—Born in New Hampshire November 23, 1804. Attended Bowdoin College in 1820. Admitted to the bar in 1827, he opened his office in Hillsboro, the town of his birth. Elected to State legislature in 1829. In 1834 he married Jane Means Appleton, the daughter of the president of Bowdoin. Served in the Mexican War. Became President March 4, 1853. He was greatly concerned for "Bleeding Kansas" as he called it. He recommended to Congress the extension of the land system over the Territories of Utah and New Mexico, with such modifications as their peculiarities would require. He died at Concord, October 8, 1869.

John Brown—Born in Torrington, Conn., May 9, 1800. His father served as a captain in the War of Independence. Family moved to Ohio when John was five. After witnessing the abuse of a small slave boy he swore eternal war against slavery. He devoted his life to abolitionistic idealogy. He hoped to establish colleges for the fugitive slaves in Pennsylvania and New England. Because of the Wilmot Proviso he felt it his duty to protect Nebraska, Utah, New Mexico and Kansas—by force of arms, if necessary—from slave holders. He is best known for his activities in Kansas and his raid on the military arsenal at Harper's Ferry. It seems ironic that he, a major factor in the war between States, should have been captured by Robert E. Lee who was to command the Confederate forces in the struggle. Brown's sons were indoctrinated with his philosophy and gave their lives (two of them anyway) for the cause. He was anxious to make a martyr of himself in an effort to arouse New England into more realistic activity than the printed page and long-winded speeches. He gave his life on December 2, 1859. His restless spirit marched through the war.

Sam Houston (1793-1863)—A native of Virginia. The family moved to Tennessee after his father's death. He preferred to live among the Cherokee Indians rather than clerk in the Maryville village store. He enlisted in the War of 1812 and remained in the service until 1818 when he resigned to study law. He hung out his shingle in Lebanon, Tennessee, and was later elected to Congress (1823). He had applied for a land grant in Texas as early as 1822 but he is better known for his work during the fight for independence. He became President of the Republic on September 5, 1836. After Texas entered the Union he became U. S. Senator (Feb. 21, 1846) and worked to help the cause of the new state. He was opposed to the Secession Convention. He died at Huntsville, Texas, July 26, 1863.

William Learned Marcy (1786-1857)—Not to be confused with various other contemporaries of the same name in the civil and military service. Captain R. B. Marcy, of the Topographical Engineers built Fort Marcy in Santa Fe and named it for the Secretary of War, William L. Marcy, a native of Mass. William made several unsuccessful bids for the Presidency. Defeated in 1852, he gave his support to Pierce who appointed him Secretary of State in 1853. After graduating from Brown University Marcy changed his residence from New England to New York where he continued to fight for the emancipation of slaves. The nation is ever grateful to him for his work with foreign powers. His dislike of Buchanan caused him to retire from political life. He died four months after his resignation.

The Gadsen Purchase—A vast tract of land embracing 45,535 square miles, purchased by the government from Mexico in 1854. This territory, bounded on the north by the Gila river, on the east by the Rio Grande, the west by the Colorado river, was acquired by treaty and the payment of $10,000,000. It included the southern parts of the present States of New Mexico and Arizona. The name derived from the fact that James Gadsden was U. S. Minister to Mexico at the time.

Benjamin Francis Stringfellow—Taught the doctrine that wherever slavery spread, the interest of the laborer and the capitalist; the slave and his master, are identical. They were in no way in conflict or opposed but rather complimented each other.

Andrew Horatio Reeder (1807-1864)—Born in Pennsylvania and practiced law at Easton before entering politics. In 1854 President Pierce appointed him first governor of the newly formed Territory of Kansas. The legislature and its allies fought him until he was removed from office August 15. He was charged with delay in reaching Kansas and in getting its government under way. He was also accused of usurpation, lack of sympathy with the people, land speculation, not submitting tamely and obediently to pro-slavery dictation. His administration ran its troubled course in less than a year. It achieved no very signal success. A stranger to border life and its ways, he never found the right approach to bring it within his grasp. President Lincoln appointed him Brigadier-General but he declined the offer saying he was too old to lead an army. He returned to Easton where he died.

New England Emigrant Aid Company—Founded by Eli Thayer of Mass. in 1854 for the purpose of sending 20,000 Free Soilers into Kansas each year. Actually Thayer hoped to make substantial profits from handling the business of prospective settlers in Kansas.

Dr. Charles Robinson—An Abolitionist from New England, he helped locate and found the city of Lawrence, Kansas, named for the secretary of the New England Emigrant Aid Company. A Free-Soiler and a Free-State man, he fought to unify Kansas hoping that there would be no pro or con questions about slavery or politics until Kansas was admitted into the Union. He was elected governor of Kansas January 5, 1856 under the Topeka Constitution. He was chief in command, with the rank of Major-General, although he had never seen military service, during the Wakarusa War. Several unsuccessful attempts were made on his life. It was agreed that he was a better medical man than a politician.

Eli Thayer (1818-1899)—A graduate of Brown University, he founded Oread Institute for Young Ladies in Worcester, Mass. He was a member of Congress from 1856 to 1861. He became an inventor of note receiving patents for a sectional safety steam boiler, a boiler cleaner and a hydraulic elevator. He favored the Wilmot Proviso and was an ardent Abolitionist.

Preston Smith Brooks (1819-1857)—A graduate of South Carolina College, he enlisted in the Mexican War as a captain of the famous Palmetto regiment distinguished for bravery and action. Elected to Congress in 1853, he took the offensive against Senator Sumner and gave him a severe beating with a gutta-percha cane. He ultimately pleaded guilty and paid a fine of three hundred dollars. He was re-elected to Congress and died in office January 27, 1857.

Charles Sumner (1811-1874)—A lawyer from Boston, famous for opposing what he considered the major side of an issue and the champion of the underdog. He opposed slavery, the Mexican War and the defiant attitude of Southern Senators. He was the recognized leader of the anti-slavery movement in Mass. As a Senator he championed the cause of Free Soilers. His debates in favor of Kansas so infuriated Brooks that this latter gave him a sound beating. He remained a political figure until death.

Robert Toombs (1810-1885)—Began practicing law under a special Act of the Georgia Legislature because he was under age, being twenty at the time and already an alumnus of three colleges. He became the leader of the States Rights Whigs of Georgia and refused to support General Scott for President. He was a U. S. Senator from 1853 to 1861. He headed the Peace Movement in Georgia in 1864 and sailed for Europe in order to avoid arrest. He refused to take the oath of allegiance and never again had the privileges of citizenship. He died in Washington, Georgia, December 15, 1885.

John Charles Fremont (1813-1890)—No story of Colorado, New Mexico, Arizona and California is completely told without Fremont, explorer, adventurer, soldier, politician. A native of Georgia he first attracts public attention for his expeditions into the Rockies. He aided in the conquest of California during the Mexican War, and as civil and military governor concluded those articles of capitulation by which Mexico gave exclusive possession of that territory to the U. S. He was the first candidate of the newly formed Republican Party in 1856, for the Presidency. He served as a major-general during the Civil War. He was governor of Arizona from 1878 to 1881. He died in New York City, July 13, 1890.

William Lewis Dayton (1807-1864)—A lawyer and Senator from New Jersey, he was proposed as Vice-President on the Fremont ticket in 1856. He was Minister to France at the time of his death, December 1, 1864.

Samuel D. Lecompte—A Kansas pioneer who claimed that partisan bias never tarnished his judicial record as Chief Justice. He was accused of neglecting his duties in favor of pro-slavery interests. Lecompton, Kansas, was named for him. He bowed out of politics and ended his days as a country lawyer.

Robert J. Walker—A native of Pennsylvania but raised in Mississippi. He was appointed by President Buchanan to succeed Geary as governor of Kansas. He was active, shrewd, lippy, intelligent and politically adroit. Small in stature, he was capable of handling big situations. He was the Senator who introduced the Bill for the American Recognition of Texas Independence. He resigned as governor because he refused to be a part of enforcing slavery laws. He advocated the Alaska Purchase and opposed the impeachment of President Johnson. He died in Washington, D. C. November 11, 1869, being sixty-eight years of age.

John Bell (1797—1869)—A native of Tennessee. He practiced law until 1827 when elected to Congress. He was Secretary of War under President Harrison. He was bitterly opposed to the Kansas-Nebraska Bill and the Lecompton Constitution.

John Cabell Breckinridge (1821-1875)—A native of Kentucky, he gave up the practice of law to serve in the Mexican War. He was a member of Congress from 1851 to 1855. He became Vice-President under Buchanan. He was a major-general in the Confederate Army and Secretary of War under President Jefferson Davis.

Chapter Two

THE TEXAS CLAIM

Ever since the days of Stephen Austin, Texans were agreed that their sympathies were in the direction pointing to slavery. Many envisioned plantations equal to the best in the South. A number of Texans resented the attitude of Northern soldiers during the Mexican War, and, while General Taylor was appreciative of the battle spirit of the Texas Rangers, he chafed at their attitude of independence and dispassionate posture toward authority; their seeming contempt for superior officers of the regular army. As President he was having his troubles with them again. At San Jacinto Santa Anna and Houston agreed that the Rio Grande should be the boundary between Mexico and the new Republic of Texas. Many were of the opinion that both generals had in mind the southern boundary; others thought it meant the Rio Grande from its very source. In the urgency of forming a government, electing a legislature, founding a capitol, charting a course, officials gave scant heed to boundaries as they sought to bring order out of chaos. When the republic realized its financial embarrassment and chased in every direction to alleviate the situation the subject was brought up. Santa Fe at the end of the trail had no right to American money for two reasons: it belonged to Texas; it was sending the money to Mexico which could in turn be converted into instruments of war against Texas. Houston was not satisfied that Santa Anna was content with the humiliation of San Jacinto. Mexico agreed to the Rio Grande as the boundary, argued those looking for an easy way out of bankruptcy, and this meant all the land to and including Albuquerque, Las Vegas and Santa Fe. Vice-President Mirabeau B. Lamar maintained that the agreement gave Texas the right to all the land up to the area included in the 36° 30′ section of the river. His was a voice crying in the wilderness until September 9, 1838, when he became President of the Republic of Texas. His scheme for the conquest of Santa Fe operated through William G. Cooke who published his request for volunteers on April 28, 1841.

"Having been authorized by His Excellency, the President, to organize a military force for the purpose of opening a commercial intercourse with the people of Santa Fe, for which purpose troops are necessary to escort the merchandise through Comanche territory, I respectfully address myself to the young men of the country. The object I have stated. The terms are: all who arm, mount, and equip themselves, will receive the pay of mounted gunmen; will serve for six months, or until the return of the expedition, and will be supplied with subsistence, etc. The companies will consist of fifty-six, rank and file, and elect their own company officers. The field and staff officers will be appointed by the President. Ten large road wagons will be furnished by the government to the merchants who desire to send their goods to that market, and the troops will secure their transportation. As this expedition will not only furnish an ample field for adventure on the march, but conduce by a successful result to the benefit of our country. I anticipate, on the part of the young men whose crops are already in the ground, a rediness to unite with us, and contribute by their loyalty, as well as their courage, to sustain the interest and the glory of our young republic. I am authorized to announce the names of Edward Burleson, Antonio Navarro, G. Van Ness and myself to represent our government with the people of Santa Fe . . ."

Manuel Armijo of Santa Fe was not without his spies. Excitement was as intense in New Mexico as it was in Texas. The governor was quite content with the "commercial intercourse" from Missouri and proceeded to offer armed resistance if necessary to dispel the illusions of might and power on the part of the young republic. Comancheros, ciboleros, mail carriers, hunters, sheep herders were all his eyes reporting every move of the advancing Texans. He dispatched messengers to Las Vegas, El Bado, Mora, Questa, Anton Chico, Albuquerque, Taos, Valencia, Belen, Socorro, Manzano, Tome calling on all to come to the defense of their country. Armijo had been suspicious of Lamar since April 1840, when he received a letter addressed to the citizens of Santa Fe in which the Texan said that he was glad that the United States and France recognized the new republic as a sister nation whose commerce "was extending with a power and celerity seldom equalled in the history of nations." He appealed to Santa Feans to give hearty co-operation in intercommercial relations and take advantage of the benefits accruing to the proximity of the neighboring republic. He hoped to send commissioners to visit Santa Fe in September to explain to the governor the vastness of the republic, its seacoast, condition of the country, and other correlative interests. Lamar, too, had his special agents. These informed him of the unrest and discontent under Armijo. He was convinced New Mexicans would receive his troops with open arms. Besides the profits of the Santa Fe trade, Lamar had an eye open for a possible route to the Pacific. He envisioned Texas merchantmen on the Rio Grande, the Atlantic and the Pacific. The economics was assuaged only by territorial expansion and an increase in seaports. This Lamar firmly believed. Mexican territory stood between the dream and fulfillment. The logical place to begin was at Santa Fe.

The boundaries of Texas as understood by Congress were approved on December 19, 1836. This Act of Congress provided that from, and after, its passage the "civil and political jurisdiction of this Republic be, and is, hereby declared to extend to the following boundaries, to wit: beginning at the mouth of the Sabine river, and running west along the Gulf of Mexico three leagues from land, to the mouth of the Rio Grande, thence up the principal stream of the said river to its source, thence due north to the forty-second degree of north latitude, thence along the boundary line as defined in the treaty between the United States and Spain to the beginning . . ." This self-same Act authorized the president to begin negotiations with the United States as soon as in his opinion the public interest required it in order to ascertain and define the boundary line as agreed upon in the said treaty.

The United States was amendable to the treaty establishing boundaries. But Mexico refused to come to terms possibly because of her own uncertain state of affairs, or, as is more likely, Santa Anna cultivated re-opening of hostilities since he declared that a state of war still existed between Texas and Mexico even though no actual fighting was taking place. He toyed with the idea of marching into Texas and would have done so if he thought it safe to leave Mexico City in the hands of a legislature seeking to oust him. To leave the capitol would be to court disaster. This is a link forged in the chain by every dictator. Only the names change. His vacillation caused Texas to breathe easier and devote more time to expansion. Another battle at this time would not be as easy nor as bloodless as San Jacinto. The boundaries, as set forth in this Act of Congress, took in a line running from the mouth of the Rio Grande "up the principal stream of the said river to its source." It was on this that Lamar based his claim over territory which had never been included in the Province of Texas by Mexico, much less by Spain in speaking of Coahuila-Texas. Military escorts along the Santa Fe Trail knew exactly where to stop so as not to set foot in foreign soil; Pike, Long and others were told in no uncertain terms where the United States ended and where New Mexico began. Santa Fe had no illusions as to the boundaries of New Mexico. Regulars were marching up from Chihuahua. Militia men were gathering from all corners. New Mexicans may have been dissatisfied with Armijo but he was preferable to the Tejanos about whom they had heard so many terrible things. Propaganda was rampant. Gossip seduced the fit and unfit. New Mexico had a hangover from tall tales for which Texas is so famous. At the moment they seemed mighty real as New Mexicans imagined their women outraged, their churches desecrated, their men killed and children strangled. A Tejano was not the same as an Americano. They had heard so many things. So, they waited.

Houston had never enforced jurisdiction over any part of New Mexico simply because he felt there was no legal basis in reality upon which to establish claim other than the contention of a few who voiced the opinion that this land was always considered a part of Texas traditionally although no one could say how the rumor started. Possibly the San Antonio de Bexar—El Paso del Norte, Ciudad Santa Fe mail route had something to do with it. Texas-New Mexico relationship was lost in antiquity. Hardly a basis for establishing a claim. Lamar was imbued with the idea that the only way to settle the claim was to adopt measures that would leave no doubt. The Rio Grande, from its very source, would be the boundary. In his annual message to Congress in 1839, he hinted at the possibility of a "Gulf of Mexico to the Pacific" Texas. Included in this was the hope or expectation of slicing off Arizona and California from the Mexican Republic and annexing it to the seaport-hungry Lone Star nation. So clear was the picture in his own mind that he expected no dissenting voice when he approached Congress for financial aid to promote the scheme. His optimism did not rub off. Rejected in the House as well as Congress he sought consolation by penning a letter to Armijo which the governor scorned to answer. Nor was the promised commission sent in September.

Anson Jones, who succeeded to the presidency, wrote in 1844: "The Santa Fe Expedition was not only unauthorized by Congress, but, in effect, positively inhibited. I voted against it on all occasions, and the project received but a few votes. The appropriations for its expenses were made without the authority of law, and by the despotic exercise of executive power, which no monarch would have dared venture upon in these times. This administration will be described by the poet in two lines:

'A chase of silly hopes and fears,
Begun by folly, closed in tears.'"

Wrote Rives: "Not only was the expedition inadequate in size but it turned out to be inadequately equipped for the hardships of the journey. The fact is that nobody knew anything about the country to be traversed. Apart from the latitude and longitude of Santa Fe, they had no notion of where they were going. A Mexican who accompanied them had been a trapper on the headwaters of the Red (Canadian) river, and had been in New Mexico, but he was utterly lost long before he reached the New Mexican settlements . . ."

News of the disaster to Texas arms filtered through to Sam Houston who was elected President. Congress was so outraged that it immediately passed an Act extending the boundaries of the Republic to include Upper and Lower California, the States of Chihuahua and Sonora, the Territory of New Mexico as well as parts of Tamaulipas, Coahuila, Durango and Sinaloa. Texas absorbed an additional population of two million people, on paper. Houston argued that the Act would serve no practical purpose. He refused to be any part of a mad scheme that would make Texas the laughing stock of the world. He promptly vetoed the bill. Nevertheless, Congress passed it over his veto. Suddenly, the matter was dropped. Shortly afterwards the Republic bowed out to join the ever growing Union of States. This action was followed by the War with Mexico and the year of Manifest Destiny saw fulfillment in a coast-to-coast America. The Hidalgo Treaty was signed near Mexico City on February 20, 1848. Under its terms Mexico renounced all claim to Texas, and agreed to recognize the Rio Grande as the boundary between the two countries. Mexico, on her part, ceded to the United States all the land now included in the States of California, Nevada, Utah, most of New Mexico (more was acquired by a later purchase), Arizona, Colorado and Wyoming. The Texas-Santa Fe Expedition disaster, or one should say the maltreatment of prisoners, converted Anson Jones to Lamar's way of thinking. He said:

"There was no subject more explicitly agreed upon, understood and settled, between Major Donelson and myself, in 1845, than that the Rio Grande, from its mouth to its source, was the true and rightful boundary of Texas, and that the United States would never agree to any other adjustment of the boundary with Mexico than the one defined by the said Act (1836). That boundary was fully recognized on the part of the United States. No other was ever dreamed of . . ."

Jones was further convinced when he saw the Treaty of Guadalupe Hidalgo. To it was appended a map showing the Rio Grande, from its mouth to its source, as the boundary of Texas. Article five of the Treaty read:

"The boundary line between the two republics shall commence in the Gulf of Mexico, three leagues from land, opposite the mouth of the Rio Grande, otherwise called Rio Bravo del Norte, or opposite the mouth of its deepest branch, if it should have more than one branch emptying directly into the sea; from thence up the middle of that river following the deepest channel, where it has more than one, to the point where it strikes the southern boundary of New Mexico, thence, westwardly along the whole southern boundary of New Mexico (which runs north of the town called El Paso) to its western termination; thence, northward along the western line of New Mexico, until it intersects the first branch of the river Gila (or if it should not intersect any branch of that river, then to the point on the said line nearest to such branch, and thence in a direct line to the same); thence down the middle of the said branch of the said river, until it empties into the Rio Colorado; thence across the Rio Colorado, following the division line between Upper and Lower California, to the Pacific Ocean. . . . In order to designate the boundary line with due precision, upon authoritative maps, and to establish upon the ground landmarks which shall show the limits of both republics, as described in the present article, the two governments shall each appoint a commissioner and a surveyor, who, before the expiration of one year from the date of the exchange of ratifications of this treaty, shall meet at the port of San Diego and proceed to run and mark the said boundary in its whole course to the mouth of the Rio Bravo del Norte. They shall keep journals and make out plans of their operations; and the result agreed upon by them shall be deemed a part of this treaty, and shall have the same force as if it were inserted therein. . . . The boundary line established by this article shall be religiously respected by each of the republics, and no change shall ever be made therein, except by the express and free consent of both nations . . ."

During the War with Mexico boundary disputes were momentarily cast aside for the more serious business of defense of country. When Governor James Pinckney Henderson realized that the United States intended to maintain the territories taken from Mexico without adjusting the claim to the source of the Rio Grande, he sent a letter of protest to the American State Department. He questioned the government's right to take what belonged to Texas. Other pressing needs commanded the Department's attention at the time so his letter was ignored. Since the nation was still at war he did not demand an explanation but asked the Texas Legislature to grant him permission to take personal command of the troops in the field. He took charge of the 2nd Texas Regiment during the Battle of Monterrey and was appointed commissioner to negotiate terms for the surrender of the city. After the war he resumed his duties as governor, refusing a second term in order to devote more time to the practice of law. Little more was said about the Texas claim during the remainder of his term as governor, although he was assured that the rights of Texas would be respected. He was given to understand that the provisional government set up in Santa Fe was temporary in character. Acting on this assumption the Second Legislative Assembly of Texas created the county of Santa Fe, Texas, and called it the Eleventh Judicial District. Judge Spruce M. Baird was dispatched as legal authority over the new district. He was kindly received. When ready to hold court he was told he was out of order and forbidden entrance to the courtroom. When this incident was relayed to Austin the State Senate was not only horrified, it was petrified. No resistance was expected especially from native New Mexicans looked upon as unfit to govern themselves or even the Pueblo

Indians. Baird arrived at a most inopportune moment. Whigs controlled the city. They were opposed to Texas control, to a man. Perhaps the only time in the history of New Mexico they were agreed. No doubt the story of the Civil War in New Mexico can be told in one volume. New Mexican politics needs a hundred more. Col. John M. Washington, commanding officer in Santa Fe at the time of Baird's arrival, took a dislike to the judge and fought him at every turn. The Texan stood his ground, determined to practice law privately until Texas and the United States arrived at an agreement. He availed himself of every opportunity to register complaints and asked the federal officials to recognize his appointment since it was their government that had unlawfully seized property belonging to the State of Texas. He took time out to wander off to Glagow, Kentucky, his birthplace, where he courted Emmacetta G. Bowdry, bringing her to Santa Fe after the marriage. It was a pinch-penny existence those first few years. When Santa Feans sought out a lawyer they did not pick Spruce Baird. He was a defiant one, but all his table pounding did not bring him what he called his rights. Gradually some sort of compromise was worked out and better days dawned. By the time the Civil War broke out he was Attorney-General of New Mexico and Indian Agent to the Navajo. He never lost his heart to New Mexico nor his loyalty to Texas. When the conflict became a reality he returned to the Lone Star State, where he recruited and commanded the 4th Regiment, Arizona Brigade, Confederate Army, serving along the northwest frontier. He was obsessed with the idea of marching his troops into Santa Fe but his superiors found means for keeping him occupied for the duration. He was paroled in 1865, and two years later opened a law office in Trinidad, Colorado, later removing to Maxwell's village of Cimarron, New Mexico, where he died June 5, 1872.

Meantime General Taylor took office. George T. Wood succeeded Henderson as governor of Texas. He took up the cudgels for Baird. He was ignored as completely as Henderson. A portion of the land claimed by Texas lay below the line included in the Missouri Compromise. It was agreed when Texas entered the Union that, with regard to territory south of that line, Texans were free to parcel it into smaller slave States if they so chose. Anti-slave groups argued that all the territory included in the Hidalgo Treaty, with the exception of Texas, was closed to slavery simply because Mexican law abolished it. Opponents countered that the region around Santa Fe was definitely within the boundaries of Texas, hence not subject to Mexican laws. The answer to this was that Texas was speaking for land over which it held no jurisdiction whatsoever. Furthermore, Mexico never looked upon the disputed area as slave. Apart from that there were no slaves in Santa Fe for Mexico to free. To substantiate their claim that Texas had no jurisdiction over the so-called Santa Fe county they sought out politically influential people and induced them to bring pressure to bear on the Federal government, stressing their contention that all the territory west of the 100th meridian was beyond a shadow of a doubt no part of Texas.

On March 6, 1849, Governor Wood addressed a fiery letter to the legislature. He recommended that all the resources of the State of Texas be placed at his disposal to be used in fighting for the rights of Texans. He would resort to arms if necessary. He was precise: "The bare denial of justice involved in an attempt to wrest from us this portion of our State is reproach enough. To succeed in that attempt would be a reproach still deeper. For Texas to submit passively to such despoilment would be the deepest reproach of all. I would recommend that ample power be conferred on the executive of the State, and ample means be placed at his disposal, and that it be expressly required of him to raise the proper issue and contest it, not by demonstrating in argument the justness of our claim, nor by reference to our statutes, but with the whole power and resources of the State. . . ."

He spoke at the proper moment. The populace was aroused and ready to back him to the last man. All of Texas now agreed that her claim to Santa Fe was as valid as its title to Point Isabel, Laredo and other Rio Grande towns. Just because Texas came into the Union was no excuse for the United States to impose boundaries. Anti-slavers brought in the further argument that Santa Fe had never been included in the territory known as the State of Coahuila-Texas, nor within the Province of Texas under Spanish or Mexican rule, nor had the Republic of Texas overtly established jurisdiction. Lamar's expedition was just what he said, not what some inferred it to be. He sought to establish trade relations with New Mexico and invited Santa Fe to protection under the Texas flag, not to seize the city as rightful

Texas property. The territory between the Nueces and the Rio Grande had been part of the State of Tammaulipas before the revolution and the Republic of Texas never exercised jurisdiction over it although claiming it from the start. This argument was relished neither by the Free Soilers nor the Federal government. Taylor was denounced as an aggressor. They implied in their arguments that his march from the Nueces to the Rio Grande was subject to investigation. The government pointed out that the march had nothing to do with the Santa Fe claim. It steadfastly maintained that New Mexico was conquered territory; not a part of Texas. Wrote the editor of the *Houston Telegraph*:

"We hope that the legislature will promptly comply with the recommendations of Governor Wood, and we are confident that the people of Texas will, to a man, sustain them with the whole resources of the State. The banner of the Lone Star shall again be unfurled—not for offense, but for defense, and those who oppose we shall crush and destroy."

Before Wood was able to organize the fight his term of office expired and he was succeeded by the even more belligerent Peter Hansborough Bell. War was inevitable. Born and reared a Southerner, Bell was a successful businessman in Petersbury, Virginia, until he interested himself in the Lone Star's bid for independence. He enlisted in the cavalry under Karnes and took part in the action at San Jacinto. After the war he continued in the service as a Texas Ranger under Jack Hays. He fought at Buena Vista in the Mexican War. He was twice elected governor of Texas. Prior to the completion of his second term he resigned, ostensibly to fill a vacancy in Congress caused by the death of David Kaufman, but really to carry on the fight in Washington. He died in North Carolina but his remains were transplanted in Texas soil in 1898. He was just as determined as Wood on insisting that the United States respect the rights of Texas. He was also willing to resort to the use of arms if necessary. The legislature, less sanguine, extended an olive branch. It asked Bell not to be so bombastic about war when perhaps a peaceful settlement was possible. It also asked Bell to appoint a commissioner to organize the counties of Presidio, Worth and Santa Fe. He selected Robert Simpson Neighbors, the man who had been named with Captain Randolph B. Marcy to make the surveys for the Indian reserves within Texas. In time he exercised greater influence over the Indians of Texas than any other white man of his generation. He was to them what William Johnson had been to the Mohawks. But negotiating for Santa Fe was not the same as bringing Indians to terms. He returned to Santa Fe not because he lacked ability but because officials in Santa Fe accorded him the same treatment meted out to Baird. He returned to his Indians and was killed by Edward Cornett (September 14, 1859).

Neighbors failed in Santa Fe for three reasons: (a) President Taylor's demand that a convention be held for the two-fold purpose of drawing up and framing a constitution as well as to apply for admission into the Union; (b) The attitude of the military and governmental officials in Santa Fe; (c) Attitude of the populace. During the convention Neighbors noted that a pronouncement was made against slavery which indicated that though the section demanded by Texas was acknowledged to be open to slavery should the people so decide, the fact remained that they were opposed. Several leaders made grandiose speeches safeguarding this action as one of grave necessity for the unity of the nation. Donaciano Vigil voiced the sentiments of the Spanish speaking when he mentioned slavery as beneath the dignity of New Mexicans. President Taylor looked to Colonel Munroe to carry out his wishes.

The convention sat from May 15 to May 25, 1850, drawing up a constitution which excluded slavery. By June 12 the work of the convention was approved by the people of New Mexico. Taylor sent Munroe a note of congratulation. The boundary issue could now be brought before the Supreme Court. Taylor proved too optimistic. He had reckoned without the opposition of Congress. Munroe watched Neighbors formulate El Paso county and strike at the organization of other New Mexico counties as requested by Texas. In his own quiet manner, greatly aided by Ortiz, Jose Antonio Martinez, Gallegos, Vigil, Delgado and Perea he organized the opposition to discomfort Neighbors.

Neighbors returned to Texas bitter and disillusioned. His report was not very complimentary to New Mexicans. Vitrol, anger, fire and brimstone punctuated his remarks. Press and people were aroused. He stirred up a hornet's nest. War and war alone would settle the issue. Texans beat to quarters. Drums sounded along the Colorado, the Nueces, the Rio Grande, the Pecos.

"We entered the Union because we wanted to; we will

leave it when we want to—and we want to now." That was the talk heard from Austin to the settlements. At mass meetings speakers demanded that the legislature draft all men of military age to march to Santa Fe and force the capitulation of Fort Marcy. They asked that all the U. S. troops be taken out of Santa Fe county—dead or alive. Governor Bell as especially vehement in his requests. He personally wished to lead Texans into Santa Fe, where he would compel New Mexicans to respect the laws of Texas and force them to fly the Texas flag. If the United States prevented such action by force of arms, Texas would not hold herself responsible for the bloodshed encumbent on patriots. If a stubborn and stupid government insisted on making martyrs of Texas then add Santa Fe to the Alamo and Goliad as the price of freedom.

The governor wrote to Taylor demanding to know why he issued orders to Colonel Munroe, and exactly what was his purpose in preventing Texas from assuming jurisdiction over territory rightfully hers. The sound of the tocsin was louder as Mars stirred from sleep. Bell summoned a special session of the legislature for August 12th. Goodwill ambassadors were sent across the sympathetic South to voice the cause of Texas. Radicals gave it dimension all out of proportion, using it as a stick against Taylor and his administration. Editors accelerated and winged catastrophe as they dressed their editorials in mourning. Cataclysm and convulsion weakened the hopes of the South for peace. In every Southern State voluntary companies drilled in preparation for the march to Texas. Mississippi sent a personal representative with a formal offer of assistance. Troops were readied. All awaited the nod from Bell.

Patiently Taylor weathered the storm. Today, tomorrow, New Mexico would have Statehood. He had the same answer for all: He no longer had the power to decide the question of boundary; there was no need for his interference; authority rested in the Supreme Court of the United States. On the other hand, the Supreme Court hesitated to act until Congress recognized New Mexico as a State. When the legislature met in Austin on August 12th, Bell recommended the adoption of such measures "as are necessary for the occupation of Santa Fe with a force ample to quell the rebellious spirit now prevailing there, and to enable us to firmly establish the jurisdiction of the State over it."

Taylor remanded the case to Congress. Senator Sam Houston, quick to resent any accusation against Texas, glared defiantly at all the assembled Senators, took the floor of the chamber and shouted to all that Texas would defend her rights. "Texas is loyal and devoted, but she is sensitive, too. She always appreciates her adversaries; she loves her friends, and when duty bids her take her stand she never counts her enemies. The Army of the United States marched there to enforce a wrong upon her, would be weak and powerless. She will not submit to wrong; she asks for nothing but what is right. . . ."

Nine years later, on July 23, 1859, he wrote: "No claim to Santa Fe or New Mexico had ever been asserted or pretended until after the battle of San Jacinto, when in my letter to General Rusk, I asserted my right to it." In the same speech in which he accused Taylor as ever having been violently opposed and prejudiced against Texas he apologized for the meeting taking place in Texas for the purpose of secession and he must ask the Senate not to interpret this action as completely the voice of Texas. Turning to the chairman he said:

"Think you, sir, after the difficulties they have encountered to get into the Union, that you can whip them out of it? No, sir. New Mexico cannot whip them out of it, even with the aid of the United States troops. We shed our blood to get into it, and we have now no arms to turn against it. But we have not looked for aggression upon us from the Union. We have looked to the Union of these States and its noble course to vindicate our rights, and to accord us what in justice we claim— what we have claimed—and less than which we can never claim."

Houston told some friends that he was ready to hasten back to Texas to take command of another army of conquerors who would march on Santa Fe.

The meeting of August 12th dissolved in talk. The meeting on December 26th denied Bell the authority to move on Santa Fe. Taylor's message to Congress on New Mexican affairs (June 17) denied any order for troops to resist the claim of Texas by force of arms. He upheld the right of the government to hold the territory under dispute until the Supreme Court pronounced its decision. The answer from Texas was that she stood by ready to "use her whole power and resources." It irked Congress to be sitting on a powder keg. News of the first shot was momentarily expected. St. Louis dispatches informed Congress (June 25) that the New Mexico Constitution was on its way.

Southern members of Congress immediately went into a huddle for concert measures. Added to the embroilio of the Wilmot Provision, the anxiety of Taylor's hopes for New Mexico as a State, the crisis of the Compromise, was the question as to whether or not New Mexico had any right to a Constitution prior to settling the Texas claim. The more radical were opposed to Taylor's New Mexico proposals as an insult to Texas; the less radical accused Taylor as using New Mexico to block the Omnibus Bill.

There was a ray of hope for Texas. She had more supporters in Washington fighting for her claim than New Mexico had fighting for Statehood. Besides, Southerners were fed up with Taylor's New Mexico policy. On July 1st, Southern Whigs selected three men—Robert Toombs, Humphrey Marshall and C. M. Conrad—to visit Taylor and prevail upon him to change his tactics for his present blandishments incited to war. They decided to make individual calls. Toombs was so worried about the interview that he was a nervous wreck before he go as far as the chief executive's office. He had just read the *National Intelligencer*, which carried a dispatch stating that Federal troops and Texas troops were about to commence hostilities in New Mexico. This would be a very sad Fourth indeed. He had also been talking to Secretary of War Crawford and learned that Taylor requested that an order be issued Col. Munroe to resist by force any attempt on the part of Texas to exercise jurisdiction in any part of the disputed territory. Crawford was opposed to violence and told the President that he would never send such an order, whereupon Taylor shouted: "Sir, in that case, I will sign it myself." Crawford met Toombs outside the executive's office and pleaded with him to expostulate and plead with the President for the peace of the nation. A. H. Stephens entered with Toombs.

Toombs used every argument at his command. Taylor was adamant. California would enter the Union at once. New Mexico would be considered upon arrival of the Constitution. Texas had no claim to the upper Rio Grande valley. "If it is a question of party expediency I shall not give up eighty-four members from the North for twenty-nine members from the South." Toombs was purple with rage. He stormed out of the office with utterings against such bullheadedness. That afternoon Stephens penned an open letter to the *National Intelligencer*, remarking:

"The first Federal gun that shall be fired against Texas, without the authority of law, will be the signal for freemen from the Delaware to the Rio Grande to rally to the rescue." He then went in quest of Toombs and together they sought out Preston, Secretary of the Navy, and found him standing in front of the Treasury building. The trio talked long, hard and loud, throwing all caution to the wind:

"If troops are ordered to Santa Fe," said the excited Stephens, "Taylor will be impeached."

"And who will impeach him?" asked the Secretary of the Navy.

"If no one else does," he answered, "I will."

Taylor got off to an awful start on Independence Day. Richie's *Union* newspaper was screaming for his impeachment. Yesterday, after Toombs and Stephens had left, Senator Hannibal Hamlin came in and found the old soldier, hands clasped behind his back, brow wrinkled in fury, pacing up and down the room. He paused a moment, turned like a bull on Hamlin, and asked:

"And what stand are you taking on the Omnibus Bill?"

"I am doing what I can to defeat it."

"Stand firm. Don't yield. That would mean disunion. You cannot understand how it hurts to hear that we have disunion men to contend with. Disunion is treason."

Hamlin, embarrassed before such an onslaught, made a hurried exit. Thurlow Tweed entered.

"Did you meet those traitors?" asked Taylor.

Tweed regretted that he had not and asked the President the reason for his agitation. Whereupon Taylor told him of his encounter with Stephens and Toombs. Also of their threats.

"I gave them to understand that if they were taken in rebellion against the Union they would be hung with less reluctance than I hanged spies and deserters in Mexico. If it is necessary I will take command of the army myself to enforce the laws."

Tweed did not think that Toombs and Stephens were advocating disunion but had a rather comprehensive plan of compromise for the preservation of the Union. When Tweed left Taylor turned to the message, still unfinished, on his desk, in which he urged Congress to admit New Mexico as well as California into the Union. He wrote that he would never permit

Texas to seize any part of New Mexico's rightful terrain. New Mexico would receive protection against any overt act on the part of Texas. He would furnish it to the last extremity. This last message, in its unfinished state, never got beyond that desk.

Bell in Texas was not without his troubles.

In his first message to the legislature the governor had recommended establishing an agency to investigate titles and claims to lands between the Nueces and the Rio Grande. The certainty of many of these claims were doubtful at best since the question interposed as to the manner in which jurisdiction graduated from Tamaulipas to Texas. This suggestion on the part of the governor caused unfavorable reaction and was not well received by the people implicated. Agitators proded and rabble rousers infiltrated with disturbing thoughts. It was the government's purpose to deprive them of their lands. Furthermore, this territory was about as much Texas as Santa Fe. It could be they were independent of Texas and not aware of it. On February 2, 1850, a meeting was held at Brownsville and preliminary steps taken to organize a separate territory. The chairman of the committee appealed to the government for admission into the Union as a State, or, if this were not feasible, as a Territory. Abolitionists in New England kept the pot boiling by pointing out that this land between the Nueces and the Rio Grande, not a part of Texas, was therefore a part of Mexico. Since a part of Mexico, then territory conquered by the United States. Slavery was forbidden in this territory by Mexican law. The U. S. government respected this law in the treaty of peace between the two nations. They were of the opinion that Texas would fare better if pretentions to Brownsville, Santa Fe and the upper Rio Grande were dropped. Bell appealed to the people of the lower Rio Grande valley to reconsider, especially since the South reiterated that it stood firm and ready to aid Texas when called upon. This new threat to organize the Territory of the Rio Grande procured for the South a firmer unity than hithertofore and solidified secession. Governor Bell, who succeeded in quieting the rumpus at Brownsville, about faced to the Santa Fe claim.

Fillmore's heritage was not an enviable one. "I herewith transmit to the two houses of Congress a letter from his Excellency, the Governor of Texas, dated on the 14th day of June last, addressed to the late President of the United States, which not having been answered by him, came to my hands on his death, and I also transmit a copy of the answer which I felt it my duty to cause to be made to that communication. Congress will perceive that the Governor of Texas officially states that by authority of the legislature of that State, he dispatched a special commissioner with full power and instructions to extend civil jurisdiction of the State over unorganized counties of El Paso, Worth, Presidio and Santa Fe, situated on its northwestern limits. He proceeds to say that the commissioner had reported to him, in an official form, that the military officers employed in the service of the United States stationed at Santa Fe interposed adversely with the inhabitants to the fulfilment of his object in favor of the establishment of a separate State government east of the Rio Grande, and within the rightful limits of the State of Texas. These four counties which Texas thus proposes to establish and organize as being within her own jurisdiction, extend over the whole territory east of the Rio Grande, which has therefore been regarded as an essential and integral part of the Department of New Mexico and actually governed and possessed by the people until conquered and severed from the Republic of Mexico by the American arms.

"The legislature of Texas has been called together by her governor for the purpose, as is understood, of maintaining her claim to the territory east of the Rio Grande and establishing over it her own jurisdiction and her own laws by force. These proceedings of Texas may well arrest the attention of all branches of the Government of the United States and I rejoice that they occur while Congress is still in session. It is, I fear, far from being impossible that, in consequence of these proceedings of Texas, a crisis may be brought on which shall summon the two houses of Congress, and still more emphatically the executive government, to an immediate readiness for the performance of their prospective duties.

"By the Constitution of the United States, the President is constituted commander-in-chief of the army and navy, and of the militia of the several States, when called into actual service of the United States. The Constitution declares, also, that he should take care that the laws be faithfully executed and that he shall, from time to time, give to Congress information of the state of the Union. Congress has power, by the Constitution, to provide for calling forth the militia to execute the laws of the Union; and suitable and appropriate acts of Congress have been passed as well for providing for calling forth the militia as for placing other suitable and efficient means in the hands of the President to enable him to discharge the constitutional functions of his office.

"The second section of the Act of February 28, 1795, declares that whenever the laws of the United States should be opposed, or their execution obstructed in any State, by combinations too powerful to be suppressed by the ordinary course of judicial proceedings, or the power vested in the marshals, the President may call forth the militia, as far as may be necessary, to suppress such combinations, and to cause the laws to be duly executed.

"By the Act of March 3, 1807, it is provided in all cases of obstruction to the laws either of the United States or any other individual State or Territory, where it is lawful, for the President to call forth the militia for the purpose of causing the laws to be duly executed, it shall be lawful for him to employ for the same purposes such part of the land or naval force of the United States as shall be adjudged necessary.

"These several enactments are now in full force so that if the laws of the United States are opposed or obstructed in any State or Territory, by combinations too powerful to be suppressed by the judicial or civil authorities it becomes a case in which it is the duty of the President either to call out the militia and naval force of the United States, or to do both, if, in his judgment, the exigency of the occasion shall so require, or for the purpose of suppressing such combinations. The constitutional duty of the President is plain and peremptory, and the authority vested in him by law for its performance clear and ample.

"Texas is a State authorized to maintain her own laws so far as they are not repugnant to the Constitution, laws and treaties of the United States; to suppress insurrections against her authority and to punish those who may commit treason against the State according to the forms provided by her own constitution and her own laws. But all this power is local, and confined entirely within the limits of Texas herself. She can hardly confer any authority which can be lawfully exercised beyond her own boundaries. All this is plain, and hardly needs argument or elucidation. If Texas militia therefore march into any one of the other States or into any Territory of the United

States, there to execute or enforce any law of Texas, they become at that moment trespassers; they are no longer under the protection of any lawful authority, and are to be regarded merely as intruders; and if, within such State or Territory, they obstruct any law of the United States, either by power of arms or mere power of numbers, constituting such a combination as is too powerful to be suppressed by the civil authority, the President of the United States has no option left to him, but is bound to obey the solemn injunction of the Constitution and exercise the high powers vested in him by that instrument and the Acts of Congress.

"Or, if any civil posse, armed or unarmed, enter into any Territory of the United States under the protection of the laws thereof, with the intent to seize individuals to be carried elsewhere for trial for alleged offenses, and this posse be too powerful to be resisted by the local civil authorities, such seizure or attempt to seize is to be prevented or resisted by the authority of the United States. The grave and important question arises now as to whether there be in the Territory of New Mexico any existing law of the United States opposition to which, or the obstruction of which, would constitute a case calling for the interposition of the authority vested in the President. The Constitution of the United States declares that 'this Constitution, and the laws of the United States, which sall be made in pursuance thereof, and all the treaties made, or which shall be made, under the authority of the United States, shall be the supreme law of the land.' If, therefore, New Mexico be a Territory of the United States and if any treaty stipulation is the supreme law of the land, it is to be maintained and upheld accordingly.

"In my letter to the governor of Texas, my reasons are given for believing that New Mexico, now a Territory of the United States, with the same extent and boundaries which belonged to it while in the actual possession of the Republic of Mexico and before the late war. In the early part of the war, both California and New Mexico were conquered by the arms of the United States and were in the military possession of the United States at the date of the treaty of peace.

"By that treaty the title by conquest was confirmed, and these territories, provinces, or departments, separated from Mexico, forever; and by the same treaty it is declared that: 'The boundary line between the two Republics should commence in the Gulf of Mexico, etc. . . .'." After describing the boundaries Fillmore continued:

"The 8th Article of the treaty is in the following terms: 'Mexicans now established in territories previously belonging to Mexico and which remain for the future within the limits of the United States as defined by the present treaty shall be free to continue where they now reside, or to remove at any time to the Mexican Republic, retaining the property which they possess in the said territories, or disposing thereof, and removing the proceeds wherever they please, without their being subjected on this account to any contribution tax, or charge whatever. Those who shall prefer to remain in the said territories may either retain the title, rights of Mexican citizens or acquire those of citizens of the United States; but they shall be under the obligation to make their election within one year from the date of the exchange or ratifications of this treaty, in the said territories after the expiration of that year without having declared their intentions to retain the character of Mexicans shall be considered to have elected to become citizens of the United States: In the said territories property of every kind, now belonging to Mexicans not established there, shall be inviolably respected. The present owners, heirs of these, and all Mexicans who may hereafter acquire said property by contract shall enjoy, with respect to it, guarantees equally ample as if the same belonged to the citizens of the United States.'

"The 9th Article is in these words: 'Mexicans who, in the aforesaid territories shall not preserve the character of citizens of the Mexican Republic conformably with what is stipulated in the preceding article, shall be incorporated into the Union of the United States and shall be admitted at the proper time (to be adjudged by the Congress of the United States) to the enjoyment of all rights of citizens of the United States according to the principles of the Constitution and in the meantime shall be maintained and protected in the free enjoyment of their liberty and property and secured in the free exercise of their religion without restriction.'

"It is plain therefore, on the force of these treaty stipulations, that all the Mexicans established in the territories north or east of the line of demarkation already mentioned come within the protection of the 9th Article and that the treaty being part of the supreme law of the land does not extend over all such Mexicans and assures to them perfect security in the free enjoyment of their liberty and property as well as in the free exercise of their religion, and this supreme law of the land being then in actual force over this territory it is to be maintained until it shall be displaced or superceded by other legal provisions; and if it be obstructed or resisted by combinations too powerful to be suppressed by the civil authority, the case is one which comes within the provisions of law, and which obliges the President to enforce those provisions. Neither the Constitution, nor the laws, nor my duty, nor my oath of office, leave me any alternative or any choice in my mode of action. The executive government of the United States has no power of authority to determine what was the true line of boundary between Mexico and the United States before the treaty of Guadalupe Hidalgo; nor has it any such power now, since the question has become a question between the State of Texas and the United States. So far as this boundary is doubtful, that doubt can only be removed by some Act of Congress, to which the assent of the State of Texas may be necessary or by some appropriate mode of legal adjudication; but in the meantime, if disturbances or collisions arise or should be threatened, it is absolutely incumbent on the executive government, however painful the duty, to take care that the laws be faithfully maintained; and that he can regard only the actual state of things as it existed at the date of the treaty, and is bound to protect all the inhabitants who were then established, and who now remain north and east of the line of demarkation in the full enjoyment of their liberty and property, according to the provisions of the 9th Article of the treaty; in other words, all must be now regarded as New Mexico which was possessed and occupied by the citizens of Mexico at the date of the treaty until a definite line of boundary shall be established by competent authority.

"This assertion of duty to protect the people of New Mexico from threatened violence or from seizure to be carried into Texas for trial for alleged offenses against Texas laws, does not at all include any claim of power on the part of the executive to establish any civil or military government within that territory. That power belongs exclusively to the legislation department, and Congress is the sole judge of the time and manner of creating or authorizing any such government.

"The duty of the executive extends only to the execution of laws and the maintenance of treaties already in force, and the protection of all the people of the United States in the enjoyment of the rights which those treaties and laws guarantee. It is exceedingly desirable that no occasion should arise for the exercise of the powers thus vested in the President by the Constitution and the laws. With whatever mildness those powers might be executed, or however clear the case of necessity yet consequences might nevertheless follow, of which no human sagacity can foresee either the evils or the end.

"Having thus laid before Congress the communication of his Excellency, the Governor of Texas, and the answer thereto, and having made such observances as I thought the occasion called for, respecting constitutional obligations which may arise in the further progress of things, and may devolve on me to be performed, I hope I shall not be regarded as stepping aside from my line of duty notwithstanding. I am aware that the subject is now before both Houses. If I express my deep and earnest conviction of the importance of an immediate decision or arrangement or settlement of the question of boundary between Texas and the Territory of New Mexico, all considerations of justice, general expediency and domestic tranquility call for this. It seems to be in its character and by position the first or one of the first of the questions growing out of the acquisition of California and New Mexico and now requiring decision. No government can be established for New Mexico, either State or Territorial, until it shall be first ascertained what New Mexico is, and what are her limits and boundaries. These cannot be fixed or known until the line of division between her and Texas shall be ascertained and established; and numerous and weighty reasons conspire, in my opinion, to show that this divisional line should be established by Congress with the assent of the government of Texas. In the first place, this seems by far the most prompt mode of proceeding, by which the end can be accomplished. If judicial proceedings were resorted to, such proceedings would necessarily be slow, and years would pass by in all probability, before the controversy could be ended. So great a delay in this case is to be avoided, if possible, such delay would be every way inconvenient, and might be the occasion of disturbances and collisions. For the same reason, I would, with the utmost deference to the wisdom of Congress, express a doubt of the expediency of the appointment of commissioners and of an examination, estimate, and an award of indemnity to be made by them. This would be but a species of arbitration which might last as long as a suit at law.

"So far as I am able to comprehend the case, the general facts are now known, and Congress is as capable of deciding on is justly and properly now as it probably would be after the report of the commissioner. If the claim of title on the part of Texas appeared to Congress to be well founded in whole or in part, it is in the competency of Congress to offer her indemnity for the surrender of that claim. In a case like this, surrounded as it is by many cogent considerations, all calling for amicable adjustment and immediate settlement, the government of the United States would be justified, in my opinion, in allowing an indemnity to Texas not unreasonable or extravagant but fair, liberal, and awarded in a just spirit of accommodation. I think no event would be hailed with more gratification by the people of the United States than the amicable adjustment of questions of difficulty which have now for a long time agitated the country, and occupied, to the exclusion of the other subjects, the time and attention of Congress.

"Having thus freely communicated the results of my reflections on the most advisable mode of adjusting the boundary question I shall nevertheless cheerfully acquiese in any other mode which the wisdom of Congress may devise. And, in conclusion, I repeat my conviction that every consideration of the public interest manifests the necessity of a provision by Congress for the settlement of this boundary question before the present session be brought to a close. The settlement of other questions connected with the same subject, within the same period, is greatly to be desired; but the adjustment of this appears to me to be in the highest degree important. In the train of such an adjustment we may well hope that there will follow a return of harmony and good will, an increased attachment to the Union, and the general satisfaction of the country."

(Signed) Milliard Fillmore.

Neither Spain nor Mexico ever considered Santa Fe as part of the Texas province. Hence, it was the prize of war resulting from the victory at San Jacinto. That, and no more. In good old American fashion, Fillmore offered a pay-off in the hopes of avoiding war. Texas was grateful. Later as a Confederate State she would march her troops into New Mexico and carve out the Confederate State of Arizona. There was the dream that should the South win, the ports along upper California might become part of Texas as originally hoped during the days of the republic. Texas might then have commerce with China and Japan as the Gulf of Mexico offered trade with Europe. Despite Fillmore's plea for an "increased attachment for the Union" a woman wrote a book that was to bring about quite the contrary. During March of 1852, the nation was introduced to Mrs. Harriet Beecher's "Uncle Tom's Cabin." Harriet was an intellectual, brought up to the sound and the fury of Revivals, song-fests, debates and pursuit of knowledge. Her preacher father had ideas about slavery as well as religion. He was a dyed in the wool abolitionist. Born in 1811, Harriet studied at her sister's school in Hartford, where she enjoyed French and Italian. She longed to be with God alone until she read Byron. She was twelve when the poet died. This so tormented her hero-worshipping soul that she ran off into the fields, throwing her little body into the wild flowers and tormenting herself over his loss. She looked up to the heavens expecting his soul to descend and engulf her in brilliant splendor. She and the heavens remained in status quo. She resolved to become a crusader. Henceforth she would devote herself to a cause to which she would give her full measure of devotion. She married Calvin Stowe, a teacher in her father's seminary, known for his ability in Greek, Arabic and Hebrew, and moved to Cincinnati. There she became a member of a literary club, wrote for magazines and raised her children. Her husband had faith in her abilities and convinced her that she could form—or reform—the mind of the West.

Her crusading spirit floated to a plantation across the river from her home wher she made observations and took notes. She moved to Maine where her husband asked her to teach at Bowdoin College, so dear to the heart of Longfellow. The Fugitive Slave Law moved her to think of the things she witnessed at the plantation. Her mind was a flambeau scintillating her mission against slavery and slave owners. She stirred as if visited by heavenly powers (Byron's spirit, perhaps?) and sat down under the hypnosis to cry out against a system rather than individuals, and contributed another factor that brought on the war. "Uncle Tom's Cabin" focused attention on slavery as nothing before or since. Fillmore and Webster thought they saw peace with the solution to the Texas claim. What they witnessed actually was the calm before the storm. Webster wrote Governor Bell on August 5, 1850:

"Sir: A letter addressed by you to the late President of the United States and dated on the 14th of June last, has, since his lamented decease, been transferred to the hands of his successor, by whom I am directed to address the following answer:

"In that letter you say that by the authority of the legislature of Texas, the executive of that state, in February last, dispatched a special commission with full power and instructions to extend the civil jurisdiction of that State over the inorganized counties of El Paso, Worth, Presidio and Santa Fe, situated upon its northwestern limits, and that the commissioner has reported to you, in official form, that the military officers employed in the service of the United States stationed at Santa Fe, interposed adversely with the inhabitants to the fulfillment of his object by employing their influence in favor of the establishment of a separate State government east of the Rio Grande, and within the rightful limits of the State of Texas. You also transmit a copy of the proclamation of Col. John Munroe, acting under the designation of civil and military governor of the Territory of New Mexico and respectfully request the President to cause you to be informed whether or not this officer has acted in this matter under the orders of his government, and whether his proclamation meets with the approval of the President of the United States.

"In the events which have occurred, the President hardly knows whether your Excellency would naturally expect an answer to this letter from him. His predecessor in office, to whom it was addressed, and under whose authority and direction the proclamation of Col. Munroe was issued, is no more, and at this time that proclamation, whatever may be regarded as its true character, has ceased to have influence or effect. The meeting of the people of New Mexico by their representatives which it invited, is understood to have taken place, although this government has not as yet received an official information of it. Partaking however, in the fullest degree, in that high respect which the executive government of the United States always entertains towards governors and governments of the States, the President thinks it is his duty nevertheless, to manifest that feeling of respect by acknowledging and answering your letter, and this duty, let me assure your Excellency, has so long been delayed only by uncontrollable circumstances and is now performed at the earliest practicable moment after the appointment of those heads of departments, and their acceptance of office, with whom it is usual, on important occasions for the President to advise.

"'In answer therefore to your first interrogatory—viz: Whether Col. Munroe in issuing the proclamation referred to, acted under the orders of the government, the President directs me to state that Col. Munroe's proclamation appears to have been issued in pursuance or in consequence of an order or letter of instructions given by the late Secretary of War, under the authority of the late President to Lieutenant-Colonel McCall. Of this order, which bears the date November 19, 1849, your Excellency was undoubtedly informed at the date of your letter. A full and accurate copy, however, is attached to this communication. Col. McCall is therein instructed that if the people of New Mexico, for whom Congress had provided no government, should manifest a wish to take any step to establish a government for themselves, and apply for admission into the Union it would be his duty, and the duty of others with whom he was associated, not to thwart but to advance their wishes. This order does not appear to authorize any exertion of military authority or of any special official or even personal interference to control or affect in any way the primary action of the people in the formation of the government, nor to permit any such interference by the subordinate officers. Col. McCall and his associates were not called upon to take a lead in any such measures, nor even to recommend anything as fit to be adopted by the people. Their whole duty was confined to what they might be able to perform subordinate to the wishes of the people. In this matter it was evidently contemplated that they were to act as the agents of the inhabitants, not as officers of the government. It must be recollected that the only government then existing in the territory was a quasi-military government; and as Congress had made no provision for the establishment of any form of civil government and as the President doubtless believed that, under these circumstances the people had a right to frame a government for themselves, and to submit it to Congress for its approval, the order was a direction that the then existing military government should not stand in the way of the accomplishment of the wishes of the people, nor thwart those wishes, if the people entertained them, for the establishment of a free, popular, republican, civil government for their own protection and benefit. This is evidently the whole purpose and object of the order. The military officer in command, and his associates, were American citizens, acquainted with the forms of civil and popular proceedings, and it was expected that they would aid the inhabitants of the territory by their advice and assistance, on their proceedings for establishing a government of their own. There is no reason to suppose that Col. Munroe, an officer as much distinguished for prudence and discretion as for gallant conduct in arms, meant to act, or did act, otherwise than in entire subordination and subserviency in the will of the people among whom he was placed. He was not authorized to do so, nor does the President understand him as intending to do anything whatever in his military character, nor to represent in any way the wishes of the executive government of the United States. To judge intellectually and fairly of these transactions, we must recall to our recollection the circumstances of the case as they then existed . . .'"

Webster goes into the War with Mexico, the invasion and conquest of New Mexico by General Kearny, the proclamation by the general to the inhabitants in which he explained that he took Santa Fe intending to hold it in all its original boundaries as New Mexico, promising the people protection against Indians, enemies and all others. On August 18, 1846 Kearny gave them a Constitution stating "that the country heretofore known as New Mexico shall hereafter be designated as the Territory of New Mexico in the United States of America." Webster also pointed out that on December 22nd of that year a copy of this Constitution was placed before the House by President Polk in the hopes of establishing a permanent territorial government. He reminded Bell that nearly four years had elapsed since this time. Besides, a treaty of peace had been concluded with Mexico by which a boundary line was established that left this conquered territory within the jurisdiction of the United States.

Letters crossed and criss-crossed from Washington to Texas. Governor Bell lamented the fact that the loss of Santa Fe dampened his hopes of an outlet to lessen the public debt. He seemed amendable to a cash settlement. Congress convened in August to fix the boundaries of the Territory of New Mexico so as to include all the region claimed by Texas west of the 100th meridian and agreed to pay Texas a cash consideration in settlement of her claim. While Governor Bell personally considered the proposal an affront to the dignity and character of the State of Texas, he secretly admitted that it was an opportunity to liquidate some of the public debt and it was tantamount to an admission by Congress that there was some justification for the claim. The Texas government had scaled down the debt to a basis in keeping with the amounts which the government of the Republic of Texas had received in incurring them. The whole subject had been a matter of controversy for some time; when the question of the claim reached a crisis, the creditors contrived to have its settlement connected with the payment of the Texas debt. Fillmore and Webster contended that the matter rested with Congress. Fillmore, less fiery than Taylor, sent a special message urging a prompt settlement of the controversy on an amicable basis. This action appeased the war mongers. The legislature adjourned and talk of armed resistance gradually died. Congress then passed the Pearce Bill which provided for the cession to the United States by Texas all of the territory lying north of the Missouri Compromise line and the territory under discussion lying west of the 103rd meridian. The consideration was fixed at ten million dolars in United States bonds, which Texas accepted. When the war eventually broke out Texas Confederate troops marched in many directions but the hope of the many was to confiscate the land that would open a pathway to the Pacific. Just what California would have done if the New Mexico-Arizona campaign proved successful is a matter of conjecture. California didn't wait to find out. Men volunteered and marched to the succor of New Mexico and remained for the duration. It is not strange that the California soldiers should fight at the side of the New Mexico soldiers; it was their way of thanking Kearny for a trade in flags and allegiance.

※ ※ ※

NOTES AND COMMENTS

Maribeau Bonaparte Lamar (1798 - 1859) — A native of Georgia, he entered the mercantile and newspaper business in Alabama but gave these up to return to his native state. Further adventures in journalism and politics brought him to Texas where he took an active part in the struggle for independence. He was elected vice-president in 1836 and president on December 10, 1838. Some regard him as the founder of Austin, Texas, as well as the Father of Education in Texas. He was active in the Mexican War. In 1857 he was named Minister to Nicaragua and Costa Rica, serving for twenty months. He died on his Richmond plantation, December 19, 1859. The middle name is more often spelled Buonaparte. It has been said that when his daughter died in 1843 her death caused such a melancholia that he sought relief in travel. His friends were ready to die for him; his enemies said he was a better poet (he wrote a book of verse) than a politician. He is remembered in Texas through Lamar county, the town of Lamar, Lamar State College and by a statue in the Hall of State at Dallas.

William G. Cooke (1808-1847)—Born in Fredericksburg, Virginia, March 26, 1808. He raised a company of New Orleans Greys to come to the rescue of Texas during the fight for Independence. He resigned from the Texas Army in 1837 to establish a drug business in Houston, but it was not to his liking and he re-enlisted as quartermaster general. His part in the ill fated Texas-Santa Fe Expedition is too well known for repetition here. He never lived down the ill treatment at the hands of Salazar. He was released from the Mexican dungeon on June 16, 1842, returning to Texas where he married Angela Navarro. He was appointed adjutant-general of the militia and served until his death on December 24, 1847. Cooke county honors him. He is buried near Seguin.

Edward Burleson (1793-1871)—A native of North Carolina, he also lived in Tennessee and Alabama before coming to Texas in 1830. He served the Republic as Brigadier-General and Congressman. He was elected Vice-President in 1841. He died in Austin, December 26, 1851. A county in Texas bears his name.

Jose Antonio Navarro (1795-1871)—Born in San Antonio, he became a lawyer, merchant, rancher, land owner and politician. He was one of the signers of the Texas Declaration of Independence. In 1825 he married Margarita de la Garza and they became the parents of seven children. He received harsh treatment from both Salazar and Santa Anna who called him a traitor to his race. He managed to escape the Acordada prison. He served Texas for the balance of his life. Four of his sons fought for the Confederacy. He died at San Antonio on January 13, 1871. Navarro county, the town of Navarro and Navarro Mills help perpetuate his memory.

George Van Ness—A native of Virginia, he became a lawyer in Texas in 1838. He suffered for his part in the Texas-Santa Fe Expedition. He was released from the Satillo prison in November 1843, but the order did not become effective until April 1844. In 1851 he was postmaster at Fort Duncan. He died some time after 1853.

Anson Jones (1798-1858)—A native of Mass., he practiced medicine at Oneida, New York. He came to Texas in 1833 and was surgeon during the fight for Independence. Married Mrs. Mary Smith McCrory at Austin May 17, 1840. He served in Congress, was appointed Minister to the United States and became President of Texas in 1844. Political reverses made him bitter, unbalanced his way of thinking, or at least his outlook, so that he took his own life, at Houston, on January 9, 1858. He founded the Medical Association of Texas in 1853. There is a beautiful statue of him in front of the courthouse at Anson, Texas. Anson is the county seat of Jones county. From a distance it looks like a miniture statue of Honest Abe in the Lincoln Memorial, due to the fact that Anson is seated very much like Lincoln.

James Pinckney Henderson (1808-1858)—A native of North Carolina, he arrived in Texas in 1836. He received a commission in the Army as Brigadier-General and was sent to the U. S. to recruit for the Republic. His success earned him several political appointments. It was while he was Minister to France that he met and married (in London) Francis Cox of Philadelphia. He was probably the only governor at the head of his troops in the Mexican War. He refused a second term in favor of his law practice. He was elected to the U. S. Senate and died in office June 4, 1858. In 1930 his remains were brought to Austin. A county in Texas was named for him.

General Stephen Watts Kearny (1794-1848)—Born in Newark, New Jersey, August 30, 1794. He left the former Kings College (Columbia University) to serve in the War of 1812. After the war he decided to make the Army his career. He was appointed commander of the Army of the West during the Mexican War and marched on Santa Fe. Several factors favored a bloodless conquest and he took possession without the loss of a man. The actual fighting broke out in Taos when he had left for California. Sterling Price put an end to the short-lived resistance movement. Difficulties in California with Fremont caused him to leave for Mexico where he served as civil governor of Vera Cruz and Mexico City but not before the battle at San Pasqual, where he was twice wounded in action. He died in St. Louis, Mo., on October 31, 1848. Raton, New Mexico, honors him with the Kearny Day Entrada each August but there is no town, no county, no public monument honoring the man responsible for New Mexico's part in the Union. The Land of Enchantment has also decided against a Centennial Celebration commemmorating Valverde, Peralta, Glorieta.

Spruce McCoy Baird (1814-1872)—a native of Glasgow, Kentucky. Taught school before coming to Texas. Practiced law and unsuccessfully attempted Texas jurisdiction over Santa Fe. Baird, Texas, in Callahan county honors him.

Robert Simpson Neighbors (1815-1859)—Born in Virginia on November 3, 1815. His parents died before he was a year old. Brought up by relatives. Arrived in Texas, 1836. He was made a Mexican prisoner by General Wool in 1844. After his release entered the Indian service. In 1854, Neighbors, together with Captain Marcy, made extensive explorations in search of sites for Indian reservations. He was shot by Edward Cornett on September 14, 1859.

Humphrey Marshal (1812-1872)—A native of Kentucky, he graduated from West Point and served in the Black Hawk War. He resigned from the Army to practice law. Served for a long time in the U. S. Congress. Became a Confederate General in the war between the States but resigned his commission to serve in the Confederate Congress. Practiced law until the date of his death.

Charles M. Conrad—a politician from Louisiana. Served in the Senate for a number of years and was Secretary of War under President Fillmore. Fort Conrad in New Mexico was named for him.

Peter Hansborough Bell (1812-1898)—Born in Spotsylvania County, Virginia, May 12, 1812. Left a business in Petersburg to get into the first for Texas Independence. Took part in the Battle of San Jacinto. Became Inspector General of the Texas Army in 1839. Fought in the Mexican War and was a Confederate Colonel in the Civil War. Married Mrs. Ella Reeves Eaton Dickens on March 3, 1857 in North Carolina. Was governor of Texas in 1849 and 1851. His remains were brought from North Carolina in 1930 and re-buried in Austin.

Mrs. Harriet Beecher Stowe (1812-1896)—"Perhaps no other American book of note has been written under so great a handicap. When Mrs. Stowe began this work, one of her large family of children was not a year old, and the others were a constant care. Nevertheless, she persevered with her epoch-making story. One of her friends has given us a picture of the difficulties in her way, the baby on her knee, the new hired girl asking whether the pork should be put on top of the beans, and whether the gingerbread should stay longer in the oven. . . . In "Uncle Tom's Cabin" Mrs. Stowe endeavored to translate into concrete form certain phases of the institution of slavery, which had been merely an abstraction to the North . . ." Halleck—*American Literature* p. 170.

"Uncle Tom's Cabin"—"The aim of the book was to create a moral revulsion, an emotional protest, against slavery. If the book had not been sentimental it would not have appealed to the millions who read it only to become embittered against slavery. If the characters had been fully drawn, the average reader would have been so lost in a maze of psychological subtleties that he would have missed the aim of the writer. If there had been no exaggeration in the novel, its appeal would have been greatly curtailed, for the emotions of many are aroused only by a vigorous shaking. But above all these weaknesses that turned out to be strong points there is one characteristic that unquestionably made for success. That was the human element, the elusive quality that makes people interested in the actions and the fate of the characters. This quality 'Uncle Tom's Cabin' had in abundance. . . . 'Uncle Tom's Cabin' is our first well known sociological novel. Its aim was the remedying of a social wrong, and its method was the method of socially minded writers of more recent days. . . . Mrs. Stowe dramatized the sorrows of negroes and the inhumanity of the institution of slavery so vividly that she did more to arouse public sentiment than any other one agitator was able to accomplish. Without the passage of the fugitive slave law that set off the explosion of Puritanical morality in Mrs. Stowe, the North might have remained unmoved against slavery until economic and political pressure became unendurable. . . ." Blankenship—*American Literature*, pp. 331-332.

With reference to the Texas claim, Senator Baldwin of Connecticut voiced this opinion (Thursday, July 25, 1850): ". . . If Texas has acquired any title to New Mexico it must have been either by conquest or cession from Mexico to Texas, or it must have been by conquest and cession to the United States for the benefit of Texas. And here, sir, I am willing to admit that if the government of the United States, in all its branches competent to decide this question, went to war with Mexico for the purpose of vindicating the title of Texas to this entire territory and acquired it in that way the government of the United States may be estopped; may by that act be restrained from setting up any title in herself, in her own right, to the territory so acquired. Not, sir, that the executive or any of the subordinate officers of the United States have the power to implicate this government by the admission that this acquisition was made for the benefit of Texas, or of any other State whatsoever. But if the government of the United States, if the legislative department of this government which alone is competent to do so, have declared war for the purpose of vindicating the title of Texas to New Mexico then it will present to question of estoppel that has been urged by Senators who have discussed the subject of that title. What then are the facts, sir? When Texas negotiated for admission into this Union it was well known that she had asserted a claim to jurisdiction up to the sources of the Rio Grande. But did the resolutions of annexation admit that claim? Not at all. Nothing could be more carefully worded to exclude any such pretense than the language of the joint resolutions. It was provided that 'the territory properly included within and rightfully belonging to Texas might be erected into a new State.' Why 'territory properly included within and rightfully belonging to Texas' if it was intended by the United States that Texas should come in with the boundaries which she had thought proper to claim? The language used in the joint resolution shows that although Congress, when they possessed it, had notice of the extent of the claim of Texas, they intended to limit her to such boundaries as she actually acquired and possessed in March, 1845, when the joint resolution was passed. . . . When, therefore, Congress in 1845 proposed to Texas to come into the Union, what did they propose? That she should come in with her rightful boundaries, and with a republican form of government to be adopted by the *people of that republic*. Who were the *people of that republic*? Were the people of New Mexico, comprising a poulation of 90,000, a portion of the people of Texas at that time? If they were, why, sir, was that constitution present to Congress as a constitution adopted by the people of Texas when the whole of the people of New Mexico were excluded from any participation in its adoption? How is it that we have presented here in December, 1845, a document purporting to have been adopted by the people of the Republic of Texas in convention when 90,000 of those who are now claimed to have constituted a portion of that people were never invited to co-operate in its formation? . . . Texas well knew at that time that no part of New Mexico was rightfully included in her limits, and, therefore, it was that she did not notify the people of New Mexico to participate in the formation of her constitution preparatory to her admission into the Union. . . . What pretense of right is there, then, if Texas did not own this territory when she accepted the proposal tended by the joint resolutions for her present claim? She has done nothing by which she could have acquired it since. The president was of the opinion that this area claimed by Texas was part of the Louisiana Purchase. He spoke of it as a re-annexation of that which had been abandoned by treaty (1819). That was the language of Mr. Polk and the friends of annexation generally. . . . It was a re-annexation of Texas. Did he mean to indicate, when he spoke of re-annexation (of Texas) as part of the Province of Louisiana; that that province had ever comprehended the capital of New Mexico, or any portion of its territory? Did anybody ever pretend that New Mexico formed a part of the old Province of Louisiana? New Mexico, which had been settled by Spaniards long before the discoveries of La Salle, which conferred upon France the title to Louisiana? Even Mr. Buchanan in a letter addressed to Mr. Slidell, November 10, 1845, eight months after the passing of the resolution of annexation writes: 'The case is different in regard to New Mexico. Santa Fe, its capital, was settled by the Spaniards more than two centuries ago; and that province has ever since been in their possession and that of the Republic of Mexico. The Texans never have conquered or taken possession of it, nor have its people ever been represented in any of their legislative assemblies or conventions. . . . This whole claim of Texas to the upper Rio Grande amounts to nothing more than this: Texas, while engaged in war with Mexico for the establishment of her own independence, was naturally desirous of extending her domain as far as the Rio Grande. She hoped, if she was successful in the conduct of the war, to be able to acquire dominion to the extent by force of her arms. She was not struggling so far as her claim to the upper Rio Grande is concerned, to vindicate her title to any territory that she then owned or had ever possessed; but she was struggling to acquire by the sword, an addition to that domain, the sovereignty over which she had already established by the sword. She had not succeeded in her effort. No army of Texas had penetrated New Mexico. No Texan, as it has already been remarked, had set his foot upon that territory in hostility to the government of New Mexico except as a prisoner of war. Mr. President, I understand that the claim which was at one time set up in behalf of Texas, growing out of the convention made with Santa Anna when a prisoner, is abandoned. . . . Congress declared that Santa Fe was no part of Texas but was in Mexico. . . . Mr. Rusk, Senator from Texas, declared that the war was declared to vindicate the title of Texas to the Rio Grande. . . . The Senator goes on to show that the lower Rio Grande was meant. He shows how General Kearny was sent to conquer New Mexico and California as part of Mexico. What object has Texas in her claim? Why, she wants an acknowledgement of her title to the sovereignty of New Mexico in order that she may transfer it to the United States for a pecuniary consideration. The government of the United States then, has waged a war with Mexico, conquered the province of New Mexico, promised liberty to its people, purchased from Mexico out of a common treasury a cession of that territory and now it is to be delivered up to Texas in order that Texas may sell it again to the United States to pay the debts of Texas which accrued during her own revolution. . . . I have endeavored to show that it (New Mexico) belongs to the United States; that Texas does not have the shadow of a claim to it. . . ."

Starkweather listened to the debates in the House. A Representative from New York, he had never been neither to California nor New Mexico but he could appreciate the confusion in those two areas as reflected in the dilemma confronting the politicos in Washington banging fists on desks, gathering in cliques about the halls, rubbing elbows in saloons, gulping down whisky as they drank in the pros and cons in fierce partisanship, dreaming, scheming, building up votes by gracious largess as they sliced off large chunks of land for their supporters and steered many into places of honor in the new domains. These were the despoilers, the graspers who came to New Mexico to build political and material empires and ruin every opportunity for Statehood for the next sixty-odd years. Appointment was less hazardous than election. So long as New Mexico remained a Territory they were on the band wagon. This was whispered in many corners of the capital and many unscrupulous men in office gained by the situation. They were so many Aaron Burrs at heart, absolute rulers too shrewd to be caught in the camp of Arnold, Wilkinson and Burr. All this Starkweather knew and his heart bled for New Mexico. Defiantly, he took the floor on February 16th and thundered against those who would make slavery the issue regarding the conquered lands.

"Unless there is some constitutional provision, some power somewhere, I see not but California and New Mexico may send up their petitions to Congress—as New Mexico has done—and pray for Territorial governments to be provided for them, to protect them against the evils of slavery in vain. In the past Presidential election people voted whether Congress had the constitutional power to make such rules and regulations in reference to the Territories of New Mexico and California as would prohibit slavery from entering there, and if so, whether such power should be exercised. Was there any other issue? Does any one pretend there was another issue? I speak of the Cass party which would not support any men for the presidency or the vice-presidency unless they would clearly and unequivocally declare that they were opposed to the principles of the provisions of the Wilmot Proviso. Southerners claim the constitutional right to enter these territories and to carry their slaves with them as property, and to hold them as such; and they deny that Congress has any constitutional power whatever to prohibit them from the exercise of this right. Nay, some gentlemen of high standing and influence maintain that slavery now exists in New Mexico and California. The Attorney General of the State of Mississippi, in reply to an invitation to address the citizens of Alabama affirmed that the act of the Mexican Congress abolishing slaves, was an act of usurpation, and therefore null and void. . . . "

When Starkweather sat down, Rep. J. B. Thompson stood up and declared: "We are at peace with all the world and there is now left for national uneasiness and anxiety the question: How shall we organize and what restrictions, if any, as to slavery shall we make in the Teritories of New Mexico and California; the interest of the government in the public lands and mineral wealth of those Territories demand of Congress a Territorial government. The people there who came under our dominion by the Treaty of Queretaro or Guadalupe Hildago, as well as our own emigrants, need and expect the protection and fostering care of our government. The organization of a Territorial government, and the enactment of suitable laws, is arrested by the question: How shall slavery there be acted upon. I know the Wilmot Proviso—that is, the proposition to forever exclude slavery from these Territories—is of Democratic origin; and I know that notwithstanding Mr. Polk signed the bill to organize the Territory of Oregon with the Wilmot Proviso, or slavery restriction in it, still, every one south of the Mason and Dixon's line—Whigs and Democrats—feel and think very much alike on this subject. The books of travelers and official explorations seem to favor and confirm the opinion expressed by the present Secretary of State (Buchanan) who, in speaking of the subject says—'In regard to New Mexico, east of the Rio Grande, the question had already been settled by the admission of Texas into the Union. Should we acquire territory beyond the Rio Grande and east of the Rocky Mountains it is morally impossible that a majority of the people should consent to the re-establishment of slavery. They are themselves a colored population (?) and among them the Negro does not belong socially to a degraded class.' (See: *Congressional Globe*—Appendix—30th Congress—2nd. Sess. New Series No. 7 pp. 95-97) . . . The recent treaty with Mexico in no way affects the institution of slavery, its existence or non-existence, as by law it stood in New Mexico and California at the acquisition. How, then, did they stand as to this species of property when we acquired them? They were parts of the Mexican confederacy, and as such, free from slavery because the Mexican government had in the year 1829, in the exercise of its supreme authority, totally abolished slavery. This law—Slavery is forever abolished in the Republic—was afterwards, in 1837, in the law providing for the payment of manumitted slaves, reaffirmed by the declarative law—Slavery is and shall remain abolished throughout the entire Republic. The transfer of those countries to us found them, shall I say Free Soil? They were without the existence of African slavery as a municipal regulation."

Rep. T. Jenkins (N.Y.) continued the discussion with: "In territories like California and New Mexico where the white population (i.e. Anglo rather than native) is comparatively small, the anxiety to gain settlers is so great that but little objection is made to slavery, and slave holders with their slaves may be considered valuable acquisitions . . ." Rep. Charles Brown (Pa.) said (February 3, 1849): "We may ask that there be no slavery in New Mexico and California because those Territories are now free and it would be encroachments on the rights of the Northern man to let the slave holder go there, but if it was not slave territory we would not ask you to abolish slavery there. . . . If slaves were to be carried to California or the higher part of New Mexico, the pressure of the whites would soon drive them out of it. But no man, North or South, that I have ever conversed with believes they will ever be carried there. The certainty that slaves will be prohibited by them when formed into States, will prevent anyone from taking slaves there if so disposed. . . ."

CHAPTER THREE

THE NEW MEXICO SCENE

"New Mexico is the anomaly of the Republic. It is a century older in European civilization than the rest, and several centuries older still in a happier semi-civilization of its own. It had its little walled cities of stone before Columbus had grandparents-to-be; and it has them yet. The most incredible pioneering the world has ever seen overran it with the zeal of a prairie-fire three hundred and fifty years ago; and the embers of that unparalleled blaze of exploration are not quite dead today. The most superhuman marches, the most awful privations, the most devoted heroism, the most unsleeping vigilance wrested this bare, brown land to the world; and having wrested it, went to sleep. The winning was the wakefullest in history—the after-nap eternal...." Charles Lummis—"The Land of Poco Tiempo" p. 1

Many spices in the brew of war bubbled to the heat of the war-mongers all over the nation. The saturation point reached from flame to brim. The pot that boiled in Washington steamed in Texas and blew the lid off in New Mexico. This latter was an unknown quantity to the United States until the proven worth of the commerce of the prairies aroused the cupidity of merchants other than the general run from Missouri. The Manifest Destiny of America would remain a dream until the land of adobe infiltrated its culture, as butter on bread, to the Atlantic. Whatever the thoughts of the Hannibal of the Southwest as he climbed the Raton Pass on his way to Santa Fe, he could not but help being impressed by the beauty of the country as his soldiers were charmed by the beauty of the senoritas and the many possibilities for future colonization in the land of sky blue reflections. After the war many returned to make New Mexico their home. A land of contrasts, it was ancient when Thomas Paine sat down to comfort the Continental Army with his "Crisis" essays; it was a beehive of acequias, pueblos, ranches, cattle branding, animal husbandry, Indian warfare before the Mayflower steered into Plymouth Rock; it was a Kingdom of the far flung Spanish empire when Shakesphere was writing his "Julius Ceasar". Yet by no stretch of the imagination could anyone imagine the setbacks and humiliations in store for this Land of Enchantment throttled by greedy politicians who acclaimed it as a land of opportunity but stiffled every opportunity for Statehood with the same old sing-song of the Wilmot Proviso, the Texas Claim, a desert, a Free-Soil conquest, a land as desolate as the manana brand of people it nurtured.

For four years following the Kearny conquest, with minor exceptions, the people were content. An exchange of flags failed to produce an exchange in the New Mexican way of life. The Anglo-Saxon eventually forced himself on the Norman-French conqueror very much as the New Mexican absorbed the American even to this day. Santa Fe, Socorro, Las Vegas, Belen, Las Cruces, even Albuquerque are unlike any cities found in the United States. New Mexico is as Spanish today as Quebec is French. Some will say its the land; others the people; others still think it is the climate. It was a land of poco tiempo even for Statehood but that was not the fault of the natives. Unscrupulous politicians sent Washington a sordid picture of the land, its people and its possibilities. These strangers who were too small for the big jobs in Washington; these office seekers sent out by their senators and congressmen because party affiliation demanded it, twisted, stormed, cursed, lamented, condoned, wondered, as they struggled to fit their way of life to the vast silences and dry arroyos. of a backward people. Anyone who couldn't speak English was backward to them. Very few sought to learn Spanish. In the end it fell to the educated ones like Gallegos, Perea, Baca, Sarracino, Jose Antonio Martinez, Alarid, Montoya and Donaciano Vigil to align the people into an understanding and need for a Constitution. Those from the East and South sought to permeate the document with Free Soil and pro-slavery laws but New Mexicans would have neither one nor the other. " We do not desire to have domestic slavery within our borders; and, until the time shall arive for admission into the Union of States, we desire to be protected against the introduction of slaves into the Territory." Thus spoke Antonio Jose Martinez, James Quinn, Donaciano Vigil, Juan Perea and Francisco Sarracino voicing the sentiments of the majority of New Mexicans.

The old Palacio was the scene of hot debates during the following year as a tug of war made a scarecrow of the Statehood-Territory issue. The majority of appointees favored a Territorial form of government simply because it was their bread and butter. Statehood would mean elections in which they would definitly be voted "out". When drafting a plan of government the delegates gave suffrage rights to all free white male inhabitants residing within the limits of New Mexico, not already citizens of the United States. Wilmot, in Washington, interpreted this to mean a recognition of slavery and he was bitterly opposed to any territory conquered during the Mexican War as having anything to do with slavery. New Mexicans were surprised as his attitude since it was directed against wild Indian tribes rather than Negroes hardly known to them until several months after the Civil War when colored troops were stationed at Fort Union and Fort Craig.

During the decade preceeding the war many with gold rush fever decided to unharness their horses in New Mexico. The wagons were not as numerous as those continuing on to the coast but they struck tap roots. They had no illusions about gold and envisioned the possibilities of the Rio Grande valley from Taos to Las Cruces. The increase in the number of military posts called for grain, wood, sheep, hide and cattle markets. Greeley's "Go West" slogan meant a livelihood for those as capable with their hands as with their tongues. One of the many opportunists to stream into New Mexico at the time was Richard H. Weightman, a retired army officer. A forceful speaker and a journalist, his platform for Statehood won him a seat in Congress. Houghton and Donaciano Vigil were right in supposing that he would do more talking than acting for Statehood was many decades away. Yet, Weightman directed the political destiny of New Mexico from 1850 to 1854. Considering the high percentage of illiteracy, the language barrier (for very few New Mexicans knew English in 1850-54), the peonage system still functioning, the pride and ambition of the ricos, the indifference of the poorer classes, the struggle against marauding Apaches, Navajos, Kiowas, Utes, Commanches and Cheyennes, this was a comparatively easy feat. Schools were still on paper. Education was obtained either from the parish priest or in Durango, Mexico City, Chihuahua, St Louis, Cincinnati or the Kaskaskia region. Few could afford to send their sons abroad. Girls were instructed by wives of the dons or of the majordomos of the parish church or the morada. In all of New Mexico there was not one convent school much less a nun. Bishop Lamy was to change all this, and the beginning was in this decade prior to Valverde and Glorieta. That he was a power in Santa Fe we recognize from the numerous appeals made to him by the Free Soilers as well as the pro-slavery groups who sought to ingratiate themselves with the totally native Catholic population (and vote) by proving themselves friends of the obispo. Because the Pueblo Indian was also affiliated with this religion it helped to be on the good side of the padre because of government contracts and expenditures through Indian agencies. Exploitation of the Indian was rampant. How many family fortunes were founded on Indian deals is a matter of conjecture.

With the rise of a Statehood Party opposing the Territorial Party, political intrigue became as involved as the days of the Borgias, and as deadly. The power of the press was as powerful then as now. The Territorial Party bought a press and printed pamphlets and broadsides that made Weightman and his followers uncomfortable. It was not an uncommon sight to see protagonists for both sides engaged in head-splitting contests in Burro Alley, on the plaza, around the Palacio, in the cantinas, gambling houses, in the homes and the parroquia churchyard. Duels, shootings and stabbings were not uncommon. Politics, family and religion are the three motivating forces in the life of a New Mexican even today, and in just that order, especially in mountain villages and communities unchanged by time. Politics is a heritage from his mother's womb; his religion comes with baptism after birth; his family ties bind as he ages. The author is no stranger to funerals resulting from political rallies. New Mexico breathes easier after election time. It has been that way since the days of DeVargas; it is a heritage from Spain.

Indians near Chaperito, La Questa (now Villanueva) Gusano (now Sands), Rayado, La Joya, Alamillo—Comanches, Jicarillas, Mescaleros, Utes, Navajos—soon became aware that all was not well with the white man. Free Soilers and Southerners may have been words they failed to understand but action proved there was a division, a disunity that made their raids easier and more frequent. They availed themselves of the opportunity to attack the settlements and the wail of sorrow was heard from Rio Arriba to Mesilla. Even Arroyo Hondo and Agua Fria but a stone's throw from Santa Fe were not spared. Crops failed, too. The cold, bleak, barren winter of 1850 did nothing to alleviate the situation. Despite Indians, famine, bitterness, cracked skulls, pistol shots, the Constitution of 1850 insisted that:

"Slavery in New Mexico is naturally impracticable, and can never, in reality, exist here; wherever it has existed, it has proved a curse and a blight to the State upon which it has been inflicted—a moral, social and political evil. The only manner in which this question now affects us is politically; and on the grounds of this character, with its general evil tendencies, we have unanimously agreed to reject it—if forever...."

Weightman, aided by his knowledge of Spanish and his vote appeal, contrived to have himself named senator-elect for New Mexico. In Washington, when Senator Foote of Mississippi, asked him the sentiments of the people of New Mexico regarding slavery, he answered: "The popular feeling is, I believe, fixedly set against that country being made the arena in which to decide political questions in which the people have no practical interest, and all attempts which have heretofore been made, or which hereafter may be made, to induce the people of that country to take sides on a question in which they are not at all interested, have been, and will, I trust, forever be utterly abortive." (*Congressional Globe*—32nd Congress 1st Sess. 755)

Unsuccessful in his fight for New Mexico Statehood that winter of 1850, Weightman returned to Santa Fe where he immediately announced his candidacy for the office of Territorial delegate. He defeated Reynolds, much to the disgust of William G. Kephart, editor of the *Santa Fe Weekly Gazette,* who insisted that Weightman had no sincere interest in Statehood for New Mexico only a good living and a berth among the politicos in Washington. Despite Houghton, Vigil and Kephart, Weightman did make a sincere effort to push through the Statehood Bill. Washington hoped that with the inauguration of Pierce in 1853, factional quarrels would cease. The Secretary of War, while anxious for peace, had little or no confidence in New Mexico as of any help to the United States. He said on January 10, of that year:

"New Mexico is so remote and so inaccessible and holds so little inducement to emigration that the struggle between the two races (Mexican and American) is destined in all probability to continue there long after it shall have ceased in every portion of the continent. By the last census the total population of New Mexico, exclusive of wild Indians, is, in round numbers, 61,000 souls; and its whole real estate is estimated (in round numbers) at $2,700,000. To protect this small population we are compelled to maintain a large military force at an annual expense nearly equal to one half the value of the whole real estate of the Territory. (Note: He included Arizona.) Would it not be better to induce the inhabitants to abandon a country which seems hardly fit for the habitation of civilized man, by remunerating them for their property in money, or in lands situated in more favorable regions? Even if the governor paid for the property quintruple its value, it would still, merely on the score of economy, be largely the gainer by the transaction and the troops now stationed in New Mexico would be available for the protection of other portions of our own and the Mexican Territory. . . . (32nd Congress 2nd Session House 103)

Had gold been discovered in New Mexico as early as in California, to the extent of a mad rush and scramble for mining districts as did happen shortly after the war, he probably would not have been so anxious to give it back to the Indians. Weightman, annoyed at these words, countered with some of his own:

"If this should be carried out what a spectacle we would see. Passing by the preparation for the departure, with tears of bitterness and sobs that would rend the heart, let us be witnesses of the exodus of the people of New Mexico. Behold the multitude! The rich, in their carriages; others in wagons and carts. See the domestic animals! The flocks and herds, the sheep and goats. The shepherd dogs are there, leading and protecting their charges. (What about the dear, little, mousy-colored burro? Comment mine)—Let me direct your attention to the poor. The patient ass (burro sounds more New Mexican) bears his part in the mournful procession. On this patient beast are laden the aged poor, the gray-haired widow and the man bowed down with years; the mother with child in arms, the sick, the lame, the halt, and the blind. No one in all that multitude has forgotten to bring with him his crucifix and his rosary, or his images, remembrances of the Savior, the Virgin, and the Saints. Few are without some memento of their homes—mayhap a fragment of the cross which stands in the camposanto (cemetery) where lie buried their fathers for two hundred years. While this vast multitude pauses on an eminence to take a last look at the land they are about to behold no more—forever, what is it they see? The uniform of the American Army! There are the dragoons, their sabres flashing in the rays of the setting sun; the serried infantry, with their bristling bayonets; the artillery troops, with their terrible batteries. All are gallant men who have covered themselves with glory in an honorable war. Who commands the army of the exodus? There is no Haynan in our Army. But were there to be an exodus, it would not be in this direction, Mr. Chairman. The people of New Mexico would flee from our limits, carefully shaking the dust from their feet as they crossed the boundary. But I am aware that it is not necessary to lay stress upon this matter. . . ."

Warming up to the subject he told them why and added "Said Col. E. V. Sumner from Santa Fe, May 27, 1852: 'Place the Territory of New Mexico in the same relation to the Government of the United States that it held toward the Mexican government before the war. Withdraw all the troops and civil officers and let the people elect their own civil officers and conduct their government in their own way, under general supervision of our government. It would probably assume a similiar form to the one we found here in 1846, viz., a civil government but under the entire control of the governor. This change would be highly gratifying to this people and I believe they would cheerfully pledge themselves never to ask for any further aid from the United States than the said appropriations that were granted to the other Territories. There would be a pronouncement or two but these would be of no consequence, as they are very harmless when confined to Mexicans alone. The New Mexicans are thoroughly debased and totally incapable of self government, (Here he contradicts himself—New Mexico managed well enough from Peralta to Armijo. Sumner had no use for native New Mexicans because he failed to understand them. He was to New Mexicans what Bascom was to Cochise and the Apaches), and there is no latent quality about them that can ever make them respectable. . . .' (All of them?)

"The people I represent are grossly calumniated by the letter of Col. Sumner. A notorious criminal who had invaded the rights of New Mexicans to such an extent that there was danger of the people forming a mob for their defense, was imprisoned by order of Col. Sumner (J. Calhoun having left). A judge of the Supreme Court issued a habeas corpus and discharged the criminal who was at that time intoxicated, Col. Sumner promptly arrested the criminal and made an order that no criminal in the future should be set at liberty whilst he was drunk, and enforced it. The judge complained that the Colonel had suspended the Habeas Corpus Act. . . ."

Judge Mower wrote from Socorro, May 25, 1852: "Whatever you may hear about a revolution in this Territory do not believe it. There is no truth in it. You know that the power and wealth of the country is in the Rio Abajo (Albuquerque-Belen area) and I have talked with every rich man in the valley and they laugh at the very idea. They say, however, a few discontented spirits may desire it but they have not the means nor the spirit to prosecute it. General Manuel Armijo (at Lemitar six miles above Socorro) says that he will send his head to the President of the United States if there is ever overt act to raise insurrection. They can do nothing. They know it. Besides, all the well informed people of New Mexico prefer American to Mexican rule. . . ."

Weightman's popularity was on the wane since his altercation with the fast riding merchant Francis X. Aubrey. Had he been more tactful and less sensitive he might have fathered New Mexico's Statehood Bill. Whatever the antecedents of Jose Manuel Gallegos, who succeeded him as Territorial Delegate, they stacked up against him because of his inability to comprehend the rapid-fire English of the Senate and the mounting concern over the Kansas-Nebraska Bill as well as the Texas Claim. Had he been as apprehensive about acquiring the language as he was fastidious about his personal appearance and popularity, he might have succeeded where Weightman failed.

Don Miguel Otero (1) of Valencia, near Tome, as adept in English as Spanish, favored the Southern cause. This of course lost him many votes. By actual count the number of slaves in New Mexico never exceeded two dozen at any one time. These belonged to politicians and soldiers. No New Mexican rico owned slaves. It was against the Mexican law prior to American invasion. Some of the Southern politicians freed their slaves in New Mexico as in the case of the Negro barber who had his shop near the cantina just off the plaza in Santa Fe. He was a popluar figure in both places. But he found it hard to make a living because of the comments from legislators and news editors who sought to convince him that he was better off as a slave.

After a rather heated and severely contested election—and which one isn't in New Mexico—Gallegos bowed out to Otero. One factor in Otero's favor was his friendship with Jefferson Davis thus winning for New Mexico many important and favorable appointments which otherwise may have proved detrimental. Before he was thirty Otero out-distanced all other competitors to find himself the most influential and powerful political figure in the Territory. Spruce M. Baird recognized this when he failed to unseat him in the elections of 1857.

It was Otero who was responsible for the passage of the law that prohibited marriage between a negro and a white in New Mexico. It was during the Otero-Baird contest that Abolitionism became an issue. Baird held that Otero was popular simply because he was backed by Secessionists, not because he was Spanish-American. That Otero was able to talk to each of his constituents in their own language seemed to make no difference to Baird. He also refused to admit that Samuel Yost, a Virginian who assumed the editorship of the *Santa Fe Gazette,* may have come in for a large share of the credit. Just a month before the Southernor took over his duties on the paper, Alexander M. Jackson, also closely associated with Jefferson Davis, arrived in Santa Fe as Territorial Secretary. Furthermore, one had but to glance at the list of appointees from Washington who became Territorial governors to know how desperately hard the South was fighting for new States and Territories to oppose the North when necessary, if only in the House and the Senate. The first governor James S. Calhoun, was from Georgia; William C. Lane (1852) was from Missouri; David Meriwether (1853) was from Kentucky; Abraham Rencher (1857) was from North Carolina; Henry Connelly (1861) while actually considered a New Mexican due to his long residence in the Territory, was a native of Virginia, despite his Free Soil sympathies. Secessionists claimed he was on their side but events proved he was definitely Union.

The appointment of Rencher was a bitter pill to swallow. Otero sought to tighten his hold by seeking the assignment for his brother-in-law, Blackwood of North Carolina. Jackson flooded Washington with letters begging the powers-that-be to further the cause of the South by filling every available political post in New Mexico with Southern sympathizers. The field was ripe. In the event of war New Mexico could be the depot between Texas and the coast. Furthermore, there was a federal arsenal at Fort Union and arms at Fort Craig. Jackson had no doubts about a divided Union. He assured his readers of a balanced contest of the South had more land. Seward, Scott and most of the men of influence in the North were holding out the olive branch; willing to make concessions favorable to the South to prevent an open eruption. Otero agreed that the North seemed to be backing down to the South for the sake of peace. Failing in his try for his wife's brother, he urged the President to name William G. Blackwood as associate justice to the Supreme Court of the Territory. The new judge lost no time in aligning the proslavery faction. Jackson meantime devoted all his spare time in drawing up a slave code to be read before the Territorial legislature. Otero kept in touch with editors of newspapers in the South as well as the popular *New York Herald* reporting proslavery activity in Santa Fe and other sections of New Mexico. Representative Pedro Valdez of Taos introduced the Bill on January 22, 1859. Several weeks later the Council adopted the Slave Code. It is interesting to note that the Territorial Council was made up of eleven native New Mexican members and two Anglo; the House comprised twenty-three New Mexicans and one Anglo. Exactly twenty-three favored the Bill in the House; all favored it in the Council. Governor Rencher immediately signed it. (For further research concerning this read the Acts of the Legislature of New Mexico in the office of the head librarian at the Museum Library, Palace of the Governors in Santa Fe) At face value some of the measures seemed ridiculous to the average New Mexican. The majority couldn't afford a new suit of clothes let alone a slave. Hence the Slave Code applied to the politicos and some ricos suspicious of Northern concessions. Some of the major measures called for:

1. Let it be a penal offense to supply false papers, either printed or handwritten, to a negro or slave.

2. To kill a slave or otherwise inflict upon him physical violence will meet with the same penalty of the law meted out to a white person.

3. To steal a slave or procure his escape is punishable by imprisonment to from four to ten years and fines.

4. Any person seeking to entice, hire, or by persuasion or inducement cause a slave to be absent from his master's services, shall be outlawed as for a penal offense.

5. To incite a slave into insurrection, rebellion or resistance against his rightful and lawful master merits the same penalty.

6. It is forbidden to gamble with slaves nor is anyone permitted to furnish them arms. Exception is made should a person have the master's written consent.

7. Any person capturing a runaway slave is entitled to claim the reward offered. Minimum reward should be twenty dollars plus ten cents for each mile from the start of pursuit to the place of capture.

8. All sheriffs are requested to receive and keep under guard such runaway slaves until lawfully claimed. Any sheriff failing in his duty in this respect is subject to a fine of not less than five hundred dollars. He may not be re-elected to office.

9. Unclaimed slaves may be sold by the sheriff to the highest bidder.

10. Any slave indicted for a felony has the right to counsel to be paid for by the master.

11. The master must procure the means to safeguard the health of his slave.

12. Masters found guilty of inhuman treatment of slaves will be prosecuted and punished.

13. No master may give the slave the use of his own time.

14. Any slave found guilty of disorderly conduct in a public place, of using abusive language, or insolent language, or make such signs to a white person may be punished by receiving thirty-nine lashes across the bared back.

15. No slave, freed negro, mulatto, may give evidence in court against a white person. They may, however, testify against each other.

16. Marriages between the two races are forbidden. Any such marriages are hereby annulled. This holds for the free as well as for the slave.

17. Any negro guilty of rape upon a white woman is punished with death.

18. No slave within the borders of New Mexico may be emancipated.

19. Any slave abroad from his master's domain without a passport will be punished with thirty-nine strokes across the bared back.

20. No freed negro is to be held as a slave. The penalty for this is not less than five and not more than ten years imprisonment and fines.

21. By slave we hereby mean a member of the African race. These laws do not apply to peons.

22. Fugitive servants, bound to their masters under contract, are to be arrested when apprehended.

23. The courts shall not interfere with the correction of such servants by their masters unless they are severely mistreated with clubs or stripes.

24. The law of 1851 prohibiting a servant quitting his master's service while in debt still binds.

25. The law of 1853 wherein a sheriff may contract a servant's services to the highest bidder when the master no longer has use for him still binds.

These laws show signs of optimism on the part of the Southerners, for they were evidently written for the future. Certainly no one thinks they were written for two dozen bewildered beings.

Flushed with their success in the legislature many ricos, with an eye more on holding their peons rather than procuring slaves, sought to interpret these laws as including captive Indians and native peon women. Captive Indians brought a bounty, not to the Territory but to the individual. I myself saw a list of one hundred and six sold at Paraje, soon to be the scene of activity between Southern Texans and Canby's men, who had no choice but accept the names imposed upon them and rejoice that they were valued at five dollars a head. Dons often sold the services of peons to other ricos especially in the Bernalillo and Socorro areas where vineyards were fast making the Territory the wine center of the nation before the industry was taken over by California. It was the policy of a rico (there were many exceptions) to employ a married couple on his ranch, pay them starvation wages, take out these wages in food, clothing and other commodities until the peons were neck deep in debt, so that they bound themselves or a son or daughter over in servitude to work it out. Thus the rico was secure of their services for many years. This system survived in the mountain areas many years following the war. It has its counterpart in our own day especially in mining areas where men cash their checks in cantinas, drinking up the whole check plus the one he still has to work for which leaves nothing for the wife and children, much less the payment of the grocery bill.

Governor Rencher, realizing the abuses that would arise in Indian captive traffic, firmly and convincingly rounded out these greedy ones in his State of the Territory message when he declared that Indians were not slaves nor was it within the legislative power of the governing body to declare them so. He did allow, however, that those Indians who were slaves at the time General Kearny's entrada, provided that the Mexican government had previously recognized them as such, came within the scope of the law. Despite his declaration, several hundred Indians were classified as slaves at the time the Civil War broke out. Even after the war captive Indians were held in bondage and it was not until almost the turn of the century that this abuse was finally stamped out.

New Mexicans were used to government by remote control. First it was Spain, then Mexico, now Washington—always a place "muy lejos." They had no fear of Spain, ignored Mexico and tolerated Washington. But Texas! Ah, Texas was another matter. The propaganda spread by Armijo, Salazar, Archuleta and others concerning the advance of the Texas-Santa Fe Expedition was able to hold its terrors almost a decade later when it was noised abroad that Texas claimed Santa Fe and was going to do something about it. Not even the show of the U. S. Army uniforms was able to squelch their terror. When Roman women wished to frighten their children they would say: "Look, Hannibal is at the door." When New Mexican mothers wished to correct their children they would say: "Look, the Texans are here to get you." It never entered the minds of the children that the Texans would get their fathers first. Mountain Men they knew and liked. Texans were another matter. Yet when the women of San Miguel, Belen, Socorro and Tome saw the pitiable plight of the Texans and the treatment accorded them by Armijo and Salazer they defied these rulers to procure them clothes and food. The Texans were not so bad after all. But propaganda has a way of working up mob hysteria. Again the forces were set in motion to convince the natives that the Texans would destroy their homes, burn their fields, rob their women, defile their holy places, enslave their children, tax the heads of families. No wonder they sighed with relief when the government paid Texas a price to relinquish her claim on Santa Fe.

Then, too, there were those who would have rejoiced to see all the Indians killed outright. Members of the Territorial Legislature were more humane. It was they, rather than General Carleton later, who originated the idea of rounding up the savage hordes and placing them on reservations. They reasoned that if the Pueblo Indians could do it, the nomads and Plains Indians should have no difficulty in following suit. They complained to Washington that there was not a corner of New Mexico that was not hemmed in by rapacious tribes who murdered and plundered at will. Cunningly, they devised methods of depriving New Mexicans of their crops and sources of subsistence. There was no reason for these tribes to roam at will when they could be rounded up and made to behave. It hurt the members of the House to think that the rest of the nation looked upon every city and town in New Mexico as frontier villages surrounded by high adobe walls to keep out the marauders, and ranchers mere sheepherders guarding flocks they could plunder at will. Said Jose Guadalupe Gallejos, President of the Council, 1854:

". . . El gran deseo de nuestro pueblo espresado ahora por medio de su Asamblea Legislativa es que las diferentes naciones barbaras que nos circundan y que anden errantes en nuestro suelo, sean reducidas a vivir dentro de limites prescriptos y convenientes, en donde sean ensenados a cultivar la tierra para conseguir su subsistencia, en vez de hacer esta, como ahora con el robo y pillaje de nuestros intereses, acaso con la creencia naturleza los ha proceido alli les seran ensenados paulatinamente el cultivo de las artes y de virtud y al trabajo, la paz, y la lealtad en sus tratados, proporcionandoles el Gobierno General los medios, etc. . . ."

("It is the wish of our people through the Legislative Assembly that the various barbarous nations that surround us and errantly be required to live within certain prescribed limits, where they will be taught to cultivate the land in order to be self-subsisting, instead of doing what they are now doing in robbing and pillaging and thus little by little they will learn to cultivate the arts, virtue and work, peace and loyalty to their treaties, the Federal Government granting the means to make this possible.")

Gallegos regretted that New Mexico was held in little or no esteem by the Federal Government because of these savages who were permitted to roam and steal as they saw fit, thus creating the impression that the Territory was in too primitive a condition for consideration by Congress as a State. If this situation was remedied the rest of the nation would not look on all New Mexicans alike as barbarians and savages. Washed of the rapacity of these tribes, New Mexico could invite in other interests to develop her resources. That Indians could steal live stock as they pleased was not as disastrous as taking captives to be sold into slavery in Mexico or to other tribesmen.

The Navajos were particularly noted for this. In October, 1858, they raided Sebolleta and took many children captive. In that same month they swooped down on Cubero carrying off sheep, women and children, going on from there to Sierra de los Ladrones where they relieved Juan Luna of over a thousand sheep after killing all his sheep herders. Their depradations during 1856 through 1860 were without number. They stole hundreds of thousands of sheep during this time, many horses, cattle, goats and milk cows. At Rio Arriba they cleaned out Juan Reyes Pino; at Sabinal they burned out Mariano Silba; at Rio Puerco they depleted the Luna brothers' stock; at San Miguel del Bado they killed all the hands at the Felix Chaves ranch. The Commanches came in from Texas and wiped out Feliciano Gutierrez at the same place.

New Mexico, prior to the Civil War, compirsed three hundred thousand square miles, a territory larger than the combined New England States, New York and Pennsylvania. Levi J. Keithley, President of the House, argued that while these recommendations impressed him, how could the government supply enough soldiers to adequately take care of the situation? There were Utes and Cheyennes to the north, Apaches and Lipans to the south, Mojaves, Utes and Yumas to the west, Lipans, Comanches, Kiowas and other tribes to the east—to say nothing of the hordes of internal tribes—Utes, Navajos, Apaches, Jicarillas and others. To track these down would require immense numbers of soldiers; but more than all this, men with a knowledge of the country, the habits of the various tribes of Indians, and spies to watch their every move.

Keithly was in favor of a civilian volunteer army. He presented a bill before the Legislature to that effect. But this was defeated because that august body could not agree on just how the money for all this was to be raised. He mapped out a series of forts—one on the San Juan river, one in the Navajo territory, one near Fort Defiance, one near Anton Chico between the Pecos River and Fort Union, one between Fort Union and Fort Stanton for the protection of wagon trains and overland mail routes, one at Pawnee Fork, one on the Canadian River, one at the headwaters of the Colorado. He suggested that the volunteers stationed at these posts be given picks and shovels and commanded to dig for minerals, which would help raise the funds to pay them. Carleton was later to fall in line with this plan, establishing posts in Arizona, Colorado and New Mexico.

President Pierce recommended to the Congress of the United States that two more regiments of mounted troops be created in New Mexico (January 31, 1855). If, and when, Congress gave the green light, Ceran St. Vrain was to head one regiment because Pierce was impressed with his civil and military record. Congress failed to pass the bill, suggesting that more men be sent to swell the garrisons already established. Besides, it seemed a waste of money to do anything for a country without a future. The appropriation could be used to better advantage elsewhere. Shortly before, in the late fall of 1854, Cheyennes and Apaches combined forces to raid within sight of Santa Fe, stealing one hundred and fifty head of horses and killing fifteen people within a stone's throw of the old San Miguel Mission. From there they went to Valencia, where they wounded Mariano Pino and killed two of his sons. They next raided the fields near Fort Union, running off five hundred head of cattle. At Bernalillo they took fifty mules and five thousand sheep from the Perea family. They stole fifty more horses and mules at Isleta.

At this time the total population of New Mexico numbered 69,307. Acting Governor Wm. S. Messervy sent prominent New Mexicans such as Gallegos, Pino, Donaciano Vigil, into San Miguel and Rio Arriba counties to raise several regiments of Territorial Militia. These were pressed into service for two months to subdue the Utes and Jicarillas around the Rayado area, who were becoming as bold as the Cheyennes and Comanches.

In 1850 Donaciano Vigil lamented the fact that of the adults in New Mexico, over twenty-five thousand interviewed said they could not read nor write. He urged that the Legislature appropriate funds for schools but it was not until December 30, 1854, that he got any response to his request. The Legislature was more concerned about county fairs at Tome, Santa Fe, Lemitar and Mesilla. Also there was the work of dividing the land acquired by the Gadsden Purchase into precincts. On February 3, 1855, Mesilla was made the Fourth Precinct, Santo Tomas de Iturbide the Fifth, and Los Amoles the Sixth. Lieut. S. D. Sturgis of the Regular Army led the Militia against the Mescalero Apaches who had raided Galisteo (1855) and commended them for their bravery and knowledge of Indian warfare. Canby was not to be of the same opinion at Valverde. Col. Thomas J. Fauntleroy, 1st Reg. Dragoons, was publicly cited for his good work against the Utes, Apaches and Jicarillas, pursuing them over the Raton mountains during snow storms, cutting off their food supplies until, half frozen to death, they sued for peace.

Leaving the Militia and the Regulars to fight the Indians, the Legislature next turned its attention to grants for possible railroads. It was hoped that the Atlantic and Pacific would reach Santa Fe by the winter of 1855. The laws governing the New Mexico Mining & Railroad Company were fixed in 1856. Then came the New Mexico Railroad Co., Inc., headed by Henry Connelly, Otero, Pino, Perea, St. Vrain and others. Again faced with the Indian problem which no amount of soldiers seemed to erase, the governor provided that any man of good character who could do so was empowered to raise a volunteer company to campaign against Indians who in any way molested private and public property anywhere within the confines of New Mexico. Such a force, however, was not to take the field unless it numbered two hundred men or over.

In an effort to replenish its fast emptying purse, the Legislature signed a contract with the Rio Grande Company of Santa Fe, headed by Samuel J. Jones, Robert P. Kelley, L. S. Owings, who were authorized to build a bridge across the Rio Grande at Mesilla. Any person wishing to cross this bridge must pay twenty-five cents. If he rode horseback he was to add an additional fee of twenty-five cents for the horse. There was a toll of fifty cents for a carriage; two dollars for a wagon and team; one penny for every sheep, hog, goat, mule, jack, horse or mare, horned cattle would not be permitted to cross without the owner paying six and one-fourth cents for each. Indians crossed free. The Legislature next voted ten thousand dollars for preparing the Santa Fe-Fort Union road. This was a rather high expenditure since just prior to the Civil War the governing body took in $9,150—spent 6,818 and was in debt $6,818 when hostilities commenced.

The officials when the Slavery question reached its height were:

  David Meriwether, Governor.
  Wm. W. H. Davis, Secretary of the Territory.
  James J. Davenport, Chief Justice.
  Kirby Benedict, Associate Justice.
  Perry E. Brocchus, Associate Justice.
  Wm. Claude Jones, U. S. Attorney.
  Charles Blummer, U. S. Marshal.
  Samuel Ellison, Translator.
  Charles L. Spencer, Treasurer.
  Horace L. Dickenson, Auditor.
  Henry Connelly, Member of the Council.
  Donaciano Vigil, Engrossing Clerk.
  Levi J. Keithly, Speaker of the House.

And it was a House Divided. Donaciano Vigil still harped on Education and dreamed his dreams for the University of the Territory of New Mexico at Santa Fe; Connelly of Peralta, was for increasing the Santa Fe Trail trade tariff; Benedict was storming against Arizona, which was preparing a Bill For Separation from New Mexico. Keithly was ready to introduce a bill repealing the Slave Act. Many felt that Arizona was not ready for independence from New Mexico, nevertheless, the Legislature said: "Let us unite in favor of the citizens of Arizona and do all in our power to procure from the Congress of the United States a separate Territory of Arizona. Let it be resolved, therefore, that Arizona be conceded a Territorial Organization and the Congress of the United States will have done a deed of justice in accepting the petition so asked." (*Diario de la Camara,* Vol. 9, p. 148.)

Keithly, a native of St. Louis, Missouri, settled in Las Vegas, New Mexico, after having lived in various parts of the Territory since 1831. As Speaker of the House he arranged with Representative Cueller y Medina of Socorro that he second Keithly's motion in favor of repeal and give a speech to the crowds in the galleries regarding the hatred Mexico always held for slavery. When Cueller finished not only people in the galleries but every legislator in the Chamber rose in applause. Shouts and cheers of "Down With Slavery," "Repeal, Repeal," filled the air. Had the voting taken place at that moment, slavery in New Mexico would have been repealed. Silently, one of the opposition who had been cheering but a moment before, asked if it would not be better to await the voting until the next day, since it was so near closing time.

In the gallery was a friend. He called to him and asked if a caucus could not be held at his home that evening. All the proslavery members as well as Keithly and Cueller were invited to attend. Liquor flowed freely, as did many tongues and later many fists. Cueller was soon convinced that he was wrong in supporting the Repeal Bill. No amount of threats would make Keithly change his mind. Eventually, the police were called in to squelch the riot. In that home that night was fought the first battle of the Civil War in New Mexico—not with guns, but with tongues, fists, knives and broken bottles. The next day Keithly was not able to make his appearance. Cueller stood up and declared the chair vacant. The resolution was passed, and adopted. Keithly was retired from the chair in absencia. Cueller was voted to take his place. Keithly's Bill was crushed. Crushed by the injustice, he resigned and returned to Las Vegas, where he became Indian Agent. Following this he returned to farming. He is buried at Las Vegas. Cueller repented his action, and when the war broke out he enlisted in the Militia under Col. Stapleton.

Meantime, action against the Indians seeming to produce no result, the need for Federal aid against them was again being brought to the attention of Congress. In 1854 a grant of $30,000 was made for the purpose of effecting treaties with the Apache, Ute and Navajo. Another grant of $25,000 was allotted for general expenses of the Indian service in New Mexico. Meriwether, in keeping with the wishes of Congress, signed treaties with a number of tribes, forwarded them to the Senate, only to learn that not one of them was ever ratified.

It was hard to ascertain just what the Senate wanted of him. Individual members seemed to be more interested in minerals, possible railroads, trading posts, private profits. What streams could be navigated? Would it be worth while for such and such a Senator to invest in warehouses along the Rio Grande? What about the possibilities of a tobacco industry? What about the wool industry? Would it be safe to invest in river boats? Would it be easier to navigate streams than send supplies over the Santa Fe Trail? It was not easy being Territorial governor.

At long last it seemed that Congress would fall in line with the reservation idea by passing the Indian Appropriation Acts of 1856 and 1857. The 1856 Act provided for the separation of the offices of governor and superintendent of Indian affairs. James L. Collins, a native of Kentucky, was named Superintendent of Indian Affairs. A pioneer in the true sense of the word he had crossed the plains to Santa Fe with pack animals, wagons and teams, an innovation along the Santa Fe Trail. Twenty-six when he first saw Santa Fe (1826) he decided to open a mercantile business in Chihuahua as more favorable than Santa Fe, remaining there until the outbreak of the Mexican War. Back in the City of Holy Faith he founded the *Santa Fe Gazette*. Active in New Mexican affairs he was a great help to President Buchanan, who appointed him to this office. Ever a protagonist for Reservations he submitted his plan to the Commissioner in January, 1858. He decided that by moving the Utes to the San Juan river, and the Apaches along the Gila, with military posts to watch their movements, they would be far enough away from the settlements for the natives not to be troubled further with these tribes. The following year Congress authorized the creation of a reserve for the Pima and Maricopa on or near the Gila. Another was authorized for the Apache in May, 1860, but unfortunately this was later returned to the public domain, possibly because treaties made by Meriwether in 1855 were suddenly made void by the reopening of hostilities.

Over in Fort Defiance Major Brooks owned a negro slave who managed at times to procure fire water both for his own and Indian consumption. One day a young buck came in, who gave the slave some argument. Not to be outdone in threats, the Indian ended by killing the negro. Angered by the rashness of the Navajo as well as sullen over the loss of his slave, Brooks, the post commander, demanded that the chief turn the culprit over to him for punishment. This he refused to do, saying that the white soldier was using this as a pretext to break the treaty. Brooks gave him a certain amount of time to give up the murderer or suffer the consequences. Declaring that a state of war now existed between the Federal Government and his tribe the chief absconded with his people into the hills. Brooks sent Col. Miles to invade the Navajo country. Reservations would have to wait another day. Miles accomplished little save gaining knowledge of the country, which was to serve him well in other campaigns. Major Electus Bacus was next sent out, but he only succeeded in destroying crops and livestock, hoping to subjugate the Indians by a scorched earth policy. Unwilling to starve to death the Navajos resorted to raids on the settlements.

Collins, angered by the action of Brooks and other undoing all his good work, contrived to have the Indians meet at Fort Defiance, where a treaty of peace was signed on Christmas Day, 1858. It proved of short duration. Colonel Bonneville, department commander, sat in on the signing.

Abraham Rencher of North Carolina succeeded Meriwether as Governor on August 17, 1857. One of his first acts was to take issue with Col. Thomas Fauntleroy, a Virginian, over authority regarding the Indians. Rencher, declaring that he as highest official in the Territory, answerable only to the President, could make certain demands on the military, sent for the protection of the populace. He relied more on native volunteers than on the regular, but insisted that Fauntleroy supply New Mexicans with ammunition to fight the Navajos. The colonel refused, whereupon the governor aired his grievance in a letter to Secretary Cass, dated at Santa Fe September 4, 1860:

"We are likely to have very serious difficulties in this Territory by the Mexicans moving in armed bodies upon the Navajo Indians, without any authority, either under the laws of the United States, or of this Territory. After the arrival of the Utah troops, and after Colonel Fauntleroy had given the Governor and the people assurances both of his ability and his determination to chastise the Navajo Indians, the people of this country held a meeting in Santa Fe, and passed resolutions . . .

"Urged on by a few ambitious or interested leaders, the people held a convention at this place on August 27th, and resolved to take matters into their own hands. They appointed officers and agreed to raise a regiment of mounted volunteers, to enter the Navajo country on September 20th in open disregard both of the laws of the United States, and of the Territory. If this movement for mounted volunteers had been made one or two months ago, when the Territory was destitute of troops, and the military commander under orders not to make war upon the Navajos, I might have assumed the responsibility of calling them out, with the hope of being approved. But now, when the Territory is full of troops, and the military commander under orders from the Secretary of War, is organizing a vigorous campaign against the Indians, I cannot see the necessity of volunteers. I have, therefore, been compelled, under a painful sense of public duty, to resist this movement, and I feel the more embarrassed in the performance of this duty, in consequence of the favor shown it by a few Federal officers, especially by the Chief Justice (William A. Davidson), whose high position on the bench must give him influence . . ."

Fauntleroy insisted that means other than war should be employed in dealing with the Navajos. Collins replied that the situation being what it was only war could cause the Navajos to sue for peace. Governor Rencher agreed with the Superintendent but still insisted that the Regular Army and not the Volunteers fight the war.

Tired of the many letters from the Governor, Secretary Cass wrote Fauntleroy commanding him to send out an expedition. Whether as a taunt against Rencher or for other reasons, Fauntleroy would not head the expedition, sending instead Lt. Col. E. R. S. Canby to invade the Navajo country in the winter of 1860-61. Marching from Fort Garland, then part of New Mexico, Canby spent months in the field in a sincere effort to negotiate peace rather than in wholesale slaughter. He was of the opinion that a reservation was the answer and several years later when hailed before the Senate about his views concerning the Bosque Redondo Reservation at Fort Sumner, his word gave Carleton the go-ahead signal to establish the reservation for the Navajos and Apaches. Second in command on this expedition was his brother-in-law, Major H. Sibley, whom he was to face as a Confederate enemy at Valverde, the battle in which Collins was also to have an active part, as well as at Johnson's Ranch at Canoncito. President Lincoln re-appointed him Superintendent of Indian Affairs. Shortly after the war he was made Receiver of the Land Office and Custodian of United States Funds at Santa Fe. It was while protecting these funds against bandits that he was shot and killed, June 6, 1869. (See the account in the *Santa Fe Gazette* at the New Mexico Museum Library, Santa Fe.)

The campaigns of the Regulars did not stop many influential

New Mexicans from forming their own companies to pursue Indians raiding the settlements. The more notable ones raised at San Miguel del Bado, Taos, Socorro, Polvadera, Rio Arriba and Abiquiu. Here Sub-agent Albert H. Pfeiffer led a party of natives and Utes into the Navajo country, capturing live stock and returning with many prisoners. It is interesting to note that many Pueblo Indians accompanied these private expeditions, serving as scouts and guides. The Utes were traditional enemies of the Navajos, which accounts for Pfeiffer's success. Had only Utes been permitted in the field against them the Navajos would have sued for peace sooner.

As time went on the Regulars concerned themselves more and more with the turn of events in their home states. Already they were dividing into North and South. Possibly Fauntleroy, Bonneville (a New Yorker) preferred the New Mexicans to raise troops against the Indians in order to save the Regulars for the inevitable conflict they knew was just around the corner. From 1851 to 1863 New Mexico was known as the Ninth Military Department of the United States. The first commander was Colonel Edwin V. Sumner, a New Englander. He had little use for New Mexican and less for the Indian. The rift between the Governor and the military, which was not to heal until Governor Connelly was appointed by Lincoln, began with Sumner, who had decided views as to how much authority was vested in the military commander of the Department. Sumner favored military posts away from cities and towns because he said these only served to corrupt the soldier. Fauntleroy succeeded Sumner. He was of the opinion that many New Mexicans instigated the Indians to rebel and that they were using the Regulars to fight battles they themselves commenced or at least instigated. He fought for the Confederacy during the Civil War, holding the rank of brigadier-general.

Colonel B. L. Bonneville succeeded Fauntleroy (who managed to have a fort named in his honor). Most of his campaigning was in territory now included in Arizona. Fauntleroy returned a second time to get into difficulties with Collins and Rencher. In 1860, Colonel W. W. Loring was given command of the Department, retaining that position until the war broke out. He resigned to join the Confederate Army.

All the great generals, with the possible exception of Lee, that fought for either the North or South, saw service in New

Mexico at some time or other during those years. How long Grant served in New Mexico I have not been able to ascertain although it was of very short duration. James Longstreet was serving in New Mexico when the war broke out. When Grant visited his brother-in-law at Fort Union he passed a remark to the editor of the *Las Vegas Optic* that New Mexico was not new to him, inferring that he had seen service there.

In New York editor Greeley published an editorial inferring that corruption played a part in the selection of Territorial officers. This angered Otero, who remained in Washington long enough following Lincoln's election to answer the charge. New Mexicans now came to see that Don Miguel was not the avowed Secessionist he professed to be, but was actually neutral, concerned only with New Mexico. His Southern wife was actually the Secessionist. Lincoln pondered Greeley's words and cast about for a reliable man to succeed Rencher. He picked Henry Connelly. Hearing of this appointment William Need wrote to Secretary Seward, August 8, 1861:

"The appointment of Dr. Henry Connelly of Peralta is one that should not have been made. In the first place, Dr. Connelly is a native of Kentucky (actually he was born in Virginia, his parents moving to Kentucky when he was four years of age); has resided in New Mexico for some twenty or twenty-five years. He is a respected citizen, fond of making money and hoarding it up. He is inter-married with a native of this country and is reputed to be rich. He has always been a pro-slavery man—was in favor of the introduction of slavery into the Territory, and owned negroes here until within a comparatively short period. A year or two ago he took the last of his slaves from this Territory to the States and sold them. He is now a professed neutral man, provided the Union cause is the strongest. According to the oral statement of Col. B. Grayson, late commissary in the United States Army (but resigned in favor of the Confederacy), a native of Kentucky, Dr. Connelly agreed with him in opinion on the slavery question, and Col. Grayson is a Secessionist, per se."

True, Connelly lent his support to the Slavery Bill when he was in the Legislature, but his New Mexican wife made him see the error of slavery and induced him to not only change his views but rid himself of the few slaves he owned. Whatever his previous convictions when he was appointed by Lincoln he remained steadfast to the Union. Rather than see the Territory fall into the hands of the Texans under Scurry of the Sibley Brigade, he moved the seat of government to Las Vegas, alerting it to be ready to remove to Fort Union should the Confederates march on Las Vegas. While a native of Virginia, where he was born on September 1, 1800, he was reared in Kentucky and educated in the study of medicine. He left Kentucky in 1820 to practice his profession in Clay County, Missouri. The sudden rise of the Santa Fe trade so interested him that he abandoned the surgical knife for the freer life of the Mountain Men and merchants who aroused his curiosity with tales of Taos, Santa Fe, Chihuahua and the open plains. There is no indication that he practiced medicine in New Mexico.

At Santa Fe his pleasing disposition won the confidence of Manuel Armijo, Juan Vigil, Guadalupe Miranda, Donaciano Vigil, and other influential New Mexicans. Like Collins, he decided to engage in the mercantile business in Chihuahua. Between that city and Santa Fe he came to have a thorough understanding of the Mexican temperament which was to serve him well when he appealed to them as governor to preserve the Union. During the years preceding the Mexican War he made a number of trips across the plains and was one of the first of the Chihuahua-Santa Fe merchants to make use of the llano stacado in a trip from Chihuahua to New Orleans. When General Kearny entered Santa Fe in 1848 Connelly chanced to be in Santa Fe and proved himself of use to the conqueror as an interpreter and in convincing him with J. W. Magoffin, of the uselessness of fighting against the Americans.

Determined now to spend the remainder of his days in New Mexico he built a home near the Chavez residence at Peralta. There in 1849 he married the widow of Don Mariano Chavez. He served New Mexico in many capacities until his appointment as Governor. He watched with interest the demands Texas made on New Mexico and the claim of that State of all the territory to the headwaters of the Rio Grande. He saw how determined the New Mexicans were to defend their land in the event of an invasion from Texas, the Texas-Santa Fe Expedition still fresh in their minds. This hard feeling between Texas and New Mexicans he was to play up when Baylor's Babies made their march from San Antonio. In the weeks following his induction into office he travelled through Rio Arriba, Taos,

Arroyo Hondo, Arroyo Seco, Las Vegas, San Miguel del Bado, Anton Chico, Chaparito, La Questa (present Villanueva) and other settlements, making them understand the situation because he used their own language. He incessantly harped upon the Texas claim to all of New Mexico east of the Rio Grande.

"Do you want them to take away your land? Did not your fathers repulse the invaders at San Miguel, Anton Chico? Were not these enemies taken in chains to Mexico? You are a fighting race. Fight for your rights and repel the invader." With such talks as these he had no difficulty in arousing them to join Kit Carson and others raising Volunteer troops for the Union.

At least so he thought. They paid attention well enough and were full of resolve when he spoke to them, but he was forced to admit that he was not as successful as he thought, for the native was always looking "with greater concern to his private and petty interests and would take steps for the defense of his land whenever he saw fit"—for this was the land of manana and they would face the problem when confronted with it, not before.

Rumors came of an advancing Texan army. The people gathered about the various plazas. Was it true that the Texans were coming? Was it true that they were at Mesilla? We want to get in the fight but we have our crops, our farms, families— who will take care of them? It is to protect them that we fight. They say that Sibley has resigned and gone over to the Texans. Yes, and Fauntleroy who would not give us ammunition to fight the Navajos; Loring, too, the boss soldier. What are we to do? Can they all be wrong? The soldiers are leaving us. Some are in Blue, the others they say wear Grey. Who will protect us against the Jicarillas, Apaches, Utes, Navajos, Comanches now? That winter, Connelly was satisfied to see the enlistments grow. Still it was not enough. He wrote to Colorado for help. Now more than ever the military cooperated with the Territorial government, but it took a war to do it.

※ ※ ※

NOTES AND COMMENTS

P. Jose Antonio Jose Martinez (1793-1867)—Politically (and that is our only concern here), P. Martinez is to New

Mexico what Savonarola was to Florence. His enemies have painted him worse than the facts in the case. Beaubien, Bent, Carlon, Quinn and others had left us a rather distorted view of an educator, publisher, presbyter, patriot and politician possibly because of his objections to their right to the Sangre de Cristo Grant. In the light of present-day research his pretensions to a Republic of Taos seem to have stemmed from their imaginations, for new light on the whole political scene shows Martinez to have been a useful and forceful figure. As a Mexican the defense of New Mexico against American invasion would have been his duty. When he learned that Kearny changed his status he did not rebel as some suspect. When Kearny sent a squad of soldiers to conduct him to Santa Fe he sent them back to the general with the message that his word was his bond. He was American because New Mexixco now flew the American flag and he would remain so. Kearny did not doubt his word. He almost lost his life in protecting Lee (brother to the one killed in the Taos Uprising) because he would not go back on his word. The Alvarez Papers and the Donaciano Vigil Papers reveal many fine qualities about this man so wronged by his opponents. He was a Free-Soiler in sentiment but was more concerned with the education of the masses. Like his friend Vigil, he decided to leave the war and the pros and cons of Union or Secession to Santa Fe and Washington. His concern was schools, reservations for Indians, government aid for the poor. He is buried in the Kit Carson Cemetery in Taos.

James Quinn—one of the early Anglo settlers in New Mexico, came to know it as a Mountain Man, trapper, Santa Fe trader and inn keeper (Taos). He eventually settled near the site of Tiptonville (later Watrous) and became quite proficient with Spanish. This helped him in his political career. In 1853 he was the president of the Territorial Legislative Assembly. After 1854 he was no longer in politics.

Francisco Sarracino—He was Jefe Politico of New Mexico from 1833 to May 1835. He fought to preserve New Mexico for A. Perez but saw the cause was lost and accepted the Revolution. He was Prefect of Bernalillo county under the Kearny Code. He continued in politics until moving into the Polvadera-Lemitar area where his descendants engage in farming. He was a Union man. He carried on the fight for Statehood all during his political carrer after the Constitution was sent on to Washington. It was suspected that pro-slavers were responsible for its long delay in reaching Washington.

Richard Hanson Weightman (1818-1861)—A native of Maryland, he had hoped for an army career until expelled from West Point for being too handy with a knife. He was captain of artillary under Kearny in the Mexican War and it was he who brought the General's commission to him shortly after the climb over Raton Pass. It was Weightman who brought the New Mexico Constitution to Washington and placed it in the hands of the President. Congress did not see it until September 9th, 1850. Donaciano Vigil and Houghton were of the opinion that Weightman was not half pleading the cause for New Mexico's Statehood and placed the blame on his shoulders. Weightman returned to work on his newspaper and to an altercation with Francis Xavier Aubrey. While acquitted of the fatal stabbing of the merchant in the old La Fonda, he was never again a happy man. He enlisted in the Civil War and was killed in the battle of Wilson's Creek, Missouri, August 10, 1861.

Edwin Vose Sumner (1797-1863)—This soldier was responsible for many of the unflattering things Congress learned about New Mexico during these years prior to the war. If he had his way he would leave it to beasts and Indians. It was no fit habitation for a soldier nor a white man. Santa Fe he considered a den of evil; Las Vegas was no better and Albuquerque was worse. He was responsible for several military posts only on the insistance of his superiors. He was anxious for both civil and military control of New Mexico in the hopes of bringing about needed reforms.

Francis X. Aubrey—A French-Canadian trapper he had some experience as a mountain Man and a Santa Fe Trader. He made a journey from Santa Fe to Missouri in eight days to win a wager. Later on he cut it down to five. A pathfinder, he convinced merchants that the trip to California was not any more difficult than the trip to Independence, Missouri. He was a Union man and might have done much for New Mexico had he not been killed by Weightman.

Miguel Antonio Otero (1829-1882)—Otero sponsored the Southern cause mostly because he recognized the concessions the North was making to the South in the hopes of avoiding war. A power such as this could do much for New Mexico. This stand gave him a certain amount of influence in Washington and many of the government expenditures during these years helped the Territory so long as this influence held. After the war it made no difference, The Huntington Library in San Marino, California has some interesting letters; in one of these Otero wrote Jackson, shortly before the war: "I have been requested by Gen. R. Davis of Mississippi to write you a letter, requesting you to draw up an act for the protection of property in slaves in New Mexico, and cause the same to be passed by our Legislature. I know that the laws of the United States, the Constitution, and the decisions of the Supreme Court on the Dred Scott case, established property in slaves in the Territories, but I think something should be done one the part of our Legislature to protect it. You will perceive at once the advantage of such a law for our Territory, and I expect you will take good care to procure its passage. . . ."

Jefferson Davis (1808-1889)—He favored expansion for the U. S. but on a basis that would equalize votes. He had hoped that New Mexico would join with Texas and Arizona in declaring for the South. He was responsible for many of the beneficial aids accruing to New Mexico from Congress during these pre-war years. New Mexico would be able to serve the South in many ways.

James S. Calhoun (1802-1852)—A native of South Carolina, his appointment as first Territorial governor of New Mexico was more than he bargained for. Hounded by Indians, native New Mexicans, Texans awaiting his decision on the Mesilla boundary dispute, Southern sympathizers, Northern Free Soilers, Comancheros, Santa Fe traders, opposition in the legislature, he became a very sick man and annoyed man indeed. He died while on the way to Washington to straighten out either himself or New Mexico.

Alexander M. Jackson—His father, also named Alexander, received land from S. Austin in 1824. Both Jacksons were from Ireland. When the elder Jackson died in 1830 he left four slaves and several children well indocrinated with pro-slavery ideas. The younger Jackson was a newspaper editor in Santa Fe and wrote editorials favoring New Mexico as a pro-slave Territory. In 1857 he became Territorial Secretary and proved very popular with the people of Santa Fe. When the war broke out he became Assistant Adjutant Gereral of the Confederate Army of New Mexico under Sibley. He predicted a slave code for New Mexico and was disappointed when New Mexico decided to stick to the Union.

William Lane Carr—He was seventy-three when appointed to fill the vacancy left by the death of Calhoun. He steered clear of partisanship saying that: "I have come among you with two objects in view, namely, to employ my time honorably to myself, and usefully to the people of this Territory. I have no other object whatsoever in view, and if I fail in these, I fail entirely. I have not come to improve my own private fortune, nor that of any other person, nor to advance the political views of any individual or party." Neither Free Soilers nor Southerners cared for him since he steered a middle course and devoted his time to solving the Indian problems confronting him. Like Calhoun, he was quite unhappy with New Mexico.

David Meriwether—A native of Virginia, but raised in Kentucky, he was fifty-three years old when he became governor of the Territory of New Mexico. Backwoodsman, hunter, trapper, trader, merchant, his life was as adventurous as that of Kit Carson. He avoided the political turmoil in Santa Fe by making repeated visits to the towns within his jurisdiction and by pow-wows with various Indian tribes. He was particularly interested in the Jicarilla Apaches. Although he was a member of the Kentucky legislature many terms and succeeded Henry Clay as U. S. Senator, he refused to involve New Mexico in a fight that belonged to the South and Southeastern States. There were no cotton plantations, no large slave gangs, nothing in common with the Southern cause nor the Northern since there were no mills, no factories, no large industries.

Thomas Turner Fauntleroy—A native of Virginia, he took part in the Black Hawk War, War of 1812, Mexican War and Frontier Wars against the recalcitrant tribes of New Mexico. He was particularly bitter against the Navajos and Jicarillas. During the civil War he was a Brigadier General in the Confederate Army. Fort Wingate in New Mexico was once known as Fort Fauntleroy. He was convinced that many of the misdeeds attributed to Indians were committed by native New Mexicans and by American settlers beginning to infiltrate along the Rio Grande from Albuquerque to Mesilla. He performed his duties well as a soldier until the war broke out. He simply resigned, and asked for a commission in the Southern Army.

William Wing Loring (1818-1896)—A soldier of fortune, lawyer, author, general, adventurer, he left his native North Carolina when he was thirteen. He enlisted in the Army to fight the Seminoles. He studied law because it was his father's wish. He played a small part in the Texas War of Independence, took part in the Mexican War and fought Indians in New Mexico and Utah. It was his ambition to turn not only all the forts of New Mexico but also the soldiers and ammunition to the South. He served in many causes but eventually died in New York.

CHAPTER FOUR

BAYLOR'S BABIES
and
THE SIBLEY BRIGADE

The Ordinance of Secession was adopted by the Texas Convention on February 1, 1861. The war now a reality, Texans proceeded to seize the United States arsenal and barracks at San Antonio. Left with no alternative General Twiggs surrendered the Federal posts in the Department of Texas. During the same month Texans confiscated government property at Brazos Santiago. Promptly vacated were Camp Cooper, Camp Colorado, Ringgold Barracks, Camp Verde, Fort McIntosh, Camp Wood, Camp Hudson, Fort Clark, Fort Inge, Fort Lancaster, Fort Brown, Fort Chadbourne, Fort Mason, Fort Bliss, Fort Quitman, Fort Davis and Fort Stockton. Never precluding the possibility of an invasion from New Mexico Colonel Van Dorn recommended that Texans set up a separate department: "In view of the fact that there are a large number of United States troops quartered in Mesilla and New Mexico, I have also mustered into service a company of foot artillery composed of old soldiers, under good officers, and put them at Fort Bliss, with instructions to throw up a small field work, and to defend it with six pieces of artillery now there. Among the officers sent to Fort Bliss were Colonel Ford and Lieutenant Colonel Baylor. With Baylor so close to Mesilla, a new phase of the history of the Civil War in New Mexico begins for all activity that smells of gun smoke, troop movement, battle and conquest centers around this warminded Texan before he turns the reins over to Sibley, his commanding officer.

W. W. Loring took over the command of the Department of New Mexico on March 23, 1861. What alarmed him at the moment was a note from Major Isaac Lynde informing him that the people of Albuquerque were planning to possess themselves.

of the government stores at the depot. This did not disturb the Federals who were more anxious about their back pay than threats of a mob. Nor were they phased by Apache inroads or talk of Baylor's Babies at Fort Bliss. The Comanches, hearing that a battle between the Texans and the Federals was imminent, made plans for depredations along the New Mexico frontier. Loring, anxious to prevent this if possible, sent Lt. McRae to visit their chiefs and smoke the peace pipe. The Comanches wished to select the location for the peace talks; the Lieutenant had orders to induce them to come to Fort Union but in the final analysis neither had to be content with the sites they wanted settling for a place between Pecos and Glorieta which was to be the locale of the battle between Sibley and the Colorado Volunteers. Lt. Col. Crittenden was sent to chastise the Mescalero Apaches.

Rather than await invasion, Texas became the aggressor by deciding to march against New Mexico. This third attempt was to prove more successful than the effort of the Texas-Santa Fe Expedition and the threat over the Santa Fe claim. Secretary of War, Simon Cameron, wrote to Caleb Smith, Secretary of the Interior, on May 20, 1861, acknowledging that New Mexico was in no shape to resist attack and that he was taking every means to alleviate the situation commensurate with the importance of the Territory. Since it did not seem to be of any importance we can understand the measures Cameron took to help safeguard New Mexico against Confederate invasion. One gets the feeling that at last a number of politicians found the answer of ridding themselves of an opressive yoke. It was the faith of men like General Carleton that eventually convinced men in Washington that New Mexico was not the bleak, barren, hopeless Territory they imagined. Loring, torn between his duty to his country and the stirrings of his conscience, tendered his resignation in favor of the latter. We discussed the situation with Major Canby who assumed command of the Northern District of the Department of New Mexico leaving the formal command with Loring who rode south to Fort Fillmore to await word from the White House regarding the acceptance of his resignation. This left him theoretically in charge, thus tying the Major's hands.

Canby showed little concern over the threat of Baylor's Babies, expecting New Mexico to follow the direction of Missouri because so many of the settlers migrated from there during the years 1852 to 1861. So long as Missouri remained pro-Union he felt assured that New Mexico on the whole would follow suit. Possibilities of threats from Sonora and Chihuahua he ignored completely. While the news from Arizona was disturbing he was confident that the small portion of the people there proclaiming for the South were not enough to cause the Federal Government any complexity. Local irregularities caused many to appeal to Canby for troops but he was in no position to render aid at the moment. He suspected that Baylor would avail himself of the chaotic condition of the region to concentrate troops there but spies could give him no conclusive evidence of Baylor's plans. All he could do was to send additional troops to Fort Fillmore, watch and wait. Meantime Loring's resignation was accepted and he dropped from the New Mexico scene completely.

The soldiers stationed at the posts in Arizona and New Mexico had not been paid for months. Many threatened to go over to Baylor unless they were paid. Major Reynolds was dispatched to Fort Fillmore and the posts in Arizona with what available funds which came in to make up part of the deficit while Major Seward was sent to Forts McLane, Breckinridge and Buchanan for the same purpose. Captain Wainwright was sent to Fort Fauntleroy to pacify the men there. On the whole the Ordinance Department proved itself capable even though in no instance did the men receive the full salary that accrued to them. Now more than ever did Canby realize that mounted men could hardly be called so from want of horses. The Quartermaster's Department blamed this on the lack of water, grass and forage that plagued New Mexico for the past two years. Beset by the threat of famine, New Mexicans were wary of selling horses to replace those worn out by constant hard service. Canby wrote out his needs in this regard urging his superior officers to see what they could do about obtaining mounts in the East since he hoped for none from New Mexico.

Brigadier General H. H. Sibley, of the Confederate Army, was in Richmond, Virginia, when he received a communication from S. Cooper, Adjutant and Inspector General, that informed him of his new duties. On July 8, 1861, the general was gratified to know that none other than President Davis selected him for the task of driving the Federals out of New Mexico because he had recently been assigned there and knew the country. The new commander was authorized to take into the service of the Confederacy all disaffected officers and soldiers on the original commissions of the former and the enlistments of the latter. He was not to delay in Richmond but to proceed at once to Texas, where in concert with Brigadier General Van Dorn he was to organize as quickly as possible troops, two full regiments of cavalry and one battery of howitzers and other such forces as he deemed necessary. It is interesting to note that in the event of his success Sibley was to organize a military government within the Territory. It was not to fall to his lot to become governor possibly because Baylor proved himself capable or he preferred to march at the head of his troops rather than sit behind a desk. Sibley could have unseated Baylor had he so chosen. Time out of mind superiors expected their subordinates to use their own judgment, circumstances being anything but the portrait painted for the superior. President Davis was so certain that Sibley would merely have to march from Texas to New Mexico to have the whole Southwest handed to him on a silver platter by sympathizers such as Magoffin of Magoffinsville, Hart of Franklin, Mowry of Arizona. Sibley was asked to be guided by circumstances and to use his good judgment regarding matters of detail that should arise. Why was he not successful? Did he believe that a man of his talent and inventive genius should have been given the Army of Virginia, or Tennessee? He was every inch a soldier yet he acted as if Baylor was the military genius. Did he leave Richmond a disappointed man? The victory at Valverde was the work of subordinates in reality although he gets the credit. Even if he master-minded the whiphand he certainly lost his grip at Peralta and Glorieta. Why? There is more to all this than meets the eye. His talent was worthy of larger fields. Lee could have used his acumen as ballast at Gettysburg. Authors are wrong in surmising that if Baylor had been at Glorieta and Peralta the Confederacy would have won rather than lost New Mexico. At the time Sibley was rounding up recruits in San Antonio neither he nor Baylor counted on California and Colorado hastening to New Mexico's aid. It is not the scope or the purpose of this book to point out the factors that brought about his seeming listlessness; we only say that the Confederacy could have used his sagacity to better purposes elsewhere.

On the same day that Sibley received his orders the Secretary of War, L. P. Walker, wrote to Governor Clark at Austin: "General Sibley has instructions from the President to proceed to Texas, there to organize a brigade of mounted troops for certain purposes. It is respectfully requested that you will extend to General Sibley such faculties in your power as will best insure his early success in raising this force." Sibley's sentiments regarding the Confederacy may be gleamed from the letter he wrote at Hart's Mill, near Fort Bliss, prior to his Richmond visit. This letter was dated June 12 and addressed to Colonel Loring:

"We are at last under the glorious banner of the Confederate States of America. It was indeed a glorious sensation of protection, hope and pride. Though its folds were modest and unpretending, the emblem was still there. The very Southern verdure and familiar foliage, as we progressed on our journey, filled us with enthusiasm and home feeling. We shall have no trouble from here down to San Antonio. The stage runs regularly semi-weekly, carrying five passengers and a reasonable amount of baggage, reaching San Antonio in six days; thence to Berwick Bay in stages, and to New Orleans by rail. Van Dorn is in command at San Antonio. He has ordered four companies of Texas troops to garrison this post. They cannot be expected to reach here, however, before the First proximo. Meanwhile Col. Magoffin, Judge Hart and Crosby are being very much exercised and concerned on account of the public stores here in their present unguarded condition.

"There are full supplies of subsistence and ammunition here for two or more companies for twelve months. The loss of these supplies by capture or destruction would occasion serious embarrassment to the cause. The gentlemen I have named have applied to me for advice in the premises. I have promised to hasten on from below by forced marches the cavalry force en route here. Meanwhile you may, by delaying your own departure a week or two, add much to the security of this property. I regret now more than ever the sickly sentimentality (I can call it by no other name) by which I was overruled in my desire to bring my whole command with me. I am satisfied now of the disaffection of the best of the rank and file in New Mexico, and that we are regarded as having betrayed and deserted them. I wish I had my part to play over again; no such peace scruples should deter me from doing what I considered a bounden duty to my friends and my cause. I do not advocate the meeting of duplicity and dishonesty by the like weapons, but if I capture the treasury building I should certainly not send back to my enemy the golden bricks.

"Should you be relieved from command too soon to prevent an attempt on the part of your successor to recapture, by a coup de main, the property here, send a notice by extraordinary express to Judge Hart. Your seat in the stage may at the same time be engaged. Movements are in contemplation from this direction which I am not at liberty to disclose. You will arrive here in time for everything and hear everything."

Sibley's stay at San Antonio was to be lengthy and prolonged for raising troops was an arduous and thankless task. Enlistments in the Sibley Brigade were not to be as fast and furious as he supposed. Since his command included the Confederate troops at El Paso and other points in New Mexico he spent much of his time keeping in touch with Lt. Col. Baylor, Judge Crosby, Judge Hart and others he knew to be favorable to the South. He ordered Baylor to make an attack on Fort Craig and to settle for nothing less than its capture. Col. Reily's regiment was already en route; Col. Green's forces following behind, with Col. Steele's men bringing up the rear. Sibley ordered Crosby and Hart to scour the countryside for supplies. Baylor's spies reported the Federals as 2,500 strong, and on the march to capture Dona Ana. The summer passed with the men acting like bees rather than soldiers. Supplies, and more supplies, seemed the order of the day. Well, in October Baylor had cause to lament that the enemy now had eleven companies of U. S. Regulars and thirteen companies of New Mexico Volunteers. He was distressed at the fact that they also had a battery of artillery and that he would have to fall back because his force was too weak against such numbers. He was ready to move his supplies to Fort Quitman and if that should prove too close, on to Fort Davis. He pleaded with Sibley in San Antonio for re-enforcements if only to protect the fruits and produce of the valley against the scorched earth policy of the Federals. He was certain that there was a fine supply of corn in the valley, enough for two or three regiments, which he sadly needed for he had no corn and but little hay. While Sibley was in favor of accumulated supplies, Baylor was not in accord for fear of an invasion. He would not be encumbered. Wagons rolled into Fort Davis loaded with corn mostly to satisfy Sibley rather than to be used by Baylor's troops. Baylor believed that he would ultimately have to bed down at Fort Davis.

Up in Santa Fe Battle, Baird and Phillips kept ears and eyes open. They talked with officers at Fort Marcy keeping Baylor informed of all they learned. Talk was that General Sumner was coming across from Guaymas to join forces with Col. Canby at Mesilla. Spies were hastened in that direction. Baylor regretted that the native population of New Mexico was decidedly pro-Federal and wished that Sibley would send him a strong force to keep them quiet. Hart wrote to Sibley on October 27th:

"It has been a week since Judge Crosby called on me in reference to supplies for your brigade. I immediately took steps to secure supplies of breadstuffs, the greater part of which must come from Sonora, as there is great scarcity in the State of Chihuahua. I sent for my Sonora agent to come to me here a month since, to meet and see what would be required of me to furnish the Confederacy. This agent was to have left about this time with a proper escort from Colonel Baylor, and some thirty or forty wagons, to commence hauling supplies from the Sonora border to the Rio Grande, which would have commenced to arrive at Fillmore by the middle of December. In the meantime my mills will furnish from the limited supplies of grain here. I have now some 40,000 to 50,000 pounds of flour and will have 40,000 to 50,000 more if the New Mexican troops do not succeed in forcing Col. Baylor to fall back beyond this place.

"The flour I have here, and may make until I am interrupted, I am now placing in a place of safety in El Paso, Mexico, as recommended by Col. Baylor in his letters which I enclose. I shall do everything in my power, and all that it is possible for a man to do in my circumstances and situation, to further the public service. This you well know, and I need not assure you of the fact. You must especially heed Judge Crosby's and Mr. Richardson's suggestions as to things here, and what you and the commanding officers of the department must do to facilitate Mr. Richardson and myself in furnishing supplies is to procure some cash funds. I can command here now from $40,00 to $50,000 —all or most of which must go to Sonora immediately to pay for flour, etc. As suggested by Col. Baylor, I have engaged an express to go into Sonora to learn if Sumner is actually coming from California via Guaymas or Fort Union. By the same express I will order the purchase of more flour, beans, salt, beef, soup, corn, etc. I have here already some 10,000 pounds of corn and 300,000 pounds of flour, all for your brigade, and awaiting your movement. I enclose herewith my last letters from Col. Baylor. His command is in peril. I hope God in His goodness, will so order things as not to make his retreat necessary from Arizona. Our express from Sonora, with intelligence from Forts Yuma and Guaymas will be back in twenty days, when you and Col. Baylor will be fully posted up as to Sumner and his movements, if he is making any, towards Arizona and California. Be easy about your supplies; we shall get all we want from Sonora—what this valley cannot furnish—until such time as you may be in full possession of New Mexico, and can avail of its resources or such part as the hungry Federals may leave for your command."

Meantime Col. Henry E. McCulloch (brother to the more dashing Ben) took command of the Department of Texas at San Antonio. He was well known to Col. Baylor who addressed himself to him rather than Sibley, still bemoaning his possible fate should his troops fall into the hands of such overwhelming forces the Federals were reputed to have. His spies reported that there were sixteen companies at Fort Craig, three within thirty miles of the fort, and that the Federals even approached Mexicans begging them to enlist. Baylor was happy to report that they were divided on the subject of making war upon Texans, or of taking any part in the war at all. The fact that the troops were disgruntled over back pay was known to Baylor who sought to capitalize on it by inviting them to join his Texans to better advantage. His spies reported also that freighters were hauling daily into Fort Craig which indicated that they would soon make a move against him. His own freighters were warned to be vigilant for at a moment's notice they might have to move to Fort Davis or Fort Quitman, from Fort Bliss. Baylor himself decided to take the offensive by pushing on to Santa Fe with his mounted troops and handing the prize over to General Sibley as a gift.

The Confederacy already divided Southern and Western New Mexico into the Territory of Arizona even before Sibley left San Antonio for Fort Bliss. The general wrote his commanding officer that he would be ready to depart for his base of operations on November 16.

"Before proceeding on this distant field of duty it appears proper that I should briefly communicate to you such facts concerning my official transactions here and touching the present condition of my forces as may be necessary for the information of your (General Cooper) office. On my arrival here, about the middle of August last, I confidently expected to be able to raise and organize my brigade within a very brief space of time, and to have been enabled by this date to have it actively employed in the accomplishment of the objects for which it was raised. Many unexpected circumstances, however, have occurred to defeat this expectation. In the first place, I was disappointed in not receiving from the executive of this State as efficient a co-operation as was desirable. This arose from no want of disposition or zeal on the part of Governor Clark to render every facility in his power for for the rapid organization of the force called for. It was the consequence simply of the very inefficient system of the State military organization to which the governor had recourse to supply the troops. He ordered sufficient number of companies which had reported to him as organized to report to me for the service of this brigade, but the most of these companies had, as it appeared, either entirely disbanded, or their numbers had become diminished below the minimum of the Confederate service. The reliance, therefore, which was placed in this mode of raising the men caused the first serious delay.

"In the second place, the designation by the governor of companies organized under the State law operated to deter other companies not so organized from offering their services to me, which many would have done at once but for the opinion, very generally prevalent, that the brigade would be filled by the companies ordered out by the governor. Although at the very earliest day that it became apparent that the companies ordered out by the governor could not be relied on, I at once resorted direct to the people themselves, yet it required the same time to counteract the effects of the misplaced reliance upon the State System.

"Another source of delay arose from the competition for men which grew out of the calls for the several regiment required for the service east of the Mississippi. I enumerate these sources of delay simply to explain the unexpected detention which I have encountered, and not as implying any imputation upon anyone whatsoever. Although I am advancing to the field of duty assigned me with the confident hope of being able to accomplish everything designed there by his Excellency, the President, yet it is proper that I should state that very great deficiencies still exist in the arms of my troops, notwithstanding every effort on my part to obviate them. Every company reported itself short of arms, and gave the sufficient reason that they were not able to be procured in their respective sections, partly in consequence of the great reluctance of the people to allow the serviceable arms to be removed from the State, for the defense of whose coast it was generally believed thy would be shortly required. The difficulty thus arising had to be surmounted in some manner. Wherefore, in virtue of the authority delegated to me in the written instruction of his Excellency, the President, I directed the purchase of serviceable firearms and the construction of lances. There not being a dollar in the hands of any of the disbursing officers of my command, I was necessitated to resort to the credit of the Government for these purchases. These liabilities are outstanding, and on the 13th of the present month I enclosed to the Chief of Ordnance the estimates of the funds necessary for their liquidation.

"I desire to invite your attention also to another matter. Shortly after my arrival here (San Antonio) General Van Dorn was relieved from duty as commander of this department, and Col. Henry E. McCullouch was left in that position. Brigadier General Herbert came within the limits of this department, but did not come on to its headquarters and assume the command, but up to very recently left Col. McCullouch to act in that capacity, so far, at least, as the depots and military affairs of this place and section were concerned. Major Maclin, Assistant Quartermaster and acting ordnance officer of this department left this place to meet General Herbert at Galveston and still remains there. Col. McCullouch also left for the same purpose shortly afterwards, and the intelligence was soon returned that he had been relieved of the command of the department by the General. The General has not yet come on here. The consequence of all this is that there is, and for the last two or three weeks has been, no officer within my reach to whom I could apply for the issues of ordnance stores absolutely necessary for my command. In this situation I assumed the responsibility of ordering and requiring from the subordinates in charge of the ordinance stores as were indispensable to my command and as could be spared from the service of the department itself. On assuming this responsibility I immediately communicated the fact to General Herbert at Galveston, with the reasons and motives for my actions, but have as yet received no reply from him. Not to have taken this responsibility would have been to incur another and an indefinite delay, which would have propably paralyzed my command for the winter, and would certainly have disabled my command for the winter, and would certainly have disabled me from arriving at El Paso, as I hope to do, in time to succor the small force there under Colonel Baylor, whose communication regarding an immediate attack by a greatly superior force I forwarded to you on the 8th inst. These facts will, I trust, vindicate me from any imputation of unwarrantable intrusion upon the powers of the department commander, which I have been scrupulous to avoid. The 4th (Col. Reily's) Regiment, being the first of this brigade, took up the line of march on the 22nd of last month (October), and at last advices was making rapid progress. The 5th Regiment (Col. Green's) being my second, took up the march on the 2nd inst., and will make all possible dispatch. I hope to arrive at El Paso in time to overtake my advance corps. Col. Steele's regiment is just now completely organized, and will probably be able to march by the 20th inst."

It was A. M. Jackson, Assistant Adjutant General of the Confederate Army of New Mexico who gave General Sibley orders to leave San Antonio on November 18, 1861. Col. Steele was to remain behind with the 3rd Regiment until other matters were cleared, after which he was to make forced marches to overtake Sibley on the road to El Paso. Col. Baylor addressed letters to friends and Southern sympathizers in California to foment revolt. Many Secessionists there waited for the vigilance of the Union men to slacken in order to escape and join his force at Dona Ana. They also had horses for sale at less than fifty dollars a head, willing to accept Confederate bonds in exchange. Fearful least the Federals would land troops at Guaymas the Colonel suggested that Confederate troops be stationed in Western Arizona to counteract this action. Some Californians did manage to escape the chary Union men reporting to Baylor that they encountered no enemy along the way but they heard rumors to the effect that the governor of Sonora received orders from Mexico City to permit the passage of Federal troops through that Mexican State. It was also reported that Union agents were in Sonora buying corn and supplies for the United States troops.

Spies were sent to watch activity at Fort Craig. They returned with the news that Federals were strongly fortifying the post and extending camps and fortifications down the Rio Grande as far south as the tiny village of Alamosa. Small pox, which plagued the fort for a time, was brought under control and while Baylor thought this an opportune time to strike he decided not to take the initiative until General Sibley made his appearance. But before the commanding officer arrived form San Antonio a skirmish took place at Mesilla, Fort Fillmore was evacuated, Union troops surrendered at Ojo de San Augustin (known as St. Augustine Springs), and the Texans were confident of capturing Fort Union, holding all of Arizona, taking over California and flying the Confederate flag over the entire Southwest.

Arm chair strategists and parlor generals will discuss the surrender of Major Isaac Lynde, commander of the 7th U. S. Infantry, till the end of time but all will agree that at no time were the hopes of the Confederacy in the Southwest so buoyant than the day when Lynde turned over his whole command to Baylor. Years later his family proved to Congress that his action was honorable, for he sought to spare his men, and placed his name back on the roll of those honorably discharged. When the news was brought to Colonel Canby at Santa Fe he refused to pass judgment remarking that it was not proper for him to express an opinion in advance of an investigation.

The evacuation of Fort Fillmore caused the commander of Fort Stanton to abandon the post in order to amalgamate with the troops at Albuquerque, the troops arriving there in two separate contingents on August 8th and 9th. Certain that the Texans would not rest until they took Fort Union, Captain Shoemaker directed the work of intrenchments, for the Federals were on the defensive and complaining of the lack of men and weapons to protect themselves against the vast army of Confederates supposedly marching against them. Fort Union could make a better stand than most since it was amply provided with artillery. Besides Canby was partial to Fort Union having spent some time there following General Sumner's stay. He boasted that Fort Union could hold against any and all Confederates sent to attack it.

Unconsciously, Major Lynde accomplished something by his surrender. He awoke the patriotism of New Mexicans. The governor of the Territory called out the militia; he appealed to the natives to arouse from their apathetic condition in forming a home guard and amassing volunteer corps; he appealed to Colorado to come to New Mexico's aid. Said Canby: "The greatest exertions are being used to organize a respectable volunteer force, but the progress does not meet with my expectations. Seventeen companies have been mustered in. Two companies are expected in a few days from Colorado Territory, and several companies of mounted volunteers are promised by the end of this week." If the cry of Sam Houston's Texans was "Remember the Alamo" the cry of Canby's New Mexicans was "Remember San Augustine Springs".

On the night of July 24th Lynde's picket brought in a deserter from Baylor's camp. He told the Major that about four hundred men led by Baylor were moving up the Rio Grande. He deserted at Willow Bar about twelve miles below the post. Expecting an attack momentarily, Lynde called in the two companies of the 7th Infantry at Santo Tomas and kept the garrison under arms until sun up. Meantime Baylor continued his progress up the river passing through the hamlet of Santo Tomas, on the opposite side of the river from the post, where he captured seven men left behind by the battalion to guard foodstuffs left behind by the hurried departure of the companies. Baylor asked the prisoners if they knew when to expect the troops from the evacuated posts of Breckinridge and Buchanan. Realizing they were of little or no value to him he let them go. They immediately crossed the river to inform the Major of their experience. Baylor made off with all the property, both public and private, that he found at Santo Tomas.

Towards evening Major Lynde decided to march against the town of Mesilla where he heard the Texans were stationed. He took six companies of the 7th Infantry, one acting as artillery, with the howitzer battery of the post and two companies of rifles. One company of infantry, with the band and convalescents, were left to garrison the post. These were commanded by Lt. Stivers and Lt. Ryan. Doctor Alden was also left behind to attend the sick. Lynde had about three hundred and eighty men on the march. Within sight of Mesilla he sent Lt. Brooks forward, with a white flag, to demand the surrender of the town.

Major Waller and Col. Herbert seeing Brooks riding towards town with the flag went out to meet him. When the Lieutenant told them that Major Lynde demanded the surrender of the town which the Texans had occupied, they told him that if Lynde wanted Mesilla he would have to fight for it. Left with no alternative but to fight, the major moved the battery forward and fired two shells at long range, but they burst in the air short of the object. The Texans and townspeople who had climbed the roofs of the flat topped adobe houses ridiculed the aim of the artillery yelling that they had to do better than that to hit anything. If they could do no better the war was as good as won. They told them to go home; the Texans wouldnt hurt them since the sight of them caused such unsteady aim. Why not just turn over New Mexico to Baylor and save the useless spilling of blood?

The command continued advancing towards the outskirts of the town. The progress was slow because the battery, which had to be moved by hand, was impeded by the heavy sand. Some of Waller's men hiding in a cornfield to the right, and others from the roof of the ranch house, opened fire on the advancing troops. Their aim was more accurate. Three men were killed; two officers and four rank and file wounded. More Texans poured into the fields on both sides. Men lined the house tops and streets; dusk fell upon the scene. Owing to the difficulty of moving through the sand, the howitzers proved useless. Lynde decided to withdraw the troops leaving Mesilla to the Texans. Back at the post he ordered the men to pile sand bags in anticipation of an attack. He sent a rider in serch of Captain Gibbs with the message to return to Fort Craig with his command as he would be in danger if he attempted to join Lynde. The Texans took possession of the road above Lynde. Messengers were sent to find the commanders of the troops from Forts Breckinridge and Buchanan in an effort to steer them around the Texans and into Fort Craig.

Baylor was sending out messengers of his own. A hundred re-enforcements arrived from Fort Bliss to augment the ever increasing numbers at Mesilla, for a number of citizens threw in with the Texans to swell the ranks to nearly seven hundred. Lynde found out that the Texans lost eleven men in killed and wounded in the exchange of fire at Mesilla and that the firing of the howitzer stampeded a number of their horses. Spies reported to the Major that the Texans were expecting a battery of artillery and that Baylor was waiting for him to move on Mesilla so that he could attack and capture the fort in his absence. This presented a serious problem for the post was perfectly commanded by sand hills for at least half the circle and the only supply of water was a mile and a half away. To remain in the fort would mean eventual surrender under the circumstances.

It was agreed to abandon the post in favor of another where there would be safety in numbers.

Lynde ordered the destruction of all the public property which could not be transferred for lack of time. Many of the men decided against throwing away good whisky, emptied their water cans in favor of the more potent liquid. They did not know it then but this action was to have telling effects on the march to St. Augustine Springs. On July 27th at one a. m. the troops took up the line of march for Fort Stanton which seemed the most practicable point to reach even though it, too, was reported threatened by Baylor's Babies. Lynde admitted he had no knowledge of the road and permitted himself to be led by guides who knew it about as much as he did. He was told that the springs were but twenty miles distant and there water could be had for all.

All went well in the cool of the night. When the sun arose the day became intensely hot as it can very well do at that time of the year in that section of New Mexico. Before long the men and horses began to show signs of fatigue. Major Lynde realized that the distance to water was a good deal farther than represented. Many of the men now wished they had kept the water. The whisky made them thirstier. Maddened at this twist of fate they threw away their flasks and canteens. Water became more precious than gold. Men vied with one another in what they would give for a swig of water. The going was to be even rougher. About six miles from the Springs the land sloped to a short ascent which formed a pass in the Organ Mountains. The climb, the intense heat, the lack of water began telling on the men and many fell unable to proceed.

As no Texans were in sight Lynde assumed he was not pursued. He decided to leave the sick and the infantry where it was while he pushed on with the mounted men in the hopes of reaching water soon. Just within reach of his goal, word came that a mounted force approached. Some said it was Captain Gibbs, others said it was the Texans. Lynde himself seemed reasonably certain it was Captain Gibbs. He rode on to the Springs where he was disappointed to find that there was scarcely sufficient water for his needs. Thinking of the men lying out in the scorching sun, he had all the mounted troops with him take an extra supply in the hopes of alleviating the suffering of most. On the way back the major became so sick he could hardly sit on his horse. It is probable he suffered a mild sun stroke. The command was asked to proceed without him. Waving goodby to Lt. Cressey, Lynde returned to the Springs. Word was soon brought him that a part of the teams had given out and could not be brought up and that large numbers of the infantry had become totally overpowered with the intense heat. As if his lot were not hard enough, an express arived at this time from Captain Gibbs with the news that eight mounted companies, supported by artillery and a large force of infantry, approached his rear guard. Lynde rode to where the infantry were and had the "Call to Arms" sounded. As he suspected only a hundred men were able to answer the call. Captain Gibbs now rode into camp with his mounted force. He verified the fact that the Texans were approaching. News was also brought in that they captured three companies of the rear guard. These men had given out and were too consumed with thirst and fatigue to put up a struggle. The four mountain howitzers that were with the wagons in the rear were also captured. These had been guarded by a company of infantry acting as artillery. Gibbs also reported that his men and horses had been without water for twenty-four hours. If there was a scarcity of water before, the captain's arrival made it even less.

 The situation seemed hopeless. Circumstances made it worse than useless to resist no matter what the fighting spirit of the few healthy or reckless ones. As Lynde later told at his hearing that honor did not demand the sacrifice of blood after the terrible suffering his troops had already undergone especially when sacrifice would prove totally useless. Sensing that it would be surrender rather than bloodshed a body of Texans followed Captain Gibbs to the vicinity of the camp to hold a parley. It was then that Lynde surrendered to Lt. Col. Baylor. The surrender included ninety-five Mounted Rifles, rank and file, and two officers; about seven full companies of the 7th Infantry, with eight officers. Wrote Lynde to Canby regarding his surrender:

 "Since I have been at Fort Fillmore my position has been of extreme embarrassment, surrounded as I have been by open and secret enemies so that no reliable information could be obtained. Disaffection prevailed even in my own command, to what extent it was impossible to ascertain, but much increased, undoubtedly, by the conduct of the officers who left their post without authority. My position has been one of great difficulty, and has ended in the misfortune of surrendering my command to the enemy. The Texas troops acted with great kindness to our men, exerting themselves in carrying water to the famishing ones in the rear; yet it was two days before the infantry could move from the camp, and then only by the assistance of their captors. The officers and men who chose to give their parole were released at Las Cruces, New Mexico" (See: *The War of the Rebellion*—Series 1 Vol. IV p. 5)

Baffled at this turn of events, Canby asked Captain Alfred Gibbs to write his version of what took place at the Springs. This he did on August 6th. The Captain left Albuquerque on July 18. At Fort Marcy he picked up supplies and beef for the men at Fort Fillmore. He arrived at Point of Rocks, twenty-seven miles from the Rio Grande, on the 26th, the day he met Lt. Lane with Company A, Mounted Rifles, and Dr. Steck, the Indian Agent, who informed him that the Texans were at Mesilla. Steck said that Baylor would do everything in his power to prevent the supplies reaching Major Lynde's men. Lane hired a guide, turned off the road, marched all that night circling around Las Cruces and Dona Ana, hoping to get into Fort Fillmore from the rear. When he got as far as El Paso de la Cueva, five miles from Ojo de San Augustin, he suddenly came upon Major Lynde's troops on their way to Fort Stanton. Joining forces with Lt. Brooks, Lynde's adjutant, they rode on to find the Major. Gibbs asked Lynde if he knew that the Texans were approaching from the rear. The Major replied that he did not but neither did he see any cause for alarm since there were two companies in the rear and the captain's seventy additional troops were sufficient to take care of the situation. He abruptly turned and hastened back to the Springs. Gibbs also stated that he counted over one hundred and fifty men lying along the road unable to rise or to carry their muskets, useless and disorganized in every way. And this was the rear guard on which he was ordered to rely! Gibbs decided to use his seventy men. Baylor swooped down on the beef cattle capturing them and two wagons. He had over three hundred men with him. Outflanked, Gibbs decided to charge with drawn pistols. Before carrying out his daring charge, he decided to send a messenger to Lynde who promptly sent word back for him to protect the wagons and fall back on the main camp. Forming three lines, the Captain began his retreat. Reporting to Major Lynde he was told to water his men and horses. The surrender had already been decided upon. The Officers resented the fact that they were not consulted. When they found out what was happening they sent up a storm of protests, all to no avail. The men were marched to Las Cruces where they turned over their wagons, arms and horses and promised to go to Fort Leavenworth for the duration via Fort Craig, Santa Fe, Las Vegas and Fort Union. How many kept their promise is a matter of conjecture. Said Lynde to the Texas commander:

"Col. Baylor, to avoid bloodshed, I conditionally surrender this whole force to you, on condition that officers and their families shall be protected from insult and private property be respected." The officers were so strenuous in their objections that Baylor, who sat on his horse patiently listening to the pros and cons, finally shouted out in his booming, deep voice, "Who is commander here? Who is responsible for the actions of the men?" (Ibid. o. c.)

Captain McNally and Dr. J. C. McKee were of the opinion that Lynde was in such a strategic position that he could have held out against three thousand Texans. The doctor said that Lynde should have sent away the women and children (one hundred and three in number) when he had the opportunity, and waited for the Texans to attack the post rather than insisting on occupying Mesilla. The officers objected to Mesilla but said that if he wanted to capture towns Dona Ana was more feasible. McNally said that when the troops arrived before Mesilla he twice persuaded Lynde to give the order to haul down the Confederate flag and just as he was ready to comply with the order, Lynde rescinded it. (See: o.c. p. 14)

The matter of the surrender was brought before the attention of Hon. G A. Grow, Speaker of the House; Simon Cameron, Secretary of War; President Lincoln; Major General McClellan —all of whom accepted the testimonies of McKee, McNally, Gibbs and Potter. Brooks, knowing the humanitarian resolve of Lynde's preventing American slaughtering American, was the only one to favor the Major. Lynde would hardly have achieved this rank in a day when it was hard to come by had he been the coward these men accused him of being. President Lincoln ordered his name erased from the roles of the U. S. Army. One man knew Lynde for the brave soldier he really was; but this man was too busy on other fronts to pay heed at the moment. After the war he was to testify for the Major and to call down the Secretary of War for condemning a man without trial or investigation. Through the efforts of General Grant and the Major's family, Lynde's name was put back on the honor roll of the U. S. Army. Wrote Col. Baylor from Dona Ana on September 21st:

"On assuming command at Fort Bliss I ascertained that the United States forces were concentrating in strong force at Fort Fillmore, and from the proximity of that post I supposed that the object of the enemy was to attack the forces under my command at Fort Bliss. I was satisfied that if I permitted them to concentrate my command was too weak to maintain my position. I therefore determined to attack the enemy in detail, and prevent, if possible, the contemplated concentration. For that purpose I sent a detachment under Major Waller to reconnoiter Fort Fillmore and see the position of the enemy pickets, also whether the fort could be approached without discovery. The report of Major Waller satisfies me that I could easily, in the night, gain a position between the fort and the river and cut off the animals as they went to water; then the enemy woud have to attack me in a strong position, thus rendering the protection afforded by the fort of no use. I accordingly took up the line of march in the night of the 23rd of July with 258 men, and in the night of the 24th succeeded in taking a position on the river near Fort Fillmore. The surprise of the enemy would have been complete but for the desertion of a private from Capt. T. F. Teel's company, who reported to Major Lynde our strength and position. The long-roll was distinctly heard, which apprised us that our approach was known to the enemy.

"On the morning of the 25th I determined to occupy Mesilla and prevent, if possible, the enemy from getting a position there, as it was one that could easily be held, and would enable them to hold the country. I reached Mesilla in the afternoon of the 25th and was soon informed that the enemy were marching to attack us. I posted my men in position and awaited the arrival of the enemy. About five o'clock in the afternoon I discovered their cavalry approaching the town by the main road, and soon after the infantry came in sight, bringing with them three howitzers. They formed within three hundred yards, and were, as near as I could tell, about six hundred strong. A flag was sent in to demand the unconditional surrender of the Texas forces, to which I answered that we would fight first and surrender afterward. The answer was followed by the enemy opening on us with their howitzers. After four or five rounds of bombs, grape and canister, the cavalry formed and marched up within 250 yards, preparatory to making a charge. Captain Hardeman's company being in position nearest the enemy, was ordered to open on them with his front rank, to see if they were within range of our guns. The fire was well directed and proved effective, killing four of the enemy and wounding seven. The cavalry was thrown into confusion and retreated hastily, running over the infantry. In a few moments the enemy were marching back in the direction of their fort; but supposing it to be a feint, intended to draw me from my position, I did not pursue them, but kept my position until the next morning, the 26th, expecting that they would attack us under cover of the night.

"The enemy not approaching I sent my spies to reconnoiter, and discover, if possible, their movements. The spies reported the enemy at work at the fort making breastworks, and evidently preparing to defend themselves. Upon hearing this, I sent an express to Fort Bliss, ordering up the artillery to attack the fort on the arrival of my re-enforcements. On the morning of the 27th, a little after daylight, my spies reported columns of dust seen in the direction of the Organ Mountains, distant fifteen miles, on the Fort Stanton road. I could, from the top of the house (I was occupying) see the movements of the enemy with the aid of a glass. I immediately ordered the command to saddle and mount, for the purpose of intercepting them at San Augustin Pass. I reached the river, distant one mile, when I received intelligence that a messenger had arrived from the fort, and stated that the enemy had fired the buildings; that it had been extinguished (Note: a heavy rain storm put out the blaze. Col. Roberts, hearing that Lynde had surrendered ordered the post abandoned and fired. He was but a short distance from the post when a storm suddenly arose and extinguished the blaze) and little had been destroyed. I at once ordered Major Waller to take a detachment of men and go to the fort, and save, if possible, the property therein, and to leave men enough to guard the post, and then overtake me as soon as possible. On reaching the foot of the mountain, distant about fifteen miles, I could see the rear of the enemy, composed chiefly of famished stragglers endeavoring to make their way to water. I disarmed and collected a number of them, and finding most of them dying of thirst, we gave them the water we had, and were compelled ourselves to go to a spring in the mountain for water, Lt. Baylor and Mr. Barnes, a citizen of Las Cruces, who acted as guide, found twenty-four of the enemy at the spring, who had from exhaustion gone to sleep, whom they captured.

"After getting water for my men I started in pursuit of the enemy, who passed through San Augustine Pass. I was delayed for some time here waiting for Major Waller, who, mistaking my orders, had arrived at Fort Fillmore, except Capt. Hardeman's company. So soon as they joined me I started in pursuit, and found the enemy's cavalry drawn up to cover the retreat of the infantry through the Pass. These I charged with Capt. Hardeman's company. They retreated in haste, leaving behind them their wagons and artillery and all their supplies. Upon gaining the summit of the Pass, a plain view of the road to San Augustine Springs was presented. The road for five miles was lined with fainting, famished soldiers, who threw down their arms as we passed and begged for water. At the Springs the enemy had drawn up in line of battle some two hundred or three hundred strong. I ordered Major Waller to charge with Capt. Hardeman's company until he reached the end of the line of the straggling soldiers, then to form and cut them off from the main body. I followed, disarming the enemy, and as fast as our jaded horses would go. On reaching Capt. Hardeman's company, who were formed, I saw Major Waller and Capt Hardeman riding into the enemy's lines. I was, in a few moments, sent for by Major Lynde, who asked upon what terms I would allow him to surrender. I replied that the surrender would be unconditional. To this Major Lynde assented, asking that private property should be respected. The articles of capitulation were signed, and the order given for the enemy to stack arms. Major Lynde's command was composed of eight companies of infantry and four of cavalry, with four pieces of artillery, the whole numbering nearly seven hundred men. My own force at the surrender was less than two hundred. I regret to report that the regimental colors were burned by the enemy to avoid surrendering them. I was delayed at the place of surrender fo two days on account of the condition of the enemy and the want of transportation. As soon as possible I marched them to Las Cruces and there paroled them, as I was informed that Capt. Moore was en route for Fort Fillmore, from Fort Buchanan, with two hundred and fifty men. I could not guard the prisoners I had and meet the coming forces. Being desirous, too, to afflict the enemy in every way, I considered that it was much better for them to bear the expense of feeding prisoners than for me to do so. . . ." (O. C. pp 19-21)

Ridding himself of the burden of prisoners, Baylor marched to the little village of Picacho, northeast of the Pass, which one may see today very much as it was then, nestled in the foothills of Lincoln National Forest. Here Baylor expected to surprise Captain Moore. It was here that he was joined by Brig. General A. S. Johnson. (Albert Sidney Johnson who had just resigned his command of the Department of the Pacific and was making his way to New Orleans and Richmond. He was made a full General and given the Confederate Department of Kentucky. He was killed in the Battle of Shiloh. His remains were taken to Austin). With Johnson were a number of officers who had also resigned their United States Commissions and a party of Californians under Captain Alonzo Ridley. Baylor turned over his command to his superior officer so that Baylor's Babies were now under the direction of one of the most famous Confederate leaders the South produced. General Johnson remained in command until he felt his services were no longer required. He sent Capt. Coopwood's spy company to meet the enemy and send him word where they were and to watch their movements and prevent any communication with them. The spies discovered them on the Miembres and reported them moving carelessly, not suspecting they were being watched. On the night of August 6th a messenger arrived at Capt. Moore's camp with the news of the surrender. The Captain was ordered to burn his transportation and supplies and to make his escape as best he could. In the event that he was able to by-pass the enemy he was to report at Fort Craig. As the mounts of the Confederates were rather jaded, the Southerners were not able to catch up with the Captain who made his way to the fort in safety.

By August 10th Baylor once again commanded his troops. The fort that was saved by a thunder storm was now occupied by a Confederate Civilian Militia composed of Southern Sympathizers from Mesilla and Dona Ana who really occupied it to see what they could salvage for themselves. The surrender also caused a panic at Fort Stanton which was immediately abandoned. Here, too, citizens living near the post took possession of it and were rewarded with valuable quartermaster's and commissary stores. Natives and Mescalero Indians gathered in large numbers demanding of the new occupants the right to pillage the post. The Southern sympathizers were too weak to resist. Besides, they were uncertain as to the whereabouts of Baylor's Babies or where to appeal for succor. They turned the post over to the Natives and Indians who made a thorough job of sacking it. Captain Walker's company was sent to hold the post for Baylor. His men went from house to house in the Bonito settlement but succeeded in recovering but a portion of the stolen property.

It was Baylor, not Sibley, who put into effect Richmond's demand for the Confederate Territory of Arizona. Believing himself secure now against attack, and knowing he would have the added support of Sibley's Brigade, Baylor issued the proclamation that made the Territory, on August 1st. Mesilla was made the capitol; Baylor was self appointed military governor. His victory was timed with that of Manassas (1st Bull Run) which certainly gave Richmond cause for rejoicing. It has never been proven conclusively that President Davis confirmed Baylor in his self-appointed position, or, if he did, he tolerated him pro tem. The editors of the Salt Lake and the San Antonio newspapers both claimed after the war that Baylor was never officially recognized by Davis as the only governor ever to rule the Confederate Territory of Arizona. Even if such proved the case, the office was short lived. Carleton and his Californians would force him to make tracks; he proves of no more use to our history as Canby and Sibley steal the scene.

Canby's demand for two additional regiments of volunteers bothered Baylor who preferred to spend this time drawing up rules, regulations, constitutions and notices the better to govern his new charges. Spies reported that the Federal Government ordered all regular troops out of New Mexico to serve on other fronts. More often as not spies brought false reports hoping to ingratiate themselves in the new government. On the strength of these reports he reported to the authorities in San Antonio that Fort Union was abandoned, the Federals taking up positions two miles above the post. He heard that there were three companies of volunteers and seven of regulars throwing up breastworks about the new position ready to defend it at all costs. He was surprised to learn that four other companies were at Santa Fe awaiting orders; four at Albuquerque and five at Fort Craig.

Indians were becoming increasingly meddlesome striking out equally against both sides, raiding settlements, stores and supplies, running off horses and sheep, plundering from Tubac to Taos. Success at Tubac caused them to attempt a try on Tucson. Baylor would have to divide his force between Indians and Federals. Now more than ever he wished Sibley would take over. Then there came rumors of men marching from California. Baylor salved his fears by saying that he would move neither against Indian nor Federal until Sibley arrived. Besides, New Mexico could be easily taken since he was held in mortal terror by every soldier still in the Territory after the affair at the Springs. Then small pox broke out among his men.

Sibley himself was concerned over Mexican help. Would Mexico recognize the Confederate States? Would they send aid and supplies? Would they take a definite stand against the Union? President Benito Juarez both admired and sought to imitate President Lincoln. Of course Sibley did not know this at the time. Nor was he aware of the internal dissentions that were to result in the intervention of France, the arrival of Maximilian, the flight of Juarez, and a thousand other reasons why Mexico had enough strife without looking across the border. Sibley arrived at Fort Bliss on December 14, 1861, taking command of all the forces of the Confederate States on the Rio Grande at and above Fort Quitman, and in all the Territory of Arizona and New Mexico designating these forces as the Confederate Army of New Mexico. At Fort Bliss he decided that the only way to conquer New Mexico was to take Fort Union. To set Baylor's mind at ease he issued General Orders No. 12—December 20th, 1861: "The general command of the forces of the Confederate States assumed by Brig. General H. H. Sibley in General Orders No. 10, from these (Fort Bliss) headquarters, and the proclamation of martial law promulgated by him, not being intended to abrogate or supercede the powers of Col. John R. Baylor, as civil and military governor of Arizona, he will continue the full exercise of the functions of that office." (O. C. p. 159) Next he prepared to send Col. Reily to Governor Luis Terrazas at Chihuahua to see what he could do about Mexican recognition of the Confederate States. The Colonel summed up his activities in a letter to Sibley on January 20, 1862:

". . . At the request of the governor I resumed my seat, when many inquires were made about the war between the South and the North, about yourself, and the number and character of your troops; to all of which I trust I gave satisfactory answers. Upon taking leave of the governor, I was escorted back to the hotel (Riddell's in Chihuahua) by Don Carlos Mayo (married to the governor's sister). He remained with me for some time, and I found him quite a friend of the South. To him I am indebted for much civilty and many kindnesses.

"The next day, at 12, Don Carlos again called for me, and, arriving at the palace, found no one with the governor but the Secretary of State and one of the judges of the Supreme Court. In a short time we were joined by Don Joaquin Durand, whose acquaintance I had previously made, and although a Mexican yet writing and speaking the English language with great fluency, having been educated in England. He came there at my request, and I was glad to avail myself of his intelligence. We almost immediately took up our communication . . . In addition to concessions made by the governor he informed me that even if President Juarez had come to him, and sanctioned by an Act of Congress, he did not think he would permit Federal troops to pass through the territory of Chihuahua to invade Texas . . . (For the state of affairs in Mexico at the time, and the president's reaction see Roeder *Juarez and His Mexico.*)

"In regard to the second point that he would not give his official sanction to the occupying of the territory of this State by foreign troops, but hoped that the Apaches of the frontier would be kept quiet, the right to pursue Indians, even into the city of Chihuahua itself, had been granted by Don Revella when governor, to Judge Simeon Hart. Upon that point, if ever rendered necessary, your troops will have no trouble. As to the right to purchase supplies in Chihuahua, embraced in the third point, the governor assured me no steps would be taken to prevent it, and, although the presence of your command would increase the price which the people of Chihuahua would have to pay, yet, independent of this, we would not be excluded. . . .

"The governor seemed anxious to have the best relation established and continued between his State and the Confederate States, and I took leave of him satisfied in my mind that he would not break, or cause to be broken, the relations that now exist. I have the honor to report that the custom-house dues I was by you instructed to have remitted were ordered by the governor to be remitted, and the governor paid me the compliment to put in my hand the order to the collector at El Paso to have the duties remitted and the bondsman released. He stated that at all times whenever necessary he would be pleased to afford protection to the persons and the property of the citizens of the Southern Confederacy. It becomes my agreeable duty to report that I took letters from no one else in Texas to Chihuahua but from Hon. Simeon Hart, and that through his introduction and his influence I received the most marked and attentive consideration. He is well known and commands high respect and great credit in Chihuahua. Permit me here again to congratulate you on having been instrumental in obtaining the first official recognition by a foreign government of the Confederate States of America. (o. c. pp 173-74)

Governor Terrazas was not the only one wishing to rid himself of Indian troubles. The history of the Civil War in New Mexico following the Battle of Glorieta ceases to be action between Confederates and Federals but between Federals (Californians and New Mexicans) against depredating tribes. During September Lt. J. R. Pullian wrote to Col. Baylor from Fort Stanton that he had sent four men—T. G. Pemberton, Joseph V. Masse, Joseph Emmanacher and Floyd A. Sanders—to scout for water and supplies. These men had explicit orders but confident that neither Federals nor Indians were in the vicinity they slackened their vigilance. They lit a fire advertising their presence near the spring. While cooking breakfast the following morning they noticed three Indians running over the adjoining hill. They saddled their horse but no sooner were they ready to take off than the attack came. Each man took up his position behind a tree, loaded their muskets, and, to their horror, found they refused to go off. They next drew their revolvers, trying a running battle, but the Indians proved too numerous. The fight lasted two hours. Sanders was able to effect his escape, jumping on his horse and galloping down an almost perpendicular mountain amidst a shower of arrows. The chase lasted ten miles. Only the fleetness of his horse saved him. Fourteen men were sent out after the Indians but not a trace of them was found. Even the three civilian volunteers with the soldiers who were known for their feats in tracking down Indians could render no assistance. The bodies of two of the men were found scalped. They were buried on the spot. The Indians had carried off their dead and wounded. Masse's body was never recovered. What the Indians did with it ramains a mystery to this day. The Indians next attacked Placito (present Lincoln which had a number of names before the present one) and fifteen Texans were dispatched there to protect the natives. Five of the Indians were killed by the Confederates. They returned to Fort Stanton at 2 A. M. amid the pouring rain. The next day the Confederates abandoned Fort Stanton in favor of Dona Ana, Arizona Territory.

To some extent Baylor had a picnic at Mesilla. He made hay while the sun favored him. He bought up all the real estate he could, knowing that Mexico would be an open market for his crops; besides, wih Sibley chasing the Federals clear to Leavenworth, with many New Mexicans proclaiming for the South, with prices taking on a new all time high, with the backing of Hart, Magoffin, Baird and others, he felt secure indeed. His real estate in Mesilla was soon to be put up on the auction block by the very forces he expected Sibley to dispose of. Carleton was marching from California.

※ ※ ※

NOTES AND COMMENTS

David Emanuel Twiggs (1790-1862)—A native of Georgia, he took part in the War against England, emerging with the rank of captain. By the end of the Black Hawk War he was a colonel and in the Mexican War he was promoted to the rank of major general. He assumed command of the Department of Texas in 1857. In February, 1861, he surrendered all the Federal forces and stores under his control to Texas Secessionist authorities. Some say that he did this under compulsion from Ben McCullough's State Troops; others say it was quite voluntary, and quite daringly, in his Union general's uniform. He was commissioned a major general in the Confederate Army but his advanced age compelled him to resign. He died in Georgia July 15, 1862.

John Salmon Ford (1815-1897)—A native of South Carolina, he served in the Texas Army from 1836 to 1838, after which he practiced medicine until 1844. He was elected to Congress and became the editor of the *Texas Democrat*. He served in the Mexican War. He also served in the State Legislature and in Texas Frontier Service against Indians. He took part in the Battle of Palmito Ranch, often called the last battle of the Confederacy. After the war he edited the *Brownsville Sentinel* and later became mayor of that city. He died in San Antonio on November 3, 1897.

John Robert Baylor (1822-1894)—He was the soul of the campaign for the conquest of New Mexico and Arizona for the Confederacy. A native of Kentucky, he was seventeen when he came to Texas to fight Comanche Indians. He was elected to the State Legislature in 1853, and was on the side that carved out Santa Fe county for Texas. As Indian Agent to the Comanches he had some disagreements with Neighbors and was dismissed. In 1859, he is reported to have led a group of men to the Brazos Indian Reservation where, as a result of the engagement, the reservation was abandoned, and the Indians taken to Nations Territory. He was living at Weatherford when he was elected delegate to the Secession Congress. President Davis confirmed him in his self-imposed position of Governor of the Confederate State of Arizona, but he almost lost his position due to his severity towards the Apaches, whom the Confederates were hoping to gain to their side. It was because of his Indian policy that he was eventually removed. He served as a member of the Confederate Congress to the end of the war. He lived for a time at San Antonio, moving to Montell, where he died February 6, 1894. Baylor maintained that he resigned not because of Apaches but because he could not get along with Sibley. It is quite possible. Both men were said to be short-tempered.

Alexander McRae—Born in North Carolina c. 1834, he graduated from West Point July 1, 1847. He was made a captain in the Mounted Rifles, June 10, 1861, having been stationed at Fort Union, Fort Conrad and Fort Craig. His death at Valverde made the rounds of the campfires from coast to coast. Said the *Daily Alta* (California, March 23): "With his artillerymen cut down, his support either killed, wounded or flying from the field, Captain McRae sat down, calmly and quietly, on one of his guns, and with revolver in hand, refusing to fly or desert his post, he fought to the last, and gloriously died the death of a hero, the last man by his guns . . ." He was buried at

Fort Craig but several years later the remains were brought to West Point. From Fort Craig to Fort Bascom he was accorded honors reminiscent of ancient Greece and Rome. It is said that his family disinherited him for his loyalty to the Union. Fort McRae in New Mexico was named for him.

Simon Cameron (1799-1889)—A newspaperman from Pennsylvania, he became involved in banking and railroading. He entered politics and was elected to the U. S. Senate. He sought the office of President and Vice-President but was able to attain neither. Lincoln appointed him Secretary of War. He remained in politics until the date of his death.

Caleb B. Smith—Republican leader from Indiana. He was opposed to sending any relief to Fort Sumter, hoping that it would at least delay the war. He wrote Lincoln letters saying it would be politically unwise to do so. He thought the best thing for the Union was the evacuation of the fort. Lincoln had appointed him Secretary of the Interior (with some reluctance) because of his work in the Republican Convention that nominated him to the Presidency. He was Seward's puppet.

Henry Hopkins Sibley (1816-1886)—A native of Louisiana, he graduated from West Point in time for service against the Seminole. He was cited for gallantry during the Mexican War. He served in Utah from 1857 to 1860. Some authors say he was Canby's brother-in-law, which Heyman, in his life of Canby questions—"The present author has found no evidence to support this assertion of their relationship. . . . The only way they could have been related is for Sibley to have been married to one of Canby's sisters, about whom little is known. It is usually claimed, however, that Mrs. Canby was Sibley's sister, which, of course, she was not." (See: *Prudent Soldier*, page 178, note 63). Sibley invented the Sibley Tent and the Sibley Stove, useful to the army on the plains and during the war. Sibley's part—or lack of it—at Valverde and Glorieta has often come under fire and is a matter of dispute to this day. Wrote one old soldier, H. C. Wright, "In the first place, Gen. Sibley was not at Glorieta. He did not even command the brigade at Valverde, a month or two before (some said a coward—others attributed it to an overdose of stimulants), and

Col. Tom Green was in command at that time. At any rate after that battle we never saw him again. . . ." (See Letter to T. L. Greer written in 1927—N.M.H.V. July, 1930.) Sibley did demand the surrender of Fort Craig but felt its defenses too solid to take by storm, which accounts for his by-passing the post. Perhaps because the Confederacy was not pleased with the outcome of the New Mexico campaigns, he was demoted to serve under R. Taylor and Edmund Kirby Smith for the balance of the war. After the surrender of Lee, he enlisted in the service of the Khedive of Egypt. After eight years he returned to the United States, broken in health and poor of purse. He died at Fredericksburg, Virginia, August 23, 1886. Had he captured Fort Union as he wished he might have been given greater military responsibility by the South. Since he had a hand in the construction of the post, he would have been on more familiar ground than Fort Craig.

Earl Van Doren (1820-1863)—Born in Mississippi, September 17, 1820, the son of P. A. Van Doren and Sophia Donelson. His uncle was President Andrew Jackson and some have said it was through him that he was able to enter West Point, from which he graduated in 1842. He took part in the Seminole War and the Mexican War. He was later cited for his care and devotion in aiding yellow fever victims in his own State. He served under Sidney A. Johnson and Robert E. Lee in Texas. He was in command of the Wichita Expedition, 1858-59. March 16, 1861, he assumed command of the Department of Texas for the Confederacy. He ordered Baylor to attack Fort Fillmore should a good opportunity present itself. He was not aware of the terrific defection of former Union soldiers and officers to the Southern cause and the exodus to the East to enlist or re-enlist in the theatre of action. Had he recognized conditions in New Mexico he may have changed his plans, possibly sending Ben or Henry McCullough into New Mexico. His early successes caused him to be promoted to major general but his losses at Pea Ridge, Corinth, Franklin, forced the Confederate Command to transfer him to Spring Hill, Tennessee. It is said that a Dr. Peters killed him out of jealousy or spite, May 8, 1863. Sheridan, who opposed him at Franklin and Spring Hill, fails to mention his sudden and violent death in his *Memoirs*.

James Wiley Magoffin (1799-1868)—A native of Kentucky, he played an important role in the history of New Mexico as well as Texas in mid-century. Whatever he paid Armijo to desist from fighting Kearny, even this would have proved a failure, according to McKnight, if Donaciano Vigil had not spoken to the people of Santa Fe, Las Vegas, Las Ruedas, Mora and San Miguel. Magoffin received $30,000 compensation from the government; Vigil received nothing. A successful trader, he was a well-known figure along the Santa Fe Trail and the Chihuahua Trail. He was arrested as a spy in Mexico but his popularity with the natives brought about his liberation. A Confederate in sentiment, he was very helpful to Baylor and Sibley. Without his aid Sibley may have postponed Valverde from lack of provisions. He enlisted in the Confederate Army in Virginia but shortly afterwards returned to Texas as Assistant Commissary with the rank of captain. His goods at Magoffinsville were seized by the Federals but recovered for the most part in 1866. He died in San Antonio on September 29, 1868.

Leroy Pope Walker—Confederate Secretary of War under Davis. He did not advocate violence, waiting for the North to fire the first shot. One of the Cabinet members said to him: "Sir, unless you sprinkle blood in the face of the people of Alabama, they will be back in the old Union in less than ten days." Yet, when he heard of the action at Fort Sumter, he said: "The flag which now flaunts the breeze here will float over the dome of the old Capitol at Washington before the first of May. . . ." He was eventually forced to resign due to ill health and lack of decision. He was from Alabama.

Edward Clark (1815-1880)—Born in Georgia, he came to Texas in 1842, after having studied law in Alabama. He served as a member of the legislature in the Republic of Texas. In the Mexican War he was on the staff of General Henderson. After the war he was secretary of state. The Secession Convention placed him in the governor's chair (vacated by Sam Houston—Clark was lieutenant governor) to complete the former governor's term. Fought in the Civil War and became a brigadier general. After the war fled to Mexico but returned to engage in business. Failed in all his undertakings until he returned to law in Marshall, Texas. He died there on May 4, 1880. He was interested in the Confederate State of Arizona and sought to renew the hope of Santa Fe country, Texas, for the Confederacy.

Josiah Frazzier Crosby (1829-1904)—Born in Charleston, South Carolina, January 3, 1829. After his father died his mother moved to Texas. He studied law and served in the legislature and as district attorney. He resigned to help establish the town of El Paso. He favored the Confederacy and his goods were seized by order of General Carleton. After the war he opened a law office in Houston. He served for a time as president of the Texas & New Orleans R. R. During the war he was on the staff of General W. Steele. He was active in the promotion of the El Paso-White Oaks (N. M.) R. R. He tried practicing law in New York but his heart was in El Paso. He returned to his beloved city and died there January 5, 1904.

James Reily (1815-1863)—A native of Ohio, he moved to Kentucky when quite young. He married Ellen Hart, the niece of Henry Clay. He settled in Nacogdoches, where he practiced law. Lamar, Houston and others availed themselves of his services as a diplomat. He served as Minister to Russia for a short time under President Buchanan. He served under Sibley but gave up his command for a diplomatic mission to Mexico. He was not successful. He had hoped to obtain permission for Mexico's help in arms as well as the use of sections of Chihuahua and Sonora as Confederate depots and training centers. He later served in Louisiana under General Banks. He was killed at the battle of Camp Bisland on Teche Bayou (part of the battle of Franklin) April 14, 1863.

Thomas Green (1814-1864)—A native of Virginia, he graduated from University of Tenessee and Princeton College. He came to Texas as a lawyer but soon found himself engaged in helping with Independence for the new nation. He returned to Tennessee for a time, returning to Texas to enter politics. He served the Republic as lawyer, judge, congressman and legislator. He served as captain in the Mexican War. He served as colonel under H. H. Sibley. As brigadier general, he took part in the re-capture of Galveston, where his cavalry dismounted and acted as marines. Transferred to Louisiana he was killed at Blair's Landing April 12, 1864. Tom Green County honors him.

William Steele (1820-1885)—A native of New York, he was twenty years of age when he graduated from West Point. He served on the frontier in New Mexico, Arizona, Utah and Texas. He served in the Mexican War. He was one of the many army officers to resign his U. S. commission for a place in the Confederate Army. He served as colonel under H. H. Sibley, later being promoted to brigadier general. He served with Tom Green at Galveston and the Red River Campaign. After the death of Green he commanded a division of artillery. After the war he became a merchant in San Antonio. He helped reorganize the Texas Rangers. He died in San Antonio, January 12, 1885.

Benjamin McCulloch (1811-1862)—A native of Tennessee he was quite friendly with Dave Crockett with whom he planned to come to Texas. He came later, in time to participate in the Texas War of Independence. He served the Republic as surveyor and as Congressman, also as scout and Indian fighter. He raised a company of Texas Rangers which was assigned as a spy company under General Z. Taylor in the Mexican War. In 1849 he went to California and was sheriff in Sacramento county before returning to Texas. In 1853 he was appointed U. S. Marshall by President Pierce. President Buchanan appointed him one of the two peace commissioners to settle the Mormon trouble in Utah Territory. He forced Twiggs to surrender in San Antonio at the outbreak of the Civil War. He became a Brigadier General in the Confederate Army winning the battle of Oak Hills, August 10, 1861. Serving under General Van Dorn in the battle of Elk Horn, he was killed by sharpshooters on the second day of battle, March 7, 1862. His body was brought to Austin for burial. McCulloch county honors him.

Henry E. McCulloch (1816-1895)—He came to Texas with his brother Ben. Like his brother he was a surveyor and Indian fighter. He served as 1st Lt. in Capt. Jack Hay's Texas Rangers and participated in the battle of the Salado in 1842. He became sheriff of Gonzolez, Texas, as well as merchant. He moved his store to Seguin. He served in the Mexican War and was Captain of Texas Rangers in 1850 to protect San Antonio from Indian raids. He served in the State Legislature. He was with his brother Ben in demanding of Twiggs the surrender of the Federal army posts in Texas at the start of the Civil War. He became a Brigadier General and took part in the battle of Millican's Bend on the Mississippi, but returned to Texas to assume command of the Northern Sub-district of Texas. After the war he was appointed superintendent of the school for the Deaf and Dumb. He died in Seguin, March 12, 1895.

Isaac Lynde—Sufficiently covered in the text. (1806-1886)

Edward Richard Sprigg Canby (1817-1873)—A native of Kentucky, the family moved to Indiana when he was five years old. He graduated from West Point in 1835. Took part in the Mexican War, served in New Mexico. Was in charge of the Department of New Mexico after Loring went over to the Confederates. When Carleton came to New Mexico Canby found use for his services elsewhere. After the war General Canby hoped to bring about peace with the Modoc Indians of northern California. A fanatic of the tribe, known as Captain Jack, killed him on April 11, 1873.

Canby was well liked in Santa Fe but failed to understand the New Mexico Volunteer. He judged them rather harshly, not taking into consideration the language barrier and their ingrained habit of fighting Indians. The New Mexican was not used to camp life and taking orders such as he expected of them nor were they aware of the seriousness of the cause against Baylor and Sibley. "On August 13, the headquarters of the army renewed its request for the withdrawal of most of the regular troops in the department. Canby was faced with a serious problem concerning the defense of the Territory. He and his Inspector-General looked askance at the citizen soldiers of New Mexico. They 'could not be relied on;' they were 'not efficient;' they were 'worse than worthless;' were 'aids to the enemy;' and were 'deficient in self-reliance and military spirit.' In addition, they were ignorant of the English language and had a 'want of capacity for instruction.' As troops they were valuable only as auxiliaries to the regulars. Canby, moreover, considered the people, as a whole, generally 'apathetic in disposition', and it has been suggested, in consequence, that he, like his predecessors in command in New Mexico, 'had a very erroneous idea' about the character of the Mexican (sic) portion of the populace. That he was influenced in this attitude by Anglo-Americans living in the

Territory, as has also been suggested, is probable. But his opinion of them was colored, primarily, by his anxiety for the safety of the Territory. . . ." Heyman o. c. p. 144.

Michael Steck (1818-1883)—A medical man, he was appointed Indian Agent by President Fillmore. He was serious in his efforts but could not get along with the governor and other officials in New Mexico and Washington. He became a successful prospector, using his gold to finance railroads. The venture proved unsuccessful and he lost all his money. He died in Virginia, October 6, 1883.

CHAPTER FIVE

THE CALIFORNIA COLUMN

Part One
(ARIZONA—THEN WESTERN NEW MEXICO)

The Military Department of California was not created because President Buchanan expected war, on the contrary, he looked for nothing more than angry exchange of words in the Senate and the House at least during his administration. The War Department acted more as a precautionary measure against Indians and unscrupulous prospectors as well as to cut down the territory of the adjoining department. The Department, created on September 13, 1858, included the territory west of the Rockies south of Oregon except as much of Utah as lay east of the 117th meridian of west longitude and of New Mexico as lay east of the 110th meridian of west longitude. It also included the Rogue river and the Umpqua districts in Southwestern Oregon. At first it was commanded by Brevet Brigadier General Newman S. Clarke, but when he died on October 17, 1860, he was succeeded by Lieutenant Colonel Benjamin L. Beall. It became known as the Department of the Pacific on January 15, 1861. (See: *War of the Rebellion* Series 1 Vol. L p. 1, herafter cited as W. R.)

Again changing hands, the Department fell to the command of Brigadier General George Wright, who vacated the position in favor of Brevet Brigadier General A. S. Johnson, much to the consternation and alarm of the Federals who insisted that if he were left in command he would turn California over to the South. The Adjutant General's office fell in line with this thinking and turned the Department over to Brigadier General Sumner, ordering him to drop what he was doing and to proceed without delay to San Francisco to relieve Johnson, who was told to entrain for Washington to await further orders. Instead, on April 9, 1861, he resigned his commission in the Army of the United States. He was not aware at the time that Sumner had been named to succeed him for he wrote that he was constrained in conscience to resign in favor of the South and he begged that a successor be appointed to relieve him as soon as practicable.

No sooner was Sumner in San Francisco than he appointed a friend of long standing, Brevet Major James H. Carleton, in command of 1st U. S. Dragoons, Companies B and K (Companies D and G at Fort Breckenridge, New Mexico), 6th U. S. Inf. Companies F and I at Camp Fitzgerald, near Los Angeles. Life during these days at the camp was very much like that of any other frontier post whose recruits were mostly from mining camps. The gold in the earth would be there when they came back from the war. No one doubted that it would be a matter of a few months, then back to prospecting. Many were not to return for six years; others like Sam Zimmerly were never to return, not because death claimed them but because they were to be captivated by the charms of the Land of Enchantment and its dark eyed Spanish beauties. Others like Captain Emil Fritz, Wm. Rynerson and Brady were to change the course of history in more than one county of New Mexico. The California Column shaped the history and destiny of the Land of the Pueblos for the next sixteen years. The gold fever was in their blood even during the war and every day they were not fighting Sibley or Indians or on guard duty they were in quest of gold, pioneering new ventures, encouraging Santa Fe trade, preparing the way for the rich strikes of the Eighties to give New Mexico a place in the sun. On August 7, Carleton received this note from General Sumner:

"Turn over your command to Captain Davidson and repair here as quickly as possible. By order of the Government you are to command the California troops on the plains, with the rank of Colonel. Captain (Winfield S.) Hancock will proceed to Washington City and report to the Quartermaster-General."

Over in New Mexico John B. Mills was apprehensive of the number of regulars leaving the Territory and wrote his friend William Nelson of Peekskill, New York, to use his influence with the President to prevent any further withdrawal of Federal troops from Arizona and Southern New Mexico. He wrote: "You are well aware that the inhabitants of that Territory are comparatively few and greatly scattered, and, therefore, in existing circumstances are dependent upon the government of the United States for protection. The latest intelligence that we have here from Arizona is that the Apaches and other tribes of Indians are very troublesome, and together with secessionists from Texas, with whom the Indians seem to be in league, are becoming more and more hostile and are committing great depredations. Robbery and murder upon an extensive scale seem to be the order of the day...." (o.c. W. R. Sept. 21, 1861)

Captain Davidson was sent to Fort Yuma to protect wagon trains against the Indians. Originally, Col. Carleton's regiment was ordered to the post for this duty but when it was ascertained that he had difficulty obtaining mounts for his soldiers, he was by-passed in favor of Davidson. However, he received orders to march his men to Warner's Ranch. As it turned out Warner's Ranch also meant Fort Yuma.

"I have sent an express to Fort Yuma with my orders, and calling for a report of the subsistence, quartermaster's medical and ordnance stores on hand. I am anxious to ascertain the amount of subsistence, particularly, as the command I am sending to that place under Colonel Carleton will far exceed in numbers that already there... Colonel Carleton is diligently engaged in preparing his regiment for the march to Warner's Ranch and Fort Yuma. It is not probable that the Colonel will reach Fort Yuma before the 1st of November...." (Col. G. Wright to Major R. C. Drum, Oct. 7, 1861).

Here are Special Orders No. 2, Headquarters District of Southern California, Los Angeles, October 7, 1861: "Col. James H. Carleton, of the First Regiment, California Volunteers, will march as soon as practicable with his entire regiment to Warner's Ranch and establish a camp at that place of four companies, under the command of a field officer. Colonel Carleton will then move with the residue of his regiment to Fort Yuma and relieve the garrison of regular troops at that place."

It took three days for Major Rigg to put all in readiness before he marched with his four companies for Warner's Ranch on the Fort Yuma road. This was a favorite stopping place for the stage, the mail, the prospector, passing caravans, the lonely traveler, the Indian. Indeed it was the first civilized stop west of the perilous Colorado Desert. General Kearney made it a resting place for his weary men on their march from Santa Fe to San

Diego. The Butterfield Stage Station was to be a historical landmark in this area. John Joseph Warner of the famous Connecticut Trumbull family was not living at the ranch at the time Rigg and Carleton encamped there but rather in Los Angeles and although he lost his interest in the property that same year the name persisted. One would say that it was rather an outpost than a ranch.

Colonel Swords made arrangements with a Mr. Banning for transportation. He supplied thirty wagons at the rate of thirty dollars a day. The contract specified that he was to haul four thousand pounds of supplies across the desert to Fort Yuma. Dr. Prentiss, the regiment surgeon, refused to move unless he were supplied an ambulance which he thought would soon be put to use since he heard that Baylor's Babies were moving in on Arizona for the purpose of attacking Fort Yuma. Once Major Riggs reached Warner's Ranch he was to empty the wagons, send them back for subsistence supplies loading at night if necessary for he was given three days to go to San Diego with the empties and four days to return with the rations. Colonel Carleton was still in Los Angeles on October 14. On that day he issued these General Orders:

"I hereby assume command of the District of Southern California.

"Lt. Col. Josept R. West, 1st Inf. Cal. Vols., with Companies E, G, and H, of that regiment, will on Wednesday morning, the 16th inst., start en route for Camp Wright, near Warner's Ranch. Having arrived at that point, Lt. Col. West, with Companies B, H, I, 1st Inf. Cal. Vol., will proceed without delay to Fort Yuma, on the Colorado river, and relieve Lt. Col. Andrews and the regular troops, officers and men, now serving at that post. Lt. Col. West will load his train with subsistence stores at Camp Wright for the garrison at Fort Yuma." (o. c. W. R.)

Colonel Wright suddenly switched Carleton to San Bernadino, canceled Col. West's leave, went to San Francisco, insisted that the remainder of the command remain at Camp Latham and ordered Carleton to pay him a visit. Two days later Carleton was still in Los Angeles. Again he wrote West reminding him that he was ordered to Fort Yuma to relieve the garrison there of its regular troops to be replaced by the California Volunteers. He urged upon him the importance of reaching the post without any further delay. He told West that promptness in executing orders must be the cardinal point in all the movements of the First Infantry. Strategically, Fort Yuma was the door to all Southern California. The Texans had to capture it to gain entrance. West had to be circumspect and guard against any possible surprise attack. West also received this soldierly advice: "If you are not surprised, your force properly managed, with the desert as an auxiliary, you will never be whipped. You will seize all ferry boats, large and small, upon the River Colorado. All the crossing of the river must be done at one point under the guns of the fort. . . ." (Ibid)

Encouraged by such leadership, West surprised everybody, including himself, by marching one hundred and forty miles within the week. At Fort Yuma he penned a note to Carleton admitting that he scarcely knew his position at the fort. He was doing his best to be a good soldier. There was a ferry boat twenty miles below the post and one thirty miles above. He would send men to appropriate them. Ferries were really of little or no use since there were many spots along the river so low that they could be forded with little or no risk. Here, too, Indians were a problem. The Cupenos were not in sympathy with West and his men, and knew how to swim the animals of pro-Southerners anxious to by-pass the Volunteers in order to join the Confederate Army. Every day conflicting reports came in from Arizona. It was said that Baylor and his men already captured Tucson. Remember, at this time Arizona was actually Western New Mexico. Even should he conquer Baylor at Tucson there was still Van Dorn at Mesilla to contend with, and after that Sibley on his way from San Antonio.

Capturing the boats along the river was not as easy as he anticipated. This caused a series of delays which contributed to hindering the Volunteers from participating in the action at Valverde. West sought to negotiate for the boats whenever possible before attempting to seize them. Messengers were dispatched to Gonzolez Ferry some thirty miles below Fort Yuma as well as to Winegar sixteen miles above the post. These were troublesome. All the other boats save a steamer sent to the mouth of the river for supplies readily acknowledged the officer's authority, the captains placing them at the disposal of the regiment. The Colonel next sent for several chiefs of the Yumas for a parley in an effort to ascertain their worth as allies. This hurt the Maricopas and Pimas at war with the Yumas and they refused to attend the meeting. Rather they donned war paint and sought measures to prevent if possible the Volunteers from passing through their territory. One of his trusted messengers was Hadji Ali, best known in American desert history for his work with the Camel Corps, a venture sanctioned by Jefferson Davis, as ill fated as the Confederacy. Hadji Ali was expressman for the West contingent. Sent to hasten the steamer already a day overdue he returned the next afternoon with the boat in tow.

Having been at Yuma long enough to study its weak and strong points, West addressed himself to Carleton with a different plan for the defense of the post. Actually it was the plan of Captain Johnson, of the steamer Cocopak. "It is an economical one," wrote West, " and permits of the retention of the command at the Warner Ranch also. Captain Johnson is of the opinion—and leaves here believing that he is prepared to contract with the Government to that end—that 300 men, with 150 tons of freight, two pieces of artillery, etc., can be landed here in ten days from San Francisco at an expense not to exceed $20,500, viz.: Charter a steamer to the mouth of the Colorado from San Francisco to carry 300 men and 150 tons of freight, $10,000; passage for 300 men from the mouth to Fort Yuma, at $10 a man; freight for the 150 tons would total $7,500. If this can be done it would, in my opinion, be a most judicious expenditure, and would, I believe, secure beyond question the possession of this post against any force the enemy can bring against it. Fort Yuma is a valuable position to be retained by the United States Government. It has cost a vast amount of money, holds a large amount of stores, and possesses great strategic importance as you are aware. Its abandonment would be equivalent to a loss of one million dollars by the United States, and contrary to the spirit that dictates the holding of all Federal property, I am not now conscious of any attempts to be made or projects entertained by the enemy for getting possession of it. . . . Three companies of the five regiments raised in California subsequent to our own could very probably be spared for the service. They are either at or convenient to San Francisco. They could be landed here by the 12th to the 15th proximo, should the department commander see the justice of my views. With six hundred men the post could be made a fortification in a short time. Now its weakness consists in its many assailable points, requiring a larger force for its successful defense than its present garrison numbers. The three additional companies could be encamped in the immediate vicinity of the post without detriment to their health, I am told by the surgeon here. The 150 tons of freight and the stores that I notified you of as being on hand will amply provide for them. They could be employed from the 15th of December to the 15th of April in defending and fortifying, and be withdrawn when the weather became too warm, and leave the place stronger than it is now. Should the enemy attempt the passage of the river I could dispute it with him fifty miles up or down. Now I dare not leave it." (o. c. W. R.)

It is hard to say what West hoped to gain by this letter. On November 18 he was recalled to Los Angeles by Carleton his vacancy filled by Major Edwin A. Rigg. Three weeks later Carleton himself was given orders to leave San Francisco and return to the Los Angeles command. Major Rigg was not long in finding out how correct West was in his surmise that there was much work to be done at Fort Yuma. One of the complaints of both settler and prospector was that Santa Fe was too far from them as a Territorial capital and they were not as interested in the war as such as they were in agitating for the separate Territory of Arizona. Their struggle was not to end until February 24, 1863, when Congress passed an Act creating the new territory. Even then other problems confronted them. Tucson, the largest city in the Gadsden Purchase area, was two hundred and fifty miles from the county seat at Mesilla and more than five hundred miles by stage from Santa Fe. No wonder the settlers struck out in 1856 for a division. Many of these settlers were from the South consequently when Baylor's Babies marched into Mesilla and declared the area Confederate country they were only too glad to elect Granville H. Oury a delegate to the Confederate Congress. Whatever the sentiments of the people of Arizona, Fort Yuma at the southwestern end of the Territory near the California border had to be fortified and prepared for defense against Confederate invasion and the protection of California.

Much of the hay needed for the horses was cut by the California Volunteers after Major Rigg signed a contract with L. J. F. Yager. This rancher agreed to let the soldiers have it at the same price paid by the Overland Mail. Yager also agreed to furnish beef for the soldiers as he had a large herd at San Felipe which could be driven to the Colorado and slaughtered as needed. He stood to lose nothing. He owned a ferry boat and the fare the men had to pay as individuals to cross and re-cross the river was rather exorbitant. Yager had come to the region in the fall of 1849 with Lieutenant A. W. Whipple and decided to settle especially since there was a report of rich strikes in California. His ferry continued to enrich him until 1877 when he sold it to the Southern Pacific Railroad.

Carleton settled with his men at Camp San Pedro, moving in from Camp Latham. Ever a stickler for detail he figured to the last pound the amount of subsistence stores his 1,600 men would need at Fort Yuma. Including ten days added for delays at Fort Yuma and contingencies on the route thither, but not comprising the five days in every seven of fresh beef to be driven on the hoof, he boiled these supplies down to 87,888 pounds. His memorandum also included three hundred six gallon water kegs, 3,000 pounds of horse and mule shoes, and he sought forage for nine hundred mules and five hundred horses to last thirty days. He adapted his calculations to a train of one hundred and fifty wagons, four hundred and twenty-five cavalry and one hundred and twenty-five artillery and officers' horses. He figured that each wagon should not start out with a load of less than 3,000 pounds. The memorandum also showed that 102,000 pounds of barley could not be transported by these wagons. This was the quantity that Carleton felt was needed to complete the forage that would be consumed in the thirty days. He felt that they could be placed upon the route by fifty teams that would be needed in the district after the expedition took the field, or by private contract, if necessary. Not one pound of these supplies or forage was to be used after leaving Fort Yuma, except the item of 10,000 pounds of pemmican. This item was prepared from pounded dried beef and beef lard.

Next Carleton prepared a list of supplies needed at Fort Yuma for a command of 1,600 men independent of its garrison, and for an expedition to last three months. He went extra heavy on the beef since the men would not have beans, rice nor potatoes with them on the march to Santa Fe. He hoped to obtain all these supplies out of San Francisco and sent men to build advance stations for them. He also wanted one large depot not too far from Mesilla or Santa Fe upon which he could draw for supplies as needed. Thus, with advance stations every two days ahead and a main depot in between the men should not want for food. No wonder Carleton was loved by his men. The ammunition for small arms and artillery, hospital stores, tools, clothing and horse and mule shoes shoes he wished shipped by sea and the Colorado, as well as 600,000 pounds of barley. He requisitioned Sharps carbines, navy revolvers, sabers, belts, carbine slings and swivels, before leaving San Pedro. He confounded the Commissary Department by asking for five thousand pounds of presents for Indians consisting of tobacco, knives, small mirrors, vermilion paint, beads, needles and thread, awls, iron arrow points, fish hooks and lines, hoes, red blankets for the chiefs and other inexpensive gifts. He wanted only the best hand made horse and mule shoes manufactured by Nelson & Duble of San Francisco. West was sent to San Francisco to make sure he received these supplies.

Meanwhile the Volunteers continued to cut grass for hay along the Gila river bank, and storing it in the deserted corrals of the Overland Stage stations. Often it was a thankless task for was the grass no sooner cut than violent storms washed it away. Once there was a flood. The river rose six inches in three hours. The soldiers worked beyond midnight to save the corrals and hay, quartermaster and commissary supplies. Fort Yuma became an island. Colorado City was washed away. The soldiers' efforts to the contrary notwithstanding, Mr. Hinton's store goods were almost entirely washed away. Samuel Wells watched his store with all its contents washed away by the flood. Gage's billiard and ten-pin alley was completely demolished. Yager had a narrow escape. The Volunteers managed to save seventy tons of government hay. The water works at the post were completely submerged. A large number of cattle were drowned. One cheerful diehard commented that at least they were safe from attack so long as they were surrounded by water. Prior to the flood Yager received this letter from his friend, Peter Brady, of Altar, Mexico:

"There is a report here that one thousand Confederate troops are on their way from Mesilla to occupy Arizona. I believe there is some truth in the rumor for the new superintendent of the Poston mine, Major Lally, has not made his appearance, but is in the Magdalena (Sonora) area waiting to see the turn of events. Mr. Palatine Robinson, of Tuscon, posted up his notices at Arivaca and at Tubac, declaring the property of Colonel Colt confiscated in Arizona, and he as a loyal citizen of the Sunny South should proceed to take possession of it. Van Alstein, Col. Colt's agent at Arivaca, objected. Pistols were drawn; the usual compliments—'sons of _____, d_____d sons of _____' were exchanged, and the parties separated without bloodshed. Van Alstein started off for Magdalena to see Major Lally. If there are one thousand Texans in Arizona they will certainly confiscate Colt's mines beyond a doubt, but I don't see how any of the Tuscon agents will be able to work it, for they have no means whatsoever. It will be a serious drawback to the country if Col. Colt's agents will not be allowed to work the mines, for the other party will do nothing I am certain."

Major Riggs asked if he might not forward this letter to Col. Carleton, to which Yager readily assented adding that the Major might annotate some comments of his own. Riggs said that he was certain that Baylor was at Tucson with at least a thousand men; that Robinson issued a proclamation declaring all property confiscated which did no belong to unqualified Southern men, including the Arizona Mining Company, Col. Colt's and all others. The Major voiced an opinion that all the hay cut from Gila to Stanwix was destroyed. He feared for the thirty tons stored at Grinnel's. He was sure Baylor knew about it. Ammi White of the Pima Villages who was known to be a loyal Union man asked protection against the possible confiscation of his goods by Baylor's Babies. Baylor went so far as to appoint a resident of Tucson as receiver of confiscated property. He only awaited the arrival of General Sibley before marching for Western Arizona for the purpose of confiscating all property not belonging to citizens of the Southern Confederacy. He seemed to think he would have complete charge of his Texans not having to turn any over to Sibley.

Alarmed by this piece of news Carleton hired a spy and ordered Rigg to send out spies to verify these rumors. Carleton's man was Federick C. Buckner who was dispatched to Fort Yuma, a make up artist of the day fitting him out in a disguise. At midnight he had ferried across the river and turned loose to wander the country. He came back with reports that confirmed their worst fears. White was taken prisonor as well as Captain McCleave and eight men sent out to patrol the area. McCleave had been at Camp Carleton when he received orders to advance to the relief of Fort Yuma. He had thirty men in his command working through the San Gorgonio Pass to the Colorado river in five days, traveling through the rough desert trail at night. Just two days before the remainder of the McCleave company, under the command of Lt. James Barrett, left San Bernadino, Captain Sherod Hunter, of the Confederate Army, entered Tucson with one hundred men. On the following day Col. James Reily with two subalterns and twenty rank and file joined Hunter. On March 1 he raised the Confederate flag over the town and pronounced the citizens members of the South promising them peace and prosperity in the name of the Confederacy. Following this Reily went across the border seeking Mexican recognition of the Confederate States. Hunter proceeded to the Pima Villages to seek out White whom he hoped to hang to the nearest tree for supplying the Federals with commodities needed for the South. Also he hoped to destroy some 300,000 pounds of wheat stored away by White.

With Sibley now moving on Fort Craig, he had sent Hunter to Tucson really to spy on the movements of the California Volunteers and to send him notice of any advance of the troops that might serve to hinder or jeopardise his return to El Paso. The impact of Valverde did not seem to stir the men at Fort Yuma who felt that this was an even more important post than either Craig or Union. When news of the disaster at Valverde was brought to Carleton his only comment was: "If so, Sibley is master of New Mexico; if not, he may have fallen back on Mesilla." Rumor also had it that Sonora defected from Mexico and joined the Confederacy. In view of the fact of the mission of Col. Reily, Carleton considered this rumor to be true. His spies told him that Sibley had four regiments of infantry, a large body of cavalry and a battery of howitzers to which he added McRae's battery captured at Valverde. Victorious below the Jornada del Muerto, Carleton felt that the Confederate would now turn in the direction of Tucson to aid Captain Hunter. Carleton set out to capture Hunter before Sibley could get to him. The force that was ordered to make it warm for Hunter was also cautioned to be on the lookout for Col. Reily, to capture him alive if possible. Carleton hoped to capture Tucson and fall back upon the Pima Villages should Sibley march to the relief of the captured town. He would leave a number of fresh troops who would come to the aid of the Pima villages if needed, or in the event Sibley's Brigade should prove too powerful the men entrenched at the Villages would fall back on Fort Yuma. Baylor he ignored completely. Sibley, he knew from Fort Union days.

He respected him as a soldier and the news from Valverde proved he had not underestimated him as a soldier.

Carleton preferred to have his cavalry at Tucson and the Pima Villages. He thought the infantry could make a better stand at Fort Yuma. Another reason: he wanted to conserve the barley at the place. The mounts could forage for themselves around Tucson. If Sibley did not take the offensive and march on Tucson, Carleton would then march his Volunteers to the Rio Grande for the purpose of re-capturing Fort Fillmore, Fort Thorn and Fort Bliss, which he said would be a harder task against Sibley's Brigade than against Baylor's Babies. He wrote his superior officer asking if he could not also have the assistance of Bowie's Regiment in taking the offensive against Sibley. Once he captured Tucson he would send men for supplies at Sonora leaving his own for Bowie. Besides the Rice and the Active could come full steam to the mouth of the Colorado with more than ample supplies for the campaign. A member of Company K, 1st Inf. Cal. Vols. wrote a letter from Stanwix (at Grinnell's home) telling his family about McCleave's capture. The family thought it should not keep the news to itself so it turned the letter over to the Sacramento Daily Union which published it on May 3, 1862:

"It was late in the evening of March 6 when McCleave knocked at the door of White's house and inquired if White was at home. He was answered in the affirmative by one of the band who in turn asked where the strangers were from. They said they were United States troops from the Colorado. The man retired as if to acquaint White with the presence of the troopers. (White was a prisoner elsewhere.) Shortly after, Hunter and about thirty of his band made their appearance and leveling a pistol at the breast of McCleave said: 'I am Captain Hunter of the Southern Army. Consider yourselves prisoners. Lay down your arms. McCleave said he would do nothing of the kind. Then Hunter remarked: 'If you make a single motion I will blow your brains out. You are in my power. Surrender immediately.' McCleave realized that it was too useless to contend against such overwhelming numbers and surrendered himself a prisoner to that guerrilla chief."

When Col. Carleton heard of McCleave's capture he could hardly believe it. He had been a fellow officer for ten years. "A whole staff could not compensate for the loss of McCleave," remarked Carleton when he heard the news. McCleave on the other hand was not so doleful. He took his capture lightly, taunting his captors that they had not won the war yet. He was taken to Tucson to await the return of Col. Reily. The men taken with him were paroled. It was while making their way to the river that they decided to rest at old Fort McLane. Here they learned of Sibley's victory at Valverde. Captain Hunter so rejoiced at this bit of information that he had his men lined up as for inspection and told them the story. An officer noticed that McCleave was not cheering and asked him to do so. The prisonor replied that his day for cheering was yet to come. This so enraged some of the privates that they would have shot him on the spot had the lieutenant not restrained them.

The contingent moved on towards Mesilla. It was during this march that Jones the expressman was captured and the Confederates learned from him the advance of the California Volunteers. Mesilla was alerted, the guard doubled, Jones and McCleave placed in jail. A week later stragglers from the Glorieta battlefield began to arrive with the news of the defeat of Sibley's Brigade by the Colorado Volunteers. The loss of their supply train of eighty wagons made the rounds. Mesilla was abandoned in favor of El Paso. Col. Reily sent for McCleave and told him that he would parole him if he promised not to take up arms against the Confederacy until exchanged. The prisoner refused. A few days later the performance was repeated. Upon his second refusal he was handed a paper signed by the adjutant which stated that he was released on his own parole of honor. He headed for Fort Craig to report for duty. En route he picked up four men, three being deserters from Sibley's Brigade. About forty miles above Mesilla they came upon Fort Thorn where they were greeted by the California Volunteers. McCleave was to serve in New Mexico for the duration.

Nor did Lt Col. West remain inactive. Col. Carleton ordered him to take Companies C and K, 1st Cal. Vols. (Infantry) and Companies A, B, and D, of the cavalry to the Pima Villages on the Gila and there establish an entrenched field work. Carleton had in mind a garrison of three companies for this post at least for the duration. This was to be his sub-depot supply center. West was cautioned to locate on a spot where there was good drinking water. He was to pick up his entrenching tools at Camp Wright and two mountain howitzers at Fort Yuma. Acting assistant surgeon Kittridge was to accompany him as medical officer. As he passed by Fort Yuma the doctor was to pick up two ambulances, three hospital tents; the flies and poles were to come from Camp Wright. Kittridge was ordered to remain at the camp established near Grinnel's, about a hundred miles above Fort Yuma, on the Gila river. Lt Col. Eyre was to command the wagons, taking with him Co. B of the cavalry. Subsistence supplies and forage for the march to the Pima Villages were to be drawn from Fort Yuma. In order not to cut too deeply into these supplies West was to take as much as possible in the thirty wagons alloted to him at Camp Wright. At Fort Yuma he was allowed five thousand pounds of pemmican. Forty-five teams were to be used to carry supplies from the fort to the Pima Villages whenever needed. For fresh beef he was to contact O'Campo and Yager. Carleton preferred that he conserve the pemmican for emergency purposes in case of a siege or for the troops used in detached service. Surgeon Prentiss was named medical officer at the Pima Villages. West was ordered to catch up with Companies A and D already on the way to Fort Yuma; these were to join his command. Befort leaving Camp Wright Captain Calloway's men were to hunt up all the empty sacks they could find as well as six gallon water kegs which West would find useful.

At Fort Yuma West was to pick up two water tanks containing six hundred gallons each which were ordered made especially for his command. Also at Fort Yuma he was to pick up more empty sacks. Carleton sought to impress upon him that he and his men would be stationed in desert country where water and forage were scarce. The sacks he was to take to the Pima and Maricopa Indians from whom he was to purchase grain. These filled sacks would also come in handy as defense walls against attack. West was also ordered to take from Fort Yuma molds to be used in making adobe bricks. Adobe would be a good substitute in case he was unable to procure willows and other bushes for making of fascines and gabions. West was given ten thousand yards of manta with which to purchase wheat and other supplies from the Indians. Out fashioned army clothing was used for the same purpose.

West was reminded that his force was but an advance guard, hence he was to risk little or no battle if any enemy approached the Pima Villages. However, if the enemy took the offensive and attacked him he was to defend himself to the last man, let the number of attackers be what they may. If he made overtures to the Indians and won them to his side he was to use them as spies. The supplies were to be stored inside the entrenchment. Men were employed in cutting hay and wheat straw for the use of the animals. The barley at Fort Yuma was to be called for only in case of extreme necessity. Carleton thought it a good idea for West to send men out to the various mining camps and ranches to live off the land as long as possible before digging into his own supplies.

One skirmish took place in Arizona that is known as the Battle of Picacho Pass. The advance guard reached the Villages on April 12th remaining there two days to rest and trade with the natives, bartering manta and clothing for flour. At this time Carleton and the main force were preparing to leave Camp Drum. It would be six weeks before they arrived at this point. Lt. James Barrett in command of a small detachment of cavalry was instructed by Capt. Calloway to move forward, and approaching Picacho Pass he was to turn off the main road to come in from the east through an opening to the left of the mountain. Lt. Baldwin, with another detachment, was ordered forward from the west. By this means the Captain hoped to cut off the retreat of the enemy's pickets who were stationed in the Pass. Barrett overstepped his instructions by moving eight miles in advance of the main body under West. Knowing that the pickets were concealed in the thicket he charged. Firing his pistol into the air he ordered them to surrender. As one of the prisoners related later, had the Lieutenant ordered the surrender without the shot they might have complied.

Instead, the Confederates answered by firing into the advancing men. Four fell at this first volley. After this the firing became general. Three of the Confederates threw down their arms and surrendered. Lt. Barrett dismounted to aid in tying them. As he lifted himself back into the saddle, a shot fired from the thicket entered his neck killing him instantly. George Johnson, 1st Cav., Co. A, was shot near the heart and died within minutes; William S. Leonard, 1st Cav., Co. D, was shot in the back, the ball ranging upwards and passing out through his mouth. He died the following day. William C. Tobin, 1st Cav., Co. B, was shot in the forehead but the brasses of his hat caused the ball to glance upwards leaving a ghastly but not fatal wound. Two others were shot in the arm and shoulder but they survived to fight the battle over a thousand times so that even their children's children repeated it in their sleep. One Confederate was killed; three were wounded; three taken prisoner; one escaped. Barrett and the others were buried side by side not far from the scene of the engagement, on the road to Tucson. So touched was Carleton by the death of the Lieutenant that he named the camp established by West at the Pima Villages Fort Barrett in his honor. He ordered that the names of the other men be called each day at roll call by their company commanders until the end of the war.

Lt. Col. West arrived at the site of the new post on April 29, too late for the medical wagon to be of any assistance. Captain Hunter and his men remained at Tucson until May 4th impervious to West and his men. He finally broke camp about the time the California Column left Fort Yuma. He marched to the Rio Grande to join forces with the Confederates retreating from Glorieta.

Carleton made arrangements that the supply trains enroute from San Pedro to Fort Yuma be so divided that not over eighty animals, whether horses or mules, be at any one point on the desert on any one day. He resorted to this measure not because he feared attack but because he learned that the water at Sackett's Wells was beginning to fail. He ordered that all the marches from Vallecito across the desert be made at night, starting from each point before six in the evening. He did this to protect both animals and men from the ever increasing intensity of the heat. Each driver was to be provided with a paper instructing him when he was to leave Vallecito, Carriso Creek, Indian Well (water to be drawn up in buckets. More can be gotten by having a man descend the well there to dip the water into buckets by a cup as fast as it runs in; this will take all day steady work to water the animals; no grass, probably no hay), Cook's Wells, Norton's Wells, Pilot Knob, Fort Yuma. The trains were to leave California a day apart. One company was to remain at Camp Wright. If the various companies and trains could not obtain beef then the commissary was to issue pork. Each company was to bring ten days rations of subsistence stores, two tents and ammunition. Under no circumstance was any officer or private permitted to bring any article of baggage, or pound's weight of baggage, not authorized by regulations for troops in the field. Every article put into the wagons was to be weighed and a list of such weight made up against every load. The Commissary Officer and the Quartermaster at Camp Wright were to remain behind until further orders. Assistant Surgeon Randle was also to remain. Brigade Surgeon Christian was to travel with either West or Major Fergusson. Each wagon was to have two water kegs. Since the marches were to be made at night, Carleton did not think the animals would be too thirsty.

Brigadier General Wright was able to report at last (April 19, 1862) that Col. Carleton was on his way. He felt that he had given the Colonel everything he needed for a successful campaign. He was happy to report that the Colonel had two hundred wagons, his own regiment (1st Inf.), First Cav. (5 companies), and Shinn's Battery. The Fifth Infantry was to remain at Fort Yuma as a reserve and a support for Carleton's command.

Each wagon of the two hundred was loaded to three thousand pounds; each drawn by six mules. The caravan was separated into four divisions numbering fifty wagons each. The four commanders of each division were Joseph Winston, William S. Veck, Gabriel Allen and N. L. Roundtree. These wagon masters were permitted three assistants each selected from among the teamsters. Every wagon was furnished with two six-gallon water kegs to prevent a water shortage along the route. General Orders No. 1 were issued on May 15th. These were the first for the Military Department of New Mexico. On that day at Fort Yuma he commanded that "The forces belonging to the United States which are now moving from the Department of the Pacific toward Arizona and New Mexico will hereafter be known as the Column from California. The following are announced as Staff Officers attached to these headquarters: viz, 1st Lt. Benjamin C. Cutler, Adjutant 1st Inf., Cal. Vols., Acting Assistant Adjutant General; Captain Tredwell Moore, Assistant Quartermaster, U. S. A., Acting Chief Quartermaster; Surg. James M. McNulty, 1st Inf. Calif. Vols., Medical Director; 1st Lt. Lafayette Hammond, Regimental Quartermaster, 1st Inf. Cal. Vols., Chief Commissary". (Ibid W. R. p. 1075)

It was not until October 14, 1863, that Acting Medical Inspector McNulty sent a full report of the history of the Column to the Surgeon-General in Washington. It was written in Santa Fe. Because he was an eyewitness it is well to recount the report in its entirety:

"On July 22, 1861, the President of the United States approved an act to authorize the employment of volunteers to aid in enforcing the laws and protecting public property. Under this act was raised in California one regiment of infantry and five companies of cavalry. These were called respectively the First Infantry and First Cavalry California Volunteers. The troops were raised for the protection of the Overland Mail Route between California and the Eastern States by way of Salt Lake City. The force was placed under the command of Bvt. Major James H. Carleton, 1st U. S. Cavalry, with the rank of Colonel.

"The regiments made rendezvous at Oakland, opposite San Francisco. During the later part of August and the month of September they had acquired nearly their full complement of men. Active preparations were making to put the command in the best condition for active field service, and by the 1st of October everything was in readiness for the movement of the troops. About this time the spirit of rebellion became manifest in California. 'Treason stalked abroad.' In the southern part of the state an open rupture was apprehended. In consequence of this condition of affairs the command of Col. Carleton was diverted from its original destination by General Sumner, department commander, and moved to the infected district. About the 1st of October the troops moved down the coast and formed a camp near Los Angeles, called Camp Latham. On the 14th three companies of the 1st Cavalry under the command of Major Eyre were ordered to relieve the regular troops stationed at San Bernadino. This place was the hot-bed of secessionism in California. On the same day orders were received to send three companies of the 1st Inf. under the command of Lt. Col. J. R. West to relieve the regulars stationed at Fort Yuma. Regular troops stationed at different parts of the state were ordered to rendezvous at San Diego and San Pedro for the purpose of embarkation.

During the two succeeding months (Sumner had been succeeded by Wright) quiet and order were restored. The distribution of the troops indicated to the disaffected the determination of the authorities to keep California firm and steadfast to the Union.

"On the 12th of January Col. Carleton was summoned to San Francisco to consult with Col. Wright in reference to the movement of troops into Utah. About this time rumors reached California that Van Dorn, of the rebel service, was fitting out an expedition for the invasion of California by way of Arizona. The fact was well established that Arizona and a portion of New Mexico were occupied by Confederate troops, and it was apparent to all that California was more accessible through Arizona by way of Fort Yuma, located on the Colorado river, on the southeastern line of the state, and is our extreme outpost. Surrounded as it is by a vast desert, if once in the possession of an enemy the key to the state is lost. In view of all these threatened dangers to the state and coast, General Wright suggested to the War Department that perhaps the government would be better served by throwing the California troops into Arizona and driving the rebels from that territory. A double object would be gained: first, an effectual guard would be kept against any invasion of the Pacific coast from that quarter; second, the California troops would fall in the rear of the Confederate forces then in New Mexico and assist the Federal forces in expelling them from that territory.

"The suggestions of General Wright were favorably received by the War Department. The feasibility of the movement was at once obtained. On the receipt of the decision of the War Department authority was granted to Col. Carleton to organize and fit out the expedition. The 5th Inf. under the command of Col. George W. Bowie, also Co. A, 3rd U. S. Artillery, with a light battery, under the command of 1st Lt. John B. Shinn, of the U. S. Army, were added to Col. Carleton's command; also Capt. Cremony's company, 2nd Cavalry, Cal. Vols. Active preparations were at once made for the movement of the column. It was important that the troops should move as soon as possible, in order that they might receive the benefit of the cool winter weather while passing over the Gila and Colorado deserts. The great distance from the Pacific Ocean to the Rio Grande, the entire and complete desolation of nearly the whole route, presented obstacles almost unsurmountable to marching a column of over 2,000 men and the same number of animals. It was well known that forage and provisions could be obtained but at two points between Fort Yuma and the Rio Grande in time of peace, and then in limited quantities, viz., the Pima Villages and at Tucson; and it being well known that the enemy occupied one, if not both, of these points, it was necessary that transportation should be made entirely independent of them. The greatest difficulty appeared to be in subsisting animals. Unless this could be done rations could not be furnished the troops, and the expedition would necessarily fall to the ground.

"With the commencement of preparations came unlooked-for difficulties. Not for twenty years had a winter of such severity occurred in California. The whole country was flooded; hundreds of horses and cattle mired down in the open plains and were lost. For weeks it was almost impossible to move a vehicle of any kind and the movement of baggage trains was out of the question. In the meantime commissary stores and forage were sent by sea to Fort Yuma, making this point a general depot and base of operations. The troops during this terrible winter lived in tents. As the rain subsided and the ground became more settled the troops were gradually moved toward Fort Yuma by companies of twos and threes. A sub-depot was formed at Oak Grove, near the edge of the Yuma desert, one hundred and twenty miles from Los Angeles, called Camp Wright. From this point to Fort Yuma (180 miles) it is a continuous desert, entirely destitute of vegetation; water very scarce and generally of bad quality. Before moving the troops on this desert Col. Carleton sent out parties and had the wells cleaned out and new ones dug, in order that every drop of water might be available. Forage for the animals was deposited at different points, between Camp Wright and Fort Yuma. The troops were marched across by companies, one day apart. At some of the wells there was so little water that it was necessary to dip it out in a pint cup, thus consuming nearly a whole night in watering one hundred animals. In order that this desert may be more thoroughly understood I quote from the notes of Lt. Col. West (the substance of which has been covered above).

". . . Contracts were made at Fort Yuma to have hay cut and deposited at different points between the fort and the Pima Villages. It was ascertained that Tucson was still in the hands of the Texans. Their pickets extended down the Rio Gila till within fifty miles of Fort Yuma. Hay deposited at different points by Col. Carleton's agents was burned. The Pima Indians are an agricultural people and cultivate large quantities of wheat. Knowing this fact and the importance of securing as much as possible, Col. Carleton had for some time been in communication with an American living ot the Villages. He was directed to purchase all the wheat the Indians had. A considerable quantity was thus accumulated, but before the advance of the Column reached that point the Texans had destroyed it all with the exception of a small quantity the Indians had cached. This is a serious loss, but the growing crops had not been molested, and Col. Carleton was enabled to secure a considerable amount for his animals. Two companies of infantry and one of cavalry were sent forward toward the Pima and Tucson. As our forces advanced the Texans fell back to Tucson. The command followed them to within a short distance of that place; but not feeling sufficiently strong to attack them, fell back to Pima. Lt. Col. West was then ordered forward with four companies of infantry. The march from Fort Yuma to the Pima Villages was fatiguing in the extreme.

"The extreme heat and alkali dust was almost unbearable; both men and animals suffered very much. As fast as possible the troops were pushed forward by way of Fort Breckenridge with four companies of infantry. The fort was re-occupied, and the Stars and Stripes again floated in the breeze. From Fort Breckenridge Col. West proceeded to Tucson by way of Canada del Oro. Our troops entered and occupied Tucson without firing a shot. At our approach the Texans made a precipitate retreat. Col. Carleton determined to collect the troops at this point for rest, drill, etc. Men and animals required rest; wagons wanted repairing. The dryness of the atmosphere and the intolerable heat had shrunk them to the point of falling to pieces. Communication was opened with Sonora for the purchase of flour, grain, etc. In the first part of June all the troops composing the Column were in and about Tucson, with the exception of a part of the 5th Inf. left to garrison Forts Yuma and Barrett. Lt. Shinn and two companies of infantry took another and more direct road from the Pima Villages to Tucson.

"Tucson is about halfway between Fort Yuma and the Rio Grande and contains a population of 400 or perhaps 500, mostly Mexicans. A few Americans and foreigners are living there, principally gamblers and ruffians, traitors to their country— secessionists. Col. Carleton received his promotion to Brigadier General of volunteers while on the desert in the early part of June. On his arrival at Tucson the Territory of Arizona was at once placed under martial law. The following proclamation was issued:

" 'The Congress of the United States has set apart a portion of New Mexico and organized it into a Territory complete of itself. This is known as the Territory of Arizona. It comprises within its limits all the country eastward from the Colorado river, which is now occupied by the forces of the United States known as the Column from California, as the flag of the United States shall be carried by this Column still farther eastward, these limits will extend in that direction until they reach the farthest geographical boundary of this Territory. Now, in the present chaotic state in which Arizona is found to be, with no civil officers to administer the law—indeed, with an utter absence of all civil authority—and with no security of life or property within its borders, it becomes the duty of the undersigned to represent the authority of the United States over the people of Arizona as well as over all those who compose or are connected with the Column from California. Thus, by virtue of his office as military commander of the U. S. forces now here, and to meet the fact that wherever within our boundaries our colors fly, there the sovereign power of our country must at once be acknowledged and law and order at once prevail, the undersigned, as military governor, assumes control of this Territory until such time as the President of the United States shall otherwise direct.

" 'Thus also it is hereby declared that until civil officers shall be sent by the government to organize the civil courts for the administration of justice, the Territory of Arizona is hereby placed under martial law. Trials for capital offenses shall be held by a military commission, to be composed of not more than thirteen nor less than nine commissioned officers. The rules of evidence shall be those customary in practice under the common law. The trial shall be public and shall be trials of record, and the mode of procedure shall be strictly in accordance with that of courts-martial in the Army of the United States. Unless the public safety absolutely requires it, no execution shall follow conviction until the orders in the case by the President shall be known. Trials for minor offenses shall be held under the same rules, except that for these a commission of not more than five nor less than three commissioned officers may sit, and a vote of a majority determine the issue. In these cases the orders of the officers organizing the commission shall be final.

" 'All matters in relation to rights in property and lands which may be in dispute shall be determined for the time being by a military commission, to be composed of not more than five nor less than three commissioned officers. Of course appeals from the decisions of such commissioners can be taken to the civil courts when once the latter have been established. There are certain fundamental rules for the government of the people of this Territory which will be rigidly enforced:

1. No man who has arrived at lawful age shall be permitted to reside within this Territory who does not without delay subscribe to the oath of allegiance to the United States.

2. No words or acts calculated to impair that veneration which all good patriots should feel for our country and government will be tolerated within this Territory or go unpunished if sufficient proof can be had of them.

3. No man who does not pursue some lawful calling or have some legitimate means of support shall be permitted to remain in the Territory.

" 'Having no thought or motive in all this but the good of the people and aiming only to do right, the undersigned confidently hopes and expects in all he does to further these ends, to have the hearty co-operation of every good citizen and soldier in Arizona. All this is to go into effect from and after this date, and will continue in force, unless disapproved or modified by General George Wright, U. S. Army, commanding the Department of the Pacific, under whose orders the Column from California has taken the field.' (Signed by Gen. Carleton)

"A number of notorious characters were arrested, examined by military commissions, and sent to Fort Yuma. Order sprang from disorder, and in a short time a den of thieves was converted into a peaceful village. In the meantime General Carleton was making active preparations to move his command to the Rio Grande; wagons were repaired, stores collected from Sonora, and everything put in as good a condition as circumstances would permit after the severe march over the Yuma and Gila deserts. No communication up to this time could be had with our forces in New Mexico. The strength of the rebels and their locality entirely unknown, the great difficulty in communicating with General Canby was on account of hostile Indians, the Apache nation occupying the whole country between the Rio Grnde and the Colorado rivers. The great distance to be traversed through their country rendered hazardous, if not impossible, for any small party to get through it. General Carleton endeavored to send an express to General Canby from Tucson. This was carried by three men. The party was attacked near Apache Pass. Two of the men were killed by Indians; the survivor was pursued some forty miles and barely escaped death. He was captured by Texans near Mesilla and the dispatches to General Canby fell into their hands. From these they learned the exact strength of General Carleton's command and the intended movement of the Column. On the 22nd of June General Carleton sent forward Lt. Col. Eyre with one hundred and forty men. This was the advance guard of the Column. With the exception of frequent skirmishing with Indians and the loss of three men killed and several wounded at Apache Pass, the party met with no other enemy before reaching the Rio Grande.

"Apache Pass is about midway between Tucson and the river. The Pass is through a spur of the Chiricahua Mountains, about three and a half or four miles long. In this Pass is a fine spring of water, and a favorite haunt of the Indians. A company of infantry and a part of a company of cavalry, with two mountain howitzers, fought the Indians at this spring for four hours. A number of the savages were killed in the fight. Our loss was three killed and several wounded. On either side of this Pass extends a plain from thirty to forty miles in width. The Indians can see parties approach, and lay in wait for them. . . ." (O. C. W. R.)

The surgeon then goes on to give the order of the line of march from California to the Rio Grande. When the Texans found out that Col. Eyre was advancing to the Rio Grande they made a hasty flight, mostly because spies magnified the strength of his forces. What they could not carry with them they destroyed. One hundred and fifty sick and wounded were left behind in the military hospital at Franklin (present El Paso) and Socorro. The Colonel crossed the river near Fort Thorn in an effort to head off the retreating Confederates. He entered Las Cruces, opposite Mesilla, and raised the American flag. He sent a detachment of men to occupy Franklin.

General Carleton, at the head of the Column, sighted the Rio Grande on August 8, having been eighteen days on the road. On the last day's march the infantry traveled forty miles without stopping for water. Carleton made the crossing exactly where Col. Eyre made it a short time before, but it was too high to be forded. Eyre's men constructed boats and two small scows to effect the crossing. A rope was attached to both sides of the boats and extended to either bank. A number of men were stationed on both banks. Thus they were able to pull the boats from shore to shore, the pullers standing in water all the time it took to transport their comrades. Each wagon was unloaded, the contents ferried across in the boats. Goods and men safely crossed, the Column marched down to Las Cruces, Mesilla and Franklin.

Taking two companies as far as Fort Quitman, Carleton called a halt for himself and one company, the other continuing on to Fort Davis. There, as at Quitman, they found the post abandoned by the Texans. One body in the state of decay was found at Fort Davis. It was pierced by arrows. The unfortunate soldier was evidently sick and left behind only to be the sport of the Comanches. He was given a military burial. Carleton had the sick and wounded Texans at Franklin and Socorro gathered together and sent under escort to San Antonio. Canby at this time commander of the Department of New Mexico was ordered East and on September 12, 1862, Gen. Carleton arrived at Santa Fe assuming command on the 18th. Incidentally, the men killed at Apache Pass were Privates James F. Keith, Peter Maloney, and Albert Schmidt. As Arizona was now a separate Territory Col. West was placed in command there. Its subsequent history is of no further interest to our story which deals with New Mexico. It is hoped that a historian of that state will one day continue its history during those war years from the time Carleton left it to the day the Confederates returned to the Union.

✠ ✠ ✠

NOTES AND COMMENTS

George Wright (1801-1865)—Born in Vermont. Graduated from West Point, 1822. Served in Wisconsin, Missouri, Kansas, Florida, Mexican War, New York. Served the District of California from 1852 to 1855. Took part in the Oregon and Washington Indian Wars from 1856 to 1861. During the Civil War he headed the Department of Oregon, Department of the Pacific and Department of California. He was transferred to the Department of Columbia in 1865. On July 27, 1865, he boarded the SS Brother Jonathan from San Francisco, with his wife to assume command of the newly created department of the Columbia with headquarters at Fort Vancouver. Near Crescent City the boat hit a rock, knocking the keel off. General Wright and his wife were among the many lost at sea. They were buried next to their son's future grave, for Colonel Thomas F. Wright was to lose his life in the Modac War on April 26, 1873, Sacramento, California.

Albert Sidney Johnson (1803-1862)—A native of Kentucky, he served in the army of the Republic of Texas. He might have achieved even greater fame than Lee had he not been killed in the battle of Shiloh.

Edwin A. Rigg—He founded Camp Wright. Stationed at Hart's Mill, he met and wooed the daughter of H. H. Cooper, the mill superintendent. She was seventeen.

John Joseph Warner—Sufficiently covered in the text.

Joseph Rodman West—Born in New Orleans, he attended the University of Pennsylvania. Served in the Mexican War. Edited a paper in San Francisco until the Civil War. Mustered out of the Army with rank of Brevet Major General of Vols. January 4, 1863. Re-enlisted to serve Department of Arkansas. Lived in Louisiana after the war where he was elected U. S. Congressman. Died sometime after 1880.

L. J. F. Yager—Had beef contracts with Overland Mail Company when it operated on the southern route. As he had large herds at San Felipe he agreed to sell to the government for the California Volunteers at Fort Yuma for the same price contracted with the Overland Mail.

William McCleave—Spent almost thirty years in the army serving at various posts from New Mexico to California. b. cir 1837 he died some time after 1883 at Berkeley, California.

Lt. Col. Eyre—Sufficiently covered in the text.

William Gilpin (1822-1894)—Attended school in England, then West Point. Was a native of Pennsylvania. Was in Seminole War, Mexican War. Editor of the St Louis Missouri Argus for a year. Friend of Benton's and influenced his enthusiasm for the West. Gilpin's political life was not as successful as his army or civilian life. He became influential as a stock holder in the Sangre de Cristo Grant and the Maxwell Land Grant. He died in Denver January 19, 1894.

John Milton Chivington (1821-1894)—Sufficiently covered in the text. It is interesting to note in passing that he died in Denver on October 4, 1894.

John P. Slough—Born Ohio c. 1820. Killed by Rynerson at Santa Fe December 17, 1867. Slough was a judge of a miner's court in Colorado when the Civil War broke out. At the time of his tragic death he was Chief Justice of the New Mexico Territorial Supreme Court. Rynerson came to New Mexico with the California Volunteers.

William Reed Scurry (1821-1864)—Born in Tennessee on February 10, 1821, became a lawyer before he was twenty-one years of age. Came to Texas in 1840 and took active part in judicial work in the Republic. Served in the Mexican War, after which he located in Clinton where he practiced law. He married Janette B. Sutton and became owner of the State Gazette in Austin, but he sold this before 1854. The Scurrys raised five children. He was a delegate at the Secession Convention. After returning to Texas from service in the Sibley Brigade, he sought to raise another army to re-capture Mesilla. He became a Brigadier General on September 12, 1863. He was in immediate command of the Confederate attack on Galveston by General John B. Magruder. He also fought at Mansfield and Pleasant Hill in Louisiana. He was killed in the battle for Jenkins' Ferry, April 30,1864. On the field he asked: "Have we whipped them?" When the answer proved to be "Yes" he spoke his last words: "Take me to a house where I can be made comfortable and die." Scurry county honors him.

Gabriel Rene Paul (1804-1886)—A native of Missouri, he entered West Point July 1, 1829. He served in the Mexican War. Commanded Fort Fillmore in New Mexico and Fort Union. A Brigadier General in the Civil War he took an active part in the action at Gettysburg. He died in Missouri, May 5, 1886.

Major Duncan lived in Las Vegas after the Civil War. He was remembered for many years for his famous Duncan Opera House theatre in that city. He took an active part in the civic interests of the community especially for his efforts at helping to obtain the present Highlands University for the city.

Lemitar and Limitar have both been accepted as proper spellings for this town according to Rand McNally's Atlas.

CHAPTER SIX

THE COLORADO VOLUNTEERS

Lt. Col Canby evinced no ebullient optimism as he studied the man before him. His spies brought word that his former friend was on the march to take the field against him. The Texas Mounted Volunteers, later known as Sibley's Brigade and the Confederate Army of New Mexico, were in training on Salado creek five miles east of San Antonio, awaiting marching orders. Scouts brought in word of ever increasing open hostilities on the part of the Apaches, Navajos, Comanches, Utes and Jicarillas. Sumner had been replaced on the coast and his successor seemed slow indeed. New Mexicans themselves seemed indifferent. Help could come from only one quarter, the North where a friend who had served with him on many a military expedition in New Mexico was now governor. He could not afford to divide his force. No, not at the moment, despite recalcitrant Indians. He would rely upon Governor William Gilpin of the Colorado Territory for help. Hence on July 6, 1861, he sent his friend this message:

"The increasing hostilities of the Indians in New Mexico will render it expedient to divert any portion of the volunteers authorized for this department for the purpose of garrisoning Fort Garland. As this post is within the limits of the Colorado Territory, I have the honor to request that you will cause two companies of infantry volunteers to be enrolled and sent to that post, to be mustered into the service of the United States at as early a period as possible. The organization of these companies should conform to that prescribed by the War Department of 1861. . . . The commanding officer at Fort Garland will be instructed to muster these companies into the service, and the arms and camp and garrison equipage necessary to equip them for service will immediately be sent to that post. No clothing can be issued at present, and the volunteers should be provided in this respect for at least three months."

Canby surmised that the Confederates would march from San Antonio to Fredericksburg over to Horsehead Crossing on the Pecos river, across to Delaware creek, skirt the Cornudas mountains into El Paso. Actually Sibley's men took the road west from San Antonio to Fort Inge, up to Howard's Wells, over to Fort Lancaster to Horsehead Crossing, up the Pecos to Pope's Crossing, then west to Fort Bliss. Canby could not be too sure. Sibley might even by-pass Fort Union, which seemed to be his objective, for the supplies at Fort Wise in Colorado Territory. He sent another letter, a message by telegraph, and still another letter to Gilpin. He also sent a dispatch to Captain Elmer Otis in charge of the Colorado post to be on the lookout for the Texans who might decide to capture the supplies at Fort Wise rather than Fort Union. The Captain replied that Kiowa spies reported three columns of Confederates moving up from Texas east of the mountains in the direction of Fort Union. Others came in with the conflicting report that the Texans had turned back. He did not know what to believe but he felt that the Kiowas were trying to give him the truth because they were on the warpath against the Texans. He ended with an urgent appeal that Canby keep him posted should he hear any rumors of Texan concentration in his direction. He would protect Fort Wise to the last man.

Canby was pleased to hear that the Captain had sent a train on to Fort Garland in an effort to strengthen that post. Since taking regulars out of Colorado might leave it vulnerable, the Colonel hoped to arm volunteers lamenting the fact that the guns he could have sent were sorely needed to arm the New Mexico Volunteers. He suggested that the Captain try Fort Leavenworth to see if arms could be shipped to him from there.

Governor Gilpin was happy to announce during the first week of September that two volunteer companies of infantry— Co. A, commanded by Capt. Slough; Co. B, by Capt. Tappan— were marching to Fort Garland to await further orders. He cautioned Canby not to overlook the difficulties in Colorado in his zeal to save New Mexico. The area was industrial (mining), and depended on the States for supplies. This meant a line of communication stretching out over eight hundred miles had to be defended against hostile Indians. For this reason he owed his primary obligations to Colorado. He asked Canby for 5,000 arms, equipment and ammunition for the infantry; ordinance and supplies and guns for two batteries of artillery. The Colonel promised to do what he could but hinted that the governor would fare better if he petitioned officials at Fort Laramie. Meantime the Captain at Fort Wise called for volunteers to relieve the troops he was anxious to send to Canby. The Colonel preferred the regulars to assist him in driving out Sibley and Baylor. Governor Connelly of New Mexico added his plea to that of Canby's particularly stressing the need for doctors and medical supplies. Gilpin penned this letter on October 26th:

"I am greatly in your (Canby's) debt for a supply of blankets and books, an attention especially apropos at a point so utterly destitute of such essentials to public business. I will respond promptly to the request of Governor Connelly and yourself for medical men who can be found here. I have further received notice from Captain Elmer Otis, Fort Wise, of the arrival there of arms for four companies of volunteers. The strong and malignant element within this Territory, added to the destitution of arms and ammunition of any kind up to this time, has rendered absolutely necessary the delay to furnish a garrison for Fort Wise. The population of the Arkansas river is not numerous enough to furnish one company, and to send them from the mining region has been impossible, from want of arms, ammunition, food, clothing, transportation, or money to procure any of these essentials. I am incessantly occupied to comply with your requisitions at the earliest moment.

"The malignant secession element of this Territory has numbered 7,500. It has been ably and secretly organized from November last, and requires extreme and extraordinary measures to meet and control its onslaught. The core of its strength has at present withdrawn to gather strength from Texas, Utah, Arkansas, and from the country of the Confederated Cherokee, Creek and other Indians. They contemplate to return with overwhelming strength and precipitate the neighboring Indians upon us. To prepare for what may be accomplished by them is my duty. This country, everywhere open to the easy, can only be defended by a sufficient force to meet the enemy in the field. It also enters into their plans to capture Fort Wise and Fort Garland; to surround New Mexico and invade it from the north. The Indian populations west of Arkansas have united with the Rebel War to the amount of 64,500, capable of furnishing an efficient army for operations upon these Territories, familiar with this country and allied to the Georgians, who sympathize with secession, and form a large portion of our mining population. You will learn that a guerilla party has been captured by Captain Otis near Fort Wise; the Captain of this band, McGee, has been in jail for several weeks in this (Denver) city." (o.c. W.R.)

New Year's Day, 1862 was not given over to celebration. Anxiety, tension, feverish pace deepened the furrows on Canby's brow. He addressed another communication to Gilpin informing him that the Texans were on the way to invade New Mexico. Would not the governor send as large a force of volunteers as he could gather to Fort Wise and Fort Garland as could possibly be spared? He was particularly interested in seeing Fort Wise strongly garrisoned. Prompt action on the part of Gilpin would aid immensely in saving New Mexico.

Gilpin wondered if Canby thought he was the only one harassed with worries. In little Denver City (pop. 3,000) over on Larimer Street, some bold, brazen soul unfurled a Confederate flag on the staff of the pole surmounting Wallingford & Murphy's mercantile establishment. Although its flapping in the breeze was short lived due to the climbing agility of one Sam Logan, it proved that Southern sympathizers were going to make their presence felt. Confederate handbills made the rounds in the mining camps; good prices were openly offered for rifles, shot guns, powder and percussion caps. How many of these found their way into enemy hands history has not recorded. Rumors— wild, fierce, strong, violent—saddened the governor's heart. What if Clark & Gruber's banking house were captured by the daring sympathizers? What if the wagon trains from Missouri were waylaid? Not yet a year in office and he inherited problems that made Canby's and Connelly's light by comparison. Actually the damage by "Johnnie Reb" as the Unionists called them was slight. True they staged a few frightening raids to break up Union enlistment meetings, obtained a non-descript pile of guns, good for hunting but useless for war; raided spontaneously as wagon trains came through, but no more than wagon bosses expected from Indians.

The Indians were convinced, more than ever before, that there was nothing superhuman about the white man. The medicine man told chiefs sitting around the council fires that they hoped the white men would wipe each other out so that the land would once again be theirs when it was all over. Desperately as the under cover Confederates worked they could never gain the upper hand and worked out the problem for Gilpin in time by going elsewhere to join General Sterling Price. This man who made swift work of the Taos Rebellion shortly after General Kearny left Santa Fe for California, was now sending men to recruit sympathizers in Colorado. Officers of the regular army sent Osage scouts to round up W. P. McClure and his contingent of Southerners. The Osages made a thorough job of it. They attacked the camp, annihilated the men, cut off their heads and rolled them at the feet of the horror stricken officers.

At 14th and Lawrence in Denver City the Methodist Church vibrated with the booming voice of the gigantic Rev. John Milton Chivington. The congregation faced the minister of beefy countenance; watched that large aquiline nose that divided eyes that pierced their souls in search of the devil. Broad faced, broad shouldered, this behemoth figure (6 ft. 5 in.) thundered against secession and sympathizers. He applied for a commission in the volunteers. Gilpin offered him a Captaincy as Chaplain of the First Colorado Regiment. He made it clear that he was not joining for the spiritual consolation of the soldiers; he meant to fight. By August 1861 he attained the rank of Colonel. He comes to the front at Glorieta.

To appeal to Washington involved delay and red tape. This Gilpin sought to avoid. The danger was imminent calling for immediate action. Colorado was in no financial position to defray the expense entailed in fitting out regiments. He would act now and ask Washington to pay the bill later. He issued negotiable drafts directly upon the national treasury in Washington to the tune of $375,000. Washington objected by removing him from office. He was replaced by John Evans of Illinois. The work of recruiting at Central City, Black Hawk, Nevadaville, Buckskin Joe, Empire City, Clear Creek and Denver City continued nevertheless for difference between heads of departments did not clear up the situation between Sibley and Canby. This tough, cosmopolitan, variegated group was to honor the name of Colorado at Glorieta, Peralta, Albuquerque and elsewhere in New Mexico.

Active for Governor Gilpin was lawyer John P. Slough who recruited Denver City's Company A. He was rewarded by receiving the appointment as company commander, then commanding Colonel of the Volunteers. The raw recruits were trained in the hastily constructed Camp Weld, named for the acting governor taking care of Colorado during Gilpin's absence in Washington. Sanmuel F. Tappan was made Lt. Col. in appreciation for his work in getting together Company B at Black Hawk and Central City. Slough insisted on guerilla like tactics while Chivington was in favor of well drilled men.

Meantime Sibley moved up the Rio Grande valley to Fort Thorn which he occupied. Realizing that Fort Craig would be his next objective, Weld sent a message to Fort Leavenworth asking General Hunt's permission to send the Colorado Volunteers south to aid that post. It was a month before he received a reply. He was advised to send all available troops to aid Col. Canby and cautioned to use discretion as to the employment of the Volunteers. Weld received this message twelve days before the action at Valverde. In camp at old Fort Bent, Tappan met Capt. Amos F. Garrison, a native of New Jersey, Commissary of the Department of New Mexico, Chief of Subsistence at Fort Union, a member of Canby's staff, now dispatched by the Colonel to find the Colorado Volunteers and urge upon them the pressing need for an immediate advance.

This was a rough time of the year for traveling the Rockies. The Raton Mountains, scenic in summer, cool in the fall, blasty in winter were tempermental in spring. As late as April one could expect the night temperatures to drop to twenty below. No sooner had the Volunteers started the climb when a bitter cold wind arose and increased in fury until it resembled a hurricane. Major Chivington's big grays and saddlemule were left where they fell dead. (cf. O. J. Hollister: *Boldly They Rode* p. 49) the men marched over the as yet undisclosed gold and coal fields of the future Elizabethtown, Baldy, Blossburg, Van Houten, Dawson which many were to come back and work in as miners years after the war. Up beyond Maxwell's ranch, the Rayado country, Fort Union, Las Vegas, Tecolote, Bernal, the site of Blanchard, Chapelle, San Miguel del Bado, San Isidro del Sur, San Isadro del Norte, over to Pecos—halting and marching. They remained at Fort Union just long enough to be reoutfitted and to observe the coldness and rift between Slough and Chivington. They left Fort Union on March 22 for Las Vegas. At Fort Union, too, there had been differences between Slough and Col. Gabriel Paul of the regular army and recently placed in charge of the post having come up from the lower Rio Grande valley.

Paul had orders to hold the fort at all hazards. He looked upon the Volunteers as part of his command. Slough thought otherwise. He insisted that he out-ranked Paul therefore was commander. Protest as Paul might, Slough left Fort Union with his own 1st Colo. Reg., Capt. Ford's company of unattached Colo. Vols., and one of the 4th Reg. New Mexico Vol., a battalion of regular infantry, three detachments of cavalry, too light batteries of four guns each, counting in all one thousand, three hundred and forty-two men. Col. Paul was left at Fort Union with a small garrison to guard the supply depot and defend the post in case of attack. It was at Coslosky's ranch near the Pecos Pueblo ruins that Col. Slough gleamed his first information as to the whereabouts of the Texans. (Coslosky—for this spelling of his name see the signature he placed on his letters to Bishop Lamy of Santa Fe in the Archdiocesan Archives at the Chancery Office in that city. This ranch is now the home of Buddy Folgeson of Dallas, Texas and his wife, Greer Garson, of movie fame. It is known as the Forked Lightning Ranch) Lt. Nelson was told to take twenty men, ride about seven miles to Pigeon's ranch (at the site of the tourist attraction advertised as the Oldest Well in America) to capture the pickets posted there. Four of them thinking Nelson's men to be fellow-Texans rode into the group suddenly to realize they were prisoners.

At Coslosky's where Chivington pitched his Camp Lewis, plans were made for his contingent of four hundred and eighteen men. The men broke camp at 7:51 A. M. advancing on Pigeon's ranch house and stage station and beyond towards Apache Canyon. They felt at home again for they were in country as mountainous as the mining regions they left in Colorado. This contingent was known as Chivington's "Pet Lambs" to distinguish them from the rest of the Pike's Peakers, as the Colorado Volunteers were generally called. The date: March 28, 1862.

Near the canyon a picket dashed back to the main body of infantry shouting: "We've got them corralled this time! Give them hell, boys! Hurrah for the Pike's Peakers." Thirty mounted Texans, led by a Lieutenant, constituting a scouting party, fell right into the arms of the advance guard. Not a shot was fired as the Federals welcomed them as prisoners. The excitement of the advance guard was communicated to the troops.

"Close up ranks," barked the officers along the line.

"Double quick." The cavalry took open orders by fours.

"This knapsack is so damn heavy," said one man as he threw it along the dusty roadside. Natives of the villages of Alamitos, Glorieta, Gonzolez, Vallecitos and Pecos came by in the wake of the hurrying Volunteers and picked up canteens, knapsacks, overcoats, clothing and cups discarded along the highway. From the looks of the cluttered road one would surmise a retreat rather than an advance. The Texans were in the field in front of Glorieta Pass near the site of the present village of Glorieta which was to spring into being with the coming of the Santa Fe Railroad. The Volunteers entered the field a little to the left of where the advance guard captured the thirty Confederates. It was here that the Sibley Brigade hoped to repeat the victory of Valverde. Anxious as the Volunteers were for battle, they were not prepared for the cannon shots from the artillery, placed near the crest of the ridge that nearly crosses, transversely, the upper part of the canyon.

The Texans unfurled their standard, the red flag of the Lone Star State. The howitzers rained shot and shell forcing the Volunteers to crowd to the left in an effort to seek shelter against the barrage of rapid fire now poured into their ranks. Like a huge, shaggy buffalo at bay, Chivington stood in his saddle shouting orders at the infantry. A pistol in each hand, one under his arm, he thundered from his equestrian pulpit, so as to be heard above the din of battle, impervious to the bullets that rained about him. His was a charmed life for the target was never hit. Captain Howland was ordered to take the mounted men to the rear for service when the Texans were in retreat. Chivington never doubted for a moment that Howland's men would see action, and soon. Captain Cook was ordered to join Howland. Captains Wynkoop and Anthony scaled the mountain side on the double-quick scattering their forces among the shrub cedar and pinons as skirmishers. Capt. Dowling's men skirmished to the right. The Pet Lambs soon made it too hot for Sibley's men who, flanked from both sides, began to withdraw. Howland failed to put in his appearance for which he was soundly rounded out by the preacher-soldier. At the far end of the field, along the rocky incline, the Texans re-formed ranks, planted the howitzers into new positions and seemed secure by reason of their more advantageous position.

From this new point the battle raged on. The first to stop a bullet was Captain Cook who was replaced by Lt. Nelson. Downing was ordered to climb the mountainside on the right above the Texan skirmishers in an effort to drive them out of the floor of the canyon. Wynkoop and Anthony were directed to do the same on the left. Nelson led his men across the arroyo at the bridge. All but one horse succeeded in making the jump. Despite the fact that Love's mount failed to negotiate the chasm, the rider managed to untangle himself from the fallen horse, and, crippled as he was, jumped over a bank to give a good account of himself for the balance of the engagement. It crippled him for life, but his action was heroic to more than his children. Three times the cavalry charged forward and back through the now disorganized, fleeing men, running over them, trampling them down, scattering them into the surrounding slopes. About fifty men remaining in the road were taken prisoner by Wynkoop and Anthony's men. The firing commenced in the afternoon and raged until darkness. Actually the fighting did not last over three hours. The loss was heavy on both sides, but minimized in official reports. Wrote Major J. M. Chivington from Camp Lewis to Canby:

". . . We marched from Bernal Springs (fourteen miles from Las Vegas on the road to Santa Fe) for Santa Fe at 3 p.m. of the 25th (of March. This letter dated on the following day) intending to surprise the enemy in small force at that place. After a march of thirty five miles, and learning we were in the vicinity of the enemy's pickets ,we halted about midnight, and about 2 a. m. on the 26th Lt. Nelson (who later resigned Aug. 31,1862) with twenty men, was sent out to surprise their pickets, which they did, and captured them at 10 a. m. The detachment again moved forward and just as we entered the (Apache) canyon discovered the advance guard of the foe and captured two Lieutenants. In a few minutes they planted their battery and began to throw grape and shell among us. In double-quick Companies A and E 1st Colo. Vols. were deployed as skirmishers to the left and on the mountain side, and Co. D was deployed as skirmishers to the right, and an order was given that the cavalry be held in readiness to charge whenever the cannon were about to retreat. Soon our men from the mountain sides made it too hot for their gunners and they fell back about one and a half miles and took another and more advantageous position, completely covering the sides of the mountains with their skirmishers to support their guns in the canyon below them.

"Having meantime assembled our skirmishers in the canyon we again deployed Co. D on the right and Co. A and E on the left, and having dismounted all the cavalry we deployed them as skirmishers except Co. F, on the left, Capt. Cook, who was ordered to charge them the moment they gave way before the fire of our Infantry. After a contest of an hour they began to prepare for another retreat, and by this time Co. D. Capt. Downing had well nigh flanked them so as to cut off their retreat, Capt Cook and Lt. Nelson and Lt. Marshall (later accidentally killed when trying to break a gun over a rock) leading the way. Co. F now made a flying charge on the enemy, running over and tramping them under the horses' feet. Capt Downing with his men and Lt. Bernard with Co. C, 3rd Cav. poured into them a sharp fire from the right which drove the enemy up a canyon on the left side of the main canyon, when Companies A and E took a large number of prisoners. It now being sundown, and we not knowing how near the enemy's re-enforcements might be, and having no cannon to oppose theirs, hastened to gather up our dead and wounded and several of the enemies, and then fell back to Pigeon's ranch and encamped for the night. Our loss was five killed and fourteen wounded. The loss of the enemy was, as we ascertained from their own accounts, thirty-two killed, forty-three wounded and seventy-one taken prisoners." (o.c. W. R. pp. 530-531)

So Dutro, Johnson, Thompson and Marshall found a resting place far from the mining camps of Colorado. The dead buried, some teams were sent out to bring in flour and corn stored a short distance away by the enemy. A messenger was dispatched to Col. Slough at Bernal informing him of the engagement. Immediately he set out for Camp Lewis. On the way he passed the prisoners being escorted to Fort Union by Lord's company of dragoons. The arrival of reserves brought about the next encounter at Pigeon's, both sides claiming victory as we gather from official reports. Col. W. R. Scurry, 4th Texas Cav. and second in command to General Sibley, wrote at Santa Fe, March 30th:

"I arrived here this morning with my command and have taken quarters for the present in this city. I will in a short time give you an official account of the battle of Glorieta which occurred on the day before yesterday in the Canyon Glorieta about twenty-two miles from this city, between the Confederate troops under my command and the Federal forces commanded by Col.

Slough, of the Colo. Vols. (Pikes Peakers), when another victory was added to the long list of Confederate triumphs.

"The action commenced at about 11 a. m. and ended at 5:30, and, although every inch of the ground was well contested, we steadily drove them back until they were in full retreat, our men pursuing them until form sheer exhaustion, we were compelled to stop. Our loss was thirty-three killed and, I believe, thirty-five wounded. Among the killed was the brave soldier and accomplished officer, Major Ragnet, and gallant and impetuous Major Sharopshire, and the daring Captain Buckholts, all of whom fell gallantly leading the men around against the enemy fire. Major Pyron had his horse shot under him, and my own cheek was twice brushed by minnie balls, each time just drawing blood, and my clothes torn in two places. . . . Our train was burned by a party who succeeded in passing undiscovered around the mountains to our rear. I regret to have to report that they fired upon and severely wounded Rev. L. H. Jones, our Chaplain, of the 4th Reg. He was holding in his hands a white flag when fired upon. The loss of the enemy was very severe, being over seventy-five killed and a large number wounded. The loss of my supplies crippled me that after burying my dead I was unable to follow up the victory. My men went for two days unfed and blanketless without murmuring. I was compelled to come here for something to eat. On last accounts the Federalists were still retiring towards Fort Union. The men at the train blew up the limber-box and spiked the 6 pounder I had left at the train so that it was rendered useless, and the cart burners left it. . . ." (o.c. W.R.)

His report on the following day was more detailed. He began with the evening of the 26th, relating how he was encamped at the village of Galisteo when an express arrived from Major Pyron telling him of a sharp conflict with the Volunteers who greatly outnumbered the Texans. As the conflict was sixteen miles away Pyron asked Scurry to come to his aid. The Confederate jumped up, shouted to his men, and in ten minutes they were on the march. The baggage train was sent forward guarded by one hundred men under the command of Lt. Taylor, of the 7th Regiment. He was to bring the train to a halt six miles in the rear of Pyron's position. Scurry marched directly across the mountains to the scene of the battle. The going was so arduous that the men pulled the artillery pieces over the mountains by hand since it was found too steep for horses. (See W.R. o.c. pp. 541-42)

At three in the morning the command united with Pyron at Johnson's ranch. The house still stands on Highway 85. After the war it was used by Santa Fe freighters as a watering place. The Las Vegas-Santa Fe stage maintained it for a time. When the railroad came through to Lamy, the mail was dumped at this place to be picked up by wagon from Santa Fe. In front of the house near the highway is a well where cool spring water may be drawn at any time. Tourists are ignorant of this fact, but people from Pecos, Rowe and Glorieta often stop here for a refreshing drink. The ranch house may still be seen near the quaint little church at Canoncito, the name of the village that sprung up in the Johnson ranch area during the railroad boom. Some day a marker will be placed on this spot.

Both sides agreed to cease fire until 8 a. m. of the 28th. Scurry occupied his time in selecting his own battleground. He wanted the Volunteers to take the offensive where he entrenched his troops. But the Coloradoans failed to put in appearance. Taking the alternative the Texan marched from his well chosen site to give battle taking portions of nine companies of the 4th Regiment, three companies of the 5th, three pieces of artillery leaving behind a small force to guard the wagon train. The Brigade numbered about six hundred men. The enemy was sighted about a mile from Pigeon's. The cavalry was ordered to dismount, form a remuda to the rear and return to the front on foot. The artillery was pushed forward to a slight elevation in the canyon opening fire immediately. The infantry was deployed into line, extending across the canyon from a fence on the left into the pine forest on the right.

Meanwhile the Peakers advanced in separate columns to the right and left of the Texans. Major Pyron was sent to check the right flank movement of the Federals; Major Ragnet was placed to block the center; Scurry took the left. A large body of infantry availing itself of a gulch that ran up the center of an enclosed field to the left of the Texans was moving under its cover past the left flank to the rear of Scurry's position. Crossing the fence on foot the Texans advanced over the clearing some two hundred yards under a heavy fire from the Peakers, and dashed into the gulch into their very midst, pistol and knife in hand. Within minutes a desperate hand to hand conflict raged along the gulch. The Colorado Volunteers gave way before the onslaught. Major Pyron was equally successful. Major Ragnet charged down the center. Lt. Bradford in charge of the artillery was carried off the field wounded. There being no other artillery officer present the three guns constituting the battery were hastily withdrawn. When Scurry heard this he sent back immediately for two of the guns. The Confederates paused to re-unite their forces which had become somewhat scattered during the last encounter. When Scurry was ready to advance again the Peakers had taken cover so that it was impossible to tell whether their main body was stationed behind a long adobe wall that ran nearly across the canyon or had taken position behind a large ledge of rocks in the rear. Private W. P. Kirk, of Capt. Phillip's Company took charge of one of the guns, and Sergeant Patrick of the artillery took over the other and brought them back to the scene of battle.

Scurry ordered them to fire the guns in the hopes of ascertaining the exact positions of the Colorado Volunteers. Major Shropshire was sent to the right with orders to move among the pines up in front until he came upon the enemy. He was to open the attack on that flank. Major Ragnet with similiar orders was sent to the left. As soon as Scurry heard the sound of their guns he would charge in front with the remainder of the command. Pyron was then sent to assist Ragnet, at the same time the center line was ordered to charge as the firing commenced on the right. Then came a lull. Scurry went to find out the cause. Major Shropshire had been killed. The soldier who shot him was a lad in his teens. The night before he had a dream that he would be killed. Captain Downing seeing him rather pensive at breakfast asked him if something troubled him. The boy replied that he had a feeling that this was his last day on earth. "We all feel that way on the eve of battle," remarked the Captain. Shot by a Texas sharpshooter just after killing Shropshire, the Captain passed by the spot where he lay. Looking up and seeing the Captain, the boy smiled and said: "I told you something would happen." He turned over and died.

Scurry took over Shropshire's command of the right flank and attacked the Coloradoans entrenched about Pigeon's ranch. Pyron and Ragnet also opened fire on the left, from the rock on the mountain side. With the center charging down the road the Volunteers were dislodged from their position moving to the ledge of rocks where they made a desperate stand. It was at this moment that three batteries of eight guns opened a furious fire of grape, canister and shell upon the advancing Texans. The Confederates pressed on determined to capture the guns. A heavy body of infantry placed itself between the guns and the advancing Texans. The Volunteers were just as determined. So furious was the fighting at this point that the right and center of the Texans united on the left. If ever a battle ground was disputed inch by inch it was Glorieta. The Volunteers saved their artillery and the guns were withdrawn to the rear. The infantry also retreated, the Confederates following. The volunteers cut loose two teams from the wagons, set fire to them in order to impede the advance. The battle lasted six hours.

Scurry reported that there were 1,400 Volunteers in the battle. During the battle a part of the Peakers succeeded in gaining Scurry's rear surprising the wagon guard, burning the wagons, taking at the same time sixteen prisoners. It was at this time also that the Chaplain was wounded. Scurry remained on the field on the 29th to bury his dead and care for the wounded. He reported that the Confederate prisoners were ordered shot should the Coloradoans be attacked as they retreated from the burning wagons. However, this may have been war talk as no one remembered ever receiving such an order.

Slough's version of the battle differs from Scurry's. To show he entertained no hard feelings towards the commanding officer at Fort Union he named his camp at Bernal, Camp Paul in his honor. From Camp Paul he marched to Coslosky's. On the 28th he marched against the Texans in two columns with a view of reconnoitering his position at Johnson's ranch. With this in mind he directed Major Chivington, with an infantry force of regulars and volunteers, to move off on the Galisteo road, attain the principal heights on the side of Apache Canyon, and occupy them. Heading the main body he moved directly into the canyon. He estimated Scurry's strength equal to his own.

The Colonel broke camp at nine in the morning arriving at Pigeon's an hour and a half later, having marched five miles. Chivington flanked off at a spot two miles beyond Coslosky's. Arriving at Pigeon's Slough ordered Capt. Chapin of the 7th Infantry to proceed forward with the cavalry and reconnoiter the position of the enemy. He got three hundred yards when the Colorado pickets were driven in and the Texans opened a fire of grape and shell from a battery placed in position on the hillside above. The batteries were ordered forward and the infantry thrown out upon the flanks. The Cavalry, with an addition of infantry, supported the batteries and firing became general. Chivington's command continued on toward Johnson's where some two hundred Texans were posted. The Pet Lambs fell upon the Confederate train of sixty wagons, capturing and destroying one 6 pounder gun and taking two officers and fifteen other prisoners. About five in the afternoon a flag of truce was sent by the Texans, and measures were taken up by both sides to care for the dead and wounded. Lt. Baker of the Volunteers had been killed; two other officers wounded; twenty-eight other men killed and forty wounded; fifteen captured. Slough thought the Confederates lost a hundred in killed and one hundred an fifty wounded. He also claimed victory. Glorieta is like Gettysburg in that the losses were heavy, the fighting fierce, both sides claiming victory when at best it was a draw.

At 5:30 p. m. Slough ordered his men to abandon their positions and return to Camp Lewis. The artillery and wagons were withdrawn, one by one. This so angered the men who wished to return to battle in order to make certain which side won that they cursed the Colonel and some even awaited the opportunity to shoot him, believing him a turn-coat. This was the so-called retreat Scurry referred to. Slough defended his action by saying that he had orders to annoy and harrass the enemy, not to annihilate him nor force his surrender. He was returning because he felt his mission was accomplished. Actually it was Chivington's action in crippling the Confederate wagon train that determined the outcome at Glorieta. If they renewed the battle after disposing of the dead and wounded the Texans would be faced with the problem of food. Supplies cut off, Scurry was forced to retreat to Santa Fe.

Camp Lewis was more of a hospital than a camp for of all the men bivouacing there one fourth were numbered among the hospitalized. The men who could march were taken to San Jose where Capt. Nicodemus brought in a message from Col. Canby for the Volunteers to fall back on Fort Union and protect it at all hazards. This command annoyed Slough who hoped to march on Santa Fe as soon as his men were refreshed. He issued his final order: "Fall back on Fort Union", then resigned. On April 11th he was still at Pigeon's. His honorable discharge arrived the following day. He made his way to Virginia where he served as Brig. General for the duration.

The troops arrived at Fort Union at 6 p. m. on April 2nd. Three days later they received orders to march south to divert the enemy's attention while Canby marched north form Fort Craig and, united, they would drive the Texans out of New Mexico. At Coslosky's they remained long enough to encourage their wounded comrades still hospitalized at Camp Lewis. Colonel Paul was in command during this march to join Canby but he resigned in favor of Lt. Col. Tappan who in turn bowed out in favor of Chivington. The fighting preacher became a Colonel on May 14, 1862. The contingent cut southwest beyond the villages of San Antonio (one of the many by that name in New Mexico), Tijeras, over the Pass south to Pajarito, Isleta, Los Lunas towards Peralta where the remnant of Sibley's Brigade had bedded for the night. There near the river bank watching the play of the moon make a sheet of silver to reflect the pointed cedars, the men were suddenly afflicted with nostalgia. Hollister mentions how he was reminded of his fathers's orchard in New England; of green-apple eating days; dreams and hopes of remembering this night near the moon-lit water and the romance of the Land of Enchantment. He would put away from him the sight of blood, the smell of rotting horse flesh, the cries of the wounded. How strange that on this eve of battle he should hold only the illusion of this blissful, peaceful hour; see only the sugar woods of the Green Mountains; envision the sparkling limpid pool of his boyhood days.

And beyond those dreams, a mile away slept men he would be forced to cut down tomorrow like cutting the micrography of an enchanted hour. Trusting privates sleeping like babes; closing their eyes to the inevitable tomorrow. The officers slept not. These men in gray thrust the war from them as they came under the spell of the river. They were living other hours as they danced the fandango with dark-eyed senoritas at Socorro, Albuquerque, Mesilla. So the night went on catering to Confederate and Federal alike.

The Volunteers had already joined Canby. It was for him to decide the time and place of battle. Dawn and Canby's bugles ushered in April 15. The Confederates accepted this as a challenge and answered with Dixie. Canby already had a brush with the Texans as we gather from a report written several days before:

"My command (860 regulars; 350 N. M. Vols.) arrived before Albuquerque on the afternoon of the 8th. I immediately made a demonstration on the town for the purpose of ascertaining the strength and position of the enemy's batteries. This demonstration was made by Capt. Graydon's Spy Company supported by the regular cavalry and developed the position of the batteries. In the skirmish Major Duncan, 3rd Cav. was seriously, but it is hoped not fatally, wounded. . . ." (W.R. o.c. p. 550)

Canby made a junction with Col. Paul's men at Tijeras on the evening of the 13th when he received word that the Texans had left Albuquerque, moving down the river. During the day and night that followed the united command marched to Peralta before the Confederates were quite aware of their presence. Thus on the morning of the 15th a mountain howitzer, a train of seven wagons loaded with supplies and escorted by a Lieutenant and thirty men fell into his hands before the Texans could ready themselves for battle. In the battle that ensued six Texans were killed, three wounded and twenty-two captured. As Canby later related that to cover this movement Col. Paul, with his column and three companies of cavalry under Captain Morris, 3rd Cav. had been detached, and, after completing it received permission to clear the bosque in front of Peralta of the Texan force then occupying it. The Colonel proved himself equal to the task only after some sharp skirmishing in which he lost a man, three others being wounded. The bosque in front and the rear of the town was then occupied by the Federals.

The position occupied by the Texans was known to be the strongest in New Mexico, with the possible exception of Fort Union. Canby had taken into consideration that the men had been without food for twenty-four hours, and many longer than that. Consequently he ordered no general attack until the area was thoroughly reconnoitered and the troops permitted time for food and rest. The reconnaissance was made on the afternoon of the same day; the points and direction of attack selected, and the camp of the command advanced to a point nearer the town where trains could be guarded by a smaller number of men. During the night the Texans abandoned their position and crossed the right bank of the Rio Grande, leaving the sick and wounded behind, with a little food to sustain them.

After detaching the staff officers attached to department headquarters to make arrangements for future operations and the train that could be spared for supplies, the pursuit was continued down the left bank of the river, Canby having in mind crossing at either La Joya, Polvadera, Sabinal or Fort Craig in the event the Texans could not be captured sooner. He camped that night five miles to the rear of the Confederates. On the following day he almost overtook the retreating men. He marched all that day in sight and almost within cannon shot of the Sibley Brigade, but on the opposite side of the river. That night the camps were directly opposite each other. The Texans abandoned most of their train, thirty-eight wagons, and hurried on into the mountains. Canby made arrangements for securing these supplies and continued on to Socorro. Here the command rested for a day, supposedly to await the arrival of the supply, still somewhat in the rear. Colonel Paul and Major Wynkoop worked out a plan of attack when Canby came to the front and squashed it, much to the disgust of the Colorado Volunteers, who wrote Peralta down in their books as the most harmless battle on record. Sibley continued his retreat on the west side of the river to the Magdalenas, through the San Mateo Mountains until he reached the dry bed of the Palomas river, down which he continued until he again struck the Rio Grande, where supplies sent out from Mesilla reached him.

At Fort Craig the Volunteers likewise awaited supplies, which, when they arrived, proved to be not provisions but vinegar and whisky. No doubt they made use of these. In August, after receiving the salary so long overdue, they prepared to return to Colorado, eating,, dancing, drinking up their newly acquired wealth as they passed Paraje, San Antonio de Senecu, Luis Lopez, Socorro, Lemitar, Polvadera. Here they rested a while before resuming the march to Belen, Jarales, Albuquerque, Alameda, Santa Ana, Algodones, up into the Pueblo country on to Santa Fe. At Albuquerque a fandango was held in their honor. They bedded at Fort Marcy while in Santa Fe. Marching again, they renewed memories at Johnson's Ranch, Coslosky's, San Jose, Bernal, Las Vegas, Fort Union. Here most of the time was spent at the little hamlet of Loma Parde, where a native whisky burned their throats and the military police were hard put breaking up the rows that occurred nightly in the cantinas. The guard house at Fort Union was soon filled with the nocturnal casanovas, the ones with the broken heads and arms living the battles over again as they recuperated at the hospital. The senoritas at Loma Parde seemed worth it. At least their native lovers gave them a better fight than they hoped for at Peralta. The remains of Lieut. Marshall were returned to caring relatives at Fort Leavenworth, Capt. Plympton, who replaced Paul as commander at Fort Union granting the necessary permission.

General Carleton replaced Canby at Santa Fe on October 18. One of his first duties was to assign Companies B, F and L to locate a new post on the Pecos (Fort Sumner), but Col. Chivington appealed to Washington and Companies B and F found themselves a mounted contingent bound for Fort Scott in Kansas, ending up instead at Denver City. The further exploits of the Colorado Volunteers belong to Colorado history, but New Mexico will never forget their action at Glorieta.

※ ※ ※

NOTES AND COMMENTS

No state in the Union can be written off as Federal to a man. Colorado was no exception. The side of the Colorado Volunteers has been repeatedly told by practically every author dealing with the war west of the Mississippi. Very few mention the hopes of the Confederacy for Colorado, especially since the rich strikes shortly before bombarding Fort Sumter. Some Southerners who came to mine in Colorado brought their slaves with them. For a brief moment a Confederate flag flew over the Wallingford & Murphy store in Denver. Billie Barnes Jensen made a study of Confederate sentiment in Colorado. He said: "Guerilla activity in the Territory of Colorado took two forms. Early in the war, bands of men were raised within the state for the purpose of capturing materials for the Confederacy and with the ultimate purpose of leaving the Territory as armed troops to join the Southern armies. Later in the war, guerilla activity consisted of the depredations of bands from outside the Territory who preyed on travelers and ranchers in sparsely settled parts of the area. . . . The imprisonment of McKee did not bring an end to the activities of his troops, for later in October a portion of the rebels raised by him moved southward. Whether

McKee was with this company or not is a disputed point among historians, yet the official records show that McKee was still confined in Denver when the events in the southern part of the Territory took place. The force that went south numbered about sixty men. The party appeared at the crossing of the Arkansas River on the trail to New Mexico, where they were probably attempting to intercept a government supply train or had already attacked it, when they were captured by a force from Fort Wise. . . ." *Confederate Sentiment in Colorado,* Billie Barnes Jensen in *The Denver Brand Book,* 1957.

"Early in February, 1862, David Hunter, in command of the department of Kansas, which then included Colorado Territory, had requested Acting Governor Weld of Colorado to send reinforcements to Colonel Canby. Accordingly, the First Colorado Regiment, commanded by Col. John B. Slough, was ordered to the scene of operations. After being assembled near the site of the present city of Trinidad, the Colorado troops marched as rapidly as possible over the snow-covered country to Fort Union, where they arrived on the evening of March 10. . . . On March 22, Col. Slough set out for Santa Fe, taking with him 1,342 men. Besides his own Colorado regiment, Col. Slough had a company of independent Colorado volunteers, a company of New Mexico volunteers, and, of regulars, at battalion of infantry, three detachments of cavalry,, and two artillery batteries of four guns each. Major John M. Chivington, with about one-third of the Colorado regiment and a force of cavalry, 418 men in all, on the afternoon of March 25 started for Santa Fe. Col. Slough having been informed that the enemy had there only about one hundred men. Late at night these troops stopped at Kozlowski's ranch near La Glorieta Pass, where they learned that a Confederate scouting party was in the neighborhood. The scouting party was captured and Major Chivington then discovered that the advance guard of General Sibly's army was at the farther end of La Glorieta Pass.

"At eight in the morning of March 26, Major Chivington's troops broke camp and marched toward the enemy. Proceeding up La Glorieta Pass, they reached the divide about two in the afternoon. Here at a sharp turn in the road, and in the midst of a thicket, the advance guard came unexpectedly upon a Confederate scouting party, consisting of thirty mounted men, led by a lieutenant. The Confederates were taken prisoner without any casualties. Major Chivington urged his men to proceed, but with caution. Three-fourths of a mile farther on, at a point where the trail turns to the right to enter Apache Canon, the west section of La Glorieta Pass, the Federal troops sighted a body of Confederates, under the command of Major Pyron. Upon seeing the Federals, the Confederates immediately halted, unfurled the 'Lone Star' flag of Texas, and planted in the road their two pieces of artillery. Without delay the Confederate gunners opened fire, throwing the Federals into momentary confusion. Major Chivington, however, proved equal to the emergency. Instructing the main body of his troops to seek cover, he sent his mounted troops to the rear, and deployed several companies as skirmishers among the pines on the mountain slopes, on either side of the Confederate guns. The fire of the skirmishers soon caused the Confederates to retire hastily to a point almost a mile from where their first stand was made. They were now at a place where the mountains drew near together and this afforded better advantages for defense. As the Confederates retired, they crossed a deep arroyo, by means of a bridge. This bridge they destroyed, in order to check the Federal onset. The guns were then posted in a defile just beyond the place where the bridge had been, and the slopes on both sides of the road were covered with troops to support the artillery. Again Major Chivington resorted to his former tactics. From the mountain sides a galling fire was poured into the Confederates, who, after sustaining the punishment for almost an hour, began to show signs of giving way. At this moment, the Federal cavalry charged, the horses leaping across the arroyo. The Confederates fled in confusion, taking their guns with them, however..."J. F. Sante, "Battle of La Glorieta Pass," N. M. H. R., October, 1932.

Confederate view:
"... In a short time we were on the march for Glorieta Pass, and arrived at the Santa Fe Trail where it enters the canyon about one hour before day. We lay on the ground until day. Soon after day the wagon train began to arrive and we began unloading in the hopes of finding our mutton, but no mutton was to be found, so we had to be content with our regular bill of fare. After breakfast we formed a battle line across the road

at the head of the canyon, and held it all day, but nothing unusual occurred that night. We had a heavy guard all night. Next morning (28th) after eating our breakfast we were told to put what we had left back in our haversacks, that we would not be back in camp till night, and in a few minutes we were on the march for Pigeon Ranch. When we were in one-half or three-fourths of a mile of the corral the picket guards began firing on us. We formed a battle line where a branch or a ravine crosses the road and we were soon under a heavy fire and a charge by the Federals. We let them charge up to about 30 yards of us, and then we rose up out of the ravine with a Texas yell, and a volley of rifle fire and drove them back, with some loss on both sides. We kept that up for some time when Colonel Scurry decided to divide us up and send about one-half of the men up on the right side, the other on the left. We kept moving up until we were opposite the old corral so we had them under a cross fire and they pulled out and left the battlefield with us. We slept in the old corral that night. As soon as they left, Colonel Scurry rode up and called for a white handkerchief, said he wanted to send a flag of truce to tell them d—d Yankees to come back and pick up their dead and wounded. No one came forward with a white handkerchief, so the old colonel "said: "—— —— ——, tear off your shirt tail, we have got to have a white flag.' I had just picked up a new beautiful white silk handkerchief off of the battlefield. I hated to give it up, but after looking around I decided there was not a shirt tail in the crowd that would do for a white flag, they would have suited better for battle flags, so I walked up and gave the colonel my much prized silk handkerchief. . . . In a couple of hours they were burying their dead. They worked all night and the next day they buried their dead and loaned us their tools to bury ours. This was the 29th and as we hadn't eaten a bite since early the morning before, so all we had to eat that day was corn we picked up in the corral the horses and mules had wasted. We had to roast the corn in the ashes of our camp fire, but it was a change and we enjoyed it. That was the last we got to eat that day. If the Union commander had only known our condition and held out until 12 o'clock the next day the Confederates would have had to surrender as we had no rations and our ammunition was about exhausted. . . . Just at dark on the 29th the bugle called us in line and Colonel Scurry made us a little speech and told us our wagons and all our supplies had been burned and our sick taken prisoners and the nearest and only place to get any supplies was in Santa Fe. . . . I think the regiment lost about 75 men and maybe more. Two of my mess mates were killed, John Manton and Willie McCormic—both were killed on the left wing of our little army, firing under Major Ragly, who was also killed. . . . Harvey Holcomb, "Confederate Reminiscences," N. M. H. R., July, 1930.

CHAPTER SEVEN

THE CONFEDERATES IN NEW MEXICO AND ARIZONA

No sooner was Colonel Baylor established in Mesilla than he sent out Roy Bean to reconnoiter and explore the possibility of recruits from the mines in Arizona as well as the frontier posts along the way. Cook Canyon, Fort Breckenridge (at the junction of the San Pedro and Arivaipa rivers, founded shortly before the war), Fort McLane, Rio Mimbres, Pinos Altos, in fact every place of habitation west of the Black Range to Yuma, wondered what Cochise and his warriors would do following the harsh treatment on the part of the military. Most looked for help from Baylor or Canby and were surprised to learn that both these officers were looking for recruits to fill the places of those in the regular army who transferred to other sections of the country and to make up the Confederate defections that confronted Baylor along the line of march to Mesilla. Captain Coopwood followed Roy Bean into the Pinos Altos country, inviting the miners and freighters to Mesilla to join Baylor.

Most of the miners merely wished to be left in peace. There seemed to be no choice. Indians, Confederates or Union—peace was out of the question. A minute company had been formed for the protection of the mines, headed by Captain Tom Helms. Coopwood made a desperate appeal to this company. Helms told the men that they had to choose for themselves according to their convictions and without resentment. Jenkins, Applezoller, Brown and Conrad elected to enlist for the North; the remaining fifty followed Coopwood to Baylor's camp. They met Captain Hardeman at Picacho and he escorted the recruits to Mesilla to introduce them to Major Waller, quartered at the Butterfield Mail Company's building, where Frank de Rider, superintendent of the mail line and one of the more prominent citizens of Mesilla, gave a speech of welcome. That night Ignacio Varela gave a fandango in their honor. War was forgotten as the men divided their time between the senoritas and the whisky. Fortunately the dance ended in the wee hours of the morning without a brawl. Tom Helms was elected captain of the new Confederate company. Shortly after this Major Lynde sent Baylor a message to take down the Confederate flag in Mesilla, as noted elsewhere. Captain Helms, noting the shortage of horses, obtained permission from Colonel Baylor to make a raid south of Mesilla and round up all the horses held by natives in their little ranches. By mere coincidence the captain chanced upon the herd from Fort Fillmore, under the care of thirty men, leading them to a grazing area for want of feed at the post itself. As Helms had no orders to attack Federals he by-passed the chance of capturing the herd and went on to the hamlets of Amolie and Chamborino near the present site of Anthony. The natives sold very few horses, Helms avoiding antagonism in an effort to purchase rather than stealing. He went back to Mesilla practically empty-handed. It was decided to send a fellow known as Jocker Jack to Fort Fillmore about getting the post horses. Jack was known at Fort Fillmore because of his beef contracts. Sergeant Hank Smith kept a diary of these days and this is the way he recorded the event:

"Jack broached the subject to Sergeant Lee and Corporal Malone and several of the men. The matter was fixed up that when Sergeant Lee was to take the herd to grass he was to talk to such men as were in sympathy with him in the matter. We were to surprise him while half of the guard were at dinner and take him and his men prisoners and take all the herd of horses and mules, but luck was not in favor of us all together. Part of the Mounted Rifles were ordered to escort a wagon train to Fort Stanton which did not take more than fifty mounted men and one company of infantry. Lee and Malone made frequent trips by night to confer with us and finally he reported that his turn would come a certain day to guard the herd, and we of course were glad to take the chances with them. Twenty-five men were detailed out of my company. We were given our chance to pick our horses out of the whole command and also all the best arms in the way of six-shooters and shot guns. Everything being ready, we stole out one night and arrived at the place of meeting before daylight. Being sort of suspicious of treachery, we were slow to make ourselves known. When they arrived with the herd about eight o'clock, Sergeant Lee was looking for some of us to meet him. Not finding anybody, he made an excuse to the corporal that he would go over to a Mexican settlement and get the news. He crossed the river and our men on guard saw him coming and reported to Lieutenant Jackson. Lee came to us and remained a few minutes, when he returned to the herd, the understanding being that while half the guard were at dinner we were to surprise him and his men while playing a game of poker; the other part of our party was to round up the herd and make a dash for the foothills of the Solita mountains on the east side of the river. Jackson not being fully satisfied with the sincerity of Lee sent me and Jack Pennington to make a reconnaissance all around the herd and within half a mile of it, but we found nothing to indicate treachery. After the guard had gone to dinner, half of our party approached the river opposite where the sergeant and his men were playing their game of poker under the shade of the cottonwoods and about twenty steps from the river bank. The opposite bank being a sand bar and covered with young growth of cottonwood and willows, they could not see us coming as the game at that particular time was very interesting. The bank on the east side of the river being a little steep we did not attempt to take our horses on top at that place. So part of the men held the horses while the others crawled up the bank and covered the party playing poker. They all jumped up, and, at the command to drop their arms, they did so quick and started laughing. By that time the other party had rounded up the herd and was ready for the start. The prisoners got their horses out of the herd already saddled. We mounted and made the run for the mountains. We made a circuit of about one hundred miles before we reached our camp at Mesilla. Lee and Malone took the oath of allegiance and joined the different companies of the command. . . ." ("With the Confederates in New Mexico," Panhandle Plains Historical Review—Vol. 2, 1929—pp. 76-77.)

With such men as Lee and Malone to contend with is it any wonder that Lynde surrendered. The colonel suffered much abuse because he seemed to vacillate between courage and cowardice. It meant very little to many of his men at this early stage of the war which side they fought for or against. The garrisons at Fort Buchanan and Fort Breckenridge, learning of the surrender, joined forces, totaling four hundred and fifty men, and marched to Fort Craig. The Indians were also aware of the situation and staged an attack on the Overland Mail wagon train. General McNees, the company manager, was bringing in the remainder of the company's property he had collected west of Tucson. The fifteen men he had with him were massacred at Stein's Pass. Baylor sent men to bury the dead. General McNees was not found, so it was presumed he remained a captive. The Confederates searched the San Simon area for traces of the general but no more was ever heard of him. This area was to be the hideout several decades later for Black Jack Ketchum and his men. Word reached Colonel Baylor that Lieutenant Lord commanded the retreat from Fort Buchanan and Fort Breckenridge. Lieutenant Jackson and a number of the men enlisting from Pinos Altos were sent to spy on his movements and were cautioned against making themselves known to the enemy. Lord camped that night at a water hole known as Soldier's Farewell. The next morning he marched on through the Burro mountain foothills, using every precaution against a surprise attack. He sent a company of dragoons one mile in advance of the contingent and a company of infantry on each side as flankers. These were midway between the dragoons and the main body of troops. They camped on the open plain beyond the hills. The next night they made camp at Cow Springs. Here the Confederates found a number of champagne bottles, empty cigar boxes and some abandoned ammunition. It seems as if the retreating Union troops were making the best of their plight. Despite the festivity Lieutenant Lord had thrown up breastworks on all four sides of the camp. The command next camped at Hot Springs, Cook's mountain and Rio Mimbres. The horses were tied to wagon wheels and picket lines. White, the sutler at both Breckenridge and Buchanan, had his supply train of thirty wagons trailing along with the troops. Smith describes the burning of these wagons:

"When we got to our position, we found everything in camp at the spring (Cook's Spring) in an uproar. Fires lighted up the whole camp and everybody in confusion. The cavalry was all ready to mount, and the infantry was in line and under arms, the artillery was limbered up and dragged to the wagon, and in less than fifteen minutes the whole camp was afire, wagons and all. The cavalry rounded up the herd of mules and started on the road to Fort Craig and the infantry bringing up the rear with three ambulances (filled with fleeing families) in the middle of the infantry. The light from the burning wagons made everything as bright as day, and the command retreating in the light of it. Lieutenant Jackson ordered ten men to start at once to the river to report the happening. The balance of the fifteen men remained to watch the final result of the conflagration. By daylight we were on the ground. We found everything burned except the hospital department, with a lot of sick men and a few camp followers—about fifteen in all—with one wagon and mules and one hospital ambulance. The artillery was partly burned, with the caisson intact. Several of the camp followers we had known in Tucson, especially Jim Turner, who told Virgil Massie (the spy who warned Lord of the advance of the Confederates) had returned from Picacho and reported the intended attack on Lord's command at that place; hence the retreat without incumbrances by Lieutenant Lord. There being good chuck and something stronger than water we enjoyed ourselves very well. The prisoners being very friendly, we had no trouble being very agreeable to them. Lieutenant Jackson finally concluded to make a move towards the river and about three o'clock in the evening we started with what we could. There were three very sick men, the hospital steward's wife, and two other women belonging to the infantry, and a Mexican woman claiming to be Jim Turner's wife. After traveling about thirty miles we were met by Captain Tom Helms with fifty men but having all that was of any account from the wreck, he thought it no use to go any further in that direction. We reached the river next day at Picacho by ten o'clock. Virgil Masterson's (Massie's?) residence being used for a hospital for the time being, we delivered the sick men to the doctor and left the steward and his wife and the other two women to take care of the sick men. The camp followers were told either to join our army or leave to rustle for themselves as we had no chuck to spare them. Col. Baylor had dispatched two hundred mounted men to San Diego Crossing (on the Rio Grande at Fort Thorne) to intercept Lieutenant Lord's retreat, but the command had passed eight or ten hours ahead of their arrival and were on their way to Fort Craig, out on the Jornada, a seventy-five-mile stretch without water and in very open country. Major Waller was in command. He thought it best not to overtake them and expose his men to an open attack on the prairie. He returned and reported the escape of Lieutenant Lord. Colonel Baylor ordered the removal of the blind battery, Fort Craig being reinforced now by the troops of Fort Bliss, Fort McLane, Fort Buchanan, Fort Breckenridge and Fort Fillmore. Colonel Baylor made his headquarters at Dona Ana and moved the whole available force to that place and keeping a close watch on the movements of old Major Lynde, who was now commander-in-chief of Fort Craig and Fort McRae...." (Smith o.c. pp. 87-89.)

This may be a discrepancy on the part of Captain Smith for Bancroft tells us that Lord moved these troops because he feared Baylor's attack following Lynde's surrender. He does add a bit of unusual information: "There was suspicion that some one at Mesilla was furnishing information to the forces at Fort Craig of our movements. Captain Coopwood, who had been sent to Point of Rocks to keep a lookout for the advance of the Federals between Point of Rocks and the San Diego Crossing of the Rio Grande, picked up three Mexicans stealing their way up the river bottom at old Fort Thorne, with a message for Major Lynde giving him all the news of our movements. The authors of the message were John Marshall and Jake Applezoller. John Marshall was one of Lord's camp followers and Jake Applezoller, Jenkins and Brown had left us at Pinos Altos some time before. Captain Coopwood reported the fact to Colonel Baylor who promptly sent a detail to Mesilla and had John Marshall and Jake Applezoller arrested and brought before him at Dona Ana where they were tried and condemned to be hung. The three Mexicans were turned loose as it turned out they didn't know for what they were sent. As they could not be implicated as spies, they returned to their families at Mesilla. John Marshall was hung as was Jake Applezoller. They were hoisted several times in order that they might reveal any news they had from Fort Craig. It was not the intention to hang them until dead, but Marshall never rallied and was found to be dead before they knew it. Jake Applezoller was resuscitated and was kept in close confinement for a long time at Dona Ana...." (Ibid p. 90)

Colonel Baylor abandoned Dona Ana for Mesilla. There a man by the name of Kelly wrote a letter to the Mesilla Times in which he accused the Colonel of cowardice in moving from Dona Ana to Mesilla because there was no real occasion for it. The Confederate officer dispatched a letter to Kelly asking him to retract and write a letter of apology which was to be printed in the paper. Kelly said he would do no such thing and thus the matter rested for a few days. About five days later Baylor was at the adjutant's office making out his reports for San Antonio and Richmond. As he returned to his own quarters he noticed Kelly coming down the street. Baylor confronted him with a second request to retract. When he refused Baylor shot and killed him. The Colonel turned the revolver over to Major Waller and considered himself under arrest. Waller ordered all the officers to convene as a court of inquiry which exonerated the leader on the grounds of self-defense. An old frontier trick. There was no prosecution. Kelly dead, shouldered the blame. What could he say in his defense? That he wasn't armed? That there was such a thing as freedom of the press? Baylor took command again and the incident forgotten. Following this Baylor ordered rations for a thirty day campaign against the Apaches depredating the Pinos Altos area. This definitely proves that Bancroft is correct in assuming that the barracks of the various posts were abandoned due to the surrender of Lynde.

The Confederates spent the first night at Picacho, the second at Rough and Ready Mail Station, the third at Good Sight Station which the Indians had burned to the ground. The following night was spent at the Santa Rita Copper Mines. The troops spent two days there prospecting and looking for Indian signs. The following night found them at Pinos Altos. Two days were spent here very much in the manner as at Santa Rita. The next camp was in the San Luis area where Mangas Coloradas (Red Sleeves) was believed to have been in camp. But there was no trace of him. The Confederates next marched to the Burro mountains where they abandoned the search for Indians in favor of wild turkey, deer and other game. The men eventually found Indians and it was Baylor's policy toward them that brought about his downfall. Major Lynde surrendered on July 27, 1861. A week later Baylor issued a proclamation organizing a provisional government under the jurisdiction fo the Confederate States of America so that the hanging of Marshall and the shooting of Kelly must have taken place some time following the surrender of Lynde but before the campaign against the Apaches.

"The social and political condition of Arizona being little short of general anarchy, and the people being literally destitute of law, order and protection, the said Territory, from the date hereof, is hereby declared temporarily organized as a military government until such time as Congress may otherwise provide. The judicial power of this Territory shall be vested in a Supreme Court, two District Courts, two Probate Courts, and justices of the peace. The two district judges shall constitute the Supreme Court, each of whom shall determine all appeals, exceptions and writs of error removed from the District Court wherein the other presides. One of the judges shall be designated as the Chief Justice of the Supreme Court. The judicial districts of the Territory shall be divided as follows: The First Judicial District shall comprise all the portion of Arizona lying east of the Apache Pass, the district and probate courts whereof shall be holden at La Mesilla. The Second Judicial District shall comprise the remainder of the Territory. The district and probate courts shall be holden at Tucson. The governor shall likewise appoint one probate judge and sheriff and the necessary justices of the peace in and for each judicial district. Each district judge shall appoint his own clerk, who shall be ex-officio clerk of the probate court within such districts. The city of Mesilla is hereby designated as the seat of the government of the Territory. Given under my hand at Mesilla on this First day of August, 1861. (Signed) J. R. Baylor, Governor and Lieutenant Colonel, Commanding."

New Mexico now had two governors—one at Santa Fe; one at Mesilla. In March, 1862, General Sibley appointed William Pelham governor to replace Connelly who was in exile at Las Vegas and ready to move to Fort Union should the Confederates prove victorious at Glorieta. Pelham is better known as the ex-Surveyor General who examined the testimony of land grant owners for clear title to lands given them under the Spanish and Mexican Governments. As Confederate governor he did not last a week. It was his intention of making Albuquerque the Confederate capital of the Territory of New Mexico as Mesilla was the capital of the Territory of Arizona. One governor sometimes presents problems enough but three can tie a territory into quite a legal knot. Fortunately Pelham remained content with the title and enacted no laws because he awaited the outcome of the action near Pecos before attempting to be sworn in office. Baylor's appointments in Mesilla obtained better results. The Enabling Act of the Confederate Congress (January 18, 1862) found no fault with Baylor's action but divided the Territory into three rather than two districts. Clerk Charles A Hoppin and Sheriff John A. Roberts were continued in office. Probate Judge Frank

Higgins was appointed by Baylor. The first order of the court (August 8, 1861) at Mesilla commanded in part that "all Collectors, Sheriffs, Clerks, Alcaldes, Constables or other persons chargeable with monies due this county (Dona Ana) be notified to appear before this Court on Thursday, the 15th day of August A. D. 1861, and render a full account of and pay into Court all monies received by or chargeable to them. All Commissioners of Roads and those acting under the Provisions of the Law relative to Vagrants appointed by the Honorable J. J. Bull, late Judge of the Probate Court of this county, be and they are hereby continued in office until further ordered. The Clerk is ordered to purchase a suitable set of books of Registry, Record, etc., for the use of this Court, the cost of which shall be paid from any unappropriated monies in the county treasury. The Tax upon Public Balls or Fandangoes is hereby fixed at three dollars for each ball, to be collected by the Sheriff."

F. DeRyther, George A. Hayward, John May, W. B. Clarke, J. W. Davis, Ramon Navarrez, Ramon Gonzolez, Jose Maria Chavez, Nestor Barela, Christian Duper, Henry Grandjean and M. Gellat were selected as jurymen for the fall term. Grandjean later moved to Monteciello and then Socorro, where he died. A fourth generation Henry Grandjean resides in Socorro today. A License Tax of three dollars was levied for each theatrical performance in town as well as for any circus traveling through. Daniel Fritz was the county treasurer. He does not seem to have been a relative of Captain Emil Fritz over whose will so much unpleasantry resulted between Murphy and McSween. Fritz showed a balance of two dollars and seventy-nine cents in the treasury. Former Justice of the Peace Rafael Vermudez showed a balance of six dollars and fifty cents. On August 20th. Raymundo Duran was appointed Pound Keeper and charged to "impound any stray animals here (in the town of Mesilla proper) and animals which may be found trespassing upon the fields or premises of the citizens of the 5th Precinct and to keep the same until their owners pay all the damages done to owners of said fields and in addition a fine of one dollar for the use of the county and twenty-five cents for the use of the Pound Keeper. "That same day Apolonio Mijares was hailed to court for assault with intent to kill. It seems that he suspected his wife of being over friendly toward Juan Avalos. The bail was set at one thousand dollars and the case was to be tried in the fall term of court. Joshua S. Sledd presented a bill for several months rent. The Confederate Courthouse belonged to him. Actually it was a hall often used for dances and meetings. Most of the cases tried by the court were for debt. Several of the jurymen asked to be excused and others replaced them. Those who refused to serve were fined and held in contempt of court. Some of the proceedings make interesting reading:

"It is ordered for the benefit of Public Health and for the purpose of cleaning the streets and plazas of the town of Mesilla that George Ackinback be and he is hereby appointed Overseer of the Markets and Special Road Commissioner in and for said town and so much of the limits of the Fourth and Fifth Precincts of the county of Dona Ana as are included within the limits of said town, and he shall have full power to collect such assessments as may be ordered to be levied for the purpose of cleaning said streets and plazas from time to time by this Court upon all persons who bring fruit, vegetables and other property usually sold in the public plaza and markets of this town, and he shall make monthly settlements with this Court of monies collected and expended by him. . . . The Market Overseer and Special Road Commissioner shall be authorized to collect the following assessments for cleaning the streets:

"On all carts and wagons of produce brought from Texas or Mexico, not less than fifty cents nor more than one dollar each.

"On all native produce (productos del pais) not less than six cents nor more than fifty cents to each individual in accordance and in proportion to the quantity he may sell or bring to sell or be sold.

"On every butcher or vender of butcher's meat, the sum of twenty-five cents for each stall or place of selling, for each day so occupied.

"Hereafter no person shall be allowed to deposit wood or other fuel upon the streets or plaza of this town for sale under the penalty of twenty-five cents for each offense. This is not to prevent the sale of wood or other fuel from carts, wagons or burros.

"It is further ordered that the practice of butchering animals upon the streets or plaza of the town for sale is prohibited and a fine for each breach of this order is assessed at fifty cents.

"Rendering or frying out tallow and lard upon the streets and plazas is declared to be a public nuisance and a fine of fifty cents shall be collected from each offender against this ordinance for every violation of the same. . . ."

Jose Maria Chavez was named Comissioner of Roads and Bridges between the plaza of Picacho and the bridge known as the Ponte de Guerras (War Bridge); Luciano Serna was appointed associate commissioner while Pablo Alvarado was ordered to attend all repairs from that bridge to the town of Mesilla. Chavez complained that he had too much to do and Jose Maria Nieto was named as his assistant. Samuel G. Bean of Picacho spoke Spanish fluently and often served as court interpreter. Roy Bean evidently did not march with Baylor in pursuit of Apaches for his name appears often in community affairs at Picacho and Mesilla. It also appears several times in a suit of attachment wherein he wishes to collect one hundred dollars from Marcial Padilla. Samuel G. Bean was also Justice of the Peace for the Fourth Precinct. The officials were interested in repairing the road from Mesilla to Fort Fillmore. Sanmual J. Jones was appointed administrator of the estate of the "late Robert P. Kelly".

"Saturday February 8, 1862—Be it remembered that on this day was held a special term of the Probate Court in and for the county of Dona Ana. Present were the Honorable John P. Deus, Judge of the Probate Court, and Charles A. Hoppin, Clerk. It is ordered by the judge presiding that the following named persons be and are hereby appointed Commissioners of Roads and Bridges within their respective precincts:

For the 2nd Precinct—Juan Bautista Montoya (at Dona Ana)
For the 3rd—Ramon Navares (at Las Cruces)
For the 4th—Pablo Alvarado (at Mesilla)
For the 5th—F. DeRyther (at Mesilla)
For the 6th—Francisco Salazar (at Santo Tomas)
For the 7th—Juan Jose Garcia (at Amoles)
For the 8th—Eligio Provencio (at La Mesa)

"It is hereby ordered that the rules and regulations for the government of the Commissioners of Roads and Bridges approved on September 15, 1861, be and are declared in force and that they be printed for the use of the said Commissioners and information of the inhabitants of the county. The Commissioners of the 4th. Precinct must notify the owner or owners of a jacal standing in the street next north of the buildings of Blas Duran and known as Calle de Medanas to remove the same, it being an obstruction of said streets. A street must be opened leading to the Rio Grande and it must be marked a public road. . . ."

Frank Higgins resigned as Probate Judge in favor of John Peter Deus who likewise resigned following the disaster to the Confederate cause at Apache Canyon. Some very interesting correspondence regarding the Confederates in New Mexico appeared in the *New Mexico Historical Review*, July, 1930. The first letter is addressed to Mr. Greer and dated from Trinity, Texas, August 5, 1927.

"The last week of July my daughter and her daughter and their husbands were in New Mexico and at your place and enjoyed the short stay there very much. They brought me several pictures and also one of your little booklets which I read with pleasure, but I told them I could give a much more correct statement about the Confederate side than the little booklet gave . . . I was in the Confederate Army for four years. To begin with, you have got the Confederate Army that took part in the battle of Pigeon Ranch over estimated. . . . In the first place General Sibley was not there and only nine companies of his brigade were there. This was nine companies of the Fourth Texas Cavalry. . . . On the morning of March 25, 1862, the nine companies left Albuquerque and left Company A, commanded by Captain Hardemann, to guard the hospitals there which were full of our sick soldiers. We had nothing to eat for several days except bread made of flour and cold water; not an ounce of meat of any kind or an eye of grease. We marched all day in a northeast direction and camped at a gold mine. . . . The next day we marched in the same direction until about the middle of the afternoon, and camped in the edge of a prairie which I think was part of the Beard sheep ranch. The hands on the ranch began to kill and bring in a large quantity of as fat mutton as anyone could wish for, so we were all happy once more, but only for a short time. We began to put our mutton on the fire, and thinking and talking about what a feast we would have in a short time, and happened to look across the prairie and saw the dust rising and it was only a few minutes until it showed to be a man. He had a paper in his hand and loped up to Colonel Scurry's tent and handed the paper to the Colonel. We were all watching and saw the Colonel gave him a paper and off he went. I was only a boy, but another man was standing by and said: 'Hell is brewing and not a mile off.' About that time Colonel Scurry came down the line with his old cap in his hand and hollowing out: 'Pack up, boys. Major Pyron has been fighting six hundred Yankees with twenty men for two days and has got a truce until twelve o'clock tomorrow and we must go to him.' The next order came in a few minutes to fall in line and leave the packing up for the teamsters, so in a short time we were on the march for Glorieta Pass, and arrived at the Santa Fe Trail where it enters the canyon about one hour before day. We lay down on the ground until day. Soon after day the wagon train began to arrive and we began unloading in the hopes of finding our mutton, but no mutton was to be found, so we had to be content with our regular bill of fare. After breakfast we formed a battle line across the road at the head of the canyon, and held it all day, but nothing unusual occurred that night. We had a heavy guard all night. Next morning after eating our breakfast we were told to put what we had left in our haversacks; that we would not be back to camp till night, and in a few minutes we were on the march for Pigeon Ranch. When we were within one-half or three-fourths of a mile of the corral the picket guards began firing on us. We formed a battle line where a branch or ravine crosses the road and were soon under a heavy fire and a charge by the Federals. We let them charge up to about thirty yards of us, and then we rose up out of the ravine with a Texas yell, and a volley of rifle fire and drove them back with some loss on both sides. We kept that up for some time when Colonel Scurry decided to divide us up and send about one-half of the men up on the right side; the other on the left. We kept moving until we were opposite the old corral so we had them under cross fire and they pulled out and left the battlefield with us. We slept in the old corral that night. As soon as they left Colonel Scurry rode up and called for a white handkerchief. He said that he wanted to send a flag of truce to tell them damned Yankees to come back and pick up their dead and wounded. No one came forward with a handkerchief so the old Colonel said: '————, tear off your shirt tail. We have got to have a white flag.' I had just picked up a new beautiful white silk handkerchief off of the battlefield. I hated to give it up, but after looking around I decided there was not a shirt tail in the crowd that would do for a white flag. They would have suited better for battle flags. I walked up and handed the Colonel my much prized handkerchief. (He never got it back). The men that followed the Yanks rode eight miles before they caught up with them. In a couple of hours they were gathering up their dead and wounded. They worked all night and the next day they buried their dead and loaned us their tools to bury ours. This was the 29th and as we hadn't eaten a bite since early the morning before, so all we had to eat that day was corn we picked up in the corral which the horses and mules had wasted. We had to roast the corn in the ashes of our camp fire, but it was a change and we enjoyed it. That was the last we got to eat that day. If the Union commander had only known our condition and held out until twelve o'clock the next day the Confederates would have had to surrender as we had no rations and our ammunition was about exhausted. We started out the morning of the 28th with a good supply of ammunition bu had used it freely all day. When Colonel Scurry would come around he never once told us to be saving our ammunition, but told us to 'give them hell, boys' which we were trying to do. If he called using bullets hell they were getting plenty of it. Just at dark on the 29th the bugle called us in line and Colonel Scurry made us a little speech and told is our wagons and all supplies had been burned and our sick taken prisoners and the nearest and only place to get any supplies was in Santa Fe which was about twenty eight miles and the only way we could get it there would be to beat the Yankees and we struck out for Santa Fe and reached there early next morning and got quarters and plenty to eat. . . . Now before closing I must not fail to give a word for that noble lady, Mrs. Canby, the Federal commander's good wife. She was living in Santa Fe when we landed there on March 30th, 1862. She lived in a large house and threw open her door and invited in all of our sick and wounded boys as long as we stayed there. At one time she was nursing fourteen of our boys. I will say that Mrs. Canby captured more hearts of Confederate soldiers than the old General ever captured Confederate bodies." (Signed) Harvey Halcomb.

    H. C. Wright wrote: ". . . Your account says they killed 1100 mules. At the outside we did not have over 500, and I for one never saw or heard of a dead one. They (i.e. the Federals) captured the mules and drove them off and burned our wagons (less than 100) and supplies. There were a lot of sick and wounded men; also cooks, drivers and camp guards. These they paroled. The most of our men marched back to Santa Fe that night and there commandered supplies. But others remained on the battlefield to care for the dead and wounded. A few provisions were found. I myself, found a lot of baled buffalo meat said to have been put up by Indians, and a number of sacks of flour. These were stored at a little place about a mile down the road from the pass. . . . Our troops remained in Santa Fe about a week and then started for Texas. Doubtless they endured hardships on the way but as for having to kill and eat their horses and mules that is all nonsense. There were but a few deaths on the way, and the fact that 1200 reached Fort Bliss only shows how greatly their numbers were overestimated in the battles. . . . I remained in Santa Fe to care for my (wounded) friend. General Canby issued us (several hundred sick and wounded) supplies and months afterwards when we were able to travel he furnished us with mules, wagons and provisions and sent us back to Texas (under parole) . . ." (Signed) H. C. Wright.

With Pelham named as governor the Confederates continued to dominate the scene in New Mexico and Arizona during those early winter months of 1862. They required everyone from Mesilla to Santa Fe to swear allegiance to the Confederate States of America or suffer the loss of property which is probably why Governor Connelly's property went up in smoke at Peralta, a loss amounting to thousands of dollars. He wrote to Seward on March 23, 1862: "I am sorry to say that the Texans have not behaved with the moderation that was expected, and that desolation has marked their progress on the Rio Grande from (Fort) Craig to Bernalillo. Exactions and confiscations are of daily occurence, and the larger portion of those who have had anything to give or to lose are here (at Las Vegas the temporary capital due to the success of the Confederates at Santa Fe) on this frontier, seeking a refuge from their rapacity, and have left their houses and contents a prey to the invaders." (See O. R. 1, 9:651) The plea of illness on the part of General Sibley during the Valverde campaign weakened the loyalty of many of his men who went about the countryside in disorderly fashion confiscating and destroying more in Indian fashion than as soldiers. The capital at Santa Fe was held by the Confederates for about a month and as at Mesilla many seeking prestige on the side of the victor pledged allegiance to the Southern cause. Most remained indifferent. Regarding the Confederates in Arizona Bancroft has this to say: "Public sentiment in Arizona was almost unanimously southern and disunion, and no secret was made of the feeling in this respect, the few union men having little or nothing to say. In 1861 a convention at Tucson seems to have formally declared the territory a part of the Confederacy, and in August of that year Granville H. Oury was elected delegate to the southern congress. It was openly asserted that the country's misfortunes were due to neglect of the government, and that this neglect arose from Arizona's well-known and patriotic devotion to the southern cause.... Early in 1862 a force of two or three hundred Texans, under Captain Hunter, marched westward from Mesilla, and in February took possession of Tucson for the Confederacy. There was of course no opposition, union men, if there were any left, fleeing across the line into Sonora. Not much is really known of Hunter's operations in Arizona so far as details are concerned, even the date of his arrival being doubtful. Besides holding Tucson, driving out men suspected of union sympathies, confiscating a few mines belonging to northerners, and fighting the Apaches to some extent, he sent a detachment to the Pima villages, and possibly contemplated an attack on Fort Yuma...." (Bancroft "Arizona and New Mexico pp. 512-515) Hunter abandoned Arizona at the approach of the California Column. The argument that Arizona sought separation from New Mexico long before the war is an old one. Time and again Tucson insisted that Santa Fe was too far away for an adequate understanding of the problems of southern and western Arizona. The hopes of obtaining this independence through the Confederacy is one of the main reasons why Baylor was successful in creating the Confederate Territory of Arizona. Walker said that "the cause of the Confederate invasion of New Mexico was the desire to annex the American Southwest and the northern States of Mexico. The advantages to be gained by this acted as subsidiary causes: an immense territory would be added to the Confederacy, including a long coast line with at least three desirable ports through which world commerce could supply the necessities of war and life; control of rich gold and silver mines would insure foreign credit and enable a navy to be launched which could meet the Federal forces on equal terms; as a result European recognition would follow; and a few soldiers and many supplies would be found in the captured country. The factors making for the success of the plan acted as contributing causes; the military forces in New Mexico were looked upon as inefficient; a majority of the inhabitants of Arizona were pro-Southern; long efforts at obtaining independent Territorial organization had resulted in failure and dissatisfaction; and the possibility that the Mexican favored the South." ("Confederate Invasion of New Mexico")

General Carleton seized the property of the pro-Southerners both in Arizona and New Mexico. Mowry complained bitterly of the Confiscation Act and the fact that United States Marshal Cutler was able to buy his mining property in Southern Arizona for $4,000 did nothing to lessen his annoyance. This seizure of property was in and out of courts throughout the balance of the war. Abraham Cutler, still United States Marshal in 1865, represented the United States as Libellant against (Sept. 2):

The property of Hugh Stevenson — The Bracitos Tract upon which Fort Fillmore is situated in Dona Ana County . . . with all the buildings thereon. The same being libeled in the United States Courts for the Third Judicial District of the Territory of New Mexico in a case of seizure and forfeiture for alleged violation of the Acts of Congress approved July 13, 1861. This is to be sold to the highest bidders on November 6, 1865.

Also the property of George H. Giddings in the town of Franklin, and a tract of land in the town of San Elizaro, county of El Paso, Texas.

Also the property of Josiah F. Crosby to wit: a certain library of law books containing one hundred copies more or less.

Also the land of Henry L. Dexter—a tract of land in the town tract of Isleta, Texas. Also the land at the place called El Brazito Chapilate.

Also the property of Samuel Maverick. All the land forty-eight miles below the town of Franklin, Texas.

Also the property of Simeon Hart. The land one and a half miles west of the town of Franklin, with a flouring mill, dwelling houses, corrals, ranch houses, stables and other buildings thereon; with all machinery attached to and used in running said mill and all other privileges thereunto belonging and known as Hart's Mill. One thousand and one hundred and fifty acres of land west of Hart's Mill.

In Franklin—Skillhorn's Blacksmith Shop and residence and all improvements in the deed of William T. Smith to said Skillhorn dated March 23, 1857.

Also the property of James C. Walker—the orchards, houses, etc., belonging to him in the town of Isleta purchased by him from Jose Juan Duran through William Claude Jones, who sold them to Walker on March 8, 1856.

Also that part of the Ponce Grant which is situated in Franklin and owned by Josiah F. Crosby, Henry S. Gillett, John S. Gillett—with all of the houses, corrals, etc., thereon.

Also the property of William C. Stanly. This property is five and one-half miles below the Mexican town of Guadalupe and about sixty-three miles from Franklin.

Also the property of the partners Samuel Maverick and William Ford—an undivided two-thirds of a certain tract of land upon which Fort Quitman is situated.

There were a number of others among whom the most notable was the Magoffin family, originally from Kentucky, later prominent in the Santa Fe trade as well as for the part played in the bloodless conquest of New Mexico by General Kearny. The story of the Magoffins is better known than most. Cutler went on to add:

"I hereby admonish and summon all persons claiming any interest in said property or knowing or having anything to say why some should not be decreed to be forfeited to the United States and be condemned and sold, to answer the prayer of said libel; that they appear before said District Court at the courthouse in La Mesilla in the said district on the sixth day of November, A. D. 1865, at ten o'clock a. m., where said cause will be heard. . . ." (See *Santa Fe Gazette Supplement,* September 3, 1865.)

※ ※ ※

NOTES AND COMMENTS

By way of contrast from the oft quoted masters Twitchell and Bancroft, this is a summary of what the Baylor family itself has to say about John Robert Baylor (found in *Frontier Times,* September, 1929):

"Colonel Baylor was born in Bourbon County, Kentucky, in 1822. His father was a physician and enlisted in the army as assistant surgeon in the 7th U. S. Infantry. His mother's name was M. Weidner. John came to Texas when in his late teens and took up residence at Marshall, where he met and wooed Emily J. Hanna. They were married in 1844. Shortly after marriage the couple moved to Fayetteville, Fayette County, where John opened a farm and cattle ranch. He was known to be quite active in all matters of public interest; waged war on disreputable characters and was frequently the people's choice in commanding expeditions against outlaws, rustlers and Indians. He came to be called Captain Baylor because of this. He was elected to the legislature in 1852, serving until 1854. He was admitted to the bar and engaged in the practice of law. In 1855 he was agent for the Comanche Indians at the reservation near Camp Cooper in what is now Stephens County. His ideas and those of people in authority clashed. He insisted that Indian horse thieves be treated as horse thieves; murderers as murderers, etc., which was not the policy of his superiors. A new agent replaced him in 1857. Baylor moved twenty miles below the agency near the Clear Fork of the Brazos and started the first cattle ranch in present Stephens County. From 1857 to 1860 he was continually at war with marauders, the biggest battle being against the Comanches in 1859. In 1860 the Indians killed one of his neighbors. He organized a few men and tracked them down. Actually there were but four men and himself. This little band succeeded in killing thirteen Indians and recapturing fifty head of horses stolen in Palo Pinto County. On February 24, 1862, he was appointed Confederate governor of Arizona and given the rank of brigadier general, but President Davis deprived him of his authority and command because of the rumors of Baylor's mistreatment of Apache Indians. He later took part in the Jay Hawkers fight on the Trinity river and in the battle of Galveston. In 1863 he was elected to the Confederate Congress. After his election he turned over his command of one hundred men (a guerilla band) to Lt. R. H. D. Sorrell. He made two trips to Richmond to explain to Davis the Apache affair in Arizona. His explanation satisfied the Confederate leader and he was exonerated. He had three sons in the Confederate Army—J. W. Baylor, W. K. Baylor, and H. W. Baylor. He settled in Waldo County in 1879."

Chapter Eight

VALVERDE

Nothing served to enliven the spirit of the Texans more than the surrender of Colonel Lynde, which was as much a surprise to them as it was to the Federals. This action behind him, Colonel Baylor focused his attention on Fort Craig with its three hundred and fifty regulars and one hundred and eighty volunteers. At least that was his idea. This vision of added glory had to give way to the stern reality; he was forced to face the facts. His horses were jaded, and the surrender at the Springs made the Indians increasingly bolder instead of intimidating them. Over near Fort Stanton, Confederates Mosse, Pemberton, Emmanaker and Sanders sent out to replenish the water supply found hostile Indians instead. After a two-hour battle three were killed and scalped. Sanders escaped. Two weeks later the Indians attacked Placito, which was again to know the ring of bullets in the Lincoln County War. Summoned to the rescue, Lt. Pulliam rode from Fort Stanton at the head of fifteen Texans and succeeded in killing five Indians.

Meantime rumors were flying regarding the California Volunteers, the Colorado Volunteers, the New Mexico Volunteers, and the Federals. Baylor decided that it might be best after all to await the arrival of Sibley's Brigade. Tired of inertia, Lt. John H. Minks of the New Mexico Mounted Volunteers took some men and rode some forty miles south of Fort Craig to a hamlet known as Canada Alamosa, where he hoped to establish a camp in order to interpose his men between the approaching Texans and the waiting Federals at the post. Also he would halt caravans going to Albuquerque and California as well as those coming from the west. He gave ten men as military escort to a wagon boss provided he would take five of his sick soldiers for hospitalization at Fort Craig. At Canada Alamosa he induced the natives to sell him fresh mounts, this taking more time than he hoped to spare. Purchasing forage was even a slower process if such a thing were possible for you have to deal with the native to realize how irritatingly slow he can be when you are consumed with hurry. Added to this Minks had to keep several small scouting parties constantly on the go. The scalps of the Federals were as prized to the Indians as those of the Confederates. Some of the privates became downright insulting when asked to use pick and shovel in order to ready the new post for habitation.

With the corral and breastworks well under way, news was brought in that riders were raising dust to the south. Six men were detailed to bring in positive information. A native civilian was asked to accompany the command as scout because of hs knowledge of the country. They returned with the report that the approaching men were part of a scouting party sent out by Captain Hubbell. Led by a man named Colisnara, these men had crossed the right bank of the river to pasture their horses. Minks felt that this was merely a pretext for abandoning their post on the Jornada del Muerto. He decided that on the morrow he would send out a detail to place them under arrest and send them back to Captain Hubbell.

Later on that evening scouts again reported men riding. Minks paid little heed to this, believing them to be the Colisnara group. Just in case he should be mistaken he ordered the men not to light fires, never to talk above a whisper, so that they could hear his voice at all times, and to be prepared to repel a night attack should the riders prove to be Texans. The teamsters who were to travel to Fort Craig were ordered to start out at 3 a. m. It was two in the morning before Minks finally felt it was safe to retire. He no sonner closed his eyes than one of the sentinels reported that he heard noises in the direction of the village. The men were aroused and prepared for battle. It was a dark, moonless night. The men were ordered to saddle their mounts, at which moment some shots were heard. Then silence. Mink asked the pickets for an explanation. They insisted that they were set upon by the enemy. Mink heard no shots but was uneasy, for the horses stampeded. Something frightened them but no one could say for certain what it was. He sent a number of the men in pursuit of the flying horses. With thirty less men to defend the camp, Mink was now concerned over the terrible Indian yell he heard in the direction of the village. He called on the remaining forty to follow him in the rescue of the town. Just as he started out, the Confederate cavalry rode up, the leader shouting: "Here's the camp. Give them hell."

The firing commenced and the surprised Texans decided to ride back to Canada Alamosa. Mink had mistaken the famous rebel yell for the Indian war cry. He thought that there were but few Texans who wished to make him believe that their forces were stronger than they actually were. He had sent Lorenzo Tobats and Felix Gallegos back to Fort Craig too soon. Not wishing to spare another man he decided to make a stand. He fell back behind some houses and fences and commanded the men to cease firing at random but to await the next move of the enemy. The lieutenant was under the impression that the Texans had actually retreated because they had not returned fire for some time. More than anything else he sought to prevent them from finding out the actual number of men he had. Taking a few trusted men with him he set out on foot to make a house-to-house search for the enemy.

He could make out nothing in the darkness. Either the enemy had evacuated the village or this was a trick to bring him out in the open. Rather than fall into a trap he returned to the camp. There he found that a number of the men went off on their own whether as deserters or for designs on the enemy he could not say. Calling Lt. Sanchez to him he asked him to see if he could find any of the men before they wandered too far afield. Hoping to ride on the town before daybreak he called on volunteers to smoke out the Texans. He determined to set fire to the outlying houses and under cover of the smoke get into Alamosa. The light from the fires would dispel the eternal darkness. Armed with matches and some dry wood he set out, followed by Lt. Medina, Sergeant Mennett and several others. The Texans were waiting. Within ten minutes Minks was driven back to the very place from which he started.

The Confederates took position at an elevation to his right, near the road leading to Fort Craig, in the hopes of cutting off his retreat. Dawn broke over the hills. Able to see at last, Minks could count not more than ten men. Still anxious to deceive the enemy Minks barked loud commands in all directions as if he had a horde. He kept the men busy firing repeatedly for an hour. John Morrin, a teamster, was wounded in the leg. Taking out his spy glass Minks could now count more than sixty mounted Confederates ready to charge. To retreat was impossible; to stand there meant to be butchered. The alternative was surrender, which he did. The Confederates burnt all the supplies they could not carry. Taken to the enemy's camp, Minks found out that he had been set upon by Captain Coopwood's Spy Company (45 men); a detachment of Captain Pyron's Company (42 men) and 24 men from another unidentified company. While the Confederates lost some horses they insisted that they had killed some of Mink's men, although he was not aware that he lost any. The lieutenant regretted that he had sent out the five scouting parties the day before. It would have proved quite an interesting battle and prevented the action at Valverde.

Word did get to Captain Henry R. Selden (later Colonel—Fort Selden honored him) that Minks was in trouble and he sent Captain R. M. Morrison from Fort Craig to render aid. Learning that the lieutenant was a prisoner he left Lt. Brady in charge of the camp near the village and took out after the victorious Confederates. Coming upon these near Fort Thorn he went into immediate action. The engagement lasted two hours without loss on either side. Ammunition running low, the captain retreated to the camp, carrying his wounded with him.

After appointing Lieutenant Poore to take inventory of the supplies taken out of Mink's camp, Captain Bethel Coopwood marched along the river road to find a suitable resting spot for the night. On the following morning while at breakfast the camp was surrounded by an estimated one hundred and ninety men from Fort Craig. The firing commenced at seven and lasted four hours.

The principal portion of the battle was fought with the Federal troops forming two lines, the shape of an angle of a square, the Confederates using the same formation within the enemy's lines. One line of Texans was composed of a detachment from Capt. Pyron's Company, Capt. Stafford's Company, all under the command of Lt. Poore, Sergeant O'Grady and Sergeant Browne. The left line was composed of a detachment from Captain Coopwood's Company and the remainder of Captain Stafford's Company. This line was under the immediate command of Lt. Sutherland, being divided into two platoons, one led by Sergeant Coutler; the other by Private Tevis who had been appointed on the spot. Although Sergeant O'Grady was severely wounded he nevertheless spurred his men forward, crying out to them never to cease firing until they avenged his blood. Also wounded were Quinn, Robinson and Lambert. At eleven the Federals suddenly ceased fire and retreated. Coopwood expected this was a ruse and awaited the renewal of battle. It never came.

At Mesilla, J. A. Lucas, president of the convention which met there on March 16, 1861, passed a resolution: That we will not recognize the present black Republican administration; we will resist any officers appointed to this Territory by the said administration with whatever means in our power. It was because of the attitude of so many at Mesilla that Col. Canby had ordered Major Lynde at Fort McLane to abandon that post and concentrate all his efforts in protecting Fort Fillmore, knowing also that the collector of customs at Las Cruces, who was also the post sutler at Fillmore, determined to turn over the government funds to the advancing Baylor's Babies. We have already seen the disastrous finale of that move. With the concentration of Southern sympathizers in the Mesilla area, Baylor selected that town as the capital of the so-called Confederate Territory of Arizona.

Canby spent the time in Santa Fe issuing orders for the protection of the Fort Smith-Anton Chico-highway; strengthening the garrisons at Albuquerque and Fort Union; raising companies of New Mexico Volunteers; insisting that a watch be kept over the actions of Hart and Magoffin in the Fort Bliss area; explaining to everyone that the war was not entirely on one side; hoping against hope that his opponent would find enough headaches in San Antonio to keep him out of New Mexico. But at Hart's Mill on June 12th Sibley was congratulating Loring and other Confederates on the glory of the Confederate cause. Van Dorn, commander at San Antonio, ordered four companies to garrison Fort Bliss. Sibley was satisfied with the subsistence stores collected by Magoffin, Hart and Crosby. He hoped to capture all the U.S. currency in the area and send it to Jefferson Davis. Lt. D. C. Smith, on his way to Chihuahua to seek the good will of the Mexican government for the Federals, was arrested with his whole command of fifteen men at Guadalupe forty miles from El Paso, by orders of Col. Baylor and his men treated as prisoners of war despite the fact that they were taken in foreign territory. W. W. Mills deplored the situation at Mesilla, sickened by the sight of the Confederate banner waving over Mesilla, as well as at the diatribes of the Confederate editor of the Mesilla Times. To make matters worse Canby was ordered to take all regular troops from New Mexico at such time and in such a manner as would not expose the Territory to conquest or invasion from Texas before the New Mexico Volunteers were properly organized, armed and posted. On this gloomy note the year 1861 ended.

The roster of fighting men as the new year dawned showed this: 352 at Fort Marcy in Santa Fe; 125 at Fort Garland; 869 at Fort Union; 623 at Albuquerque; 2,065 in the Fort Craig area; 297 at Cubero; 151 at Abo famous for its mission ruins; 39 at Hatch's Ranch; 107 at Camp Connelly; 53 on the outskirts of Santa Fe; 70 near Fort Wise. Sibley, who was aware of these numbers, issued a proclamation offering amnesty to any who would lay down their arms and don the grey of the Confederacy. Canby's spies kept him posted reporting every move the Sibley Brigade made. United now with Baylor's Babies this aggregate of 3,500 men was known as The Confederate Army of New Mexico. In keeping with his policy of obtaining supplies for his own men and for the Confederacy, Sibley decided to march on Fort Union whose supplies he evaluated at $275,000. Canby on the other hand was opposed to his brother-in-law taking the offensive and marched south of Fort Craig to select a battleground of his own choosing. Seven miles from the post, in the Rio Grande valley, was the village of Valverde.

Sibley marched out of Fort Bliss heading Riley's and Green's regiments, five companies of Steele's, five of Baylor's Babies; Teel's and Riley's batteries; three independent companies which would have amounted in all to about three thousand men had not four hundred been in sick bay. Canby had five companies of the Fifth, three of the Seventh and three of the Tenth Infantry; two companies of the First and five of the Third Cavalry; McRae's Battery (G of the 2nd and I of the 3rd Cav.) and a company of Colorado Volunteers. The New Mexico troops consisted of the 1st Reg. (Kit Carson's); seven companies of the 2nd; seven of the 3rd; one of the 4th; two of the 5th; Grayson's Spy Company and about one thousand hastily collected and unorganized militia giving him to face Sibley an aggregate of 3,810 men. The opposing forces met near Valverde on February 21st, 1862.

To begin with, Canby's frame of mind was not conducive to victory. He had no confidence in the New Mexico Volunteers; the New Mexico Militia he considered a burden, undisciplined, untrained, unfit. Army life meant little or nothing to them. They knew the secrets of Indian warfare but all this was new to them. Besides they were brooding about whether or not they could get back to their fields to till the soil for their early crops. Also they sensed their commander's lack of confidence in them. He had planned from the very beginning to bring on a battle in which the New Mexico troops would not be obliged to maneuver in the presence of, or under the fire of, the Confederates. Nor was he ever too certain as to how many were actually Southern sympathizers.

Several authors in writing of the engagement at Valverde bring out the fact that New Mexicans fled the battlefield. Willing to brand them as cowards, they failed to analyze the New Mexican mind. Men whose forebears marched with Coronado, Espejo, Sosa, Onate, Peralta and other Conquistadores of note; men whose forefathers came to New Mexico as soldiers; who had ever to be vigilant against the menace of roving Indians; whose ancestors were ever one jump ahead of the Saracens; who proved they could hold frontiers against overwhelming odds; whose sons and grandsons were to win glory in the Spanish American war and both World Wars—these could hardly be the type to flee the sight of gunsmoke at Valverde. Taunted by the members of the regular army, mistreated by superiors, held in disdain by Canby, they could hardly be expected to hold the spotlight in the face of the odds against them. Besides, they were being constantly reminded that they were members of an inferior race because of the barrier of their native tongue which they insisted on using at every available opportunity. New Mexico is bi-lingual to this day. Had the New Mexico Volunteers and the Militia faced Indians that day the story of Valverde would have been differently written.

Just two days previous Sibley had fallen back from his advanced position and crossed to the east bank of the river, in an effort, like Canby, to select his own battleground. From Paraje, about seven miles below Valverde, to a point immediately opposite Fort Craig, the Rio Grande in those days before Elephant Butte Dam, was bounded on the east by a basaltic mesa ranging from forty to eighty feet in height, good for bridle paths but unfit for army wagons. Only at one point could a road be serviceable for artillery use. Directly opposite Fort Craig a point of the pedregal projected into the valley and at a distance of about one thousand yards held an advantage of an attack against Fort Craig, tenable only should the aggressor be prevented in locating batteries on that point. Two and a half miles above the fort the Contradero Mesa—about three miles long and two miles wide—ascended a height of three hundred feet above the level of the valley. At the southern and northern ends of the mesa the valley of the river proved accessible, favorable at both points for the establishment of a camp beyond the reach of the artillery and covered in front by the Rio Grande itself. The pedregal (mal pais) is traversed by ridges of drifting sand, broken in places by protruding beds of lava and parallel in their general direction to the valley of the river. The canyons between these ridges, natural covered ways, gave the Texans advantages not lost on them. They especially aided in concealing Sibley's movements and secured him from attack by the impracticable character of the country between him and Canby.

The main force of the Confederate Army of New Mexico moved up one of these canyons on February 20th. At four in the afternoon it reached a position which would have been to Canby's advantage should he assume the offensive even though the ground at his front was rather uneven for manuevers of cavalry or artillery. Canby set out to attack this force while on the march although the main body of his troops had already been thrown across the river and advanced into the vicinity of the ravine up which the Confederates were moving. Preparations for the attack were made, and the skirmishers thrown forward for the purpose of drawing the fire of the Confederate batteries. Canby insisted that this manuever was accomplished and would have resulted in victory had not Pino's New Mexico Volunteers been thrown into confusion by a few, what he termed, harmless cannon shots, that it was impossible to restore them to any kind of order. This and then near approach of night rendered it inexpedient to continue the attack.

Colonel Roberts was ordered out with the cavalry in an effort to mask Canby's intentions and to keep the Confederates in their position as long as possible during which time the infantry troops were withdrawn and posted so as to prevent them from effecting a lodgment during the night at a point opposite the post, after which the cavalry and artillery crossed the Rio Grande towards Fort Craig.

At eight o'clock on the 21st scouts reported that Sibley's men were moving in the direction of the upper ford. Col. Roberts was sent with the regular and volunteer cavalry to occupy and hold the ford. Behind him came two sections of McRae's battery and two Hall's 24 pounder howitzers, supported by Brotherton's Company of the 5th, Ingraham's of the 7th and Mortimore's and Hubbell's selected companies of Volunteers. Grayson's Spy Company and five hundred mounted militia under Col. Pino and Col. Stapleton had already moved to the eastern bank of the river to watch the Confederates, threaten his flanks and rear, and to impede his movements.

As the Confederates concentrated more in the direction of the upper ford Selden's battalion, eight companies of regular infantry and one of the Colorado Volunteers, were recalled from the opposite side of the river and sent forward to re-enforce Col. Roberts. Kit Carson's eight companies of New Mexico Volunteers followed immediately afterwards. By noon all of Sibley's Brigade and Baylor's Babies (headed by Col. Pyron and now known as Pyron's Rangers), with the exception of five hundred men, was moving towards the upper ford.

Leaving two companies of volunteers, a regiment under Col. Armijo, and some detachments from the regulars to garrison Fort Craig should Sibley succeed in by-passing him, Canby ordered Pino's regiment from its position on the opposite bank, and moved with Co. G, 1st Cav. and the balance of McRae's battery, to the upper crossing. Here he was amazed to learn that the Texans had already gained the crossing prior to his advance. He endeavored to effect a lodgment that would command the ford. Major Duncan, 3rd Cavalry, in command of the immediate advance, swiftly crossed the river, dismounted his men, and in a sharp but spirited skirmish, drove the Confederates from their positions, thus enabling Col. Roberts to establish his batteries in positions to drive Sibleys men from the dense bosque in the rear of the ford.

Artillery and small arms kept up incessant firing for two hours. The Texans fought with great determination. These were under the leadership of (later General) Pyron who received reinforcements at 10 a. m., the battle having commenced at eight. Green's Regiment was next ordered to the front to support

Pyron, together with Teel's and Reily's batteries. Col. Sutton's battalion from the 7th and other troops were formed in battle line behind them. At the end of two hours the Confederates were repulsed. Shortly after the noon hour, General Sibley became ill and turned the command over to Green. At two in the afternoon Selden's command reached the field and under Col. Robert's direction immediately crossed the river to attack the Texans who had now taken up a new position. The Confederate cavalry bore down on Roberts, but he held his ground. The batteries were now crossed to the east bank of the river. Hammered by McRae, Hall, Selden and Duncan, the Confederates sought shelter behind the sand dunes. Three of their guns were put out of commission.

Earlier Green's men had formed in line on horse back, the line extending from the mesa to the river but Col. Carson's men gained the heights of the mesa and fired down upon them killing a great number of horses. The men were ordered to dismount. They all had long knives made by the blacksmiths back home. These knives were about eighteen inches long and now proved of service as the men dug into the loose sand to make fox holes as a shelter against the Federal batteries. Union gunners, annoyed by the Confederate sharpshooters hidden in the bosque or thicket of alamogordo trees, had to move the guns to the north. By noon they drove the Texans back from the bosque into the arroyo and again the Confederates took shelter behind the low ridges of sand.

In the afternoon Canby relieved Benjamin S. Roberts and ordered an encircled movement against both wings of the Texas line. The position occupied by Sibley's men was one of great natural strength. They were behind a sand ridge nearly parallel to the course of the river which sheltered them from Federal fire and concealed their movements. The Texans abandoned the train giving additional strength of five hundred men. Direct attack would prove disastrous to Canby who decided to force the left side of the line where McRae's battery was located. Selden and Carson were at the center; Hall and Duncan at the right. Pino and Valdez were held in reserve.

Canby hoped to advance the right and center, pivot to the left, enfilade his position behind the sand hill and drive the enemy from the field. Captains Lord and Claflin were ordered to hold themselves in readiness as cavalry reserve. Plympton's four companies of regulars and the Colorado Volunteers as well as Pino's regiment were ordered to cross the river as reserves for the left and as an additional support for McRae's battery. While completing these arrangements Canby was informed that the enemy had opened up on Hall's battery. Major Duncan sent such urgent and repeated messages for help that Canby sent Ingraham's Company, followed by Wingate's battalion to support him. Carson's men now entered the thick of the fighting. The Confederates abandoned the first range of sand hills and lodged behind the second. It has been said that five companies of the Second New Mexico Reg. refused to obey the command to cross the river and aid in the defense of the right wing, leaving a weakened line that Green was not long in discovering. He placed Major Henry Ragnet against this wing and concentrated the larger portion of his army in the opposite direction ordering Captain Lang and his lancers to attack the Federal left wing. This insubordination on the field of battle does not appear in the official records, although Twitchell and others mention it. A furious attempt was made to take the guns under Kit Carson and it has been said that he shot several of his men when they took to their heels under heavy fire. Captain Lang died a few days later in the military hospital (pro tem) at Socorro as a result of wounds suffered in this encounter. (Major Ragnet died on the field of battle, at Johnson's Ranch, Canoncito.)

At this moment a storming force supported by several pieces of artillery estimated at a thousand men suddenly marched from behind the ridge making for McRae's battery. Canby saw that Plympton's men were entirely unsuspicious of the new danger and made haste to close up the defense but before he could get to Plympton the Volunteers gave way communicating their panic to the regulars. The main body of Plympton's command however, rushed into the battery and engaged in a gallant and desperate attempt to repel the Confederates. The advance of the storming party was driven back, and under cover of this repulse the first fugitives from the battery crossed the river with but little loss.

Company A, 2nd Colo. Vols. was on the extreme left, new uniforms bright in the New Mexico sun. The sight of these new uniforms gave the Confederates the impression that these were raw New Mexico recruits. Mounted lancers were dispatched to impale them. Of the hundred men charging with their nine foot lances, three rode back to Green unharmed. The Coloradoans shot the horses rather than the men. Shot at that burst of speed the riders had no time to throw themselves from their mounts consequently many suffered broken arms and legs. The Texans now opened on them with cannon forcing them to retreat to the river, not without severe loss.

Lord's squadron was ordered to make a junction with Claflin's and protect the battery but finding himself in the cross fire of both Union and Confederate troops he veered to the left without making the charge. Another officer riding into the conflict at the moment called upon him to hold his ground but Lord kept on. Even abusive language failed to halt him. The capture of the artillery seemed to be the objective of the Texans. They reasoned that as long as the battery was in action the battle would be lost. Col. Greene, Col. Scurry and Major Lockridge told the men that their fight was vain unless the artillery of the enemy was silenced. They called for volunteers and fifteen hundred men resolved to storm the six hundred yards between death and victory. "Take that battery or lose the day," shouted Scurry. Out of the earth they sprang like so many grey phantoms—some on horse, some on foot, no longer hearing the commands of their officers, no longer thinking as rational men, just so many automatons feeding cannon as one in every three fell in their tracks. Yet, they inflicted heavy damage. Ninety-three Federals fell in the eight minutes that Col. Scurry led the charge. On they came—heedless of life, order, death.

First they made for Hall's battery. The reserve between flew to its support. From the moment that it made its appearance the storming party was met by a terrible fire of grape and double canister from the battery and the musketry of the infantry. The Texans, like a wounded bear, retreated to lick its wounds. Just for a moment. Revolvers in hand, knives in teeth, they now concentrated on McRae's battery. Flailing sabres and side arms they followed the devil-may-care Lockridge into the very jaws of death. Step by step they fought with fury, bravery, fate or any other name you wish to call it, seeing only the battery that they had to silence; one track minds puffing their way to McRae. At last Lockridge laid his hand on one of the big guns; took off his hat to wave it in signal of victory. McRae, already wounded, cried in a loud voice: "Shoot the ———." Those were his last words. A bullet silenced his voice forever. Nor did Lockridge escape. His body covered McRae's.

Wingate's battalion, coming up on the double quick, poured

a rapid and destructive fire on the Confederates. So great was the confusion that resulted that it looked as if the Confederate charge was in vain. But others came to their aid and the battle raged on another two hours, centered around the fallen Lockridge and McRae. To Col. Canby all seemed confusion. Rather than witness any more useless slaughter he ordered Selden to fall back slowly and cover the retreat. He sent orders to the other commanders to re-cross the river. Pino's Regiment, of which only Sena's Company and part of another could be induced to cross the river, was in wildest confusion and no efforts of their own officers or of the regular staff could induce them to restore order. Canby reported that more than one hundred men from this regiment deserted from the field. Under cover first of Selden's column and afterwards the regular cavalry, the stragglers were collected, arrangements made for the removal of the dead and care provided for the wounded; the beef herds driven in, public property collected and removed. General Sibley assumed command at seven and ordered pursuit abandoned. Col. Roberts later said that in proportion to the numbers engaged the losses were unexampled in any single battle ever fought in this continent. Canby marched on to Fort Craig.

The next morning under a flag of truce, Sibley sent Lt. Col. Scurry, Lt. Ochiltree and Captain D. W. Shannon to demand the surrender of the post. Canby refused. Scurry reported to Sibley that he thought the fort too strongly garrisoned to be captured at the time. Sibley bivouaced on the ground two days while burying the dead, caring for the wounded, and debating with himself as to the advisability of storming Fort Craig. Private Smith said years later when questioned about the burial of the Texans: "We dug a ditch four feet deep, wrapped forty of our boys in their blankets, placed them into the earth without so much as marking the spot." Lord was able to account for his action or lack of action to the satisfaction of the judges in the court martial held at Fort Craig. As official reports on both sides minimized their losses we shall never know exactly how many men fell in the action at Valverde.

Sibley left most of his wounded at Socorro and marched on to Albuquerque. Troops were sent to Cubero to gather supplies stored there for the Federals. Captain H. M. Enos, hearing that the battle of Valverde was not to favorable for Canby, and that the Texans were approaching, ordered all such provisions that might fall into their hands burned. The natives did what they could to prevent this salvaging molasses, vinegar, soap, candles, saddles, carpenter tools and furniture. It was at this time that Carleton's buildings were destroyed.

Leaving a few companies to garrison Albuquerque the Confederate commander left for Santa Fe on March 3rd. Major Donaldson evacuated the city on the orders of Canby. Governor Connelly and the Territorial Legislature moved the capital to Las Vegas to be near Fort Union. General Canby was at Socorro when the Colorado Volunteers went into action at Glorieta. Governor Connelly writing to Secretary Seward on March 11, said: "The New Mexico Militia have all dispersed and have gone to prepare their lands for the coming harvest and this is by far the best use that could be made of them." On that very day Canby at Fort Craig wrote Col. Paul: "Place no reliance on the New Mexican troops except for partisan operations, and then only when the main operations will not be affected by the result." Two months later over five hundred of the deserters from the New Mexico Volunteers availed themselves of the conditional pardon offered them; the others, fearing thy would be sought out by Canby, formed guerilla bands raiding the settlements for food, and making themselves as obnoxious as the Indians, until Pino, Sena and others induced them to behave themselves.

Col. Nicholas Pino and part of the 2nd Reg. New Mexico Militia left Fort Craig on the night of February 22nd. The Colonel's heart was heavy because of the way some of his men acted at Valverde. He knew Canby would never forgive them and he wished to get the men away from the taunts of the others. The detachment, consisting of two hundred and eighty men, passed through Socorro two days later. Six miles above Socorro was the town of Lemitar where Governor Manuel Armijo ended his days. There Pino met Lt. Cooley with letters from General O. P. Hovey, ordering him to fall back on Socorro. Pino sent Major Ribera on ahead to Polvadera another six miles beyond Lemitar, with a file of deserted volunteers and militiamen that had been picked up along the road on the march from Fort Craig. Pino himself started back to Socorro. Major C. E. Wesche and Lt. Col. Baca went on ahead to select a site for a camp. Captain Gutierrez and fourteen men were sent to Los Huesos near Luis Lopez below Socorro to graze the horses. No sooner on the road than word came that Confederates were approaching. Baca and two companies were sent to unite with Gutierrez and investigate. Lt. Co. McNeill and his Texans took their positions on an elevation southwest of Socorro. Captain Frazier was sent to go around the town and hold the road to Lemitar. About eight p. m. the Confederates fired a cannon ball over Socorro. This so alarmed the men that many felt they would have another battle on their hands when they wanted to get to their spring plowing that they took advantage of the darkness to desert. Captain Ignacio Montoya was sent to Camp Connelly with a note asking for help. Wesche and the others were ordered back from Lemitar. These were employed in going from house to house in asking the citizens to come to the aid of the militia. Don Pedro Baca, an influential citizen, was said to have remarked that the government had only proven a curse to the Territory of New Mexico and he hoped that the Texans would take possession of the town. McNeill sent an officer to the alcalde's house asking him to make arrangements for the surrender of the town, and to induce Col. Pino to surrender his men. Pino was in favor of a battle on the plain south of the town and prepared for it but so many of his men deserted that the final outcome of a parley the next morning in a home on the street near the big mission church of San Miguel resulted in Pino's resolution to visit the Confederate camp for terms of surrender. When it was noised abroad that Pino had surrendered over one hundred and fifty volunteers came out of hiding and took the neutrality oath. The Colonel and his officers were paroled. The Confederates marched on to Belen and Albuquerque and Glorieta.

NOTES AND COMMENTS

Concerning the Battle of Valverde, "The American Annual Cyclopaedia And Register of Important Events of The Year 1862," echoing Canby's sentiments, had this to say: "The slave laws of the Territory were repealed in December 1861. New Mexico during the year 1862 was the theatre of some of the most desperate and hard fought battles of the war. On the 4th of January, 1862 it was ascertained that a Texan force 1,500 strong, under the command of the Confederate General Sibley, were approaching Fort Craig two hundred miles south of Santa Fe, which Col. E. R. Canby held with about 1,000 regular troops and 1,500 volunteers. Finding the Federal force too strong to be attacked, Sibley and his Texans fell back and did not again approach Fort Craig until they had been largely re-enforced. In the last days of January having received re-enforcements which brought his force to fully 3,500, the Confederate General again advanced toward the fort. Col. Canby, hearing on the 18th of February from scouts and deserters, that the enemy were within thirty miles from Fort Craig, sallied out with a large force to meet and attack them, but could find no trace of them, and returned to the fort. On the 18th the Confederates appeared in front of the fort about 2,000 strong, but retired the same day and it was supposed commenced a retreat. Col. Canby dispatched Major Duncan with a squadron of dragoons and mounted men, to follow and harass them. The Texans retreated down the valley of the Rio Grande to a ravine about eight miles below the fort where they had a battery of eight guns strongly planted. From this, after a sharp skirmish, Major Duncan was recalled. (Duncan after the war figured largely in the civic affairs of Las Vegas. The Duncan Opera House was named for him. His grandchildren carry on the work in the Meadow City, one married to a prominent grocer whose civic pride matches that of the Duncans.) On the 19th and 20th the Texans attempted to cross the Rio Grande in order to take possession of the height opposite Fort Craig but were driven back by the Federal forces without material losses on either side. On the 21st a desperate battle was fought lasting most of the day at a place called Valverde about ten miles below Fort Craig. Early in the morning the Federal forces captured 200 mules belonging to the Texans and burned many wagons and soon crossed the Rio Grande to attack them with a battery of six pieces and two mountain howitzers. Both parties fought with the greatest desperation, the Texans to capture the battery, the deadly execution of which cut them off from access to water, for want of which they and their animals were near perishing, and the Federal troops to hold the ground they had gained. The two howitzers were under command of Lt. Hall who successfully, and with great courage, repulsed their attempts to capture them; the six gun battery was commanded by Capt McRae, and to the capture of this the main efforts of the Texans were directed. They would not have succeeded had not the New Mexican Volunteers (Col. Pino's Regiment) been panic stricken and fled in great disorder, and the regulars refused to obey their commander.

The Texans, repeatedly repulsed by the terrible fire of the battery, which was admirably served by Capt. McRae, finally came up to the charge, armed with only their long bowie knives and Colt revolvers and though more than half their number fell before they reached it, they finally succeeded in killing all the gunners and capturing the batteries. The brave McRae and Bell stood at their guns when all the rest had fled and defended themselves with their revolvers till they were killed. The loss of this battery compelled Col. Canby to fall back to Fort Craig. His loss of 62 killed and 140 wounded; that of the Confederates was very much greater, and effectively crippled their subsequent operations. They did not attempt to capture Fort Craig but proceeded up the Rio Grande to Albuquerque and Santa Fe, both of which towns were evacuated by our forces which fell back to Fort Union, one hundred miles east of Santa Fe, a strong position where the government stores for the Department were concentrated. Col. Canby intercepted and captured a force of 400 Texans on their way north to re-enforce General Sibley. Col. Slough in command of a force of 1,300 Colorado Mounted Volunteers, reached Apache Pass on the 26th of March on his way to re-enforce Col. Donelson (?—meant Canby or Gabriel at Fort Union) . . ."

Williams in his book, "With the Border Ruffians," is not very complimentary: "It was now the end of October, 1861, and General Sibley was organizing his Texan Brigade of 3,000 mounted men, or three regiments in all, for expedition to New Mexico. There it was supposed the Northern forces were weak, and that he would easily overrun the country; with the result that probably the far western States, including Arizona, and even California, might join the Confederacy. It was a foolhardy scheme to send the flower of our Texan youth on a march like this of 800 miles, into a country where they had no base of operations and could get no reinforcements, and no help, unless they met with complete success. But our leaders were crazy, I think, in those days, and believed they had the game in their own hands; so no enterprise was too rash for them to undertake. I saw the gallant force march away, with drums beating and flags flying, and every man, from the General downwards, confident of victory. Alas! A few months after, I saw the first detachment of the remnant come straggling back on foot, broken, disorganized, and in an all together deplorable condition. The tale of disaster is soon told. The march in the fall rains was a most arduous one, but the men and horses were of the best, and struggled through it bravely.... At this time the remnants of Sibley's Texan Brigade began to straggle back from New Mexico in woeful plight. It was in the end of October in the previous year that it had marched out, three thousand strong, the flower of Texan youth, with high hopes of victory; and now it was a broken, disorganized rabble, ragged and half starved. The horses had nearly all died, and such of the men as returned had tramped hundreds of miles with scarce a whole boot among them. The whole business had been shamefully mismanaged by General Sibley, who was absolutely incompetent, and yet was entrusted with a command like this!"

Ladd, in his little known book on New Mexico, has this to say about Valverde: "A serious loss overtook the Texans in the night. Their animals being imperfectly guarded, broke loose and ran wildly to the river for water. More than 200 horses and mules were captured and brought into the fort (Craig). This interfered seriously with the movements of the Confederate supply train, part of which was abandoned, while the rest was moved over the sand hills. But the wagons thus lost contained all the blankets, books, papers and camp utensils of the 4th Texan Cav. Reg., commanded by Col. Wm. R. Scurry, one of the most effective portions of their little invading army.

"On the morning of the 21st the Texans held the position assigned to them the night before, and Gen. Sibley, who had been too ill to direct the preliminary movements, now assumed command in person, taking the saddle at daybreak in order to bring on a battle at the crossing without delay. The 5th and part of the 7th Reg. of cavalry and Teel's battery were ordered to make a strong movement on the fort, while an equal force under Col. Scurry was directed to make a careful but steady approach toward the upper ford of the Rio Grande. At eight o'clock the movement of the Texans toward the river was discovered by Gen. Canby, who ordered Col. Roberts, with the U. S. regular and volunteer cavalry to occupy the ford.

"He was followed by four pieces of McRae's battery, two twenty-four-pounder howitzers, two companies of infantry and two selected companies of volunteers, while Graydon's Spy Company and 500 mounted militia ware dispatched to the eastern bank of the river to threaten the Confederate flank and watch their movements.

"No Federals were seen in the vicinity of the river when Pyron's battalion of 250 Texan cavalry reached its banks, and they proceeded to water their horses, which for twenty-four hours had been without water. The groves of pine and cottonwood in the Valverde bottomlands near the river concealed the movements of the opposing forces from each other. A portion of Col. Roberts cavalry having reached the crossing at the ford of the upper mesa, forded the river, and dismounting, posted their horses behind a sand ridge about eighty yards from the river and parallel to it. These troops were commanded by Major Duncan, who soon had his men under cover of the low sand hills, logs and scattering trees, where they began a lively skirmish with the Texans, whom they quickly drove out of the woods at the crossing, and Duncan planted his guns in the heavy timber where they could shell the Texans and command the ford by their fire.

"The Texans endeavored to ascertain the number of troops thus holding the ground, but were repelled by the sharp-shooters, and left in doubt as to the strength of the Federals. The Texans, however, soon began to concentrate on this point, the reinforcements which were coming down from the mesa. Finding that it was an exceedingly important position, a vigorous fight began to secure and hold it. On this position turned the final issue of the battle. Three attempts to dislodge Roberts and Duncan were made during the forenoon. Pyron's battalion and Scurry's 4th Reg. dismounted, for two hours fought the Federals, who effectively used their guns and howitzers to resist their assault and silence a light gun of the Texans.

"At one o'clock in the afternoon the Confederates brought up their two heavier guns, under the command of Capt. Teel, and severely pounded the Federal left. The artillery firing grew more fierce since the Federals soon had eight pieces in action, disabling all but five gunners at the Texan guns. The Texans brought up some howitzers which did effective service during the day, and Scurry held his right with two pieces till he was supported by another regiment of Texan cavalry.

"Gen. Sibley was obliged early in the afternoon to give the command to Col. Green, through exhaustion from recent sickness and the constant strain of the forenoon's battle. His troops were in a strong position behind a sand ridge, which covered his guns and men from the Federal shots, and shielded them from observation.

"Gen. Canby attempted to force the Confederate left flank by a strong force of artillery, dismounted cavalry and regular infantry, with a mounted squadron of volunteers in reserve. Pivoting on the left of his line Canby's right and center were moving up to enfilade the position of the Confederates, when Lang's 5th Texan Cav. made a charge on Duncan's Federal battalion. This attack of the lancers was bravely resisted and caused them great loss; but the Federals being brought under the fire of the Confederate guns, suffered greatly while pursuing the Texans to the second range of hills, and were forced to retreat. Carson's New Mexican troops also repelled a column of Texans, charging upon a twenty-four-pounder gun, and severely beat them. Shortly before sunset an order came to the Confederates to charge all along the line. Suddenly darting from behind the ridge, the Texans dashed with ringing shots upon McRae's battery of six guns, which was supported by columns of infantry and cavalry, from which grape, canister and musket balls were pouring upon their foes impetuously advancing upon them.

"The Texans were approaching in a circular segment half a mile long, enveloping the left, front and part of the right of the battery. Armed only with double-barrelled fowling pieces and revolvers, with daring unsurpassed, they faced the deadly hail of missiles. General Canby ordered Plympton with four companies of regulars and one company of Colo. Vols. to hasten to the support of McRae's guns. The volunteers supporting this battery on the other side gave way in panic, and rushing through Plympton's line, carried his ranks away with them in their flight. Some of the regulars, however, rushed in upon the battery and drove the storming party back for a little distance, protecting the fugitives who were crossing the river. Lord's squadron of cavalry now charged upon the Texans, who had regained the battery, and the cavalry flinched under the fire of the guns. The artillery men contended with revolvers, and the infantry with muskets, at close quarters, till half the Federals supporting the batteries had fallen, and they were driven from the ground by fresh troops of the Confederacy. But Wingate's battalion now came forward on the double-quick, making the Texans recoil before their unexpected attack and sharp firing. Reinforcements, however, opportunely arrived to steady their confused ranks. Col. Roberts had led the Federal right to far toward the sand hills, in pursuit of the Texans. His lines were broken, and Gen. Canby ordered a retreat, protecting the troops from other parts of the field as they crossed the river. Roberts skillfully directed this withdrawal from the face of the enemy. The wounded were borne back from the hills; the ammunition wagons and even the arms of the fallen men were saved. On the west bank of the river the regular troops, who had retreated from the fighting on the other side, were collected and ordered into the fort. Pino's New Mexican Vols. were in terrible disorder, and could not be rallied into line. Only one regiment had entered into the fight across the river. A hundred men had deserted from his command and fled to the hills. The regular cavalry gathered in the stragglers and, under a flag of truce, removed the dead and wounded, and the whole command were returned to the protection of the fort. . . ."

CHAPTER NINE

THE CALIFORNIA COLUMN

Part Two

IN NEW MEXICO TO THE YEAR ENDING 1862

While Confederate Colonel Scurry was fighting the Battle of Glorieta Sibley was enroute to Santa Fe where he made provision for the sick and the wounded and where he was greeted as a liberator by Southern sympathizers and by Confederate General William Pelham rcently liberated from the guard house at Fort Union. Sibley remained at Santa Fe nearly a month when he realized that supplies were not coming in as well as he expected. He decided to move the Brigade to Manzano, a village of five hundred souls, southeast of Albuquerque and known until recent days for its famous apple orchard. The name itself suggestive of the fruit, and the good crop of wheat raised there that spring, as well as the fact that it was more centrally located for expresses to Fort Craig, Fort Union, Fort Stanton and Albuquerque, Sibley decided to evacuate Santa Fe in favor of the apple village. As Sibley had made Albuquerque the supply depot of the Confederate Army of New Mexico due to the generosity, of the merchants Rafael and Manuel Armijo, who placed goods to the amount of two hundred thousand dollars at his disposal, he was now alarmed to learn that Canby decided to leave Fort Craig to advance on Albuquerque and Santa Fe. Sibley was confronted with the choice of fighting the Federals at Fort Union where they seemed to be concentrating or evacuate the country with the scant supplies on hand. Col. Scurry effected a crossing of the Rio Grande at Los Lunas after which followed the Battle of Peralta which Sibley dismissed in his report as a "day occupied at Peralta in ineffectual firing on both sides." (W. R. o. c. Series I Vol. 9, p. 510).

After nightfall he gave orders for recrossing the Brigade to the west bank of the river, the Federals being on the opposite shore. The transportation of the artillery became a problem which irritated Sibley because he was anxious to demolish the now weakened garrison at Fort Craig. Col. Green could not find a convenient crossing thus defeating Sibley's plan which likewise had to be abandoned as was the one for the lush fields of Manzano. Major Bethel Coopwood, who knew the country better than either Green or Scurry, suggested that they march through the mountains, avoid Fort Craig and strike the river again below the post. Sibley fell in with the plan and the feat over mountains with the men helping to pull the heavy guns was accomplished in ten days on seven days rations. The Confederate commander regreted that he had to leave his wounded in hospitals at Santa Fe, Socorro and Albuquerque. Now that he was abandoning New Mexico he had little good to say for it although he was all praise when he took over as head of the Confederate Army of New Mexico. " I should express the conviction, determined by some experience, that, except for its political geographical position, the Territory of New Mexico is not worth a quarter of the blood and treasure expended in its conquest. As a field of military operations it possesses not a single element, except in the multiplicity of its defensible positions. The indispensable element, food, cannot be relied on. During the past year, and pending the recent operations, hundreds of thousands of sheep have been driven off by the Navajoes. Indeed, such were the complaints of the people in this respect that I had determined, as good policy, to encourage private enterprises against that tribe and the Apaches, and to legalize the enslaving of them." (W.R. o.c.—pp. 511-12)

Over at Cubero, west of Albuquerque, Doctor F. E. Kavenaugh saw no reason why he and three other Southern sympathizers could not capture Captain Francisco Aragon and the forty two New Mexicans guarding the surgical and other stores at the post there. The entered Aragon's quarters and gave him ten minutes to make up his mind to resist or surrender. Valverde seemed to make him feel invincible. Aragon decided to turn over the post with its valuable medicines, its sixty arms, its three thousand rounds of ammunition to Dr. Kavenaugh. The men were permitted to return to Albuquerque with rifles for defense against Navajos and on the promise that once they arrived there they would report to the Confederates at that place. Richmond

Gillespie was dispatched to summon aid and Captain A. S. Thurmond with twenty-five men was sent from Albuquerque to receive the post for the Confederacy. George Gardenhier, one of Kavenaugh's men was appointed commissary; the third man, R. T. Thompson, a Virginian, was known to have Southern sympathies but Aragon never thought he would so bring them into the open. It was probably the first and last time in the history of New Mexico that a four man army took over a complete town (pop 500) and post and held it until the relief forces arrived. Sibley was prompt to make use of the supplies captured at Cubero. Wrote Sibley:

"We have been surrounded with every description of embarrassment, general and individual. Whole trains had been abandoned, and scantily provided, as they had originally been, with blankets and clothing, the men had, without a murmur, given up the little left them. More than all this, on the representation of their officers that forage could not be procured with one accord the regiment agreed to be dismounted. The battle of Glorieta was fought March 28 by detached troops, under the command of Lt. Col. Scurry, and Federal forces, principally Pike's Peakers, under the command of Col. Slough; the one having 1,000 men and the other estimated at 1,500 or 2,000. Pending the battle the enemy detached a portion of his forces to attack and destroy our supply train, which he succeeded in doing, thus crippling Col. Scurry to such a degree that he was two days without provisions or blankets. The patient, uncomplaining endurance of our men is most remarkable and praiseworthy. Our loss was thirty-three killed, thirty-five wounded. Among the killed were Majors Ragnet, Shropshire and Capt. Buckholts. Col. Scurry had his cheek twice grazed by Minnie balls, and Major Pyron had his horse killed under him. In consequence of the loss of his train Col. Scurry has fallen back upon Santa Fe. I must have re-enforcements. The future operations of this army will be duly reported. Send me re-enforcements." (W.R. o. c. p. 541)

Colonel Benjamin S. Roberts of the 5th New Mexico Infantry, re-occupied Santa Fe and Albuquerque in April, leaving a garrison in each place. On March 31st Canby was still at Fort Craig, which had become the temporary headquarters of the Military Department of New Mexico since the Confederates occupied Santa Fe, debating whether or not to pursue the Texans through the Abo Pass—Anto Chico route or by way of Albuquerque-Galisteo. He was still fuming, for his last remark to the Adjutant General was: "The New Mexico Volunteers cannot be relied on for any purpose of this kind." Yet he placed Kit Carson in charge of Fort Craig allowing him to retain seven companies of his own regiment, two of the 2nd and one of the 4th Reg. N. M. Vols., leaving also all the convalescents which were to add to his strength as they recovered. Carson was admonished to hold the post at all costs should he be attacked.

On April 12, 1862, Col. Paul wrote to Governor Connelly from Galisteo that it was safe for him to remove the seat of the government from Las Vegas back to Santa Fe. Following the engagement at Peralta this Colonel who now headed the 4th New Mexico Volunteers, was assigned to the command of the field force operating in the neighborhood of Fort Craig. Canby himself returned there leaving for Santa Fe on April 27th when he saw that it would be useless to engage the fleeing Brigade in another battle. By the first week of May he was back in Santa Fe ordering supplies for the depots at Peralta and Fort Craig should the Confederates decide to make a stand after all. Two companies of the 2nd Kansas Regiment were sent to strengthen Fort Union. Captain J. C. McFerran was also sent there to superintend the Quartermaster Department. Surgeon was told to divide his time between Santa Fe and Fort Union to administer the needs of the sick. Alarmed that more troops would be sent to New Mexico Canby wrote to Washington:

"I have learned through the newspapers that five regiments of volunteers have been ordered from the East to this Territory. If this force is intended only for the defense of New Mexico and the re-occupation of Arizona, the whole of it will not in my judgement be necessary. Two regiments, in addition to the troops now here, will, I think, be amply sufficient, if at the same time arrangements are made to severe our communication with the East by arming and garrisoning strongly the posts between Fort Union and Fort Riley. The difficulty of securing supplies of all kinds in this country makes it important that no greater force should be sent here than is absolutely necessary. No operations can be carried on with advantage from New Mexico against any part of the South as all supplies for such operations must be brought from the East, as no reliance can be placed upon the resources of this country, Arizona, or Chihuahua. . . ." (W.R. o.c. 670)

What Canby did not know was that General Lee was preparing to send two companies of cavalry to Sibley following the news of Glorieta, and that President Jefferson Davis was collecting supplies at Richmond to be sent to the Sibley Brigade. Both the President and the General sent Sibley letters of congratulation for his work with the Confederate Army of New Mexico. Unable to supply his own troops with provisions, much less the hundreds of Confederate prisoners, Canby, on May 12 ordered the Confederates paroled. Capt. J. Graydon of the New Mexico Mounted Volunteers followed in the wake of Sibley's retreating command and was amazed to learn that they marched from Nugales to Rio Puerco—over a hundred miles—in five days. Governor Connelly went to Peralta to ascertain how the Confederates treated his home and property. The two days vandalism on their part he estimated at $30,000. It was not until June 21sh that Canby made mention of the approach of the troops from California. Carleton's advance caused alarm among the remaining Texans at Fort Bliss and Fort Fillmore occupied by General Sibley and Greene respectively. Col. Steele was at Dona Ana where he was told to await further orders. Major Pyron had already left Fort Bliss for San Antonio. Wrote Canby at Santa Fe, June 11th:

"The 2nd Regiment (Greene's) is scattered in parties of fifteen or twenty along the road between Dona Ana and Franklin, committing outrages upon the inhabitants they meet upon the highway. They are almost on the point of starvation, receiving as a ration one pound and a quarter of beef and twelve ounces of flour. The Mexican population are much enraged against them on account of their rude treatment. There are no provisions to be bought in this valley, for they are not to be had. Sibley has pressed all the spare provisions on the American side of the river, and has given orders to take all the necessary transportation and provisions from the villages below. No army can subsist in this valley this year unless they bring the necessary supplies along, for there is no supply, not even of live stock, and there will be a scanty wheat crop—no live stock—to say the best of it. It is believed here that there will be a famine among the people at Mesilla, Las Cruces, Dona Ana, and Picacho. The Confederate paper money is selling at twenty cents on the dollar, and large amounts could be bought for less if there were any purchasers. Captain Hunter's company returned from Tucson. They report a large Federal force near that place when they left." (W.R. o.c. p. 678)

Lt. Col. West took possession of Tucson on May 20th, Carleton arriving later and remaining to establish law and order until July 23rd when he moved on to Las Cruces with one company of Infantry and two of Volunteer Cavalry. The Chiricahua Apaches proved hostile especially at Apache Pass where the Indians had the habit of lying in ambush for troops and teamsters coming for the fresh water found there. To eliminate this menace Carleton founded Fort Bowie at the Pass leaving a garrison of one hundred rank and file of the 5th Cal. Vol. Infantry, and thirteen rank and file of the 5th Cal. Vol. Cavalry. Thus was inaugurated the work which was to occupy the California Column for the next few years—that of Indian Fighters.

Carleton arrived at the Rio Grande, three miles above Fort Thorn, on August 7, 1862, marched fifteen miles south to the crossing known as San Diego where he found two small leaky boats. The river ran high with rather rapid flow but the men stripped off their clothes and pulled the supply wagons across the roaring stream by sheer brute strength. At San Diego crossing a larger and more reliable transport was built. The California Column, headed by Carleton, marched into Las Cruces on August 10th. Lt. Col. Eyre had already arrived. The commander of Fort Craig was kind enough to send him four companies of 5th U. S. Inf. and two companies of regular cavalry at the request of Canby but these for some unaccountable reason were marched back to Fort Craig just the day before the arrival of General Carleton. Eyre, feeling that he was under obligation to Chivington and Howe of the Colorado Volunteers, who occupied Fort Craig at the moment, placed himself under their orders. Chivington was prompt to command him not to march any further south than Las Cruces although Eyre had hoped to go on to either Fort Fillmore or Fort Bliss in an effort to overtake Col. Steele of the Sibley Brigade.

Upon the arrival of General Carleton Eyre quartered his men at Fort Thorne. It was the timely arrival of Eyre that saved Mesilla and Las Cruces from being reduced to ashes by the retreating Confederates. He had with him Captain Fritz (over whose will the Lincoln County War in which Billy the Kid starred was later to be fought) Lt. Haden and Lt. Baldwin, 1st Cal. Vol. Cav. and one hundred and forty rank and file. It was because of what happened to some of Eyre's men at Apache Pass that Carleton formulated his Indian Policy that culminated in Bosque Redondo. As the Colonel told it in his own words:

"About 12, (June 26th) I being engaged at the spring superintending the watering of animals it being necessary to dip it with tin cups—four shots were heard in the vicinity of where the horses that had been watered were being grazed under a strong guard. Immediately thereafter it was reported that Indians were in sight and that the guard had fired to give the alarm. Almost immediately thereafter it was reported that Indians were in sight waving a white flag. I at once started for them, taking with me a white flag, and Mr. Newcomb, as interpreter. At the end of about an hour I succeeded in getting sufficiently near one of them to be understood. I explained to him what I desired and asked for the chief. At this time at least seventy-five or a hundred Indians were in sight, many of them mounted on good looking horses and all of them armed with fire arms, some with rifles and six-shooting pistols. Of the latter I observed a great number and occasionally single-barreled shot-guns. When the chief came forward I told him we were Americans, and that our Great Captain lived in Washington; that we wished to be friends of the Apaches; that at present I was only traveling through their country; and desired he would not interfere with my men or animals; that a great captain was at Tucson with a large number of soldiers; that he wished to have a talk with all the Apache chiefs and to make peace with them and make them presents. He professed a great desire to be friendly with the Americans, and assured me that neither my men nor animals should be molested. He asked for tobacco and something to eat. I gave him all that could possibly be spared, and we parted, with a request on his part that I would meet him at the same place at sunset. On my return it was reported to me that three of the men were missing. A party of thirty were at once sent out in the vicinity where the firing was heard, and after an hour's search the bodies of the missing men were found stripped of all their clothing and two of them scalped. Each was shot through the chest with fire-arms and lanced through the neck. They were victims of their own imprudence, the entire command having been repeatedly warned by me not to wander from camp. It appears they had started, leading their horses from the spring where the watering was to be done, over the ridge into another gulch, when they came on the Indians and were murdered. The Indians succeeded in getting one horse. When the bodies of the murdered men were found instant pursuit of the Indians was made, some of whom were seen on a hill half a mile distant; but being unable to come up with them a return to camp was ordered, carrying in the dead bodies, which were buried, the entire command being present. The animals now being all watered, or as much as could be obtained for them, and there being very little grass in the pass, at 6 p.m. left camp; marched out and made a dry camp on the plain two miles beyond the canyon. At eleven p.m. a volley of six or eight shots was fired into camp, wounding Acting Assistant Surgeon Kittredge in the head and killing one horse at the picket line." (W.R. o. c. pp. 586-587)

Of course the three were interested in availing themselves of the opportunity of locating a rich strike to which they would return following the war. It has been said that when Carleton went on his expedition to the Gran Quivira the purpose was actually a quest after hidden treasure. Many of the California Volunteers complained that the reason they did so much digging in New Mexico was in the hopes that they could find a gold vein or silver mine for General Carleton or other officers. Many used all their free time as prospectors without benefit of Carleton or any other officer. The probability of gold or copper kept many in New Mexico for the balance of their lives.

Eyre reoccupied Fort Thorn on July 5 and immediately sent Captain Fritz to Col. Steele to ask him what prisoner Canby had that he wanted in exchange for Captain McCleave. White who was captured at the Pima was released. Two lieutenants of Steel's regiment were given in exchange for McCleave who was dispatched to Fort Craig for supplies. Eyre left Fort Thorn on July 13th for San Diego. He now had the added strength of Captain Howland's 3rd U. S. Cavalry troops of one hundred men. Chivington sent orders from Fort Craig that he was to scout the area to find out all he could about the strength of the remaining Confederates for Canby decided he would not come to Fort Thorn until he could come in force. Chivington himself was ordered to Santa Barbara with sixteen companies of infantry and a battery of six four-pounder guns and two 24-pounder howitzers and an additional cavalry force to support the advance of General Carleton and to cooperate with the forces under his command in a united effort to re-occupy the Mesilla valley.

This hurt Eyre who could read between the lines that Chivington was telling him to stay where he was (back at Fort Thorn) and leave the glory of advancing on Mesilla and Fort Fillmore to the commander of the Colorado Volunteers who had been appointed commander of Fort Craig and the Southern Military District of New Mexico by Canby. This position was later to be given West by Carleton. Consulting with Capt. Fritz, Capt. Howland and Capt. Tilford, Eyre, on their advice, decided that he was not disobeying orders if he marched on Mesilla despite Chivington. He sent wagonmaster Black with some men to San Diego to ascertain whether or not the river had receeded enough to get the train of thirteen wagons across at that point. Black came back with a favorable report and on August 15 Eyre marched his entire command to San Diego. The boat to be used in the crossing was constructed at Fort Thorn and hauled eighteen miles by mule train. Meantime Col. Howe was appointed commander of the Southern Military District of New Mexico and his first order was to have Lt. F. Van Vliet intercept Eyre before he made the crossing with the command that he was not to cross until further orders. But the message arrived too late. Eyre was already across the Rio Grande. McCleave arrived with supplies from Fort Craig and Eyre decided to push on to Robledo or Dona Ana to await further orders and to write an apologetic note to Howe explaining that he had not received Van Vliet's note in time. Finding neither food for the men nor forage for the animals at Dona Ana Eyre decided to push on to Las Cruces. There the officers occupied the houses left vacant by the fleeing Southern sympathizers who expected reprisals at the hands of the California Volunteers. Here also he found that a goodly portion of Confederates were still at Fort Bliss (Franklin) gathering all the government property which they had secreted and planning to sell it to a prominent citizen of El Paso. Eyre was all for marching on Fort Bliss but was hindered by a positive order from Col. Howe who told him to remain at Las Cruces until further notice. Eyre did take down the Confederate flag at Las Cruces and supplemented it with that of the United States, as he did at Fort Thorn, Fort Fillmore, Mesilla and Fort Bliss.

At Las Cruces Carleton caught up with Eyre who gave him a full report of his activities from the monent he left Tucson for which Carleton recommended that Washington military officials give him his own regiment. Canby wrote Carleton at Las Cruces that he agreed to furnish the California Column all the subsistence stores they would need together with $30,000 subsistence funds. He hoped that Carleton would agree with him that all the United States regular troops be removed from New Mexico and that California be the supply base to furnish volunteers for the duration. He even gave Carleton the right to station his troops where he saw fit in Arizona and Southern New Mexico. Col. Steele ordered the sale of all public property that could not be carried back to San Antonio. As a result he was able to raise $830 in specia and enough food to see his men safely home. He left the money and a letter for Carleton telling him that he had to leave his wounded behind, the money to be spent on their behalf, which he did. Carleton next left for Franklin (present El Paso) where he found a surgeon of the Confederate Army and twenty-five sick and disabled soldiers. These, according to Canby's instructions, he took prisoner. Next he went to El Paso, Mexico, to recover twelve wagons of stores hidden there by the Texans. These were sent to the newly established depot at Mesilla. Taking three companies of cavalry with him Carleton marched down the Rio Grande valley to restore the confidence of the people, treating them not as marauders, but paying a fair price for all the supplies he bought of them. On August 22nd they entered Fort Quitman where they hoisted the Stars and Stripes. Captain John C. Cremony of Co. B, 2nd Cal. Vol. Cav. was placed in charge pro tem. Capt. Shirland, like Cremony, a resident of Sacramento, of the 1st Cal. Vol. Cav. was directed to proceed another one hundred and forty miles to Fort Davis to re-occupy it in the name of the United States Government. At Las Cruces Carleton issued these orders:

"Commanders of towns will at once establish sanitary regulations, and require them to be observed by the inhabitants and by the troops, so far as the policing of the streets and the keeping of their dwellings, quarters, stores, corrals, etc. in a state of cleanliness may be necessary to their health and comfort. Frequent inspections will be made by commanding officers or by a medical officer under his direction, to see that in all respects these regulations are followed. It is expected that all of the inhabitants living along the Rio Grande southward from the Jornada del Muerto to Fort Bliss, in Texas, will, at the earliest practicable moment, repair their dwellings and clean up their streets. The people may now rest assured that the era of anarchy and misrule—when there was no protection to life and property—when there was the plunder of the wealthy, when the poor were robbed and oppressed, when all were insulted and maltreated, and when there was no respect for age or sex—has passed away; that now, under the sacred banner of our country, all may claim and receive their just rights. Therefore let the burden of anxiety be lifted from their hearts; and once more let them pursue their avocations with cheerfulness, and with all the confidence that the protection which now shelters them from injustice will always be stronger in proportion as they shall be powerless to protect themselves." (W.R. o.c. p. 602)

While orders came for General Carleton to relieve Brig. Gen. Canby as Commander of the Department of New Mexico, on August 26th, it was not until September 18th that Canby turned over the office to his successor. Carleton sat down and wrote out a list of appointments and office hours. The period of enlistment for Companies D and H, 1st Inf. Cal. Volunteers; Companies E and C, 1st Cav., Cal. Volunteers having expired Carleton asked Col. Rigg to have them recalled from the San Marcial and other areas where they were busily engaged in trailing Apaches, to Fort Craig either for discharge or re-enlistment. All re-enlisted. It is interesting to note that Carleton showed no partiality to his California men, when it came time to appoint commanders to the various military posts. While West was given the honor as head of the Southern District at Mesilla, Lt Col. T. H. Dodd, 2nd Colo. Vols. was appointed commander at Fort Marcy in Santa Fe; Major A. H. Mayer, 1st N. M. Vols. at Fort Garland in Colorado; Capt. P. W. L. Plympton, 7th U. S. Inf. at Fort Union; Capt. W. R. Shoemaker retained the Ordnance at the same post; Capt. H. B. Bristol, 5th U. S. Inf. took over at Peralta; Capt. J.C. Shaw, 1st N. M. Vols. at Cubero; Col. Christopher (Kit) Carson, 1st N. M. Vols. at Los Lunas; Major Arthur Morrison, 1st N. M. Vols. at Polvadera; Capt. J. D. Sena, 1st N. M. Vols. at Galisteo; Capt. Samuel Archer, 5th U. S. Inf. at Fort Craig; Capt J. Updegraff, 5th U. S. Inf., the area near Tucson; Major E. W. Wynkoop, 1st Colo. Vols., the area near Fort Craig; Capt H. R. Selden, 5th U. S. Inf., at Fort Wingate to releive Major E. W. Eaton. Col. West received the resounding title of Commander of the District of Arizona. On September 21st Carleton wrote a note of thanks to the California Column regretting that his new position would remove him from immediate association with the troops. In October Col. Carson was ordered to Fort Stanton to quiet the Indians in that area. Canby went East to other fields. A California Volunteer, Captain John C. Cremony, receives the honor with Capt. Updegraff, as co-founder of Fort Sumner, on the Pecos river, having been commanded to do so by General Carleton in the fall of 1862.

The balance of the year 1862 was spent in Indian campaigns in New Mexico and Arizona. The Volunteers accustomed themselves to life in New Mexico, many becoming acquainted with native women whom they married. Sam Zimmerly started the Zimmerly dynasty in Socorro. His grandchildren have gone far afield in railroading and petroleum engineering. The record of his exploits may be found in the family archives at Socorro. Every available opportunity was taken by the Volunteers to obtain furloughs secretly for the purpose of digging in the hills for rich strikes. Many of the miners and prospectors who worked at Baldy, Bland, Elizabethtown, Magdalena, Shakesphere, Silver City and other famous gold fields marched with Carleton from California to save New Mexico for the Union. The history of the California Column is so inter-woven with that of the Regulars, the New Mexico Volunteers and the New Mexico Militia for the balance of the war that the rest of their history is told by years rather than by separating each command and its particular feat or service. As related in a previous chapter the work of the Column in Arizona beyond the time it separated from New Mexico is not our concern here. True, many of the men complained bitterly that they had entered service to fight the Confederates, not Indians. Gradually factions pro and con Carleton made themselves heard and found champions. As much as they wished, in many instances, to re-enlist elsewhere where troops were actually employed against Confederates, a way was always found to retain them in New Mexico.

What many of them did not know was that never for a moment did some die-hards like Col. Hart of the Confederacy, Baird, Mculloch, Magruder, Scurry, Hubbell, and others never gave up hope until the last shot was fired that New Mexico could be captured for President Jefferson Davis. When Major-General John B. Magruder assumed command at San Antonio, replacing Brigadier-General Herbert (November 29, 1862) he addressed all letters from Headquarters of The District of Texas, New Mexico and Arizona, never once admitting that Arizona and part of New Mexico no longer flew the banner of the Stars and Bars. From his first day in office he made plans to arm another brigade to take Santa Fe from Carleton and his California Column. This Carleton knew but kept to himself and his staff. The men were kept in trim fighting Indians to be in shape for the day when Baird and his Arizona Brigade would make the move to wrest New Mexico from the Union.

※ ※ ※

NOTES AND COMMENTS

Henry R. Selden (1816-1865)—A native of Vermont, he graduated from West Point in 1839. Took part in the Mexican War. Was stationed on the frontier until the Civil War. Took active part in action at Valverde. While in command of Fort Union let a cold go too long. Died at the post hospital February 2, 1865. Fort Selden was named in his honor.

Peter William Livingston Plympton (1821-1866)—A native of Missouri, he graduated from West Point in 1843. Served in the Mexican War and on the frontier. Was at Fort Marcy, Santa Fe, when the Civil War broke out. Served with distinction at Valverde. Was commander at Fort Union in 1862. Died at Fort Marcy, August 11, 1866.

Benjamin Wingate—A native of Indiana. He served in the Mexican War. Died as the result of a wound sustained at Valverde. Fort Wingate honors him. It was formerly known as Fort Fauntleroy.

William Beck Ochiltree (1811-1867)—A county on the Texas plains honors him. Perryton is the county seat. He was a lawyer from North Carolina, serving the Republic of Texas in many capacities. Ill health forced him to resign from the Confederate Army in 1863.

Oliver P. Hovey—Seems to have come to Santa Fe about the time the American troops marched over Raton Pass. He was a journalist and printed a small newspaper for the soldiers. He also printed the Kearny Code. He was still active in newspaper work when the Civil War broke out. He also served in the Territorial Legislature. He became a general in the Territorial Militia. He also had a law office in Santa Fe serving for a time as a judge. He was quite popular with the Americans and the Spanish speaking of the city, being one of the first to come to their defense against segregation.

Nicolas Pino (1819-1896)—He was the son of Pedro Bautista Pino, the only person ever to represent New Mexico in the Courtes of Spain. Nicolas was well educated, lived a full life, having witnessed the Revolt of 1837, the Taos Rebellion, the Mexican War and the Civil War. Besides the active part he took in the Civil War as one of the leaders of the New Mexico Volunteers, he served for many years in the New Mexico legislature. He did much to promote the cause of education and alleviate the condition of the poor. He is buried in Galisteo, New Mexico.

Colonel Francisco Pera (1830-1913)—Born in Los Padillas, New Mexico, January 9, 1830. Attended the Sena school in Santa Fe but, it closed when the teacher went to join Manuel Armijo in suppressing the Rebellion of 1837. After furthering his education in the Benevidez school at Los Ranchos de Albuquerqe, he went back to Bernalillo to teach his younger brothers and sisters. Went to college in St. Louis, Missouri. He, Aubrey and others drove a herd of 50,000 head of sheep to California in 1853. He was stationed in Albuquerque after enlisting in the Union Army, and commanded the garrison there in the winter of 1861-62. He took part in the battle of Glorieta. Shortly afterwards he was elected to Congress. He was sitting near Abraham Lincoln when the President was shot in the Ford Theatre. He married Dolores Otero on March 15, 1851 and had eighteen children, many of whom died in infancy. His wife died in 1866. He married Gabriela Montoya in 1875. Of this union eighteen children were also born, ten of them surviving their father. He objected to Kirby Benedict's treatment of General Carleton and gave his wholehearted support to the unpopular general. This cost him his seat in Congress. He failed to win re-election. Perea ranks with Donaciano Vigil as among the great figures of New Mexico history. It was the work of such men as Vigil and Perea who saved New Mexico for the Union.

Benjamin S. Roberts—Sufficiently covered in the text.

John C. Cremony—Sufficiently covered in the text. He is best known for his book "Life Among the Apaches" published in New York in 1868. He prided himself on his knowledge of Apache which he said was acquired from the prisoner, Red Sleeves. As the Smithsonian gave General Carleton credit for the Apache language manuscript, Cremony commented that it was to be expected since Carleton was a General and he was only a Captain.

J. Shaw came to New Mexico in 1852. He established the Baptist church in Socorro but for some reason he was dropped from the rolls for disobedience. He took to the study of law, served in the N. M. Vols. during the war, and returned to Socorro to his law office. He was twice married.

Captain Updegraff—Sufficiently covered in the text.

W. R. Shoemaker—William Rawlee served in the Ordnance Department from 1841 to 1866. The village of Shoemaker between Watrous and Optimo honors him.

Eaton W. Eaton—Born in New York State October 10, 1827. He attended various schools before coming West for gold in 1849. Taking one look at Santa Fe he decided to go no further. He obtained a job clerking with a mercantile concern. He married Marcelina Chavez and bought a land grant near Galitseo. During the Civil War he served under Kit Carson. He moved to Socorro in 1875, where he opened a drug store. He took charge of the Vigilantes to rid Socorro of undesirables. He engaged in mining activities at Kelly, and in a mercantile business at San Marcial. His family returned to Socorro after the San Marcial flood of 1928.

Captain Skillman—Came to New Mexico with Col. Doniphan in 1846. He was sent as a spy to Chihuahua and also took part in the engagement at Sacramento. Had a business in Mesilla and took up for the Confederacy. Sought to raise troops with Baird and Scurry to be known as the Confederate Army of Arizona to re-capture Tucson and Mesilla for the Confederacy.

Henry Whiting Stanton—Killed by Apaches while on a scouting trip through the Sacramento Mountains. Fort Stanton honors him. Date of death: January 19, 1855.

Albert H. Pfeiffer (1822-1881)—Born Friesland, Holland, October 22, 1822. His father was a Lutheran minister; his mother a native of Scotland. He was twenty-two when he came to America. He entered the army serving along the New Mexico frontier, using his spare time to assist in newspaper work. In 1852 he married a girl from Abiquiu, being stationed at the military post there for some time. Three children were born of this marriage. He was in command of Fort McRae when he took ill and hearing of the curative powers of the hot springs some six miles from the garrison he took his wife, some servant girls and a small escort to the springs. No sooner in the water when the Apaches attacked. The soldiers, surprised and stunned, took to their heels to seek cover. A poisoned arrow entered the Captain's left leg and side. He managed to swim, escape, obtain medical aid. The Indians killed his wife. He first saw the Del Norte country in Colorado while out on a scouting expedition in 1851. He decided he would come back to live there some day. After the war he built his home here. His old wound bothering he finally succumbed April 6, 1881. He often went to Pagosa Springs in Colorado for the medicinal value of the waters. He was adopted by the Utes and known to them as Ta-ta—Father—a name also given Lucien B. Maxwell.

F. McCabe—Sufficiently covered in the text.

Red Sleeves—Sufficiently covered in the text.

J.C. Knapp (1805-1888)—A native of Cayuga county, New York, he became a Methodist minister. He was instrumental in the founding of several theological schools and colleges. He became a missionary in Wisconson working mainly among the Indians of the Six Nations at Green Bay. He became a journalist, politician and lawyer. In 1861 he was appointed a judge of the New Mexico Territorial Supreme Court. His difficulties with General Carleton caused him to be removed from office. He died in Florida in July 1888.

A. H. French—Settled down to ranching after the war. He wrote a book telling of his experiences. Black Jack Ketchem is said to have worked on his ranch.

Emil Fritz—For more about him see the chapters on the N. M. Vols. & Gen. Carleton.

Jose D. Sena—Sufficiently covered in the text.

L. D. Murphy—Best known for his part in the Lincoln County War.

H. A. Greene (also appears in records as Green) Sufficiently covered in text.

Irvin McDowell (1818-1885) Sufficiently covered in text.

George Brinton McClellan (1826-1885) Sufficiently covered in text.

Captain Deus—Sufficiently covered in text.

General Crocker—Sufficiently covered in text.

William Quantrell (c. 1816-1864)—A guerrilla best known for his Lawrence, Kansas, raid. He was killed in Kentucky in 1864.

Daniel B. Haskell—Sufficiently covered in the text.

John Pope (1822-1892)—A native of Illinois, he graduated from West Point in 1842. Served in the Mexican War. In 1853 he was in New Mexico, employed in surveys for the projected Pacific railway. He explored the plains and the Rockies. He was the first to use to advantage artesian wells to irrigate western arid land. He was in command of the Federal forces in the second engagement at Bull Run (Manassas). He died in Ohio, September 23, 1892.

Kirby Benedict—Judge Benedict, active in the New Mexico Territorial Supreme Court for many years, was one of the organizers of the New Mexico Historical Society. Some of his pronouncements were rather dramatic. He insisted that New Mexico could get along without the aid of the California Volunteers. It was one way of making the N. M. Vols. and N. M. Militia more self reliant.

Sylvester Mowry—Sufficiently covered in the text. (1830-1871)

Ben C. Cutler (1834-1867)—Born in Mass., raised in Brooklyn where his father was Episcopalian minister. Benjamin came to California in the hopes of a rich strike. Served as Carleton's adjutant general. Died in Santa Fe Oct. 18, 1867.

Lt. Col. Francisco Chavez—Son of Don Mariano Chavez who was once governor of New Mexico under the Mexican flag. Born in 1831, Francisco studied medicine in the United States but never took up practice. Don Mariano's widow, the daughter of Don Pedro Perea of Bernalillo, became Governor Connelly's wife. Francisco served in the Territorial Legislature and passed laws to ameliroate the condition of the working classes. He sought to destroy imprisonment for debt except in the case of fraud. He was well known to Lucien B. Maxwell, Kit Carson, and others of note in his day.

CHAPTER TEN

THE CAMPAIGNS OF 1863

Governor Connelly summed up the work the California Volunteers had cut out for themselves when he wrote Secretary Seward that nothing new transpired in the Territory at the moment except the Navajo War just beginning. It was to the credit of General Carleton that he was able to place twelve hundred men in the field to hunt down the Indians, which were all he could spare due to the necessity of keeping a garrison at Fort Craig, Pinos, Albuquerque, Fort Stanton, Fort Garland, and Fort Union. Magruder, Scurry, Hart, Baird, Burgess and Skillman were interested in only one thing as the New Year dawned: The return of Arizona with New Mexico to the fold of the Confederacy. Carleton would keep the men disciplined and prepared under the guise of Indian wars.

Kit Carson was selected to lead the men against the Navajo following his good work against the Mescaleros in the fall and winter of 1862. Actually, Carleton was worried about the battery of artillery the father-in-law of Simeon Hart sold to the Mexican government at Chihuahua with the stipulation that these and other guns were to be sold back to the Confederates when they again marched against New Mexico. The General wrote a letter of protest to the Governor of Chihuahua demanding to know why a friendly power purchased arms of an enemy of the Federal Government. The protest was ignored. There was no other recourse than to re-occupy Fort Stanton, chase Indians and watch the border. He wrote to Colonel Carson:

"Enclosed you will find a confidential communication to Col. West, commanding the District of Arizona; . . . it directs him to send two expeditions against the Mescalero Indians, starting them on the 15th of next month (November). I desire you to send one of your mounted companies down to the junction of the Rio Hondo with the Pecos, to act as an outpost to this country, to keep scouts well down the river toward Delaware Creek, to see that no force advances up the Pecos from the direction of Fort Lancaster, in Texas, without your having timely notice of the fact, so that you can send me word.

"As your scouts from this company come near the mouth of the Penasco they will doubtless find plenty of Mescaleros. It was near that point where Captain H. W. Stanton was killed by them. In this case you could, if you thought it advisable, move the company down to the mouth of the Penasco, to produce an impression upon the Indians; at the same time guard the approaches to New Mexico by the way of the Pecos; but under no circumstances will it leave the valley of the river unwatched. The other three companies you can divide as you please, but with these you will make war upon the Mescaleros and upon all other Indians you may find in the Mescalero country, until further orders. All Indian men of the tribe are to be killed whenever and wherever you can find them; the women and children will not be harmed, but you will take them prisoners and feed them at Fort Stanton until you receive other instructions about them. If the Indians send in a flag and desire to treat for peace say to the bearer that when the people of New Mexico were attacked by the Texans, the Mescaleros broke off their treaty for peace and murdered innocent people and run off their stock; that now our hands are untied and you have been sent to punish them for their treachery and their crimes; that you have no power to make peace; their chiefs and twenty of their principal men must come to Santa Fe to have a talk there; but tell them fairly and frankly that you will keep after their people and slay them until you receive orders to desist, from these headquarters; that this making of treaties for them to break whenever they have an interest in breaking them will not be done anymore; that time has passed by; that we have no faith in their promises; that we believe that if we kill some of their men in fair, open war they will be apt to remember that it will be better for them to remain at peace than to be at war. I trust that this severity, in the long run, will be the most humane course that could be pursued toward these Indians.

"You observe that there is a large force helping you. I do not wish to tie your hands by instructions. The whole duty can be summed up in a few words: The Indians are to be soundly whipped, without parleys or councils except as above. Be careful not to mistake the troops from below for Texans. If a force of rebels come you know how to annoy it—how to stir up their camps and stock by night; how to lay waste the prairies by fire; how to make the country very warm for them and the road a difficult one. Do this, and keep me advised of all you do." (Santa Fe, October 12, 1862 W. R. Oo c. p. 579)

In his letter to West, Carleton notified the Colonel that he ordered Carson to re-occupy Fort Stanton, asking him to work with him yet independent of him. Captain McCleave was to take one company of California Volunteers plus his own company and twenty native spies and guides for an expedition against the Mescaleros. They were not to return prior to December 31st. Captain Roberts was to lead another expedition. He was to seek out twenty first-rate Pueblo Indian guides at Socorro del Sur, and San Elizario who were to be commanded by Don Gregorio Garcia of San Elizario while on the march. Seventy-five pack saddles were shipped down from Fort Union for the use of the two expeditions. These movements were to remain military secrets. Carleton wanted neither the Texans nor the Indians to know of these plans. Captain Willis, with a portion of his company, and Lt. Whittemore were to remain behind to guard Hart's Mill.

Col. Carson had some very able and capable men on his staff: Capt. A. B. Carey, of the regular army; Lt. R. S. Barrett, of the Cal. Vols., who served as chief commissary; Lt. L. G. Murphy, Adjutant, 1st N. M. Vols. He was the first volunteer to sign up at Fort Union when the war broke out. His Civil War record was better than his record later on in the Lincoln County War. Major Joseph Cummings, 1st N. M. Vols; Major Arthur Morrison, 1st N. M. Vols.; Dr. Allen F. Peck, 1st N. M. Vols. was surgeon; Rev. Domacio Talarid replaced Padre J. A. Martinez as chaplain mostly because this latter was having difficulties with ecclesiastical authorities at the time and because Carson and he could not get along, although both were of the same faith. Nine companies, an aggregate of seven hundred and thirty-six men made up the balance of the command. The following captains headed companies: F.P. Abreu; E. Everett; J. D. Sena; J. Birney (A B C D); J. L. Barbey (G); A. H. Pheiffer (H); J. Thompson (K) F. McCabe (L); C. Deus (M). Carson founded Fort Canby near the Navajo country which would be his supply depot and Pueblo Colorado, west of Fort Defiance, his headquarters.

The first contingent of Mescaleros arrived at Fort Stanton on January 4, 1863. Carson was informed that one hundred members of the tribe would arrive within the next week to try out the reservation plan Carleton now had in mind. Sick, beaten, hunted, starved, Chiefs Mancos Son, Se-ha-thi, Ojo Blanco, Janero, Viejo, Janero Pablo, Janero Francisco, Jose la Pas, surrendered their people at the post. However, they availed themselves of every opportunity to kill soldiers as was proven when two privates from Co. M, 1st N. M. Vols., left picket duty in favor of a hunting expedition, orders to the contrary notwithstanding. Attacked by Indians, one named Strunk, was killed.

The Gila Apache Chief, Red Sleeves, became a controversial figure, not because of his life, but rather because of his tragic death. As early as 1852 he had dealings with Greiner and Sumner at Acoma where he refused to sign a treaty because he declared that no sooner would he sign than New Mexicans would take the field against him. The Indian was known to Gerard Kearny with whom he had made a treaty several years before. Red Sleeves offered to attach his Gilas with some of Kearny's men and capture Chihuahua and Sonora for America. Kearny gently refused the offer which offended the Indian who promptly declared that the Americans were not the brave fighters they made themselves out to be. With Red Sleeves free to roam the Miembres and the Gila, Carleton felt that travel between New Mexico and Arizona would never be safe. He would breathe easier if the Indian were on a reservation. Several expeditions sent against him failed to capture him. Eventually he was taken into custody near Pinos Altos, by Capt Shirland of the Cal. Vols., and marched to Fort McLane where he was imprisoned. The guards reported that between midnight and one a. m. he made three attempts to escape, consequently, they were compelled to shoot him (January 17, 1863). *The Santa Fe New Mexican* for April 14, 1865, carried this interesting item by Judge J. G. Knapp of Mesilla, who not only objected to Carleton's Indian Policy but to the man himself becoming so vitrolic that he had to be removed from office:

"But little more than two years have passed since Mangas Coloradas (Spanish for Red Sleeves), the most powerful of all the Apache chiefs, voluntarily came into one of your forts and agreed to deliver himself and a band of Apaches to your control. He was confined in the guardhouse. That night he was aroused from his sleep. Some say that a soldier threw something and hit him; others that he was punched with a pole, and because he raised himself up to see what had disturbed his sleep, he was instantly perforated with bullets and killed. The next morning at dawn his lodge was attacked, and his wife and daughter shared the fate of husband and father. Not content with having killed a prisoner of war without cause your soldiers tore the scalp from his head and severed his head from his body and after boiling the flesh exhibited the skull as a badge of honor, while the scalps of himself, his wife and daughter are worn as ornaments. This single violation of all the laws of civilized warfare has kept from your possession the most powerful of all Apache bands. He may have been as cruel and wicked as he is reported to have been but that will not justify such treatment after he had voluntarily placed himself in the possession of your troops. . . ."

The hunt after Indians continued. Captain Shirland tracked down some Apaches to their rancheria, surprised and defeated the warriors, killing nine and wounding many more. What added fury to the Captain's attack was the fact that he saw some mules stolen from the Apache Pass post in the Indian remuda. The rancheria and all that pertained to it was destroyed.

During that same month of January Captain Wm. McCleave started from Fort McLane on an expedition to the Pinos Altos mines where he came upon some of Red Sleeves warriors. Eleven were killed in the attack that followed. It was in this encounter that the chief's wife was wounded. Some horses were captured but were in such poor shape for traveling that the Captain decided to leave them with the miners. Shortly afterwards Indians attacked two hunting parties of Co. A, 5th Inf. Cal. Vols., in the vicinity of the mines, killing Private William Hussey and wounding Sergeant T. B. Setton. The Indian loss was twenty killed and fifteen wounded.

The Navajos vied with the Apaches in giving the California Volunteers trouble. They ranged over a wide area including in their raids each new settlement as it was founded—San Miguel del Bado, Paraje (old Fra Cristobal at the end of the jornada from Socorro), Alamillo, La Joya, Contreras, San Acasio, Las Vegas—to the resentment of the Apaches who considered these places as rancherias being cultivated for them to swoop upon at will as they needed produce and live stock. Plundering the settlements was an established practice long before Carleton marched his men in from California. Because both tribes took their turns in divesting the native of his livelihood, the General, who should have known better since he was an old frontier fighter himself, much of his experience being here in New Mexico, had the impression that both tribes spoke the same language and could live very well together on the reservation he planned for them. Forcing the Navajos and Apaches to live at Bosque Redondo did more to defeat his purpose that the diatribes of Judge Knapp, the editor of the *Santa Fe New Mexican,* Sylvester Mowry, Magoffin and Hart who were opposed to Carleton's very breathing. The reason why neither Navajo nor Apache never wiped out any of the settlements was because they looked upon the native as a natural herdsman and farmer who would raise stock and produce for him to take at will, for he was as stubborn and determined as he was hardy and tireless. No loss was great enough to drive him off his land. He had migrated from Santa Fe, Albuquerque, Belen, Sabinal, Socorro, Los Corrales, Taos, Luis Lopez to till the land the government gave him and no Indian was going to drive him off it. Drought, disease, rust, the elements could not do it—he would be darned if he would let the Indians succeed where nature had failed. Which the Indian enjoyed. He knew on which side his bread was buttered. Now these soldiers were here to cut off this continuous supply. Neither Apache nor Navajo would permit it. Their very survival was at stake. They had depredated too long to make their own living of the soil.

In February, a party of Navajos encircled Lemitar and drove off four thousand sheep. About twelve miles above this town, on the same trail, they stopped at Alamillo (Santa Ana de Alamillo near San Acasio on the Rio Grande moved to higher ground after the war following a flood that almost wiped out the village.) to add two thousand more to the ever increasing herd—having already plundered San Antonio, Luis Lope and Socorro. Angered at the daring of the maruaders, Luis Maria Baca ran to the padre at the San Miguel church in Socorro, petitioned and obtained permission to ring the large bell, asking for volunteers of the crowd that assembled. The Indians were pursued to the Sierras Oscuras where they were forced to make a stand. Three were killed, several wounded, and the sheep were headed home, wagging their tails behind them. Resting a week to recover from the shock of their loss, they headed for Pope's Artesian Well, rode on another twenty-five miles where they found six thousand sheep which they appropriated without much ado, then started back to Socorro and Lemitar to get back the one they lost in the

Oscuras. In addition to the sheep they took three hundred head of horses. Above San Lorenzo de Chamisal near Sabinal they took two thousand more sheep. Again Baca rounded up men—Socorro, Polvadera, Sabinal, Lemitar, Luis Lopez, San Antonio. Just south of San Antonio along the Jornada the Indians were surrounded and the stock recovered. One thing they were discovering: The native was becoming increasingly more determined in keeping his stock and produce. The day that the tribesmen could take at will was coming to an end.

On March 18, two expressmen traveling from Fort Stanton to Fort Union came upon a group of Navajos leading a large flock of sheep in the direction of Fort Defiance. Realizing they were discovered the Indians left the live stock to give pursuit to the two fleeing soldiers who would certainly give the alarm at Fort Union if permitted to escape. Instead, the men took the trail back to Fort Stanton where they reported to Captain F. P. Abreu who immediately dispatched Lt. D. McAllister and thirty men, with ten days rations, to run off the Navajos and bring in the stock. The Indians succeeded in covering their tracks in the Oscuras nor was the Lieutenant able to tell what happened to the sheep. He returned to Fort Stanton empty handed.

To prove that the presence of the soldiers meant little or nothing to them the Gila Apaches chose the afternoon of March 22 to make a raid on the public herd at Fort West. When they left the post was minus sixty head of horses. McCleave, now a Major, took Lt. French, Lt. Latimer, forty men of Co. A, twenty-five of Co. B, fourteen of Co. C, of the Cal. Vols., trailing the Indians westward, then down the Gila to the Rio Negro where he found a rancheria. Thirty of the men were mounted on the only serviceable animals the Indians failed to take. The mounted Volunteers were placed under the command of Lt. Latimer; the Major led the others. Latimer's men rode twelve miles down the left side of the stream. There they rested. All during this time the rain came down in torrents. It was an uncomfortable night to say the least. It was a determined lot that attacked at dawn. McCleave's men, hidden in the bluffs about the village, poured lead, thick and fast, into the lodges of the thoroughly startled, still slumbering, Indians.

Within twenty minutes the Indians acknowledged themselves to be whipped. Twenty-five of them lay dead; those that could flee did so. The Volunteers rounded up all the horses they could find, both government and Indian. The lodges, provisions, fields in back of the village were put to the torch. Private J. Hall of Co. B was the only Volunteer wounded in the fight. Returned to his own camp, McCleave rested long enough for lunch before starting on a return trip over another route. This led up a canyon from the sides of which the Indians attacked the rear guard of the command, wounding Lt. French, killing two horses and wounding one. As soon as the attack was made the Californians ascended the perpendicular walls by climbing one over the other as they dodged shower after shower of arrows. When they reached the top the Indians fled in every direction.

McCleave was proud to report the superiority of the Volunteers over the Apaches at their own style of fighting as was proven in the case of Corporal C. E. Ellis of Co. A, who crawled unseen to a rock behind which a buck had been giving his men a rough time. The Corporal gave a short cough. When the Indian raised his head, alerted by the sound, Ellis finished him off with a bullet through the brain. The Indians lost three men before deciding to give up the fight. Provisions running out, McCleave sent some men back to the fort for supplies, subsisting on horse meat until their return. Within twenty-four hours Hall died and was buried there in the canyon.

Major Morrison heading Capt. A. H. Pfeiffer's Company of New Mexican Volunteers en route from Fort Stanton to Fort McCrae found a wounded native near Ojo de San Nicolas. He belonged to the caravan owned by Martin Lujan of Socorro del Sur. He told the Colonel that the train was attacked as they stopped to water the animals and nearly the entire party wiped out. Wounded in three places he was left behind because the Indians believed him dead. Taking Lt. L. A. Bargie and eighteen men with him, the Major went into action. They found ten abandoned wagons at the salt marshes, and within a circuit of three miles discovered seven dead New Mexicans whose bodies were placed in a common grave. The trail led to the Sacramento Mountains, then to the Sierra Blanca, where they encountered a party of natives from Tularosa bent on the same mission. A wounded New Mexican had ridden into town for help. As the Indians already had twenty hours start and were well hidden in the mountain recesses, he abandoned the trail and returned to Ojo de San Nicolas.

Spring in the air, it was not only plant life that was moving.

John D. Burgess wrote to Scurry, now a Brigadier General: "I have understood privately from Capt. Skillman that the presumption was that your command would move toward Arizona and New Mexico this spring. Should such be the case, I am in such a position here that should you require any army supplies, such as flour, corn, beans, soap, shoes, etc., I would be glad to furnish the same, for which I am willing to take cotton at a fair price in exchange, as you are aware that it requires specie to purchase those things in this country. . . ." (W.R. o.c. p. 1065—March 17, 1863)

Spruce Baird, Colonel of the Arizona Brigade, Confederate Army, was alarmed to think that the army he worked so hard to keep together was joining forces with the Sibley Brigade to work in Louisiana. Sibley's Brigade would now be equally as formidable on the sea as at Valverde. Undaunted, Baird continued trying that there was still time since things were not materially changed in New Mexico and Arizona. About the time that the Texans were marching off to Louisiana Capt. Benjamin F. Harrover, 5th Inf. Cal. Vols. attacked a band of Apaches at Apache Pass. Since the Indians felt secure by the sheer force of numbers (200) they kept up the battle for two hours. Despite all the firing the tally finally showed three Indians dead and Private M. B. Wilcox of Co. E wounded, before the Apaches retreated.

Major Joseph Smith, commander of Fort Stanton, during May of that year, went in pursuit of a party of Comanches who had come in from Texas to raid the farmers at Ruidoso, killing a rancher named Harding, and running off his twelve head of stock. The Major failed to apprehend the culprits. Cesario Duran, who had a ranch near Dona Ana, angered at the Indians for stealing his sheep, rounded up a number of New Mexicans, trailed the Indians to the San Andreas Mountains where he killed many. He lost two men in the engagement. The men under Lt. Col. J. F. Chavez, 1st N. M. Vols. captured a famous chief known as Gordo (Fatty) turning him over to Lt. B. Shivers. The Indian boasted that he would soon be free. The sentinel at the guardhouse was amazed to see Gordo not only free of his ropes but making for the clump of trees to the west. He placed his rifle against his shoulder, aimed and fired. The Indians tallied up the death of Gordo as another act to be avenged. Hearing of a large train coming up from Chihuahua, and hoping there would be guns in the wagons, they intercepted the caravan near the border but wagonmaster Charles Hayden outwitted them and they gave up the idea after losing eleven men and their leader Chief Copinggan.

Captain T. T. Tidball, 5th Inf. Cal. Vols. enlisted the aid of some civilians to attack a rancheria in Canon de Arivaypa. His own command numbered twenty-five. The expedition marched five days without lighting a fire, maintaining silence throughout, hiding by day, following native guides by night, they were later pleased to learn from the Indians themselves that no white man had ever set foot in this region before. Fifty of the Apaches were killed. The Captain lost Private Thomas McClelland.

Six miles above Las Vegas is the site of the Montezuma Hot Springs. The Fort Union-Fort Stanton Trail passed these springs. In early June the Navajos attacked the freighters resting at this spot before proceeding to Fort Union. In order to save their lives the men fled to cover in the Gallinas Mountains. The Indians made off with wagons and supplies. During that same month Lt. Bargie was attacked along the Jornada as he escorted two prisoners to Mesilla. Giving the men rifles he told them to use them in self defense but to return them if the Indians were beaten off. The Lieutenant was killed during the struggle. Also killed were Sergeants Pena of Sapello, Ulibarri of Las Vegas and Lucero of La Questa (present Villanueva). The two prisoners marched to Mesilla, reported the action and surrendered the rifles.

Near Fort McRae was a hot spring of which Capt. A. H. Pfeiffer, his New Mexican wife, two servant girls, and an escort of six men of the 1st N. M. Vols. decided to take advantage by bathing and wading. No sooner enjoying the warm water than twenty Apaches surrounded the spring. Privates Nestor Quintana and Juan de Dios Maestas were killed outright. Capt. Pfeiffer was wounded in the side. Private Dolores Montoya and a citizen named Betts who was with the wounded. The war party went off with the women. Wounded as he was, the Captain headed for Fort McRae where he enlisted the aid of the commander, Major Morrison, who picked twenty men and started after the fleeing Indians. When the Indians realized they were being trailed, they put arrows through the three women because they slowed their pace. The Captain's wife and one of the servant girls died. The Apaches escaped.

A week later Indians raided the remuda at Fort Stanton. Pursuit proved ineffectual and the army had to send to Fort

Union for more mounts. Shortly afterwards John Hinckley was attacked and killed; Nicolas Quintana was carried off to be burnt at the stake. Captain Rafael Chacon, 1st N. M. Vols. went in pursuit of Indians who ran off some horses and oxen at Fort Wingate. The oxen were soon left behind because they could not attain the speed the captors wished. For three days Chacon followed the trail determined not to return until he wiped out the raiders. Caught up with at last, the Indians gave the soldiers a two hour battle before they broke ranks and fled. The number killed was not determined; one private was wounded.

Elsewhere Captain N. J. Pishon of the Cal. Vols. was sent after eight Indians who boldly rode to the remuda at Fort Craig, cut out a hundred and twenty horses and headed for the Mogollons. He overtook them west of the garrison, killed four and recovered the animals. The Indians put up a stiff fight wounding a captain and two privates. Captain A. H. French saw a band of Apaches near Fort Thorne. Outnumbered three he nevertheless decided to attack. Ten Indians were killed; two of his men wounded. Sgt. E. W. Hoyt, Co. D, 1st Inf. Cal. Vols. had charge of four wagons en route to Las Cruces. He was attacked at Cook's Pass losing three wagons. Four men were wounded.

Lt. Juan Marquez, 1st N. M. Vols., was on a scouting expedition near Cabeza de Caballo on the Rio Hondo when his camp of fifteen men was attacked by fifty Indians. Abandoning the camp the men sought cover, driving the Indians across the river by their rapid fire. The fight lasted several hours. All during the fighting more and more of the enemy swelled the ranks of the original fifty until Marquez had two hundred to contend with. The ammunition giving out, he ordered the men to break their rifles rather than have them fall into the hands of the Indians, and asked the men to make their escape as best they could. Fourteen reported at Fort Stanton. Jose Chavez was killed. Capt F. P. Abreu and Capt. Emil Fritz rode from the post to overtake the Apaches who, warned of the approach of the soldiers, split into so many directions that the captains were baffled and returned without so much as the comfort of a shot at the redskins.

In July the Navajos took twenty thousand sheep from Las Vegas, Chaperito, Anton Chico and La Questa. These were never re-captured. Lt. John Lambert, 5th Inf. Cal. Vols., was attacked at Cook's Canyon. Two of his men were wounded. One (Private

Queen) eventually died. Lt. Col. McMullen's ambulance was attacked near Paraje. Assistant Surgeon E. S. Watson and Private Johnson, Co. G, were killed almost instantly. The Indians succeeded in capturing McMullen's horse. Three of the attackers were killed and several wounded before the Indians finally called it off. Lt. B. Stevens, on the way to Fort Wingate, came upon seven Navajos who surprised him by giving themselves up.

In August a war party of Utes, Mohuaches and Tabahuaches killed nine Navajos and ran off twenty-two of their horses. Captain E. H. Bergman reported that a party of Co. I, 1st N. M. Vols., in charge of a herd of beef cattle, were attacked by Navajos near Conchos Spring. Sergeant Jose Lucero, Privates Juan F. Ortiz and Jose Barreras, protected by some old fallen limbs, were able to stave off a massacre keeping up the fight for eight hours, when the Indians succeeded in killing Lucero and Ortiz. Barreras, although bleeding from eight arrow wounds, gathered up the muskets and pistols of his dead companions, and under cover of darkness threw them into the spring. Angered at the loss, the Indians fractured his skull with rocks, leaving him for dead, but he regained consciousness towards morning and staggered into Chaparito to tell his story. Even Canby would have to marvel at such courage. Conquistadores must have applauded from their graves. Unable to fish the guns from the spring the Indians had to be content with the cattle. Further on they added ten thousand sheep to the herd. Capt. Bergmann mounted thirty men hoping to intercept them at the crossing of the Pecos. Corporal Martinez caught up with the rear guard, killing two and wounding several others. He destroyed their camp regaining possession of three beeves for all the effort.

Meantime the Utes kept up their warfare against the Navajo. They reported to Superintendent Steck that they had killed thirty of the enemy, and brought sixty children into the agency, as well as thirty horses and two thousand re-captured sheep. This certainly shows the confidence they had in Steck since they could have very nicely appropriated the prisoners and live stock.

On August 5 the Col. Kit Carson broke camp near Rio Bonito for a prolonged expedition against the Navajos. On the first day he sent Sergeant Romero and fifteen men after two seen lingering in the area. Romero returned with one captured horse. The Indians escaped. Captain Pfeiffer rounded up some Indian women, one of whom was killed in attempting to escape. Could he have been thinking of another woman who sought to escape her captors? It was while on this expedition with Carson that Major Cummings, 1st N. M. Vols., was shot through the abdomen by a concealed Indian, and died instantly. Fort Cummings was later to be erected in his honor.

Captain H. A Greene, 1st Inf. Cal. Vols., learning that a war party crossed the Rio Grande with a large herd of sheep, on August 8th, mounted twenty men in pursuit. He dogged their trail for two hundred miles and just when they felt safe he opened fire. The surprised Indians fled at the first volley. Almost two thousand sheep were recovered. These the captain drove back to Fort Craig. Several days later Navajos attacked the government herd at Fort Union driving off eighteen mules. Captain V. Drescher, 1st Inf Cal Vol. trailed Indians that stampeded the herd at Fort West. Not one animal was recovered. Toward the end of the month Indians attacked the mail stage along the Jornada near the place known as Point of Rocks. The mail was scattered, the men killed, the mules run off. Captain Greene had some men bring in the stage and as much of the mail they could gather. The Indians were found near the Rio Grande. Lt. Fountain (years later to be killed with his son near the white sands of Alamogordo) led the charge across the river. Private George Dickey saw an Indian jump into the river and wounded him. The Indian turned and shot Dickey—the only shot fired by the Indians in the skirmish. Dickey was buried along the banks of the Rio Grande.

General Carleton had his mind made up. The answer to all these Indian troubles lay in a reservation near a military post where the soldiers could keep strict watch on them. Col. Carson, an old Indian fighter, was appointed for the task. If he could prove to the Indians that Canon de Chelly was not as impenetrable as they thought, the backbone of their resistance would be broken. Secreting Captain Pfeiffer in the canon, the movements of the enemy were under constant surveilance. Fearing discovery by two approaching Indians, the captain's men fired upon them, wounding them, but not sufficiently enough to prevent their escape to sound the alarm. The men returned to Fort Canby. The Indians were crestfallen. They realized that their natural fortress was not as safe against the white man as they thought it was, and, for the first time there was talk of surrender. But the majority agreed that they were not licked yet. They would fight on until compelled to surrender either by starvation or lack of arms. Hearing that a wagon train of wood—so necessary for cooking and warmth against the chilly August nights in the mountains— a large band was sent to intercept the train before it reached Fort Wingate. Private Luciano Pais was wounded, but was able to get word to Captain Rafael Chacon at the post. Forty men were sent after the hundred and fifty Indians. Chacon seemed to know his business, for he soon had the Navajos on the run, capturing seven children and a native named Agapito Apodaca (of Socorro), recovering the wood, sheep, goats, horses, mules, burros and colts that the Indians were taking to the canon. Apaches raided the remuda at Fort Bowie making off with six horses. Captain Tidball went in pursuit but was unable to regain the mounts.

Captain Joseph P. Hargrave, 1st Cal. Vols., was sent from Fort Wingate in early September. Indians had bee running off sheep too close for comfort. While he succeeded in regaining the sheep near the Little Colorado, the Indians retaliated by stealing his mounts. About the same time the Governor of the Jemez Pueblo led a united band of Utes and Pueblos agains the Navajos killing nine.

Captain J. J. Whitlock, 5th Inf. Cal. Vols., surrounded a Navajo camp only to find it abandoned. Destroying the mescal, blankets and other material found there, he trailed the Indians for several days but accomplished little when he found them. His guide was wounded in the fifteen minute battle that followed before the Navajos fled. Not an Indian was wounded or hurt in any way. When Indians attacked Puertecito de las Salinas three natives were so angered that they brazenly went in pursuit, lacking wit but not courage. Laughingly, the Indians made short work of them. Captain Henry A. Green, commander of Fort McRae, went after Indians said to be at Canada Palomas near Alamosa. While he found some stock, there was not an Indian in sight. Lt P. A. J. Russell, 1st Inf. Cal. Vols., took four mounted men and a party of Pueblos to Valles Grandes along a trail that led from there right into the village of Jemez. The battle was short and fierce. Eight Navajos were killed, twenty women taken prisoner, horses and sheep re-captured.

Baltazar Montano of Pecos led some civilians after Navajos who had stolen his sheep. He killed two, wounded five and brought the stock back safe and sound.

Again Col. Carson made an attempt against the Navajos but the broken down condition of his mounts caused him to abandon the project for another day. He did succeed in destroying a village on the way back. Some of his men were attacked five miles from Fort Canby. One was killed, one wounded. It proved to the Colonel that the Indians were watching him just as closely as he was watching them. Early in October Pueblos from Taos, Jemez, Picuris and Santo Domingo went on the war path against the Navajos, killing twenty-two, capturing fifty-one and returning with over a thousand sheep. Their successes must have shamed the soldiers. Major Edward B. Wills, 1st Inf. Cal. Vols., led an expedition from Fort Wingate but succeeded in destroying several fields of pumpkins and watermelons where he thought he would really wipe out the enemy. He took prisoner the two Indians he found at Jacob's Well.

On October 2nd, two wagons sent a mile from Fort Craig for wood, were attacked by Indians. The non-commissioned officer, five men and teamsters, ran at the first volley, leaving one musket, ten mules and the wagons to the aggressors. The train of Don Miguel Romero, of Las Vegas, who was delivering his hay contract to Fort Canby, was attacked by Indians, but the hay was delivered, although two of the men were wounded. Lt. T. Henderson, 1st Cav. N. M. Vols., attacked a group of Indians raiding along the Fort Stanton-Santa Fe road. The Indians escaped, leaving a herd of government mules to the soldiers. Two days later (October 18) Lt. Dowlen of the same contingent attacked a party of Indians near Laguna Negra, killing two of them. Next Capt. Chacon went in pursuit of Indians who ran off stock at Fort Wingate. All he recovered were two mules and two horses. Lt. Nicolas Hodt, 1st N. M. Vols. at Fort Canby had no better luck. Lt. E. Latimer, 1st Cav. N. M. Vols., left Fort Union on October 31st to take twenty-one Indian prisoners to Fort Sumner. Camping along the Gallinas, sixteen of the prisoners managed to elude him. Pursuit proved ineffective in that mountainous country. He marched into the fort with five. At Sierra Negra beyond Fort Wingate, civilians tired of the ineffectiveness of the soldiers, took matters into their own hands, killing a number of Navajos in battles at Sierra de Schsca and Sierra Negra. Captain Anderson led an expedition along the Gila but accomplished little or nothing.

Captain Green left Fort McRea for Rio Plumas but finding no Indians returned to the post. Sergeant Rhodes left behind their hiding place, eventually came up with them near Vidette Station. In the fight that followed one of his men was wounded; one Indian killed. Captain Tafoya found some Indians near the site of Datil. They escaped, leaving the stock. General Estanislado Montoya attacked Indians at Tres Hermanos but accomplished nothing.

Early in November Col. Carson left Fort Canby for the country west of the Oribi villages. A detachment under Sergeant Andres Herrera overtook a small war party near the camp. He succeeded in wounding two and in capturing a number of sheep. Later on he came upon some stragglers left in two villages. These latter he destroyed. The sheep, women and children were taken to Colonel Carson. Roman A. Baca left Ceboyetta with a party of one hundred and sixteen New Mexicans. About fifty miles from Chusca they encountered about two hundred Indians, who retreated after losing nine men in killed (6) and prisoners (3). Lt. J. Laughlin on the way to Los Pinos from Fort Wingate surprised a band of Indians at Rio Puerco. These fled, leaving seventy head of cattle. Soldiers from Fort McRea overtook a flock of sheep near the site of Caballo south of the Jornada. Major Henry D. Wallen, commander of Fort Sumner, was awakened on the morning of December 16th by Mr. Labadie and Rev. Fialon, who reported to him that a large number of Indians with an immense herd of sheep were at the Carritas. The men were awakened, given two days' rations, thirty Apache guides and sent in pursuit. Labadie and Rev. Fialon refused to be left behind. The mounted men, in advance of the foot soldiers took up the trail on the west bank of the Pecos river, coming upon the Indians about thirty-five miles below the post. A hundred and thirty well armed Indians gave battle. Twelve were killed and a number wounded before they decided to abandon the field. Over five thousand sheep were recovered, as well as nearly all the effects stolen from Labadie's train. Rev. Filion was in the thick of the fight. Whether he hit anything he never said.

Apaches led by Chiefs Ojo Blanco (White Eye) and Codetta, and a Navajo named Alazan, hearing some pistol shots just before reaching the Pecos river, abandoned about five thousand sheep. Lt. McDermott, with ten mounted men and six Apaches, sent to bring back the sheep, managed to wound Alazan, who died before he reached Fort Sumner. The others were either captured or surrendered later when the reservation was definitely established. A party of thirty-five Navajos, tired of war, surrendered at Fort Wingate just before Christmas.

Lt. D. Montoya, sent out by Col. Carson at Fort Canby, encountered a blinding snow storm, but following orders did not return until he had attacked an Indian encampment, killing one and taking a number of prisoners. Near Pueblo, Colorado, the command pursued a few fleeing Indians and captured them not before they wounded Corporal Marcos. Three days before Christmas Capt. John Thompson left Fort Canby with one hundred men but did not find any until December 26th, where the enemy engaged Sergeant Romero in a battle at the Mesa de Baca. On the same day Sergeant Dorsette found some Indians in another direction. The other two Indian engagements for 1863 were led by civilians from San Miguel del Bado. They surprised the enemy near Pecos and recovered their stock. Col. Carson spent most of this time completing arrangements for his attack on Canon de Chelly.

NOTES AND COMMENTS

It was during 1863 that small parties of Navajos and Apaches committed many depredations in the area about Anton Chico, Villanueva, Las Vegas and within sight of Fort Union. In October of that year they were such a menace around the post where there was no cavalry that General Carleton sent Captain Emil Fritz to take command of Fort Union and subdue the Indians in that area. Colonel Carson as commander of the 1st N. M. Vols. was in charge of Fort Union for a time in 1862 and it is interesting to read his provision return sheet (Sheet No. 2—No. 2 Provision Return for April and May, 1862). "I hereby certify that I have compared the within abstract with the original return now in my possession and find that they amount to:

    6,433 rations of fresh beef
  10,325 rations of flour
    3,692 rations of bacon

    6,845 rations of beans
    1,818 rations of rice
    1,382 rations of desiccated vegetables
  10,180 rations of coffee
      297 rations of tea
  10,405 rations of sugar
  10,045 rations of vinegar

Also rations of candles (adamantine), soap and salt.

The chronological order of skirmishes for 1863 may be found in the War Records as well as in the article "Volunteer Soldiers of New Mexico and Their Conflicts with Indians in 1862 and 1863," by Estelle Bennett Burton, in *Old Santa Fe Magazine* for April, 1914. This is the report of Adj. Gen. Ben C. Cutler to the Secretary of the Interior—Feb. 24, 1864:

January 4—Col. Carson, commanding Fort Stanton, reported arrival of two Mescalero Indians who stated that in six days one hundred Mescalero Indians would deliver themselves up at Fort Stanton; that this number comprised all the Mescaleros not already at Bosque Redondo.

January 8—Captain Updegraff, commanding Fort Sumner (evidently there was a distinction between the California Column and the New Mexico Vols.), reported that two men of the picket stations at Bosque Grande (Redondo?) left the picket contrary to orders, to hunt, and that one of them, Private Samuel Strunk, Company M, 1st N. M. Vols., was killed by Indians; that the number of Indians then at Bosque Redondo was 248.

January 17—Col. Carson reported the arrival at Fort Stanton of 100 Mescaleros mentioned in his communications of the 4th inst., under the following named chiefs: Ojo Blanco, Janero Viejo, Janero Pablo, Janero Francisco, Jose La Paz, Mancos Son, Schat-hi.

January 17—Capt. E. D. Shirland, 1st Cav. Cal. Vols., brought Mangas Coloradas, an Apache chief, into Fort McLean, a prisoner. On the morning of the 18th, in attempting to escape (?), Mangas was killed by the guard.

January 19—Capt. Wm. McCleave, 1st Cav. Col. Vols., reported that in obedience to orders, he started from Fort McLean and proceeded to the Pinos Altos mines; arriving at the latter place a party of Mangas Coloradas' band of Apaches approached the men who were ordered to attack them, which was done;

eleven Indians were killed and one wounded; the latter proved to be the wife of the chief, Mangas Coloradas. Three horses were captured, but, being in poor condition, the people at the mines were permitted to keep them.

January 20—Capt. Shirland came upon an Indian rancheria, surprised and defeated the Indians, killing nine and wounding many more, and capturing from them thirty-four head of stock, a portion of which were government mules. The rancheria and all that pertained to it was destroyed.

January 29—The Indians attacked two hunting parties of Company A, 5th Cav. Cal. Vols., at Pinos Altos mines, killed Private Hussey and wounded Sergeant Sitton. The Indians were driven off with a loss of twenty killed and fifteen wounded. Sergeant Sitton behaved gallantly in this affair.

February 16—L. M. Baca reported that 4,000 sheep were stolen from the neighborhood of Limitar (several miles north of Socorro) by Navajos, and reported that the Navajos stole 2,000 sheep which he recaptured at the Sierras Oscuras, killing three and wounding several Indians, and capturing all their saddles, provisions, etc.

February 25—Jose L. Perea reported that a band of forty Navajos attacked and drove off 6,000 sheep twenty-five miles south of Pope's artesian well.

March 4—L. M. Baca reported that since Feb. 26th three hundred and ten head of horses and cattle had been stolen by Indians from the neighborhood of Limitar.

March 5—Major Morrison reported departure of Indians mentioned in Col. Carson's communication of Jan. 17, from Fort Stanton to Bosque Redondo; also the departure of fifteen additional Indians who had given themselves up.

March 12—Indians captured near Sabinal (in the area of Belen) 2,300 head of sheep; were followed by Mexicans who recaptured them on the Jornado (south of Socorro) on the night of the 12th.

March—A band of forty Indians pursued two expressmen going from Fort Stanton to Fort Union. These Indians had a large herd of sheep. Captain Abreu, commanding Fort Stanton, sent Lt. McAllister and thirty men, with ten days' rations, to the Sierras Oscuras, to intercept them. The expedition failed to recover the stock.

March 22—The Gila Apaches (in the afternoon) made a descent upon the public herd which was grazing near Fort West (in Arizona) and succeeded in running off some sixty head of horses. At 8 p. m. the gallant Major Wm. McCleave started in pursuit, with a command consisting of Lt. French and Lt. Latimer, 1st Cav. Cal. Vols., forty men of Company A, twenty-five men of Company B, and fourteen men of Co. C, 1st Cav. Cal. Vols. Major McCleave followed the trail of the Indians in a westerly course about seventy miles, and down the Gila five miles, then across a divide to Rio Negro, where he arrived at 9 a. m. on the 26th, and then moved up the stream a short distance; signs at this point indicated the close proximity of Indians and a rancheria. During twilight the command moved up the stream two miles and made camp. Thirty men were mounted on the only serviceable animals left, under Lt. Latimer, and thirty dismounted, under Major McCleave, started in search of the rancheria, leaving the remainder of the command, with Lt. French, in charge of broken-down animals, pack-animals, provisions, etc. Leaving the camp at 8 o'clock p. m. the command ascended a mountain on the west side of the stream and traveled about twelve miles without meeting with any success. Here the command rested from one o'clock of the 27th until dawn of day, it raining all the time. When light enough to see, Major McCleave discovered, from an elevated position, trees, which indicated the presence of water, and a horse grazing in the neighborhood also indicated that the rancheria was near by. Lt. Latimer was ordered ahead with his command; discovered ranchera and gallantly charged upon it. Part of the dismounted men immediately commenced gathering in and guarding the horses, to prevent the escape of the Indians, while the others were skirmishing and fighting on the bluffs. The fight lasted twenty minutes and resulted in the complete routing of the Indians, the capture of all our own horses that could be found, and many Indian horses, the killing of twenty-five Indians, and the complete destruction of the rancheria, provisions, and all they possessed. Private Hall of Co. B, 1st Cal. Vols., was wounded in this fight. The command then returned to camp and soon after noon started on the return trip by a route supposed to be more direct than the one by which the Indians were followed from the fort. This route led up a canyon from the sides of which the Indians attacked the rear guard of the command, wounding Lieutenant French, killing two horses and wounding one. As soon as the attack was made, the soldiers ascended the perpendicular walls of the canyon by climbing one over the other. This was done amidst showers of arrows. As soon as they reached the top the Indians fled in every direction. The superiority of the Californians over the Apaches at their own style of fighting was shown in the case of Corporal Ellis of Co. A, who crawled unseen to a rock behind which was an Indian, and gave a short cough. The Indian raised his head to discover its cause, when a bullet from Ellis's rifle dashed through his brain. The Indians lost in this attack, three killed.

On the 30th, provisions giving out, a sergeant and five men were sent to the fort for a supply. Until their return the party subsisted on horse flesh. On the 4th of April the command reached the fort. On the 5th Private Hall died from the wounds received in the fight. Indian loss; twenty-eight killed. The troops lost one.

March 24—Major Morrison, with Captain Pfeiffer's company of New Mexico Volunteers, en route from Fort Stanton to Fort McRae, at San Nicolas spring came upon a wounded Mexican who stated that he belonged to a train belonging to Martin Lujan of Socorro (del Sur) Texas; that the train had been attacked by Indians and nearly all the party killed, he being wounded in three places and being left for dead. Major Morrison, with Lt. Bargie and eighteen men of the company, went in pursuit, came to the salt marshes at day break of the 25th, found ten wagons stripped of everything portable, and, within a circuit of three miles, seven bodies of Mexicans, which they buried. They then followed the trail of the Indians towards the Sacramento mountains, then towards the Sierra Blanca until noon, when they met a party of Mexicans from Tularosa, in pursuit of the same Indians; they had been informed of the massacre by another wounded Mexican who had escaped. The Indians had at this time twenty hours start and were hidden in the recesses of the Sierra Blanca. Major Morrison returned to San Nicolas spring, arriving there on the evening of the 25th, having traveled one hundred and fifty miles. Lt. Bargie's conduct is spoken of as deserving of praise. Estimated number of Indians, forty-five in all—twenty of whom were warriors; arrows indicate they were Apaches; seven Mexicans killed and seventy head of cattle stolen.

April 25—Capt. Benjamin F. Harrover, 5th Inf. Cal. Vols., reported that he attacked, at Apache Pass, a band of Apache Indians, numbering about two hundred, thirty of them mounted and several of them armed with guns. At the first fire the Indians fell back, but kept up the fight for nearly two hours. In this affair Private Wilcox of Co. E, 5th Inf. Cal. Vols., was wounded. Indian loss: three killed, wounded unknown; troops, one private wounded.

May 1—Cesario Duran, a citizen, reported that a party under his command had a hard fight with the Apaches in the San Andres mountains and succeeded in killing and wounding many Indians. The party lost two men killed; the party recovered several animals and captured seven horses.

May—Major Joseph Smith, commanding Fort Stanton, reported that a party of Indians made a descent on the farmers of Ruidoso and killed a man named Harding, robbed his house and drove off ten or twelve head of stock.

May 8—Lt. Col. J. F. Chavez, 1st N. M. Vols., reported that an Indian named Gordo was seized and turned over to Lt. B. Stevens (three days later May 11). The Indian unbound himself and attempted to escape; the sentinel in charge shot and killed him.

May 15—Navajos stole six head of horses from the Jemez Indians.

May—Charles T. Hayden, citizen, reported that the Indians attacked his train near the line of Chihuahua; they were defeated with a loss of eleven killed including the renowned Copinggan. Three horses were captured in this fight.

May—Capt. T. T. Tidball, 5th Inf. Cal. Vols., with twenty-five men of his company and a small party of citizens attacked a rancheria in Cajon de Arivaypa killing over fifty Indians, wounding as many more, taking ten prisoners and capturing sixty head of stock, with the loss of only one man—Thomas McClelland. The party marched five days without lighting a fire, maintaining silence, hiding by day and traveling by night over a country hitherto untrod by white men.

June—Major Joseph Smith, commanding Fort Stanton, reported that the Indians attacked the expressmen on the 21st of June, near the Gallinas and compelled them to abandon their mules and express matter and to take to the mountains; the mules and express lost.

June 20—Capt A. H. Pfeiffer, wife, and two servant girls, with escort of six men of the 1st U. M. Vols., were attacked by a party of Apache Indians numbering fifteen or twenty, at a hot spring near Fort McRae. The Captain was bathing at the time, when the Indians made a rush upon the party, killing two men, Privates Nestor Quintana and Maestas. Capt Pfeiffer was wounded in his side by an arrow, and Private Dolores———— received two shots in his right hand and arm. A citizen named Betts, who was with Capt Pfeiffer, was also wounded. The remainder of the party, except the women, succeeded in reaching Fort McRae unharmed, and reported the facts to Major Morrison, commanding the post. He immediately started in pursuit, with twenty mounted men, but did not succeed in overtaking the Indians. Mrs. Pfeiffer and the servant girls were found on the trail, badly wounded. Mrs. Pfeiffer and one of the servants died. Loss in this affair: two privates killed, two women mortally wounded; one officer, one private, one woman and a citizen wounded; seven horses and two mules taken by the Indians. Indian loss unknown.

June 24—Major Morrison reported an attack on Lt. Bargie and escort on the Jornada, in which Lt. Bargie, while fighting gallantly, was killed. The conduct of Sergeants Pena and Ulibarri and the two prisoners they had in charge is highly praised.

June 26—Major Morrison reported further, in regard to the fight on the Jornada, that Private Lucero, 1st N. M. Vols., was killed.

June 27—Major Joseph Smith, commanding Fort Stanton, reported the loss of part of his herd of horses and mules stolen by Indians. An Infantry company was sent in pursuit.

June 28—Lt. W. H. Hogdon, 5th Inf. Cal. Vols., reported that on his way from Fort Stanton to Santa Fe, near Gallinas Springs, he found the bodies of Privates Nicolas Quintana, of Co. A, 1st N. M. Vols., and John Hinckley of Co. A, 5th Cal. Vols., who had been murdered by the Indians. The Indians had evidently wounded Private Quintana, tied him to a stake and burned him. Some legal tender notes and several letters were found near the body of Hinckley.

July 2—Lt Col. Chaves reported that Capt. Rafael Chacon, 1st N. M. Vols., with twenty men, was sent in pursuit of a band of Indians who had stolen some horses and oxen from Fort Wingate. The oxen were recaptured near the post; the troops followed the trail of the Indians for three days and finally overtook them when a sharp fight ensued. The Indians fought with great bravery, but were finally driven from their cover and fled. The conduct of Sergeant Antonio Jose Fresquez in this affair is highly spoken of by Capt Chacon. Indian loss unknown; troops: one private wounded.

July 4—Capt. N. J. Pishon reported that with twenty-seven men of his Co. D, 1st Cav. Cal. Vols., he pursued a party of eight Indians who had driven off one hundred and four government mules from Fort Craig, overtook them a few miles from the post, killed four Indians and recovered all the mules. Capt. Jules L. Barbey who accompanied the command was shot through the wrist by an arrow. Privates Jackson and Bancroft were also slightly wounded.

July 12—Capt. A. H. French, 1st Cav. Cal. Vols., with twenty-seven men of his company, attacked and routed, near Fort Thorne, a band of Apache Indians supposed to number sixty-four warriors. Indian loss, ten killed and four horses captured. Sergeant Walsh and Farriers Burns were wounded.

July 11—Sergeant E. W. Hoyt of Co. D, 1st Inf. Cal. Vols., with three men of Co. B, and three men of Co. D, 1st Inf. Cal. Vols., having in charge four wagons en route to Las Cruces, was attacked by Indians in Cook's Pass, forced to abandon three wagons and nineteen mules, and had four men slightly wounded. Sergeant Hoyt acted with the greatest coolness in this affair.

July 19—Lt. Juan Marquez, 1st N. M. Vols., while returning from Horse Head crossing of the Pecos, with fifteen men of Co. A, 1st N. M. Vols., was attacked at the Rio Hondo by about fifty Indians, while in camp at that point. The Indians gained possession of the camp but were finally driven across the river, carrying with them their wounded. They soon after re-crossed the river and charged on the herd but were again driven back with loss. In this charge Private Jose Chavez was killed. The fight was continued for several hours; the Indian force rapidly increased and at last numbered two hundred. The ammunition gave out and the soldiers were ordered to break their rifles and make their escape, which they did. Lt. Marquez reports the conduct of the following men as worthy of mention: Corporals Brigaloa and Jose Gonzolez and Privates Santiago Torres, G. Romero, Antonio Archuleta, Jose D. Fresquez and J. Lopez. All the public animals (including ten mules) were lost in this affair. Indian loss, six killed.

Lt. Col. McMullen's ambulance was attacked by Indians near Paraje and Assistant Surgeon E. S. Watson and Private Johnson, Co. G, both of 1st Inf. Cal. Vols., were killed. The escort killed two Indians and wounded others. Col. McMullen's horse was captured by the Indians. Our loss, one commissioned officer and one private killed; one horse lost. Indian loss, three killed and wounded unknown.

July 22—Capt. F. P. Abreu, 1st N. M. Vols., and Capt. Emil Fritz, 1st Cav. Cal. Vols., with a detachment of N. M. Vols., left Fort Stanton for the Rio Pecos to overtake and chastise the Indians who attacked Lt. Marquez. After following the Indians for forty-five miles. Capt. Fritz came upon their camp and captured two horses, six mules, and all the plunder of the camp. The Indians made their escape.

July 30—Lt. W. H. Higdon reported that on the 30th of July, en route from Fort Union to Fort Stanton, he saw about seventy-five Indians driving a large herd of sheep judged to number twenty-thousand. Believing his party too small to attack so large a band of Indians, they were allowed to pass unmolested.

July 24—Lt John Lambert, 5th Inf. Cal. Vols., reported that the Indians attacked a detachment under his command in Cook's Canyon; at the first fire Sergeant Hance of Co. H. 5th Inf., was wounded in the shoulder and hand; soon after, Private Queen, of Co. F, was mortally wounded. Two wagons were abandoned to the Indians, also twelve mules. Private Queen died befor the fight ended.

Aug. 4—Lt. B. Stevens, 1st N. M. Vols., reported that when he was returning from Cuvero to Fort Wingate, he came upon a party of Navajo Indians, seven men and two boys, took them prisoners and placed them in the guard house at Fort Wingate.

Aug. 6—M. Steck, Supt. of Indian Affairs, reported that a portion of the Utes, Mohuaches and Tabahuaches had killed nine Navajos and captured twenty-two horses.

Capt. E. H. Bergmann reported that a party of Co. I, 1st N. M. Vols., in charge of a herd of beef cattle, were attacked by a body of Navajos on the 22nd. of July, near Conchas Spring. The party consisted of Sergeant Jose Lucero and Privates Juan F. Ortiz and Jose Barreras, who fought the Indians from 11 a.m. until after sundown, killing and wounding several of them. The

Indians succeeded in killing Sergeant Lucero and Private Ortiz. Private Barreras, being severely wounded by eight arrow shots, gathered up the muskets and pistols of his dead comrades and threw them into the spring. The Indians fractured his skull with rocks and left him for dead but he recovered towards morning and made his way to Chaparito. The Indians drove off the cattle; number not stated. Captain Bergmann, learning that the Indians had driven off ten thousand sheep, mounted thirty men and endeavored to intercept them at the crossing of the Pecos. Corporal Martinez came close to their rear and succeeded in killing two and wounding several. The Corporal destroyed their camp utensils and captured three beeves.

Aug. 11—M. Steck reported that the Utes during the last ten days had killed thirty Navajos and captured and brought in sixty children of both sexes and captured thirty horses and two thousand sheep. On the 11th inst. four Utes came in with three scalps and six captives. Total: thirty-three killed, sixty-six captured and thirty horses and two thousand sheep taken.

Aug. 19—Col C. Carson reported that he left camp near Canyon Bonito, Aug. 5th on a scout for thirty days. On the first day he sent out Sergeant Romero with fifteen men after two Indians seen in the vicinity; captured one of their horses. The Indians made their escape. On the night of the 4th Capt. Pfeiffer captured eleven women and children besides a woman and child killed while attempting to escape (the child being killed accidently). Capt. Pfeiffer's party also captured two other children, one hundred sheep and goats and one horse. The Utes captured in the same vicinity eighteen horses and two mules and killed one Indian. Capt. Pfeiffer wounded an Indian but he escaped. On the 16th a party sent for some pack-saddles, brought in one Indian woman. At this camp the brave Major Cummings, 1st N. M. Vols., was shot through the abdomen by a concealed Indian and died instantly. One of the parties sent out from this camp captured an Indian woman. Total Indians killed, three, captured fifteen; wounded, one; twenty horses, two mules and one hundred sheep and goats captured. Troops: one commissioned officer killed.

Capt. Henry A. Greene, 1st Inf. Cal. Vols., having received information that a party of Indians with a large herd of sheep had crossed the Rio Grande on the morning of the 8th, mounted twenty men and started in pursuit and after following their trail for nearly two hundred miles, came upon them and opened fire. The Indians fled, and the command recovered 1,600 to 1,800 sheep and drove them to Fort Craig.

Aug. 24—Capt. W. Craig reported that a party of sixteen Indians attacked his herders near Fort Union and drove off eighteen government mules.

Aug. 27—Capt V. Drescher, 1st Inf. Cal. Vols., reported the horses and mules at Fort West were stampeded by Indians; animals not recovered; Indians not pursued. Twenty-six mules and one horse lost.

Aug. 29—Capt. Henry A. Greene, 1st Inf. Cal. Vols., reported that the Indians attacked the mail stage on the Jornada near the Point of Rocks, and captured seven mules. As soon as the information was received fifteen mounted men were sent in pursuit and nine detailed to escort the stage through. The mounted party, on coming in view of the Rio Grande, saw three Indians on the bank; the balance of the bank were back in the brush; the three Indians were fired upon; one of them fell but recovered again. A part of the command under Lt. Fountain charged across the river; the Indians ran and concealed themselves. The party then dismounted and commenced to skirmish through the bushes. While on this duty Private George Dickey was mortally wounded by the only shot fired by the Indians during the affair. Dickey saw an Indian jump into the river and shot him; the Indian turned after being shot and gave Dickey the wound which caused his death. Indian loss, one killed, three wounded. Our loss, one private killed.

Aug.—Col. C. Carson with his command left Pueblo Colorado on the 20th day of Aug. for Canon de Chelly wih the main force, secreting twenty-five men under Capt. Pfeiffer in the canon to watch for Indians. Soon after, two Indians were seen approaching the canon and were fired upon, and, although badly wounded, succeeded in getting away. On the same day the advance guard pursued and killed an Indian. On the 31st the command returned to Fort Canby. Indian loss, one killed, two wounded.

Aug. 27—Two Navajo Indian prisoners attempted to escape from the guard house at Fort Defiance; one was killed by the guard and the other mortally wounded.

Aug. 23—Capt. R. Chacon, 1st Cav. N. M. Vols., left Fort Wingate with forty enlisted men on a scout after Indians. On the 27th, when near the salt lakes, the party espied a band of Navajos and succeeded in killing two and capturing eight. On the same day one of the Indians, in attempting to escape, was killed by the soldier who had him in charge. On the 28th the party attacked one hundred and fifty Indians who fled in all directions; the party here captured seven children and recovered a captive Mexican boy named Agapito Apodaca, killed three Indians and captured 1,500 head of sheep and goats, seventeen head of horses, mules, burros and colts. On this scout there were six Indians killed, fourteen captured, one Mexican boy rescued.

Aug. 27—Capt. T. T. Tidball, 5th Inf. Cal. Vols., commanding Fort Bowie (in the Arizona Territory) reported that the Apache Indians ran off six horses and one mule from that post.

Aug. 31—Lt. Col. Chavez, commanding Fort Wingate, reported that a large party of Navajos attacked the escort to the wood wagons about five miles from the post, wounding Private Luciano Pais and driving off twelve mules. The Indians were pursued, but not overtaken. Our loss, one man wounded, twelve mules taken.

September 5—M. Steck reported that a party of Utes had killed nine Navajos and captured forty children and that the Pueblo Indians had killed a Navajo warrior and that the Governor of the Jemez had killed one Navajo; Indian loss, eleven killed, forty captured.

Captain J. H. Whitlock, 5th Inf. Cal. Vols., reported that he found an Indian camp, surprised it and captured two mules, one Sharp's carbine, one U. S. blanket, one thousand pounds of mescal; burned the camp including all that pertained to it. On the 8th of Sept. he found Indians in force and had a spirited fight with them for fifteen minutes. One man and a guide severely wounded and one horse killed. Indian loss unknown. Our loss, one soldier and one citizen wounded; one horse killed.

September 8—The Indians made an attack on Puertocito de las Salinas. The three Mexicans who went in pursuit of them were killed.

September 26—Capt. Henry A. Greene, the indefatigable, commanding Fort McRae, learning that a band of Indians with ten head of stock had crossed the Rio Grande near the Rio de Los Alamosos, and that Corporal August, with three men, had gone in pursuit, immediately mounted eight men and started for the town of Alamosa; arriving at this point, eighteen mounted Mexicans joined his party. The whole party then traveled to Canada Polomas crossing. At this point the stock was found, having been abandoned by the Indians. Corporal August and Privates Daniel D. Tomkins, Alonzo C. Mullen and William Lockhart are highly praised by Capt. Greene for their zeal and energy on this occasion.

September 27—Lt. P. A. J. Russell, 1st Inf. Cal. Vols., with four mounted men and a party of Pueblo Indians, started for Valles Grandes on the trail of a band of Navajos who had stolen a lot of stock from the Pueblos. The trail was followed into the town of Jemez where the party re-captured one hundred and twenty-five head of sheep and two horses. Killed eight Navajos and took twenty women prisoners.

September 28—Baltazar Montano, citizen, reported the result of a campaign against the Navajos as follows: Two Indians killed, five wounded, eleven or twelve animals captured; two horses and one mule lost.

October 5—Col. Carson reported that on the 22nd of Sept. his command pursued a party of Indians, but owing to the broken down condition of the animals they only succeeded in capturing one. On the 2nd of Oct. discovered a small Indian village which had just been abandoned; this was destroyed, nineteen animals captured, seven of which got away. Three men left camp to hunt up the animals which had escaped; did not return until after the command had returned to Fort Canby. They stated that they were attacked by a party of Indians when within five miles of the post, one of whom they killed. One of the men, named Martin, was severely wounded and the Indians captured his mule. On the 3rd of Oct. Lt. Postle discovered an Indian, pursued him and wounded him in three places; the Lt. was slightly wounded by the Indian. Indian loss, one killed, one wounded, one captured, twelve animals captured; our loss, one officer and one private wounded and one mule lost.

Ramon Luna, agent for the Pueblo Indians, reported that the Pueblos in a recent campaign against the Navajos killed 22 of them, captured 51 prisoners, 1,200 sheep and forty mules; some of the mules had the U. S. brand.

October 6—Major Edward B. Willis, 1st Inf. Cal. Vols., left for Fort Wingate on the 15th of Sept. on an expedition against the Indians, with forty men each of Co. H, 1st Inf., Cal. Vols., and Co. F, 1st N. M. Vols. At the Cienega Alarilla the command captured one horse and one mule; at Jacob's Well wounded a few Indians and captured two of them. At this point found and destroyed several fields of pumpkins and watermelons. The command then returned to Fort Wingate. Major Willis in his report said: 'I cannot speak in too high terms of the officers and men of this command; no men could be more anxious to do their duty or more cheeerfully incur the hardships of a campaign; after a march of twenty-five or thirty miles, the whole command would cheerfully volunteer and march the whole night on the slightest prospect of doing any service.' Two Indians, one horse, one mule captured.

October 13—Two wagons which had been sent about a mile from Fort Canby for wood, in charge of a non-commissioned officer and five men, were attacked by Indians; the escort and teamsters ran at the first fire leaving the wagons and teams in the possession of the Indians; ten mules were lost, two mules and the wagons were left. One of the soldiers, in his hurry to escape, left his musket at the wagons; the Indians carried it off.

October 15—Miguel Romero's wagon train was attacked by Indians while on its way from hay camp (Romero was hay contractor) to Fort Canby; the non-commissioned Officer in charge of the escort was wounded and one teamster severely wounded. The Indians drove off five mules and one pony.

October 16—Lt. Thomas Henderson, 1st Cav., N. M. Vols., reported that while enroute from Fort Stanton to Santa Fe he met three Indians with a lot of mules, near the Buffalo Spring. The Indians, on being discovered, abandoned nineteen mules and escaped.

October 18—Lt. Dowlin, 1st Cav., N. M. Vols., reported that a party under his command killed two Indians near Laguna Negra.

October 22, Capt. Rafael Chacon, with his company, pursued a band of Indians who had run off stock near Fort Wingate and captured from them two mules and two horses.

October 21—Lt. Nicholas Hodt, 1st N. M. Vols., with forty men, left Fort Canby October 21st on a scout against the Indians. On the 22nd saw a party of Indians who succeeded in escaping to the mountains; near Canada Colorada the command captured one woman.

October 25—Lt. Charles H. Fitch, on an Indian scout, captured two horses and one mule.

October 31—Lt. E. Latimer, 1st Cav., Cal. Vols., left Fort Union with a detachment of nine men for Fort Sumner, having in charge twenty-one Indian prisoners. On the night of October 4th while encamped at the mouth of the Gallinas river, sixteen of the Indians succeeded in making their escape. They were pursued but not re-captured.

November 4—Capt. A. L. Anderson reported that while in camp on the Gila river near the Pimal mountains, the Indians crept to within range of his picket line and discharged several volleys of arrows at the animals, sentinels and the men sleeping near. Four horses were so badly wounded that it became necessary to kill them. A squad of men was left concealed in the camp and after the column had marched they succeeded in killing one of a party of Indians who approached them. Indian loss, one killed; our loss, four horses killed.

November 5—Capt. Henry A. Greene, commanding Fort McRae, reported that a band of Indians crossed the Rio Grande near Rio Plumas, with several hundred sheep, on the night of November 4th. As soon as the information was received at Fort McRae, Capt. Greene mounted seven men and started for the point it was reported the Indians had crossed; arriving there he found that the men at the vidette station had already started in pursuit. Capt. Greene took up the trail, and on the 5th overtook the men from the station. After traveling with them one hundred and fifty miles, Capt. Green returned to Fort McRae, leaving Sergeant Rhodes and Corporal——?? to follow the trail. On the 12th of November Sergeant Rhodes returned and reported that he overtook the Indians about two hundred and twenty-five miles from the Rio Grande and after a sharp skirmish routed them and recovered 170 sheep. Private Atkinson was wounded by an arrow in this affair. The sergeant and the men who were with him are highly recommended by Capt. Greene. Indian loss, one killed and four wounded. Capt. Green states that the Indians could not have crossed the river with the sheep, within two miles of Lt. Whitemore's camp, had that officer used proper vigilance. Our loss, one private wounded.

Lt. Nicolas Hodt, 1st Cav., N. M. Vols., left Fort Canby Oct. 27th on a scout after Indians. Results of his scout: four government mules worn out and shot.

E. Montoya reported that his party attacked a band of Indians at the "Tres Hermanos" and recovered forty-two head of cattle. The Brigadier General of the N. M. Militia (Montoya) reported that Capt. Tafoya overtook a party of Indians near Sierra del Datil and took from them twenty-six head of cattle, four burros and three horses.

November 9—A party of Mexicans passed through Fort Wingate on Nov. 1st in pursuit of Indians. At the Sierra Negra the party had a fight with a band of Navajos; killed five and took sixteen prisoners. About two leagues from Sierra Negra the party had another fight with Indians; killed two and took two prisoners, twenty horses and mules and twenty-five sheep and goats. At Carriso Springs the party came upon a band of Indians numbering from two to three hundred, with several thousand head of stock; the captain of the party being fearful of losing his prisoners, allowed this band to pass unmolested. Indian loss, seven killed, forty-two prisoners; twenty horses and mules and twenty-five sheep and goats captured.

November 15—Col. Carson with his command left Fort Canby for the country west of the Oribi villages for the purpose of chastising the Navajo Indians inhabiting that region. On the 16th a detachment under Sergeant Andres Herrera overtook a small party of Indians, two of whom were killed and two wounded; fifty sheep and one horse were captured. Col. Carson speaks in high terms of the zeal and energy displayed by Sergeant Herrera. On the 25th the command captured one boy and seven horses and destroyed an encampment; on the same day captured one woman and one child and destroyed an Indian village. On the 3rd of December surprised an Indian encampment, capturing one horse and four oxen. The Indians escaped. Indian loss, two killed, two wounded, three captured; 550 sheep and goats, nine horses and four oxen captured.

November 4—Ten head of cattle belonging to the command at Valles Grandes were driven off by the Indians.

November 9—Jose Ignacio Valencia, in charge of a herd of sheep, had a fight with Indians at Canoncitas de las Conchas. One Indian was killed.

November 27—Roman A. Baca reported that he left Cebolleta with a party of 116 mounted Mexicans and travelled in a northwesterly direction for six days; when about fifty miles from Chusca, on the sixth day out, the party encountered about two hundred Indians; killed six and took three prisoners who are now in the custody of Lt. Stevens. The party also captured three Indian ponies.

November 30—Lt. J. Laughlin, while enroute from Fort Wingate to Los Pinos on the night of November 30 surprised a party of six or seven Indians at the Rio Puerco; the Indians fled leaving seventy head of cattle which were taken to Los Pinos and turned over to the owner.

December 1—Capt. H. A. Greene receiving information that a band of Indians crossed the Jornada with 200 sheep, took seven of his men and started on their trail. The party overtook the sheep on the summit of Sierra Caballo on the east side of the Rio Grande. The sheep were taken to Fort McRae.

December 7—Lt. Benjamin F. Stevens reported that he saw three Mexicans near Cebolleta having three Indian captives in their possession; the whole party were taken prisoners by him. The Mexicans soon made their escape. The Indians were sent to Fort Sumner.

December 6—Navajos ran off some cows from the Santa Ana Pueblo; the Indians of the pueblo went in pursuit, recovered their stock and killed two Navajos.

December 11—Jose Maria Martin, with a party of Mexicans, went in pursuit of Navajos who had been stealing stock; the stock was recovered and two Indians killed.

December 16—Major Henry D. Wallen, U. S. 7th Inf., commanding Fort Sumner, reported that on the morning of the 16th Mr. Labadie and Rev. A. Fialon reported to him that a large number of Indians with an immense herd of sheep were at the Carretas. The officers and men of Co. D, 5th, and Co. C, 7th Inf., were awakened and prepared to take the field with two days rations; a Lieutenant with eight mounted men of Co. B, 2nd Cav., Cal. Vols. was also got in readiness. Mr. Labadie and Rev. Fialon, with thirty Apaches also started in pursuit. The party left the post at 5:30 A. M. for the Carretas; the mounted men and Indian Agent, with the Indians, outstripped the party on foot and took up the Navajo trail on the west bank of the Pecos. At thirty-five miles northwest of Fort Sumner they overtook the Navajos, in number about 130, ten mounted and twenty armed with rifles. A severe contest ensued in which the Navajos lost twelve killed and left on the field, and a number killed and wounded who were carried off; one prisoner taken, all the sheep recovered, amounting to 5,259 burros, four rifles, one horse; their provisions, blankets, 150 pairs of moccasins and nearly all the effects taken from Mr. Labadie's train. Major Wallen calls the attention of the General commanding to the gallant conduct of Mr. Labadie, Privates Loser and Osier of Co. B, 2nd Cav., Cal. Vols. Ojo Blanco, Cadeta, the chiefs of the Apaches; Alazan, an Apache who was badly wounded and the Apaches generally who rendered signal service. Lt. Newbold, with three men, pursued the flying Navajos three miles beyond the scene of action but owing to the exhausted condition of his animals was obliged to desist from further pursuit. The Navajos, just before reaching the Pecos, were alarmed by some pistol shots discharged from a wagon train and abandoned 4,630 sheep which were secured by the Mexicans attached to the train. Lt. McDermott, with ten mounted men and six Apaches, was sent to collect the herd and bring it to the post. Before reaching the camp, Alazan died.

Thirty-five Navajos were sent to Fort Sumner today. They gave themselves up at Fort Wingate as prisoners of war.

December 20—1st Lt. D. Montoya, 1st Cav., N. M. Vols., in accordance with instructions received from Col. Carson, left Fort Canby in pursuit of a party of Navajo Indians. On the second day out he marched through a heavy snow storm. On the third day came upon an Indian encampment, attacked it, and succeeded in killing one Indian and capturing thirteen women and children beside a lot of Navajo blankets, moccasins, etc. Near the Pueblo Colorado the command pursued two Indians and captured the woman. Lt. Montoya recommends to the notice of the Colonel commanding the good conduct and soldierly bearing of 1st Lt. C. M. Hubbell, 1st Sgt. Antonio Mora of Co. C, 1st Cav., N. M. Vols., who was severely wounded in the last affair. Corporal Marcos of Co. C was particularly conspicuous on this scout; he was also wounded. Sgt. Jose Ortiz was also very active in pursuing and engaging the Indians.

December 22—Capt. John Thompson, 1st Cav., N. M. Vols., left Fort Canby with one hundred men on a scout after Indians. On the 26th at Mesa la Baca he sent out Sgt. Romero with thirty men, who came upon a party of Indians; killed one and captured twelve. On the same day under Sgt. Dorsette discovered two Indians; wounded one, captured the other.

December 28—The people of San Miguel (del Bado) and

Pueblo (two miles from San Miguel on the present road to Sena or Puertecito as it was then known) overtook and surprised a party of Indians and recovered a lot of cattle and took the arms of the Indians."

CHAPTER ELEVEN

1864

1864 was the greatest year in the eventful life of Col. Kit Carson. It opened with Canon de Chelly (or Chelle as he spelled it) and closed with Adobe Walls—both victories, both proving him to be the undisputed engineer of telling expeditions against the Indian—neither engagement took place in New Mexico as we know it. Canon de Chelly, today a National Monument, is north of Fort Defiance, just across the New Mexico line in Arizona; Adobe Walls, to achieve fame again in buffalo hunting days, is in the Texas Panhandle, near Borger. Both engagements took place in cold weather. Whatever the romantic touch in dime novels regarding Indian endurance in cold weather, Carson knew this did not apply to Navajos. The Colonel would use all weapons at his command—cold and starvation proved his allies.

Canon de Chelly, Canon del Muerto and Monument Canyon form a series of long, deep gorges cut in red sandstone of the Defiance Plateau by streams that carry off the major part of the runoff from the Lukachuhai, Chuska and Tunitcha mountains. The perpendicular smooth walls of the canon parallel each other for miles, often attaining heights surpassing one thousand feet. In niches in their sides the remains of prehistoric dwellings seemingly hang by a thread. There is good bottom land along the floor of the canon. Here the Navajos had fruit trees, fields of maize, pumpkin, squash and watermelon. Here water flowed. In the summer. With plenty of wood and food high up in those cliff dwellings, they could withstand and hold out against Grant's army if sent against them.

For a long time Carson studied the topography as more and more roving bands of Navajos sought this natural fortress. Fall succeeded summer as the Indians wondered why he had not attacked. Then came the heavy snows. Carson was ready. On January 6th he issued marching orders to fourteen commissioned officers and 375 enlisted men. Through the snow they marched —three full days—from Fort Canby to Canon de Chelly. In the summer it would have taken a day, but the Navajos would have had the advantage. Carson halted at Pueblo, Colorado, long enough to meet the supply train driven by oxen. This was under the command of Major Jose D. Sena and was sent out shortly after the New Year before the troops readied themselves so as to be at this precise spot by the 9th. The going was rougher than Carson anticipated for it took the train five days to make the 25 mile journey, and 27 oxen were lost along the way. Compelled to lighten the loads, the Colonel left behind ten days rations to be guarded by twenty-five men. Three days later he arrived at the west mouth of the canon de Chelly. Camping there for the night the following day he made a detour to the right of the line of march taking his staff and an escort with him. Six miles from the mouth he decided to reconnoiter before giving battle. He proceeded up the canyon on the south side for another five miles but finding no possible means for descending to the floor he decided to turn back. Indians on the north side watched his movements breathing easier when they saw that they were out of range of his small arms.

Meantime Sergeant Andres Herrera had been sent out the night before with fifty men to locate signs of fresh trails. At daybreak he followed tracks in the snow overtaking the Indians as they were about to enter the canyon. He attacked, killing eleven Indians, capturing some prisoners and sheep and goats before he re-joined Carson just returning from his unsuccessful efforts at descent. The next day the Colonel changed his tactics. He sent out two commands to operate each side of the canyon. Each had haversacks filled with three days rations. Carson, while not a well read man, was a well informed man. Canby and others told him that Major General Irvin McDowell lost the First Battle of Bull Run (Manassas) because he failed to take into consideration that the rations which he ordered cooked on the 18th of July and put into haversacks on the following day might not be cooked because brigade and regiment commanders would find other matters to occupy their time. As it turned out the cooking was done on Sunday, July 20th, and the day lost gave Beauregard and Johnston the time they needed. Rations were a primary consideration with Carson. Here in the dead of winter they would make the difference between success and failure. This Navajo

Rock of Gibraltar would not be another Manassas. Yet the plan in many respects followed the pattern mapped out by McDowell for Manassas and makes one wonder whether or not Carson received some sound advice from the regular army officers serving with his command. Unlike McClellan he took it. Humility was characteristic of the old Indian fighter who was not destined to survive the war by many years. He was more corpulant now than in the days when he went on scouting expeditions with Maxwell, Abreu, St. Vrain, Fremont and others, but his brain was alert and was to remain so till the end of his days. He was not only a born leader; it was thrust upon him.

The first command he sent out under the leadership of Captain A. B. Carey, 13th U. S. Inf., consisted of Companies B and G, 1st Cav., N. M. Vols. The second headed by Captain Joseph Beney, 1st Cav., N. M. Vols., marched along the north side of the canyon. Carson marched with Carey mostly because he was a bit apprehensive about Captain Pfeiffer sent out from Fort Canby to operate from the east opening of the canyon with a view of adding to the knowledge of the topography in that direction. Carson was under the impression that no white man had ever penetrated this region before especially the section known as Canon del Muerto. In 1805, Baca, Montoya, Torres, Apodaca and others from Socorro, Belen, La Joya, San Acacia, Polvadera, Alamillo and Lemitar banded together in retaliation for a raid on their sheep, trailing the Navajos to what became known as Massacre Cave in the Canon del Muerto. Marks made by the bullets that ricocheted when fired into the interior may be seen to this day. Women and children were not spared. The Indians realized then that this natural fortress proved ineffectual when the natives were aroused. Now, sixty years later, the white man was again sufficiently maddened to track the enemy to his hideout.

Carson came upon the bodies of the dead and wounded left there by Sergeant Herrera the day before. The Navajos were too stunned to pick up the wounded under cover of the night and Dr. Shout marveled that they hadn't frozen to death. Two died before he was able to give medical attention; three recovered under his skillful care. Asked later why they did not care for their wounded or bury their dead they replied that they were told by traders and Comancheros that this was a war of extermination. No quarter would be given neither to man woman nor child. This they readily believed because Carson kept after them, hunting them down like wild animals, allowing no time for provisioning themselves, applying the scorched earth policy, keeping them on the move without food or clothing or a place to lay their heads—relentless in his aim to starve them out, burn them out or bury them. Their villages were razed, their live stock taken, their children captive. Only this Gibraltar of Navajodom was left. Now even that was gone.

Carson continued his march to a point in the canyon that afforded an unobstructed view of the eastern outlet, anxiously hoping to see some signs of Pfeiffer. Neither a soldier nor an Indian was in sight. Under the fresh snow the barren ground yielded no grass for the mounts. He had no choice but to return. His only satisfaction was in knowing that the south side of the canyon could be flanked from east to west without much trouble, there being no interesting canyons of any extent. Back in camp he rejoiced to find that Pfeiffer had accomplished his mission without casualty and performed the rare feat of passing through the canyon from east to west in good order. He had killed three Indians, brought in nineteen prisoners, buried two other Indians found frozen to death. When an Indian can freeze to death in his own country it speaks well for these strangers so open to attack. The Captain had this to say about his progress through the Canon del Muerto:

"For the first twelve miles my travel through the canyon was accomplished on the ice of the bed of the stream which courses through it. Lt. C. M. Hubbell, who was in charge of the rear, had a great deal of trouble in proceeding with the pack trains, as the mules frequently broke through the ice and tumbled down with their loads. All the Indian prisoners taken thus far were half starved and naked. The canyon has no road except the bottom of the creek. We traveled mostly on the ice, our animals breaking through every few minutes, and one mule split completely open under the exhausting fatigue of the march. We traveled eight miles on the 12th and had several skirmishes with the Indians who were on both sides of the canyon whooping, yelling and cursing, firing shots and throwing rocks down upon my command. Killed two buck Indians in the encounter and one squaw, who obstinately persisted in hurling rocks and pieces of wood at the soldiers. Six prisoners were captured on this occasion. . . . Here the Navajos sought refuge when pursued by the invading force, whether of neighboring tribes or the arms of the Government, and here they were enabled to jump about on the ledges of the rocks like mountain cats, hallowing at me, swearing and cursing and threatening vengeance on my command in every variety of Spanish they were capable of mastering; a couple of shots from my soldiers with their trusty rifles caused the redskins to disperse instantly...." (W.R. o.c.)

As Carson made his way back to the main camp he was joined by three Indians with a flag of truce. They said that they wished to submit and requested permission to bring their people to the camp. The Colonel told them that they could come unmolested up to ten o'clock the next morning. If they did not show up by that time they would be hunted down and the work of destruction continued. The next morning sixty Indians surrendered. Carson explained to them that they would have to go to the Bosque Redondo location that Carleton had selected for them. They made it clear that they had no choice. They were in the state of starvation; many of their women and children had already died of neglect and for want of nourishment. A reservation was better than extermination. After eating the meat placed before them they requested permission to return to their caves to tell the others. Perhaps any other man would have expected deception at this point. Carson gave them ten days to convince their tribesmen.

Captain Carey was sent to destroy the peach orchards and the dwellings. An artist accompanied him in order to make some sketches of the canyon for the government. Carey was to return from west to east. A number of Navajos asked to accompany him. What they thought as their peach trees and homes went up in smoke has not been recorded. Captain Berney returned with his command after killing two Indians. It is to the credit of these Captains as well as to Major Jose D. Sena and Colonel Carson that they did not slaughter nor massacre when every opportunity presented itself. If victory is gauged not in the number killed but by the number of prisoners taken then Carson's was a tremendous one. How many Navajos would have reached the Bosque Redondo under a different leader is something that will keep arm-chair generals busy for generations to come as they argue the whys and wherefores.

Carson returned to Fort Canby to receive the Indians as they arrived and to send out other expeditions to prosecute the campaign and to effect the speedy removal of all the Indians north and west of the Little Red River. No sooner in camp than four Indians overtook him explaining that they were from the vicinity of the Juanico Mountains where there were some rich Navajos who would like to come in and surrender themselves but were afraid that they would be deprived of their possessions. Carson held no assurance. He was only in charge of the campaign; other officials regulated what they could or could not take to the Bosque. Leaving his prisoners at the post, and three companies to guard them, Carson went out a second time remaining away sixteen days. When he returned he found Capt. Carey with one hundred and ten additional prisoners waiting for him. Lt. L. G. Murphy of Lincoln County War fame accompanied Carson on this expedition. On January 23rd, Major Sena in charge of the supply train, returned to Fort Canby with over three hundred more Navajos. Chief Cabeza Blanco was with him. He reported that he expected over a thousand of his people would come in shortly to give themselves up. Already Fort Canby had more Navajos than soldiers. Near Cienaga Juanico some of Captain Pfeiffer's soldiers saw smoke in a distance. He sent Sergeant Trujillo to investigate. It was a camp fire made by eight Navajo women and children in eighteen inches of snow. All were in the state of starvation.

Carson was in favor of dispersing the Indians very much as the Utes did with their captives. While these latter sold them to Mexican families, Carson was in favor of giving them away free so that they could have food to eat and clothes to wear. He told General Carleton that if they were disposed of in this manner they would be no expense to the government and they would be domesticated in time. They would be better off among the natives than at Bosque Redondo. Carleton would not hear of it and wanted every prisoner accounted for. He was going to prove to the whole world that he had the answer for he was positive he could make agrarians out of the nomads.

On January 17th the Navajos took over the express station at Ojo de Oso. Sergeant J. Martin Bud, Co. K, 1st Cav., N. M. Vols., was sent to attack the station. After a short but lively battle the Indians fled. He succeeded in capturing six. These were turned over to Lt. Bishop who took them to Fort Wingate. Next the Navajos attacked Rio Arriba where they ran off stock. Citizens of the town trailed them to Canon de Chelly but were unable to find neither stock nor Indians. The one Navajo they chanced upon was speedily dispatched without much ado. The trek known to the Navajos as El Paseo Largo (The Long Walk) began during the first week of March when Captain Carey sent 2,103 Navajos to the Bosque Redondo under the supervision of Captain John Thompson, 1st Cav., N. M. Vols., with the aid of five non-commissioned officers and 22 privates of Company K, N. M. Vols. The Indians could have overpowered them by sheer force of numbers. Perhaps the thought of food during those winter months, or the fact that they were tired of hiding away deterred them for the moment.

Wagon-master Russell was well known and well liked by both the California and New Mexico Volunteers. When the Navajos attacked his train and killed him a howl of protest reached Carleton. Captain Francis McCabe was sent to track them down. His disciplinary measures were even more rigid than those of Carson's. At no time during the expedition were the men permitted to talk above a whisper. No smoking was allowed much less a fire. All traveling was done at night; the day was given to sleeping and resting the mounts. The Indians were found at Rio Puerco. Rather than hazard a battle they fled. McCabe returned with one hundred and twelve prisoners.

Indians alone did not occupy Carleton's time. In March he wrote to General H. W. Halleck in Washington for the sum of one hundred thousand dollars to be drawn on the Bank of San Francisco for supplies for the California Volunteers. Tired of waiting for the Texans to attack, Carleton decided to take the offensive. Just how well Carleton knew General George McClellan I have not been able to determine. Both had served in the Southwest and seemed to have crossed each other's path in the decade preceding the war. When one studies McClellan's plan and tactics for moving the Army of the Potomac to Yorktown he begins to wonder whether the General was a pen pusher or a sword pusher. This much they both seemed to have in common: letters to superiors and feeling superior to the one to whom the letter was addressed. With the possible exception of Antietam McClellan did not cover himself with glory. Indeed failure to follow up his victory cost him his command. Carleton did not see one major nor even minor engagement from the first day of the war to the last. Anxious to meet Sibley or Baylor in an exchange of fire, the only shots he was able to fire were through letters to superiors as perfectionists are wont to do. No perfectionist ever lived who did not make enemies in his own ranks, and McClellan and Carleton are good examples of the destruction of delayed action. Always going to, when I get more supplies, more men, more guns, more this and more that—much to the joy of the enemy who capitalizes on all these useless preparations that set the stage for inactivity. Carleton could not afford Pinkerton men as did Mc Clellan but he did have his spies and these told him that the Texans were ready to march on New Mexico. Meantime he expanded his pet project—a reservation for Navajos and Apaches. But what of the Utes, Commanches, Kiowas, Cheyennes, and other tribes that raided the frontier settlements, and even the interior, at will? For the moment even the Navajos had to be put aside for the more important task of readying the troops for an attack against Texas.

Captain P. W. L. Plympton was sent to Chihuahua to plead with the governor for beef, flour, corn, mules and horses. Of all the times to ask aid of Mexico! When the advance columns of the French army under Generals Douay and Bazaine were marching on Pueblo, and Mexico would need all the supplies and mounts to check the ambitions of Maximilian. Mexico, too, was at war. It was fighting to preserve its unity of States. When Juarez at this very time sought refuge in the city of Chihuahua the crowds invaded his lodging and forced him to accompany them to the site where Hidalgo met his death and to make a speech at the base of the monument, for they looked to him as the Liberator. How then could they give to another army when their own was in want? Even Plympton could understand this. If, however, the Federals would give guns in exchange, then perhaps both parties would arrive at a fairly satisfactory agreement. Exchange for guns! This would involve international treaties, letters to the Secretary of War, so many more delays which Carleton could ill afford especially since five companies of the First California Volunteers would be mustered out of service during July, August and September. Carleton knew they were anxious to get back to California to re-enlist in other fields where battles against the Confederates were taking place. He must give them cause to re-enlist in New Mexico.

He would send these companies to General West at Mesilla. West was to march into Texas and attack General K. Smith. He was to attach his command with that of General Banks and together unite in crushing the Texan who still insisted that New Mexico and Arizona were part of the Confederate States. For this purpose he needed $150,00 in coin for the Quartermaster's Department, and the same amount for the Subsistence Department, all of which could be drawn either at New York, St. Louis or San Francisco. If he could not obtain food and mounts from the Governor of Chihuahua he could at least request permission for General West to enter his troops through Mexican territory in the march from El Paso to El Paso del Norte so as to cut off the road leading from El Paso del Norte to San Antonio. This offensive action must be kept very secret. The men were not to be told where they were going. One thousand men would be stationed at Seaton's opposite El Paso del Norte; from there they would march to Eagle Pass, Monclova in Coahuila, on to San Antonio.

The plan was a bold one, at least as mapped out for General Halleck. What he sought to arrange with General Lorenzo Thomas was something different entirely. He wrote that while Confederate General K. Smith should be attacked, and General Banks could use the aid of the California Volunteers for this purpose, nevertheless, the situation was such that these troops were really needed to protect Arizona, which was having as much difficulty with Indians as New Mexico, as well as to round up the remaining Navajos still holding out against the Bosque Redondo project. There were now six thousand Indians at the reservation but there was room for more.

During the first week of April Governor Goodwin wrote General Carleton that the Indians were becoming increasingly bolder and he needed troops to wipe them out. Generals Halleck and Thomas both agreeing that General Banks might be able to take care of the situation in Texas without the aid of General West, Carleton arranged to have five hundred of the Volunteers start from Las Cruces and move into Arizona. Meantime Lt. Nelson was sent to scout around in Texas should any movement be contemplated against New Mexico when these troops left Las Cruces. He succeeded in rounding up a few prisoners from Captain Skillman's company taking them to Santa Fe for questioning. Carleton was convinced more than ever that vigilance was to be the by-word since the Texans were awaiting an opportunity to re-capture Mesilla and Tucson.

Despite Judge Knapp's attacks on Carleton the Bosque

Redondo project seemed to sound off very nicely. There were two hundred Navajo children attending school at the reservation; the Indians were planting corn, orchards, making adobes, and otherwise usefully employed. Over a thousand more still awaited transportation from Fort Canby. In secret they were home sick for their own country. They resented being forced to live with their enemies, the Apaches, at Bosque Redondo. Carleton thought they were being particular in wanting the reservation to themselves, for there was no reason why Indians from various tribes could not live as harmoniously together as white men of different nationalities.

Lt. Henry H. Stevens was sent into Arizona Territory to stop the depredations of the Indians there. He had forty-seven enlisted men, a detachment of one Corporal and ten California Volunteers of Company C, 5th Infantry, accompanied by Juan Arrozas of Rio Mimbres as guide. He steered them right into an ambush of one hundred Apaches at Steen's Peak. Steven's horse was killed, one man mortally wounded, and three slightly wounded at the first volley. The battle lasted for forty-five minutes. When the smoke cleared away ten Indians lay dead and thirty wounded. The march after Confederate General Smith would have to wait.

In Washington Senator Doolittle presented Senate Bill No. 226 in which he asked that $100,000 be sent to help the Indians at the Bosque Redondo. Honorable J. P. Usher, Secretary of the Interior, was asked to investigate the necessity of placing such funds in Carleton's care. Secretary of War, Edwin M. Stanton, was not too sure that the Indians were worth that much. He called in General Canby asking him the advisability of such generousity. Canby told him that the government had spent eight years trying to herd the Navajos but had nothing to show for all the expense of the campaigns. Now that Carleton had them at the Bosque Redondo it would be worth the government's efforts to pass the Bill. When placed before the Committee for a vote 24 were in favor; eleven voted no. The Indians got the money. It was also decided to move Fort Whipple to a new location the better to deal with the recalcitrant Apaches. Colonel Carson was sent to Fort Sumner to take charge of the post and to deal with the Indians at the Bosque.

Dr. J. M. McNulty had charge of the funds privately collected by the Volunteers from California to take care of needs other than military. He had over seven thousand dollars. A meeting was called as to how to dispose of these funds. It was decided to build a hospital in Santa Fe at Fort Marcy, to be placed in the care of the Sisters of Loretto at Our Lady of Light Academy. Lt. C. H. De Forrest drew up the blue prints for the project and forwarded them to Washington. The blue prints were rejected. Eventually the Sisters of Charity built St. Vincent's Hospital near the post (See: *Santa Fe Gazette* July 2, 1864). Fearful that he would lose too many soldiers wishing to muster out for service elsewhere, Carleton appealed to them at Fort Craig, through the voice of the editor of the *Santa Fe Gazette* (August 18):

"California Volunteers: Are you aware that your adopted State has done much for her sons who are now enlisted in the service of their country? As soon as you are mustered out of the service you will receive a duplicate certificate of discharge, which, with the addition of your signature, you can forward in a letter to Brig. General George S. Evans, Adjutant General of the State of California, and he will remit you at once the amount of your five dollars bounty. Request him to return you the marked value and for your three years term of service he will send you the full amount, less ten percent, in gold coin, or the equivalent in notes which runs to about three hundred dollars.

"In addition to this, the last legislature of our State passed an Act giving a bounty of three hundred dollars to each and every one of her brave soldiers who may re-enlist. This last amount you can likewise obtain from the Adjutant General of the State of California, who is a soldier's true friend. He will do all in his power to aid and assist you in procuring, free of charge, every allowance to which you are, or may be, entitled.

"As soon as you re-enlist a roll will be made out and forwarded to California of all the men re-enlisting, and you will at the same time receive a copy of enlistment papers, which, on being forwarded to General Evans, will enable you to obtain, at once, without cost, the three hundred dollars bounty for re-enlistment. This, when converted into notes, will amout to very nearly six hundred dollars.

"In addition to this your five dollar bounty will continue as heretofore. From all of which you will preceive that instead of doing less than some of the Eastern States, California is doing more as may be shown from the following figures:

Amount of $5.00 Bounty due	$180
Amount of $5.00 Bounty for re-enlistment	$300
Amount of $5.00 Bounty to Veterans	$180
Total in gold coin	$600

"This is worth to you, here at least, one thousand dollars in notes."

While the signature affixed was that of Oscar M. Brown, Col. 1st Cal. Cav., Cal. Vols., commanding Fort Craig for the moment, the wording was that of the editor of the Gazette who favored Carleton throughout his struggle with Judge Knapp simply because the editor of the rival *Santa Fe Weekly News* was opposed to Carleton, Bosque Redondo, and the General's Indian policy. Although the Volunteers were divided between loyalty to Carleton and a chance to fight Confederates rather than Indians, the sum proved a tempting morsel to many. As many said: if it were a question of fighting Indians there were many closer to home; they did not have to come to New Mexico for that, for, as they understood it, they enlisted because Sibley was preparing to attack Arizona and New Mexico.

During the last week of July the Apaches again went on the rampage attacking Trujillo, La Cuesta, Anton Chico and Chaparito, taking women and children prisoners, running off live stock and killing men and youths that opposed them. Captain Emil Fritz took eighteen men with him from Fort Sumner but lost the trail in the Gallinas Mts. Again Carleton appealed to the Volunteers not to forsake New Mexico for California. The chance to get at the Confederates was close at hand if they would be patient. He wrote an open letter to them and all the people of New Mexico which was published in the July 15th issue of the *Santa Fe Gazette*:

"The condition of affairs in the Department of New Mexico having reference to the proximity of Texas, and to the fact that the Confederate forces have spies hovering about our boundaries and prowling in our midst, where they have many friends and correspondents, of which we have positive proof; and considering the fact that the commander of the Confederate forces in Texas still claims this Territory and that of Arizona as belonging to his Department, and still flaunts at the head of his orders and letters—Head Quarters Department of Texas, New Mexico and Arizona—thereby making either a puerile and ridiculous vaunt, or indicating a standing claim on this country which he is only awaiting a favorable opportunity to enforce; and considering the fact that bands of guerrillas and robbers, claiming to be Confederate troops, hover along the throughfares leading to to New Mexico, from the east, which bands doubtless have their emissaries in our midst to give information when the trains of our wealthy citizens start with funds for the purchase of goods in the States, so that these trains may be waylaid and robbed at points of the road favorable to such enterprises as has been recently done, it continues to be a military necessity that the persons traveling through this Department shall be provided with passports by which they can be identified and distinguished from spies and traitors and rebels. The General in Chief of the Army in alluding to this matter sums up in a few words why the police regulations are necessary here.

"In a Department like that of New Mexico and Arizona, of great geographical extent and a sparce population mostly strangers to each other, with a small military force mostly at isolated and remote stations, and with numerous spies and traitors scattered throughout the country measures of military police somewhat stringent in their character are sometimes necessary to preserve peace and order. No good and loyal citizen can object to them. All such can comply with the rule without inconvenience or loss of dignity. I mention in this connection that I, myself, and the officers of my staff, have be required to procure, in Washington and St. Louis, passports from our inferior officers, the Provosts Marshals, for our identification to enable us to pass the guards in the streets and public roads. In times of war and public danger, this is a proper and necessary measure of military police, and no officer, military or civil, no matter what his rank can object to it in places where the public safety requires its adoption. Officers of this Department are not to be thrown off their guard against the machinations of rebels who in reality covert the gold fields of Arizona and the silver mines of New Mexico. We must guard against traitors in our midst. Passports will be furnished at Franklin, Las Cruces, Fort McRae, Fort Craig, Los Pinos, Albuquerque, Santa Fe, Fort Sumner, Fort Union, Fort Bascom and other places. Non-residents of New Mexico are required to take the oath of allegiance to the United States before being furnished with a passport."

Captain Emil Fritz, seeing that he would avail nothing in

pursuing the large war party of Apaches raiding the settlements, returned to Fort Sumner, where the commanding officer, Captain H. B. Bristol, sent Captain F. McCabe with 43 enlisted men of Company L, N. M. Vols., six Navajo spies and guides, to track down the marauders believed heading south from the Gallinas to the Sierra Oscura Mountains. Lt. H. C. Gilbert said that he had traced them there. He and the eight men left him by Fritz for that purpose joined McCabe near the Mal Pais country. They traveled on to Ojo de Loma, Sierra Oscura, Jornada del Muerto, Ojo Alamo where they found Sanchez, the post guide of Fort Stanton, who thought he was trailing Major Chacon. At Tularosa thirteen citizens joined the group. Lt. Gilbert was sent on with twenty men to follow the trail for the Indians were now definitely proven to be Coyoteros Apaches heading for their own country. He was ambushed by seventy of the party and killed. The Indians fled to the San Francisco Mountains. Captain H. A. Greene, still in command of Fort McRae, went on the trail of the party that split from the main group to head the six thousand sheep they had taken from Anton Chico into the San Andres Mountains. The Indians escaped under cover of darkness leaving the Captain the sheep to be restored to their rightful owners. McCabe kept on the trail of the others on to the Guadalupe Mountains. A snow storm forced him to return to Tulerosa. He had marched eighteen hundred miles in 88 days to be halted by a snow storm. Lt. Gilbert was buried with appropriate honors. He was neither scalped nor mutilated. His grave was on the highest peaks in the Sacramento Mountains.

Colonel Chacon joined his forces with those of McCabe. At the Sacramento river they had a skirmish with some Indians, other than the ones they were trailing. One private was killed, one wounded. Four deserted under cover of the heavy exchange of shots. Three of the Navajo scouts took sick as well as five other men. These McCabe sent back to Fort Sumner with Col. Chacon who felt that since McCabe had the orders to trail the Apaches he should not interfere. Next the Indians raided Cimarron Crossing stealing one hundred and thirty mules. Asst. Inspector General N. H. Davis went in pursuit but was not able to overtake neither mules nor Indians. General Carleton went to Fort Union for ten days to personally supervise the departure of the main body of troops he was sending into the Plains country to stop the Commanches, Kiowas and Cheyennes. Indeed Carleton spent the fall of 1864 visiting all posts south, east and west of Santa Fe down on to Franklin. It was at Las Cruces on December 16th that he penned a letter to all the people of New Mexico defending his treatment of the Navajos at Bosque Redondo. At Franklin he was especially interested in finding out whether there were any signs of approaching Confederates. Ascertained that there were none he attended the ball in his honor breathing freer than he had for months.

Colonel O. M. Brown left Fort Craig for the Sierra Blanca Mountains on October 1st. He took with him Captain Wm. Ayers, 1st N. M. Vols., and twenty of his men; Captain W. H. Lent, 1st N. M. Infantry and thirty of his men; Lt. L. F. Sanburn, Co. H, 1st Cal. Vols., Mounted, and fifty of his men together with five packers and herders, two guides, one interpreter, 42 pack mules, and a month's rations. Guides Felipe Gonzoles and Antonio Santillanes of Limitar led him to the Little Colorado river where they came upon a rancheria to uncover several old men, women and children, the rest having fled. On November 7th he arrived at San Vicente (present Silver City) the Indians always retreating before him. Winter in the Black Range mountains becoming too severe, he returned to Fort Craig.

Colonel Kit Carson, relieved of duties at Fort Sumner, was given new orders. He was to lead the expedition from Fort Union into the Plains country. General Carleton had spent much time with him and Lucien B. Maxwell going over details. Maxwell favored the use of Utes and Jicarillas living on his famous grant as guides and warriors since they were the traditional enemies of the Indians Carson was being sent to conquer. Carleton admitted the wisdom of their plan. Over in the extreme eastern corner of New Mexico was a post founded the year before by Captain Peter William Livingston Plympton who staffed it with one hundred and twelve men before he was succeeded by Captain Bergmann, who left the post with fifty men in an effort to again track down the marauders. This post was known as Fort Bascom and was built to protect the Cimarron cutoff of the Santa Fe Trail against the Comanches who used this route in traveling from Santa Fe to the Arkansas river. Late in August Captain Bergmann left the post with fifty men in an effort to find forage for his mounts somewhere near Fort Union and to clear the trail of Indians. It was at Fort Bascom that Carson made his final plans.

It was the dead of winter and a blinding snowstorm held him up for two days. Arrived at the post with 75 Utes and Jicarillas; he also assembled the following men:

Captain E. Fritz's Company B, 1st Cav., Cal. Vols.—60 men.
Capt. Wilhorn's Company M, 1st Cal. Vols., Mtd.—30 men.
Lt. Heath—part of Company K, 1st Cal. Vols.—38 men.
Captain Deus—Company M—1st Cav., New Mexico Vols.
Lt. Bishop and 69 men.
Captain Buney—Company D—1st Cav., New Mexico Vols. —39 men.
Lt. Edmeston with 58 men of Company A, 1st Vet. Cal. Vols.
Lt. Pettis—Company K—1st Inf., Cal. Vols. and 27 men.
Two mountain howitzers.

The infantry was placed under the command of Lt. Col. F. P. Abreu, 1st Inf., N. M. Vols.; the cavalry under Major William McCleave, 1st Cav., Cal. Vols., while the Indians were commanded by Lt. Charles Haberhorn, 1st Cav., N. M. Vols. In all Carson had fourteen officers (counting the medical staff) and 321 men besides the Indians. The supply train followed the troops to a place known as Adobe Fort two hundred miles east of the post, better known to us as Adobe Walls in the Texas Panhandle near the site of Borger. He was twice delayed along the Canadian river due to snow storms. At Arroyo de la Mula, about thirty miles from Adobe Walls, he dispatched two Ute spies with instructions to proceed a short distance down the river and return the same evening if they saw any fresh signs of the enemy. They returned about an hour after sunset to report signs of Kiowas and Comanches in the area. All the wagons were immediately loaded and placed in charge of Lt. Col. Abreu. Taking the infantry and dismounted cavalry force and Lt. Peter's howitzers, Carson marched fifteen miles that night before making camp. Again he sent out spies. They returned two hours before daybreak. Breaking camp Carson continued the line of march along the Canadian.

About an hour after sunup the old Indian fighter discovered a party of Indians on the opposite bank, calling for him to cross and take him if he dared. Major McCleave and Captain Deus were ordered to take their men, cross the river and give battle. Carson continued along the river. Word came of an Indian encampment five miles further along the stream. Captain Fritz was ordered to advance with his company and act in conjunction with the Major still on the opposite side of the river. The Indians opened on Fritz who shortly received the aid of Lt. Heath and his men. Carson followed with the artillery and two other companies. The Indians abandoned their camp of about one hundred and fifty lodges but hotly contested the ground between there and Adobe Walls, a distance of about four miles. At this point they took a position and made a stand. Across the river they made several charges on Major McCleave's command before Carson's arrival, but the Major had the situation well in hand having repulsed the charges. When the howitzers were placed into position the Indians ceased fire wondering what was going to happen next.

The mounts playing out, Carson ordered all firing to cease and in the face of the enemy told the men to rest and have their breakfast. While the men ate, Carson took out his spy glass, focused it at a point about three miles east of Adobe Walls where there was another Indian village of 350 lodges, and spotted a horde advancing on his command. The men were ordered to mount. No sooner were the men in position than Carson was surrounded by a thousand Indians riding better horses than he had ever hoped to see. They charged from different points, invariably repulsed with great loss. Lt. Pettis took over the howitzers whose telling effect drove the enemy out of range. The Indians decided on a siege. Rather than have the Indians carry off provisions during the night in abandoning their lodges, Carson determined to destroy the village.

Captain Fritz was ordered to protect the right flank, Captain Witham and Captain Deus the left, Captain Birney and Lt. Heath the rear. In this formation Carson marched on the villages. The Indians interposed themselves between the lodges and the advancing men. The real battle began. The Indians charged so repeatedly, and with such desperation, that Carson began to entertain doubts about the safety of the rear, but Captain Birney seemed to be holding his own as his men poured volley after volley into the adamant lines, causing them to break on every occasion with great slaughter. Their charges proving of no avail, the Indians set fire to the valley in the rear, swept of snow by the high winds such as can still blow in the Texas Panhandle. The fury of the fire caused the rear to close up at double quick. Carson retaliated by setting fire to the grass in front of him, retiring to a stretch of elevated ground on the right to be out of danger of the fire. The Indians advanced under cover of the smoke and fire only to be repulsed by the howitzers.

The fighting was constantly kept up in the rear until Carson arrived within five hundred yards of the village. The Indians again charged only to give way before the artillery. The entire village and stores amounting to one hundred and fifty lodges of the best manufacture, a large amount of dried meat, berries, buffalo robes, powder, cooking utensils and the property of the Kiowa Chief Sierrito fell into his hands. Carson admitted that the Indians acted with more daring and bravery than he had ever before witnessed. He was saddened at the sight of so many rifles of the latest make evidently sold to the Indians by unscrupulous traders and Comancheros. The battle lasted until sunset. What the Indians shot at mostly was horses possibly in order to prevent the soldiers from riding into the village. At the end of the battle Carson found that two of his men were killed, ten wounded, a large number of horses wounded. Of the allies one Ute was killed, five wounded. Of the enemy he estimated the casualties as sixty in dead and wounded. The really savage fighting took place between the Indian allies and the enemy. The Utes and Jicarillas cut off a force of Comanches and Kiowas, disobeyed Carson's orders by crossing the Canadian, pursued the fugitives deep into the Nations territory returning with many scalps and dancing their victory dance on Red Deer creek near the site of Miami in Roberts county. They never reported the scalps hung up to dry. It was a long time before Comanches and Kiowas attemped any more raids in New Mexico. Rations having been issued to December 31st, 1864 Carson left Fort Bascom for Fort Union. Camp Nicholas which he established at the bequest of General Carleton proved of little or no purpose and was shortly abandoned. Several other posts founded under the supervision of the General proved of more permanent value. Surgeon Courtwright was thankful he was not overworked with wounded out there in the biting wind that howled over the Texas Panhandle. (For an account of this engagement See W. R. also *Santa Fe Gazette* and *Rodeo Town* pp 10-21.

1864 was also the year that witnessed the second march of Missouri Volunteers into New Mexico, the first being under General Kearny (Col. Doniphan's men) in the year of Manifest Destiny. Special Orders No. 17, isued by General Carleton concern these men from Missouri: "The exigencies of the public service requires that Co. H, Eleventh Cavalry, Missouri Vols., take post at Fort Union, N. M., until further orders. The commanding officer at the post is charged with personally seeing that this company is put into a state of drill, discipline and good order. He will have two drills a day every week day—one on foot and one mounted—will have the officers recite in tactics to himself three times a week, and have the non-commissioned offcers recite in tactics to his adjutant three times a week, and will report when the company is properly instructed and ready at all points for field service. . . ."

Since there seemed little danger of a Confederate invasion in New Mexico in 1864 many of the native volunteers were permitted to go to their farms for the seasonal planting. This is why the official lists fail to tally with the actual count of men in the service. Also Carleton, Cutler, Bergmann and others seemed to be concerned with reports involving the Regulars and the California Column so as to make it appear that outsiders were protecting New Mexico when in point of fact more New Mexico Volunteers were in uniform than Regulars and the California Column combined. Here is the list sent to the War Department for troops in New Mexico in May, 1864. Not one name of a native New Mexican appears yet Estanislao Montoya's command from San Antonio (N. M.) and Stapleton's command from Socorro were afield rounding up Apaches. No soldier in any war has suffered the injustices of the New Mexican Volunteer; none ever caught in such a hopeless rope of sand nor accorded the Silent Treatment as he was; he was behind the Iron Curtain of his time. Perhaps it was the language barrier or the propaganda built up but a little over a decade before had not time to simmer down. The last time the United States was at war was against these very people. Carleton, Cutler, Brotherton, Plympton, Greene never let them forget it.

Santa Fe	Commander	Headquarters—Officers 22	Rank & File
Albuquerque	Capt. D. H. Brotherton	3	88
Fort Bascom	Capt. E. H. Bergmann	4	131
Fort Canby	Capt. P. W. Plympton	5	233
Fort Craig	Major C. E. Bennett	9	165
Fort Marcy	Capt. R. M. Crandal	2	100

Fort McRae—Capt. H. A. Greene	1	24
Fort Stanton—Capt. Wm. Brady	3	74
Fort Sumner—Major H. D. Wallen	8	219
Fort Union—Lt. Col. Wm. McMullen	13	392
Fort Wingate—Major E. W. Eaton	1	103
Fort Cummings—Capt. V. Dresher	1	38
Las Cruces—Capt. G. T. Witan	2	65

Dog Canon (Canyon) is mentioned repeatedly in reports since much of the Apache concentration took place there from the time the California Column entered New Mexico to the opening of the military reservation at Bosque Redondo. Here is a letter written at Dog Canon August 27, 1864 by Captain Francis McCabe, of the 1st N. M. Vols., to Assistant Adjutant General Ben Cutler at Santa Fe: "I have the honor to report that in obedience to verbal orders received from H. Bristol, Commanding Officer at Fort Sumner, New Mexico, I left Sumner on the 6th Inst. with 43 enlisted men of my Company L, 1st N. M. Cav. and six Navajo Indians as guides and spies, to pursue and capture an Apache war party which had lately committed various murders and robberies in the vicinity of Chaparito. On reporting to Col. Carson, Agent and Superintendant at Fort Sumner, I was instructed by him to march to Fort Stanton and after obtaining provisions and other supplies at the post, to proceed to find the Indians' trail and follow it to the village.

"The Colonel likewise advised me to go to Tulerosa and if possible to employ competent guides and a small company of citizens at that place and from there to proceed to Dog Canon where he supposed the Indians would be found with their plunder. I started accordingly and on the 11th inst. arrived at Fort Stanton where I was advised that the same body of Indians had attacked Mr. Parker's train near Gallinas Springs, and run off his mules. I could find no guide here but on the morning of the 12th as I was ready to start Lieut. H. C. Gilbert, 1st Cav., N. M. Vols., and eight men who had been sent out to pursue the Indians returned with the information that he had followed their trail until he overtook them at a point in the Sierra Oscura and that he judged their village was but a short distance from that point. Lieut. Gilbert stated that he returned for reinforcements to attack the rancheria. I accordingly started that afternoon with Lt. Gilbert and his party of eight men attached to mine. After marching all night I halted at a point thirty-six miles north of the Sierra Oscura mountains. At 12 o'clock on the 13th I left camp and marched until sundown, when I halted at a (rain) water hole about eight miles east of Mal Pais. Here I was informed by one of my Navajo guides that he knew where the Apache village lay, and that by marching all the next day he could reach it. I accordingly marched at daylight and crossed Mal Pais, which being a belt of disrupted and broken rocks, with no other known trail, the passage was exceedingly difficult and many of my horses and mules were badly cut by the sharp projecting rocks.

"I reached El Ojo de la Loma, a spring in the desert between the Siera Blanca and the Sierra Oscura ranges about 2 p. m. and having watered and unsaddled my animals I sent forward the Indian to reconnoitre the Apache village. He returned at dark stating that it was about five or six leagues off. I then marched the next day to the point that Lieut. Gilbert reported having seen the Apaches and after having passed through many canyons I reached it at 3 p. m. The Indian guides pronounced the trail to be eight or ten days old. I started the same evening and followed it until dark when I was obliged to halt for the night. At daylight the next morning my Navajo guide informed me that the trail passed over the spur of the Sierra Oscura mountains to the village. We marched to this place and reached it at noon but found that it had not been occupied by Indians recently. I returned the same day and encamped at a hole of water in the rocks and at daylight the next morning resumed the search for the trail, which was found running in a westerly direction along the base of the Sierra Oscura. I marched all that day and all night passing a deep canyon in the mountains twenty miles long which opens on the Jornada del Muerte. The night march was conducted in a severe thunderstorm which lasted several hours. Having halted at daylight I rested until 12 o'clock noon and marched again on the trail which took a direction south. At 6 p. m. I halted in a fine valley where grass was abundant but not water for the animals, and next day resumed the march at daylight and at 12 noon found a little water in holes, sufficient for the men but not for the animals. At 3 p. m. I found water and good grass at Ojo Alamo in a deep canyon in the mountains. Here I was joined by Sanchez, the post guide of Fort Stanton, who informed me that he had mistaken my trail for that of

Major Chacon who was a day's march in the rear. I started the next morning taking the guide with me whom I sent about six hundred yards ahead with five men to trail. By this time my Navajo guides stated that the mountains were unknown to them and they believed that the Indians (we were pursuing) were Coyotero Apaches. I found water this day twice on the trail before 12 o'clock, and after a severe march of 45 miles I encamped without water within ten miles of a point where the trail entered the desert in the San Andres mountains. My guide was totally ignorant of the country and a few of my men proved better trailers than the guide. On the morning of the 22nd. I started for the point where the canyon opened on the desert sending the guide and trailers in advance in search of water. No water was found until we searched the salt lake called Salina toward which my guide led me assuring me that the water was potable. On reaching there I found to my mortification that the water was salt. I had to saddle up and march toward the San Nicolas mountains. I found a hole of water near that point and found the mule and sheep trail running across the desert toward Dog Canon. After a short rest I marched across the desert and next morning arrived at the water tanks having marched sixty miles in 24 hours.

"Half of my command's horses were still on the desert when I reached the tanks and I immediately sent back water for their relief and at noon marched to a stream called Rio Alamo. I found here that most of my horses had broken down. They were abandoned by my order. Several of my men were very sick. I rested that day and sent my guide to Dog Canon to look for the trail. He returned the next morning and informed me that the trail led into the canon, and the Indians were there. I immediately formed my men, mounted and dismounted, and marched to the canon determined to enter it and attack the Indians. I found on entering the mouth that the Indians had (merely) entered it (for the purpose of) watering their horses and had left and started for the Sacramento river four days before. I detailed Lieut. Gilbert with twenty men to follow the trail instructing him to use caution and diligence in the pursuit, and marched my broken down men and horses to a camp near Tulerosa to recruit.

"On reaching Tulerosa I called for guides and a party to take a new direction to the laguna where I supposed the Indian village to be located. Mr. Parker reached me yesterday morning informing me that Major Chacon had arrived and I started with sixteen of my men and fourteen citizens besides to follow the Indians. On my way to this place I received a messenger who informed me that Lieutenant Gilbert had a fight with the Indians yesterday near Rio Milagro and that the Lieutenant was killed at the first discharge. All the horses were killed and wounded by the Apaches, and a guide and one man mortally wounded. Corporal Gallegos behaved well and brought off the wounded. He was of Co. L. The fourteen Apaches whom we were pursuing had been joined by a large number of others, who, we have been informed by our Navajo guide, are Coyoteros. I have sent out water and wagons to relieve and bring in my wounded, and I will march in half an hour with the remainder of my command and about twenty citizens to attack the Apaches. Major Chacon and Lieut. Cook will march tonight also. Although repulsed the men of Lieut. Gilbert's party behaved very nobly and he fell very gallantly himself at the head of his men. I deeply regret his fall and will avenge it if possible. The Indians are said to be about seventy in number. It is closing dark and I can't be more explicit for want of time. . . ."

McCabe discovered that Lieutenant Gilbert was not scalped either because the Indians respected his heroism in also killing his opponent or because the Apache was not given to scalping as zealously as other tribes or simply be for lack of time, nevertheless, the Captain was grateful that the body was not mutilated. The Lieutenant was buried with full military honors. His body was carried to the highest peak of the Sacramento mountains where, wrote the Captain, "We raised a small monument of stones over his resting place and his name is cut in a small stone and placed fronting the trail leading to the Sacramento river." He went on to add that the citizens of Tulerosa who marched with him were under the command of a Mr. Gregory. They found a quantity of mutton left by the Apaches at the Sacramento river. He failed to find the Apaches and even lost four men by desertion. Lieutenant Gilbert remained unavenged. His descendants still live in Socorro, proud of the name they bear.

NOTES AND COMMENTS

Christopher Carson (1808-1868)—Trapper, Mountain Man, Scout, soldier, rancher, Indian Agent, husbandman, adventurer, his life has so many slants, despite the number of books already written, that the surface seems unscratched. His Adobe Walls campaign against the Comanche brought a torrent of criticism but he weathered the storm, always with the same question—"Where were you when we were fighting the Comanches?" Many of his critics claimed that he was soundly beaten and only the long range guns as well as the fighting spirit of the Jicarillas and Utes saved his retreat from becoming a massacre or a rout. Carson claimed a victory. Only the dimension of time will tell. It will make a nice thesis for a student of history anxious to get away from the Lincoln county affair, gunslingers, cattle trails and other run of the mill Westerns. He died in Colorado several months after his wife Josefita Jaramillo of Taos. He had often expressed to his friend, Lucien B. Maxwell, that he wished to be buried next to her. Consequently, Maxwell brought his remains to New Mexico. They reposed in the earth near the Maxwell house in Cimarron for a time but since the Grant was sold, the remains were brought to Taos. Some travelers speak of two graves in Maxwell's yard in 1869. It is possible that Maxwell brought Josefita's remains to rest beside those of her husband's during those few months before the gold strike at Willow creek caused Maxwell to move since he did not relish the stampede. It was the story of Sutter in California all over again, only Maxwell salvaged more than Sutter. Merchants, movies, T. V., publishers, manufacturers will profit by a resurgence and a boom in Kit Carson "coon" caps, sweaters, songs, books as happened a few years ago when kids discovered Davy Crockett.

General Orders No. 4—Headquarters Department of New Mexico—Santa Fe, February 18, 1865.

The following record of combats with Indians on the part of the troops, as well as on that of citizens of New Mexico and Arizona, during the year 1864, is published for the information of all concerned. Only those operations are mentioned which were attended with results either in our favor or against us, and they are about as one to four, so that the account which follows shows but a faint idea of the work performed. It is possible that there may have been some robberies, which are not mentioned here; but if so, no authentic report of them has been received. The number of Indians on the reservation at Bosque Redondo, as shown by General Orders No. 3, series for 1864, from these headquarters, was 703 Apaches and Navajos on the 31st of December of that year.

January—Major Sena, First N. M. Vols., with his command, arrived at Fort Canby, bringing in 344 Navajo prisoners.

January 3—Wagonmaster Russell's train enroute to Fort Canby, N. M., was attacked near the Puerco by about 150 Navajo Indians. Mr. Russell was killed; Mr. Strong and two teamsters wounded. The three lead wagons were cut off and twenty mules were taken by the Indians, together with some corn, blankets, etc. This information was forwarded to the Commanding General of the Department by Major John C. McFerran, Chief Quartermaster, with the following remarks: "Respectfully referred to the Department Commander for his information. This Wagonmaster Russell is Powell Russell, who entered the service of the Quartermaster's Department as a teamster, a poor, illiterate boy, in 1853. By his honesty, industry, modesty, truth, and energy, he rose to be the principal or head wagonmaster in the Department. This position he has filled to the perfect satisfaction of everyone, and has now fallen like a true man, as he was, at his post and doing his duty. It will be very, very difficult to replace him."

January 5—Major Edward B. Willis, 1st Inf., Cal. Vols., acommanding Fort Whipple, Arizona, reports that the Penal Apaches ran off eleven head of government cattle at Walker's mines. A party under Captain Hargrave was sent in pursuit, but failed to overtake the Indians.

January 6—Capt. Julius C. Shaw, 1st Cav., N. M. Vols., commanding Fort Wingate, reports that four Navajo Indians surrendered themselves at that post.

January 6—Major Henry D. Wallen, U. S. 7th Inf., commanding Fort Sumner, N. M., reports that on the morning of the 5th inst. the Navajos ran off the Apache herd from that post. Lt. Newbold, 5th U. S. Inf., with ten men of the 2nd Cav., Cal. Vols., and 5th Inf. were sent in pursuit, accompanied by Mr. Labadie, Indian Agent, Mr. Carrillo, Mr. Whittenmore and 25 Apaches from the reservation. Capt Calloway and his Co. I, 1st Inf., Cal. Vols., was directed to follow the trail of the mounted party. Lt. Newbold encountered over 100 Navajos, mounted and on foot, about twelve miles from the post. A sharp fight ensued, in which nine Navajos were left dead on the field. The Navajos then broke into two parties and fled, and a running fight was kept up for about ten miles. Part of the force pursued one party to the Pecos river. Of this party only eight escaped. Of the other party of Indians only seventeen escaped, and some of these were wounded. Forty Indians were reported to have been left dead on the field, and at least twenty-five wounded. It is believed that nearly all the Navajos would have been killed had it not been for the extremely cold weather. The mercury was ten degrees below zero. The men could with difficulty cap their pieces, their fingers being so numb. Some were frost-bitten. About 50 head of horses and mules were recovered in this fight, all belonging to the Apaches. Major Wallen calls the attention of the General commanding to the handsome manner in which Lt. Newbold managed this successful engagement, also to the meritorious conduct of the soldiers, citizens, and Apaches engaged.

January 8—Mr. George Cooler, wagon and forage master at Fort Craig, N. M., with 10 infantry and a party of (New) Mexican citizens, while on a scout after Indians, recovered one (New) Mexican boy named Vicente Urban (from near Pecos), who was stolen by the Indians near the Pecos river; one rifle and 58 goats. On the 11th inst. came upon a party of Indians and succeeded in killing one and capturing one squaw and one child. In this skirmish two of Cooler's party were wounded; one of them, Jose Garcia, died the next day. On the 12th found seven horses and one mule, and captured two Indian women.

January 12—Capt. Julius C. Shaw, 1st Cav., N. M. Vols., commanding Fort Wingate, reports that Lt. Jose Maria Sanchez, with a detachment of Co. F, 1st Cav., N. M. Vols., attacked a party of Indians near the Datil mountains (later the homestead of Agnes C. Morley and Eugene M. Rhodes, famous New Mexican writers—both now departed) and killed three men, captured two women and one boy and 18 Navajo horses and 62 head of sheep and goats. The chief, Sordo, was killed in this fight. Captain Shaw also reports that 60 Navajos had given themselves up at that post since the 1st Inst.

January 14—Sgt. Joseph Felmer, 1st Cav., Cal. Vols., reports that he recovered seven head of cattle while in pursuit of a party of Indians and turned them over to Don Pablo, of La Joya, N. M.

January 15—Serafin Ramirez, a citizen of N. M., reports that the Navajo Indians drove off 12 head of cattle and two mules belonging to him, between the 25th of Dec. and the 9th of Jan. and during the same time they killed three of his cattle.

January 21—Capt. Julius C. Shaw, commanding Fort Wingate, N. M., reports that 23 Navajo Indians have surrendered at that post since his last report.

January—On the 6th inst. Col. Christopher Carson, commanding the Navajo Expedition, left Fort Canby, N. M., with 14 commissioned officers and 375 enlisted men, on an expedition to the Canon de Chelly. On the 8th inst. one warrior was killed by the Colonel's escort. On the 12 Sgt. Andres Herrera, with 50 men, who was sent out the previous night, returned bringing into camp two women, two children, prisoners and 130 head of sheep and goats, and reported that his command had killed eleven and wounded five Indians. On the 14th inst. Capt. Pfeiffer and party, who had been sent out from Fort Canby some days previous to operate in the east opening of the canon, came into camp and reported having passed through the canon without a single casualty in his command. He killed three Indians and brought in 19 prisoners, women and children. On the 15th inst. 60 Indians arrived in camp and surrendered themselves as prisoners. On the same day a party under the command of Capt. Joseph Berney killed two Indians and captured four. One hundred and ten Indians surrendered to Capt. Carey's command while upon its return march to Fort Canby. Result of this expedition: 23 Indians killed, 5 wounded, 34 prisoners, 200 voluntarily surrendered—and 200 head of sheep and goats captured.

January 24—A party of 30 Americans and 14 Maricopa and Pimo Indians under Col. King S. Woolsey, aid to the governor of Arizona, attacked a band of Gila Apaches sixty or seventy miles northeast of the Pimo villages, and killed 19 of them and wounded others. Cyrus Lennon, of Woolsey's party, was killed by a wounded Indian.

January 26—Lt. Thomas A. Young, 5th Inf., Cal. Vols., with one Sgt. and eleven privates of the Cal. Vols., started from Fort Craig, N. M., on a scout after Indians. On the 28th the party was attacked by about 60 Indians, who wounded Lt. Young, Sgt. Thomas Richards, and Privates Harvey McConkey, Thomas Clark and Louis Mann of Co. D, 1st Cav., Cal. Vols. In this affair 7 Indians were killed. The party, not being strong enough to continue the fight, returned to Fort Craig, on the 30th inst.

January—The militia of Socorro Co., N. M. under General Stanislaus Montoya, on a scout near Sierra Datil, killed 20 Indians and took 20 prisoners.

February 2—Major E. W. Eaton, commanding at Fort Wingate, sent 200 Indians from that post to Los Pinos, en route to the Bosque Redondo. The chief, Delgadito, arrived at Fort Wingate this day with 680 Indians.

February 14—Capt. A. B. Carey, U.S.A., commanding Fort Canby, N. M., reports the arrival at that post of Soldado Surdo, with his herd; also, that there are now 1,000 prisoners now at that post.

February 14—Capt. Joseph Berney, 1st Cav. N. M. Vols., arrived at Los Pinos this day, bringing in 175 Navajo prisoners.

February 24—Capt. A. B. Carey, commanding the Navajo expedition, reports that he has forwarded 175 Navajos to the Bosque Redondo since last report, and that there are now 1500 Navajos at Fort Canby awaiting transportation.

Lt. Martin Mullins. U. S. S., commanding Los Pinos, N. M., reports that to present date 2019 Navajos have arrived at that post enroute to Fort Sumner, and that there are 1445 now at that post awaiting transportation.

February 24—Capt. James H. Whitlock, with 21 men of his Co. F, 5th Inf., Cal. Vols., left camp on the Mimbres, N. M., on the 24th of Feb., on a scout after Apache Indians. About 5 p. m on the 25th came up to a party of 19 Indians, attacked and killed 13 and wounded the others, and captured one Indian pony.

February 25—Three Indian women escaped from the detachment commanded by Lt. W. R. Smith, 1st Inf., Cal. Vols., while enroute from Fort Union to the Bosque Redondo.

February 28—Capt. A. B. Carey reports that there are 2500 Navajos at Fort Canby awaiting transportation to the Bosque Redondo.

March 4—2138 Navajos were this day forwarded from Fort Canby to the Bosque Redondo, having in their possession 473 horses and 3,000 sheep. 126 Indians died at Fort Canby between Feb. 20 and March 4th.

March 7—Lt. Hodt, 1st Cav., N. M. Vols., with 25 enlisted men, left Fort Canby on a scout after Indians who had stolen 18 horses and mules from Caballo Prieto, chief who had surrendered. The thieves, four in number, were captured near Zuni, and eleven head of the stock recovered.

March 8—Capt. Quirino Maes, from Conojos, Colo. Terr., with an independent company of 67 men, arrived at Pueblo, Colo. This company had been operating against the Navajos since the 1st of Jan. 1864, and had killed 26 Indians and had captured four. Five horses were taken from the Indians.

March 14—Capt. Joseph Berney arrived at Fort Sumner with 1430 Navajo prisoners. Ten Indians died on the road from Los Pinos.

March 18—Major Edward B. Willis, 1st Inf., Cal. Vols., with 40 enlisted men and 14 citizens, fell in with a party of Apaches near the San Francisco river (present Reserve, N. M.) Arizona, killed 5 Indians and lost one man—Private Fisher, Co. D, 1st Cav., Cal. Vols.

March 18—Eight mounted Indians made an attack on a government herd near Cow Springs, N. M. and drove off 68 mules, four government and two private horses. The Indians were pursued by Lt. H. H. Stevens, 5th Cal. Inf., with nine men, for a considerable distance, but they escaped with the stock.

March 27—55 Navajos surrendered at Fort Canby, N. M., eight of whom died. They had 62 head of sheep and goats.

March 29—86 Navajos arrived at Los Pinos, N. M., enroute to Fort Sumner, having with them 6 horses and 2 mules.

March—The Apache Indians attacked Mr. Goodhue and four other persons, between the Hasiampa and Granite creek. Goodhue was killed. The men with him succeeded in driving the Indians off. The Indians also attacked a train of wagons near Weaver, Arizona, and mortally wounded a Mr. Rykman and a Mexican; another of the party was slightly wounded. The Indians took all the stock, and plundered the wagons.

April 3—86 Navajos surrendered at Fort Canby, two of whom died. These Indians had 120 sheep and goats, and six horses.

April 5—Capt. Francis McCabe, 1st Cav., N. M. Vols., arrived at Los Pinos, N. M., bringing 720 Navajo Indians.

April 7—Capt. James H. Whitlock, 5th Cav., Cal. Vols., with a command of 26 enlisted men of Co. F and 20 enlisted men of Co. L under Lt. Burkett, and 10 enlisted men of Co. C, 1st Cav., Cal. Vols., attacked about 250 Indians near Mt. Grey or Sierra Bonita, Arizona, and after a spirited fight of over one hour routed the Indians, killing 21 left on the ground, and wounding a large number. 45 head of horses and mules were captured from the Indians, and all their provisions and camp equipage destroyed.

April 10—78 Navajos surendered at Fort Canby, having in their possession one horse and 150 head of sheep and goats.

April 11—Major Edward B. Willis, commanding Fort Whipple, Arizona, reports that Col. King S. Woolsey, with his party, surprised an Indian rancheria, killing 14 Indians, who were left on the ground, and wounding others who escaped. A small party of Cal. Vols., who were sent with Col. Woolsey, behaved well—Privates Beach and Holman, of Co. F, killing 5 Indians.

April—Lt. Martin Quintana, 1st Cav., N. M. Vols., reports that while enroute from Moqui to Fort Canby four Indians delivered themselves up to his command.

April 24—192 Navajos surrendered themselves at Fort Canby since last report, making the total on hand at that post 623. They have 320 head of horses and 650 head of sheep.

May 1—40 Mescalero Apaches including Ojo Blanco, escaped from the Indian reservation at Fort Sumner, and returned to their own country. (This party voluntarily returned Sept. 16—Shortly afterwards Chief Ojo Blanco died.)

May 3—Lt. Henry H. Stevens, 5th Inf., Cal Vols., with a command of 54 men, Cal. Vols., while on the march from Fort Cummings to Fort Bowie, Arizona, was attacked in Doubtful Canon, near Stein's Peak, by about 100 Apaches. The fight lasted nearly 2 hours, and resulted in the killing of 10 Apaches, who were left on the ground, and the wounding of about 20. The troops lost in this affair, one man missing and five wounded—one mortally; one horse killed and one wounded.

May 9—Capt. Charles P. Marion reports that while on a scout near Zuni, 500 Navajos surrendered themselves to his command. These Indians had in their possession 1000 horses and over 5000 sheep and goats.

May 11—The Apache Indians ran off two horses from the ranch of Mr. Stipich, a farmer on the Rio Bonito. They were pursued by 2nd Lt. S. L. Snyder and 13 men of Co. A, 1st Cav., N. M. Vols., but were not overtaken.

May 13—777 Navajo Indians arrived at Fort Sumner this day.

May 25—Lt. Col. Nelson H. Davis, Asst. Inspector General, U. S. A., with Capt. T. T. Tidball, 5th Inf., Cay. Vols., two commissioned officer and 102 enlisted men, Cav. and Inf., started from Fort Bowie on a scout after Indians. On the 25th inst. surprised a rancheria, and killed one Indian; later the same day, one woman and two children were captured. On the 28th captured 5 women and 2 children.

May 29—Capt. George A. Burkett, with 33 enlisted men of Co. I, 5th Inf., Cal. Vols., surprised an Indian rancheria on the Rio de Mescal, and killed 13, wounded 13; took 3 prisoners; captured one mule, 3 horses, one Sharps carbine, one saddle and saddle bags, one ton of mescal, and a small quantity of powder. The command destroyed some fields of corn and wheat. A portion of mescal was kept to feed the prisoners; the balance was destroyed.

May 29—The command surprised a rancheria, killed 36, wounded 4, took two prisoners; captured $660 in gold coin, one Sharps carbine, one Colt's revolver, one shotgun, one saddle, 1000 pounds of mescal, a lot of horse equipments, powder, powder-horns, etc. Sgt. Charles Brown, Co. K, 5th Inf., Cal. Vols., is mentioned in Capt. Tidball's report for his zeal and energy in this scout.

June 3—550 Navajos arrived at Los Pinos this day. They had 190 horses, 294 sheep and goats. These Indians, with 200 others were forwarded to Fort Sumner.

June 3—The Apache Indians attacked a party of 5 miners near Fort Whipple, Arizona, and wounded every man of the party.

June 7—Capt. Julius C. Shaw, 1st Cav., N. M. Vols., with his command, attacked a rancheria near Apache spring. Two Indians were mortally wounded.

June 11—Four Apaches attacked a party of soldiers under Capt. T. T. Tidball, near San Pedro crossing, but did not succeed in doing any damage. The troops wounded one of the Indians.

June 20—Major Edward B. Willis, 1st Inf., Cal. Vols., reports that a detachment under his command attacked a party of

Apache Indians near Salinas river, Arizona, and killed four of them.

June 20—The express escort between Camp Goodwin and Fort Bowie was attacked by a party of Indians while crossing the Chiricahua mountains. The Indians were whipped off by the escort. Several Indians were reported wounded.

June—Capt. Henry M. Benson, 1st Inf., Cal. Vols., left Fort Whipple, Arizona Territory, with his Co. F, 1st Cal. Inf., on a scout after Indians. Five Indians were killed and two wounded by his command, and large quantities of corn and beans destroyed.

June—Capt. Albert H. Pfeiffer, 1st Cav, N. M. Vols., with one Lieutenant and 64 enlisted men, attacked a band of Indians near the Colorado Chiquito, Arizona, and in a running fight of eight miles killed five and wounded seven of them. After the fight was over two Indians came into camp with signs of peace, but in a moment fired their guns, severely wounding Capt. Pfeiffer and Private Pedro Rael. The Indians were instantly killed. When the shots were fired, a large party of Indians came running toward the camp. A volley was fired into them, when they scattered in all directions. This volley wounded several.

June 28—Capt. James H. Whitlock, commanding Camp Miembres, reports that he left the post on 21st inst. on a scout after Indians. On the 22nd, came upon a party of 3 Indians, two of whom were killed, the third captured.

July 10—Lt. Antonio Abeyta, 1st Cav., N. M. Vols., while enroute from Fort Wingate to Los Pinos, N. M., with 26 Navajo and 7 Apache prisoners, came upon a party of Navajos at Fish spring, numbering 375, coming in to surrender themselves and go to the reservation. They had 300 horses, 16 mules, 1085 sheep, 350 goats. This party was turned over to the commanding officer at Los Pinos.

July—Capt. Saturnino Baca, 1st Cav., N. M. Vols., with 53 enlisted men, left Fort Canby on the 9th ist. on a scout after Indians. Marched to the Little Colo. river. He returned to Fort Canby on the 21th inst. On this scout 6 Indians were killed and six taken prisoners; two horses and two mules were captured, and large quantities of corn, wheat, beans, etc. were destroyed.

August 1—Capt. T. T. Tidball, 5th Inf., Cal. Vols., returned from a scout of 23 days. He reports that he saw but few Indians, and killed but one—an Apache chief called Old Plume.

August 1—Four (New) Mexican citizens are reported as having been killed by Apache Indians on the Conchas.

August 1—1209 Navajos and 12 Apaches left Los Pinos, N. M., for Bosque Redondo. They had 357 horses, 19 mules, 2000 sheep and goats.

August 3—A band of Apache Indians, having captives, sheep, horses, burros and cattle, were discovered near Alamo Gordo by Delgadito Chiquito, Navajo chief, who sent a messenger to Fort Sumner to inform the commanding officer of the fact. 35 men of the Cal. Cav. were sent in pursuit; also a strong party of Navajos from the reservation. In the meantime Delgadito's party attacked the Apaches and were defeated with a loss of one killed and 3 wounded, among the latter Delgadito himself. The party of Navajos from the post came upon the Apaches and took from them 500 sheep and 13 burros.

August 6—Mr. Charles G. Parker's train enroute to Chihuahua, Mexico, was attacked by the Mescalero Apaches, twenty miles below the Gallinas mountains. The Indians drove off about 50 mules. They were followed by the wagonmaster and some teamsters, but succeeded in driving off the animals. Two men were severely wounded.

August 5—Sgt. B. F. Fergusson, of Co. E, 5th Cal. Vols., with a party of men, attacked 15 Apaches who were seen approaching the camp on the Rio Carlos, and killed 5 of them.

August—The command which left Fort Cummings on Aug. 5th on a scout to Lake Guzman, killed one Indian near the Florida mountains. Very few Indians were seen, they evidently having deserted the country on the approach of the troops, who, on this scout, marched 1200 miles.

August 12—Lt. Henry Becker, 1st Cav. N. M. Vols., left Fort Canby, N. M., with 92 Indian prisoners and 800 head of sheep. On the route to Los Pinos he was joined by 151 Indians, having in their possession 700 sheep and 85 horses. Indians and stock were turned over to the commanding officer at Los Pinos.

August—Col. King S. Woolsey reports that while on a scout after Indians near the Rio Prieto, one of his men, named J. W. Beauchamp, was waylaid and killed by the Apache Indians.

August—Major Thomas J. Blakenney, 1st Cav., Cal. Vols., on a scout of 30 days after Apache Indians, killed ten and captured two Indians, and destroyed 20 acres of corn and large quantities of pumpkins, beans, etc.

August—Capt. Henry A. Greene, 1st Inf., Cal. Vols., on a scout after Indians from Fort McRae, N. M., killed 5 Indians and captured 6. Nineteen head of beef cattle were recovered from the Indians.

August—Capt. John S. Thayer, 5th Inf., Cal. Vols., left Fort Goodwin, Arizona, with his company, on a scout after Indians. On the 4th day out the company destroyed about 70 acres of corn, also several small fields of beans and pumpkins. On the 6th day came upon a party of Indians—wounded several and captured one, who was afterwards shot while attempting to escape. A (New) Mexican captive was rescued from these Indians. On the 8th day out attacked a party of Indians and killed six and wounded two.

August 25—Capt. Francis McCabe, 1st Cav., N. M. Vols., reports that while on a scout after Indians in the Sacramento mountains, he detached a party under Lt. Henry W. Gilbert, of the same regiment, to follow the trail of the Indians. Lt. Gilbert took with him 20 men. The party, although warned by a guide, marched in a body directly into an ambush, when Lt. Gilbert was killed at first fire. The guide Sanchez and Private M. Sandoval were killed and three men wounded. One Apache killed and five wounded. The command was leading the horses when the attack was made. The men after the fall of their leader, shamefully abandoned their horses. The Indians got the most of the horses and equipments.

September 19—Lt. Patrick Healy, 1st Inf., N. M. Vols., with a detachment of ten men, while in pursuit of Indians, entered the town of Canada de Alamosa, N. M., where 5 Indians were captured. One of the Indians afterwards made his escape.

September 25—Capt. Wm. Ayers, 1st Inf., N. M. Vols., learning that a party of Indians were at Canada de Alamosa, started in pursuit of them and succeeded in capturing one man, four women and children. The others escaped to the mountains.

October 20—A band of Navajo Indians attacked Mr. Huning's train on the Colorado Chiquito and succeeded in driving off seven or eight hundred head of sheep, the property of Capt. Joseph P. Hargrave.

November 6—Some Indians are said to have run off 500 head of sheep from the headwaters of the Rio Puerco, belonging to Don Ynez Perea.

November 8—On the 8th of Nov., some Navajos and Apaches from the west ran off 3000 head of sheep belonging to Don Jose Pino y Baca, four miles from Limitar, N. M., and killed four herders who had the sheep in charge. Their names were Antonio Gallegos, Romaldo Peralta, Francisco Capillo, Leoncio Sarcilla (Garcia?). Instructions were sent to Major Eaton, commanding Fort Wingate, to cross the country to the Rio Quemado and endeavor to cut the trail of the Indians.

November 9—A Navajo found lurking near the government herd at Fort Sumner was arrested by the herd guard, and in attempting to make his escape was killed.

November 25—Col. Christopher Carson, 1st Cav., N. M. Vols., with a command consisting of 14 commissioned officers, 321 enlisted men, 75 Indians, Apaches and Utes, attacked a Kiowa village of about 150 lodges, near the adobe fort on the Canadian river, in Texas, and after a severe fight compelled the Indians to retreat, with a loss of sixty killed and wounded. The village was then destroyed. The engagement commenced at 8:30 a. m. and lasted without intermission until sunset. In this fight Privates John O'Donnell and John Sullivan, of Co. M, 1st Cav., Cal. Vols., were killed, and Corporal N. Newman, Privates Thomas Briggs, J. Jameson,—Mapes, Jasper Winant, J. Horseley of Co. B, and Holygrafer, of Co. G, 1st Cav., Cal. Vols., Antonio Duran, Antonio Sanchez of Co. M, and Hilario Romero of Co., I, 1st Cav., N. M. Vols., were wounded. Four Utes wounded.

Col. Carson in his report, mentions the following officers as deserving the highest praise: Major McCleave, Capt. Emil Fritz and Lt. Heath, of the 1st Cav., Cal. Vols.; Capt. Deus and Capt. Berney, 1st Cav., N. M. Vols.; Lt. Pettis, 1st Inf., Cal. Vols., Lt. Edgar, 1st Cav., N. M. Vols., and Asst. Surgeon George S. Courtright, U. S. Vols. The command destroyed 150 lodges of the best manufacture; a large amount of dried meats, berries, buffalo robes, powder, cooking utensils, etc., also a buggy and spring wagon, the property of Sierrito, or Little Mountain, the Kiowa chief.

November 27—Col. Oscar M. Brown, 1st Cav., Cal. Vols., with 100 men, returned from a scout to the Apache country. Four squaws were captured by Col. Brown's command. Although this scout of nearly sixty days was unsuccessful, it was one of the hardest of the year.

December 2—1020 Navajos, having in their possession 3500 sheep and goats, 400 horses and 30 mules, arrived at Fort Sumner.

December—Major E. W. Eaton, 1st Cav., N. M. Vols., on a scout after Indians, came upon their camp, near Red river; killed one Indian and took two prisoners and recovered 175 sheep, one horse and one burro. These were the Indians who helped to run off sheep from Limitar on Nov. 8.

December 15—Capt. John Thompson, 1st Cav., N. M. Vols., with a small party of men, attacked an Indian rancheria near Weaver, Arizona, killed eleven and wounded four.

December 24—Lt. Paul Dowlin, 1st Cav., N. M. Vols., reports that on his return trip from Fort Whipple, Arizona, the Navajos ran off 14 of his mules.

December 25—A band of Apache Indians made an attack on the town of Rincon, near Fort McRae, N. M.; took a (New) Mexican boy prisoner, and drove off nine head of cattle. A party was started in pursuit and succeeded in recovering three head of cattle. The (New) Mexican's body was found, lanced in several places.

December 29—Capt. William Brady, 1st Cav., N. M. Vols., reports that he found the body of Reyes Flores, the guide, near the Tuleroso sawmill. Whether he had been killed by Indians or others is not certain.

December 31—Lt. Samuel L. Barr, with Co. F, 5th U. S. Inf., and a detachment of 1st Cav., N. M. Vols., surprised an Indian camp near Sycamore Springs, Arizona; killed four Indians and captured two head of cattle.

Chapter Twelve

1865

General Carleton was alarmed at the quality of the guns and the ample amount of ammunition the Comanches and Kiowas used in the battle at Adobe Walls. He soundly rounded out traders and citizens in general who went into Indian country to speculate. Talking to them through the editor of the Santa Fe Gazette he said "These guns killed our soldiers; they were used in raids against our wagon trains; the people selling these guns to Indians are traitors to their country. Henceforth no one will trade with the Comanches nor the Kiowas without a special passport for the purpose. These will be obtained from Lt. Col. Abreu, the commanding officer at Fort Bascom (who in January, 1865, succeeded Captain Bergmann) who will inquire into the nature of their business." Abreu complained that the traders and others found a way to steal by the pickets at night so that the order was useless. Carleton thereby put a complete ban on any dealings with either tribe until a treaty of peace was signed. The Comancheros ignored this command also. Carleton's enemies continued to denounce his Indian policy. Rather than answer them he appealed to the people of New Mexico.

He told them that time out of mind the Navajos subsisted on the flocks of their fathers; thought nothing of reducing wealthy families to poverty; murdering and plundering. The Spaniards fought them to no avail. Following Kearny, Doniphan, Washington, Sumner, Bonneville, Miles, Canby and others always trusted them ending their visits to them by treaties. But the Navajo chiefs always considered these men weaklings because they preferred peace talks to gun smoke. They jeered and sneered each treaty intending to break all their promises. Carleton reminded them that when he succeeded Canby as head of the Department of New Mexico he could have sent the California Volunteers back but he kept them in New Mexico to wipe out the Navajo.

In the zeal of his appeal he forgot to tell them that actually they were kept to keep an eye on the Texas Confederates who even now were assembled to march on Mesilla and Tucson. He did tell them that when eighteen Navajo chieftains approached him in Santa Fe suing for peace and asked for a treaty he sent them home telling them to return when they were sincere. It was then that he conceived the notion that the best place for them to keep a treaty would be on a reservation. He sent campaign after campaign out after them to bring in prisoners and seemed satisfied that two hundred years of treaty breaking was at an end.

He had decided on the Bosque Redondo country in the spring of 1863 for he saw that here was water, fertile soil, beautiful country. It was also sufficiently removed from the settlements to keep them in line. In the fall of that year he wrote to the War Department which agreed that after all the Indians were giving up a country larger than the State of Ohio for a few acres at the Bosque. True the crops failed in 1864 (and in 1865) but that was not the fault of the Navajos. The high cost came not because of the prices the government was paying to feed these thousands of Indians but because of the general crop failure of the year before. If the price of mutton, beef, wheat, alfalfa was reaching to the skies, so was the price of groceries, coffee, wood, hay. It was the result of war. Besides the people of New Mexico had no complaint since they fed and clothed the Navajos by plunder long before the advent of the California Volunteers. What if the government gave Lucien B. Maxwell a good price for thousands of sheep and other commodities? He had them to sell. He was not especially selected but his prices were fairer.

The Indians planted a fine crop of corn and were ready to pluck it when corn worm destroyed the entire crop. This destruction was not the work of the army for the purpose of keeping up the high price. The Indians were safe off the route to California, the Arizona mining fields, the New Mexico silver fields, where they especially liked to attack because unsuspected attacks always produced guns and ammunition. Despite the cost, feeding these Indians was cheaper than fighting them. The Navajos are enemies of the Kiowas and Comanches. Bosque Redondo was just ninety miles from their territory. In time Carleton hoped to have 25,000 thousand Navajos trained by his soldiers as a forward wall and a stumbling block to these tribes and thus cut off this menace to bring peace to the settlements. If this was not working for the good of the people of New Mexico, he did not know what was. (See: *Santa Fe Gazette* through December, 1854 and January, 1865).

Carleton hoped to get the "rico" Navajos to submit. Besides, Manuelito and three hundred of his people still held out against the Bosque Redondo reservation. Major E. W. Eaton, commander of Fort Wingate, sent two runners and interpreters to the chief to induce him to change his mind. He refused saying that he was happy where he was; he was harming no one. Rio Bonito was his home; there he would stay. The runners noted about 3,000 sheep, 500 head of horses, 30 warriors, 6 "ricos" and 100 old people at the village. Asked where he got the sheep Manuelito replied that they belonged to the tribesmen and were not stolen. The six "ricos" had lived on the headwaters of the Red river, but seeking safety in numbers came to live with him. If any stealing was being perpetrated let the soldiers look for the twenty warriors living at Red river under the leadership of Chief Cabeza Blanco. The runners told him that Captain Hargrave's sheep were stolen as well as Lt. Dowlin's mules and the Santillanes sheep from Limitar. They had permission to search the camp. The men returned to Fort Wingate empty handed.

General Crocker who was in charge of the Bosque Redondo and Fort Sumner in the early part of 1865 was ordered back to the States to report for new duties but he took sick before he could obey the order, died and was given a military burial at Fort Sumner. Manderfield and Tucker, editors of the *Santa Fe New Mexican* newspaper were opposed to Carleton mostly because he catered to their chief rival, the *Santa Fe Gazette*. When the California Volunteers of the 1st Reg. were discharged at Mesilla, and met to reorganize for re-enlistment, they wrote a letter which the New Mexican was glad to carry for weeks after the original first appeared. While the meeting took place on September 15, 1864, it was not until some time later that it first appeared in print. John M. Kerr was chairman at the meeting, and Charles Soule, secretary. He seems to have worded the document:

"Three years ago, buoyant with hope and full with anticipation that we would be led against the common enemy of our country, we left our homes and all that was near and dear to us; sacrificed our personal interests and took up the line of march. Nothing of importance characterized this march until our arrival at Fort Yuma, on the Colorado river. At this point commenced that series of gross dereliction of duty, frauds, unwarranted delays, marches, and counter marches, without any progress, which facts, when they receive the awful sentence of history, will forever shroud the name of James H. Carleton in the darkest obloquy and disgrace.

"General Carleton, whilst at Tucson in Arizona Territory, knowing that the rebels were on the Rio Grande, plundering and robbing the citizens of that valley, for no good cause whatsoever persistently delayed and refused to follow and punish them when fully within his power to do so, although both men and officers were clamorous to be led forward, and it is an indisputable fact that he never moved from that point towards the Rio Grande until he was positively informed that the enemy had retired.

"And on the arrival of the column on the Rio Grande, instead of being, as we desired, sent against hostile Indians who were murdering and robbing citizens and devastating the country, a large number of us were shut up in towns and compelled to do police duty over loyal citizens who heroically suffered from the common enemy, and who had, unsolicited and unsupported, taken up arms and resisted the occupation of the country by them.

"General Carleton has established a military surveillance over these same citizens, imprisoned and brutally treated their judges, inaugurated martial law, established courts of his own creation and compelled citizens to answer before them for offenses unknown to the laws, has fined and compelled citizens to labor without conviction or trial, has taken private property without just compensation, and has encouraged his subordinates in resisting ministerial officers in the service of process by the civil courts.

"These are but a few of the many outrages perpetrated by General Carleton under the specious pretext of serving his country, during our stay in New Mexico, and, while the citizens have been denied their rights, the soldiers, too, have likewise suffered from his tyrannical conduct. We cannot better close this public expression of our sentiments than by saying that we believe the interests of the government which we volunteered to defend cannot be better served than by dispensing with the services of General Carleton. As an officer he is incompetent. He is wanting in all those qualities which endear and endow the citizen and characterizes the true soldier, and on the eve of our departure for our homes we thank the people of New Mexico for their kindness. . . ."

The three signatures affixed to the letter were those of William Jones, Co. E, Cal. Vols.; Howard Morrison of the same company, and John Collins of Company H. Carleton knew that it was next to useless and hopeless to answer minds poisoned against him. He was already heavily burdened with the charges of Sylvester Mowry, who, if he won his case, would leave the General destitute. Also other disturbing news came from Franklin. Captain D. H. Brotherton, 5th U. S. Infantry, commander of the post at Franklin, went out on a scouting expedition and came upon a band of twenty Confederates who said they were on their way to Franklin as deserters. Their story confirmed what Carleton always believed: The Texans never abandoned hope of marching into New Mexico. J. Davis had served the Confederacy in Col. Johnson's battery. He and the nineteen others lived in Johnson county, Texas. They were approached by Col. S. Baird's agents and signed up at Gainesville for service in New Mexico.

General Scurry and Col. Baird petitioned Brig. General Henry McCullough permission to raise a battalion of Confederate troops to range the direction of New Mexico with the intention of recapturing Mesilla and of driving Carleton out of Santa Fe. Davis did not mind fighting for the Confederacy until he saw the type of men Baird's agents were enlisting. Men were coming in by the hundreds. Bushwhackers, joining the companies at Gainesville and Fort Belknap; men who had plundered with William Quantrell and were left without a leader when he was killed the year before. They had been with him during his depredations at Lawrence, in western Missouri and Kentucky. Other bushwhackers had served under Anderson. Davis found nine companies assembled when he enlisted. There was no question that several thousand men were assembled ready to swoop on New Mexico. Baird had promised much and the men looked forward to the fulfillment of those promises. Already they raided caravans going to Chihuahua, California, Arizona and New Mexico. A man named Frank Martin had been sent the winter before to live in Las Cruces and keep his eyes and ears open. He was now back in Texas and was to act in the capacity of guide and scout for the expedition. Baird but awaited the growth of grass to begin his march. He had nursed old grudges and had spent these many months preparing to settle the score with a number of people. Davis and his companions were upset at the type of men Baird enlisted for service in New Mexico. Pillage and rampage was not his idea of war. The twenty decided to avail themselves of the first opportunity to warn the people of New Mexico. As for themselves they would move to either Arkansas or Missouri where the bitterness was the bitterness of war, not of personal animosity. They were not prepared to fight an individual's battles; they wished to fight for the Confederacy. Nor did they wish to see Baird turn into another Quantrell. Thus by the 3rd of May Carleton knew the whole story. Secretly, he hoped the Texans would strike soon to stop the complaints of the California Volunteers who claimed they hadn't seen a grey uniform from the day they enlisted.

General Carleton left for Franklin to spend the next few weeks in making preparations to locate a new post to be named Fort Selden thus honoring one of the heroes of Valverde. Col. N. H. Davis was sent to make a treaty with the Gila Apaches under Victorio. The attempt proved fruitless and he returned without accomplishing a thing save in strengthening the Apache's resolve to hold out against the white man. On May 25, 1865 the garrison at Las Cruces was moved to Roblero where active operations were at once commenced towards building the new fort. Another band of Texans, about a hundred strong, arrived at Franklin about this time. These deserters had been with Col. Baird and were on the road six weeks subsisting on mule and horse meat. They confirmed the Davis testimony that a force of over a thousand men had been raised for the purpose of raiding New Mexico, and cutting off and plundering the trains on the plains. Carleton hoped to garrison the new post with enough troops to weaken the advance on Fort Craig and if they succeeded in getting by Franklin, Mesilla, Fort Selden, Fort Craig, he would make a stand at either Limitar or Polvadera. Like McClellan he believed in elaborate preparations and would like to have three men for every one Baird would send against him.

On April 12, 1865, Lee's men laid down their arms at Appomattox. General Dick Taylor did not surrender his army to General Canby until May 3rd. He commanded all the Confederate troops in Alabama, Mississippi and eastern Louisiana. Texas surrendered shortly afterwards which accounts for the fact that hostilities between Baird and Carleton were pending almost to June. Glad that the nation was no longer at war, Carleton again turned his attention to his pet project at Bosque Redondo, from which a number of Indians succeeded in making their escape in the middle of June placing Santa Fe and the settlements on the alert. Soldiers were sent in pursuit while the chorus of "I told you so" made Carleton anxious for their capture. Ambrosio Armijo's company of guides and spies were sent out to capture the notorious highwaymen and outlaws Nicanor Bustos, Epimenio Chavez, and Juan de J. Anaya, deserters from the New Mexico Volunteers and pocket size editions of Quantrell. These were captured at Tajique by Don Inez Perez of Armijo's company. Because they were guerrillas, bandits, murderers and dangerous men they were taken to Albuquerque in chains and lodged in the jail there. On June 25th, a mob of civilians congregated before the jail, broke down the door, and hung the trio in front of the court house portico. Carleton never did get one name of the self-appointed vigilantes. The trio were said to have killed thirty Americans and ten natives. Captain Wm. Brady, 1st N. M. Vols. caught up with Chief Cabeza Blanco and Chief Juanico in the San Nicolas Mountains. Rather than return to the Bosque they fought the Captain to a finish. Two chiefs were buried where they fell. Brady returned to Fort Selden to have his horses shod after which he took up the trail from where he left off, this time with less success. On July 4th, 1865, Carleton issued general orders No. 17 which abolished martial law in New Mexico. Three days later Lt. J. S. Crouch sent this letter to Col. Rigg, commander of Fort Craig:

"I have the honor to report that I received the order to return to Fort Craig on the 4th inst. I immediately sent an express to Abo Pass for my cavalry which I had sent there on the 3rd. One of my men has just got in from Abo and informs me that Lt. Strong, N. M. Vols., arrived at the pass shortly after my men did, and that yesterday Strong attacked over two hundred Indians at La Sufetura. A hard fight ensued. He drove the Indians away from the springs. He killed two Indian men and one squaw, and took one squaw and four children prisoners. Five or six animals were captured. Strong thinks the Indians will be forced to come in to Abo, or the river, for water, as there is none at La Sulfeltura or Gibolo Springs. After receiving this information I thought it best not to return to the fort until I heard from you. I have sent an express to all my stations with orders to carefully guard all the crossings. Signs of Indians were seen in the mountains east of here yesterday. Had I not received the order to return I should have proceeded to Abo today with the men under my command. Lt. Strong, with my men, can hold Abo Pass. Captain _____ of N. M. Cav. Vols., is at Manzano, or near there. If I hear of Indians anywhere on the river I will pack the team of mules and follow them. There can be no doubt but that some two hundred or three hundred Indians are still in these mountains. . . ." (Quoted in the *Santa Fe Gazette*)

Lt. Crouch reinforced his pickets as far down as Tajo, with militia and soldiers. He next went up the river with a number of militia distributing them at all points where he thought the Indians would likely cross. As none were reported attempting to cross he began to wonder if he had made a mistake. Sergeant Blanchard came in to his camp from Abo Pass and gave an official report of the action at Sulfeltura. Blanchard was of the opinion that the Indians were digging for water when Strong attacked them. He thought they numbered two hundred. The Indians scattered into the mountains. Strong decided to remain at Abo to see if they would collect together for an attack. Shinn was sent southeast of Abo in search of any that might congregate there. Crouch was a bit put out because Strong made no effort to write him an official report of the action nor did he make any attempt to run down the fleeing Indians. As Crouch's cavalry was close at hand they would have gladly aided Strong if he but asked. Crouch's hope that they would cross the Tajo was never realized for the Indians went westward through the mountains to assemble at the Gila where they felt comparatively safe for a time.

When General Kirby Smith surrendered at Galveston and General Carleton took advantage of the surrender to abolish martial law for New Mexico, the editor of the *Santa Fe New Mexican* used the action to advantage by lambasting Carleton in the abuse that went on under the name of martial law. He reminded his readers that General Canby first established the law on October 20, 1861; then Carleton adopted Canby's Order No. 53 with additions and modifications, as suited his purpose. Said the editor:

"This order of General Carleton was among one of his first acts in assuming the command of this Department of the Army, which he undertook to create a law, and which his subordinates, by his direction, enforced at the point of the bayonet, over a

Territory then fully officered and legislated for by its representatives, acting under, and by virtue of, Acts of Congress and in which all the judges were present, and the Courts of the Territory and the United States were open, and some of them in actual session at the time. It may well be doubted if a stronger case of usurpation can be found. The Texans (note the date) passed Fort Craig on their return from Santa Fe on April 25, 1862, and only stopped in the Mesilla valley because of the neglect of General Canby to follow them. But their power was broken and on July 4 of the same year they abandoned all their positions in New Mexico and by the date of Carleton's order, re-proclaiming martial law (September 25) the last of the armed rebels of the invading army had reached San Antonio." (See Santa Fe New Mexican for October and November 1865)

The editor went on to enumerate the abuses. He could not understand why New Mexicans endured the law for the three years they did since the object of the law was to protect them from the Confederates who seemed to exist in the mind of General Carleton. The law was not needed for fighting Indians, for New Mexicans fought Indians long before Carleton was born and would continue to do so long after he was dead. Carleton kept eight thousand Indians at the Bosque Redondo. And at what a price. He had to lord it over someone and since the white man objected and since the war was over he would continue to dominate the Navajo, although he did make attempts to dictate to all of the Territory of New Mexico. The day of reporting news as such was yet to come. Partisanship, personalities, opinions, dogmas, made up the paper. Nor was there anything like an Associated Press. Something that happened in June or July could very likely make the headlines in September, or not at all according to the editor's likes or dislikes. New Mexico was the last place where guns were silenced. Indians were pursued even beyond the turn of the century.

General Estanislao of Socorro started from Fort Craig with Captain Vigil of the Territorial Militia, and thirty men, on an expedition to round up Indians still hesitant about Bosque Redondo. He traveled as far as El Sierrito de Pedernal. Finding no water there he continued on to Alamitos. The water hole there was also dry. High winds and dust storms impeded the movement of the troops and made the quest for water of primary importance. Indians were relegated to the background. He went on another thirty-eight miles to Caballo Mountain where Captain Trujillo was stationed. He had enough water to satisfy the wants of men and animals. Montoya remained at Caballo to give the horses a rest. He sent Trujillo on towards San Diego to investigate the report that Indians were seen in that locality. Evidently the Indians must have heard that he was on the way for by the time he got there they vanished. Trujillo trailed them into the San Andreas Mountains where he met a scout on the way in to report to Montoya that Indians were on the way to attack him at Caballo. Rather than take the defensive Montoya went out to give battle. He took all their equipment, captured seven horses, a young child, hoping to capture more. But the Indians fled. He pursued them forty-nine miles back into the mountains where he discovered thy had a village but it was too strongly fortified for him to attack. Sending to Fort Craig for assistance the messenger brought back orders for him to return to the post. It would be left to the California Volunteers to attack the rancheria. By the time the Volunteers took over the Indians abandoned the village for other parts.

Captain Daniel B. Haskell, 1st Veteran Infantry, California Volunteers, had come through many an Indian skirmish unscathed He had thirsted in the desert and hungered on the plain. The war over, he remained at Fort Craig following the old routine of chasing Apaches, Navajos, Comanches and Kiowas. He had enlisted in 1861 and when the old regiment mustered out he re-registered. He was married and had three children. On May 8, he decided to take a swim in the Rio Grande. Suddenly, he cramped, went under, the body being fished out two days later. The post was in mourning for Haskell was well liked. Lt. Col. Edwin A. Rigg, commander of Fort Craig, led the funeral procession. The officers of the post paid the deceased high tribute. Staffing Fort Craig at the time were: Capt. William F. French, Lt. George H. Pettis, Asst. Surgeon George S. Courtwright, Capt. Thomas P. Chapman, Captain L. J. J. Nissen, Lt. John S. Crouch, Lt. A. B. John, Lt. L. F. Sanburn, Lt. James J. Billings, 2nd Lt. Richard Hudson and 2nd Lt. William Oman. Several weeks later Captain French was sent to command Fort McRae.

Toward the latter part of the month of July the Navajo chief, Jose Pillon, who escaped from the Bosque Redondo, returned to Fort McRae and surrendered to Captain French. He said that he had been on the road twenty days. He had ten men,

27 children, 40 horses, two mules and four guns at the time he gave himself up. He said that there were others coming to surrender but when they got to the Jornada del Muerte they changed their minds and decided to raid Paraje and Valverde. French sent troops out after them. When they saw Lt. Slater they hid themselves in the bosque near Valverde. The Lieutenant rode by them without being aware of their presence. They killed a horse for food after which they decided that they were better off back at the Bosque Redondo so they rode on to Fort McCrae and surrendered to Captain French.

Up at Fort Sumner Captain S. A. Gorham went in pursuit of Indians who left the reservation. Since he had only ten men with him he sent to Fort Stanton for more. Captain Wm. Brady and fifty New Mexico Vols. came to his aid. They trailed the Indians to Fort Craig and found them encamped in the mountains beyond the post. The camp was attacked and forty warriors were killed. Darkness setting in, the soldiers waited until the next day before resuming the attack. During the night the Navajos had buried thirty of their dead. Chief Cabeza Blanco (Some reports call him Caballo Blanco—White Horse but the majority Cabeza Blanco—White Head—which name I retained) The trail now pointed in the direction of Las Cruces. Near there the Navajos surrendered. The sheep and goats were turned over to Lt. Jennings, Quartermaster at the post in Las Cruces; the Indians were taken back to Bosque Redondo.

All was quiet up Fort Union way so General Carleton issued orders for Captain Patrick Healy, 1st Inf., N. M. Vols., to take men and rations and repair the road from the post to Raton Pass. The men worked from July 22nd to August 22nd, wishing that they would be sent out after Indians. It took a little time for the Captain to convince them that the work they were doing was just as important. (See *Santa Fe Weekly Gazette* Sept. 16, 1865) Fort Sumner at this time was flying its flag at half mast due to the death of General M. M. Crocker. To prove that the government was not stinting in feeding the Indians at Bosque Redondo, Major Wm. McCleave wrote out the following expenditures:

March	$70,578.30
April	72,704.97
May	70,861.15
June	53,519.04

July	60,610.94
August	65,773.68
September	58,308.90

$452,356.98

By 1869 Congress was ready to agree that the Bosque Redondo reservation proved a dismal failure and the Indians were permitted to return to their own country where their efforts at rehabilitation made the last state worse than the first. But that story belongs elsewhere. (For an account of their after life during the hard years that followed their return to their own country see: Wm. Keleher, *Turmoil in New Mexico*—Book Four, The Long Walk.

On November 1, 1865, the Military District of New Mexico was transferred from the Department of the Pacific to the Department of Missouri, commanded by General Pope, no stranger to New Mexico. He had served at various posts in the Territory, and boasted the fact at a dinner given in his honor at Las Vegas when the Santa Fe Railroad started the New Town there. It is a well known fact that when he took over the command along the Potomac he sought to toughen the men according to the standards of the frontier posts in New Mexico. The first pronouncement he made was that he wished the California Volunteers to return to California because he felt that he had no jurisdiction over them. He also sought to muster out one regiment of New Mexico Volunteers without any provision being made for replacements. The governor was alarmed. This would leave only one regiment of Volunteers and a few of the 5th U. S. Infantry —about 900 men to garrison the entire frontier.

A meeting was held at Santa Fe. The people petitioned Secretary of War, E. M. Stanton, to ask General John Pope to change his mind. Judge Kirby Benedict refused to sign saying that the war was over and Pope had enough experience to know what he was doing. The governor insisted that the California troops were essential to the protection of New Mexico. Pope eventually ordered the force to be reduced to 1516 men with an active force of 952 to take care of the Indians at the reservation and elsewhere. Many of the California Volunteers refused to go back. Efforts were made to accommodate both. Thus it is that names like Zimmerly, Campbell, Snyder and others persist there to this day. Before they returned to the west coast the soldiers sent an open letter of appreciation to the people of New Mexico in gratitude for the hospitality they found here during the several years they lived in the Territory.

Donaciano Montoya, Captain 1st Cav., N. M. Vols., went on an expedition after Navajos to Datil, Quemado, Cienega Amarilla, Zuni, Fort Canby, Bear Spring, Rio Puerco. His trip proving fruitless, he reurned to Fort Craig. Thus the year ended and the Civil War became a thing of the past. There would be countless other trips after Indians who became even bolder with the opening of new mining camps. Victorio, Geronimo, Nana, Cochise were to spread a reign of terror what would make Pope sorry he rid New Mexico of the Volunteers. But the Indian Wars in New Mexico are not part of this story. Some day New Mexico will erect monuments to honor the brave men from California and Colorado who gave up much to preserve the Territory for the Union. The New Mexico Volunteers and the New Mexico Militia still await commemorative shafts in the Land of Enchantment.

1865 was the year of decision for General Carleton. On the heels of the announcement that General Lee surrendered, he issued orders for the erection of Fort Seldon (April 25). General Orders No. 12, given at the General's headquarters in Santa Fe, read as follows:

"To provide for the better protection of the Mesilla Valley, and to lessen the perils of the Jornada del Muerto, a military post to be known as Fort Selden to perpetuate the memory of the late, lamented Col. Henry R. Selden will at once be established at Roblero, New Mexico, on the site already selected by Lt. Col. Nelson H. Davis, Assistant Inspector General, U. S. A. This post will be built of adobes and have a capacity for a company of Infantry and a company of Cavalry with 60 horses. For the present its garrison will consist of Captain Whitlock's Co. C, 1st Veteran Infantry, Cal. Vols., and Captain Cook's Co. F, 1st Inf., N. M. Vols. Captain James H. Whitlock will be commanding officer and Captain Rufus C. Vose, 1st Cav., Cal. Vols., will be the Quartermaster and Commissary. The troops designated will move at once upon the ground. Col. John C. McFerran, U. S. A., Chief Quartermaster of this Department, will give orders in detail as to the plan and the construction of the work and will furnish all the necessary employees, funds, tools, means of transportation and supplies, which in his judgment may be necessary to have the post completed at the earliest practicable day. The troops will assist in the work as far as possible. Lt. Col. N. M. Davis, U. S. A. will mark out as much ground contiguous to the site already selected as will be necessary for the military reserve at Fort Selden. The ground will not be settled upon by persons not connected with the military establishment at Fort Selden."

Carleton himself lived at Franklin nearby during the first few weeks of the work on the new post to make certain that Davis would lose no time in building. He was especially anxious after learning from deserters that Judge S. Biard was readying over a thousand men in Texas to raid New Mexico, plunder the Santa Fe Trail caravans, cut off supplies to southern New Mexico and force the Territory to recognize the Texas claim on all the land from the headwaters of the Rio Grande, east and south to the Mesilla valley. Meantime Davis fitted out an expedition in search of Chief Victorio and his Gila Apaches in the hopes of a peace council at least until the fort was constructed. His search proved vain and he returned to Las Cruces. It was not until Monday, May 21, 1865 that the garrison at Las Cruces was able to move to Roblero to begin construction. Several weeks later Col. McFerran was transferred for duty in the East. He had been in New Mexico since 1862 and Governor Connelly regretted the change. He escorted the departing Colonel to Arroyo Hondo near Santa Fe where he delivered a farewell speech to the assembled crowds. McFerran had made himself quite popular in Santa Fe. For the balance of the year Carleton was to be torn between criticism for his Bosque Redondo Reservation and praise for his years of service in New Mexico.

NOTES AND COMMENTS

Most of 1865 was taken up with the pros and cons of General Carleton's pet project at Bosque Redondo. The plan was sound and might have worked had he not encountered so much opposition. Even nature worked against the project, for the work of the Indians went to naught when the drought, grasshopper, corn borer, beetle and weevil got through with the nicely growing crops. Many criticized Carleton for merely transplanting the Indians from the western part of New Mexico to the eastern without solving the problem of keeping them from marauding and killing. Las Vegas, Tulerosa, Anton Chico, Chaperito, Mora, Sapello, La Questa, Las Ruedas, Gusano, Pecos, Los Trigos. Las Colonias, Los Lunes, Socorro, Bonito were embittered because previously they encountered Comanches, Kiowas, Jicarillas, Utes; now, because of Bosque Redondo their sheep and cattle herds were further exposed to the inroads of discontent and malcontent Mescaleros and Navajos. New Mexico was one vast arena of military posts, prospectors, Comancheros, Indian exploiters, Pueblos and tribesmen all being chased about by ambitious politicians who blamed Carleton for all the tears, bloodshed, robberies and failures. For every five who came to his defense there were twenty-five waiting to tear it down. His enemies eventually won.

Carleton's Defense before Doolittle, Foster and Ross sent to investigate the Bosque Redondo project—Santa Fe, July 3, 1865:
"I am Brigadier General of volunteers and Major of the 6th regiment U. S. cavalry. I have been in the service twenty-five years. I first came to this Territory with General Sumner in 1851, and left in the fall of 1856. I returned again in the summer of 1862, and have been here ever since. I have been in command of this department since the 18th of September 1862. My principal duties have been in connection with Indian affairs. According to the best of my information, the facts stated in my printed pamphlet, dated December 16, 1864, are correct, and express my present opinion; and I offer that letter as part of my present statement. The Navajo country is a country of elevated mesas, destitute of water, and has some few ranges of mountains. Between these mesas are some low lands, whereon some springs and streams are found. These springs or streams are a great distance from each other, as compared with the frequency of water found elsewhere. These waters are of a limited extent and volume; and the best of them sink in the earth at a short distance from their source. There are two exceptions to this general remark. One is the San Juan, a tributary of the Colorado of the West. Along this river are intervals of some extent, but separated from each other by ranges of mountains and mesas that abut upon the river. No one of these intervals is large enough for a reservation for one-quarter of these Navajos. Formidable ranges of moun-

tains are near by, in which they could hide, and no force of troops could keep them together. This is on the supposition that a reservation were selected on the San Juan river. Now, the cost of transporting supplies on the San Juan river. Now, the cost of transporting supplies from the Rio Grande to that point to subsist the Indians and to provide for the troops necessary to guard them in that locality would be immense, because the country to be traversed is difficult for the passage of wagons, and has long stretches through sage plains without water in one or two instances from forty to sixty miles.

"The San Juan runs through a country bearing gold, which will soon attract miners to that region; and even if the Indians were placed there they would soon come into conflicts with that kind of men, and great difficulties and complications would result therefrom. The other exception to which I alluded is that of the Colorado Chiquito or Flax river. This is affluent to the Colorado of the West further down than San Juan. It is subject to very great floods from the melting snows on the Mogollon mountains at its source. When these floods have passed by the river is very low, and its valleys become gradually covered with saline effloresence, fatal to the growth of corn along its banks, which may be considered as some evidence that it would not be a good place for a reservation. The distance to the Colorado Chiquito is nearly as great as to the San Juan, and the cost of transportation as much.

"There is no unoccupied place in the Territory as large as the Bosque fit for cultivation and capable of irrigation. I should say that there is at least 10,000, and perhaps 15,000 acres of land that could be put under water at the Bosque. The Pueblo Indians compare favorably with the lower classes of the other inhabitants of the country. I think the Navajo Indians are all pagans with the exception of the Cebollatanos. In Castenada's narrative of the first expedition into New Mexico under Vasquez de Coronado, it is set forth that Indians were found in pueblos as at present day. Among these Pueblos doubtless Catholic missionaries established churches and schools, and the Indians of those pueblos became christianized and civilized. This has raised them very much above the nomadic Indians of the country in point of intelligence and gentleness. With the exception of one or two intervals of a few years each, there has been a constant state of hostility between the people of New Mexico and the Navajo Indians.

Even in these intervals occasional forays were made into the settlements to capture sheep and cattle. The Mexicans would follow them into their country to recapture the stolen stock, and would kill some of he Indians and would capture some of the women and children and make slaves of them. But in times when open hostilities existed these efforts were increased on each side to capture stock and women and children, so that the country was kept in a continual state of commotion. This was the state of things when we acquired the Territory from the Republic of Mexico. To the best of my recollection Col. Doniphan (who came here with General Kearney) made the first expedition into the Navajo country in 1846. Col. Washington made an expedition into their country in the year 1849; General Sumner in 1851. From 1851 until 1859 there was a period of comparative quiet, interrupted, as I have said, by occasonal forays, particularly on the part of the Navajos. In 1859 war again broke out, and in 1860 the Navajos attacked Fort Defiance. About this time Col. Miles made an expedition into their country, and also Col. Bonneville; and finally General Canby made a long campaign against them, leading his troops in person. When the Texan invasion occurred, after General Canby's campaign against the Navajos, and when every soldier was employed to repel that invasion, then the Navajos, as well as the Apaches, rode over the country rough-shod. This was in the winter of 1861 and in the spring and summer of 1862. I relieved General Canby in command of the department; and this was the condition of the Navajos and Apaches at that time. The Indian difficulties in New Mexico, since the treaty with Mexico, have obliged the United States to keep in that Territory a force whose average strength has been at least three thousand men, employees and all reckoned in. This covers a period of eighteen years. A large portion of these troops have been cavalry, the most expensive arm in the military service, especially in New Mexico where forage is very expensive. The horses required as remounts for this cavalry have to be brought accross the plains from the States at great risk and expense. Sometimes large numbers have been stampeded and have never been heard from since. Many die before they reach this country. The same holds true of the mules, more numerous necessarily than the cavalry horses, by reason of the extent of the country over which supplies have to be hauled to subsist and clothe the troops. Those which arrive here it takes at least a year to acclimate; and after this the loss of horses by death, by being broken down, and lost on scouts, and killed in action, and stolen by Indians, is enormous compared with losses of cavalry horses in any other country. In my opinion the entire expense of maintaining a mounted regiment here amounts to what follows. With the exception of the troops employed to repel the Texas invasion, there has been but little necessity for troops in this country since we acquired it in 1848, unless to fight Indians. And if it should so happen that the nomadic Indians can be placed on reservations and kept there until they become sufficiently domesticated to be contented in that condition of life, I cannot see any reason why troops would be more necessary in New Mexico than Illinois, except, perhaps, a small police force kept along the boundary line of Mexico. While it is difficult to say exactly, my opinion is, that about one-half of the forces employed have been necessary by the difficulties with the Navajos. I should say that 400 cavalry and 200 infantry would be amply sufficient to keep the Navajos and Apaches on the reservation at the Bosque Redondo. The Apaches of the bands of the Jicarilla, Mescalero and Mimbres not yet captured, number, say, 1300 souls, more or less. These are all of the Apaches that properly belong in New Mexico; but there are other Apaches in Texas, Chihuahua (Another 15 years are to pass before Mexico concentrates on the Apache menace) Sonora and Arizona, who make inroads into New Mexico, and against whom a military force is necessary here. There are also bands of Ute Indians in New Mexico which need military surveillance. They occupy the northern part of New Mexico, but are mainly located in Utah. If the Apaches who properly belong in New Mexico were settled with other Apaches at Bosque Redondo, 900 additional troops of the proper proportion of the different arms of the service would be sufficient for police purposes along the boundary line and to prevent inroads from exterior Apaches, provided the troops in Arizona are sufficiently numerous and do their duty. In my opinion, if the nomadic Indians of Arizona and New Mexico were settled on reservations, no more force would be required in this country than sufficient to guard them and to act as a police (force) along the boundary, as before stated. In this connection I feel constrained to say that much of the hostility manifested by many of the people of New Mexico against the reservation system grows out of the fact that when this system goes into successful operation there will be no more tribes from which they can capture servants, and the military force being reduced to a very small number, the millions of dollars annually expended here on account of the military establishment will, in a great measure, cease. I believe that the Indians upon the reservation at the Bosque Redondo will soon be able to raise sufficient breadstuffs for their support, and I thought that they would be enabled to produce, besides this, enough corn and fodder to sustain a cavalry force in the winter time at that point, should it be necessary to have one there to operate against the Indians of the plains in the summer. Some complaints have been made that there is not sufficient fuel at or near the Bosque Redondo to supply the Indians. In answer to these complaints I will say that with the extensive fields of mesquite in that neighborhood, the timber along the southern side of the Staked Plain near by and the cedar and pinion up the river, which can be floated down, there is enough fuel to last a great many years; during which time trees should be cultivated along all the asequias and in other suitable places upon the reservation to supply the demand when all the other fuel referred to has become exhausted. The mesquite is a species of acacia, which produces the gum-arabic. In New Mexico the tree becomes dwindled to a dwarf shrub; in Texas it attains its full height from 15 to 30 feet, and is there a fine tree. This shrub in New Mexico has very large roots proportionate to what grows above ground, and these roots are dug for fuel. Mesquite roots make a very hot and excellent fire, and but little is wanted in any one lodge.

"Whilst the Navajo country does not possess, in my opinion, any one place large enough for a reservation for that tribe, it is singularly well adapted to pastoral pursuits The land of the lower as well as the upper levels are clothed with very nutritious grasses. The places where flocks and herds could come to get water are sufficiently numerous for that purpose, and near them are arable lands enough to raise bread for the shepherds and herdsmen. There is no doubt but that the northern portion of that country is very rich in the precious metals, particularly in gold (which, if the truth must be told, is the real reason for moving them from their own land to the Bosque Redondo—strange, too, that in our own day this should be the land with the uranium).

"The Mescalero Apaches are, like the Navajo, nomadic. They are also a patriarchal people, the band being divided into small communities. They are very fierce, brave, daring and perfidious, and experience has shown that treaties or bargains with them had no effect to restrain them from hostilities and depredations. So that when once they were gotten in hand by war, I, as commander of this department, felt that it was due to the people and the government not to trust them any more, and so I sent all those who were captured, or who voluntarily surrendered themselves, to the reservation.

"The number of Indians—men, women and children—who have been captured or bought from the Utes, and who live in the families in the Territory, may be safely set down as at least 3,000. So far as my observation has gone the (New) Mexicans treat these Indians with great kindness. After a while they become conversant with the language, become attached to the families they live in, and very seldom care to run away. If they should attempt to run away I believe they would be captured by their owners. They are held as 'servants'; as 'hewers of wood and drawers of water.' In my judgment, three out of four of these servants are Navajos. These servants do not inter-marry much with the Mexicans, but the women bear children from illicit intercourse. The offspring of this intercourse are considered as peons. The Indians upon the reservation, if properly cared for by the military commander, run no risk of being stolen or attacked.

"An Indian named Pino Baca, now at the Bosque Redondo, was captured at Cibolleta, and on the road to the reservation escaped from the guard and ran back to his own country. He was ordered to be recaptured or killed. He was recaptured, taken to Fort Wingate and placed in irons, with a view of sending him to the reservation should an opportunity occur. He again broke loose, was again captured, sent to the Bosque, where he was kept in irons for three or four months. He was charged, among other things, with having sold two Navajo children, and was considered a very great scoundrel. Since his release on the 16th of last April, it is said that he has behaved himself very well. This selling of children by Navajos, especially of orphan children, is said to be of not unfrequent occurrence. . . ."

SECTION TWO

CHAPTER ONE

GENERAL CARLETON

Looking at a photograph of General Carleton, the first thing that strikes you is the severity of his features. Eyes defiant, cold, penetrating; nose aquiline, four deep furrows above the bridge, creating an impression of sternness; receding forehead—and that unruly hair parted to the right—face weatherbeaten, as bronzed as an Indian's. Mutton chop whispers and the mustache above the rather wide mouth, for their very style affix a date. You are looking at a New Englander and a soldier. Somehow you know it. Here is the man who ruled New Mexico from 1862 to 1872. No monument tells you this; no hostel bears his name; no town perpetuates it. There are Entrada Days for Coronado, markers for Espejo, fiestas for Kearny—for Carleton there is silence. Today, to many New Mexicans the name Carleton would be as unfamiliar as a tidal wave.

Underneath the cold exterior was a positive love for New Mexico. He had opportunities for fame with armies better known and equipped than the California Volunteers, the New Mexico Militia, the Colorado Volunteers, the New Mexico Volunteers, but this corner of the land flew the American flag and here he was as prepared to shed his blood as others at Manassas, Petersburg, Gettysburg and Marvern Hill. Brought face to face with war, deceit, hatred, bitterness, rancour, ambition, the family life that he loved, the responsible position he held as head of the New Mexico Military Department, caused him to relegate his tender nature to the background to adopt a front really foreign to his make up. He could not have had the many friends he did if he were really the cold, conniving, calculating, ambitious grasper his enemies made him out to be.

Intelligent, alert, progressive, he had more confidence in the future of New Mexico than Daniel Webster, Stanton, Cass, and officials in Washington, who thought it ought to be given back to the Indians. As a soldier in Fort Union, Albuquerque, Fort Marcy, he converted his hard-earned salary into real estate long before the conflict between the States. Here he lived the best years of his life with Sophia Garland Wolfe, his wife. Here his children—Eva, Henry Guy and Maud—lived their lives as best they could as children of a frontier officer. It was his fatherly instinct that caused him to buy property in Albuquerque, the better to provide security for these nomads who followed him from garrison to garrison. Only to lose all in the war. He did not come from California to protect his interests —the fortunes or misfortunes of war, would take care of that. He came because he loved New Mexico and would save the Territory for the Union. He was a composite of McClellan and Pope. He had to be something. And he asked his friends to take him for what he was. It has been said that his report to the Smithsonian Institution on Abo was merely a cover up in his quest for a treasure said to be buried there. Buried Treasures were at Chilili, Abuquiu, Taos, Mesilla, La Questa, Anton Chico, and a hundred other places in New Mexico. Why did he not search after the war when he had more time on his hands? Why did he not become a prospector like hundreds of the Volunteers who served under him, leaving their bones to dry in the earth above Socorro, Elizabethtown, Baldy, Shakesphere, Hillsboro, Bland, Parkview, Silver City, Santa Rita, and other mining villages. His friends from Manassas to Appomattox blazoned their names forever on the pages of history—both for the North and the South—he preferred the obscurity of this outpost because even this was part of the America he loved. He used the Navajos at the Bosque Redondo to prove that New Mexico could rank high among the agricultural centers of the nation. He saved the Southwest for America, and for that he lives in oblivion. Only the state of Civil War and the intrusion of the French in Mexico saved that nation from making a deal with the Confederacy for all that land taken back by General Kearny in exchange for supplies, guns and ammunition. Carleton saw that the threat was always there as well as the threat of a second Texan invasion. He would stand at the helm to pilot the ship safely through these devastating storms. It was one of those rare cases in history where everybody was really out of step but Charlie.

Southwest of Campobello Island, on the mainland, one hundred and nineteen feet above sea level, and facing the Atlantic, is the little Maine town of Lumec that manages to survive as a port of entry, a tourist attraction and a fisherman's paradise. Here on December 27, 1814, James Henry Carlton was born. A war was in progress at the time, as an Indian War was to be in progress at the time of his death, and in his lifetime he was to be sandwiched between the Black Hawk War, the Civil War, and countless Indian wars. So, with war in his blood, he was to grow up a soldier, not at West Point, which he never attended, not at a military institute, but as a normal American youth who selected the army precisely because he was born near the sea. Already during the Black Hawk War he was drilling with the Maine Militia, and on August 20, 1838, he received his lieutenant's commission. At the time no young man in Maine would think of going through life without a little knowledge of Greek, Latin and the humanities. Even blacksmiths in the days of Longfellow, Lowell, Whittier, were qualied to teach these subjects and more. Servant girls spoke German, French, Latin, Greek, with the fervor of a teenager discussing her latest heart throb in Hollywood. Carleton didn't need college, circumstances forced book learning on him.

The new lieutenant was called to the Aroostook Valley, where a boundary dispute between Great Britan and the United States looked as if America would have her third war with England. His superior officer becoming ill, Carleton commanded a battalion for the first time in his life. The Aroostook War settled on paper, Carleton marched his men to Bangor in May, 1839, where they were mustered out of service. Pleased at the lieutenant's conduct during the whole affair, the governor pointed him out to Joel Poinsett, Secretary of War, and recommended him for a position in the Regular Army. Examination passed, he was sent to the Cavalry School of Practice at Carlisle, Pennsylvania, commanded by Captain E. V. Sumner, who was to be his lifelong friend. Thus, on October 18, 1839, Carleton began his military career as a 1st Lt. in the U. S. 1st Dragoons. In March, 1841, he left Carlisle at the head of one hundred recruits for the Fort Gibson, Indian Territory post. He had a year to study the habits of the Creeks, Seminoles and Cherokees. It is interesting to note that his company commander was Burgwin, who was to lead the attack on the Taos Pueblo during the insurrection following Kearny's march to California.

Carleton was instrumental in the construction of Fort Croghan on the site of Council Bluffs, Iowa. About this time he met Audubon, the Naturalist, and the two became warm friends. The Pottawatomies at Council Bluffs were disappointed to learn that Carleton was to return to Fort Gibson to stand trial at a court martial involving the permitting of a fellow officer who was a murderer to escape. The full details are clothed in mystery, but it is more than likely that it really amounted to the age old jealousy between a West Point man and a non-West Point man. Whatever the cause, Carleton was suspended by the President of the United States and sentenced to serve six months without pay, much to the disappointment of Lt. Col. R. Mason, who wished to see him dishonorably discharged.

In 1843 he was stationed at Fort Leavenworth, where he mingled with Delawares, Kickapoos and Shawnees. During the following year he worked among the Pawnees and the Plattes, holding council meetings, preparing the way for treaties. Major Clifton Warton, in command of this expedition was pleased with his work. Next came the Otto, Missouri, Iowas, Sacs and Foxes. On March 17, 1845, he was promoted to the rank of 1st Lt., serving under Col. Kearny in an expedition across the Great Plains to the Rockies. Again there were pow-wows with the Ogallalla, the Brule Sioux, the Dodge Pole Creek, Cheyennes, Arapahoes and the Comanches. Promoted to the rank of 1st Lt. he did not lord it over the more favored graduates from the school on the Hudson, who were surprised indeed, for it was not often that a non-West Pointer received promotion in those days. He now began to keep a careful journal, noting fauna, birds, animal and plant life, possibly due to his contact with Audubon. He made a collection of mineralogical and geological specimens which Harvard University was grateful to receive.

In 1846 Carleton's company was ordered to San Antonio, Texas, to be alerted for war with Mexico. When the war broke out he was a member of General Wool's staff as aide-de-camp. Wool and even Scott could have done much for Carleton had he so wished, when the Civil War broke out years later, for both stood high in Lincoln's estimation, the President often going to West Point for Scott's advice.

The part he took in the battle of Buena Vista brought him

the rank of brevet major for gallant and meritorious conduct. Shortly afterwards he was ordered to Scott's army, which was approaching Mexico City from Vera Cruz. Enroute he became ill and was sent to Washington to rest and regain his health. Never inactive he spent the time writing a *History of the Battle of Buena Vista*, published by Harper Brothers, and considered by many historians the best account of the engagement to date. His health restored, he was ordered to Fort Leavenworth, then Fort Kearny, back to Fort Leavenworth, and to Fort Laramie. He seems to have been married while stationed at Fort Leavenworth. He arrived at Fort Union in April, 1853. His oldest child, Eva, was either born here or at Fort Laramie. Henry Guy was born at Fort Union in 1856. While in New Mexico Carleton worked among the Apaches, Utes, Navajos, Pueblos and Movjaves (one of the various spellings for this tribe). In New Mexico, too, he became very well acquainted with Beaubien, Maxwell, Carson, Abreu, Keithly, and many others who were to prove serviceable during the great conflict. He was with Kit Carson when the Dragoons trailed the Jicarillas to the summit of Fischer's Peak between Raton Pass and Trinidad, Colo. Carleton had lost a wager to Kit Carson as to the time when the Indians would be overtaken. The Indian fighter from Taos received a fine black beaver hat from Boston. Years ago when I visited the Carson home in Taos a picture of the scout hung on the north wall. He was wearing the hat. Carleton's associations in New Mexico proved that he was not the stuffed shirt his enemies later made him out to be. Nor would a man with the severe New England turn of mind, a blue nose, have stooped to bet with a scout and Indian fighter, much less associate with him.

In 1854 he invested all his savings in a group of adobe structures located between the plaza and the Rio Grande, just beyond the old San Felipe church, in Albuquerque. The government was interested in establishing a post in this locality. As a military man he could not rent to the government, so the government paid his wife, in whose name the contract was signed, the sum of one hundred and twenty-five dollars a month for the use of the buildings as shops, stables, store houses and hospital. (For a full account of Carleton's deal with the government, see Wm. Keleher's *Turmoil in New Mexico*.)

In 1856 Carleton was again in Washington, where he was ordered to study Captain George B. McClellan's reports of military life and activity in Europe. He was to pattern much of his later military life after the celebrated McClellan. This work over, General Scott sent him back to Fort Union with four hundred recruits. He no sooner had them safely tucked away at the post than he was ordered back to Virginia to recruit his own regiment of 1st Dragoons. These were transferred from New Mexico to California, where Carleton joined them in the fall of 1858. Here at Fort Tejon he continued his work among the various Indian tribes. In 1860, he was stationed along the Mojave River to watch the surly Pah-Utes who were blamed for the Mountain Meadows massacre. Carleton, who had the job of burying the victims, was of the opinion that it was the work of white men aided by a few redskins. (See his account in Document No. 605, House of Representatives, 57th Congress, First Session.)

Many of the officers in New Mexico did not have slaves, because they could obtain the services of the natives and even friendly Indians at practically no cost to them save food. Others, like Carleton, preferred at least one slave. Indeed, the two dozen slaves (round figures) found in New Mexico at the time the war commenced were those for the most part belonging to these officers. When the war broke out Carleton and two companies of dragoons were ordered from Fort Tejon to Los Angeles, to keep an eye on Southern sympathizers. On July 9, he received orders from General E. V. Sumner to go to San Bernardino disguised as a civilian to investigate the report of secessionist activities carried on at that place. Returning to Sumner with his findings he went back to Los Angeles but was told to turn his command over to another and report for further orders at San Francisco. He was to command the California Volunteers. The new Department Commander, Brig. Gen. George Wright, hoped to use these troops to reopen the Southern Mail Route; as it turned out they were to police New Mexico for the duration.

Even when marching thorough Arizona Carleton took time out to hold pow-wows with the Maricopa, the Pima, the Papago. One might say that Indians were an avocation or an obsession. As early as 1844 he had informed a wide audience as to the hardships of a dragoon among the Pawnees. New Yorkers gulped it up, as they still do, whenever tales of Indians, outlaws and frontiersmen hit the pulp stands. Carleton knew how to dramatize for the benefit of his audience. He would have been successful on TV or in Hollywood. Every governor from Calhoun to Connelly called him friend. Nor did he ever forget a friend, as is testified in Forts Canby, Cummings, Whipple, Sumner, among others. He could never condone the action of any officer or former military man sympathizing with the South. That is why he was so severe with one Sylvester Mowry. At the time the California Column marched through Arizona in an effort to meet Sibley, Mowry was a mining engineer. Carleton had him arrested on the charge of treason.

Hailed before a court martial tribunal at Tucson, Mowry was found guilty and taken to Fort Yuma. Carleton seized his mine in the name of the government. Released after a second trial proved the evidence inconclusive, Mowry went to California to open legal proceedings against Carleton and others, suing them for the sum of $1,129,000 for damages sustained in closing the mine. Carleton hired the law firm of Hall & McAlister of San Francisco to defend him. Mowry enlisted the aid of Senator Conness and Senator Sprague to come to his defense. Mowry was a graduate of West Point and a classmate of Gen. U. S. Grant. He wrote to the general and asked in the name of all that was decent, and for the good of the Union cause to get rid of Carleton.

California proving of no aid, Mowry went to New York, where he soon had the ear of the editor of the *New York World* (Telegram added much later). Despite the diatribes against Carleton, the Federal government seized the mines, eventually selling them for $2,000 under the Confiscation Act. Carleton said that the fact that the mines could only bring $2,000 proved that they were all Mowry claimed them to be. And since the government sold them Mowry must have been a Secessionist. When Santa Feans read the articles in the *New York World* they held two mass meetings and gave Carleton a vote of confidence for his work in New Mexico. The Territorial Legislature followed suit. When the Governor of Arizona wrote to Carleton for help against the Indians, Mowry wrote to Grant that he hoped that Carleton would not be in command of the troops, for he would get nothing done, and would Grant please give the command to his old schoolmate. Grant wisely ignored the letter. In 1865 Mowry was living at the Union Club in New York. Three weeks after Appomattox he again wrote to Grant, denouncing Carleton as a man without honor and without courage. He reminded Grant that during the years 1862-63, he built and held a place in Arizona without the sign of a trooper in the area to give him protection; yet, he was able to defend himself without their aid. He also brought out the point that Carleton never faced a Confederate throughout the Civil War. (See *Santa Fe New Mexican*, May 10, 1865.)

The advance of the California Column has been treated elsewhere. Suffice it to say that the natives showed a marked resentment towards the Confederates ever since Sibley's retreat. They refused to recognize Confederate money, were sullen and moody over Steele's forages for food and clothing, even to the extent of organizing guerilla bands to oppose him, killing one captain and several soldiers who insisted on carrying off grain and food. The Texans themselves were so disgusted with the state of affairs in the Confederate Territory of Arizona that they threatened mutiny unless ordered back to San Antonio, and Jefferson Davis was forced to abandon the idea of a coast-to-coast Confederacy. (See W. R. Series 1, Vol. L, Part 2.)

At Apache Pass, Carleton established Fort Bowie (named after Col. George W. Bowie, Commander of the District of Arizona, then at Franklin or present El Paso, Texas). Carleton arrived at Fort Thorn on August 7, his appointment as Brigadier General having become effective as of April 28, 1862. While still in the Mesilla valley he received news that he was selected to replace Brig. Gen. Canby as head of the Department of New Mexico. Assuming command on September 18, he issued the following order:

"The following staff officers are announced: 1st Lt. Ben C. Cutler, 1st Cal. Inf., acting as Asst. Adjutant General; Major Henry D. Wallen, 7th U. S. Inf., Acting Inspector General; Capt. A. W. Evans, 6th U. S. Cav., Acting Assistant Inspector General; Captain John C. McFerran, U. S. Army, Chief Quartermaster; Capt. A. F. Garrison, U. S. Vols., Chief Commissary of Subsistence; Surg. E. I. Bailey, U. S. Army, Medical Director; Surg James M. McNulty of the 1st Cal. Vols. Inf., in addition to his duties as medical director of the column from California, is assigned to duty as Acting Medical Inspector of the Department of New Mexico, and will be governed in the performance of his duties by such instructions as he may receive from these headquarters, Major William J. Martin, U. S. Army, Chief

Paymaster; Captain Wm. H. Rossell, 10th U. S. Inf., will continue to perform the duties of disbursing officer of the fund for collecting, drilling and organizing volunteers; Captain Wm. R. Shoemaker, military store-keeper of ordnance, will perform the duties of Chief of Ordnance at Fort Union. The orderly hours at Department Headquarters will be from 9 to 10 a. m. for chiefs of departments and officers on duty, and from 10 a. m. to 12 noon for citizens on business. All orders and instructions from Headquarters, Department of New Mexico, unless hereafter modified or repealed, will remain in full force; and particular attention is directed to Department General Orders of July 7, 1862." (W. R. o.c. p. 116.)

Colonel J. R. West was placed in command at Mesilla. Before leaving for Santa Fe he left these interesting orders reflecting his love of cleanliness. He has often been quoted as hating and belittling the natives as an unsanitary and uneducated lot, but really, while he did not like the dirt, he did like the native. He would have shook the dust of the Land of Enchantment long since had he not. If ever an opportunity presented itself for him to be elsewhere, it was the Civil War:

"Commanders of towns will at once establish sanitary regulations and require them to be observed by the inhabitants and by the troops, so far as the policing the streets and keeping of their dwellings, quarters, stores, corrals, etc., in a state of cleanliness may be necessary to their health and comfort. Frequent inspections will be made by commanding officers or by a medical officer under his direction, to see that in all respects these regulations are followed. It is expected that all the inhabitants living along the Rio Grande southward from the Jornada del Muerto to Fort Bliss in Texas, will at the earliest practicable moment repair their dwellings and clean up the streets. The people may now rest assured that the era of anarchy and misrule—when there was no protection to life or property, when the wealthy were plundered, when the poor were robbed and oppressed, when all were insulted and maltreated, and when there was no respect for age or sex—has passed away; that now, under the sacred banner of our country all may claim and shall receive their just rights." (W. R. o.c. p. 144.)

Carleton felt the loss of his property at Albuquerque. Col. Kit Carson, Capt. Henry Selden, Lt. A. Anderson met at Santa Fe to discuss and estimate the amount of damage to Carleton.

While they priced his damages at $8,600, Carleton was not so much upset by this Act of War as by the fact that his hopes of providing security for his wife and children vanished with the smoke. Twenty-eight years were to pass before his heirs would be helped by the government he loved and served so well. Shortly after Carleton assumed command at Santa Fe eighteen Navajo chieftains paid him a visit.

"And to what do I owe this honor?" asked the general.

"We wish a treaty."

"What do you want of a treaty?"

"So that we may hereafter have peace."

"And what do you know of peace? If this be true, as you say, go home. Stay there. Attend to your affairs. Commit no more robberies, nor murders, upon my people. Do this and you shall have peace."

"These murders you speak of, they are not our doing. Young bucks stir up the tribesmen. Our heads are bowed in grief."

"If you cannot control them, what good would it do to speak of a treaty? You have had so many. Not one have you kept. I am not a child. You cannot deceive me. You come for gifts that are part of a treaty. Go. If you murder or rob any of the people of New Mexico so surely as the sun rises you shall have a treaty you shall not soon forget."

For a moment the chiefs stood—stunned, shocked, discomfitted by what the interpreter told them. Said the spokesman:

"We have visited white chiefs many times. We have made many treaties. Never have we been so treated. No white chief ever refused us a treaty before. But we will show this new chief that we are good Indians. We will return to our country and talk to our young men that there must be no more war."

Murders, robberies, depredations on New Mexicans were mild up to this time compared to what followed. Some well-disposed chief sent word that none of these things were to their liking but they could not prevent them. Carleton replied that since they all lived together he had no way of separating the good from the bad. Thus the idea of the Bosque Redondo Reservation was born. Let the friendly ones separate from the unruly and live on the land the Great White Father in Washington would give them, then he would know which to treat as his children and which to punish as his enemy. He would see to it that they would want for nothing. Not an Indian—good, bad or indifferent—showed his face. Carleton sent another message begging them to reconsider. The Indians replied that all Carlton had was big talk like Kearny, Bonneville, Canby and others before him. Angered by their indifference, the General told them that if they showed no dispositions for peace by July 20th he would assume that a state of war existed between New Mexico and the Navajos. Again the Indians taunted him. They were immune to such threats, having heard them for years —nor did they scare easily. Carleton was all bark and no bite. Thus it was that Carleton brought Kit Carson into the picture. It has been said that the general became part owner of the *Santa Fe Gazette* because he sought to convince the public that his Bosque Redondo policy was the best for the Navajo and the best for New Mexico.

Oddly enough the campaigns did not open against the Navajo but the Apache. Carleton felt safe in employing his troops in Indian warfare for his spies reported that the contemplated Texan advance was still just so much paper talk. He wrote to Washington, February 1, 1863:

"I consider the possibility of such an advance (from Texas) so remote that I feel justified in employing the troops under my command in chastising the hostile tribes of Indians by which the settled portions of the Territory are surrounded. The Mescalero Apaches have been completely subdued. I now have 350 of that tribe at Fort Sumner and en route thither. These comprise all that are left of those Indians, except a few who have either run off into Mexico or joined the Gila Apaches. I shall try to settle what have come in on a reservation near Fort Stanton and have them plant fields for their subsistence the coming year. The expedition ordered into the Gila country has already been quite successful. Mangas Coloradas, doubtless the worst Indian within our boundaries, and one who has been the cause of more murders and more torturing and of burning at the stake in this country than all others together, has been killed (January 19), but in a guard house not a battle. He was shot presumably attempting to escape, and in one battle a few days since over twenty of his followers were killed and quite an amount of stock captured. Among this stock were found some U. S. mules captured from one of our trains in an attack made upon it by these Indians last November on the Jornada del Muerte. Hostilities (last November) against the Gila Apaches are now prosecuted with vigor (by Col. West, who was sent out against them before Carleton called in Kit Carson) and will be productive of lasting benefits." (W. R. Series 1, Vol. XV, p. 670.)

Nevertheless he kept the men in trim over and against the day the Texans would attempt to recapture Mesilla. A man of Carleton's vision and foresight made enemies. To give such rich bottom land to Indians who had no heart nor stomach for the new location; to spur the cattle industry as he did—Chisum was to move from Texas to be near a land of forts and beef contracts—to bring about a radical change in prices of corn, wheat, wool, mutton, pork, alfalfa and wood, was more than these enemies, headed by Knapp and Mowry, could stand. The New York papers charged the general with tyranny, oppression and speculation. A committee was named in Santa Fe to undo the harm of the New York papers. Governor Connelly was elected president; Simon Delgado and Ceran St. Vrain, vice-presidents; Joab Houghton and John T. Russell, secretaries. They said in effect:

"We have known the private, public and official character of the said Carleton for many years and such charges and imputations against him meet us as new and surprising, having been unheard of by us who reside constantly in this Territory. These charges have no foundation in the opinion of our inhabitants. He is regarded by us and the people of this Territory as an able, patriotic and faithful commander and one who is earnestly, actively and disinterestedly devoting his time, abilities and means in his hands to chastise and subdue the hostile Indians, to preserve the integrity of the Government and Union, and to promote and advance the highest and best interests of the Territory and her people. The military administration in this Territory, in all its branches and operations has never been more honestly, fairly, energetically and usefully conducted than by General Carleton. The official acts of General Carleton as commander of this Department in sustaining and aiding the Civil Departments of this Territory, the Executive as well as the Judicial, in the discharge of their duties, meets with our hearty approval."

Let us give some direct quotes from the *Santa Fe Gazette*, whether Carleton owned a partnership in it or not, or was using it as his mouthpiece, the editorials do reflect the attitude of Carleton's friends and preserve for us the flavor of the bombastic, name calling, tongue in cheek frontier journalism. The editor said what he had to say, the way he wanted to say it, no holds barred, hurting whomsoever he pleased to hurt in favor of what he believed to be the truth, although it meant the loss of friends, prestige, property, money and even life. These editorials were usually one long paragraph, sometimes covering an eight-column page. But they were read. They were discussed in the cantina, around the acequias, arroyas, homes, milpas, campos, vegas, court rooms, parlors, church, forts, shops, fandangos, funciones, fiestas, visperas, adobe brick yards—everywhere and anywhere two caballeros got together for a platica. Those who could not read listened to those who could. Politicos were revered as padres when they discussed such affairs.

"A feeling of grief and indignation pervaded the reflecting inhabitants of this place upon finding after the arrival of the mail upon Thursday of last week, that General Carleton commanding this Department was furiously and vindictively and, as is believed here, calumniated in an exceedingly unjust, abusive, false and injurious manner in the *New York World* and *Journal of Commerce* and other papers. The general was then (when the mail arrived) absent upon official business (at Franklin, Texas) in the lower part of the Territory (the editor thought he was at Mesilla). The citizen portion of the community felt the wrong no less than the military. The political status of the papers referred to was known, but at the same time they have a general circulation and have a large number of readers, and a wide influence. The inhabitants felt and believed that a very deeply premeditated and concerted effort was made in some quarters by some persons to malign, discredit and otherwise injure by far the most active, efficient and successful commanding officer known in New Mexico since the Territorial Organization (1851).

"All here too, know that the class of men designated, when made to feel their inferiority and delinquencies resort to low, creeping and malignant modes to gratify their spleen, malice and motives. One of the common modes of such men in New Mexico is to procure caluminous assaults and aspersions to be published in the States against they cannot and dare not reach where their acts and conduct are known. These are men who will smile and fawn upon Carleton like 'purps' to his face, and then creep like low and malicious 'hounds' to falsify, misrepresent and detract from his conduct and character, and in the dark . . ." (See the editorials in the *Santa Fe Gazette* for January and February of that year and for February, 1864.) To convince his readers that his editorials were not mere bombast, the editor carried the news of the reception accorded Carleton at Franklin:

"General Carleton, staff and escort, arrived here on the 30th of January. Never were the feelings and sentiments of gladness and welcome more clearly expressed than they were upon the faces of every soldier and citizen of this town. As soon as the news reached the city of El Paso, Mexico, the principle citizens of that pleasant and growing place came in large numbers to pay him their respects and offer him their friendly hands. Don Juan Zubiran, Dr. Samaniego and other prominent residents of El Paso, wishing to extend the hostelities of their city to the general and the gentlemen with him, promptly arranged a grand baile at the residence of the doctor. Cards of invitation were soon distributed for the ball to be given upon the night of February 1st. The ball came off and it was one of the most brilliant and richerche displays of the kind ever seen upon these frontiers. It was indeed hard to realize that an entertainment so perfect in all its appointments could be procured in this isolated and far away country. The spacious hall of the doctor's was filled with handsome and graceful ladies richly and gracefully dressed. Col. Bowie's brass band from Franklin reached the city in advance of the guests and, after serenading some of the principal families, prepared to the doctor's at ten o'clock in the evening, the dancing began and from that hour until clear daylight the gay movement of the glad feet was incessant. Each dance succeeded the other as fast as the quadrilles, cotillions and waltzes could be formed, and, if possible, the last set and figure was gone through with, with more zeal than the first. I have never witnessed so much real good feeling and so many happy faces as on this occasion. The supper was a grand banquet. The table was mounted with the purest wines, choice fruits and all the varieties of sweetmeats. In the center was a pyramid cake of an enormous size; from the top floated the national colors of the United States and Mexico, beautifully commingling. At two in the morning supper was announced, and the ladies were escorted by detachments of from ten to fifteen at a time. When one party left the table another filled their places; so the dancing went on undisturbed. The arrangement was excellent and worked to a charm. After supper was over, the table was stuffed of everything but sandwiches, cakes and hot coffee which were served during the remainder of the night. All kept up to the dancing pitch. No one seemed to feel the necessity of liquor stimulants. The only look of sorrow visible was when daylight forced all to say a hurried 'goodbye.' The general and his party and all who attended this dance are unanimous in its praise and will remember it as one of the 'green spots' in their future lives."

The editorial for March 5, 1864, was just a heady: "We are not the apologist nor the eulogist of this commander. Others have assailed his official conduct. So far as we are informed and believe, his assailants have been governed by motives growing out of malice and esteem. This being our (i.e., editor W. H. Manderfield) clean conviction, a sense of truth and justice impels us not to remain silent. Carleton presents himself to us as a public officer charged by the government with a large amount of military power and business, to be by him administered. From lawful authority he has these in his hands. These might have been placed in the hands of another and Carleton left to his chances of power and destruction. Fortunately for New Mexico they were not left to another. He is in command of this Department by virtue of the power and decision of the government, and could the voice of the mass of the inhabitants be heard and heeded, no other officer, bearing a commission, with their consent, be furnished to displace him.

"The people had no choice in his selection, but it was one of the cases in which the selection and the man corresponded to the wishes and opinions of those for whom he was to use military means and authority for their benefit and welfare and not for personal consideration. He was one of the military servants of the government, and the government is the trustee, and at all times, is supposed to be the friend of the people, their rights and honor.

"This country in the winter and and spring of 1862 was overrun by invaders from Texas. If any portion was not formally seized by them it was not because they were prevented until they met the Coloradans with the U. S. Military in this Territory. The Coloradans came to assist the soldiers and officers and citizens in driving away the enemy and restoring the authority of loyal men, and loyalty as well is what made the combined forces compel them to leave the land and people they had imprudently violated and wronged.

"The Coloradans were sent here for a temporary but essential and glorious service. They came to sacrifice their lives or drive away the Texan invaders. Too much honor never can be given to the Coloradans for their enterprise, services and success. Every just man of brains who knows the facts will acknowledge the high utilities and results they so signally rendered and effected to this Territory and the government. While they were acting, the loyal and brave men of California were moving. A column formed there to march here for permanent service in the Territory. It was approaching Mesilla when the Texans fled for safety. Who believes they would have gone from Arizona had they not known that the Californians would either kill, capture or drive them away? No legitimate government, with lawful officers, had been in Dona Ana county for some time.

"When Carleton arrived with his column all was anarchy, and had been. It was his duty to restore order. And he did! Necessity, the most imperious, was upon him. He was equal to the times.

"It is easy to judge the events after they are passed. The narrow, conceited, mean, malicious heart finds pleasure in seeking to find out and aggravate some error or fault in a great public movement where the scope, aim and results are eminently for the public and general good. When Carleton arrived no one knew the Texans would not be reinforced and attempt a reconquest. Their marauders and bandits were known to be hovering and lurking in places about our frontiers. They left warm, devoted and useful friends in New Mexico. For a long time the people, officers and troops were alive with excitement and apprehension that another invasion was at hand, and Carleton provided to meet and repel it. The great rebel disasters of the Southwest in the first portion of 1863 doubtless prevented it. In view of this situation and the circumstances then pending, Carleton would have been highly culpable not to have adopted means and precautions so as to be able to know and destroy the designs and movements of the rebels and their friends against this Territory. . . .

". . . The rebels have as much as they can to maintain themselves in their own countries without invading more, and bringing their wrongs upon this people. Guerrilla bands need not be feared. That class of foul, brutal wretches left the country with the Texans. Outside of New Mexico the precautionary rules adapted, and the sleepless vigilance practised by General Carleton are known. These of themselves tend to keep guerrillas and evil doers from the attempts upon the peace, safety and prosperity of the inhabitants. But for these this Territory would have been overrun by the violent vagabonds and scoundrels nature and the times have bred. Carleton's policy, energy and military regulations have chiefly kept the swarm of outside villains away. On the other hand, Carleton's bringing promise of safety from Indians, when once completely accomplished, the farmer, stock grower, and all the citizens, will be advanced in prosperity; stock will be secure to the owners; the Indians will be confined and provided for. Citizens should not complain if the government provides for the Indians in order to give security to the people, their property, their homes. When the Indians voluntarily submit or are made prisoners, they cannot, in the face of the world and Christianity, be destroyed. To turn them loose again upon their promises, in the forms and ceremonies of treaties would only be repeating the oft-repeated blunder and folly so often proven a failure. Carleton now has at Fort Sumner about 3,500 Indians. Provisions such as corn, meal, flour, etc., they must have from the government for a time. This will increase greatly the necessity or demand for these articles. Prices will be favorable to the producer. If Carleton is not obstructed, if he shall have time to carry his Indian policy to completion, if enlarged views and motives shall prevail, and the counsels of the Lilliputsian, the Chinaware, shall pass for what they are really worth, New Mexico will take up a line of march greater and truer than any former period. . . ."

Tucker of the *Santa Fe New Mexican* was not as favorable. Part of his August 11, 1865, editorial ran: "Carleton took his military hand from the throats of the people of New Mexico, whose liberties he had garroted for three years, not because he was wholly or even partially imbued with a returning sense of justice, but because martial law had been abrogated in the States where war had already existed in all its envenomed fury, and for that reason General Carleton in a written order abolished martial law in New Mexico. The *Gazette*, in publishing the abrogating order puts the responsibility of robbing the people of New Mexico of their liberties upon the shoulders of General Canby, etc...."

On March 13, 1865, Carleton was breveted Lt. Col. and Colonel for meritorious services in New Mexico, despite the voices of his enemies. On the same date he was breveted brigadier general, U. S. Vols., for gallant service in the Northwest, and also breveted major general, U. S. Vols., for meritorious service during the war. Mustered out of volunteer service, April 30, 1866, he was breveted Lt. Col. U. S. Cav. on July 31st of that year. He retained command of the Department of New Mexico until April 30, 1866. He then went to Washington and Eastport to renew old acquaintances and for the rest he earned. On June 1, 1868, he was assigned to San Antonio, Texas. He contracted a cold shortly before Christmas but refusing to dampen his family's spirits during the Yuletide season, he neglected it. Pneumonia resulted, causing him to take to his bed on December 27th. On January 7, 1873, his death was announced to the people of San Antonio.

※ ※ ※

NOTES AND COMMENTS

The name Carleton dates at least from the Norman Conquest, 1066. The Carleton Dynasty in America, as we know it, begins with the return from England of John Carleton and his wife, Hannah Jewett, to the Rowley estate in New England about forty years after the landing of the Pilgrims.

General Carleton's parents were John Carleton and (Mrs.) Abigail Phelps, widow of Rufus Hallowell.

The General's father died in 1830.

James Henry Carleton first saw service as a lieutenant in the Aroostook War during the Maine boundary controversy.

It was John James Audubon who first interested Carleton in Antiquarian and Naturalistic studies. Audubon described the young lieutenant as a "fine companion and a perfect gentleman."

It was when he was camped near the home of Spruce Baird, seven miles from Albuquerque, on the road to Manzano and

Abo in December, 1853, that Carleton penned his sentiments regarding New Mexico and New Mexicans, his spirits dampened by the mud, rain, wind and cold. These sentiments were used against him a decade later by his enemies and helped remove him from office. Carleton seems to have liked his comfort. He was also a bit cocky as Cremony and others testify, and had a bit of the McClellan in him. He expected his subordinates to perform as perfectly as himself. When things went wrong, they were to blame. This is his picture of New Mexico: "The dirty little villages through which we passed have generally turned out their inhabitants en masse to get a sight of us. This gave us a sight of them. Men, women and children exhibited themselves to us in groups picturesque as well as grotesque. Some were blanketed; some with white-washed faces and some with scarlet-dyed; some with rebozos, some nearly naked; some on housetops, shading their eyes with their hands and others peering through chinks and crannies in the mud walls of their dwellings; but all were curious as to whence we came and whither we were going. The national expression of quien sabe appeared deeply written on every face.

"In no rancho or village have we seen a solitary indication of industry, cleanliness, or thrift since we left Albuquerque; and it may be remarked that we have yet to see in that town the first evidence of these cardinal virtues. Indolence, squalid poverty, filth and utter ignorance of everything beyond their corn fields and asequias seem to characterize the inhabitants who are settled along the east bank of the river. We have seen nothing denoting energy on the part of anyone save that shown by old man Chavez and his sons-in-law. On the contrary, we could but observe amongst them what seemed to be a universal proclivity for rags, dirt and filthiness in all things. Sheer laziness and listlessness mark their every movement. It may be said that the people whom we saw were of the lower order, but we were justified in coming to that conclusion from not seeing any of a better class...." (See: Hunt's *James Henry Carleton*, p. 146.)

That Carleton and Cremony did not seem to get along we gather from a letter written by Carleton at Santa Fe to Major Waller at Fort Sumner, December 24, 1863: "If Captain Cremony, when out on a late scout, did not exercise energy in his pursuit of Indians, as is indicated in your letter, your duty is plain. It is very expensive keeping cavalry at Fort Sumner. He has a fine company, and if his men are properly led and handled would be of great service. You must keep that lower country free of hostile Navajos. If Cremony is not the man to be at the head of his men to lead them, you must get some other leader. . . ."

General Carleton thought as much of Capt. E. Fritz as he did Cremony. It was over the Fritz will that the Lincoln County troubles developed some years after the war. Carleton is said to have remarked, after some Indians escaped from Bosque Redondo: "If Fritz is chasing them they will never be caught." (See: Correspondence of Secretary of Interior for the years 1863-1864.)

Here is a sample of one letter—Santa Fe, August 26, 1863, to Major Joseph Smith, Commander of Fort Stanton: "The Indians (are) beginning to be troublesome about Fort Union, where there is no cavalry. I have been obliged to order Capt. Fritz's company to that post. . . . Let Capt. Fritz transfer his new horse equipments complete to Capt. Abreu; he will have them replaced at Fort Union. Capt. Fritz will also transfer to Capt. Abreu, of the new horses which he has received, enough to mount sixty of Capt. Abreu's men. . . ." The general then goes on to mention all the sheep stolen by Navajos near Fort Union—adding: "I hope and trust this flock will not GET BY YOU . . ." Meaning he didn't expect Fritz to capture it or that he let such a thing happen in the past. While Carleton had Cremony transferred to California, he relented against Fritz and later commended his work.

Carleton was 58 when he died of pneumonia, January 7, 1873, at San Antonio, Texas. His body was shipped to Mt. Auburn Cemetery, Cambridge, and buried by the side of his first wife, Henrietta.

In a letter addressed to Lt. Col. Wm. McMullen, Commander pro tem of Fort Union, written at Santa Fe, December 19, 1863, Carleton said: "Tell Capt. Fritz, for once, I hope he will catch the Indians."

CHAPTER TWO

THE NEW MEXICO VOLUNTEERS

Centuries of awareness against the inroads of the Utes, Navajos, Kiowas, Comanches and Apaches gave the New Mexican an adeptness for frontier fighting. Each alcalde summoned the citizens when an Indian raid threatened, passed out arms, selected a leader, and the fight or the chase was on. If the settler possessed a better gun than the old musket or lance passed out by the alcalde he was permitted to carry it to battle. Mexico was too involved with problems of its own to equip the frontier with up-to-date weapons and too concerned for its own safety to build up a citizen's army. Hence when the Civil War broke out the idea of regiments, companies, systematized method of warfare was as strange to them as their language was to the regular soldier. When Romero, Vigil, Alarid, Montoya raised companies the men went about it very much as their ancestors before them out to punish Indians. This accounts for the varieties of enlistments encountered in the muster rolls during the first few months of the war. Many of the men had never fired a gun before simply because they never owned one. Uniforms were an innovation. Army regulations beyond their comprehension for only at the military posts did they see such things. They were frontier fighters accustomed to fighting Indians. Valverde confused them. They were not cowards as some authors would have us believe. Cowards did not hold the settlements against marauders for centuries and still survive. Most of the volunteers at Valverde were in the service a month and at best three months. By December, 1861, there were 3,500 New Mexico volunteers in the field for service. One must always remember the language barrier. Few officers could give commands in English. They had the will but lacked the training and knowledge for the field at Valverde. History dismissed these men after the battle so that many believed that the Territory was

387

protected solely by the California Volunteers. The National Archives in Washington disclose that New Mexican Volunteers served until 1867. Again it is a matter of language. All the reports are written in English. Much of the story of New Mexico from the Mexican War to comparatively recent date was written by men who refused to recognize that the war with Mexico was over, and people with less refinement, culture, bigotry, prejudice and artistic temperament than the New Mexicans they wrote about usually sought to paint them as peons, unprincipled, lazy, cowardly, cheats, robbers, ignorant and stupid. True, they lacked schools and learning but they had natural ability. To simply write off the New Mexican Volunteer as cowardly in the action at Valverde is not to tell the whole story. Proportionately more New Mexicans gave their lives at Bataan than the rest of the nation put together. This is because the boys were trained for warfare and proved their true metal which stems from the conquistadors. The miracle of Valverde is that there were any New Mexicans there to fight at all. Very few understood the reason for the Civil War and many cared less; not one had ever seen Lincoln or any member of his cabinet; Fort Sumter was not a rallying cry for the native New Mexican still confronted with the problem of licking the Comanche, Apache and Navajo. That the invasion was from Texas he could understand having had the experience in the Texas-Santa Fe Expedition and the near threat of another invasion because of Texan claims to the Rio Grande. The Texan seemed more the enemy than the Confederate. Nor had there even been organized war for the New Mexicans since the days of the conquistadores. Each plaza solved its own Indian problem. The presidio at Santa Fe and the quasi presidios at Albuquerque, Taos, Del Bado, Las Vegas and Socorro were lacking both in arms and men to ever organize a militia sufficient to cope with the needs of the frontier settlements until the arrival of the Americans. With forts strung along the Rio Grande from north to south, from Fort Bliss to Fort Union, the New Mexican very graciously left all the fighting to the regular army, only occasionally following the old method of dashing after Indians in the wake of a raid or horse stealing party. This system of an independent company is found in the records during the first year of the war. An alcalde or a man the citizens respected went about the plaza recruiting troops, signing them up for a month, and as long as six months. Also he was a man with political aspirations.

Romero, Alarid, Tafoya, Montoya were captains not by military service but through the generosity of the Territorial Legislature, still struggling for recognition as a State. In proportion to population, the percentage was definitely higher than most States in the Union. More blood was shed at Valverde than in any battle of the first year of the Civil War anywhere in the country, the ratio of participants being considered. The work of the New Mexico Volunteers has been minimized simply because New Mexico was not as important to the United States in 1861 as it was in 1846-48, when the nation was looking toward a coast-to-coast expansion. The very fact that the soldiers were called from the garrisons in New Mexico to posts elsewhere indicates that the Territory was left to its own military resources. The Union Army eased its conscience by insisting that the California Column continue duty in New Mexico for the duration. General Carleton was left to shoulder the responsibility and to ward off any further attack from Texas. The troops found that they were Indian fighters. If they wanted to fight Confederates they would have to move to the Kansas area or east of the Mississippi. In protecting the settlements against the Indians the California Column and the New Mexican Volunteer was preserving New Mexico for the Union. Basically, the Indian was a Confederate ally. His work was the work of destruction just as if Jefferson Davis commanded him to do so. Had there been railroads in New Mexico at the time perhaps Confederate troops might have done more fighting on New Mexico soil. Santa Fe, Albuquerque, Las Vegas, Mesilla combined did not make up the population of Richmond nor Washington, D. C. Yet, they were the largest towns in New Mexico. Government archives show that the New Mexican Volunteer served with distinction until 1867. There were several shape-ups which came under the heading of Old Organization (O.O.) and New Organization (N.O.). Concerning the New Mexican list, the Government has this to say:

"The supposedly correct name of a Union Soldier from New Mexico may not appear in this index for several reasons: (a) He may not have served in a New Mexico unit; (b) He may have served under a different name or used a different spelling of his name; (c) proper records of his service may not have been made, or, if made, may have been lost or destroyed in the confusion that often attended the initial mobilization or subsequent military operations and disbandment of troops; (d) The references to the soldier in the original records may be so vague that it has not been practicable to determine his correct name or the unit in which he served; (e) The soldier may have served in the regular army instead of a volunteer organization. The index cards in this copy are part of a body of records in the National Archives designated as Record Group 94, Records in the Office of the Adjutant General. The compilation of service records of Union Soldiers was begun in 1890 under the direction of Captain Fred C. Ainsworth, head of the Record and Pension Division of the War Department. Records of the Staff Officers are maintained in a separate alphabetical series. Records of scouts, guides, spies are found among the records of the Provost Marshall General in the National Archives . . . ."

The spellings found in this list of the New Mexico Volunteers are the original; anything found in parenthesis is for the sake of clarification. O. O. means Old Organization but not necessarily the battle of Valverde. N. O. means New Organization. The rank given is usually the rank the soldier held at the termination of his service. Those listed for 1861-62 are the Volunteers who saw action at Valverde, Peralta, Albuquerque, Glorieta, Pigeon's Ranch, Apache Pass, Kosloskie's Ranch belong to the story of the Colorado Volunteers. Several books have been published containing the lists of the California Column and the Colorado Column. The story of the Confederate Soldiers belongs to the history of the Civil War in Texas. This is the first time that the list of the New Mexico Volunteers has ever been published. The names follow the order found in the index at the National Archives in Washington. Those wishing more details concerning a particular Volunteer, especially if he gave his life for the Cause, should contact the director of the National Archives at Washington. Most of these served for the duration which dispells the charge that the duty of policing New Mexico during the war was left entirely to the California Column.

The New Mexico Volunteers are not to be thought of in the light of the action at Valverde any more than the Union Army is to be judge by the Battle of Bull Run. War, as directed from books and commands from Washington, was a new experience. Uniforms, arms, ammunition even for volunteers were unheard of. Time out of mind it was just a question of a campaign against marauders, then home again. Or, if the fields beckoned, then wait until after the harvest. Furthermore, with the exception of a few volunteers from Mora, Chacon, Guadalupita, they never had to face their own kind in battle before. It seemed useless to shoot at a white man for no particular reason. While they marched against the Texans in 1842, and collected to resist Kearny in 1846, in neither instance was there any battle. The only bloodshed was the result of over-zeal, or mercenary, on the part of Salazar. He had hoped for a prize for the ears of the Texans. Even the Revolution of 1837-38 was mostly against the Taos Indians. The rampage against Bent, Lee and others was the work of the Pueblo Indians of Taos who repented their violence when Sterling Price marched against them. Actually, it was with the arrival of Carleton that the New Mexican Volunteers realized that the Civil War was a national affair, not an isolated skirmish against Indians. Had Carleton been in command at Valverde, perhaps the New Mexicans might have made a better showing. He immediately began the practice commenced after First Manassas of mingling the troops and placing them under command of experienced officers of the regular Army as well as the California Volunteers. On November 9, 1862, Carleton was able to write to General Lorenzo Thomas in Washington, D. C.:

"You are aware of the hostile attitude of the Mescalero Apaches, the Pino Alto Apaches, and the Navajos, and also of the rumors of another Texan raid. I shall endeavor to accomplish everything possible with the handful of men which are left. Five companies of Col. Carson's regiment are now at Fort Stanton and in the Mescalero country, and four companies of Col. Vols. enter that country from Fort Fillmore and from Franklin (now El Paso), Texas. These nine companies will, I trust, punish the Mescaleros well. Already in one small affair, Carson's men have killed Jose Largo and Manuelito (notorious depredators), two of the principal chiefs, and nine of the men, besides wounding several, and besides capturing, as I learn, some seventeen horses. . . ."

Even this battle was criticized and Carleton wrote to Carson, in order to still those who resented anything the New Mexican's did: "If you are satisfied that Graydon's attack on Manuelito and his people was not fair and open, see that all the horses and mules, including the two said to be in the hands of a Mr. Beach, of Manzano, are returned to the survivors of the Manuelito band...." After Major Arthur Morrison reported that the Mescaleros wiped out the Lujan train sent to the plains near Fort Stanton for salt, Carleton wrote to Carson: "You will be sure to have slain every Mescalero Indian who may be met with at large in the vicinity of your post. No woman or child of the tribe will be injured but such will be sent as prisoners to Fort Sumner. Send Captain Abreu's company out, or as much of it as can be spared, and endeavor to recover the stock of Mr. Lujan, of Socorro (del Sur), Texas, a very worthy man." One favorable comment is found in Carleton's letter to General Halleck, May 10, 1863: "Do not despise New Mexico as a drain upon the general government. The money will come back again." To Col. Rigg, at Fort Craig, Carleton wrote: You will send the eleven troops, 1st N. M. Vols., who arrived at your post to Los Pinos at the first opportunity. You will forward to the same point all recruits for that regiment received from below as soon as practicable their arrival at Fort Craig. They are much needed in the Navajo country.... The troops must be kept after Indians, not in big bodies, with noises and smokes, and the gleam of arms by day, and fires and talk and comfortable sleep at night; but in small parties moving day after day with a fixedness of purpose that never gives up. In this way as large a command as that at Craig ought not to be run over or hooted at by a few naked Indians armed with bows and arrows. Some flour, bacon, a little coffee and sugar, thrown on a pack mule, with men carrying say, two or three days rations in their haversacks, and it will surprise the country what a few resolute men can do. If a hunter goes after a deer, he tries all sorts of wiles to get within gunshot of it. An Indian is a more watchful and more wary animal than a deer. He must be hunted with skill; he cannot be blundered upon; nor will he allow his pursurers to come upon him when he knows it, unless he is the stronger.... I once, in this country, with some good trackers under Kit Carson, followed a trail of Apaches for over a fortnight. I caught them. Others can do as well."

The letter Carleton sent to General Thomas in Washington, August 16, 1863, registered alarm: "You are aware that the Territories of New Mexico and Arizona are more extensive say, than five or six States such as Ohio; that they swarm with hostile Indians; that the wealth of the country, consisting mainly in flocks and herds, is greatly exposed to depredations on a large scale. A man may have twenty thousand dollars worth of stock, the result of a life of watching and care, and in one night becomes a beggar from a raid by a dozen Navajo or Apaches. Since Col. Carson took the field many small bands of Navajos have come into the settlements and are committing some murders and many robberies. I have all the troops in the field which can be spared from the various posts, but men on foot, in an open country, are not successful against these mounted savages. If I could have the full regiment of cavalry asked for, and could have authority to raise one independent company of native mounted volunteers in each county, to scout in that county, I really believe the Indian wars in New Mexico could be brought forever to a close. Pray send the regiment and grant the authority. These companies could be discharged as soon as their services were no longer required. The men of each county being familiar with all the trails and watering places of their own county, and being near the flocks and herds of their own neighbors, to get notice and give chase the moment hostile Indians have made their appearance would in my opinion, be a cheap and efficient auxiliary to the operations by the more permanent organized troops. We have rumors of a guerilla force having been organized at San Antonio, Texas, under the notorious Baylor, to come here on a robbing and murdering expedition. This may be so; and if so, you can see, as well as I, the greater necessity of sending more troops here. Whatever is done should be done at once...."

General Tomas recognized in this the same tactics of McClellan. He thought New Mexico had enough man power to defend itself against all comers. It was just a question of depending on New Mexicans to rally to the colors. Thomas wrote to the governor asking his aid in raising the volunteers that Carleton needed. the *Santa Fe New Mexican* for November 7, 1863, carried this item: "Now is a good time to enlist as a volunteer. A regiment is being raised, by authority of the government. Many a poor, healthy man, is now working as a peon, for scarcely anything worthy to be called wages, and for equally scanty food and clothing. When a soldier, and is sick, a physician attends him. His officers are bound to treat him with care and justice. He received thirteen dollars a month, as pay, with good and abundant food and clothing. When mustered into service, he received some portion of his pay in advance. He becomes entitled to a bounty of one hundred dollars. He will stand his chances, for the future favors, liberality and justice of the government. When discharged, there will be no danger of his having to pay a portion due him to some person not entitled to anything, under pretense that such person procures his pay from the government. The laboring man can find no mode so easy, creditable and profitable to discharge himself from poverty and servitude, as enlisting as a volunteer. The duties of the service promote patriotism, punctuality, courage and manliness."

Carleton had reasons for believing that the governor would receive no response to his proclamation. Again he wrote to General Thomas (Sept. 13, 1863): "Authority has been received by the governor of New Mexico to raise in the Territory two regiments more of troops, but it is very doubtful if even one can now be raised;

1. Due to the real scarcity of men;
2. Because other more profitable pursuits interpose;
3. Because nearly all the floating population will go to the new gold fields.

"An effort will be made to raise one regiment of infantry, as there are not horses in the Territory which can be spared from other labor to mount a regiment of cavalry. If a full regiment of cavalry could be sent at once from the States I could whip the Indians and protect the miners. . . ." Carleton would also furnish them fresh horses which he wouldn't to native New Mexicans. With such treatment, such contempt on the part of the officers of Anglo extraction, how could they hope to induce enlistment much less a spirit of patriotism. New Mexicans did not actually feel they were fighting the Civil War any more than the California Volunteers. They were still stalking Indians. Californians were anxious to go home since they arrived too late for Valverde, as did the Coloradans after Glorieta.

To the commander at Los Pinos, N. M. Carleton wrote (Dec. 25, 1863): "It is important that you send a force, say of twenty mounted men, under a reliable energetic officer, who, if he gets upon a trail of Indians, will not wish to turn back without results (a dig at Cremony), to the Abo Pass, to remain there and in that neighborhood twenty days, to watch for Navajos coming from the direction of the Pecos, with or without stock, and to attack any and all parties it may find of these Indians. There are small bands of these Indians coming through to cross near the mouth of the Puerco. These may be intercepted. If Casa

Colorado would be a better point, with pickets patrolling out towards the mountains to cut trails going east or west, you can send the party there...." In a letter to General Thomas dated August 24, 1864, Carleton is concerned over the approaching mustering out date for many of the New Mexico Volunteers, which shows how he greatly valued their services despite his comments about them: "I (again) call your attention to the condition of this department with reference to its rapidly diminishing force from the mustering out of service now, and between this time next November, of most of the 1st Cav., N. M Vols., of five companies of the 1st Cav., and 1st and 5th Regiments of Infantry, Cal. Vols. As you see this leaves the department in a helpless condition. The Indians upon the plains are attacking our trains and killing our people. We are in active hostilities with the Apaches of Arizona, and have 7,641 Indian prisoners upon the reservation (at Bosque Redondo) which, for the present, we are obliged to guard. I heard a rumor that it was the intention of the War Department to send Col. Ford's Cal. Vols. for service in this department. If that regiment, now in Missouri, could be sent at once across the plains to New Mexico, the moral effect upon the hostile Indians en route would doubtless be so great that they would leave the road and thus let our trains come through in safety...."

General Thomas pigeon-holed the letter and Carleton, ever ready with a pen, again wrote: "If you will give me 2,000 efficient men from the States, Ford's Colo. Regiment as part of them, and give me authority to employ our Utes, Apaches and Navajos, I feel quite sure that the Kiowas and Comanches, to say the least, can be so roughly handled as to make them refrain from these depredations for years to come. The season is rapidly advancing, and unless the troops arrive here by the end of October their stock will be unfit for service this fall and winter...." As usual, Thomas ignored him. Carleton had to rely on Lucien B. Maxwell, Kit Carson, Donaciano Vigil, Estanislao Montoya, Carlos Beaubien, Eaton, Chavez, Baca and Connelley to talk the New Mexicans into re-enlisting for another two years. It was Carson and Abreu who eventually silenced the Comanches and Kiowas. The New Mexican Volunteers gave a good account of themselves. South of Albuquerque General Montoya and his volunteers moved back the Apache hordes. In summing up the activities for 1864, Adjutant General Ben C. Cutler remarked:

"During the year 1864, the few troops serving within the department of New Mexico were obliged to undergo extraordinary labors, privations and hardships in following their line of duty. Early in the year, while the country was still covered with snow, their marches in pursuit of Navajo Indians, in continuation of the campaign begun in the summer of 1863, the frequent combats with bands of that tribe, not only in the Navajo country but in the open plains to the east of the Rio Grande, exhibited courage, self-denial, perseverance, ability, and the will to encounter and endure protracted hardships, on the part of both officers and men, which would be very creditable to any troops in the army. It was often their lot to be compelled, from the nature of the country, and sometimes from the limited means of transportation, to carry their blankets and provisions on their backs, and to struggle for days through deep snows, over mountains, through forests, and down through the deep mazes of the most wonderful canons in the world, in pursuit of a wily and active enemy, who was familiar with every rod of that distant and, in many places, hitherto considered inaccessible regions. It was their lot to feel that even though they were successful in their efforts, far beyond the success which had attended the labors of others who had preceded them in campaigns against these Indians, still they would win none of the eclat which those receive for, perhaps, no harder service on other fields. It was their lot to show fidelity and integrity and earnestness in their labors for the public good—prompted to this course, not by the expectation of applause or advancement, but by a feeling honestly to discharge their duty, though no approving eye witnessed their labors or their sufferings, and they had no credit save that shown in the mirror of a clear conscience, or by the approval of their own hearts. The results which followed such labors will be considered as remarkable in the annals of Indian warfare.

"The Navajos soon found that they had no place of security from such determined adversaries, and, being pressed on every hand by unexampled rigor, the spirit of the tribe was soon broken. Many were captured, and more voluntarily surrendered, when, in bands of fifty to one and two thousand, they commenced their pilgrimage to the Bosque Redondo, a place selected for them by the government, and situated upon the open plains east of the Rio Grande, and more than four hundred miles from their native valleys and mountains. The exodus of this whole people, men, women and children, with their flocks and herds, leaving forever the land of their fathers, was an interesting but a touching sight. (Eventually they returned to the land of their fathers")

Then came the operations of the troops against the Apaches of Arizona. To those acquainted with the difficulties of campaigning in that distant country—formidable against the movement and supply of troops in every way in which a country can be formidable, whether considered on account of its deserts, its rugged and sterile mountains, its frequent and often impassable defiles, and, in widely extended regions, the scarcity of water and grass—the wonder will be that the troops were ever able to overtake the Indians at all. Although the results of operations in that Territory were not so great as hoped for, yet they were creditable, and were won at an expense of toil and privation of which any description could give but a faint idea to one who had never traversed this very singular country. The marches of the troops were long and sometimes repaid by but poor results. For example: on one expedition, under one of our most distinguished officers, the troops marched 1,200 miles, and actually killed but one Indian. Oftentimes long scouts would be made, and not an Indian, or even the track of one, would be discovered; yet the movements of the troops in every direction through the country of the Arizona Apaches, and a few partial encounters with them, attended by great good fortune, gave us the morale over them, until now they are inclined to flee at the sight of our armed parties, and scatter in all directions, and not to stand upon hilltops and crags and jeer at our men by insulting cries and gestures, as they did when we first began war upon them. It is hoped that in a short time they too will be sufficiently subdued to surrender and go upon a reservation.

"While all this was doing, the Indians of the plains commenced their attacks upon the trains of the government and of citizens coming out with supplies. This required that troops should be sent out to help these trains past the points of danger. Once this was done, and the most of the trains secure, an expedition was formed to punish even these Indians for their conduct. The Kiowas had been the most hostile, and had committed some of the most atrocious of the murders. It so happened that in Col. Carson's brilliant affair with the Comanches and Kiowas, on the 25th of November, the Kiowas suffered the most loss, and had their beautiful village of 150 lodges together wtih all their property and reserve of food, entirely destroyed.

"Not only have the troops thus followed and punished the Indians, but they have opened new roads, repaired others which had become destroyed by floods, have built posts, guarded trains through the interior of Arizona and New Mexico, and conducted the thousands of captive Indians from the old Navajo country to the reservation, and not only guarded them there, but have directed their labors in opening up what will be one of the most magnificent farms in the United States. The general commanding the department takes great pleasure in being able to congratulate the troops on such a record. The increased security of life and property throughout the widely extended department, attests the beneficial results which spring from these efforts. The prosperity of New Mexico and Arizona will be sure to follow. So it must ever be a source of gratification and pride to every officer and soldier engaged in this great labor to know that the people for whom he has toiled are getting to be more secure in their lives, and to be better off in their worldly condition. All this has been done quietly and without ostensation on the part of the troops. In the great events which have marked the struggle of our country to preserve intact the Union of all the States, it was not expected that such labors would receive the attention of the general government; but the fact that two great States will yet date their rise, progress, and the commencement of their prosperity from this subjugation of hostile Indians, will always be most gratifying to remember by those who so nobly did the work." Santa Fe, N. M. Feb. 18, 1865.

Years after the war, Lt. Col. J. F. Chavez, when asked why the Volunteers panicked, remarked that it was a new type of fighting for the men, and that there were no groves or shelter for the men, nor trees for the concealment of their movements. Several other officers however, mentioned trees. It is possible that these were stationed where the bosque was and the others in the barren sand hill area. Col. Roberts said: "On reaching the crossing at the foot of the mesa of the Contadero, I discovered that the Confederate forces had already reached the river and occupied the large bosques in the Valverde bottom, with quite heavy forces of cavalry and several guns. Major Duncan, commanding the regular cavalry in advance, promptly crossed the ford, and dismounting his force, commenced the action by skirmishing on foot, and in a spirited and sharp skirmish with the Confederates, cleared the bosque of their forces, enabling me to establish the batteries, to cover the crossing and to shell the enemy from the heavy timbers he had already seized. . . ." Major Thomas Duncan, 3rd U. S. Cav. said "I was directed by Col. B. S. Roberts, commanding column, to cross the river and hold the bosque on the opposite side, so as to prevent the enemy from reaching water. . ." Col. Kit Carson said "My column, supported by the gun on the right, was moving forward to sweep the wood near the hills, when I received the order to retreat and recross the river. . . ."

CHAPTER THREE

OFFICIAL LIST OF NEW MEXICO VOLUNTEERS

This is a sample record sheet—parenthesis my own:
JUAN A. DURO (DURAN), Age 42
Enlisted Santa Fe, New Mexico, July 1, 1861
Mustered in July 8, 1861
For three years, 1st New Mexico Volunteers
Company F—1st N. M. Vols., July 8, 1861
Discharged February, 1862 (possibly because wounded at Valverde)
At Camp Connelly May 3, 1862. Regiment re-organized May 10, 1862
Made Provost Marshal of Polvedera District May 9, 1862
Mustered out August 31, 1863

* * *

To give the record sheet of all the Volunteers would be to make the book too bulky, nor would the information prove of interest to any save the family group of the soldier. All information here will be brief and exactly as on the index sheet. All are privates unless otherwise indicated.

Abeita, Alejandro, Co. E, 1st N. M. Cav.
Aveita, Desiderio, Co. D, 1st N. M. Cav.
Abeita, Petro, Co. I, 1st N. M. Cav.
Abalos, Catarino, Batt. D, N. M. Vols., 1866-67.
Abarado, Francisco, Co. L, 1st N. M. Vol. Cav.
Alvarez, Anselmo, Co. A, 1st. N. M. Inf.
Alvares, Dominguez, Co. C. Batt'n, N. M. Vols., 1866-67.
Abeita, Jose, Co. E, 2nd N. M. Inf.
Abeita, Alejandro, Co. B, 1st N. M. Cav.
Abeita, Antonio, Co. G, 1st N. M. Vols., Lieutenant.
Abeita, Candido, Co. G, 1st N. M. Vols.
Abeita, Casimiro, Co. C, 1st N. M. Cav.
Abeita, Felipe, Alarid's Independent Co., N. M. Mil. Inf., 3 mos. Service, 1861-1862.
Abeita, Jesus, Co. F, 1st N. M. Inf.

Abeita, Jose, Co. D, 1st N. M. Inf.
Abeita, Jose Emilio, Co. D, 1st N. M. Inf.
Abeita, Jose Ignacio, Co. A, 1st N. M. Vols.
Abeita, Longino, Co. G, 1st N. M. Inf.
Abeita, Manuel G., Vigil's Independent N. M. Mounted Vols., 3 mo. 1861.
Abeita, Miguel, Co. A, N. M. Vols.
Abeita, Norbeto, Co. K, 2nd N. M. Inf.
Abeita, Pablo Antonio, Co. D, 1st N. M. Inf., Sergeant.
Abeita, Pedro, Co. I, 1st N. M. Cav.
Abeita, Rafael, Co. D-A-E, 2nd N. M. Inf.
Abeita, Ignacio, Co. A, 1st N. M. Inf.
Abeitia, Benito, Co. D, 1st N. M. Inf., 3 mo. 1861-62.
Abilez, Juan, Co. H-D, 2nd N. M. Inf.
Abilonsea, Jose Antonio, Co. B-C, 1st N. M. Cav.
Abeyta, Jose, Co. F-B-C, 2nd N. M. Inf.
Abeita, Alejandro, Co. B-1, 1st N. M. Cav.
Abeyta, Antonio, Co. B-K, 1st N. M. Cav., 2nd Lieutenant.
Abeita, Bernadino, Co. A, 1st N. M. Inf.
Abeita, Casimiro, Co. A, 1st N. M. Cav.
Abeita, Desiderio, Co. F, 2nd N. M. Vols. Inf.
Abeita, Jesus Maria, Co. C-1, 1st N. M. Militia Inf., 3 mo. 1861-63.
Abeita, Jose, Co. E-C, 1st N. M. Cav.
Abeita, Jose Ignacio, Co. A, 1st N. M. Inf.
Abeyta, Jose Miguel, Co. A, Batt'n N. M. Vols., 1866-67; Co. E, 1st N. M. Cav. (early part of war).
Abeita, Pedro, Co. F-H, 1st N. M. Inf.
Abeita, Aniceto, Co. C, 2nd N. M. Inf.
Abeita, Antonio, Co. B-K, 1st N. M. Cav., 1st Lieutenant.
Abeytia, Bernadino, Co. C. 1st N. M. Inf.
Abeytia, Camero (Carmen), Co. B, Batt'n N. M. Vols., 1866-67.
Abeytia, Diego, Co. C, 2nd N. M. Vols. Inf., Sergeant.
Abeyta, Jose, Co. E-C, 1st N. M. Cav.
Abeyta, Jesus Ignacio, Co. C, 2nd N. M. Inf.
Abeita, Pablo A., Co. G, 1st N. M. Inf.
Abeita, Candido, Co. G, 1st N. M. Inf.
Abeita, Andres, Hubbell's Independent N. M. Mounted Vols., 3 mo. 1861.
Abidris, Francisco, Co. D, 1st N. M. Cav.
Abila, Eulogio, Co. A, Batt'n N. M. Vols., 1866-67.
Abila, Jose Eulogio, Co. C, 1st N. M. Inf.
Abila, Jose Salvador, Co. I, 1st N. M. Inf.
Abila, Juan de Jesus, Co. I, 1st N. M. Inf.
Abila, Domingo, Co. G, 1st N. M. Inf.
Avila, Manuel, Co. A, 1st N. M. Cav.
Avila, Lorenzo, Co. G, 1st N. M. Inf.
Avila, Vicente, Co. I-K, 1st N. M. Inf.
Abilez, Juan, Co. H-D, 1st N. M. Inf.
Abilez, Juan Lorenzo, Co. D, 1st N. M. Cav.
Abilos, Pablo, Co. D, 1st N. M. Cav.
Abilonsea, Jose Antonio, Co. C, 2nd N. M. Inf.
Abrego, Apolonio, Co. A, 1st N. M. Cav.
Abreu, Francisco, Co. C, 1st N. M. Inf., Colonel.
Abiate, Andres, Hubbell's Independent Company, N. M. Vols.
Albares, Francisco, Co. A, 1st N. M. Cav.
Abeyta, Jose Miguel, Co. A, N. M. Vols., 1866-67.
Abeyta, Jesus, Co. C-B, 1st N. M. Militia Inf., 1 mo. 1861; Co. F-B-E, 2nd N. M. Inf.
Abeyta, Jose, Co. H, 3rd N. M. Mounted Inf., 8 mo. 1862.
Abreu, Jose Maria, Co. A, 2nd N. M. Mt. Inf.
Abreu, Norberto, Co. A, 2nd N. M. Inf., Sergeant.

Acunio, Dionicio, Co. D, 1st N. M. Cav.
Acosta, Estanislao, Co. A, 2nd N. M. Inf.
Acosta, Refugio, Co. A, 2nd N. M. Inf.; Co. H-L, 1st N. M. Cav.
Acune, Clemente, Co. A, 1st. N. M. Inf., N. O.
Acuna, Eulogio, Co. E, 1st N. M. Inf.
Acuna, Jesus, Co. A, Batt'n N. M. Vols., 1866-67
Acuna, Jose, Co. A, 1st N. M. Cav.
Acuna, Leandro, Co. L-A, 1st N. M. Cav.
Adams, Alonzo, Co. E, 4th N. M. Inf.
Adams, James S., Transfer for 1st N. M. Cav. from 1st Calif. Cav., California Column.
Adams, John M., Co. F, 1st N. M. Inf., O. O.
Adas, Patricinio, Co. H, 1st N. M. Cav.
Aguilar, Luis, Co. I-D, 2nd N. M. Inf.
Aguilar, Roque, Co. B-A, 2nd N. M. Inf.; Co. C, 1st N. M. Cav.
Agires, Herman, Co. L, 1st N. M. Cav.
Aguilar, Prudencio, Co. A, 1st N. M. Cav.
Aguilar, Luis Maria, Co. L, 1st N. M. Cav.
Aguello, Toribio Pedro, Co. B, 1st N. M. Cav.; Co. K, 1st N. M. Inf., O. O.
Aguirrez, Fermin, Co. L, 1st N. M. Cav.
Aguero, Antonio, Co. B, 1st N. M. Cav.; Co. A, 1st N. M. Inf., O. O.
Aguero, Felipe, Co. A, 1st N. M. Inf., O. O.; Co. A, 1st N. M. Cav.
Aguero, Jose, Co. A, 1st N. M. Inf., O. O.
Aguero, Nicolas, Co. B, 1st N. M. Cav.; Co A, 1st N. M. Inf., O. O.
Aguilar, Julio, Perea's Batt'n., N. M. Militia Infantry, Sergeant.
Aguilar, Marcelino, Simpson's Independent Co., Mounted Spies and Guides.
Aguilar, Nestor, Co. A, 1st N. M. Cav.
Aguilar, Pablo, Co. K, 1st. N. M. Inf., O. O. Sergeant.
Aguirre, Amado, Co. F, 2nd N. M. Inf.
Aguirre, Romo, Co. A, 1st N. M. Inf.
Alarcon, Demetrio, Co. H, 3rd N. M. Mt. Inf., 6 mos., 1861-62.
Alarid, Incarnacion, Alarid's Independent Co., N. M. Mt. Inf., 6 mos., 1861-62, Capt.; Co. D, 1st N. M. Inf., N. O. Captain.
Alarid, Juan Antonio, Co. L-I, 1st N. M. Cav.
Alarid, Jose Antonio, Co. C-I, 1st N. M. Inf., O. O.
Alarid, Juan, Alarid's Independent Co., N. M. Mt. Inf., 6 mos., 1861-62.
Alarid, Luis, Co. F, 1st N. M. Inf., O. O.
Alarid, Pedro, Romero's Independent Co., Co. A, Militia Inf., 6 mos., 1861-62.
Alarid, Jose Clemente, Co. C, 3rd. N. M. Inf.
Albares, Antonio, Co. D, 1st N. M. Cav.
Albares, Mirando, Co. A, 1st N. M. Inf.
Albares, Pedro, Perea's Batt'n., N. M. Militia Inf., 6 mos., 1861-62.
Alarid, Jesus, Co. A-D-E, 1st N. M. Inf.
Alaris, Demetrio, Co. I, 1st N. M. Inf.
Alaris, Ramon, Co. B, 5th N. M. Inf.
Alarid, Benito, Sena's Co. A, 1st N. M. Inf., 2 mos., 1861.
Alarid, Francisco, Alarid's Independent Co., N. M. Militia Inf., 3 mos., 1861-62.
Alarid, Gaspar Cruz Y, Alarid's Independent Co., N. M. Mt. Inf., 3 mos., 1861-62, Captain.
Albares, Polonio, Co. A, 1st N. M. Cav.
Albares, Prexedes, Co. D, 1st N. M. Cav.
Albarez, Amadeo, Co. I, 1st N. M. Inf.
Albedrez, Dionicio, Co. A, 1st N. M. Cav.
Alberia, Silvester, Perea's Independent Co., N. M. Vols. 60 days, 1862.
Albetia, Jesus, Co. F, 1st N. M. Inf., N. O.
Albeteia, Jose Alejandro, Co. A, 2nd N.M .Inf.

Albetia, Miguel, Co. A, 1st N. M. Inf., N. O.
Alberes, Nicomedes, Co. H, 1st N. M. Cav.
Albeyas, Esteban, Co. A, 1st N. M. Cav.
Albidrez, Casimiro, Co. H-G, 1st N. M. Inf.
Abeitia, Jose Alejandro, Co. A, 1st N. M. Inf.
Albilez, Juan, Co. H-D, 1st N. M. Inf.
Abillar, Esteban, Co. I-D, 2nd N. M. Inf.
Abillar, Eleofas, Co. I, 1st N. M. Cav
Abiluces, Jose Antonio, Co. B-C, 1st N. M. Cav.
Alcainia, Jon, Co. C, 1st N. M. Cav.
Alcavas, Rumualdo, Co. A, 1st N. M. Cav.
Aldais, Jose, Co. A, 1st N. M. Cav.
Aldarete, Silvester, Co. D, 1st N. M. Vols, Batt'y.
Aldarete, Manuel, Co. B, 1st N. M. Vols., Batt'y.
Aldan, Patricinio, Co. A, 1st N. M. Cav.
Aldeya, Jesus, Co. A, 1st N. M. Inf.
Alderete, Francisco, Co. D, 1st N. M. Inf.
Alderete, Jose Maria, Co. D, 2nd N. M. Inf.
Analla (Anaya) Bernardo, Co I, 1st N. M. Inf., O. O.
Analla, Concepcion, Co. C, Batt'n N. M. Vols., 1866-67.
Analla, Dolores, Co. A, 1st N. M. Inf., N. O.
Analla, Jose Dolores, Co. I, 1st N. M. Inf., N. O.; Co. G, 3rd N. M. Mt. Inf., 6 mos., 1861-62.
Aanya, Jose, Co. D-E, 3rd N. M. Inf., 6 mos., 1861-62, Sergeant.
Anaya, Jose Antonio-Balles Co., Perea's Batt'n, N. M. Mt. Inf., 3 mos., 1861-62.
Analla, Juan de Jesus, Co. C, 1st N. M. Inf., N. O.
Anaya, Nestor, Del Balles Co., Perea's Batt'n, N. M. Militia Inf., Corporal.
Anaya, Pablo, Co. A, 2nd N. M. Inf.
Anaya, Severiano, Co. G, 3rd N. M. Mt. Inf., 6 mos., 1861-62.
Analla, Sencion, Co. I-D-F, 2nd N. M. Inf.
Anaya, Ambrosio, Co. G, 2nd N. M. Inf.
Analla, Bernardo, Co. I, 1st N. M. Inf., O. O.
Anaya, Pedro, Co. C, 4th N. M. Inf.
Anaya, Jose, Alarid's Independent N. M. Militia, 3 mos., 1861-62; Co. A, 1st N. M. Inf.
Anaya, Juan, Co. K, 1st N. M. Inf., N. O.
Anaya, Pablo, Co. C, 1st N. M. Cav.
Anderson, George, Co. K, Batt'n N. M. Vols., 1866-67; Co. C, 4th N. M. Inf.; 1st. N. M. Cav. N. M. Vols.
Anderson, Joseph D., Co. M, 1st N. M. Cav.
Andrada, Atanacio, Co P, 1st N. M. Cav.
Andrada, Jose, Co. F, 1st N. M. Inf., N. O.; Co. H, 2nd N. M. Inf.
Andreas, Jose, Co. I, 1st N. M. Inf.
Andrada, Candelario, Co. C, 1st N. M. Cav.
Andrajo, Porfirio, Co. H, 1st N. M. Inf.; Co. A, 1st N. M. Cav.
Angel, Francisco, Co. F, 1st N. M. Militia Inf.
Angel, Jesus, Co. C, 1st N. M. Inf., O. O.
Angel, Jose Inocencio, Co. B, 1st N. M. Inf., O. O.
Angel, Juan, Co. E, 1st N. M. Inf., N. O.
Angel, Juan Isidro, Co. I, 1st N. M. Cav.
Angel, Luis, Co. A-E, 2nd N. M. Inf.
Angel, Alorgio, Co. E, 3rd N. M. Militia Inf.
Anilla, Sencion, Co. I, 1st N. M. Cav.
Anna, John, Co. G, 1st N. M. Cav.
Anaya, Juan Pablo, Co. K, 1st N. M. Cav.
Anaya, Concepcion, Co. B, 1st N. M. Inf., N. O.
Antellotti, Joseph, Co. F, 1st N. M. Inf., Corporal.
Atentio, Juan Antonio, Alarid's Independent Co., N. M. Militia Inf., 3 mos., 1861-62.

Atencio, Manuel, Alarid's Independent Co., N. M. Militia Inf., 3 mos., 1861-62.
Atencio, Juan Pedro, Co. D, 1st N. M. Inf.
Apodoca, Juan M., Co. G, 1st N. M. Inf.
Apodoca, Nicolas, Co. K, 1st N. M. Inf. N. O.
Apodoca, Porfiro, Co. M, 1st N. M. Inf.
Apodoca, Juan, Co. D, 1st N. M. Inf.; Co. E-K, 3rd N. M. Militia Inf., 3 mos., 1861-62.
Apodoca, Juan Jose, Co. A, 3rd N. M. Militia Inf., 6 mos. 1861-62, Co. L, 3rd N. M. Inf.
Apodoca, Juan Pablo, Co. D, 1st N. M. Inf., O. O.
Apodoca, Lorenzo, Co. I, 5th N. M. Inf.; Co. H, 1st N. M. Cav., Corporal.
Apodaca, Manuel, Co. B, 3rd N. M. Militia Inf., 6 mos., 1861-62.
Apodaca, Marcellius, Co. H-A, 3rd N. M. Militia Inf., 6 mos., 1861-62.
Apodoca, Mariano, Jaramillo's Co. of Perea's Batt'n, N. M. Mil. Inf., 3 mos. 1861-62.
Apodaca, Nicanor, Co. D, 1st N. M. Inf., Aragon's Co. of Perea's Batt'n, N. M. Mil. Inf. 3 mos., 1861-62.
Apodaca, Nicolas, Co. K, 1st N. M. Inf.; Co. E, 3rd N. M. Mt. Vols., 6 mos., 1861-62; Co. B, 4th N. M. Inf.
Apodaca, Pedro, Graydon's Independent Co., N. M. Militia Inf., 3 mos., 1861-62; Co. H-D, 3rd N. M. Inf.; Co. B, 4th N. M. Inf.
Apodoca, Perjulio, Co. A, 1st N. M. Inf. O. O.
Apodoca, Rafael, Co. D, 1st N. M. Cav.
Apodoca, Ramon, Co C, 1st N. M. Cav.; Co. D-H, 3rd N. M. Inf.
Apodaca, Jose Ramon, Co. D-H, 3rd N. M. Mt. Inf.
Apodaca, Rosario, Co. D, 1st N. M. Mil. Inf. N. O.
Apodaca, Ruperto, Co. D, 1st N. M. Inf., O. O.
Apodaca, Santiago, Co. D, 3rd N. M. Mt. Inf., 6 mos., 1861-62.
Apodaca, Isidro, Co. H, 1st N. M. Cav.
Apodaca, Vicente, Gonzolez Independent Co., N. M. Militia, 3 mos., 1861.
Apodaca, Dolores, Co. L-K-D, 1st N. M. Cav.
Apodaca, Felipe, Co. D, 1st N. M. Cav.
Apodaca, Jesus, Hubbell's Independent Co., N. M. Militia Vols., 3 mos., 1861.
Apodaca, Jose Maria, Graydon's Independent Co., N. M. Militia Cav., 3 mos., 1861.
Apodaca, Manuel, Co. I, 1st N. M. Cav.
Apodaca, Alojio, Hubbell's Independent Co., N. M. Militia Vols., 3 mos., 1861.
Apodaca, Pedro, Graydon's Independent Co., N. M. Militia Vols., 3 mos., 1861.
Apodaca, Rafael, Co. C, 1st N. M. Inf.
Apodaca, Ysidro, Co. A, 5th N. M. Inf.
Apodoca, Eulogio, Co. A, 1st N. M. Inf., N. O.
Apodaca, Guillimo, Co. A-D, 1st N. M. Inf,, 3 mos., 1861-62.
Apodaca, Juan de Dios, Co. D, 1st N. M. Cav.
Apodaca, Alvirio, Co. F-D, 4th N. M. Inf.
Apodaca, Antonio, Hubbell's Co. H, Perea's Batt'n, N. M. Militia Inf., 3 mos. 1861-62.
Apodaca, Bautista, Co. B, 4th N. M. Inf.
Apodaca, Zenida, Montoya's Co., Perea's Batt'n, N. M. Militia Inf., 3mos., 1861-62.
Apodaca, Romualdo, Co. H, 1st N. M. Inf., N. O.
Apodaca, Victor, Co. D, 3rd N. M. Mt. Inf., 3 mos., 1861-62.
Apodaca, Desiderio, Co. E, 3rd N. M. Mt. Inf., 6 mos., 1861-62; Co. F, 4th N. M. Inf.; Co. D, 1st N. M. Cav.
Apodaca, Dolores, Co. L-K, 1st N. M. Cav., Sergeant.

Apodaca, Domingo, Co. C, 1st N. M. Cav.; Co. E, 3rd N. M. Mt. Inf., 6 mos. 1861-62.
Apodaca, Eulogio, Jaramillo's Co., Perea's Batt'n, N. M. Militia, 3 mos., 1861-62.
Apodaca, Francisco, Del Balle's Co., Perea's Batt'n, N. M. Militia Inf., 3 mos., 1861-62; Co. H, 1st N. M. Inf., N. O.; Co. E, 3rd N. M. Mt. Inf., Sergeant.
Apodaca, Gregorio, Del Balle's Co., Perea's Batt'n, N. M. Militia Inf., 3 mos., 1861-62.
Apodaca, Jesus, Co. B, 1st N. M. Cav.; Co. E, 2nd N. M. Inf.
Apodaca, Jose, Jaramillo's Co., Perea's Batt'n, N. M. Militia Inf. 3 mos., 1861-62, Corporal.
Apodaca, Jose Maria, Graydon's Independent Co., N. M. Militia Co. Vols., 3 mos., 1861-62.
Apodaca, Jose Materio (Mateo?) Del Valle's Co., Perea's Batt'n, N. M. Militia Inf., 3 mos., 1861-62.
Apodaca, Juan Rafael, Co. I, 1st N. M. Inf., N. O.
Aguirra, Silverio, Co. H, 1st N. M. Cav.
Aguirrez, Fermin, Co. I, 1st N. M. Cav.
Aracon (Aragon?), Demetrio, Co. H, 3rd N. M. Militia Inf.
Aragon, Pedro Antonio, Co. D, 1st N. M. Inf., N. O.; Co. B, 1st N. M. Inf.
Aragon, Eusebio, Montoya's Co., Perea's Batt'n, N. M. Militia Inf., 3 mos., 1861-62.
Aragon, Berejildo, Co. K, 1st N. M. Cav.
Aragon, Emilio, Co. K, 1st N. M. Cav.
Aragon, Clemente, Co. A-E, 2nd N. M. Inf.
Aragon, Cruz, Co. B, 1st N. M. Cav.
Aragon, Atanacio, Co. C-E, 1st N. M. Inf.
Aragon, David, Montoya's Co., Perea's Batt'n, N. M. Militia Inf., 3 mos., 1861-62.
Aragon, Desiderio, Co. E, 3rd N. M. Mt. Inf., 3 mos., 1861-62.
Aragon, Encarnacion, Co. D, 1st N. M. Inf., N. O.
Aragon, Esteban, Co. G, 3rd N. M. Mt. Inf., 6 mos., 1861-62.
Aragon, Evaristo, Hubbell's Independent Co., N. M. Militia Vols., 3 mos., 1861.
Aragon, Francisco, Co. B, 4th N. M. Inf.
Aragon, German, Co. I, 1st N. M. Cav.; Co. K, 1st N. M. Inf., O. O.
Aragon, Herman, Hubbell's Independent Co., N. M. Militia Vols., 3 mos., 1861.
Aragon, Ignacio, Co. A, 3rd N. M. Mt. Inf., 6 mos., 1861-62.
Aragon, Isidro, Co. I, 1st N. M. Mil., 3 mos., 1861-62.
Aragon, Jesus, Co. I, 1st N. M. Inf.; Co. G, 2nd N. M. Inf.
Aragon, Jose Antonio, Co. F, 4th N. M. Inf.
Aragon, Jose de los Angeles, Co. D, 4th N. M. Inf.
Aragon, Jose de la Cruz, Co. K, 3rd N. M. Inf.
Aragon, Jose Dolores, Co. F, 1st N. M. Cav.
Aragon, Jose Lino, Mink's Independent Co., N. M. Vols., 3 mos., 1861.
Aragon, Jose Leon, Co. H, 3rd N. M. Mt. Inf., 6 mos., 1861-62.
Aragon, Jose Manuel, Co. E-B, 3rd N. M. Mt. Inf., 6 mos., 1861-62.
Aragon, Juan Bautista, Alarid's Independent Co., N. M. Militia Inf., 3 mos., 1861-62.
Aragon, Julian, Co. C, 1st N. M. Cav.; Co. F, 4th N. M. Inf., Sergeant.
Aragon, Jose Manuel, Hubbell's Co., Perea's Batt'n, N. M. Militia Inf., 3 mos., 1861-62; Co. I, 1st N. M. Cav.
Aragon, Antonio Manuel, Co. G, N. M. Mt. Inf., 6 mos., 1861-62.
Aragon, Nabor, Co. A, N. M. Mt. Inf., 6 mos., 1861-62.
Aragon, Pedro, Hubbell's Co., Perea's Batt'n, N. M. Militia Inf., 3 mos. 1861-62.
Aragon, Quirino, Co. A-E, N. M. Mt. Vols., 6 mos., 1861-62.
Aragon, Ramon, Co. E-B, 3rd N. M. Mt. Vols., 6 mos., 1861-62.

Aragon, Sisicio, Co. B-C, 4th N. M. Inf.
Armento, Juan, I Batt., N. M. Vols., 1866-67.
Armijo, Juan, Co. I, 1st N. M. Cav.
Armijo, Antonio, Co. E, 1st N. M. Cav.
Andrada, Diego, Co. A, 1st N. M. Militia Inf., 3 mos., 1861-62.
Aranda, Ignacio, Co. I-H, 2nd N. M. Inf.; Co. I, Batt'n N. M. Vols., 1866-67.
Arando, Jose Gabriel, Co. E, 2nd N. M. Inf.
Arando, Isidoro, Co. A, 1st N. M. Cav.
Arando, Antonio, Del Balle's Co., Perea's Batt'n, N. M. Militia Inf., 3 mos., 1861-62, Corporal.
Andrada, Anatonio Jose, Jaramillo's Co., Perea's Batt'n, N. M. Militia Inf., 3 mos., 1861-62.
Atencio, Edebiges, Co. B, 1st N. M. Mt. Vols.
Alcarjo, Jose, Co. C, 1st N. M. Cav., Trumpeter.
Arce, Mauricio, Co. A, 1st N. M. Inf., O. O.
Archiveque, Jose, Co. E, 1st N. M. Cav.; Co. C, Batt'n N. M. Vols. 1866-67.
Archiveque, Cristobal, Co. I, 2nd N. M. Inf.
Archiveque, Arcadio, Aragon's Co., Perea's Batt'n, N. M. Militia Inf., 3 mos. 1861-62.
Arcia (Garcia?) Luis, Co. L, 1st N. M. Cav.
Archiveque, Antonio, Co. F, 3rd N. M. Mt. Inf., 6 mos., 1861-62.
Archiveque, Aniceto, Co. C, 1st N. M. Inf. N. O.
Archuleta, Antonio, Co.A,Co.A,1stN.M.Cav.
Archuleta, Benito, Co. K, 3rd N. M. Vols., 6 mos., 1861-62.
Archuleta, Catarino, Co. E, 3rd N. M. Mt. Inf., 6 mos. 1861-62.
Archuleta, Crecencio, Co. B, 1st N. M. Inf., O. O.
Archuleta, Cristobal, Co. E, 2nd N. M. Inf.
Archuleta, Culas (Nicholas?) Co. E, 4th N. M. Inf.
Archuleta, Diego, Co. F, 1st N. M. Mil. Inf., 3 mos., 1861-62.
Archuleta, Donaciano, Co. D, 3rd N. M. Mt. Inf., 6 mos. 1861-62.
Archuleta, Encarnacion, Co. H, 1st N. M. Inf., 3mos., 1861; Vigils Independent Co., N. M. Militia Vols.
Archuleta, Epifacio, Co. G-I, N. M. Inf., N. O.
Archuleta, Florencio, Co. A, 1st N. M. Inf., O. O.
Archuleta, Francisco, Co. A, Batt'n N. M. Vols., 1866-67.
Archuleta, Jesus Maria, Co. E, 3rd N. M. Mt. Vols., 6 mos., 1861-62.
Archuleta, Joaquin, Co. C, 1st N. M. Cav.
Archuleta, Jose, Co. H, 1st N. M. Cav.
Archuleta, Jose Cleto, Simpson's Independent Co., N. M. Spies and Guides.
Archuleta, Luciano,. Vigil's Independent Co., N. M. Militia Vols., 3 mos., 1861.
Archuleta, Jose Miguel, Co. I, 1st N. M. Inf., O. O., Wagoner.
Archuleta, Juan Andres, Co. C, 1st N. M. Cav.; Co. D, 1st N. M. Militia Inf., 3 mos., 1861-62.
Archuleta, Juan de Jesus, Co. G, 1st N. M. Inf., N. O.
Archuleta, Juan, Co. D, 1st N. M. Inf., O. O.
Archuleta, Juan de Mata, Mink's Independent Co., N. M. Militia Vols., 3 mos., 1861.
Archuleta, Juan Nep, Vigil's Independent Co., N. M. Militia Vals., 3 mos., 1861-62.
Archuleta, Juan Julio, Co. E, 2nd N. M. Inf.
Archuleta, Juan Rafael, Co. F, 1st N. M. Militia Inf., 3 mos., 1861-62.
Archuleta, Lucio, Co. I, 1st N. M. Inf., N. O.
Archuleta, Luciano, Vigil's Independent Co., N. M. Militia, 6 mos., 1861-62.
Archuleta, Luis, Co. L, 1st N. M. Cav.
Archuleta, Marco, Co. H, 9rd N. M. Mt. Inf.

Archuseta, Miguel, Co. A, 1st N. M. Cav.; Co. A, Batt'n N. M. Vols., 1866-67.
Archuleta, Nabor, Co. G, 1st N. M. Inf. N. O.
Archuleta, Nicolas, Co. C, 1st N. M. Cav.
Archuleta, Panteleon, Co. F-G, 1st N. M. Inf. O. O.
Archuleta, Pastor, Co. C, 3rd N. M. Mt. Inf., 6 mos. 1861-62.
Archuleta, Pedro, Co. A, 1st N. M. Inf., N. O.
Archuleta, Teodoro, Co. E, 7st N. M. Inf., N.O.
Archuleta, Toribio, Co. D, 1st N. M. Inf., O. O.
Archuleta, Vivian, Co. B, 1st N. M. Inf., O. O.
Archuleta, Vicente, Co. D, 1st N. M. Inf.
Archuleta, Pedro, Co. I, 1st N. M. Inf., N. O.
Archuleta, Mariano, Co. B, 1st N. M. Inf., O. O.
Archuleta, Jose Ciatino, Co. F, 1st N. M. Cav.
Archuleta, Juan Ignacio, Co. A, 1st N. M. Cav.
Archuleta, Julian Ignacio, Co. D, 1st N. M. Inf.
Archuleta, Lucio, Co. D, 1st N. M. Inf., N. O.
Arcibia, Antonio, Co. D, Batt'n N. M. Vols., 1866-67, Sergeant.
Aragon, Dario, Del Valle's Co. Perea's Batt'n N. M. Militia Inf., 1861-62.
Arellano, Manuel, Co. K, 1st N. M. Cav.
Arellano, Juan Domingo, Co. D, 1st N. M. Militia Inf., 3 mos. 1861-62.
Arellano, Inocencio, Co. B, 1st N. M. Inf., O. O.
Arey, Catarino, Co. F, 1st N. M. Cav.
Arguello, Juan Jose, Co. A, 1st N. M. Militia Inf., 3 mos. 1861-62.
Arguello, Juan Manuel, Co. E-D, 1st N. M. Inf., O. O.
Arguello, Juan Reyes, Co. B, 1st N. M. Inf., O. O., Corporal.
Arguello, Mandrido, Co. E, 1st N. M. Cav.
Arguello, Mateo, Co. E, 1st N. M. Cav., Corporal.
Arguello, Mauricio, Co. K, 1st N. M. Cav., O. O.
Arguello, Salvador, Co. E, 1st N. M. Cav.
Arguello, Torivio, Co. E, 1st N. M. Cav., Corporal.
Arias, Enrigal, Co. K, 1st N. M. Cav.
Arias, Diega, Co. F, 1st N. M. Inf.
Arias, Jesus, Batt'n N. M. Vols., 1866-67; Co. B, 1st N. M. Inf., O. O.; Co. B, 1st N. M. Cav., N. O.
Arias, Jesus Fer., Co. H-L, 1st N. M. Cav., Sergeant.
Arian, Juan de Jesus, Co. K, 1st N. M. Inf., O. O.
Arias, Ramon, Co. I, 1st N. M. Cav.; Co. B, Batt'n N. M. Vols., 1866-67.
Arias, Diego, Co. B, 1st N. M. Cav., Sergeant.
Arias, Juan Luis, Co. E-B, 3rd N. M. Militia Inf., 6 mos. 1861-62.
Angel, Jesus, Co. B, 1st N. M. Inf., O. O.
Arios, Florencio, Jeramillo's Co. Perea's Batt'n, N. M. Militia Inc., 3 mos., 1861-62.
Arios, Jesus Maria, Co. H, 1st N. M. Inf., O. O.
Arios, Roman, Co. H, 1st N. M. Inf., O. O.
Armenta, Luciano, Co. B, 1st N. M. Cav.
Armijo, Benigno, Alarid's Independent Co., N. M. Inf., 3 mos., 1861-62.
Armijo, Antonio, Co. D, Batt'n N. M. Vols., 1866-67; Co. D, 1st N. M. Inf., N. O.
Armijo, Francisco, Min's Independent Co., M. M. Militia Vols., 3 mos., 1861-62.
Armijo, Jesus, Montoya's Co., Perea's Batt'n, N. M. Militia Inf., 3 mos., 1861-62.
Armijo, Jose, Co. D, 4th N. M. Inf.
Armijo, Jose Manuel, Co. E, 2nd N. M. Inf.
Armijo, Juan, B Battery, N. M. Vols., 1866-67; Co. C, 1st N. M. Cav.
Armijo, Luciano, Co. D, Batt'n N. M. Vols., 1866-67.
Armijo, Romualdo, Montoya's Co., Perea's Batt'n, N. M. Militia Inf., 3 mos., 1861-62.

Armijo, Antonio, Romero's Independent Co., A, N. M. Militia Inf., 3 mos., 1861-62.
Armijo, Jose Manuel, Co. E, 1st N. M. Inf.
Armijo, Ambrosio, Perea's Independent Co., N. M. Vols., sixty days, 1862.
Armijo, Antonio, Co. A, Batt'n N. M. Vols., 1866-67; Co. E, 1st N. M. Cav.; Graydon's Independent Co., N. M. Militia Vols., 3 mos., 1861-62.
Armijo, Antonio Maria, Tafoya's Independent Co., N. M. Militia Iif., 3 mos., 1861-62, Corporal.
Armijo, Benito, Co. K, 3rd N. M. Mt. Vols., 6 mos., 1861-62.
Armijo, Bengino, Alarid's Independent Co., N. M. Militia Inf., 3 mos., 1861-62, Corporal.
Armijo, Vicente, Montoya's Co., Perea's Batt'n, N. M. Militia Inf., 3 mos., 1861-62.
Armijo, Vivian, Co. A-E, 3rd N. M. Mt. Inf., 6 mos. 1861-62.
Armijo, Bonifacio, Co. D, Batt'n N. M. Vols., 1866-67.
Armijo, Cristobal, Perea's Independent Co., N. M. Vols., 60 days, 1862.
Armijo, Eduardo, Romero's Independent Co. A, N. M. Militia Inf., 3 mos., 1861-62.
Armijo, Francisco, Jaramillo's Co., Perea's Batt'n, N. M. Militia Inf., 3 mos. 1861-62.
Armijo, Francisco, Tafoya's Independent Co., N. M. Militia Inf., 3 mos., 1861-62.
Armijo, Guadalupe, Hubbell's Independent Co., N. M. Militia Vols.
Armijo, James, Perea's Independent Co., N. M. Vols., Sixty days, 1861.
Armijo, Jesus, Gonzolez Independent Co., N. M. Militia Inf., 3 mos., 1861.
Armijo, Jesus Maria, Hubbell's Independent Co., N. M. Militia Inf., 3 mos., 1861, Corporal.
Armijo, Jose, Jaramillo's Co., Perea's Batt'n, N. M. Militia Inf., 3 mos., 1861-62.
Armijo, Jose Antonio, Gonzolez Independent Co., N. M. Militia, 3 mos., 1861.
Armijo, Jose Domingo, Sena's Co. H, N. M. Militia, 2 mos., 1862.
Armijo, Juan, Graydon's Independent Co., N. M. Militia Vols., 3 mos., 1861-62.
Armijo, Luis, Gonzolez Independent Co., N. M. Militia, 3 mos., 1861.
Armijo,g Manuel, Co. L, 1st N. M. Cav.
Armijo, Mateo, Jaramillo's Co., Perea's Batt'n, N. M. Militia Inf., 3 mos., 1861-62.
Armijo, Matias, Tafoya's Independent Co., N. M. Militia, 3 mos., 1861-62.
Armijo, Nepomiceno, Co. A, Batt'n N. M. Vols., 1866-67; Co. A, 1st N. M. Inf., O. O.
Armijo, Pablo, Romero's Independent Co. A, N. M. Militia, 3 mos., 1861-62.
Armijo, Pedro, Graydon's Independent Co., 1st N. M. Militia Vols., 3 mos., 1861-62.
Armijo, Rafael, Perea's Independent Co., N. M. Vols., 60 days, 1862.
Armijo, Remigio, Co. B, 3rd N. M. Mt. Inf., 6 mos., 1861-62, Corporal.
Armijo, Salvador, Perea's Independent Co., N. M. Vols., 60 days, 1862.
Armijo, Gregorio, Co. D, 1st N. M. Inf.
Armijo, Bonifacio, Co. F, 1st N. M. Cav.; Batt'n N. M. Vols., 1866-67.
Arnaux, Edmund, Co. A, 1st N. M. Inf., Lieutenant.
Aronda, Teodocio, Co. A, 1st N. M. Cav.
Anaya, Cruz, Co. A-E, 3rd N. M. Mt. Inf., 6 mos., 1861-62.
Arrez, Catarino, (Also listed as Arias), Co. F, 1st N. M. Cav.

Arroyo, Juan, Graydon's Independent Co., N. M. Mt. Vols., 3 mos., 1861-62.
Arse, Jose, Co. G, 2nd N. M. Inf.
Arse, Maurencio, Co. C, 1st N. M. Inf.
Artago, Valentino, Romero's 3rd. N. M. Independent Co., 6 mos., 1861-62.
Artiago, Jose Maria, Co K, 1st N. M. Cav.
Artiago, Juan, Co. H, 2nd N. M. Inf.
Artin, Lewis R., Co. B, 1st N. M. Cav.
Areyanas, Thomas, Co. H, 1st N. M. Inf., O. O.
Areyanas, Jose A., Co. C, 1st N. M. Cav., Corporal.
Asebia, Louis, Co. L, 1st N. M. Cav.
Aseba, Andres, Co. D, 1st N. M. Inf., N. O.
Ashton, John, Co. B, 1st N. M. Cav., O. O.
Atencio, Atanacio, Co. B, 3rd N. M. Mt. Vols., 6 mos., 1861-62.
Avalas, Tomas, Co. E, 1st N. M. Inf.
Avalia, Jose Salvador, Co. I, 1st N. M. Inf., O. O.
Avalia, Catarin, Co. B, 1st N. M. Inf., N. O.
Avarista, Henriquez, Co. A, 1st N. M. Cav.
Avellana, Manuel, Co. E1I, N. M. Mt. Vols., 6 mos., 1861-62.
Avillas, Calisto, Co. F, 1st N. M. Inf.
Ager, Edward E., Co. I, 1st N. M. Inf., N. O. 2nd Lieutenant.
Ayers, John, Co. I, 1st N. M. Inf., 1st Lieutenant.
Ayres, William, Co. D, 1st N. M. Inf., N. O., Captain.

Babbitt, Robert, Co. K, 1st N. M. Cav.; 4th N. M. Inf.
Babbitt, William W., Co. D, 1st N. M. Cav., Colonel.
Baca, Armendaris, Y. Sena's Co., 1st N. M. Militia, 3 mos., 1862.
Baca, Antonio, Co. D, Batt'n N. M. Vols., 1866-67; Co. C, 1st N. M. Cav.; Co. F-G, 1st N. M. Inf., O. O.
Baca, Antonnio Maria, Hubbell's Co., Perea's Batt'n, N. M. Militia Inf., 3 mos., 1861-62.
Baca, Antonio Martinez y, Co. A-E, 3rd N. M. Mt. Inf., 6 mos., 1861-62.
Baca, Bernardo, Co. C, 1st N. M. Cav.; Co. A, Batt'n N. M. Vols., 1866-67.
Baca, Vicente, Tafoya's Independent Co., N. M. Militia, 3 mos., 1861-62.
Baca, Bictoriano, Co. H-E, 1st N. M. Cav.
Baca, Camilio, Gonzolez Independent Co., N. M. Militia, 6 mos., 1861-62.
Baca, Casildo, Gonzolez Independent Co., N. M. Militia, 3 mos., 1861.
Baca, Catarino, Co. L, 1st N. M. Cav.
Baca, Crecencio, Co. K-C, 1st N. M. Cav.; Co. A, 3rd N. M. Mt. Vols., 3 mos., 1861-62.
Baca, David, Co. D., 3rd N. M. Mt. Vols., 6 mos., 1861-62.
Baca, Dolores, Del Balle Co., Perea's Batt'n, N. M. Militia Inf., 3 mos., 1861-62.
Baca, Eliseo, Co. L, 3rd N. M. Mt. Vols., 1861-62, 6 mos.
Baca, Enriques, Hubbell's Co., Perea's Batt'n, N. M. Militia Inf., 3 mos., 1861-62.
Baca, Esquipula, Co. D, 3rd N. M. Mt. Inf., 6 mos.. 1861-62.
Baca, Fabian, Co. E-D, 2nd N. M. Inf.
Baca, Facundo, Romero's Independent Co. A, N. M. Militia Inf., 3 mos., 1861-62.
Baca, Felipe, Aragon's Co., Perea's Batt'n N. M. Militia Inf., 3 mos., 1861-62.
Baca, Felipe, Tafoya's Independent Co., N. M. Militia Inf., 3 mos., 1861-62.
Baca, Francisco, Gonzolez Independent Co., N. M. Militia Inf., 3 mos., 1861.

Baca, Francisco, Tafoya's Independent Co., N. M. Militia Inf., Co. C, 3 mos., 1861-62.
Baca, Jesus, Montoya's Co., Perea's Batt'n, N. M. Militia Inf., 3 mos., 1861-62.
Baca, Jesus Maria Sena y, Co. F, 1st N. M. Inf.; Co. B, 1st N. M. Cav., Captain.
Baca, Jose, Capt. Gonzolez's 3rd N. M. Mounted Infantry, 6 mos., 1861-62.
Baca, Jose Antonio, Co. G, 1st N. M. Inf.
Baca, Jose Francisco, Co. F, 1st N. M. Mt. Inf., 3 mos., 1861-62.
Baca, Jose Geronimo, Sena's Co. A, N. M. Militia, 2 mos. 1862.
Baca, Jose Isidoro, Co. F, 1st N. M. Cav.; 4th N. M. Inf.
Baca, Jose Maria, Co. C, 1st Reg. N. M. Cav.; Gonzolez Independent Co., N. M. Militia, 3 mos., 1861; Co. E, 1st N. M. Cav.; Co. D, 2nd N. M. Inf.
Baca, Jose Natividad, Romero's Independent Co. A, N. M. Militia Inf., 3 mos., 1861-62.
Baca, Jose Rafael, Sena's Co., N. M. Militia, 2 mos., 1862.
Baca, Juan, Montoya's Co., Perea's Batt'n, N. M. Militia Inf., 3 mos., 1861-62; Co. C, 1st N.M. Cav.; Co. H-M, 1st N. M. Cav.
Baca, Juan Andres, Co. H, 2nd N. M. Inf.
Baca, Juan Antonio, Co. M, 1st N. M. Cav.
Baca, Juan Baca y, Sena's Co. A, N. M. Militia, 2 mos., 1862.
Baca, Juan Chavez y, Co. E, 2nd N. M. Inf.
Baca, Juan de Dios, Organizer Baca's Co., Perea's Batt'n, N. M. Militia Inf., 3 mos., 1861-62, Captain.
Baca, Juan Jose, Aragon's Co., Perea's Batt'n, N. M. Militia, 3 mos., 1861-62; Co. D, 1st N. M. Cav.
Baca, Juan Nepomoceno, Co. E-H, 3rd N. M. Mt. Vols., Bugler, 3 mos., 1861-62.
Baca, Juan de Dios, Sena's Co. A, N. M. Militia, 3 mos., 1862.
Baca, Julian, Co. E, 1st N. M. Inf., N. O.; Co. B, 1st N. M. Inf., O. O.; Co. H, 2nd N. M. Mt. Vols., 6 mos., 1861-62; Co. B, 4th N. M. Vols.
Baca, Lino, Co. A, 2nd N. M. Inf.
Baca, Lorenzo, Co. A, 2nd N. M. Inf.
Baca, Manual, Tafoya,s Independent Co., N. M. Militia, 3 mos., 1861-62.
Baca, Manuel Co. H, 3rd N. M. Mt. Inf., 6 mos., 1861-62; Co. A, 4th N. M. Inf.
Baca, Manuel Maria de J., Vigil's Independent Co., N. M. Mt. Vols., 3 mos., 1861.
Baca, Marcelino, Co. D, 1st N. M. Inf., O. O.
Baca, Mariano, Co. K, 2nd N. M. Inf., Corporal.
Baca, Martin, Co. E, 2nd N. M. Inf., Corporal; Co. K, 3rd N. M. Mt. Inf., 6 mos., 1861-62.
Baca, Nicolas, Mink's Independent Co., N. M. Mt. Vols., 3 mos., 1861.
Baca, Nicolas, Montoya's Co., Perea's Batt'n, N. M. Vols., 3 mos., 1861-62.
Baca, Pablo, Co. K, 2nd N. M. Inf., Capt. Romero's Co., 3rd N. M. Mt. Inf., 6 mos., 1861-62.
Baca, Patrocinio, Co. E, 2nd N. M. Inf., Corporal.
Baca, Perfecto, Co. A, 3rd N. M. Mt. Inf., 6 mos., 1861-62.
Baca, Pablito, Co. D-A, 2nd N. M. Inf.
Baca, Rafael, Capt. Romero's Co., 3rd N. M. Mt. Inf. 6 mos., 1861-62.
Baca, Roman, Gonzolez Independent Co., N. M. Militia, 3 mos., 1861, Corporal.
Baca, Roman, Montoya's Co., Perea's Batt'n, N. M. Militia, 3 mos., 1861-62; Co. F, 1st N. M. Inf., N. O.
Baca, Santiago, Capt. Romero's Co., 3rd N. M. Mt. Inf., 6 mos., 1861-62, Corporal.

Baca, Santos, Tafoya's Independent Co., N. M. Militia, 3 mos., 1861-62.
Baca, Saturnino, Co. F-E, 1st N. M. Cav., Captain.
Baca, Simon, Capt. Romero's Co., 3rd N. M. Mt. Inf., 6 mos., 1861-62.
Bachicha, Trinidad, Co. A-H, 3rd N. M. Mt. Inf., 6 mos., 1861-62.
Baia, Jesus Maria, Co. K, 2nd N. M. Inf.
Baldonado, Elejandro, Co. B, 1st N. M. Cav.
Baker, Oliver, Co. J, 1st N. M. Cav., Corporal.
Baker, George, Graydon's N. M. Mt. Vols., 3 mos., 1861-62; Co. A, 3rd N. M. Mt. Vols., 6 mos., 1861-62.
Baker, Henry, Co. H-M, 1st N. M. Cav., 1st Sergeant.
Belesquez, Jose Antonio, Hubbell's Co., Perea's Batt'n, 3 mos., 1861-62.
Balverde, Juan Jose, Co. G-I, 1st N. M. Inf., N. O.
Baldonado, Alejandro, Co. A, 1st N. M. Cav.
Baldonado, Epifanio, Co. I, 1st N. M. Inf., N. O.
Baldonado, Pedro, Co. F, 1st N. M. Inf., N. O.
Baldez, Brigido, Co. F, 3rd N. M. Mt. Inf., 6 mos., 1861-62.
Baldez, Jose Antonio, Co. I, 1st N. M. Inf., N. O.
Baldez, Jose Miguel, Co. F, 3rd N. M. Mt. Inf., 6 mos., 1861-62.
Baldez, Jose Rafael, Co. I, 1st N. M. Inf., N. O.
Baldez, Alejandro, Graydon's Independent Co., No M. Mtd. Vols., 3 mos., 1861-62.
Baldez, Francisco, Co. D, 1st N. M. Cav.
Baldez, Julian, Co. D., 1st N. M. Inf., N. O.
Baldez, Manuel, Co. C, 1st N. M. Inf.
Baldonado, Ignacio, Co. L, 3rd N. M. Mt. Inf., 6 mos., 1861-62.
Baldonado, Pedro Co. F, 1st N. M. Inf., N. O.
Baldonado, Benigno, Co. C, 1st N. M. Inf, N. O.
Baldwin, Charles R. Co. C, 1st N. M. Cav., Corporal.
Balegos, Jose, Baca's Co., Perea's Batt'n, N. M. Vols.
Balencia, Antonio, Co. A, 1st N. M. Cav.
Balencia, Felipe, Co. C, 3rd N. M. Mt. Inf., 6 mos., 1861-62.
Balencia, Guadalupe, Doran's Co., N. M. Militia.
Balencia, Jesus Maria, Co. H, 3rd N. M. Mt. Inf., 6 mos., 1861-62.
Balencia, Jose Antonio, Co. A-Co. I, 1st N. M. Cav., N. O.
Balencia, Jose Lauriano, Co. C, 1st N. M. Inf., N. O.
Balencia, Locario, Co. H, 1st N. M. Cav.
Balencia, Manuel, Co. H, 3rd N. M. Mt. Inf., 6 mos., 1861-62.
Balencia, Marcos, Co. H, 3rd N. M. Inf., 6 mos., 1861-62.
Balegos, Marcos, Co. H, 3rd N. M. Inf., 6 mos., 1861-62.
Balegos, Nerio, Co. B, 1st N. M. Inf., N. O.; Co. H, 3rd N. M. Mt. Inf., 6 mos., 1861-62.
Balegos, Regiano, Baca's Co., Perea's Batt'n, N. M. Vols., 3 mos., 1861-62.
Balensuelo, Catarino, Co. E, 1st N. M. Inf., N. O.
Balensuelo, Gregorio, Perea's Independent Co., 60 days, 1862.
Balensuelo, Antonio, Co. B, 1st N. M. Militia—Inf., 3 mos., 1861-62.
Balerio, Jose Miguel, Co. C, N. M. Cav.; Co. B, 2nd N. M. Inf.
Ballejos, Pedro, Co. F, 1st N. M. Inf., N. O.
Ballejos, Antonio, Co. A, 5th N. M. Inf.
Ballejos, Donaciano, Co. D, 1st N. M. Inf., N. O.
Ballejos, Jose Dolores, Co. I, 1st N. M. Cav.
Ballejos, Jose Francisco, Co. F, 1st N. M. Inf.
Ballejos, Manuel, Co. D, 1st N. M. Inf.
Ballejos, Pablo, Co. A, 1st N. M. Inf.
Ballejos, Pedro, Co. D, 1st N. M. Cav.
Ballejos, Valentino, Grayson's Independent Co., 3 mos., 1861-62.
Ballejos, Jesus, Hubbell's Co., Perea's Batt'n, N. M. Vols., 3 mos., 1861-62.
Ballejos, Antonio, Co. H, 1st N. M. Cav.

Ballejos, Jose Chavez y, Gonzolez Independent Co., N. M. Militia, 3 mos., 1861.
Ballejos, Jose Jaramillo y, Co. D, 1st N. M. Vols.
Ballejos, Prudencio, Co. F, 1st N. M. Cav., N. O.
Ballejos, Manuel Graydon's Independent Co., N. M. Mt. Vols., 3 mos., 1861-62, Corporal.
Balverde, Juan Jose, Co. G, 1st N. M. Cav., N. O.
Benavides, Florentino, Co. M-E, 1st N. M. Cav.
Banderas, Juan, Co. D-C, 1st N. M. Cav.
Borrego, Gabino, Co. C, 1st N. M. Cav.
Bannaghan, Michael, Co. H, 1st Calif. Inf.; 1st N. M. Inf., N. O.
Banuelos, Jose T., Co. E, 1st N. M. Inf., N. O.
Barela, Pancho, Co. E, 1st N. M. Cav., Bugler.
Barela, Juan, Co. F, 1st N. M. Cav.
Barancas, Anesito, Co. D, 1st N. M. Cav.
Baranca, Juan, Co. D, 1st N. M. Cav.; Co. K, 3rd N. M. Mt. Inf., 6 mos., 1861-62.
Baranca, Juan, Co. D, 1st N. M. Cav.
Baranca, Juan Pedro Martin y, Co. E, 1st N. M. Inf.
Baranca, Leon P. Montoya's Co., Perea's Batt'n, N. M. Militia Inf., 3 mos., 1861-62.
Baraza, Manuel, Co. A, 1st N. M. Cav.
Barby, Jules, Co. J, 1st N. M. Cav., Captain.
Barela, Aristeo, Co. D, 1st N. M. Cav.
Barela, Desiderio, Co. B, 1st N. M. Mt. Inf., 3 mos., 1861-62.
Barela, Encarnacion, Co. H, 1st N. M. Inf., N. O.
Barela, Eustacio, Co. C, 1st N. M. Inf., N. O.
Barela, Francisco, Co. E, 1st N. M. Inf.
Barela, Jesus Maria, Co. H, 1st N. M. Cav., Sergeant.
Barela, Jose, Co. D, 1st N. M. Mt. Inf., 6 mos., 1861-62.
Barela, Jose Samuel, Capt., Romero's 3rd N. M. Mt. Inf., 6 mos., 1861-62.
Barela, Jose Maria, Co. K, 3rd N. M. Mt. Inf., 6 mos., 1861-62.
Barela, Juan, Co. F, 1st N. M. Cav.
Barela, Juan Pedro, Co. K, 1st N. M. Inf., N. O.
Barela, Librado, Co. B, 1st N. M. Inf., N. O.
Barela, Manuel, Co. E, 1st N. M. Cav.
Barela, Maximo, Co. D, 1st N. M. Cav.
Barela, Migual, Simpson's Independent Co., Mt. Spies and Guides; Perea's Independent Co., 60 days, 1862.
Barela, Octaviano, Captain Romero's 3rd N. M. Mt. Inf., 3 mos., 1861-62, Sergeant.
Barela, Pancho, Co. E, 1st N. M. Cav., Bugler.
Barela, Rafael, Del Valle's Co., Perea's Batt'n, N. M. Vols., 3 mos., 1861-62.
Barela, Roman Co. H, 1st N. M. Inf., Corporal.
Barela, Teodosio, Capt. Romero's 3rd N. M. Mt. Inf., 3 mos., 1861-62.
Barela, Inez, Co. H, 2nd N. M. Cav.
Barela, Hilario, Co. A, 1st N. M. Cav.
Barela, Maximo, Co. D, 1st N. M. Cav.
Barela, Francisco, Co. E, 1st N. M. Mt. Inf., N. O.
Barela, Jesus Maria, Tafoya's Co., N. M. Militia, 3 mos., 1861-62.
Barela, Joaquin, Co. F, 1st N. M. Inf.
Barela, Juan, Tafoya's Independent Co., N. M. Militia, 3 mos., 1861-62; Co. K-F, 1st N. M. Inf.
Barela, Librado, Co. B, 1st N. M. Inf., O. O.; Co. K, 1st N. M. Cav.
Barela, Ramon, Co. F, 1st N. M. Inf., N. O.
Barela, Valentin, Tafoya's Independent Co., N. M. Militia, 3 mos., 1861-62.
Barela, Encarnacion, Co. A, 1st N. M. Cav.
Barela, Pedro, Co. F, 1st N. M. Inf., N. O.

Barela, Marcos, Baca's Co., Perea's Batt'n, N. M. Vols., 3 mos., 1861-62.
Bargas, Vicente, Co. B, 1st N. M. Cav.
Bargas, Jose, Co. E, 1st N. M. Inf., N. O.
Bargas, Juan, Co. A, 1st N. M. Cav.
Bargas, Nonato, Co. C, 3rd N. M. Mt. Inf., 6 mos., 1861-62.
Bargas, Pablo, Co. B, 1st N. M. Cav.
Bargas, Esias, Co. E, 3rd N. M. Mt. Inf., 6 mos., 1861-62.
Barila, Desiderio, Co. B, 1st N. M. Inf., 3 mos., 1861.
Barila, Joaquin, Co. F, 1st N. M. Inf., N. O.
Barila, Juan, Co. F, 1st N. M. Inf., N. O.
Barila, Juan Pedro, Co. K, 1st N. M. Inf., N. O.
Barila, Agapito, Co. C, 1st N. M. Cav.
Barila, Moses, Co. K, 1st N. M. Cav.
Baron, Jose, Co. C, 1st N. M. Inf., N. O.
Baron, Juan de Dios, Co. F, 1st N. M. Cav.
Baron, Roman, Co. C, 1st N. M. Cav.
Barr, James C., Co. C, 1st N. M. Cav.
Barrate, Romelo, Hubbell's Independent Co., N. M. Mt. Vols., 3 mos., 1861-62.
Barros, Lorenzo, Alarid's Independent Co., N. M. Militia Inf., 3 mos., 1861-62.
Baraza, Manuel, Co. A, 1st N. M. Cav.
Baraza, Gabino, Co. B, 1st N. M. Inf.
Barreria, Miguel, Co. A, 1st N. M. Inf., N. O.
Barela, Jose Manuel, Capt. Romero's Co., 6 mos. 1861-62.
Barela, Teodocio, Capt. Romero's Co., 6 mos., 1861-62.
Barruntos, Saturnino, Co. A, 5th N. M. Inf., Captain.
Barros, Francisco, Co. H, 1st N. M. Inf., N. O.
Barros, Jose Desiderio, Co. F, 1st N. M. Cav.
Barros, Ramon, Co. C, 1st N. M. Inf.
Bartlett, Thomas, Co. C, Batt'n N. M. Vols., 1866-67, 1st Lieutenant.
Barvero, Miguel, Co. C ,1st N. M. Inf., N. O.
Basquez, Felipe, Co. E, 1st N. M. Vols.
Basquez, Francisco, Co. E, 1st N. M. Cav.
Basquez, Juan, Co. J, 1st N. M. Inf., N. O.
Basquez, Lorenzo, Mink's Independent Co., N. M. Vols., 3 mos. 1861, Sergeant.
Basquez, Miguel, Co. E, 1st N. M. Cav.
Basquez, Cleto, Co. E, 3rd N. M. Mt. Inf., 6 mos. 1861-62.
Basquez, Pablo, Co. A, 1st N. M. Mt. Inf., 3 mos. 1861-62.
Basquez, Balentin, Co. F, 3rd N. M. Mt. Inf., 6 mos. 1861-62.
Basquez, Andres, Co. E, 1st N. M. Cav.
Baum, Benjamin, Co. I, 1st N. M. Inf.
Barera, Miguel, Co. C, 1st N. M. Inf., O. O.
Baxter, Eldridge D., Co. G, 1st N. M. Cav.
Bagejo, Filbiersio, Tafoya's Independent Co., N. M. Vols., 3 mos. 1861-62
Mamirez (Ramirez?), Cruz, Co. E, 1st N. M. Inf., N. O.
Benavidez, Miguel, Co. E, 1st N. M. Inf.
Beard, Samuel, Co. K-L, Tarrier-Blacksmith.
Beauregard, John, Co. G, 1st N. M. Cav.
Bechtol, Samuel, Co. M, 1st N. M. Cav.
Beck, John M., Co. A, 1st N. M. Inf.
Berry, Thomas, Co. C, 1st N. M. Vols.
Bega (Vega), Catrino, Co. E, 1st N. M. Inf., N. O.
Bega (Vega), Cruz, Co. H, 1st N. M. Cav.
Brila, Juan, Gonzolez Independent Co., N. M. Militia, 3 N. M. 1861.
Beilia, Francisco, Co. K, 2nd N. M. Mt. Inf.
Bejil (Vigil), Cesario, Romero's Independent Co. A. N. M. Mil., 3 mos. 1861-62.

Bejil, Juan, Co. H, 5th N. M. Inf.
Bejil, Martin, Co. I, 2nd N. M. Inf.
Bela (Blea?), Juan T., Co. F, 1st N. M. Inf., O. O.
Belarde, Antonio, Co. K, 1st N. M. Inf., O. O., Corporal.
Belarde, Gregorio, Co. E, 1st N. M. Cav., Sergeant.
Belarde, Jesus, Co. C, 1st N. M. Cav.
Belarde, Ambrosio, Co. H, 2nd N. M. Inf.
Balesquez, Francisco, Co. K, 1st N. M. Inf.
Balesquez, Isidro, Co. D, 1st N. M. Inf., O. O.
Balesquez, Agostin, Vigil's Independent Co., N. M. Mt. Vols., 3 mos., 1861.
Balesquez, Jose Antonio, Hubbell's Co., Perea's Batt'n N. M. Vols., 3 mos., 1861-62.
Balesquez, Pablo, Co. C, 1st N. M. Mt. Inf., 3 mos. 1861-62.
Balesquez, Juan, Baca's Co. Perea's Batt'n, N. M. Vols., 3 mos. 1861-62.
Balesquez, Miguel, Co. A, 3rd N. M. Mt. Inf., 6 mos. 1861-62.
Balesquez, Norberto, Mink's Independent Co., N. M. Mt. Vols., 3 mos. 1861-62.
Balesquez, Ambrosio, Co. H, 2nd N. M. Inf., Corporal.
Bellejos, Donaciano, Co. D, 1st N. M. Inf., N. O.
Beltran, Dolores, Co. I, 1st N. M. Cav.
Beltran, Francisco, Co. E, 1st N. M. Inf.
Beltran, Cristobal, Sena's Co. A, 1st N. M. Mil., 2 mos. 1862.
Benavides, Jesus Maria, Co. A, 1st N. M. Vols.; Co. G, 3rd N. M. Mt. Inf., 6 mos. 1861-62.
Benavides, Antonio Jose, Co. F, 3rd N. M. Mt. Inf., 3 mos., 1861-62.
Benavides, Francisco, Co. F, 2nd N. M. Inf.; Vigil's Independent Co., N. M. Mt. Vols., 3 mos., 1861.
Benavides, Manimiano, Co., 2nd N. M. Inf.
Benavides, Jose Maria, Co. I, 2nd N. M. Inf.
Benavides, Julian, Co. K, 1st N. M. Inf., N. O.
Benavides, Miguel, Co. K, 1st N. M. Cav.
Benavidse, Pedro, Co. K, 1st N. M. Inf.
Benavides, Sixto, Co. I, 2nd N. M. Inf.
Benavides, Isidro, Co. C, Batt'n N. M. Vols., 1866-67.
Benavides, Leandro, Co. A, 3rd N. M. Mt. Inf., 6 mos., 1861-62.
Benavides, Flores, Co. E, 2nd N. M. Inf.
Benavides, Gregorio, Romero's Independent Co. A, N. M. Militia Inf., 3 mos., 1861-62.
Benavides, Gamericindo, Graydon's Independent Co., 3 mos., 1861-62.
Benavides, Jinio, Co. D, 1st N. M. Cav.
Benavides, Jose, Alarid's Independent Co., 3 mos., 1861-62.
Benavides, Doroteo, Romero's Independent Co. A, N. M. Militia Inf., 3 mos., 1861-62.
Benavides, Teodocio, Co. H, 1st N. M. Inf., O. O.
Benavides, Jose Lazaro Hubbell's Co., Perea's Batt'n N. M. Vols., 3 mos., 1861-62.
Benavides, Julian, Co. K, 1st N. M. Inf.
Benavides, Santiago, Hubbell's Co., Perea's Batt'n, N. M. Vols., 3 mos,. 1861-62.
Benavides, Victorio, Hubbell's Co., Perea's Batt'n, N. M. Vols., 3 mos., 1861-62.
Benavides, Miguel, (1st), Co. D, 1st N. M. Cav.
Benavides, Miguel (2nd), Co. D, 1st N. M. Cav.
Benavides, Guadalupe, Co. A, 5th N. M. Inf.
Bennett, Joseph, Co. A, 1st N. M. Cav., 2nd or Lt. Colonel.
Benavides, Ramon, Co. E, 3rd N. M. Mt. Inf., 6 mos., 1861-62.
Bensinger, Carlos, Co. B, 5th N. M. Inf.; Co. A, 3rd N. M. Inf., 6 mos., 1861-62.
Benetes, Miguel, Co. G, 2nd N. M. Inf.

Bergen, Charles, Co. F-G, 1st N. M. Inf.
Berger, Federick, Co. E-H-G, 1st N. M. Inf.-N. M. Cav., 1st Sergeant.
Bergmann, Edward H., Co. A, Batt'n Vols., 1666-67, Captain; Co. I-M, N. M. Cav., Major; Co. C-H, 1st N. M. Inf. O. O.
Beltran, Dolores, Co. D, 1st N. M. Cav.
Bermudas, Jesus, Graydon's Independent Co., N. M. Mt. Vols., 3 mos., 1861-62.
Bernal, Alejo, Co. K, 3rd N. M. Mt. Inf., 6 mos., 1861-62.
Bernal, Antonio Jose, Co. C, 4th N. M. Inf.
Bernal, Guadalupe, Co. D, 1st N. M. Cav.
Bernal, Jose Pablo, Co. A, 1st N. M. Cav.
Bernal, Rafael, Co. J, 1st N. M. Inf., N. O.
Besca, (Baca?) Jesus, Co. F, 1st N. M. Inf., O. O.
Besera, Jose Maria, Tafoya's Co., N. M. Militia, 3 mos., 1861-62.
Bialfrando, Jose Leon, Co. F, 3rd N. M. Mt. Vols., 6 mos., 1861-62.
Bialfrando, Diego, Co. C, 4th N. M. Inf.
Bea, Nuevo, Co. E, 1st N. M. Inf., O. O.
Billa (Villa), Alba Jose Clemente Co. C, 1st N. M. Inf.
Billapondo, Augustino, Baca's Co., Perea's Batt'n, N. M. Vols., 3 mos., 1861-62.
Billapondo, Sencion, Co. H, 1st N. M. Inf.
Billeges, Donaciano, Co. D, 1st N. M. Inf., N. O.
Bialpondo, Diego, Co. D, 1st N. M. Vols.
Bishop, Peter, Co. H, 1st N. M. Cav., Captain.
Bitalen, Victoriano, Co. I-B, 1st N. M. Cav.
Blais, Jose Miguel, Co. A, 1st N. M. Cav.
Blanco, Jesus, Baca's Co., Perea's Batt'n, N. M. Militia Inf., 3 mos., 1861-62.
Balesco, Jesus, Co. I, 2nd N. M. Inf.
Blakenship, Benson, Co. C, 1st N. M. Cav.
Blansevilla, Catarino, Co. B, Batt'n N. M. Vols., 1866-67.
Blas, Jose Miguel, Co. B, Batt'n N. M. Vols., 1866-67.
Blea, Abelino, Co. C, 1st N. M. Inf.
Blea, Amado, Co. A, 1st N. M. Inf., N. O.
Blea, Benino, Romero's Independent Co., N. M. Militia, 3 mos., 1861-62.
Blea, Cornelio, Co. D, 1st N. M. Cav.
Blea, Francisco, Co. D, Batt'n N. M. Vols., 1866-67.
Blea, Jose Andres, Romero's Independent Co., N. M. Militia Inf., 3 mos., 1861-62.
Blea, Juan Francisco, Co. B, 1st N. M. Cav.
Blea, Jose Maria, Co. D, 1st N. M. Inf., O. O.
Blea, Matias, Co. F, 1st N. M. Cav.
Blea, Miguel, Romero's Independent Co., N. M. Militia Inf., 3 mos., 1861-62.
Blea, Pilar, Co H, 1st N. M. Cav.
Blea, Ramon, Co. J, 1st N. M. Inf., N. O.
Blea, Sencion, Co. C, 1st N. M. Inf., N. O.
Bobete, Norberto, Co. F, 1st N. M. Inf., 3 mos., 1861-62.
Borgorque, Ruperto, Co. C, 1st N. M. Inf. O. O.
Barrego, Gabino, Co. C, 1st N. M. Cav.
Bomar, Patrick, Co. E, 1st N. M. Inf., O. O.
Bonny, Santiago, Co. A, 1st N. M. Cav., O. O.
Bensall, William, Co. I, 1st N. M. Inf.
Boosh, L. C., Co. F, 1st N. M. Inf., O. O.
Booth, Linley E., Co. B, 1st N. M. Cav.
Borden, John M. Co. F, 1st N. M. Inf., O. O.
Borgerquez, Ruperto, Co. I, 1st N. M. Inf., O. O.
Borrego, Gabino, Co. C, 1st N. M. Inf.; Co. B, 2nd N. M. Inf.
Borrego, Inocencio, Co. B, 3rd N. M. Mtd. Inf., 1861-62, 6 mos.
Boteras (also listed as Gutierez, Miguel), Co. M, 1st N. M. Cav.

Boulden, Joseph L. Lewis, Co. M-I, 1st N. M. Cav., Quartermaster Sergeant.
Bourke, Michael, Co. B, 1st N. M. Inf., O. O.
Bowen, George, Co. B-K, 1st N. M. Inf., O. O.
Brady, Peter, Co. K, 1st N. M. Cav.
Brady, William, Co. I-G-A. 1st N. M. Cav., 1st Lieutenant—Captain; 2nd N. M. Vols., Bvt. Major; Co. B, 1st N. M. Inf., Private, Lt., and Adjutant 1st N. M. Cav., (later of Lincoln Co. War fame)
Branch, Alfred, Co. G-B, 3rd N. M. Mtd. Inf., 1st Lt.
Branch, Almer Wallace, Co. M, 1st N. M. Cav., 1st Sergeant.
Branch, Richard, Co. G, 3rd N. M. Mtd. Inf., Capt., 6 mos., 1861-62.
Branden, Richard, Co. K, 1st N. M. Cav.
Brey, Julius C., Co. F-J, 1st N. M. Cav., Assistant Surgeon.
Bricton, Jose Feliz, Duran's Co., N. M. Militia Inf., Corporal.
Brifalba, Blas, Co. D-E, 1st N. M. Inf., O. O.
Brigalla & Brigalba—(same as above).
Brigalba, Simon, Gonzolez Independent Co., N. M. Militia Inf.
Briggs, George Otis, Co. M, 1st N. M. Cav.
Brigalba, Francisco, Co. A-D, 2nd N. M. Inf.
Brito, Albino, Co. E, 1st N. M. Cav.; Co. I, 1st N. M. Inf., O. O.
Brito, Anastacio, Co. B, 1st N. M. Inf., O. O.; Co. I, 1st N. M. Militia, Sena's Co., 60 days, 1852, Sergeant.
Brito, Juan Antonio, Co. A, 1st N. M. Militia, Sena's Co., 60 days, 1862.
Brito, Jose Miguel, Montoya's Co., Perea's Batt'n, N. M. Militia Inf., 3 mos., 1861-62.
Brito, Juan, Co. C, 4th N. M. Inf.
Brooks, William H., Co. I, 1st N. M. Cav., 1st Lt.; Co. H, 1st N. M. Inf., O. O.
Brosee, John, Co. F, 3rd N. M. Mtd. Inf., 6 mos., 1861-62.
Brown, A. L., Co. D, 1st N. M. Cav. See also: 1st Cav. Colo.
Brown, Charles, Co. D, Batt'n N. M. Vols., 1866-67; Co. B, 1st N. M. Cav., Farrier (i.e., one who took care of horses and their shoeing). Co. D, 1st N. M. Cav.
Brown, John, Co. L-K, 1st N. M. Cav.
Brown, William, Co. G, 1st N. M. Cav.
Broterman, William, Co. G, 1st N. M. Cav.; Co. I, 1st N. M. Inf.
Brubacker, John Wesley, Co. M, 1st N. M. Cav., Trumpeter.
Brueno, David, Co. A, 1st N. M. Militia Inf., 3 mos., 1861-62.
Bruno, John, Co. K, 1st N. M. Inf., O. O.
Bruste, Maximio, Tafoya's Independent Co., N. M. Militia, 3 mos., 1861-62.
Brustes, Jesus Maria Tafoya's Independent Co., N. M. Mil., 3 mos., 1861-62, Musician.
Bruno, Antonio, Co. I, 1st N. M. Inf., N. O.
Bruno, Jose, Co. H, 1st N. M. Cav., Corporal.
Baca, Jacinto Baca's Co., Perea's N. M. Mil., Inf., 3 mos., 1861-62.
Buchan, John A., Graydon's Independent Co., N. M. Mounted Vols., 3 mos., 1861-62.
Buciago, Pedro, Co. C, 1st N. M. Inf., O. O.
Buck, John, Co. A, 1st N. M. Cav.; Co. C, 1st N. M. Inf.
Buena, Bautista, Co. A, 1st N. M. Cav.
Buena, Jose Mateo, Co. I, 1st N. M. Inf., N. O.
Buena, Rafael, Co. D, 1st N M. Cav.
Buena, Pascal, Co. A, Batt'n N. M. Vols., 1866-67.
Buena, Dabi (David), Co. K, 1st N. M. Inf., N. O., Sergeant.
Bueno, Jesus, Co. C, 1st N. M. Cav.; Co. E-D, 4th N. M. Inf.
Bueno, Jose, Co. H, 1st N. M. Cav., Corporal.
Bueno, Jose Antonio, Co. I, 1st N. M. Inf., O. O.
Bueno, Jose Rafael, Co. D, 1st N. M. Cav.
Bueno, Juan Bautista, Co. A, 1st N. M. Cav.

Bueno, Juan Isidro, Co. F, 4th N. M. Inf.
Bueno, Pablo, Co. A, 1st N. M. Mil. Inf., 3 mos., 1861-62.
Bueno, Pablo, Co. D, 3rd N. M. Mtd. Inf., 1861-62.
Burnella, Crecencio, Co. A, Batt'n N. M. Vols., 1866-67.
Balerio, Antonio, Co. F, 1st N. M. Cav., 3 mos., 1861-62.
Bunker, Marvin S., Co. A, Batt'n N. M. Vols., 1866-67, 1st Sgt.; Co. C, 1st N. M. Cav., 1st Serg.
Burciago, Francisco, Duran's Co., N. M. Mil. Inf.
Burciago, Pedro, Co. C, 1st N. M. Inf., N. O., Sergeant.
Burk, John, Co. C, 1st N. M. Inf., O. O.
Burk, Richard, Co. K, 1st N. M. Cav., Farrier.
Burns, Joseph, Co. G, 1st N. M. Cav.
Burns, Michael, Co. K, 1st N. M. Cav., Corporal; Co. C, 4th N. M. Inf.
Burrett, Johnson, Co. I, 1st N. M. Cav., Quartermaster Sergeant.
Burt, Darwin Snell, Co. M, 1st N. M. Cav.
Burt, William, Co. M-A, 1st N. M. Cav., Blacksmith.
Buscher, Fritz, Co. C-D, 1st N. M. Inf., O. O.
Bustamonte, Francisco, Co. F-B, 1st N. M. Cav., Sergeant.
Bustamonte, Andres, Co. H, 2nd N. M. Inf.
Bustamonte, Antonio Jose, Alarid's Independent Co., N. M. Mil. Inf., 3 mos., 1861-62.
Bustamonte, Antonio, Hubbell's Co., Perea's Batt'n, N. M. Mil. Inf., 3 mos., 1861-62, Corporal.
Bustamonte, Jose de los Reyes, Graydon's Independent Co., N. M. Mt. Vols., 3 mos., 1861-62.
Bustamonte, Cayetano, Co. B, 1st N. M. Mil. Inf., 3 mos., 1861-62.
Bustos, Juan, Co. K-F, 3rd N. M. Mtd. Inf.
Bustos, Francisco, Co. D, 3rd N. M. Mtd. Inf., 3 mos., 1861-62.
Bustos, Jesus, Co. A, Batt'n N. M. Vols., 1866-67.
Bustos, Jose Antonio, Co. F, 1st N. M. Cav.
Bustos, Maugricio, Co. E, 3rd N. M. Mtd. Inf., 6 mos., 1861-62.
Bustos, Pedro Jose, Co. I-F, 3rd N. M. Mtd. Inf., 6 mos., 1861-62.
Bustos, Sirilio, Co. G, 1st N. M. Inf., N. O.
Bustos, Soledon, Montoya's Co., Perea's Batt'n, N. M. Mil. Inf., 3 mos., 1861-62.
Bustos, Teofolio, Co. I, 1st N. M. Inf., O. O.
Butierez, Jose de Jesus, Romero's Independent Co., N. M. Mil. Inf., 6 mos., 1861-62.
Butierez, Juan Bautista, Co. I, 1st N. M. Inf., O. O.
Butierez, Miguel, Co. A, Batt'n N. M. Vols., 1866-67.
Butierez, Vidal, Simpson's Independent Co., N. M. Mtd. Spies and Guides.
Butierez, Abran, Co. D, 1st N. M. Cav.
Butierez, Egenio, Co. D, 1st N. M. Cav.
Butierez, Monico, Co. K, 3rd N. M. Mtd. Inf., 6 mos., 1861-62.
Butler, Dennis, Co. A, 1st N. M. Cav.
Butler, Eugene, Co. D, 1st N. M. Cav.
Butterlin, Paul, Co. K, 1st N. M. Cav., Bugler-Trumpeter; Co. D, 4th N. M. Cav., Musician.

Caballero, Bernardo, Co. A, 1st N. M. Cav.
Candelario, Jose, Co. F., 1st N. M. Inf., O. O.
Candelario, Ferdinando, Co. A, 1st N. M. Cav.
Candelario, Jose Antonio, Co. F, 1st N. M. Mil. Inf., 3 mos., 1861-62.
Candelario, Pedro, Co. H, 1st N. M. Inf.
Caballos, Tomas, Co. K, 3rd N. M. Mtd. Inf., Sergeant.
Chavez, Juan de Jesus, Co. H, 1st N. M. Mtd. Inf., 6 mos., 1861-62.
Cabillero, Jose C., Co. F, 1st N. M. Inf.
Cassias, Jose Dolores, Co. E, 1st N. M. Cav.
Cassias, Jose Victor, Co. F-D, 4th N. M. Inf.
Cassias, Tomas, Co. I, 1st N. M. Cav.

Cassias, Jose Maria, Co. H, 1st N. M. Inf.
Coca, Ignacio, Co. B, 3rd N. M. Mtd. Inf., 6 mos., 1861-62.
Cadena, Andres, Co. C-B, 1st N. M. Inf., O. O.; Co. A-B, 1st N. M. Inf., N. O.; Co. F, 2nd N. M. Inf.
Cadena, Sabino, Co. F-B-D, 2nd N. M. Inf.
Cady, Richard, Co. F, 1st N. M. Cav.
Cadagon, James W., 1st N. M. Inf., Steward, O. O.
Cady, Michael, Co. F, 1st N. M. Cav.
Calderon, Magdaleno, Co. G, 2nd N. M. Inf.
Calderon, Ramon E., Co. G, 1st N. M. Inf., N. O.
Caldwell, John C., Co. F, 1st N. M. Inf., O. O.
Calhoun, John, Co. K, 1st N. M. Inf., N. O.
Callan, Patrick H., Co. K, 1st N. M. Inf., N. O.
Calles, Juan, Co. E, 4th N. M. Inf., Sergeant.
Comacho, Antonio, Aragon's Co., Perea's Batt'n, N. M. Vols., 3 mos., 1861-62.
Camaduran, Bentura, Co. I, 1st N. M. Cav.; Co. C, 1st N. M. Cav.; Co. D, 4th N. M. Inf.
Comonez, Ynez, Co. C, Batt'n N. M. Vols., 1866-67, Corporal.
Campos, Francisco, Co. K-F, 1st N. M. Cav.
Campbell, George, Co. B, 1st N. M. Cav.
Campos, Florentino, Co. E, 1st N. M. Inf., N. O.
Campos, Francisco, Co. K-D-G, 1st N. M. Cav.
Campos, Jose de la Luz, Co. L, 1st N. M. Cav.
Campos, Pedro, Romero's Co., 3rd N. M. Mtd. Inf., 4 mos., 1861-62.
Conung, Ines, Co. C, Batt'n N. M. Vols., 1866-67, Corporal.
Candelario, Felix, Co. E, 2nd N. M. Inf.
Candelario, Jose, Co. F, 3rd N. M. Inf.; Co. G, 3rd N. M. Mtd. Inf., 6 mos., 1861-62.
Candelario, Juan, Co. F-B-C, 2nd N. M. Inf.
Candelario, Francisco, Romero's Co., 3rd N. M. Mtd. Inf., 6 mos., 1861-62.
Candelario, Vicente, Co. K-I-D, 2nd N. M. Inf.
Candelario, Jesus Maria, Co. G, 3rd N. M. Mtd. Inf., 6 mos., 1861-62, Corporal.
Candelario, Juan Francisco, Romero's Co., 3rd N. M. Mtd. Inf., 6 mos,. 1861-62.
Candelario, Pablo, Co. P, 5th N. M. Inf.
Candelario, Pedro Miguel, Co. D, 1st N. M. Cav.; Co. F-I-B, 2nd N. M. Inf.
Candelario, Ramon, Co. B, 5th N. M. Inf.
Candelario, Santos, Co. F, 1st N. M. Cav.
Candelario, Basilio, Aragon's Co., Perea's Batt'n, N. M. Vols., 3 mos., 1861-62.
Candelario, Bicente, Montoya's Co., Perea's Batt'n, N. M. Vols., 3 mos., 1861-62; Co. K-D, 2nd N. M. Inf.
Candelario, Francisco, Montoya's Co., Perea's Batt'n, N. M. Vols., 3 mos., 1861-62; Co. D, 2nd N. M. Inf.
Candelario, Jesus Maria, Co. I, 1st N. M. Inf.; Co. G, 3rd N. M. Mtd. Inf., 6 mos., 1861-62.
Candelario, Jose, Del Balle's Co., Perea's Batt'n, N. M. Mil. Inf., 3 mos., 1861-62; Co. D, 2nd N. M. Inf.
Candelario, Jose Amador, Co. F, 1st N. M. Cav.
Candelario, Jose Antonio, Co. C, Batt'n, N. M. Vols., 1866-67.
Candelario, Macario, Aragon's Co., Perea's Batt'n, N. M. Mil. Inf., 3 mos., 1861-62.
Candelario, Miguel, Del Balle's Co., Perea's Batt'n, N. M. Mil. Inf., 3 mos., 1861-62.
Candelario, Pablo, Co. L, 1st N. M. Cav.
Candelario, Pablo, Co. L, 1st N. M. Cav.

Candelario, Pascual, Del Balle's Co., Perea's Batt'n, N. M. Mil. Inf., 3 mos., 1861-62.
Candelario, Tomas, Co. D, 4th N. M. Inf.
Candelario, Felipe, Jaramillo's Co., Perea's Batt'n, N. M. Mil. Inf., 3 mos., 1861-62.
Candelario, Francisco, Co. F, 1st N. M. Mil. Inf., 3 mos., 1861-62.
Candelario, Geronimo, Co. F, Batt'n N. M. Vols., 1866-67.
Candelario, Seyba, Co. A, 1st N. M. Mil. Inf., 3 mos., 1861-62.
Candelario, Manuel, Jaramillo's Co., Perea's Batt'n, N. M. Mil. Inf., 3 mos., 1861-62.
Candelario, Pablo, Graydon's Independent Co., N. M. Mtd. Vols., 3 mos., 1861-62.
Candelario, Pablo, Jaramillo's Co., Berea's Batt'n, N. M. Mil. Inf., 3 mos., 1861-62; Co. I, 1st N. M. Cav.
Candelario, Roque, Co. A, 5th N. M. Inf.
Candelario, Santos, Co. I, 1st N. M. Cav.; Co. D-E-A, 2nd N. M. Inf.
Candelario, Ignacio, Jaramillo's Co., Perea's Batt'n, N. M. Mil. Inf., 3 mos., 1861-62.
Candelario, Tomas, Co. A, Batt'n N. M. Vols., 1866-67; Co. C-L, 1st N. M. Cav.
Candelario, Vicente, Co. F, 2nd N. M. Cav.
Canillo, Pedro, Co. A, 3rd N. M. Inf.
Cannon, James D., Co. K, 1st N. M. Inf., N. O., 1st Lieut.; See also 1st Cav. Cal. Vols.
Canonez, Inez, Co. L, 1st N. M. Cav.
Capland, see—
Copeland, John A., Co. F, 1st N. M. Cav.
Carabajal, Francisco, Co. F-B, 2nd N. M. Inf.
Carabajal, Hombono, Co. F, 2nd N. M. Inf.
Carabajal, Manuel Montoya's Co., Perea's Batt'n, N. M. Mil. Inf., 3 mos., 1861-62.
Carabajal, Merejildo, Co. G, 1st N. M. Inf., N. O.
Carabajal, Salamon, Co. F, 1st N. M. Cav.
Carabajal, Todocio, Co. K, 1st N. M. Inf., N. O.
Casados, Jose Refugio, Co. B, 1st N. M. Inf., 6 mos., 1861-62.
Correlas, Vicente, Co. G, 1st N. M. Inf., N. O.
Carasco, Fernando Tafoya's Independent Co., N. M. Mil. Ind., 3 mos., 1861-62.
Carasco, Bicente, Co. F, 1st N. M. Cav.
Caravajal, Jose Dolores, Co. L, 3rd N. M. Mtd. Inf., 6 mos., 1861-62.
Caravajal, Juan, Aragon's Co., Perea's Batt'n, N. M. Mil. Inf., 3 mos., 1861-62.
Carcias, Jose de Jesus, Co. I, 1st N. M. Inf., N. O.
Cardenas, Antonio Abran, Co. F, 1st N. M. Cav.
Cardenas, Andres, Co. I, 1st N. M. Inf., N. O.
Cardenas, Jose Manuel, Co. F, 1st N. M. Cav.
Cardenas, Jose Simon, Co. E, 1st N. M. Mil. Inf., 3 mos., 1861-62.
Cardenas, Jose Carmel, Co. F, 1st N. M. Cav.
Cardenas, Jose Dolores, Mink's Independent Co., N. M. Mtd. Vols., 3 mos., 1861.
Cardenas, Juan Andres, Co. D, 1st N. M. Mil. Inf., 3 mos., 1861-62.
Cardenas, Jose Manuel, Co. D, 3rd N. M. Mtd. Inf., 6 mos., 1861-62.
Cardenas, Juan Matias, Co. B, 3rd N. M. Mtd. Inf., 6 mos., 1861-62.
Cardenas, Juan Pascual, Co. C, 3rd N. M. Mtd. Inf., 6 mos., 1861-62.
Cardenas, Manuel, Co. B, 3rd N. M. Mtd. Inf., 6 mos., 1861-62.
Cardenas, Quirino, Co. A-G, 1st N. M. Inf., N. O.
Cardenas, Jose Matias, Co. B, 3rd N. M. Mtd. Inf., 6 mos., 1861-62.
Cardenas, Antonio Simon, Co. B, Batt'n, N. M. Vols., 1866-67; Co. C, 1st N. M. Inf., N. O.
Cordova, Antonio, Co. F, 1st N. M. Cav.
Cordova, Salvador, Co. A, 1st N. M. Mil. Inf., 3 mos., 1861-62.
Cordova, Jose, Co. I, 1st N. M. Cav.

Cordova, Jose Bicente, Co. D-E, 1st N. M. Inf.
Carillo, Luis, Co. C, 2nd N. M. Inf.
Cariago, Jesus, Co. E-F, 2nd N. M. Inf.
Carillo, Rafael, Co. A, Batt'n N. M. Vols., 1866-67.
Carillo, Ramon, Alarid's Independent Co., N. M. Mil. Inf., 3 mos., 1861-62.
Carillo, Francisco, Co. H, 1st N. M. Inf., N. O.
Carillo, Juan, Co. K-I-D, 3rd N. M. Mtd. Inf., 6 mos., 1861-62.
Carillo, Mateo Gonzolez, Independent Co., N. M. Mil. Inf., 3 mos., 1861.
Carillo, Teodocio, Co. L, 1st N. M. Cav.
Carillo, Tomas, Co. D-K-I, 3rd N. M. Mtd. Inf., 3 mos., 1861-62.
Casias, Jose Victor, Co. B, 3rd N. M. Mtd. Inf., 6 mos., 1861-62.
Carrion, Jesus, Co. G, 2nd N. M. Inf., Sergeant.
Carrion, Manuel, Romero's Co. L, 3rd N. M. Mtd. Inf., 6 mos., 1861-62.
Carrion, Mariano, Co. H, 1st N. M. Cav.
Caris, Francisco, Alarid's Independent Co., N. M. Mil. Inf., 3 mos., 1861-62.
Carlyle, Charles, Co. I-H, 1st N. M. Inf., N. O.
Carmody, John, Co. I, 3rd N. M. Mtd. Inf., 6 mos., 1861-62, First Sergeant.
Carragee, Jesus, Co. F, 1st N. M. Cav.
Carrasco, Pedro, Co. B, 1st N. M. Inf., N. O.
Carrasco, Ygnes, Co. H, 1st N. M. Cav.
Carrelas, Bicente, Co. G, 1st N. M. Inf.
Carrillo, Matias, Tafoya's Independent Co., N. M. Mil. Inf., 3 mos., 1861-62, Corporal.
Carrillo, Jose, Hubbell's Co., Perea's Batt'n, N. M. Mil. Inf., 3 mos., 1861-62.
Carrion, Francisco, Co. H, 1st N. M. Cav.
Carro, Ines, Co. E, 1st N. M. Inf.
Carroll, Patrick, Co. K, 1st N. M. Inf., N. O.
Carson, Christopher, Co. F-I, Batt'n, N. M. Vols., 1866-67, Lt. Col., Bvt. Brig. Gen., U. S. Vols.; Co. F-1, 1st N. M. Cav.; Co. F, 1st N. M. Inf., O. O.; Co. F-I, 4th Batt'n N. M. Vols., Lt. Col.
Carson, Robert, Simpson's Independent Co., N. M. Mtd. Spies and Guides.
Castigo, Cecilio, Co. B, 1st N. M. Inf., N. O.
Cortinas, Juan, Co. F, 1st N. M. Cav.
Casadas, Juan, Co. E, 1st N. M. Cav.
Casados, Carlos, Romero's Independent Co. A, 3 mos., 1861-62, Sergeant.
Casados, Jesus, Co. D, 3rd N. M. Mtd. Inf., 6 mos., 1861-62.
Casados, Jose Antonio, Co. D, 3rd N. M. Mtd. Vols., 6 mos., 1861-62.
Casados, Jose Manuel, Sena's Co. A, 1st N. M. Militia, 3 mos., 1862.
Casados, Jose Maria, Co. I, 1st N. M. Inf., N. O.
Casados, Jose Refugio, Co. B, 3rd N. M. Mtd. Inf., 6 mos., 1861-62.
Casados, Juan Nepumeceno, Mink's Independent Co., N. M. Mtd. Vols., 3 mos., 1861.
Casados, Julian, Co. H, 3rd N. M. Mtd. Vols., 6 mos., 1861-62.
Casados, Polonario, Alarid's Independent Co., N. M. Mil. Inf., 6 mos., 1861-62.
Casados, Roman, Co. C, 1st N. M. Inf., O. O.
Caseas, Tomas, Co. I-E, 1st N. M. Cav.
Casias, Jose Jesus, Co. I, 1st N. M. Inf., Corporal.
Casias, Jose Victorio, Co. B, 3rd N. M. Mtd. Inf., 6 mos., 1861-62.
Casias, Jose Dolores, Co. K, 1st N. M. Inf., O. O.
Casias, Jose Maria, Co. I, 1st N. M. Cav., Corporal.
Casillo, Toribio, Hubbell's Co., Perea's Batt'n, N. M. Mil. Inf., 3 mos., 1861-62.
Cassidos, Roman, Co. A, 1st N. M. Cav.
Castello, Cecilia, Co. B, 1st N. M. Inf.

Castillo, Antonio Jose, Co. D, 1st N. M. Inf.
Castillo, Juan, Co. D, 1st N. M. Inf., N. O.
Castillo, Sisto, Co. H, 1st N. M. Inf.
Castenada, Eusebio, Co. I-D, 2nd N. M. Inf., Sergeant.
Castenada, Jose de la Cruz, Co. H, 1st N. M. Inf., N. O.
Castenada, Jose Maria, Co. A-E, 2nd N. M. Inf.
Castenada, Sabriano, Co. F, 1st N. M. Cav.
Castenada, Antonio, Co. H, 2nd N. M. Inf.
Castenada, Francisco, Jaramillo's Co., Perea's Batt'n, N. M. Mil. Inf., 3 mos., 1861-62.
Castenada, Francisco, Romero's 3rd N. M. Mtd. Inf., 6 mos., 1861-62, Sergeant.
Castenada, Jose, Graydon's Independent Co., N. M. Mtd. Vols., 3 mos., 1861-62.
Castenada, Jose Francisco, Co. A, Batt'n, N. M. Vols., 1866-67.
Castenada, Manuel, Hubbell's Independent Co., N. M. Mtd. Vols., 3 mos., 1861; Co. A-E, 1st N. M. Cav.
Castenada, Jesua Maria, Co. A, 1st N. M. Inf., N. O.; Co. A-E, 2nd N. M. Inf.
Castenada, Juan Ignacio, Co. B, 1st N. M. Inf., O. O.
Castenada, Juan Jose, Co. L, 1st N. M. Cav.
Castenada, Mateo, Gonzolez Independent Co., N. M. Mil. Inf., 3 mos., 1861.
Castenada, Nestor, Co. G, 3rd N. M. Mtd. Inf., 6 mos., 1861-62, Sergeant.
Castenada, Nicolas Baca's Co., Perea's Batt'n, N. M. Militia, Inf., 3 mos., 1861-62.
Castenada, Patricio, Graydon's Independent Co., N. M. Mtd. Vols., 3 mos., 1861-62.
Castenada, Gormecindo, Graydon's Independent Co., N. M. Mtd. Vols., 3 mos., 1861-62.
Castenada, Romstene, Tafoya's Independent Co., N. M. Mil., 3 mos., 1861-62.
Castenada, Sobriano, Co. F, 1st N. M. Cav.
Castenada, Sisto, Co. H, 1st N. M. Inf.
Castorano, Jose Antonio, Hubbell's Independent Co., N. M. Vols., 3 mos., 1861, Corporal.
Castro, Domingo, Co. A, 1st N. M. Cav.
Castro, Donaciano, Co. I, 1st N. M. Cav., O. O.; Co. H, 1st N. M. Inf.
Castro, Ignacio, Co. B, 1st N. M. Cav.; Co. F, 1st N. M. Inf., O. O.
Castro, Juan de Dios, Co. A, Batt'n N. M. Vols., 1866-67.
Castro, Luciano, Co. G, 1st N. M. Cav.
Catt, William, Co. I, 1st N. M. Cav.
Calbedon, Isidro, Co. G, 1st N. M. Cav.
Chavez, Catarino, Co. L, 1st N. M. Cav.
Cedillo, Bartolo, Hubbell's Co., Perea's Batt'n, N. M. Mil. Inf., 3 mos., 1861-62.
Cedillo, Iasinto, Hubbell's Co., Perea's Batt'n, N. M. Mil. Inf., 3 mos., 1861-62.
Cedillo, George, Hubbell's Co., Perea's Batt'n, N. M. Mil. Inf., 3 mos., 1861-62.
Cedillo, Lorenzo, Jeramillo's Co., Perea's Batt'n, N. M. Mil. Inf., 3 mos., 1861-62.
Celler, John, Co. F, 7st N. M. Inf., O. O.; Co. E, 1st N. M. Cav., Corp.
Cervantes, Pascual, Co. D, 1st N. M. Inf., O. O.
Carcas, Bartolo, Co. H, 1st N. M. Inf., N. O.
Carcas, Tomas, Co. G, 1st N. M. Inf.
Cerna, Francisco, Aragon's Co., Perea's Batt'n, N. M. Mil. Inf., 3 mos., 1861-62.
Cerna, Jose Alcario, Co. E, 1st N. M. Cav.
Carlijo, Cecilio, Co. B, 1st N. M. Inf.
Cervantes, Margarito, Co. C, 1st N. M. Inf.

Chavez, Antonio, Co. I, 2nd N. M. Inf., Corporal.
Chavez, Eusebio, Co. H-D, 2nd N. M. Inf.; Co. A-B, 1st N. M. Cav., Corporal.
Chavez, Guadalupe, Co. F, 2nd N. M. Inf.
Chavez, Isidro, Co. H, 1st N. M. Cav.
Chavez, Jesus Garcia y, Co. K, 1st N. M. Inf.
Chavez, Jose Amado, Co. G, 2nd N. M. Inf.
Chavez, Jose Manuel, Co. K, 2nd N. M. Inf.
Chavez, Jose Maria, Co. D-E, 2nd N. M. Inf.
Chavez, Jose Gonzoles y, Co. D-H, 2nd N. M. Inf.
Chavez, Juan Montoya's Co., Perea's Batt'n, N. M. Mil. Inf., 3 mos., 1861-62.
Chavez, Juan Gallegos y, Co. H, 2nd N. M. Inf.
Chavez, Manuel, Co. F-K, 2nd N. M. Inf.
Chavez, Manuel Sanchez y, Co. H, 2nd N. M. Inf.
Chavez, Pedro, Co. H, 2nd N. M. Inf.
Chavez, Ramon, Co. H, 1st N. M. Cav.
Chavez, Ynez, Co. G, 2nd N. M. Inf.
Chavez, Cristobal, Del Balle's Co., Perea's Batt'n, N. M. Mil. Inf., 3 mos., 1861-62, First Lieutenant.
Chavez, Jose Dolores, Del Balle's Co., Perea's Batt'n, N. M. Mil. Inf., 3 mos., 1861-62.
Chavez, Juan, Del Balle's Co., Berea's Batt'n, N. M. Mil. Inf., 3 mos., 1861-62.
Chavez, Yginio, Del Balle's Co., Perea's Batt'n, N. M. Mil. Inf., 3 mos., 1861-62.
Chacon, Antonio, Co. K-E, Inst. N. M. Cav.; Co. C, 3rd N. M. Mtd. Inf., 6 mos., 1861-62; Co. B-C, 4th N. M. Inf.
Chacon, Antonio, Co. A, 1st N. M. Inf.
Chacon, Cornelio, Vigil's Independent Co., N. M. Mil., Vols., 3 mos., 1861.
Chacon, Diego, Vigil's Independent Co., N. M. Mil. Vols., 3 mos., 1861.
Chacon, Jose Jesus, Co. B, Batt'n N. M. Batt'n Vols., 1866-67.
Chacon, Jose Maria Vigil's Independent Co., N. M. Militia Vols., 3 mos., 1861.
Chacon, Juan de Dios, Co. H, 3rd N. M. Mtd. Inf., 6 mos., 1861-62.
Chacon, Manuel, Gregorio Co. C, 3rd N. M. Mtd. Vols., 6 mos., 1861-62.
Chacon, Panteleon, Co. E-D, 4th N. M. Inf.; Co. C, 1st N. M. Cav.
Chacon, Rafael, Co. E, 1st N. M. Cav., Major; Co. K,, 1st N. M. Inf., Captain, O. O.
Chacon, Tomas, Vigil's Independent Co., N. M. Mil. Vols., 3 mos., 1861-62.
Chacon, Atanacio, Co. H, 1st N. M. Cav.
Chacon, Manuel, Co. G, 3rd N. M. Mtd. Inf., 3 mos., 1861-62.
Chacon, Jose Rafael, Co. D, 2nd N. M. Inf.
Chacon, Mose Maria, Co. E-B, 3rd N. M. Mtd. Cav., 3 mos., 1861-62.
Chacon, Marcos, Co. C, 4th N. M. Inf.
Chacon, Francisco, Co. H, 1st N. M. Inf.
Chacon, Jesus, Co. L, 1st N. M. Cav.
Chacon, Teodoro, Co. C, 1st N. M. Cav., Bugler.
Chacon, Benjamin F., Co. D, 1st N. M. Cav., Farrier.
Chacon, Albino, Romero's Independent Co., N. M. Mil. Inf., 3 mos., 1861-62.
Chacon, Amado, Perea's Batt'n, N. M. Mil. Inf., 60 days, 1862, Sergeant.
Chacon, Ambrosio, Co. C, 1st N. M. Inf., N. O.
Chacon, Aniseto, Simpson's Independent Co., N. M. Mtd. Spies and Guides.
Chacon, Anselmo, Baca's Co., Berea's Batt'n, N. M. Mil. Inf., 3 mos., 1861-62.

Chavez, Diago Antonio, Co. F, 1st N. M. Cav.
Chavez, Antonio J. C., Co. L, 1st N. M. Cav.
Chavez, Augustin, Co. G, 3rd N. Mtd. Inf., 6 mos., 1861-62.
Chavez, Bernard, Tafoya's Independent Co., N. M. Mil. Inf., 6 mos., 1861-62.
Chavez, Bitrino, Co. B, 4th N. M. Inf.
Chavez, Blas, Co. C-D, 1st N. M. Cav.; Co. E-D, 4th N. M. Inf., Corporal.
Chavez, Blas Griego y, Jaramillo's Co., Perea's Batt'n, N. M. Mil. Inf., 3 mos., 1861-62.
Chavez, Brito, Co. G, 3rd N. M. Mtd. Vols., 6 mos., 1861-62.
Chavez, Carlos, Co. L, 3rd N. M. Mtd. Inf., 6 mos., 1861-62.
Chavez, Carpion, Tafoya's Independent Co., N. M. Mil. Inf., 3 mos., 1861-62.
Chavez, Cantino, Co. F, 3rd N. M. Mtd. Inf., 3 mos., 1861-62.
Chavez, Catrino, Co. B, 3rd N. M. Mtd. Inf., 6 mos., 1861-62.
Chavez, Concepcion, Romero's Independent Co. A, N. M. Mil. Inf., 6 mos., 1861-62.
Chavez, Cruz, Tafoya's Independent Co., N. M. Mil. Inf., 3 mos., 1861-62.
Chavez, Diego A., Co. E, 2nd N. M. Inf., Corporal.
Chavez, Dionicio, Co. L, 3rd N. M. Mtd. Inf., 6 Mo., 1861-62.
Chavez, Domingo, Co. C, 1st N. M. Cav.
Chavez, Doroteo, Romero's 3rd N. M. Mtd. Inf., 6 mos., 1861-62.
Chavez, Espamino, Co. B, 5th N. M. Inf.
Chavez, Eugenio, Co. I, 1st N. M. Cav., Farrier.
Chavez, Faustin, Co. B, 1st N. M. Inf., O. O.
Chavez, Felipe, Tafoya's Independent Co., N. M. Mil. Inf., 3 mos., 1861-62.
Chavez, Francisco, Co. A-E, 2nd N. M. Inf.
Chavez, Geronimo, Hubbell's Independent Co., N. M. Mtd. Vols., 3 mos., 1861-62.
Chavez, Jesus, Gonzolez Independent Co. A, N. M. Mil. Mtd. Inf., 3 mos., 1861-62.
Chavez, Jesus Maria, Sena's Co. A, 1st N. M. Mil. Inf., 3 mos., 1861-62.
Chavez, Jose Francisco, Co. F, 1st N. M. Inf., O. O.
Chavez, Jose, Gonzolez Independent Co. A, N. M. Mil. Inf., 3 mos., 1861.
Chavez, Jose, Hubbell's Independent Co., N. M. Mtd. Vols., 3 mos., 1861; Co. D, 1st N. M. Inf.; Co. E, 1st N. M. Cav.; Co. K-I, 1st N. M. Cav.
Chavez, Jose Amado, Co. G, 2nd N. M. Inf.
Chavez, Jose Angel, Baca's Co., Perea's Batt'n, N. M. Mil. Inf., 3 mos., 1861-62.
Chavez, Jose Hilario, Co. D, 1st N. M. Cav.
Chavez, Jose Ramon, Tafoya's Independent Co., N. M. Mil. Inf., 3 mos., 1861-62.
Chavez, Jose Roque, Co. K, 1st N. M. Cav.
Chavez, Juan, Alarid's Independent Co., N. M. Mil. Inf., 3 mos., 1861-62.
Chavez, Juan, Hubbell's Co., Perea's Batt'n, N. M. Mil. Inf., 3 mos., 1861-62.
Chavez, Juan Antonio, Romero's Co., 3rd N. M. Mtd. Inf., 6 mos., 1860-61, Corporal.
Chavez, Juan Baca y, Co. D, 1st N. M. Cav.
Chaves, Juan de Dios, Co. E, 1st N. M. Cav.
Chavez, Juan de Jesus, Co. F, 1st N. M. Inf.; Co. H, 3rd N. M. Mtd. Inf., 6 mos., 1861-62.
Chavez, Juan J., Hubbell's Co., Perea's Batt'n, N. M. Mil. Inf., 3 mos., 1861-62, Sergeant.

Chavez, Juan Jose Tafoya's Independent Co., N. M. Mil. Inf., 3 mos., 1861-62.
Chavez, Jose de los Reyes, Co. D-E-A, 2nd N. M. Inf.
Chavez, Juan y Manuel, Hubbell's Independent Co., N. M. Mtd. Vols., 3 mos., 1861.
Chavez, Justo, Co. D, 1st N. M. Cav.; Co. F, 2nd N. M. Inf.
Chavez, Lamterino, Gonzolez Independent Co., N. M. Mil., 3 mos., 1861.
Chavez, Leonicio, Co. G, 1st N. M. Cav.
Chavez, Manuel Hubbell's Co., Perea's Batt'n, N. M. Mil. Inf., 3 mos., 1861-62.
Chavez, Manuel, Vigil's Independent Co., N. M. Mtd. Vols., 3 mos., 1861.
Chavez, Manuel Sanchez y, Co. H, 2nd N. M. Inf.
Chavez, Manuel Gonzolez y, Co. H, 2nd N. M. Inf.
Chavez, Maximiano, Hubbell's Independent Co., N. M. Mtd. Vols., 3 mos., 1861, Corporal.
Chavez, Mariano Chavez y, Hubbell's Independent Co., N. M. Mtd. Vols., 1 mo., 1861; Co. B, 5th N. M. Inf.
Chavez, Martin, Co. K, 1st N. M. Cav.
Chavez, Mauricio—1st, Co. F, 1st N. M. Inf., N. O.
Chavez, Mauricio—2nd, Co. F, 1st N. M. Inf., N. O.
Chavez, Melquiades, Hubbell's Independent Co., N. M. Vol. Vols., 2 mos., 1861, Sergeant.
Chavez, Melquiades, Jaramillo's Co., Perea's Batt'n, N. M. Mil. Inf., 3 mos., 1861-62, 2nd Lieut.
Chavez, Merejildo, Tafoya's Independent Co., N. M. Mil., 3 mos., 1861-62.
Chavez, Miguel, Jaramillo's Co., Perea's Batt'n, N. M. Mil. Inf., 3 mos., 1861-62.
Chavez, Miguel A., Gonzolez Independent Co., N. M. Mil., 3 mos., 1861.
Chavez, Juan Montoya y, Co. A-E, 2nd N. M. Inf.
Chavez, Alojio, Romero's Co., 3rd N. M. Mtd. Inf., 6 mos., 1861-62.
Chavez, Pablo, Hubbell's Independent Co., N. M. Mtd. Vols., 2 mos., 1861.
Chavez, Panteleon, Co. E, 1st N. M. Inf., N. O.
Chavez, Pedro, Gonzolez Independent Co., N. M. Mil., 3 mos., 1861, Sergeant.
Chavez, Pedro, Perea's Independent Co., N. M. Vols., 60 days, 1862.
Chavez, Rafael, Hubbell's Independent Co., N. M. Vols., 2 mos., 1861, Sergeant.
Chavez, Rafael Ortiz y, Co. A-E, 2nd N. M .Inf., Captain.
Chavez, Rells, Hubbel's Independent Co., N. M. Mtd. Vols., 3 mos., 1861.
Chavez, Rufino, Hubbell's Independent Co., N. M. Mtd. Vols., 3 mos., 1861.
Chavez, Tomas, Romero's Independent Co., N. M. Mil. Inf., 3 mos., 1861-62.
Chavez, Valentine, Co. D, 1st N. M. Cav.
Chavez, Victoriano, Co. H-G, 1st N. M. Cav.
Chavez, Isidro, Co. H, 1st N. M. Cav.
Chavez, Escuipula, Aragon's Co., Perea's Batt'n, N. M. Mil. Inf., 3 mos., 1861-62, Corporal.
Chavez, Gregorio, Co. C-A, 2nd N. M. Inf.
Chacon, Jose, Co. C, 1st N. M. Inf., N. O.
Chacon, Panteleon, Co. D-E, 4th N. M. Inf.
Chirina, Felix, Co. B, 3rd N. M. Mtd. Inf., 6 mos., 1861-62.
Crespin, Viterbio, Montoya's Co., Perea's Batt'n, N. M. Mil. Inf., 3 mos., 1861-62.
Cisneros, Francisco, Co. E, 4th N. M. Inf.

Cisneros, Eliseo, Jaramillo's Co., Perea's Batt'n, N. M. Mil. Inf., 3 mos., 1861-62.
Cisneros, Nestor, Co. D, 1st N. M. Mil. Inf., 3 mos., 1861-62.
Cisneros, Augustin, Co. K, 1st N. M. Cav.
Cisneros, Jose, Aragon's Co., Perea's Batt'n., N. M. Mil. Inf., 3 mos., 1861-62.
Cisneros, Juan, Co. K, 1st N. M. Inf., N. O.
Cisneros, Victorio, Gonzolez, Independent Co., N. M. Mil., 3 mos., 1861.
Clark, C. B., Perea's Independent Co., N. M. Vols., 60 days, 1862.
Clark, John, Co. B, Batt'n N. M. Vol.s 1866-67, Farrier—Sgt.
Clark, Michael, Co. C, 1st N. M. Inf., O. O.
Cline, August, Co. D, 1st N. M. Cav.
Coca, Antonio, Co. A, 4th N. M. Inf., Bugler.
Coca, Benito, Co. D, 3rd N. M. Mtd. Inf., 6 mos., 1861-62.
Coca, Bicente, Co. D, 4th N. M. Inf.
Coca, Ignacio, Co. B, 3rd N. M. Mtd. Inf., 3 mos., 1861-62.
Coca, Jose de la Cruz, Romero's Independent Co. A, N. M. Mil., 3 mos., 1861.
Coca, Juan Jose Roque, Co. C, 1st N. M. Mil. Inf., 3 mos., 1861-62, Corporal.
Coca, Juan Bautista, Mink's Independent Co., N. M. Mtd. Vols., 3 mos., 1861, Sgt.
Coca, Juan de Jesus, Duran's Co., N. M. Mil.
Caffield, John, Co. K, 1st N. M. Cav.
Coffin, Martin V. B., Co. I, 1st N. M. Cav.
Coughlin, Thomas, Co. A, Batt'n N. M. Vols., 1866-67, 1st Lt.
Caldwell, J. C., Co. F, 1st N. M. Inf.
Cole, William, Co. D, 1st N. M. Cav., Sgt.
Colombo, Rosalio, Co. I-D, 2nd N. M. Inf., 1st Sgt.
Comins, Ralph C., Co. F, 1st N. M. Inf., N. O.; Co. K, 1st N.M. Cav., 2nd Sergeant.
Conway, William, Co. K-H, 1st N. M. Cav.; Co. C, 4th N. M. Inf.
Canone, Ynez, Co. L, 1st N. M. Cav.
Conklin, Carlos, Duran's Co., N. M. Mil., 2nd Lt.
Connelly, Henry, Perea's Independent Co. N. M. Vols., 60 days, 1862. Sergeant.
Connover, Addison, Co. H, 1st N. M. Inf., Trans. from 1st Inf., Cal. Volunteers.
Contreras, Jesus, Co. C-D, Batt'n N. M. Vols., 1866-67, Corporal.
Contreras, Abinicio, Co. H, 1st N. M. Cav.
Contreras, Juan Cristobal, Co. K, 1st N. M. Inf.
Contreras, Pedro, Del Balle's Co., Perea's Batt'n, N. M. Mil. Inf., 3 mos., 1861-62.
Cook, George W., Co. D, 1st N. M. Cav., Sgt.; Co. F, 1st N. M. Inf., Captain; Co. E-D, 4th N. M. Inf., 1st Lt.
Cooley, Corydon E., Co. C, 1st N. M. Inf.
Copeland, Edward, Co. K, 1st N. M. Cav., Sgt.
Copeland, John H., Co. A, 3rd N. M. Mtd. Vols., 6 mos., 1861-62.
Corales, Refugio, Co. G, 2nd N. M. Inf.
Coronado, Cicilio, Co. F, 1st N. M. Cav.
Cordero, Inez, Co. H, 1st N. M. Inf.
Cordova, Antonio, Co. A, 1st N. M. Mil. Inf., 6 mos., 1861-62.
Cordova, Felipe, Baca's Co., Perea's Batt'n, N. M. Mil. Inf., 3 mos., 1861-62.
Cordova, Henrique, Co. A, 1st N. M. Cav.
Cordova, Jose, Co. C, 3rd N. M. Mtd. Inf., 6 mos., 1861-62.
Cordova, Jose Miguel, Co. A, 1st N. M. Mil. Inf., 3 mos., 1861-62.
Cordova, Juan Esteban, Co. A, 1st N. M. Inf.
Cordova, Juan Santiago, Co. E, 1st N. M. Cav.
Cordova, Salvador, Co. A, 1st N. M. Inf.
Cordova, Profilo, Co. E, 3rd. N. M. Mtd. Inf., 6 mos., 1861-62.

Cordova, Anastasio, Co. F, 1st N. M. Mil. Inf., 3 mos., 1861-62.
Cordova, Francisco, Co. D, 1st N. M. Cav.
Cordova, Ignacio, Co. F, 2nd N. M. Inf.
Cordova, Jesus Maria, Co. K, 1st N. M. Inf.
Cordova, Jose Francisco, Co. E, 4th N. M. Inf.
Cordova, Jose Bicente, Co. D, 1st N. M. Inf., O. O.
Cordova, Juan, Co. A, 1st N. M. Inf., O. O.
Cordova, Juan de Jesus, Co. E, 4th N. M. Inf.
Cordova, Juan Esteban, Co. I, 1st N. M. Cav.
Cordova, Juan Francisco, Co. H, 1st N. M. Inf., O. O.
Cordova, Juan Rafael, Co. D, 1st N. M. Inf., N. M.
Cordova, Juan Ramos, Co. D, 1st N. M. Inf., O. O.
Cordova, Juan Santiago, Co. A, 1st N. M. Cav.
Cordova, Mariano, Co. D, 1st N. M. Militia Inf.; Co. I, 1st N. M. Cav.
Cordova, Quirino, Co. D, 3rd N. M. Mtd. Inf., 6 mos., 1861-62.
Cordova, Rafael, Co. B, 1st N. M. Mil. Inf., 3 mos., 1861-62.
Cordova, Roman, Co. B, 1st N. M. Mil. Inf., 3 mos., 1861-62.
Cordova, Santiago, Co. C, Batt'n N. M. Mtd. Vols., 1866-67.
Cordova, Senovio, Graydon's Independent Co., N. M. Mtd. Vols., 3 mos., 1861-62.
Cordova, Tomas, Co. C, Batt'n N. M. Mtd. Vols., 1866-67.
Cordova, Vicente, Co. E, 1st N. M. Mil. Inf., 3 mos., 1861-62.
Cordova, Jose Enriquez, Co. D, 1st N. M. Inf., O. O.
Cordova, Jose Rafael, Co. I, 1st N. M. Inf., N. O.
Cordova, Juan de Jesus, Co. I, 1st N. M. Inf.
Cordova, Jesus Maria, Co. I, 1st N. M. Inf. O. O.
Cordova, Crecencio, Graydon's Independent Co. N. M. Mtd. Vols., 3 mos., 1861-62.
Cordova, Jose Maria, Tafoya's Independent Co., N. M. Mil., 3 mos., 1861-62.
Cordova, Francisco, Co. D, 1st N. M. Inf.
Cordova, Juan Jose, Graydon's Independent Co., N. M. Mtd. Vols., 3 mos., 1861-62.
Camillo, Anastacio, Graydon's Independent Co., N. M. Mil., 3 mos., 1862, Musician.
Coris, Felipe, Co. B, 1st N. M. Cav.
Coris, Filimeno, Co. F, 1st N. M. Inf., O. O.; Co. B, 1st N. M. Cav.
Coris, Jose, Co. C, Batt'n N. M. Vols., 1866-67.
Coris, Juan Jose, Co. F, 1st N. M. Inf., O. O.
Carmody, John, Co. D, 1st N. M. Cav.
Coronado, Juan, Co. E, 1st N. M. Inf.
Corrales, Bicente, Co. G, 1st N. M. Inf.
Cortez, Francisco, Co. K, 1st N. M. Inf.
Cortez, Crecencio, Co. H, 1st N. M. Inf.
Cortez, Jose, Co. E, 1st N. M. Militia Inf., 3 mos., 1861-62.
Cortez, Jose Antonio, Co. E, 1st N. M. Mil. Inf., 3 mos., 1861-62.
Cortez, Jose Emanuel, Co. E, 1st N. M. Mil. Inf., 3 mos., 1861-62.
Cortez, Jose Guadalupe, Co. E, 1st N. M. Mil. Inf., 3 mos., 1861-62.
Cortez, Librado, Co. F, 1st N. M. Inf., N. O.
Cortez, Concepcion, Co. I-D, 3rd N. M. Mtd. Inf., 6 mos., 1861-62, Corporal.
Cortines, Juan, Co. F, 1st N. M. Cav.
Costa, Julian, Co. F, 1st N. M. Cav.
Castenada, Eusebio, Co. I-D, 1st N. M. Inf.
Costello, Jose, Antonio, Del Balle's Co., Perea's Batt'n, N. M. Mil. Inf., 3 mos., 1861-62.
Costello, Jose Miguel, Co. D, 1st N. M. Inf., N. O.
Castro, Juan de Dios, Co. B, 2nd N. M. Inf.
Cota, Juan, Co. A, 1st N. M. Inf., O. O.
Cox, George, Co. F, 1st N. M. Inf., Trans. 1st Cav. Cal. Vols.
Coyle, Stephen, Co. M, 1st N. M. Cav. Lt.
Crane, Alfred A. Co. F, 4th N. M. Inf., Assistant Surgeon.

Crespin, Antonio, Romero's Independent Co. A, N. M. Militia Inf., 3 mos., 1861-62, Corporal.
Crespin, Benito, Co. A, 3rd N. M. Mtd Inf., Corporal.
Crespin, Diego, Co. D, 1st N. M. Cav.
Crespin, Jesus, Co. A, 1st N. M. Inf.
Crespin, Jose, Co. C, 1st N. M. Inf., N. O.
Crespin, Jose Aniseto, Co. A, 3rd N. M. Mtd. Vols., 6 mos., 1861-62.
Crespin, Juan, Co. D, Batt'n N. M. Vols., 1866-67.
Crespin, Julian, Romero's Independent Co. A, N. M. Mil. Inf., 3 mos., 1861-62 Drummer.
Crespin, Nasario, Jaramillo's Co. Perea's Batt'n N. M. Mil. Inf.; 3 mos. 1861-62.
Crespin, Viterbo, Montoya's Co., Perea's Batt'n, N. M. Mil. Inf., 3 mos., 1861-62.
Crespin, Isidro, Montoya's Co., Perea's Batt'n, N. M. Mil. Inf., 3 mos., Drummer.
Cronin, Michael, Co. A-I, 1st N. M. Cav.
Cross, Elisha, Co. I, 1st N. M. Cav., O. O.
Crowley, William, Co. I, 1st N. M. Inf., O. O.
Cruz, Felipe, Co. F-D, 4th N. M. Inf.
Cruz, Jacinto, Co. D-F, 4th N. M. Inf.
Cruz, Marcos, Co. G, 1st N. M. Cav.
Cruz, Jose Santos, Co. A, Batt'n, N. M. Vols., 1866-67.
Cruz, Juan Ignacio, Co. D-E, 1st N. M. Inf., Sgt.
Cruz, Diego Antonio, Vigil's Independent Co., N. M. Mtd. Vols., 3 mos., 1861.
Cruz, Jose Dolores, Co. I, 1st N. M. Inf., N. O.
Cruz, Jose Felipe, Co. I, 1st N. M. Inf.
Cruz, Jose Leon, Co. B, 3rd N. M. Mtd. Inf., 6 mos., 1861-62.
Cruz, Jose Manuel, Co. B, 3rd N. M. Mtd Inf., 6mos., 1861-62.
Cruz, Jose Prudencio, Co. D, 1st N. M. Mil. Inf., 3 mos., 1861-62.
Cruz, Norberto, Co. B, 3rd N. M. Mtd. Inf., 6 mos., 1861-62.
Cummings, Joseph, Co. I-K, 1st N. M. Cav., Fort Cummings was named for him. Major.
Cusack, Phillip, Co. B, 1st N. M. Inf., N. O.
Cushing, James Henry, Co. M-E, 1st N. M. Cav.
Cussman, Pablo, Co. D, 1st N. M. Cav.

Daguebara, Placido, Co. H, 1st N. M. Cav.
Daguero, Juan, Co. F, 1st N. M. Mil. Inf.
Dalo, Thomas, Co. A, 1st N. M. Cav.
Dalton, John, Co. D, 3rd N. M. Mtd. Inf., 6 mos., 1861-62.
Damours, Augustine P., Co. F-E, 1st N. M. Cav.
Dunigay, Timothy, Co. F, 1st N. M. Inf., N. O.
Darling, George, Co. F, 1st N. M. Inf., N. O.
Dates, James, Co. D, 1st N. M. Cav.
Davila, Julian, Co. A-E, 3rd N. M. Mtd. Inf., 6 mos., 1861-62.
Davis, David A., Co. A, 1st N. M. Inf., N. O. Trans. 1st Cav., Cal. Vols.
Davis, Jefferson H., Co. E, 1st N. M. Inf. N. O.
Dan, John, Co. H, 1st N. M. Cav., 2nd Lt.
Daguero, Antonio, Co. K, 1st N. M. Inf.
Daguero, Felipe, Co. B, 1st N. M. Cav.
Daguero, Nicholas, Co. B, 1st N. M. Cav., O. O.
Daguero, Toribio, Co. B, 1st N. M. Cav.
Dearmond, Alexander, Co. K, 2nd N. M. Inf.
DeForrest, Cyrus H., Co. D, Batt'n N. M. Vols., 1866-67, 1st Lt.
Daguero, Demetrio, Montoya's Co., Perea's Batt'n, N. M. Mil. Inf., 3 mos., 1861-62.
DeGuebara, Ignacio N., Co. H, 1st N. M. Cav., Farrier.
DeHague, Joseph L., Co. L, 1st N. M. Cav., 1st Lt.
DeLeon, Juan, Co. F, 1st N. M. Cav.
DeHerrera, Felipe, Co. A, 3rd N. M. Mil. Inf.

De-la-O, Fernando, Co. E, 1st N. M. Inf., N. O.
De-la-O, Tomas, Co. E, 1st N. M. Inf., O. O.
De-la-Riba, Cristobal, Co. C, 1st N. M. Inf., N. O.
De-la-Riba, Luis, Co. F, 1st N. M. Inf.
De-la-Torre, Eusebio, Co. E, 1st N. M. Inf., N. O.
Del Balle, Augosto, Del Balle's Co., Perea's Batt'n, N. M. Mil. Inf., Captain, 3 mos., 1861-62.
DeLeon, Juan, Co. D, Batt'n N. M. Vols., 1866-67.
Delgado, Antonio J., Co. F, 1st N. M. Mil. Inf., 3 mos., 1861-62.
Delgado, Manuel Baca y, Co. D, 2nd N. M. Inf., Captain.
De Luna, Miguel, Jaramillo's Co., Perea's Batt'n, N. M. Mil. Inf., 3 mos., 1861-62.
Dominguez, Delfido, Co. F, 3rd N. M. Mtd. Inf., 6 mos., 1861-62.
Dominguez, Juan C., Co. A, 1st N. M. Inf., O. O.
Dominguez, Rafael, Co. K, 1st N. M. Inf.
Depeu, Edmund, Co. D, 1st N. M. Cav., 2nd Lt.
Derma, Antonio M., Co. I, 1st N. M. Inf., O. O.
Derma, Antonio Jose, Co. I, 1st N. M. Inf., O. O.
Derma, Jose Seledon, Co. I, 1st N. M. Inf., O. O.
Derma, Rafael, Co. K, 1st N. M. Inf., N. O.
Derma, Cecilio, Co. K, 1st N. M. Inf., N. O.
De Soto, Prospero, Co. G, 3rd N. M. Mtd. Inf., 6 mos., 1861-62. Sgt.
Deus, Charles, Co. M, 1st N. M. Cav., Captain.
Devero, Jose, Co. D, 3rd N. M. Mtd. Inf., 6 mos., 1861-62.
Devine, James, Co. L-K, 1st N. M. Cav.
Dias, Emilio, Co. F, 1st N. M. Inf.
Dias, Dionisio, Co. A, 1st N. M. Mil. Inf., 3 mos., 1861-62.
Dias, Evaristo, Co. G, 2nd N. M. Inf.
Dias, Geronimo, Co. H, 1st N. M. Inf.
Dias, Jose Trinidad, Co. A, 1st N. M. Inf.
Dias, Luis, Co. C, 1st N. M. Cav.
Dias, Luis, Co. C, 1st N. M. Inf.
Dias, Miguel, Co. A, 1st N. M. Cav.
Dickens, Louis, Co. C, 1st N. M. Inf., O. O.
Dillon, Edward, Co. D, 1st N. M. Cav.
Dillon, James, Co. K, 1st N. M. Cav.
Dias, Miguel M., Co. D, Batt'n N. M. Vols., 1866-67.
Diosa, Manuel, Baca's Co., Perea's Batt'n, N. M. Mil. Inf., 3 mos., 1861-62.
Divine, James, Co. L-K, 1st N. M. Inf.
Dodd, William John R., Co. G, 1st N. M. Inf.
Dodson, Wilson, Co. G, 1st N. M. Cav.
Dominguez, Juan Jose, Co. H, 1st N. M. Cav.
Dominguez, Antonio, Co. B, 1st N. M. Cav.
Dominguez, Estanislado, Co. D, 1st N. M. Cav.
Dominguez, Francisco, Co. D, Batt'n, N. M. Vols., 1866-67.
Dominguez, Juan, Co. D, Batt'n, N. M. Vols., 1866-67.
Dominguez, Pomiciendo, Graydon's Independent Co., 3 mos., 1861-62.
Dominguez, Rafael, Co. A, 2nd N. M. Inf.
Dominguez, Delifdo, Co. I, 1st N. M. Inf.
Dominguez, Gabriel, Alarid's Ind't Co., N. M. Mil. Inf., 3 mos., 1861-62.
Dominguez, Cayetano, Co. K, 3rd N. M. Mtd. Inf.
Dominguez, Delgado, Co. B, Batt'n, N. M. Vols., 1866-67.
Dominguez, Juan Jose, Co. E, 1st N. M. Cav.
Dominguez, Julio, Co. K, 1st N. M. Inf.
Dominguez, Yomas, Co. F, 1st N. M. Inf.
Dominguez, Pedro, Co. F, 1st N. M. Inf.
Dominguez, Rafael, Co. L, 1st N. M. Cav.
Dominguez, Rosario, Co. C, 1st N. M. Inf.
Dominguez, Tomas, Co. F, 3rd N. M. Mtd Inf.
Dominguez, Victoriano, Co. A, 1st N. M. Cav., N. O.
Dominguez, Juan Dionicio, Co. A, 1st N. M. Inf.

Dominguez, Antonio, Co. B, 1st N. M. Cav.
Dominguez, Nepoceno, Romero's Independent Co. A, N. M. Mil., 6 mos., 1861-62.
Donoho, Joseph, Co. K, 1st N. M. Cav.; Co. C, 4th N. M. Inf.
Donoho, William, Co. E; D, 4th N. M. Inf., Sgt.
Donoho, Michael, Co. K, 1st N. M. Inf., Sgt.
Dorame, Joseph, Co. C, Batt'n N. M. Vols., 1866-67; Co. L, 1st N. M. Cav.
Dorsette, John W., Co. C, 4th N. M. Inf., Sgt.
Dowlin, John W., Co. F, 1st N. M. Cav., Sgt.
Dowlin, Paul, Co. K, 1st N. M. Cav., Captain.
Dowling, J. B., Co. F, 1st N. M. Cav.
Drennan, John, Co. I, 1st N. M. Inf.
Dreufas, Adolph, Co. F, 1st N. M. Inf., N. O., Ord., Sgt.
David, Samuel, Co. B, 1st N. M. Inf.
Drum, George, Co. G, 1st N. M. Cav.
Durante, Francisco, Co. D, Batt'n N. M. Vols., 1866-67.
Dubois, E. Leon, Co. F, 1st N. M. Inf., N. O.
Dunn, Albert W., Co. L, 1st N. M. Cav.
Dunn, George, Co. G, 1st N. M. Cav.
Duran, Agapito, Co. F, 3rd N. M. Inf.
Duran, Andres, Co. F, 1st N. M. Cav.; Co. E, 3rd N. M. Mil. Vols., 3 mos., 1861-62.
Duran, Antonio, Del Balle's Co., Perea's Batt'n, N. M. Mil. Inf., 3 mos., 1861-62.
Duran, Basilio, Co. L, 1st N. M. Cav.
Cruz, Vicente, Co. L, 1st N. M. Cav.; Del Balle's Co., Perea's Batt'n. N. M. Mil. Inf., 3 mos., 1861-62.
Duran, Donaciano, Co. E, 1st N. M. Cav.
Duran, Doroteo, Co. A, 1st N. M.: Inf.
Duran, Francisco, Co. K, 1st N. M. Inf.
Duran, Gregorio, Co. B, 1st N. M. Inf., N. O.
Duran, Ignacio, Co. A, 1st N. M. Cav.
Duran, Jesus, Co. B, 1st N. M. Cav.
Duran, Jesus Maria, Co. F, 1st N. M. Cav.
Duran, Jose Mink's Independent Co., Mtd. Vols., 3 mos., 1861-62; Co. D, 1st N. M. Cav.
Duran, Jose Abran, Co. A, 1st N. M. Mil. Inf., 3 mos., 1861-62.
Duran, Jose Antonio, Co. D, 1st N. M. Cav.
Duran, Jose Antonio Juan, Mink's Independent Co., N. M. Mtd. Vols., 3 mos., 1861.
Duran, Jose Cosme, Co. C, 3rd N. M. Mtd. Inf., 3 mos., 1861-62.
Duran, Jose Dolores, Co. C, 3rd N. M. Mtd. Inf., 6 mos., 1861-62.
Duran, Jose E., Duran's Co. N. M. Mil., Captain.
Duran, Jose Ignacio, Co. A, 1st N. M. Inf.
Duran, Jose Manuel, Vigil's Independent Co., N. M. Mtd. Vols., 3 mos., 1861.
Duran, Jose Nasario, Co. E, 1st N. M. Cav.
Duran, Jose Ramon, Co. D, 1st N. M. Cav.
Duran, Juan, Co. D, 2nd N. M. Inf.
Duran, Juan Cristobal, Co. L, 1st N. M. Cav.
Duran, Juan de Jesus, Aragon's Co., Perea's Batt'n, N. M. Mil. Inf., 3 mos., 1861-62.
Duran, Juan Isidro, Co. D, 1st N. M. Inf.
Duran, Juan Jose, Co. B, 3rd N. M. Mtd. Inf., 3 mos., 1861-62.
Duran, Lino, Co. G, 1st N. M. Cav.
Duran, Luciano, Del Balle's Co., Perea's Batt'n, N. M. Mil. Inf., 3 mos., 1861-62.
Duran, Loreto, Co. H, 3rd N. M. Mtd. Inf., 6 mos., 1861-62.
Duran, Luis, Co. D, 1st N. M. Mil., 6 mos., 1861-62.
Duran, Manuel, Co. E, 1st N. M. Cav.
Duran, Marcelino, Co. B, 3rd N. M. Inf.

Duran, Miguel, Graydon's Independent Co., N. M. Mtd. Vols., 3 mos., 1861-62.
Duran, Rafael, Co. D, 3rd N. M. Mtd. Vols.
Duran, Juan Antonio, Co. D, 1st N. M. Mil. Inf., 3 mos., 1861-62.
Duran, Ramon, Duran's Co., N. M. Mil.
Duran, Damian, Graydon's Independent Co., N. M. Mtd. Vols., 3 mos., 1861-62.

Eaton, Ethan U., Co. D-F-I, 1st N. M. Cav., Capt., Lt., Col.
Escudero, Filiciano, Co. B, 1st N. M. Mil. Inf., 3 mos., 1861-62.
Edgar, Edward, Co. G-A, 1st N. M. Cav., 2nd Lt.
Edgar, James, Co. I-G-D, 1st N. M. Cav., 2nd Lt.
Edgar, John B., Co. K, 1st N. M. Cav.
Atencio, Edubigen, Co. D, 1st N. M. Cav.
Eich, Peter, Co. L-K, 1st N. M. Cav., Corp.
Edaco, Jose Marino, Co. A, 1st N. M. Cav., Corp.
Eldridge, Norman, Co. A, 1st N. M. Cav., Corp.
Elbet, Charles, Co. A, 1st N. M. Inf., O. O.
Elliot, John Collins, Co. M, 1st N. M. Cav.
Etlas, John Millian, Co. D, 1st N. M. Inf., N. O.
Ellsworth, George H., Co. K, 1st N. M. Cav.
Encinias, Luis, Co. D, 1st N. M. Cav.
Engle, Peter, Co. M, 1st N. M. Cav., Sgt.
Ennis, James, Simpson's Independent Co., N. M. Mtd. Spies and Guides.
Ennis, James, Simpson's Independent Co., N. M. Mtd. Spies and Guides.
Encinias, Jesus, Co. A-D, 3rd N. M. Mtd. Inf., 3 mos., 1861-62.
Encinias, Juan de Dios, Co. B, 1st N. M. Inf., N. O.
Encinias, Miguel, Romero's Independent Co. A, N. M. Mil. Inf., 3 mos., 1861-62.
Herrera, Jose, Co. E, 1st N. M. Inf., O. O.
Herrera, Jose Amador, Co. E, 1st N. M. Inf.
Ulibarri, Paublino, Co. K, 1st N. M. Cav.
Ernandez, Jesus, Co. E, 1st N. M. Inf.
Espinoza, Tomas, Co. E, 4th N. M. Inf.
Herrera, Antonio, Jaramillo's Co., Perea's Batt'n, N. M. Mil. Inf., 3 mos., 1861-62.
Herrera, Luis, Co. E, 1st N. M. Inf., N. O.
Herrera, Teodore, Co. K, 1st N. M. Cav.; Co. B, 4th N. M. Inf.
Erwin, John, Co. C, Batt'n N. M. Vols., 1866-67.
Escalante, Nieves, Co. I, 1st N. M. Cav.; 2nd N. M. Inf.
Escalante, Ramon, Co. K, 1st N. M. Inf.
Escalante, Santiago, Co. D, 1st N. M. Cav.
Escalante, Jose Maria, Aragon's Co., Perea's Batt'n, N. M. Mil. Inf., 3 mos., 1861-62.
Escarate, Reyes, Co. I-D, 2nd N. M. Inf.
Escarate, Jose de la Luz, Co. E, N. M. Inf.
Escobedo, Tomas, Co. A, Batt'n N. M. Vols., 1866-67; Co. E, 1st N. M. Cav.
Escobar, Jose Maria, Co. D, 1st N. M. Cav.
Esquivel, Tomas, Co. A, 1st N. M. Cav., Sgt.
Espinosa, Jose Maria, Co. H, 2nd N. M. Inf.
Espinosa, Jose Dolores, Co. I, 1st N. M. Inf.
Espinosa, Agapito, Co. G, 1st N. M. Inf., N. O.
Espinosa, Basilio, Co. D-F, 4th N. M. Inf.
Espinosa, Delfido, Co. D, 4th N. M. Inf.
Espinosa, Donaciano, Co. D, 1st N. M. Inf., Sgt.
Espinosa, Encarnacion Co. A, 2nd N. M. Inf.
Espinosa, Francisco, Co. D, 1st N. M. Cav.
Espinosa, Francisco Antonio, Co F, 4th N. M. Inf.
Espinosa, Gregorio, Co. K, 2nd N. M. Inf.

Espinosa, Jesus, Co. A, 1st N. M. Cav., Corp.
Espinosa, Jose Abeita, Co. D, 1st N. M. Cav., Corp.
Espinosa, Jose Antonio, Co. E, 1st N. M. Inf.
Espinosa, Jose de Jesus, Co. I, 1st N. M. Cav.
Espinosa, Jose Domingues, Co. F, 4th N. M. Inf., O. O.
Espinosa, Jose Pedro, Co. E, 1st N. M. Inf., O. O.
Espinosa, Jose Isidro, Co. I, 1st N. M. Cav.
Espinosa, Juan, Tafoya's Independent Co., N. M. Mil., 3 mos., 1861-62; Co. B, 2nd N. M. Inf.
Espinosa, Juan, Co. F, 3rd N. M. Mtd. Inf., 6 mos., 1861-62.
Espinosa, Juan de Jesus, Co. F, 3rd N. M. Mtd. Inf., 6 mos., 1861-62.
Espinosa, Julian, Co. D, 1st N. M. Inf., O. O.
Espinosa, Lionicio, Co. D, 3rd N. M. Mtd. Inf., 6 mos., 1861-62.
Espinosa, Luis, Co. D, Batt'n N. M. Vols., 1866-67; Co. B, 1st N. M. Cav.
Espinosa, Bicente, Minks Independent Co., N. M. Mtd. Vols., 3 mos., 1861; Co. B, 2nd N. M. Inf.
Espinosa, Agapito, Co. G, 1st N. M. Inf.
Escudero, Pedro, Alarid's Independent Co., N. M. Mtd. Vols., 3 mos., 1861-62.
Esquivel, Dionicio, Montoya's Co., Perea's Batt'n, N. M. Mil. Inf., 3 mos., 1861-62.
Esquivel, Encarnacion, Romero's Co. A, N. M. Mil. Inf., 3 mos., 1861-62.
Esquivel, Jesus, Romero's Co. A, N. M. Mil. Inf., 3 mos., 1861-62.
Esquivel, Jose, Romero's Co. A, N. M. Mil. Inf., 3 mos., 1861-62.
Esquibel, Jose Pedro, Co. B, 1st N. M. Cav., O. O.
Esquival, Juan, Co. H, 1st N. M. Inf., O. O.
Esquibel, Juan de Jesus, Co. D, 4th N. M. Inf.
Esquivel, Juan Manuel, Vigil's Independent Co., Mtd. Vols., 3 mos., 1861-62.
Esquivel, Miguel, Co. E, 3rd N. M. Mtd. Inf., 3 mos., 1861-62.
Esquivel, Miguel Antonio, Co. H, 1st N. M. Inf., O. O.
Esquivel, Rafael, Co. C, 1st N. M. Cav.
Estrada, Jose Candelario, Montoya's Co., Perea's Batt'n, N. M. Mil. Inf., 3 mos., 1861-62.
Estrada, Ramon, Co. G, 1st N. M. Inf.; Co. F, 3rd N. M. Mtd. Inf., 3 mos., 1861-62.
Estrada, Teodoro, Co. F, 3rd N. M. Mtd. Inf., 3 mos., 1861-62.
Estrada, Luciano, Co. B, 1st N. M. Inf., O. O.
Erlecia, Benino, Co. L, 1st N. M. Cav.
Edward, R. H., Perea's Independent Co., N. M. Vols., 60 days, 1862.
Eyre, Percy, Co. K, 1st N. M. Cav., 1st Lt.

Fajardo, Naciso, Tafoya's Independent Co., N. M. Mil., 3 mos., 1861-62.
Fajardo, Pifanio, Tafoya's Independent Co., N. . Militia, 3 mos., 1861-62.
Fajardo, Pablo, Gonzolez Independent Co., N. M. Mil., 3 mos., 1861-62.
Farjardo, Romoceno, Gonzolez Independent Co., N. M. Militia, 3 mos., 1861-62.
Falck, Earnest, Co. M, 1st N. M. Inf., O. O.
Fajardo, Ejifanio, Co. F, 1st N. M. Inf., O. O.
Jaramillo, Crecencio, Co. D, 2nd N. M. Inf.
Jaramillo, Jose Dolores, Co. D, 2nd N. M. Inf.
Faringly, Louis C., Co. D, 1st N. M. Cav., 1st Lt.
Farley, John, Co. G, 1st N. M. Cav.
Farley, Thomas, Co. H, 1st N. M. Inf.
Rubio, Faustin, Co. H, 1st N. M. Inf. O. O.
Feary, John William, Co. L, 1st N. M. Cav., 1st Lt.
Felliner, Ludwig G., Co. G, 1st N. M. Cav.
Felliner, Joseph, Co. I, 1st N. M. Inf., N. O.

Felsenthal, Louis, Co. G, 1st N. M. Inf., O. O.
Fenorio (Tenorio?)
Jose Rafael, Co. B, 3rd N. M. Mtd., Inf., 6 mos., 1861-62,Corp.
Ferio, John M. Co. I, 1st N. M. Inf., See: Cal. Vols.
Fernandez, Francisco Antonio, Co. G, 1st N. M. Inf.
Fernandez, Susano, Co. A, 1st N. M. Cav.
Fernandez, Antonio, Co. I, 1st N. M. Mil. Inf., 3 mos., 1861-62.
Fernandez, Joaquin, Minks Independent Co., 1st N. M. Mtd. Vols., 3 mos., 1861-62.
Fernandez, Jose Domingo, 3rd N. M. Mtd. Inf., 6 mos., 1861-62.
Fernandez, Estanislado, Mink's Independent Co., N. M. Mtd. Vols., 3 mos., 1861.
Fernandez, Juan, Mink's Independent Co., N. M. Mtd. Vols., 3 mos., 1861.
Fernandez, Refugio, Co. M, 1st N. M. Cav.
Fersher, John, Co. A, 1st N. M. Cav.
Fielder, Eugene, Co. M, 1st N. M. Cav.
Fuentes, Tiburcio, Co. C, 1st N. M. Cav.
Figeroa, Edwardo, Co. E, 1st N. M. Inf., N. O.
Fimbres, Jose, Co. A, Batt'n N. M. Vols., 1866-67.
Finnet, John P., Co. D, 1st N. M. Inf., 1st Lt.
Finn, Michael, Co. H, 1st N. M. Inf., N. O.; Co. D-E, Batt'n N. M. Vols., 1866-67.
Fitch, Charles H., Co. K, 1st N. M. Cav., 2nd Lt.
Flannigan, William, Co. G, 1st N. M. Cav.; Co. I, 5th N. M. Inf.
Flores, Nicolas, Co. K, 1st N. M. Cav.
Flyn, Joseph, Co. D, 1st N. M. Cav.
Flores, George W., Co. A, 1st N. M. Cav.
Flores, Cecilio, Co. F, 1st N. M. Cav.
Flores, Camelio, Co. F, 1st N. M. Mil. Inf., 3 mos., 1861-62.
Flores, Dimas, Co. I, 2nd N. M. Inf.
Flores, Francisco, Co. D, 1st N. M. Cav.
Flores, Jose de Garcia y, Co. H, 1st N. M. Cav.
Flores, Jose Guadalupe, Co. D, 3rd N. M. Mtd. Inf., 6 mos., 1861-62.
Flores, Jose Dario, Co. H, 3rd N. M. Mtd. Inf., 6 mos., 1861-62.
Flores, Jose Luis, Co. F, 1st N. M. Cav.
Flores, Julian, Co. H, 3rd N. M. Mtd. Inf., 6 mos., 1861-62.
Flores, Lucillo, Co. F, 1st N. M. Cav.
Flores, Luis, Co. M, 1st N. M. Cav.
Flores, Luis Jose, Co. B, 1st N. M. Inf., O. O.
Flores, Magdaleno, Co. B, 1st N. M. Inf., O. O.
Flores, Manuel, Co. F, 1st N. M. Inf. Mil., 3 mos., 1861-62.
Flores, Melquiades, Romero's Independent Co. A, Mil. Inf., 3 mos., 1861-62.
Flores, Pedro, Co. E, 1st N. M. Cav.
Flores, Romualdo, Romero's Independent Co., N. M. Mil. Inf., 3 mos., 1861-62.
Flores, Salvador, Co. G, 1st N. M. Cav.
Flores, Sostenes, Co. D, 1st N. M. Cav.
Flores, Francisco, Co. D, 1st N. M. Cav.
Flowers, Carl W., Co. G, 1st N. M. Cav., Bugler.
Flowers, George, Co. B, 1st N. M. Inf., N. O.
Flores, Juan Chavez y, Co. D, 1st N. M. Cav.
Cortez, Juan, 3rd N. M. Mtd. Inf., 6 mos., 1861-62.
Ford, John, Co. K, 1st N. M. Cav., Sgt.
Ferris, Santiago, Co. K, 1st N. M. Cav.
Foster, John, Co. B, 1st N. M. Cav., Corp.
Foster, Orlando G., Co. M, 1st N. M. Cav., Corp.
Foster, James, Co. M., 1st N. M. Cav.
Foster, William, Co. G, 1st N. M. Cav., Sgt.
Fay, John, Co. B, 1st N. M. Inf., O. O. See also 2nd U. S. Inf.
Jiminez, Francisco, Co. M, 1st N. M. Cav.

Frank, Peter, Co. I, 1st N. M. Cav.
Freeman, William, Co. G, 1st N. M. Cav.
Fresquez, Jose F., Co. D, Batt'n, N. M. Vols., 1866-67.
Fresquez, Jose Dolores, Co. A, 1st N. M. Cav.
Fresquez, Jose Tomas, Co. A, 4th N. M. Inf.
Fresher, John, Co. C, Batt'n N. M. Vols., 1866-67.
Fresquez, Bartolo, Co. M, 1st N. M. Cav.
Fresquez, Guadalupe, Co. F, 3rd N. M. Mtd. Inf., 6 mos., 1861-62.
Fresquez, Jose, Co. I, 1st N. M. Inf.
Fresquez, Jose Antonio, Co. E, 1st N. M. Cav.
Fresquez, Jose Ignacio, Co. B, 1st N. M. Mil. Inf., 6 mos., 1861-62.
Fresquez, Jose Maria, Co. H, 1st N. M. Inf., N. O.
Fresquez, Tomas, Co. D, 1st N. M. Mil. Inf., 3 mos., 1861-62.
Fresquez, Lionicio, Co. H, 1st N. M. Inf., N. O.
Fresquez, Pedro, Co. H, 1st N. M. Inf.
Fresquez, Timoteo, Co. C, 1st N. M. Inf., N. O.
Fresquez, Vicente, Co. E, 1st N. M. Cav.
Fresquez, Candelario, Co. F, 1st N. M. Mtd. Inf., 6 mos., 1861-62.
Fresquez, Carpio, Co. D, 3rd N. M. Mtd. Inf., 6 mos., 1861-62.
Fresquez, Esquipula, Co. E, 1st N. M. Mil. Inf., 3 mos., 1861-62.
Frujillo (Trujillo?) J. Julian, Duran's Co., N. M. Mil., Sgt.
Frujillo, Pedro Jose, Co. B, 1st N. M. Cav.
Fuentes, Roman, Graydon's Co., N. M. Mtd. Vols., 3 mos., 1861-62.
Fuentes, Tiburcio, Co. D-E, 1st N. M. Cav., Bugler.
Fuller, S. D., Co. D, 1st N. M. Cav., Sgt., See also Mounted Rifles,
Funk, Augustine Charles, Co. D, 1st N. M. Cav., See also 1st Cal. Inf.

Galbadon, Rufino, Co. D, 1st N. M. Inf.
Galbadon, Epifanio, Co. D, 1st N. M. Cav.
Galbadon, Apolonio, Co. I, 1st N. M. Inf.
Galbadon, Antonio, Baca's Co., Perea's Batt'n, N. M. Mil. Inf., 3 mos., 1861-62.
Galbadon, Francisco, Gonzoles, Independent Co., N. M. Mil., 3 mos., 1861-62.
Galbadon, Jose Nieves, Hubbell's Independent Co., N. M. Mtd. Vols., 3 mos., 1861.
Galbadon, Juan, Baca's Co., Perea's Batt'n, N. M. Mil. Inf., 6 mos., 1861-62; Co. K, 2nd N. M. Inf.
Galbadon, Esteban, Montoya's Co., Perea's N. M. Mil. Inf., 3 mos., 1861-62.
Galbadon, Juan Pascual, Co. B, 3rd N. M. Mtd. Inf., 6 mos., 1861-62.
Galbadon, Rufino, Co. A, 1st N. M. Cav.
Galbadon, Nolasco, Co. I, 1st N. M. Inf., O. O.
Galbadon, Eufrasio, Co. I, 1st N. M. Inf.
Gana, Matias, Co. H, 1st N. M. Inf., N. O., Sgt.
Gana, Rafael, Co. H, 1st N. M. Inf.
Galendo, Ricardo, Co. I, 1st N. M. Inf.
Galendo, Santiago, Co. H, 1st N. M. Inf.
Galiz, Carlos, Co. D, 1st N. M. Inf., O. O.
Galiz, Florenzo, Romero's Independent Co. A., N. M. Mil. Inf., 3 mos., 1861-62.
Galliger, Thomas, Co. A, 3rd N. M. Mtd. Inf., Farrier, 6 mos., 1861-62.
Galliger, Bernard, Co. I, 1st N. M. Inf., N. O.
Gallegos, Pablo, Baca's Co., Perea's Batt'n, N. M. Mil. Inf., 3 mos., 1861-62.
Gallegos, Feliz, Co. B, 1st N. M. Inf.
Gallegos, Doroteo, Co. K, 2nd N. M. Inf.
Gallegos, Francisco, Co. B, 1st N. M. Inf.
Gallegos, Juan, Co. G, 1st N. M. Inf.
Gallegos, Bicente, Co. F, 1st N. M. Cav.
Gallegos, Luis, Co. A, Batt'n N. M. Vols., 1866-67, Q. M. Sgt.
Gallegos, Melquiades, Co. C, Batt'n N. M. Vols., 1866-67.

Gallegos, Pedro Jose, Co. C, 4th N. M. Inf.
Gallegos, Albino, Co. E, 3rd N. M. Mtd. Inf., 6 mos., 1861-62.
Gallegos, Andres, Co. E, 3rd N. M. Mtd. Inf., 6 mos., 1861-62.
Gallegos, Antonio A., Co. K, 1st N. M. Inf.
Gallegos, Antonio Domingo, Co. M, 1st N. M. Cav.
Gallegos, Atenacio, Co. A, 1st N. M. Inf., O. O.
Gallegos, Cacio, Co. H, 3rd N. M. Mtd. Inf., 6 mos., 1861-62., Corp.
Gallegos, Dolores, Co. E, 3rd N. M. Mtd., Inf., Sgt.
Gallegos, Doroteo, Co. K, 2nd N. M. Inf.
Gallegos, Felipe, Co. C, 1st N. M. Inf.
Gallegos, Gregorio, Co. C, 1st N. M. Inf., N. O.
Gallegos, Guadalupe, Co. K, 3rd N. M. Mtd. Inf., 6 mos., 1861-62.
Gallegos, Isidro Antonio, Co. F, 1st N. M. Mil. Inf., 3 mos., 1861-62.
Gallegos, Jose, 1st, Jaramillo's Co., Perea's Batt'n, N. M. Mil. Inf., 3 mos., 1861-62.
Gallegos, Jose, 2nd, Jaramillo's Co., Perea's Batt'n, N. M. Mil. Inf., 3 mos., 1861-62; Co. E, 2nd N. M. Inf., Sgt.
Gallegos, Jose Manuel, Co. C, 1st N. M. Inf.
Gallegos, Jose Rafael, Co. D, 2nd N. M. Inf.
Gallegos, Jose Ramos, Co. K, 3rd N. M. Mtd. Inf., 6 mos., 1861-62.
Gallegos, Juan, Montoya's Co., Perea's Batt'n, N. M. Mil. Inf., 6 mos., 1861-62.
Gallegos, Juan, Co. F, 1st N. M. Mil. Inf., 3 mos., 1861.
Gallegos, Julian, Montoya's Co., Perea's Batt'n, N. M. Mil. Inf., 6 mos., 1861-62.
Gallegos, Luis, Hubbell's Co., Perea's Batt'n, N. M. Mil. Inf., 3 mos., 1861-62.
Gallegos, Lucas, Co. D, 2nd N. M. Inf., Musician.
Gallegos, Luis Maria, Co. C, 1st N. M. Cav.
Gallegos, Manuel, Co. B, 2nd N. M. Inf.
Gallegos, Martin, Graydon's Independent Co., N. M. Mtd. Vols., 3 mos., 1861-62.
Gallegos, Miguel, Jaramillo's Co., Perea's Batt'n, N. M. Mil. Inf., 3 mos., 1861-62.
Gallegos, Nestor, Co. F-B, 2nd N. M. Inf.
Gallegos, Pedro, Co. F, 1st N. M. Cav.
Gallegos, Pedro Jose, Co. C, 4th N. M. Cav.
Gallegos, Pedro Maria, Co. C, 1st N. M. Inf., N. O.
Gallegos, Prudencio, Co. F, 1st N. M. Inf.
Gallegos, Ramon, Co. M, 1st N. M. Cav.; Co. C, 1st N. M. Militia Inf., 3 mos., 1861-62.
Gallegos, Santiago, Co. G, 3rd N. M. Mtd. Inf., 3 mos., 1861-62.
Gallegos, Lino, Co. I, 1st N. M. Inf., O. O.
Gallegos, Agapito, Co. F, 4th N. M. Inf.
Gallegos, Atanacio, Co. A, 1st N. M. Inf., O. O.
Gallegos, Basilio, Co. D, 1st N. M. Inf., O. O.
Gallegos, Blas, Vigil's Independent Co., N. M. Mtd. Vols., 3 mos., 1861-62.
Gallegos, Canuto, Co. A, 1st N. M. Inf.
Gallegos, Dolore, Co. E, 2nd N. M. Inf.
Gallegos, Donaciano, Alarid's Independent Co., N. M. Mil. Inf., 3 mos., 1861-62.
Gallegos, Felix, Mink's Independent Co., N. M. Mtd. Vols., 3 mos., 1861.
Gallegos, Gabriel, Co. E, 1st N. M. Inf., O. O.
Gallegos, Gavino, Co. E-D, 4th N. M. Inf.
Gallegos, Gregorio, Co. D, 3rd N. M. Mtd. Inf., 3 mos., 1861; Co. D, 1st N. M. Inf.
Gallegos, Guadalupe, Co. K, 3rd N. M. Mtd. Inf., 6 mos., 1861-62.
Gallegos, Ignacio, Vigil's Independent Co., N. M. Mtd. Vols., 3 mos., 1861.
Gallegos, Isidro, Co. D, 1st N. M. Inf., O. O.

Gallegos, Jacinto, Co. D, 2nd N. M. Mtd. Inf.
Gallegos, Jesus, Co. H, 3rd N. M. Mtd. Inf., 6 mos., 1861-62.
Gallegos, Jose, Baca's Co., Perea's Batt'n, N. M. Mil. Inf., 3 mos., 1861-62.
Gallegos, Jose Andres, Co. D, 4th N. M. Inf.
Gallegos, Jose Angel, Co. D, 1st N. M. Inf., O. O.
Gallegos, Jose B. Martin y, Vigil's Independent Co., N. M. Mtd., Vols., 3 mos., 1861-62.
Gallegos, Jose Bruno, Co. D, 1st N. M. Mil. Inf., 3 mos., 1861.
Gallegos, Jose Desiderio, Co. E, 1st N. M. Cav.
Gallegos, Jose Francisco, Co. D, 3rd N. M. Mtd. Inf., 6 mos., 1861-62, Colonel.
Gallegos, Jose Jacinto, Duran's Co., N. M. Militia.
Gallegos, Jose Maria, Co. C, 1st N. M. Inf., O. O.
Gallegos, Nestor, Co. C, Batt'n N. M. Vols., 1866-67.
Gallegos, Nicolas, Co. C, 2nd N. M. Inf.
Gallegos, Pablo, Co. G, 3rd N. M. Mtd., Inf., 6 mos., 1861-62.
Gallegos, Pascual, Aragon's Co., Perea's Batt'n, N. M. Mil. Inf., 3 mos., 1861-62.
Gallegos, Polito, Co. D, 3rd N. M. Mtd. Inf., O. O.
Gallegos, Prudencio, Co. G, 1st N. M. Inf.
Gallegos, Juan Nepumeceno, Co. G, 1st N. M. Inf.
Gallegos, Juan Pablo, Co. H, 1st N. M. Inf.
Gallegos, Julian, Montoya's Co., Perea's Batt'n, N. M. Mtd. Vols., 1861-62, 3 mos.
Gallegos, Marcelino, Romero's Independent Co. A, N. M. Mil. Inf., 3 mos., 1861-62, Corp.
Gallegos, Marcos, Co. E, 2nd N. M. Inf.
Gallegos, Nofrio, Co. F, 3rd N. M. Mtd. Inf., 3 mos., 1861-62.
Gallegos, Rafael, Co. G, 3rd N. M. Mtd. Inf., 6 mos., 1861-62.
Gallegos, Roman, Co. D, 1st N. M. Inf., O. O.
Gallegos, Limio, Co. I, 2nd N. M. Cav.
Gallegos, Timoteo, Montoya's Co., Perea's Batt'n, N. M. Mil. Inf., 6 mos., 1861-62.
Gallegos, Tomas, Gonzolez Co., N. M. Mil., 3 mos., 1861.
Gallegos, Ysidro, Co. B. 4th N. M. Inf.
Galligan, Peter, Co. C, 4th N. M. Inf.
Gamboa, Jesus, Co. D, 2nd N. M. Inf.
Ganten, Henry, Co. H, 1st N. M. Inf., O. O.
Gonzolez Desiderio Co. I 1st N. M. Cav.
Gonzolez, Eligio, Co. B, 1st N. M. Inf.
Gonzolez, Jose Ignacio, Co. I, 1st N. M. Inf., O. O.
Gonzolez, Santos, Co. D, 1st N. M. Cav.
Guanes, Juan Pablo, Co. M, 1st N. M. Cav.
Garcia, Abran, Co. A, 1st N. M. Cav.
Garcia, Ildefonso, Co. B, 1st N. M. Inf.
Garcia, Alejandro, Co. E, 1st N. M. Cav.
Garcia, Albino, Hubbell's Co., Perea's Batt'n, N. M. Mil. Inf., 6 mos., 1861-62; Co. D, 1st N. M. Inf., Corp.
Garcia, Ambrosio, Co. H, 1st N. M. Inf., N. O.
Garcia, Atanacio, Co. C, 1st N. M. Mil. Inf., 3 mos., 1861-62; Co. J, 3rd N. M. Inf., Corp.
Garcia, Atanacio, Co. G, 3rd N. M. Mtd. Inf., 6 mos., 1861-62.
Garcia, Andres, Baca's Co., Perea's Batt'n, N. M. Mil. Inf., 3 mos., 1861-62; Co. A, 1st N. M. Inf., N. O.
Garcia, Antonio Andres, Co. D, 1st N. M. Mil. Inf., 3 mos., 1861-62.
Garcia, Anistacio, Co. A, 4th N. M. Inf., and 1st N. M. Cav.
Garcia, Antonio (1st), Montoya's Co., Perea's Batt'n, N. M. Mtd. Inf., 3 mos., 1861-62.
Garcia, Antonio (2nd), Montoya's Co., Perea's Batt'n, N. M. Mtd. Inf., 3 mos., 1861-62.
Garcia, Antonio Abran, Co. H, 1st N. M. Inf., O. O.

Garcia, Antonio Jose, Co. B, 1st N. M. Inf., O. O., and 1st N. M. Cav., and 2nd N. M. Inf.; Co. B, 3rd N. M. Mtd. Inf., 6 mos, 1861-62; Duran's Co, N. M. Mil., Sgt.
Garcia, Adan, Co. F, 1st N. M. Cav.
Garcia, Bernardo, Co. C, Batt'n N. M. Vols., 1866-67.
Garcia, Bidal, Co. C, 1st N. M. Inf., N. O.
Garcia, Bictor, Co. D, 2nd N. M. Inf., Sgt.
Garcia, Candelario, Co. E, 2nd N. M. Inf., 1st Lieut.
Garcia, Catalino, Co. K, 1st N. M. Cav., Co. C, 4th N. M. Inf.
Garcia, Cecilio, Tafoya's Independent Co., N. M., Militia Inf., 3 mos.,
Garcia, Cleto, Del Balle's Co., Perea's Batt'n, N. M. Mil. Inf., 3 mos., 1861-62.
Garcia, Cornelio, Co. F, 1st N. M. Inf., N. O.
Garcia, Crespin, Co. D, 3rd N. M. Mtd. Inf., 6 mos., 1861-62.
Garcia, Desiderio, Co. C, 1st N. M. Inf., N. O.; Co. B, 1st N. M. Mil. Inf., 3 mos., 1861-62.
Garcia, Demetrio, Montoya's Co., Berea's Batt'n, N. M. Mil. Inf., 3 mos., 1861-62.
Garcia, Diego, Co. B, 1st N. M. Cav.
Garcia, Dolores, Co. A, 1st N. M. Cav.
Garcia, Domingo, Graydon's Independent Co., N. M. Mtd. Vols., 3 mos., 1861-62, 1st Sgt.
Garcia, Domingo, Perea's Batt'n, N. M. Mil. Inf., Montoya's Co., 3 mos., 1861-62; Co. C, 1st N. M. Cav.
Garcia, Felix, Co. F, 1st N. M. Cav.
Garcia, Felipe, Alarid's Co., N. M. Mil. Inf., 3 mos., 1861-62.
Garcia, Felipe, Hubbell's Co., Perea's Batt'n, N. M. Mil. Inf., 3 mos., 1861-62; Co. H, 1st N. M. Cav. and Co. A, 5th N. M. Inf.
Garcia, Feliz Andres, Co. E, 1st N. M. Mil. Inf., 3 mos., 1861-62.
Garcia, Fernandez, Graydon's Independent Co., N. M. Mtd. Vols., 3 mos., 1861-62.
Garcia, Francisco, Romero's Independent Co. A, N. M. Mil. Co., 3 mos., 1861-62; Co. B, 1st N. M. Cav.; Co. F, B, 2nd N. M. Inf.; Co. C, 4th N. M. Inf.; Co. B, 5th N. M. Inf.
Garcia, Francisco Antonio, Del Balle's Co., Perea's Batt'n, N. M. Mil. Inf., 3 mos., 1861-62.
Garcia, Genero, Montoya's Co., Perea's Batt'n, N. M. Mil. Inf., 3 mos., 1861-62.
Garcia, German, Co. K-E, 3rd N. M. Mtd. Inf., 6 mos., 1861-62.
Garcia, Guadalupe, 1st N. M. Mil., Sena's Co. A, 2 mos., 1862.
Garcia, Guadalupe (1st), Co. A, 1st N. M. Mil. Inf., 3 mos., 1861-62, Corp.
Garcia, Guadalupe (2nd), Co. B, 1st N. M. Mil. Inf., 3 mos., 1861-62.
Garcia, Ildefonso, Co. B, 5th N. M. Inf.
Garcia, Inocencio, Co. A, 4th N. M. Inf. and Co. F, 1st N. M. Cav.
Garcia, Jacinto, Simpson's Independent Co., N. M. Mounted Spies and Guides.
Garcia, Jesus, Co. B, Batt'n N. M. Vols., 1866-67; Graydon's Independent Co., N. M. Mtd. Vols., 3 mos., 1861-62; Co. C, 1st N. M. Cav. and Co. C, 4th N. M. Inf.
Garcia, Jesus Maria Chavez y, Co. B-A, 2nd N. M. Inf. and Co. B, 5th N. M. Inf.
Garcia, Jose J., Co. G, 3rd N. M. Mtd. Inf., 6 mos., 1861-62; Co. D, 1st N. M. Inf., O. O.; Co. G, 2nd N. M. Inf.
Garcia, Jose Tafoya's Independent Co., N. M. Mil., 3 mos., 1861-62.
Garcia, Jose Antonio, Co. F, 1st N. M. Mil. Inf., 3 mos., 1861-62.
Garcia, Jose de Jesus, Co. D, 2nd N. M. Inf.; Co. C, 3rd N. M. Mtd. Inf., 6 mos., 1861-62.
Garcia, Jose de la Luz, Alarid's Independent Co., N. M. Mil. Inf., 3 mos., 1861-62.
Garcia, Jose Dolores, Co. I, 3rd N. M. Mtd. Inf., 6 mos., 1861-62; Co. L, 1st N. M. Cav.

Garcia, Jose Guadalupe, Co. C, 1st N. M. Cav., Co. A, Batt'n, N. M. Vols., Co. A, 1866-67.
Garcia, Jose Manuel, Jaramillo's Co., Perea's Batt'n, N. M. Mil. Inf., 3 mos., 1861-62.
Garcia, Jose Manuel, 1st N. M. Mil. Inf., 3 mos., 1861-62.
Garcia, Jose Pablo, Co. I, 1st N. M. Inf., O. O., Corp.
Garcia, Jose Prudencio, Co. F, 1st N. M. Cav., Sgt.
Garcia, Jose Rafael, Co. F, 1st N. M. Cav. and Co. A, 4th N. M. Inf., Bugler.
Garcia, Jose Ramon, Co. C, 1st N. M. Cav. and Co. A, 2nd N. M. Inf.
Garcia, Jose Seferino, Co. C, 1st N. M. Cav.
Garcia, Juan Alarid's Independent Co., N. M. Mil. Inf., 3 mos., 1861-62.
Garcia, Juan, Hubbell's Independent Co., N. M. Mtd. Vols., 3 mos., 1861.
Garcia, Juan, Baca's Co., Perea's Batt'n, N. M. Mil. Inf., 3 mos., 1861-62.
Garcia, Juan, Jaramillo's Co., Perea's Batt'n, N. M. Mil. Inf., 3 mos., 1861-62.
Garcia, Juan, Tafoya's Co., N. M. Mil., 3 mos., 1861-62.
Garcia, Juan Cristobal, Co. D, 3rd N. M, Mtd. Inf., 6 mos., 1861-62.
Garcia, Juan de Dios, Co. D, N. M. Mil. Inf., 3 mos., 1861-62.
Garcia, Juan Jesus, Co. B, 1st N. M. Cav.; Co. D, 1st N. M. Mil. Inf., 3 mos., 1861-62.
Garcia, Juan Jose, Graydon's Independent Co., N. M. Mtd. Vols., 3 mos., 1861-62.
Garcia, Juan Jose, Aragon's Co., Perea's Batt'n, N. M. Mil. Inf., 3 mos., 1861-62.
Garcia, Juan Pablo, Co. E, 3rd N. M. Mtd. Inf., 6 mos., 1861-62.
Garcia, Julio, Co. H, 3rd N. M. Mtd. Inf., 6 mos., 1861-62.
Garcia, Lorenzo (1st), Co. B, 1st N. M. Cav.
Garcia, Lorenzo (2nd), Co. B, 1st N. M. Cav. and Co. I, D, 2nd N. M. Inf.
Garcia, Luciano, Romero's Co., A, N. M. Mil. Inf., 3 mos., 1861-62.
Garcia, Luis, Gonzolez Independent Co., 1861, 3 mos.
Garcia, Luis, Jaramillo's Co., Perea's Batt'n, N. M. Mil. Inf., 3 mos., 1861-62.
Garcia, Manuel Jaramillo's Co., Perea's Batt'n, N. M. Mil. Inf., 3 mos., 1861-62; Co. D, Batt'n N. M. Vols., 1866-67, Corp.
Garcia, Manuel, Del Balle's Co., Perea's Batt'n, N. M. Mil. Inf., 3 mos., 1861-62, Corp.
Garcia, Marcelino, Co. K, 1st N. M. Cav.
Garcia, Margarito, Co. G, 2nd N. M. Inf.
Garcia, Merigeldo, Gonzolez Co., N. M. Militia, 3 mos., 1861-62.
Garcia, Miguel, Jaramillo's Co., Perea's Batt'n, N. M. Mil. Inf., 3 mos., 1861-62.
Garcia, Miguel, Aragon's Co., Perea's Batt'n, N. M. Mil. Inf., 3 mos., 1861-62.
Garcia, Meliton, Co. K, 1st N. M. Inf., and Co. F, 4th N. M. Inf.
Garcia, Narciso, Co. L, 3rd N. M. Mtd. Inf., 6 mos., 1861-62, Corp.
Garcia, Nepomoceno, Co. B-C, 4th N. M. Inf.
Garcia, Nestor, Co. B, 1st N. M. Inf., N. O.
Garcia, Nivian, Tafoya's Independent Co., N. M. Mil. Inf., 3 mos., 1861-62.
Garcia, Ologio, Co. M, 1st N. M. Cav.
Garcia, Pablo, Jaramillo's Co., Perea's Batt'n, N. M. Mil. Inf., 3 mos., 1861-62.
Garcia, Pedro Antonio, Vigil's Independent Co., N. M. Mtd. Vols., 3 mos., 1861-62.
Garcia, Ramon, Co. C, Batt'n N. M. Vols., 1866-67.
Garcia, Reyes, Co. K, 1st N. M. Inf., N. O.
Garcia, Arcardo, Co. F, 1st N. M. Inf., N. O.

Garcia, Romualdo, Co. G, 2nd N. M. Inf.
Garcia, Romo, Alarid's Independent Co., N. M. Mil. Inf., 3 mos., 1861-62.
Garcia, Romolo, Co. F, 1st N. M. Inf., N. O.
Garcia, Santiago, 3rd N. M. Mtd. Inf., 6 mos., 1861-62, Lieut.
Garcia, Santos, Montoya's Co., Perea's Batt'n, N. M. Mil. Inf., 3 mos., 1861-62.
Garcia, Simon, Alarid's Independent Co., N. M. Mil. Inf., 3 mos., 1861-62; Co. F, 1st N. M. Cav.
Garcia, Sotero, Co. E, 1st N. M. Cav.
Garcia, Susito, Simpson's Independent Co., N. M. Mtd. Spies and Guides.
Garcia, Tomas, Hubbell's Co., Perea's Batt'n, N. M. Mil. Inf., 3 mos., 1861-62.
Garcia, Timoteo, Graydon's Independent Co., N. M. Mtd. Vols., 1861-62.
Garcia, Toribio, Co. D, 1st N. M. Mil. Inf., 3 mos., 1861-62.
Garcia, Vicente, Co. L, 3rd N. M. Mtd. Inf., 6 mos., 1861-62.
Garcia, Victor, 3rd N. M. Mtd. Inf., 6 mos., 1861-62, Lieut.
Garcia, Jesus Luis, Co. D, 1st N. M. Inf., N. O.
Gordonio, Jesus, Co. M, 1st N. M. Cav., Recruit.
Gardino, Antonio, Albino, Co. K, 1st N. M. Inf., Corp., O. O.
Garella, Jose—See Gurule.
Garcia, Macario, Co. B, 5th N. M. Inf.
Garamillo (Jaramillo), Matias, Co. D, 2nd N. M. Inf., Sgt.
Garza, Salome, Co. H, 1st N. M. Inf., N. O.
Gurule, Antonio A., Co. E, 1st N. M. Inf., O. O.
Gurule, Casimiro, Co. D, Batt'n N. M. Vols., 1866-67.
Gurule, Juan, Montoya's Co., Berea's Batt'n, N. M. Mil. Inf., 3 mos., 1861-62.
Gurule, Pablo Antonio, Co. C, 1st N. M. Cav.
Gurule, Jose Maria, Co. C, 1st N. M. Cav.
Gannes, Juan Pablo, Co. M, 1st N. M. Cav.
Ganna, Rafael, Co. F, 1st N. M. Mil. Inf., 3 mos., 1861-62.
Gaus, Gottfield, Co. B, 3rd N. M. Mtd. Inf., Hosp. Steward
Gayelachowski, Alexander, Co. F-J, 2nd N. M. Inf., Chaplain
Gonzolez, Jose M., Co. K, 1st N. M. Inf., N. O.
Gonzolez, Guadalupe, Co. K, 1st N. M. Inf., N. O.
Gerote (Gurule), Ternino, Graydon's Independent Co., N. M. Mtd. Vols., 3 mos., 1861-62.
Giallo, Jose C., Gonzolez Independent Co., N. M. Mil., 3 mos., 1861.
Gilbert, Henry W., Co. A, 1st New Mexico Cav., 1st Lieut.
Gillegros (Gallegos), Neston, Co. D, 1st N. M. Cav.
Giminez (Jiminez), Manuel, Co. F, 1st N. M. Mil., 3 mos., 1861-62, Captain.
Gorgobia, Turnio, Co. H, 1st N. M. Cav., Sgt.
Giron, Bictor, Co. A, 4th N. M. Inf.
Giron, Francisco, Baca's Co., Perea's Batt'n, N. M. Mil. Inf., 3 mos., 1861-62.
Giron, Jesus, Co. K-D, 2nd N. M. Inf., Corp.
Giron, Jose Alejo, Tafoya's Independent Co., N. M. Mil., 3 mos., 1861-62.
Giron, Jose de Jesus, Co. E, D, 1st N. M. Inf., O. O.
Giron, Pablo, Co. A, 1st N. M. Inf., N. O.
Glancy, Thomas, Co. K, 1st N. M. Inf., N. O., Lieut.
Glazer, Jose Andres—See Salazar.
Glenn, John, Co. M, 1st N. M. Cav.
Glenn, James, Co. G, 1st N. M. Cav.
McCarthy, Michael, Co. D, 1st N. M. Inf., N. O.
Galbadon, Michael, Graydon's Independent Co., N. M. Mtd. Vols., 3 mos., 1861-62, Corp.

Gold, Moses A., Baca's Co., Perea's Batt'n, N. M. Mil. Inf., 3 mos., 1861-62, Sgt.
Gonzolez, Anicleto, Duran's Co., N. M. Mil.
Gomez, Agapito, Co. I, 1st N. M. Inf., Corp.
Gomez, Alvino, Co. D, 1st N. M. Cav.
Gomez, Anastacio, Duran's Co., N. M. Mil.
Gomez, Antonio, Co. M, 1st N. M. Cav.; also Duran's Co., 1st N. M. Mil.
Gomez, Desiderio, Duran's Co., N. M. Mil., Corp.
Gomez, Felipe, Vigil's Independent Co., N. M. Mtd. Vols., 3 mos., 1861.
Gomez, Francisco, Co. I-D, 2nd N. M. Inf.
Gomez, Gregorio, Duran's Co., N. M. Mil.
Gomez, Gertrudis, Co. H, D, 2nd N. M. Inf.
Gomez, Jesus, Jose H, Co. F, 1st N. M. Cav.
Gomez, Jose Gregorio, Mink's Independent Co., N. M. Mtd. Vols., 3 mos., 1861-62, Corp.
Gomez, Juan, Co. C, 3rd N. M. Mtd. Vols., 6 mos., 1861-62.
Gomez, Juan de Dios, Co. F, 1st N. M. Cav. and Duran's Co., N. M. Mil.
Gomez, Juan Domingo, Co. D, 1st N. M. Cav.
Gomez, Juan Jose, Co. F, 1st N. M. Cav.
Gomez, Lorenzo, Co. I, 1st N. M. Inf.
Gomez, Manuel Antonio, Co. C, 1st N. M. Cav.
Gomez, Pedro, Co. D, 1st N. M. Inf., 3 mos., 1861-62.
Gomez, Santiago, Duran's Co., N. M. Mil.
Gomez, Zenobio, Hubbell's Co., Perea's Batt'n, N. M. Mil. Inf., 3 mos., 1861-62.
Gomez, Bicente, Co. F, 1st N. M. Mil. Inf., 3 mos., 1861-62.
Gomez, Miguel, Alarid's Independent Co., N. M. Mil. Inf., 3 mos., 1861-62.
Gomez, Ramon, Co. F, 1st N. M. Cav.
Gomez, Rafael, Co. F, 1st N. M. Inf., N. O.
Gonzolez, Jose Santos, Co. D, 1st N. M. Cav.
Gonzolez, Antonio, Co. G, 1st N. M. Inf., Corp.
Gonzolez, Ambrosio, Co. G, 1st N. M. Inf.
Gonzolez, Basilio, Co. B, 5th N. M. Inf.
Gonzolez, Binino, Co. D, 1st N. M. Cav.
Gonzolez, Bicente, Co. D, 1st N. M. Cav., Corp.
Gonzolez, Claudio de Jesus, Co. B, 1st N. M. Mil. Inf., 3 mos., 1861-62.
Gonzolez, Desiderio, Co. H, 1st N. M. Inf., O. O.
Gonzolez, Diego, Co. D, H, 1st N. M. Inf., O. O.
Gonzolez, Donaciano, Co. D, 4th N. M. Inf.
Gonzolez, Eligio, Co. A, 1st N. M. Inf.
Gonzolez, Encarnacion, Co. I, 1st N. M. Inf.
Gonzolez, Esquipula, Co. B, 1st N. M. Inf., 3 mos., 1861-62.
Gonzolez, Eugenio, Co. H, 1st N. M. Cav.
Gonzolez, Teodocio, Mink's Independent Co., 1st N. M. Mtd., Vols., 3 mos., 1861.
Gonzolez, Felipe, Co. L, 3rd N. M. Mtd. Inf., 6 mos., 1861-62.
Gonzolez, Francisco, Del Balle's Co., Perea's Batt'n, N. M. Mil. Inf., 3 mos., 1861-62.
Gonzolez, Francisco, Simpson's Independent Co., N. M. Mtd., Spies and Guides.
Gonzolez, Hilario, Co. A, 1st N. M. Inf., 3 mos., 1861-62, Sgt.
Gonzolez, Gregorio, Gonzolez Independent Co., N. M. Mil., 3 mos., 1861.
Gonzolez, Guadalupe, 1st N. M. Mil., Sena's Co. A, 2 mos., 1862.
Gonzolez, Higinio V., Co. I, 1st N. M. Cav.
Gonzolez, Ignacio, Co. H, 1st N. M. Inf., N. O.
Gonzolez, Encarnacion, Co. D, 1st N. M. Inf., N. O.

Gonzolez, Jesus, Graydon's Independent Co., N. M. Mtd. Vols., 3 mos., 1861-62.
Gonzolez, Jose M., Graydon's Independent Co., N. M. Mtd. Vols., 3 mos., 1861-62.
Gonzolez, Jose Miguel, Romero's Independent Co. A, 1st N. M. Mil. Inf., 3 mos., 1861-62.
Gonzolez, Jose (1st), Co. F, 1st N. M. Cav.
Gonzolez, Jose (2nd), Co. F, 1st N. M. Cav.
Gonzolez, Jose Alcario, Co. F, 1st N. M. Mil. Inf., 3 mos., 1861-62.
Gonzolez, Jose Amador, Co. H, 3rd N. M. Mtd. Inf., 6 mos., 1861-62.
Gonzolez, Jose Aniceto, Co. E, 2nd N. M. Inf.
Gonzolez, Jose de Jesus, Co. D, Batt'n, N. M. Vols., 1866-67.
Gonzolez, Jose de la Cruz, Gonzolez Independent Co., N. M. Mil. Co., 1861, 3 mos.
Gonzolez, Jose Dolores, Co. E, 1st N. M. Mil. Inf., 3 mos., 1861-62.
Gonzolez, Jose Escularia, Gonzolez Independent Co., N. M. Mil., 3 mos., 1861.
Gonzolez, Jose Ignacio, Co. K, 1st N. M. Inf., N. O.
Gonzolez, Jose Ildefonso, Co. K, 3rd N. M. Mtd. Inf., 6 mos., 1861-62.
Gonzolez, Jose Leon, Co. F, 1st N. M. Cav.
Gonzolez, Jose Manuel, Co. E, 1st N. M. Cav.
Gonzolez, Jose Maria, Co. A, 2nd N. M. Inf.
Gonzolez, Jose Refugio, Co. L, 1st N. M. Cav.
Gonzolez, Juan, Gonzolez Independent Co., N. M. Mil. Inf., 3 mos., 1861, Corp.
Gonzolez, Juan, Montoya's Co., Berea's Batt'n, N. M. Mil. Inf., 3 mos., 1861-62.
Gonzolez, Juan, Romero's Independent Co. A, 1st N. M. Mil. Inf., 3 mos., 1861-62.
Gonzolez, Juan de Dios, Mink's Independent Co., N. M. Mtd. Vols., 3 mos., 1861.
Gonzolez, Juan Esteban, Romero's Independent Co. A, N. M. Mil., 3 mos., 1861-62.
Gonzolez, Juan Manuel, Mink's Independent Co., N. M. Mtd. Vols., 3 mos., 1861.
Gonzolez, Juan Lorenzo, Co. F, D, 4th N. M. Inf.
Gonzolez, Loretto, Co. D, 1st N. M. Inf., N. O.
Gonzolez, Luis, 3rd N. M. Mtd. Inf., 6 mos., 1861-62.
Gonzolez, Manuel, Co. D, B, 2nd N. M. Inf.
Gonzolez, Marcelino, Co. E, 1st N. M. Cav., 1st Sgt.; Alarid's Independent Co., N. M. Mil. Inf., 3 mos., 1861-62.
Gonzolez, Marcos, Alarid's Independent Co., N. M. Mil. Inf., 3 mos., 1861-62.
Gonzolez, Marcos, Romero's Independent Co., A, N. M. Mil. Inf., 3 mos., 1861-62.
Gonzolez, Matias, Co. L, 1st N. M. Cav.
Gonzolez, Miguel Antonio, Co. B, 1st N. M. Cav., Corp.
Gonzolez, Anastacio, Co. E, 1st N. M. Cav.
Gonzolez, Nestor, Gonzolez Independent Co., N. M. Mil., 3 mos., 1861, Captain.
Gonzolez, Nicanor, Gonzolez Independent Co., N. M. Mil., 3 mos., 1861.
Gonzolez, Nieves, Co. C, 1st N. M. Inf., N. O.

Herramanus, Jose Pablo, Co. K, 1st N. M. Cav., Bugler.
Hammel, Alois, Co. G, K, 1st N. M. Cav., Bugler.

Jaramillo, Eluterio, Co. H, 3rd N. M. Mtd. Inf., 6 mos., 1861-62.
Jaramillo, Pablo, Co. G, 3rd N. M. Mtd. Inf., 6 mos., 1861-62.
Jaramillo, Ramon, Co. G, 3rd N. M. Mtd. Inf., 6 mos., 1861-62.
Jaramillo, Santiago, Co. E, 2nd N. M. Inf.
Harder, Frank, Co. C, H, 1st N. M. Inf., N. O., Captain.

Hardison, Charles, Co. G, 1st N. M. Cav., Sgt.
Hargus, Simpson, Co. M, 1st N. M. Cav.
Jaramillo, Mauricio, Co. K, 2nd N. M. Inf.
Jaramillo, Loreto, Co. K, 2nd N. M. Inf.
Harker, John L., Co. D, E, 1st N. M. Inf., O. O.
Harvey, William A., Co. I, 1st N. M. Cav.
Harrin, John, Co. M, 1st N. M. Cav., 1st Sgt.
Harris, George, Co. E, D, 4th N. M. Inf.
Harris, James, Co. K, 1st N. M. Cav.
Harrison, Henry, Co. L, K, 1st N. M. Cav., Sgt.
Harrison, Hezekiah, Co. C, E, 1st N. M. Inf., N. O., 2nd Lt.
Harton, Charles, Co. B, 1st N. M. Cav.
Harwin, John, Co. M, 1st N. M. Cav.
Hawey, Squire Henry, Co. L, M, 1st N. M. Cav., Saddler.
Hessbrook, Daniel, Co. G, 1st N. M. Cav.
Haskins, Wiley, Co. K, 1st N. M. Cav., Corp.
Hasslet, Thomas, Co. B, 1st N. M. Inf., O. O.
Hawkins, Joseph, Co. E, 1st N. M. Inf., O. O.
Hay, Yldefonso, Co. I, D, 2nd N. M. Inf., Captain.
Hayes, William, Co. M, 1st N. M. Cav., Sgt.
Hildago, Luz, Co. E, 1st N. M. Inf.
Fernandez, Luciano, Co. A, 1st N. M. Cav.
Hermosillo, Loteto, Co. G, 1st N. M. Cav.
Henderson, Addison Clark, Co. M, 1st N. M. Cav.
Henderson, Thomas, Co. B, 1st N. M. Cav., Captain.
Herrera, Florentino, Co. B, 1st N. M. Inf., N. O.
Herrera, Jesus Maria, Vigil's Independent Co., N. M. Mtd., Vols., 3 mos., 1861, 1st Sgt.
Herrera, Santiago, Co. B, 1st N. M. Inf.
Herrera, Vicente, Co. B, 1st N. M. Inf.
Herrera, Diego Antonio, Co. C, Batt'n, N. M. Vols., 1866-67.
Herrera, Luis, Co. C, Batt'n N. M. Vols., 1866-67.
Herrera, Andres, Co. B, 2nd N. M. Inf., Sgt.
Herrera, Jesus, Co. D, 1st N. M. Cav.
Herrera, Rafael, Co. B, 2nd N. M. Inf.
Herrera, Seledon, Co. B, 1st N. M. Cav.
Herrera, Vivian, Romero's Independent Co. A, N. M. Mil. Inf., 3 mos., 1861-62.
Herman, Joseph, Co. B, Batt'n N. M. Vols., 1866-67.
Herman, Paul, Co. M, 1st N. M. Cav.
Hernandez, Lauterino, Co. C, Batt'n, N. M. Vols., 1865-66.
Martinez, Hermeigildo, Co. H, 1st N. M. Inf., Corp.
Hernandez, Fabian, Co. E, G, 1st N. M. Inf.
Hernandez, Gertrudis, Co. H, 1st N. M. Inf.
Hernandez, Jesus Maria, Co. L, 3rd N. M. Mtd. Inf., 6 mos., 1861-62.
Hernandez, Jose Silvestre, Co. D, 4th N. M. Inf.
Hernandez, Marcelino, Co. F, 2nd N. M. Inf., Wagoner.
Hernandez Ramon, Co. D, 1st N. M. Cav.
Hernandez, Simon, Co. B, Batt'n N. M. Vols., 1866-67.
Hernandez, Francisco, Co. A, 5th N. M. Inf., Co. A.
Heron, Bitor, Co. A, 3rd N. M. Mtd. Inf., 6 mos., 1861-62.
Herrera, Albino, Co. A, 3rd N. M. Mtd. Inf., 6 mos., 1861-62.
Herrera, Antonio, Co. H, 1st N. M. Inf., N. O.
Herrera, Antonio, Co. A, 3rd N. M. Mtd. Inf., 6 mos., 1861-62.
Herrera, Diego Antonio, Co. B, 1st N. M. Cav.
Herrera, Joaquin, Co. H, 1st N. M. Inf., N. O., Sgt.
Herrera, Miguel Antonio, Co. A, 3rd N. M. Mtd. Inf., 6 mos., 1861-62.
Herrera, Andres, Co. B, 2nd N. M. Inf., Sgt.
Herrera, Amador, Co. F, 1st N. M. Mil. Inf., 3 mos., 1861-62.
Herrera, Concepcion, Co. D, 1st N. M. Mil. Inf., 3 mos., 1861-62.
Herrera, Duardo, Co. F, 1st N. M. Mil. Inf., 3 mos., 1861-62.
Herrera, Felipe de, Co. A, 1st N. M. Mil. Inf., 3 mos., 1861-62.

Herrera, Florentin, Co. B, 1st N. M. Inf., N. O.
Herrera, Francisco de, Co. B, 1st N. M. Mil. Inf., 3 mos., 1861-62.
Herrera, Gabriel, Co. K, 1st N. M. Inf., N. O.
Herrera, Ignacio, Co. G, 3rd N. M. Mtd., Inf., 6 mos., 1861-62.
Herrera, Jesus, Co. F, B, 2nd N. M. Inf.
Herrera, Jose Santos, Co. A, 1st N. M. Cav.
Herrera, Juan Antonio, Vigil's Independent Co., N. M. Mtd. Vols., 3 mos., 1861.
Herrera, Juan Bautista, Co. B, 1st N. M. Mil. Inf., 3 mos., 1861-62.
Herrera, Juan Jose, Co. A, 3rd N. M. Mtd. Inf., 6 mos., 1861-62.
Herrera, Juan Pablo, Co. E, 1st N. M. Mil. Inf., 3 mos., 1861-62.
Herrera, Luis, Co. C, Batt'n, N. M. Vols., 1866-67.
Herrera, Manuel, Romero's Independent Co. A, N. M. Mil. Inf., 3 mos., 1861-62.
Herrera, Marcelino, Co. C, 1st N. M. Inf., N. O.; Alarid's Independent Co., N. M. Mil. Inf., 3 mos., 1861-62.
Herrera, Marcos, Romero's Independent Co. A, N. M. Mil. Inf., 3 mos., 1861-62, Corp.
Herrera, Pablo, Co. G, 1st N. M. Inf., N. O.
Herrera, Paulino, Co. C, 1st N. M. Cav.
Herrera, Rafael, Co. D, E, 1st N. M. Inf., O. O.
Herrera, Santiago, Co. B, C, 1st N. M. Inf., N. O.
Herrera, Seledon, Co. D, 1st N. M. Cav.
Herrera, Teodoro, Co. G, 1st N. M. Inf., N. O.
Herrera, Vicente, Co. B, 1st N. M. Inf., N. O.
Herrera, Vivian, Romero's Independent Co. A, N. M. Mil. Inf., 3 mos., 1861-62.
Hildago, Guadalupe, Co. A, 1st N. M. Cav., Corp.
Hildago, Jose B., Co. F, 1st N. M. Cav.
Hildago, Jose Leon, Co. A, 1st N. M. Inf., O. O.
Hildago, Luz, Co. E, 1st N. M. Inf., N. O.
Hill, Ruben A., Co. K, 1st N. M. Inf., N. O., Captain.
Hill, Thomas W., Co. C, 1st N. M. Cav.
Hilton, Albert, Co. M., 1st N. M. Cav.
Henchley, William S., Co. K, 1st N. M. Cav., Com. Sgt.
Hinojioso, Juan, Co. A, E, 3rd N. M. Mtd. Inf., 6 mos., 1861-62.
Hirsch, William, Co. D, 1st N. M. Mil. Inf., 3 mos., 1861-62, 2nd Lt.
Hirsch, Wm. H. P., Co. K, E, B, C, 1st N. M. Inf., O. O., Wagoner.
Hodt, Nicolas, Co. C, D, B, 1st N. M. Cav., Captain.
Hodge, Andrew, Co. K, D, 1st N. M. Inf., N. O., 1st Sgt.
Holford, Hannibal, Simpson's Independent Co., N. M. Mtd. Spies and Guides, 1st Lt.
Holibos, Apariso, Co. E, 1st N. M. Inf.
Holmes, Henry M., Co. A, 1st N. M. Cav., 2nd. Lt.
Holmes, Michael, Co. E, 1st N. M. Inf., O. O.
Hohmes. Thomas, Co. K, F, G, 1st N. M. Cav., 1st Lt.
Honey, Thomas, Co. K, 1st N. M. Cav. and Co. D, 4th N. M. Inf.
Hinojiod, Juan, Co. A, 3rd N. M. Mtd. Inf., 6 mos., 1861-62
Hopping, Charles, Co. F, 1st N. M. Cav., Musician 1st Class.
Howard, W. H., Co. B, 1st N. M. Cav.
Hamlett, George, Co. I, 3rd N. M. Mtd. Inf., 6 mos., 1861-62.
Hubbell, John R., Hubbell's Co., Perea's Batt'n, N. M. Mil. Inf., Captain.
Hubbell, Charles M., Hubbell's Independent Co., 3rd N. M. Mtd. Vol., 3 mos., 1861 1st Lt.; Co. H, I, 1st N. M. Cav., Captain.
Hubbell, Santiago L., Hubbell's Independent Co., N. M. Mtd. Vols., 3 mos., 1861, Captain; Co. B, 5th N. M. Inf., Captain.
Hubbell, William, Co. L, K, 1st. N. M. Cav.
Hughman, John, Co. D, Batt'n N. M. Vols., 1866-67.
Hughes, Nicolas, Co. D, 1st N. M. Inf., Corp.
Humbert, Elias, Co. E, 1st N. M. Inf., N. O.

Hunning, Henrique, Del Balle's Co., Perea's Batt'n, N. M. Mil. Inf., 3 mos., 1861-62.
Hunt, Hamilton, Co. G, 1st N. M. Cav., Corp.
Hurban (Urban), Jose, Co. L, 1st N. M. Cav.
Hurtado, Agapito, Co. D, H, 1st N. M. Inf., O. O.
Moria, Jose, Co. H, 1st N. M. Cav., Bugler.
Moria, Nicolo, Duran's Co., N. M. Mil.
Hurtado, Tomas, Co. F, 3rd N. M. Mtd. Inf., 6 mos., 1861-62.
Hult, Nicolas, Co. C, 2nd N. M. Inf., 2nd Lt.
Hoy, Ildefonso, Co. I, D, 2nd N. M. Inf.
Hyath, Ruben Henry, Co. M, 1st N. M. Cav.
Hynes, Charles, Co. I, 1st N. M. Inf., Sgt.

Ide, Ezra B., Co. F, 1st N. M. Inf., N. O.
Iliz, Dionicio, Co. B, 1st N. M. Inf., N. O.
Incinas, Luis, Co. H, 3rd N. M. Mtd. Inf., 6 mos., 1861-62.
Irwin, John, Co. G, 1st N. M. Cav., O. O.
Irwin, Robert, 1st N. M. Inf., O. O. See: U. S. Infantry list.
Isco, Cristobal, Co A, 1st N. M. Inf.
Isena, Jesus Sandoval y, Co. I, 1st N. M. Inf., O. O.

Jackson, Charles, Co. F, 1st N. M. Cav. See: U. S. Artillery List.
Jackson, William, Co. J, K, 1st N. M. Cav. See: U. S. Infantry List.
Jacobs, Henry, Co. D, E, 1st N. M. Inf., O. O., Sgt.
Jacques, Jesus, Co. A, 1st N. M. Inf.
Jaeñ, Carlos, Co. A, 2nd N. M. Inf.
Jaramillo, Jose, Co. D, Batt'n N. M. Vols., 1866-67.
Jaramillo, Manuel, Co. D, Batt'n N. M. Vols., 1866-67.
Jaramillo, Anastacio, Co. B, Batt'n N. M. Vols., 1866-67; Hubbell's Co., Perea's Batt'n, N. M. Mil. Inf., 3 mos., 1861-62.
Jaramillo, Antonio, Co. H, 2nd N. M. Inf.
Jaramillo, Jose, Co. F, 1st N. M. Mil. Inf., 3 mos., 1861-62; Co. A, 1st N. M. Cav.
Jaramillo, Jose Matias, Co. D, 1st N. M. Inf.
Jaramillo, Jose Dolores, Co. D, A, 2nd N. M. Inf., Corp.
Jaramillo, Juan Lovato y, Alarid's Independent Co., N. M. Mil. Inf., 3 mos., 1861-62.
Jaramillo, Donacio, Co. D, E, 1st N. M. Inf.
Jaramillo, Francisco, Co. I, 1st N. M. Cav.
Jaramillo, Jesus Maria, Co. K, F, 3rd N. M. Mtd. Inf., 6 mos., 1861-62.
Jaramillo, Lino, Co. I, 1st N. M. Cav.
Jaramillo, Luciano, Co. B, 3rd N. M. Mtd. Inf., 6 mos., 1861-62.
Jaramillo, Miguel, Co. D, E, 1st N. M. Inf., O. O.
Jaramillo, Teofilo, Co. B, 1st N. M. Mil. Inf., 3 mos., 1861-62, Corp.
Jaramillo, Crecencio, Co. D, 2nd N. M. Inf.
Jaramillo, Cruz, Jaramillo's Co., Perea's Batt'n, N. M. Mil. Inf., 3 mos., 1861-62.
Jaramillo, Eluterio, Co. G, 3rd N. M. Mtd. Inf., 6 mos., 1861-62.
Jaramillo, Donacio, Co. D, E, 1st N. M. Inf., O. O.
Jaramillo, Faustin, Jaramillo's Co., Perea's Batt'n, N. M. Mtd. Inf., 3 mo., 1861-62.
Jaramillo, Francisco, Co. I, 1st N. M. Cav., O. O.
Jaramillo, Jesus, Co. A, 2nd N. M. Inf.
Jaramillo, Jose Dolores, Co. D, A, 2nd N. M. Inf., Corp.
Jaramillo, Dolores, Co. B, 1st N. M. Inf., O. O.
Jaramillo, Jose Guadalupe, Co. B, 1st N. M. Cav.
Jaramillo, Jose Ignacio, Co. D, 1st N. M. Inf., O. O.
Jaramillo, Jose Manuel, Co. D, Batt'n N. M. Vols., 1866-67.
Jaramillo, Jose Maria, Jaramillo's Co., Perea's Batt'n, N. M. Mil. Inf., 3 mos., 1861-62.
Jaramillo, Jose Hilario, Co. C, B, 1st N. M. Mil. Inf., 3 mos., 1861-62.
Jaramillo, Juan, Co. B, 1st N. M. Inf., N. O.

Jaramillo, Co. C, 1st N. M. Inf.
Jaramillo, Juan Jose, Aragon's Co., Perea's Batt'n, N. M. Mil. Inf., 3 mos., 1861-62.
Jaramilo, Lino, Co. D, 1st N. M. Inf.
Jaramilo, Matias, Co. D, 2nd N. M. Inf.
Jaramillo, Miguel, Aragon's Co., Perea's Batt'n, N. M. Mil. Inf., 3 mos., 1861-62.
Jaramillo, Miguel, Montoya's Co., Perea Batt'n, N. M. Mil. Inf., 3 mos., 1861-62.
Jaramillo, Nestor, Co. E, 1st N. M. Cav., Jaramillo's Co., Perea's Batt'n, N. M. Mil. Inf., 3 mos., 1861-62, Captain.
Jaramillo, Nicolas, Co. B, 5th N. M. Inf., Corp.
Jaramillo, Pablo, Hubbell's Co., Perea's Batt'n, N. M. Mil. Inf., 3 mos., 1861-62.
Jaramillo, Ramon, Co. G, 3rd N. M. Mtd. Inf., 6 mos, 1861-62.
Jaramillo, Relles, Co. K, 1st N. M. Inf., N. O.
Jaramillo, Santiago, Co. F, 1st N. M. Inf., N. O.
Jaramillo, Sisto, Graydon's Independent Co., N. M. Mtd. Vols., 3 mos., 1861-62.
Jaramillo, Teofilo, Co. B, 1st N. M. Mil., 1861-62, 3 mos., Corp.
Jaramillo, Eusebio Trujillo y, Mink's Independent Co., N. M. Mtd. Vols., 3 mos., 1861.
Jaramillo, Venturo, Jaramillo's Co., Berea's Batt'n, N. M. Mtd. Inf., 3 mos., 1861-62.
Jaramillo, Vicente, Hubbell's Co., Perea's Batt'n, N. M. Mil. Inf., 3 mos., 1861-62.
Jaramillo, Pedro, Vigil's Independent Co., N. M. Mtd. Vols., 3 mos., 1861.
Jaramillo, Roman, Co. G, 3rd N. M. Mtd. Inf., 6 mos., 1861-62.
Jeanet, Gabriel, Co. D, 1st N. M. Mil. Inf., 3 mos., 1861-62, Lieut.
Jefts, George, Co. D, 1st N. M. Cav.
Jiminez, Francisco, Co. H, 1st N. M. Cav., Bugler.
Jiminez, Gregorio, Co. I, D, 2nd N. M. Inf., Musician.
Jewell, Lucian, Co. F, 1st N. M. Inf., O. O., Musician, Leader of Band, Bandmaster for 1st N. M. Cav.
Jiminez, Jesus, 1st N. M. Mil., Sena's Co. A, 2 mos., 1862.
Jiminez, Francisco, Co. H, D, 1st N. M. Cav., Wagoner.
Johnson, Felix, Co. M, E, 1st N. M. Cav.
Johnson, George, Co. K, 1st N. M. Cav.
Johnson, John R., Co. G, 2nd N. M. Cav, 1st Lieut.
Johnson, Leonard D., Co. G, 1st N. M. Cav.
Jones, Samuel, Co. K, 1st N. M. Cav.
Jones, Sylvester, Co. D, 1st N. M. Inf., Corp.
Jaramillo, Magrino, Co. K, 2nd N. M. Inf.
Joyola, Pascual, Gonzolez Independent Co., N. M. Mil. Inf., 3 mos., 1861, Sgt.
Joyola, Camillo, Tafoya's Independent Co., N. M. Mil. Inf., 3 mos., 1861-62, 2nd Lt.
Joyola, Bentura, Gonzolez Independent Co., N. M. Mil. Inf., 3 mos., 1861.
Joyola, Claudio, Gonzolez Independent Co., N. M. Mil. Inf., 3 mos., 1861.
Juarez, Anselmo, Co. H, 1st N. M. Cav.
Juarez, Francisco, Co. H, 1st N. M. Inf., N. O.
Juarez, Aniseto, Co. H, 1st N. M. Co. H, 1st N. M. Inf.
Juarez, Ignacio, Co. E, D, 1st N. M. Inf., N. O., Bugler.
Juarez, Martin, Co. H, 1st N. M. Inf., N. O.
Juarez, Jose Albino, Co. C, B, 1st N. M. Mil. Inf., 3 mos., 1861-62, Sgt.
Juyse, Francisco, Co. F, 1st N. M. Inf., N. O.
Juyse, Juan, Perea's Independent Co., N. M. Vols., 60 days, 1862.
Jurado, Hilario, Co. D, 1st N. M. Inf.

Jurado, Inocente, Co. F, 1st N. M. Cav.
Jurado, Mauricio, Co. F, 1st N. M. Inf., O. O.

Kane, Charles W., Co. D, 2nd N. M. Inf., Sgt.
Knouse, Abram Morris, Co. M, 1st N. M. Cav., 1st Lt.
Kast, Charles, Co. D, 1st N. M. Cav.
Kaulback, William, Co. G, 1st N. M. Cav.
Kearns, Thomas, Co. E, 1st N. M. Cav., 2nd Lt.
Keis, Joseph F., Co. C, 4th N. M. Inf.
Kelly, James, Co. G, 1st N. M. Cav., Saddler.
Kelly, John, Co. G, 1st N. M. Cav., Corp.
Kelley, George, Co. A, 1st N. M. Inf., N. O.
Kelly, Lewis, Co. F, 1st N. M. Inf.
Kelly, Michael, Co. K, H, 1st N. M. Cav., Sgt. Major.
Kelly, Thomas, Simpson's Independent Co., N. M. Mtd., Spies and Guides.
Kelsey, Louis A., Co. M, 1st N. M. Cav.
Kemp, Northrop, Co. H, 1st N. M. Inf., Capt.
Kennedy, Michael, Co. D, 1st N. M. Cav., Sgt. See: U. S. Army Rolls.
Kenny, James, Co. B, 1st N. M. Inf., O. O.
Keesler, Jerome, Co. K, 1st N. M. Cav.

Labade, Jesus, Co. A, 1st N. M. Cav.
Labadi, Juan, Co. H, 2nd N. M. Inf.
Lobato, Jesus M., Co. F, 1st N. M. Inf.
Lobato, Alcario, Co. C, 3rd N. M. Mtd. Inf., 6 mos., 1861-62, Corp.
Lobato, Antonio, Co. B, 1st N. M. Cav.
Lobato, Cornelio, Co. B, 1st N. M. Inf., Corp.
Lobato, Dionicio, Co. F, 1st N. M. Inf., O. O.
Lobato, Doris, Co. H, 3rd N. M. Mtd. Inf., 6 mos., 1861-62.
Lobato, Gregorio, Co. B, 1st N. M. Cav.
Lobato, Jose de la Luz, Co. B, D, 1st N. M. Cav.
Lobato, Juan Antonio, Co. D, 1st N. M. Cav.
Lobato, Lino, Co. G, 2nd N. M. Inf.
Lobato, Manuel, Co. C, 3rd N. M. Mtd. Inf., 6 mos., 1861-62.
La Biean, Alexander. See: California Volunteers.
Lucero, Doroteo, Co. H, 1st N. M. Inf., N. O.
Lackey, William S., Co. E, K, 1st N. M. Inf., N. O., Corp. See: California Vols.
Lacroix, Baptiste, Co. K, 1st N. M. Inf., N. O.
Lacroix, Martin, 1st N. M. Inf., Corp.
Lafont, Antonio, Co. D, 1st N. M. Mil. Inf., 3 mos., 1861-62, Corp.
Lujan, Rafael, Co. K, 3rd N. M. Mtd. Inf., 6 mos., 1861-62.
Lujan, Tomas, Co. K, 3rd N. M. Mtd. Inf., 6 mos., 1861-62.
Lampscht, Otto. See: U. S. Infantry rolls.
Larranaga, Jose, Co. C, 1st N. M. Inf., Corp.
Lopez, Jose Maria, Co. H, 1st N. M. Inf.
Laquella, Fransuello, Co. K, 1st N. M. Inf.
Lara, Cipriano, Co. H, 3rd N. M. Mtd. Inf., 6 mos., 1861-62., Sgt.
Lara, Francisco, Co. B, 1st N. M. Inf.
Lara, Juan, Co. H, 1st N. M. Inf., N. O.
Lovato, Lorenzo Sanchez y, Co. E, 2nd N. M. Inf., Musician.
Laranago, Jose, Co. A, 1st N. M. Cav., Com. Sgt.
Lariba, Cristobal, Co. K, 3rd N. M. Mtd. Inf., 6 mos., 1861-62.
Lariba, Nabor, Co. C, 1st N. M. Cav., Sgt.
Larria, Jochim, Co. A, 3rd N. M. Mtd. Inf., 6 mos., 1861-62.
Lasch, Thomas, Co. C, Batt'n N. M. Vols., 1866-67, Corp.
Lucero, Macedonio, Co. G, 2nd N. M. Inf.
Laner, Henry W., Co. A, 1st N. M. Inf., N. O., Capt.
Laughlin, Daniel, Co. M, 1st N. M. Cav.
Laughlin, Joseph, Co. E, 1st N. M. Cav., 2nd Lieut.
Lauterbach, John H., Co. K, 1st N. M. Cav.

Lavadi, Jesus, Co. C, 1st N. M. Inf.
Leahy, Patrick, Co. J, 1st N. M. Cav.
Leal, Benito, Co. A, 1st N. M. Inf., O. O.
Leal, Bentura, Co. I, 3rd N. M. Mtd. Inf., 6 mos., 1861-62.
Leal, Jose Dolores, Co. A, 1st N. M. Inf., N. O.
Leal, Jose Isidro, Co. I, 3rd N. M. Mtd. Inf., 6 mos., 1861-62, Bugler.
Leal, Pedro, Co. I, 3rd N. M. Mtd. Inf., 6 mos., 1861-62.
Letchuza, Felipe, Co. D, 1st N. M. Cav.
Letchuza, Francisco, Co. F, 4th N. M. Inf.
Ledesme, Pablo, Co. M, 1st N. M. Cav.
Lee, Ismael Hadden, Co. M, 1st N. M. Cav., Sgt.
Legra, Antonio, Co. H, 3rd N. M. Mtd. Inf., 6 mos., 1861-62.
Legra, Jesus, Co. A, 3rd N. M. Mtd. Inf., 6 mos., 1861-62, Corp.
Leiba, Atilana, Montoya's Co., Perea's Batt'n, N. M. Mtd. Inf., 3 mos., 1861-62.
Leiba, Jesus, Co. E, 1st N. M. Cav., Corp.
Leiba, Jose Inocencio, Co. B, F, 1st N. M. Cav., Sgt.
Leiba, Jose Ignacio, Co. F, 1st N. M. Inf., N. O.
Leiba, Jose Nestor, Co. B, 1st N. M. Inf., O. O.
Leiba, Juan M., Co. B, 1st N. M. Cav.
Leiba, Manuel, Co. A., 4th N. M. Inf.
Leiba, Pedro, Co. E, 1st N. M. Cav.
Leiba, Antonio, Co. H, 3rd N. M. Mtd. Inf., 6 mos., 1861-62.
Lemon, George W., Co. C, 1st N. M. Cav., Com. Sgt.
Lent, William, Co. E, 1st N. M. Inf., Captain.
Lente, Juan, Vigil's Independent Co., N. M. Mtd. Vols., 3 mos., 1861.
Leon, Jose Maria, Co. K, 2nd N. M. Inf.
Leon, Juan D., Co. D, 1st N. M. Cav.
Lenon, Juan, Co. K, 1st N. M. Cav.
Lerma, Nepomoceno, Co. K, 3rd N. M. Mtd. Inf., 6 mos., 1861-62, Sgt.
Lerma, Francisco, Co. F, 1st N. M. Inf., N. O.
Leroux, Louis W., Co. A, N. M. Mil. Inf., 3 mos., 1861-62, Captain.
Lerskof, Nelson, Co. M, 1st N. M. Cav.
Lucero, Tomas, Co. C, Batt'n N. M. Vols., 1866-67.
Lewis, James M., Co. M, 1st N. M. Cav., Corp.
Lewis, John, Co. D, 1st N. M. Cav., 1st Lieut.
Leyba, Domingo, Co. B, 1st N. M. Cav.
Leyba, Jose Nestor, Co. C, 1st N. M. Inf., Corp.
Leyba, Juan Matias, Co. B, 1st N. M. Cav.
Leyba, Pedro, Co. E, 1st N. M. Cav.
Leyba, Jose Antonio, Co. H, 1st N. M. Inf., N. O., Corp.
Light, John, Co. B, 1st N. M. Cav.
Leon, Juan, Co. D, 1st N. M. Cav.
Chofe, Jose Maria, Co. K, 2nd N. M. Inf.
Lippe, Justo, Co. B, 1st N. M. Cav.
Lobato, Catarino, Co. D, 1st N. M. Cav.
Lobato, Jose de la Luz, Co. B, 1st N. M. Cav.
Lobato, Lino, Co. G, 2nd N. M. Inf.
Ladoux, Felipe, Co. A, 3rd N. M. Mtd. Inf., 6 mos., 1861-62.
Loe, George A., Co. B, 1st N. M. Cav. Sgt.
Libermore, Ira S., Co. M, 1st N. M. Cav., Farrier.
Lobato, Bartolo, Aragon's Co., Perea's Batt'n, N. M. Mil., 3 mos., 1861-62.
Lobato, Benino, Montoya's Co., Perea's Batt'n, N. M. Mil. Inf., 3 mos., 1861-62.
Lobato, Bernado, Duran's Co., N. M. Mil.
Lobato, Cornelio, Co. B, 1st N. M. Inf., N. O., Corp.
Lobato, Co. D, 3rd N. M. Mtd. Inf., 6 mos., 1861-62.
Lobato, Diego, Co. I, 1st N. M. Cav.
Lobato, Dionicio, Co. H, 1st N. M. Inf., O. O.
Lobato, Filomeno, Co. K, 2nd N. M. Inf.

Lobato, Francisco, Baca's Co., Perea's Batt'n, N. M. Mil. Inf., 3 mos., 1861-62.
Lobato, Gregario, Co. B, 1st N. M. Cav.
Lobato, Jose Ribera y Romero's Independent Co. A, N. M. Mil. Inf., 6 mos., 1861-62, Sgt.
Lobato, Julian, Mink's Independent Co., N. M. Mtd. Vols., 3 mos., 1861.
Lobato, Leandro, Co. E, 3rd N. M. Mtd. Inf., 6 mos., 1861-62, Corp.
Lobato, Manuel, Co. B, I, 1st N. M. Cav., Bugler.
Lujan, Elejandro Hilario, Co. B., Batt'n N. M. Vols., 1866-67.
Lujan, Jose Bentura, Co. C, 1st N. M. Cav.
Lujan, Nicolas, Co. B, K, 1st N. M. Inf.
Long, George, Co. F, 4th N. M. Inf.
Longmuir, John, Graydon's Independent Co., N. M. Mtd. Vols., 3 mos., 1861-62, 2nd Lieut.
Lopez, Antonio, Co. H, 1st N. M. Cav., Corp.
Lopez, Telesforo, Co. H, 1st N. M. Cav.
Lopez, Antonio Jesus, Co. D, 1st N. M. Cav., Corp.
Lopez, Bicente, Co. G, 1st N. M. Inf., N. O., Corp.
Lopez, Blas, Co. B, 1st N. M. Mil. Inf., 3 mos., 1861-62.
Lopez, Sisto, Co. K, 1st N. M. Inf.
Lopez, Damacio, Aragon's Co., Perea's Batt'n, N. M. Mil. Inf., 3 mos., 1861-62.
Lopez, Doroteo, Hubbell's Independent Co., N. M. Mtd. Vols.
Lopez, Felipe, Co. D, 1st N. M. Inf.
Lopez, Francisco, Co. D, 1st N. M. Mil. Inf., 3 mos., 1861-62.
Lopez, Geronimo, Co. G, 2nd N. M. Inf.
Lopez, Jesus Maria, Co. I, 1st N. M. Cav.
Lopez, Jose Enriques, Co. D, 1st N. M. Inf., O. O.
Lopez, J. M. Esquipula, Co. A, 1st N. M. Inf., O. O.
Lopez, Juan Bautista, Co. F, 1st N. M. Inf.
Lopez, Juan de Dios, Co. B, 1st N. M. Mil. Inf., 3 mos., 1861-62.
Lopez, Julian, Co. G, 2nd N. M. Inf.
Lopez, Juan Albino, Mink's Independent Co., 3 mos., 1861-62.
Lopez, Manuel, Co. A, 3rd N. M. Mtd. Inf., 6 mos., 1861-62.
Lopez, Marcelino, Co. H, 1st N. M. Cav.
Lopez, Miguel, Co. H, 1st N. M. Inf., N. O.
Lopez, Nasario, Co. B, 1st N. M. Mil. Inf., 3 mos., 1861-62.
Lopez, Pablo, Del Balle's Co., Perea's Batt'n, N. M. Mil. Inf., 3 mos., 1861-62.
Lopez, Donaciano, Co. H, 1st N. M. Cav., Corp.
Lopez, Ruperto, Co. H, 1st N. M. Cav.
Lopez, Salvado, Co. D, 1st N. M. Inf.
Lopez, Santos Jose, Co. G, 2nd N. M. Inf.
Lopez, Simon, Co. K, 1st N. M. Cav., Corp.
Lopez, Telesfor, Co. C, 1st N. M. Inf.
Lopez, Tranquilino, Co. G, 1st N. M. Inf.
Lopez, Isidro, Duran's Co., N. M. Militia.
Lopez, Guadalupe, Co. G, 1st N. M. Inf., N. O.
Lopez, Ignacio, Co. A, 3rd N. M. Mtd. Inf., 6 mos., 1861-62.
Lopez, Ynez, Co. B, 1st N. M. Cav.
Lopez, Lazaro, Co. G, 1st N. M. Inf., Bugler.
Lopez, Lorenzo, Graydon's Co., N. M. Mtd. Vols., 3 mos., 1861-62.
Lopez, Manuel Graydon's Independent Co., N. M. Mtd. Vols., 3 mos., 1861-62.
Lopez, Marlin, Co. C, 1st N. M. Inf., Sgt.
Lopez, Sabino, Co. C, 1st N. M. Inf., Corp.
Losano, Jesus Maria, Co. B, 1st N. M. Inf.
Losano, Rito, Co. D, 2nd N. M. Inf.
Louis, John, Co. D, 1st N. M. Cav., 1st Lieut.
Lucero, Abran, Co. D, 1st N. M. Cav., and 4th N. M. Inf.
Lucero, Agapito, Co. A, Batt'n N. M. Vols., 1866-67.

Lucero, Alfonso, Co. D, 1st N. M. Mil. Inf., 6 mos., 1861-62.
Lucero, Ambrosio, Co. A, 4th N. M. Inf. and Co. G, 1st N. M. Mil. Inf., 6 mos., 1861-62.
Lucero, Anastacio, Romero's Independent Co. A, N. M. Mil. Inf., 3 mos., 1861-62; Co. A, Batt'n N. M. Vols., 1866-67.
Lucero, Antonio, Montoya's Co., Perea's Batt'n N. M. Mil. Inf., 6 mos., 1861-62.
Lucero, Antonio Jose, Co. H, 2nd N. M. Inf.
Lucero, Boleriano, Hubbell's Co., Perea's Batt'n, N. M. Mil. Inf., 6 mos., 1861-62.
Lucero, Cesario, Graydon's Independent Co., N. M. Mtd. Vols., 3 mos., 1861-62.
Lucero, Cornelio, Co. A, 1st N. M. Inf., O. O.
Lucero, Cristobal, Montoya's Co., Perea's Batt'n N. M. Mil. Inf., 6 mos. 1861-62.
Lucero, Diego, Hubbell's Independent Co., N. M. Mtd. Vols., 3 mos., 1861.
Lucero, Dolores, Co. D, 2nd N. M. Inf.
Lucero, Doroteo, Co. H, 1st N. M. Inf.
Lucero, Encarnacion, Co. E, 1st N. M. Cav.
Lucero, Faustin, Romero's Independent Co. A, N. M. Mil. Inf., 6 mos., 1861-62.
Lucero, Francisco, Co. H, 1st N. M. Inf., O. O.; Co. E, 3rd N. M. Mtd. Inf., 6 mos., 1861-62.
Lucero, Gabriel, Co. E, 1st N. M. Mil. Inf., 3 mos., 1861-62.
Lucero, Gervatio, Co. D, E, 1st N. M. Inf., O. O.
Lucero, Gregorio, Co. C, 1st N. M. Cav., Corp.
Lucero, Hurlano, Co. D, 3rd N. M. Mtd. Inf., 6 mos., 1861-62.
Lucero, Ignacio, Del Balle's Co., Perea's Batt'n, N. M. Mil. Inf., 6 mos., 1861-62.
Lucero, Jesus, Co. D, 3rd N. M. Mtd. Inf., 6 mos., 1861-62, Sgt.
Lucero, Joaquin, Co. C, 1st N. M. Mil. Inf., 3 mos., 1861-62.
Lucero, Jose, Aragon's Co., Perea's Batt'n, N. M. Mil. Inf., 6 mos., 1861-62.
Lucero, Jose (1st), Co. C, 4th N. M. Inf.
Lucero, Jose (2nd), Co. C, 4th N. M. Inf.
Lucero, Jose (3rd), Co. C, 4th N. M. Inf.
Lucero, Jose Abran, Co. G, 1st N. M. Inf., N. O.
Lucero, Jose Antonio, Co. A, 1st N. M. Cav., Corp.
Lucero, Jose Estanislado, Jaramillo's Co., Perea's Batt'n, N. M. Vols., 3 mos., 1861-62.
Lucero, Jose de la Cruz, Aragon's Co., Perea's Batt'n, N. M. Vols., 3 mos., 1861-62.
Lucero, Jose de Jesus, Co. E, 4th N. M. Inf.
Lucero, Jose Carlos, Co. E, 2nd N. M. Inf.
Licon, Juan Senon, Co. B, 4th N. M. Inf.
Licon, Pedro, Co. A, 1st N. M. Inf., N. O.
Light, John, Co. E, 1st N. M. Cav.
Lucero, Jose Francisco, Co. F, 3rd N. M. Mt. Inf., 6 mos., 1861-62.
Lucero, Jose Gonzolez y, Alarid's Co., Perea's Batt'n, N. M. Mil. Inf., 3 mos., 1861-62.
Lucero, Jose Gregorio, Co. I, 1st N. M. Inf., O. O.
Lucero, Jose Ramon, Co. E, 1st N. M. Cav.
Lucero, Jose Simon, Co. D, 1st N. M. Cav.
Lucero, Juan, Jaramillo's Co., Perea's Batt'n, N. M. Mil. Inf., 3 mos., 1861-62.
Lucero, Juan, Gonzolez Independent Co., N. M. Mil., 3 mos., 1861.
Lucero, Juan, Del Balle's Co., Perea's Batt'n, N. M. Mil. Inf., 3 mos., 1861-62.
Lucero, Juan Andres, Jaramillo's Co., Perea's Batt'n, N. M. Mil. Inf., 3 mos., 1861-62.
Lucero, Juan Bautista, Co. F, 1st N. M. Inf., N. O., Corp.

Lucero, Juan Cristobal, Montoya's Co., Perea's Batt'n, N. M. Mil. Inf., 3 mos., 1861-62.
Lucero, Juan de Jesus, Co. H, 3rd N. M. Mtd. Inf., 6 mos., 1861-62.
Lucero, Juan Ignacio, Co. K, 1st N. M. Inf., N. O.
Lucero, Juan Francisco, Romero's Independent Co. A, N. M. Mil. Inf., 3 mos., 1861-62, Sgt.
Lucero, Juan Nepumoceno, Co. A, 1st N. M. Inf., N. O.
Lucero, Julian, Co. A, 1st N. M. Inf.; Montoya's Co., Perea's Batt'n, N. M. Mil. Inf., 3 mos., 1861-62.
Lucero, Leon, Del Balle's Co., Perea's Batt'n, N. M. Mil. Inf., 3 mos., 1861-62.
Lucero, Luciano, Gonzolez Independent Co., N. M. Mil., 3 mos., 1861.
Lucero, Marcelino, Co. D, 1st N. M. Inf.
Lucero, Meterio, Co. B, Batt'n N. M. Vols., 1866-67.
Lucero, Miguel, Co. G, 3rd N. M. Mtd. Inf., 6 mos., 1861-62.
Lucero, Miguel Antonio, Co. L, 3rd N. M. Mtd. Inf., 6 mos., 1861-62.
Lucero, Nasario, Co. E, 1st N. M. Inf.; Co. B, 1st N. M. Mil. Inf., 3 mos., 1861-62, Lieutenant.
Lucero, Nestor, Co. B, C, 4th N. M. Inf.
Lucero, Pablo, Simpson's Independent Co., N. M. Mtd. Spies and Guides.
Lucero, Pablo, Romero's Independent Co. A, N. M. Mil. Inf., 3 mos., 1861-62.
Lucero, Pedro, Jaramillo's Co., Perea's Batt'n, N. M. Mil. Inf., 3 mos., 1861-62.
Lucero, Ramon, Co. H, 3rd N. M. Mtd. Inf., 6 mos., 1861-62.
Lucero, Ramon, Hubbell's Co., Perea's Batt'n, N. M. Mil. Inf., 3 mos., 1861-62.
Lucero, Salvador, Del Balle's Co., Perea's Batt'n, N. M. Mil. Inf., 3 mos., 1861-62.
Lucero, Santiago, Co. E, 1st N. M. Inf.
Lucero, Tesesfor, Montoya's Co., Perea's Batt'n, N. M. Mil. Inf., 3 mos., 1861-62.
Lucero, Tomas, Co. H, 1st N. M. Inf.; Co. C, 3rd N. M. Mtd. Inf., 6 mos., 1861-62.
Lucero, Vicente, Aragon's Co., Perea's Batt'n, N. M. Mil. Vols., 3 mos., 1861-62.
Lucero, Vivian, Co. A, 1st N. M. Inf.
Lujan, Aniceto, Co. H, 1st N. M. Cav.
Lujan, Cristobal, Co. I, 3rd N. M. Mtd. Inf., 6 mos., 1861-62.
Lujan, Domingo, Co. K, 1st N. M. Inf., N. O.
Lujan, Faustin, Co. A, 2nd N. M. Inf.
Lujan, Vidal, Co. H, 3rd N. M. Mtd. Inf., 6 mos., 1861-62.
Lujan, Antonio, Co. F, 1st N. M. Mil. Inf., 6 mos., 1861-62.
Lujan, Bicente, Montoya's Co., Perea's Batt'n, N. M. Mil. Inf., 3 mos., 1861-62.
Lujan, Casimiro, Hubbell's Co., Perea's Batt'n, N. M. Mil. Inf., 3 mos., 1861-62.
Lujan, Diego, Co. I, 1st N. M. Inf., N. O.
Lujan, Domingo, Co. D, 1st N. M. Cav.
Lujan, Eluterio, Alarid's Independent Co., N. M. Mil. Inf., 3 mos., 1861-62.
Lujan, Francisco, Co. E, 2nd N. M. Inf. and Duran's Co., N. M. Mil., Sgt.
Lujan, Baltazar, Co. I, 1st N. M. Cav.
Lujan, Elejandro Hilario, Co. B, Batt'n N. M. Vols., 1866-67.
Lujan, Ignacio, Co. D, Batt'n N. M. Vols., 1866-67.
Lujan, Jose Ynes, Co. F, 3rd N. M. Mtd. Inf., 6 mos., 1861-62.
Lujan, Jose Venturo, Co. C, 1st N. M. Cav.
Lujan, Juan, Co. B, 1st N. M. Cav.
Lujan, Julian, Romero's Independent Co. A, N. M. Mil. Inf., 6 mos., 1861-62.

Lujan, Manuel Alarid's Independent Co., N. M. Mil. Inf., 3 mos., 1861-62.
Lujan, Nicolas, Co. K, 1st N. M. Inf., N. O., Musician; Mink's Independent Co., N. M. Mtd. Vols., 3 mos., 1861.
Lujan, Rafael, Co. K, 1st N. M. Mil. Inf., 6 mos., 1861-62.
Lujan, Vidal, Co. H, 3rd N. M. Mtd. Inf., 6 mos., 1861-62.
Lujan, J. Nepomoceno, Co. A, 5th N. M. Inf.
Lujan, Manuel Sanchez y, Mink's Ind. Co., N. M. Mtd. Vols., 3 mos., 1861.
Lull, Morris, Co. F, 2nd N. M. Inf., Q. M. Sgt.
Luna, Andres, Co. K, 1st N. M. Inf.
Luna, Antonio Jesus, Perea's Independent Co., 60 days, 1861.
Luna, Benceslao, Perea's Independent Co., N. M. Vols., 60 days, 1861.
Luna, Florenso Geronimo, Co. G, 3rd N. M. Mil. Inf., 6 mos., 1861-62.
Luna, Jesus, Romero's 3rd N. M. Mtd. Inf., 6 mos., 1861-62.
Luna, Jose Graydon's Independent Co., N. M. Mtd. Vols., 3 mos., 1861-62.
Luna, Jose, Baca's Co., Perea's Batt'n, N. M. Mil. Inf., 3 mos., 1861-62.
Luna, Jose Tafoya's Independent Co., N. M. Mil., 3 mos., 1861-62.
Lune, Jose, 3rd N. M. Mtd. Inf., 6 mos., 1861-62, Corp.
Luna, Juan Graydon's Independent Co., N. M. Mtd. Vols., 3 mos., 1861-62.
Luna, Juan, Romero's Co. A, 3rd N. M. Mtd. Inf., 6 mos., 1861-62, Corp.
Luna, Maximiliano, Co. H, 1st N. M. Inf., Musician.
Luna, Marcos, Baca's Co., Perea's Batt'n, N. M. Mil. Inf., 3 mos., 1861-62.
Luna, Macedonio, Co. I, 1st N. M. Cav.
Luna, Pablo, Baca's Co., Perea's Batt'n, N. M. Mil. Inf., 3 mos., 1861-62.
Luna, Rafael, Perea's Independent Co., N. M. Vols., 60 days, 1861.
Luna, Vicente, Co. A, Batt'n N. M. Vols., 1866-67.
Luna, Camillo, Co. K, 2nd N. M. Inf.
Luna, Manuel, Co. K, 2nd N. M. Inf.
Luna, Antonio, Co. F, 1st N. M. Mil. Inf., 3 mos., 1861-62.

Martinez, Vicente, Mink's Independent Co., N. M. Mtd. Vols., 3 mos., 1861.
Maes, Juan, Co. I, 1st N. M. Inf., Sgt.
Maes, Pablo Trinidad, Co. I, 1st N. M. Inf., O. O., Sgt.
Machowitz, Bonificio, Co. I, 1st N. M. Cav., Lieut.
Macegra, Antonio, Co., 1st N. M. Inf.
Markey, William, Co. G, 1st N. M. Cav.
Machlegray, John, Co. I, 1st N. M. Inf.
Macrae, Nathaniel, Co. I and F, 1st N. M. Inf., 1st Lieutenant.
Macure, George, Co. F, 1st N. M. Inf., O. O.
Medina, Antonio, Co. H, 1st N. M. Inf., O. O.
Medina, Antonio Jose, Co. H, 1st N. M. Inf., O. O.
Medina, Juan Remegio, Co. I, 1st N. M. Inf., O. O.
Medina, Jose Jesus, Co. I, 1st N. M. Inf., O. O.
Medina, Jose Maria, Co. I, 1st N. M. Inf., N. O.
Medina, Juan de Jesus, Co. I, 1st N. M. Inf.
Madero, Camillo, Co. B, Batt'n N. M. Vols., 1866-67.
Medina, Jose de Jesus, Co. I, 1st N. M. Inf., N. O.
Medina, Juan Ignacio, Co. B, 1st N. M. Inf.
Medina, Juan Patricio, Co. I, 1st N. M. Inf.
Medina, Florencio, Co. I, 1st N. M. Inf., N. O.
Medina, Jose Mateo, 1st N. M. Inf.
Medina, Pedro J., Co. C, 1st N. M. Inf., O. O.
Medina, Victor, Co. I, 1st N. M. Inf., N. O.
Medrano, Quirino, Co. D, 1st N. M. Cav.; Co. A, Batt'n N. M. Vols., 1866-67.

Medrano, Florentino, Co. G, 1st N. M. Inf., N. O.
Madrid, Eugenio, Co. I, 1st N. M. Cav.
Madrid, Jose Maria, Co. C, 1st N. M. Cav.
Madrid, Marcos, Co. I, 4th N. M. Inf.
Madrid, Agapito, Co. C and F, 1st N. M. Militia Inf., 4 mos., 1861-62.
Madrid, Benito, Co. E, 1st N. M. Mil. Inf., 3 mos., 1861-62.
Madrid, Desiderio, Co. D, 3rd N. M. Mtd. Vols., 6 mos., 1861-62.
Madrid, Eugenio, Co. D, 1st N. M. Cav.; Co. H, 1st N. M. Inf., O. O.
Madrid, Feliz, Co. A, 1st N. M. Inf., N. O.
Madrid, Jesus Maria, Co. D, 4th N. M. Inf. and 1st N. M. Cav.
Madrid, Jose, Co. C, Batt'n N. M. Vols., 1866-67; Co. A, 1st N. M. Cav.; Co. B, 1st N. M. Inf.
Madrid, Jose Felipe, Co. B, 1st N. M. Inf., O. O., Wagoner.
Madrid, Jose Ignacio, Co. E, H, 3rd N. M. Inf., 6 mos., 1861-62.
Madrid, Juan, Co. F, 1st N. M. Inf.; Co. K, 1st N. M. Cav.; Co. B, 1st N. M. Inf.
Madrid, Juan de Dios, Co. I, 1st N. M. Inf.; Co. D, 4th N. M. Inf.
Madrid, Mariano, Co. D, Batt'n N. M. Vols., 1866-67.
Madrid, Tranquilino, Co. A, 1st N. M. Mil. Inf., 4 mos., 1861-62.
Madrid, Jose Maria, Co. P, 1st N. M. Cav.
Madrid, Agapito, Vigil's Independent Co., N. M. Mtd. Vols., 1861, 3 mos.
Madrid, Alejandro, Vigil's Independent Co., N. M. Mtd. Vols., 4 mos., 1861.
Madrid, Antonio, Co. C, 1st N. M. Inf., N. O.
Madrid, Benito, Co. E, 1st N. M. Mil. Inf., 3 mos., 1861-62.
Madrid, Jose, Co. C, Batt'n N. M. Vols., 1866-67.
Madrid, Jose, Co. A, H, 1st N. M. Cav.
Madrid, Rafael, Co. M, 1st N. M. Cav.
Maes, Anastacio, Co. D, 1st N. M. Mil. Inf., 3 mos., 1861-62.
Maes, Maria Antonio, Co. A, 1st N. M. Cav.
Maes, Desiderio, Co. A, C, 1st N. M. Cav.
Maes, Bernardo, Co. D, 1st N. M. Mil. Inf., 3 mos., 1861-62.
Maes, Facundo, Co. D, Batt'n N. M. Vols., 1866-67.
Maes, Felipe, Co. A, 1st N. M. Cav.
Maes, Bernardo, Co. A, 3rd N. M. Inf., 4 mos., 1861-62.
Maes, Jesus, Co. B, 4th N. M. Inf., and 3rd N. M. Inf.
Maes, Jose Manuel, Co. H, 1st N. M. Inf.; Sena's Co. A, 1st N .M. Mil. Inf., 3 mos., 1862.
Mares, Juan, Co. H, 1st N. M. Inf., 6 mos., 1861-62; and 3rd N. M. Mtd. Vols.
Maes, Juan, Co. B, 4th N. M. Inf.
Maes, Juan Ramon, Co. C, Batt'n N. M. Vols., 1866-67.
Maes, Julio, Co. E, 2nd N. M. Inf.
Maes, Manuel Antonio, Romero's Independent Co. A, N. M. Mil. Inf., 3 mos., 1861-62.
Maes, Matias, Co. A, 3rd N. M. Mtd. Inf., 6 mos., 1861-62.
Maes, Julio, Co. A, 3rd N. M. Mtd. Inf.
Maes, Pedro, Co. B, 2nd N. M. Inf.; Co. C, 1st N. M. Cav.
Maes, Felipe, Co. A, 3rd N. M. Mtd. Inf.
Maes, Rafael, Co. F, 3rd N. M. Mtd. Vols., 6 mos., 1861-62.
Macias, Jesus, Mink's Independent Co., N. M. Mtd. Vols., 3 mos., 1861-62.
Maese, Julio, Co. E, 2nd N. M. Inf.
Maese, Pablo, Mink's Independent Co., N. M. Mtd. Vols., 3 mos., 1861.
Maestas, Casimiro, Co. A, 1st N. M. Cav.
Maestas, Jose Maria, Co. B, 2nd N. M. Inf.
Maes, Fabian, Gonzolez Independent Co., N. M. Mil., 3 mos., 1861.
Maes, Juan Ramon, Co. C, 2nd N. M. Inf.
Maes, Santiago, Co. D, 4th N. M. Inf.
Maes, Jesus, Co. B, Batt'n N. M. Vols., 1866-67; Co. E, 1st N. M. Inf.
Maes, Bernabe, Co. A, 1st N. M. Inf.

Maja, Juan Maria, Co. A, 1st N. M. Inf.
Medrano, Damacio, Co. G, 1st N. M. Inf.
Maldonado, Jose, Co. C, Batt'n N. M. Vols, 1866-67.
Maldonado, Juan, Co. C, Batt'n N. M. Vols., 1866-67.
Maldonado, Concepcion, Tafoya's Independent Co., N. M. Mil. Inf., 4 mos., 1861-62.
Maldonado, Dolores, Perea's Batt'n, N. M. Mil. Inf., 4 mos., 1861-62.
Maldonado, Jesus, Co. D, 1st N. M. Cav.; Co. H and B, 2nd N. M. Inf.; Co. H, 3rd N. M. Mtd. Inf.
Maldonado, Jose, Co. F, B, 2nd N. M. Inf.
Maldonado, Juan, Perea's Batt'n, N. M. Mil. Inf., 3 mos., 1861-62.
Maldonado, Pedro, Mink's Independent Co., N. M. Mtd. Vols., 3 mos., 1861; 3rd N. M. Mtd. Inf.
Maldonado, Ramon, Perea's Batt'n, N. M. Mil. Inf., 3 mos., 1861-62.
Maldonado, Teodocio, Co. I, B, 2nd N. M. Inf.
Maldonado, Tomas, Co. F, 1st N. M. Inf., O. O.
Maldonado, Jose, Co. F, B, 1st N. M. Inf.
Maldonado, Pablo, Co. E, 4th N. M. Inf.
Maldonado, Juan Maria, Co. A, B, 4th N. M. Inf.
Maldonado, Pedro, Co. F, 1st N. M. Inf., O. O.
Mallat, Robert, Co. C, 4th N. M. Inf.
Manjuio, Jesus, Co. A, 5th N. M. Inf.
Manzanarez, Antonio, Co. I, 1st N. M. Vols.
Manchaca, Juan, Co. D, B, 1st N. M. Inf.
Manchago, Pedro, Co. I, 1st N. M. Inf., N. O.
Manchego, Juan Jesus, Co. A, 3rd N. M. Vols., 4 mos., 1861.
Manzanares, Pedro, Co. I, 1st N. M. Inf., O. O., Sgt.
Mansice, William A., Co. E, D, 4th N. M. Inf.
Montoya, Jose, 1st N. M. Vols., 6 mos., 1861-62, Aragon's Co.
Martinez, Roque, Perea's Batt'n, N. M. Mil. Inf., 3 mos., 1861-62.
Mantle, William, Co. D, 1st N. M. Inf., O. O.
Manzanares, Jesus, Vigil's Independent Co., Mtd. Vols., 3 mos., 1861; Co. I, 1st N. M. Inf., O. O.
Marquez, Antonio, Co. G, 1st N. M. Inf.
Marquez, Santiago, Co. G, 1st N. M. Inf., 6 mos., 1861-62.
Moreno, Antonio, Co. A, B, 1st N. M. Inf., N. O.
Marquez, Gaspar, Co. D, 1st N. M. Inf., N. O.
Marquez, Jose Augustin, Co. P, 5th N. M. Inf.; Co. D, 1st N. M. Inf., N. O.
Marquez, Juan, Co. D, 1st N. M. Inf., N. O.
Marquez, Martin, Co. B, 1st N. M. Inf., N. O.
Marquez, Merejildo, Co. E, 1st N. M. Inf., N. O.
Marquez, Ramon, Co. I, 1st N. M. Inf., N. O.
Marquez, ———, Co. I, 1st N. M. Cav.
Naranjo, Antonio, Co. H, 1st N. M. Cav., O. O.
Moreno, Ambrosio, Co. C, 2nd N. M. Inf.
Moreno, Juan, Co. A, 1st N. M. Cav.
Mares, Alfonso, Co. K, 1st N. M. Inf.
Mares, Antonio, Perea's Batt'n, N. M. Mil. Inf., 3 mos., 1861-62; (after 1862 enlisted as Antonio Montoya).
Mares, Jose Antonio, Co. C, 1st N. M. Inf., N. O.
Mares, Benito, Co. F, 1st N. M. Cav.; Co. A, 3rd N. M. Mtd. Inf., 6 mos., 1861-62; Co. A, 1st N. M. Inf.
Mares, Esquipula, Co. H, D, 2nd N. M. Mtd. Inf. and 1st N. M. Vol. Cav., Co. A.
Mares, Francisco, Co. G, 1st N. M. Inf., N. O.
Mares, Gabriel, Co. C, 1st N. M. Cav.; Co. C, A, 2nd N. M. Inf.
Mares, Jesus, Co. H, 1st N. M. Inf., 6 mos., 1861-62.
Mares, Juan, Co. K, 4th N. M. Inf., N. O.; Co. H, 3rd N. M. Mtd. Inf., 6 mos., 1861-62.
Mares, Manuel, Co. A, 3rd N. M. Mtd. Vols., 6 mos., 1861-62.

Mares, Pedro, Jaramillo's Co., Perea's Batt'n, N. M. Mil. Inf., 3 mos., 1861-62.
Mares, Rumualdo, Aragon's Co. A, Perea's Batt'n, N. M. Mil. Inf., 3 mos., 1861-62.
Mares, Santos, Co. C, A, 2nd N. M. Inf.
Mares, Simon, Co. D, 1st N. M. Inf.
Marquez, Antonio, Co. D, 1st N. M. Inf., N. O.; Co. G, 3rd N. M. Mtd. Vols., 6 mos., 1861-62.
Mariega, Antonio Domingo, Co. D, 1st N. M. Cav.
Marino, Jesus, Co. G, 3rd N. M. Mtd. Inf., 6 mos., 1861-62.
Marino, Vicente y Aragon, Perea's Batt'n, N. M. Mil. Inf., 6 mos., 1861-62.
Mares, Agapito, Co. E, 4th N. M. Inf.
Mares, Carlos P., Co. A, C, 1st N. M. Cav., Captain.
Mares, Alfonso, Co. K, 1st N. M. Inf., N. O.
Mares, Francisco, Co. G, 1st N. M. Vols., N. O.
Mares, Jose Antonio, Co. C, 1st N. M. Inf., N. O.
Mares, Jose Maria, Co. D, 1st N. M. Cav.
Mares, Simon, Co. D, 1st N. M. Inf.
Marquez, Guadalupe, Co. D, 1st N. M. Cav.; Co. E, F, 2nd N. M. Inf.
Marquez, Jesus, Romero's Independent Co. A, N. M. Mil. Inf., 6 mos., 1861-62.
Marquez, Juan, Co. C, 1st N. M. Inf., O. O., Sgt.; Co. E, 2nd N. M. Inf., Wagoner.
Marquez, Juan Manuel, Co. I, 1st N. M. Mil. Inf., 6 mos., 1861-62.
Mares, Marcos, Co. I, 1st N. M. Mil. Inf., 3 mos., 1861-62.
Marquez, Ramon, Co. B, Batt'n N. M. Vols., 1866-67, Bugler.
Marquez, Santiago, Co. G, 3rd N. M. Mil. Inf.
Marquez, Augustin, Co. H, 1st N. M. Inf., N. O.
Marquez, Tranquilino, Co. B, 1st N. M. Cav.
Marquez, Julian, Tafoya's Independent Co., N. M. Mil., 3 mos., 1861-62.
Marr, William, Co. A, 1st N. M. Inf., O. O.
Naranjo, Juan de Dios, Co. K, I, 1st N. M. Cav.
Marino, Jose Antonio, Hubbell's Independent Co., N. M. Mtd. Vols., 3 mos., 1861.
Manualia, Jose Concepcion, Co. I, 1st N. M. Inf., N. O.
Martin, Ambrosio Montoya y, Perea's Batt'n, N. M. Mil. Inf., 3 mos., 1861-62.
Martin, Antonio Juan de Dios, Co. G, H, 1st N. M. Inf., Batt'n N. M. Vols., 1866-67; N. M. Mil. Inf., 6 mos., 1861-62.
Martin, Antonio, Co. K, 1st N. M. Inf. and Co. F, D, 4th N. M. Inf.
Martin, Antonio Domingo, Co. A, 3rd N. M. Mtd. Inf., 3 mos., 1861-62, Corp.
Martin, Apolonio, Co. F, 3rd N. M. Mtd. Inf., 3 mos., 1861-62.
Martin, Baca y, Co. K, 3rd N. M. Mtd. Inf., 3 mos., 1861-62.
Martin, Basilio, Co. D, 5th N. M. Inf.
Martin, Baltazar, Vigil's Independent Co., N. M. Mtd. Vols.
Martin, Benigno, 1st N. M. Militia, Sena's Co. A, 2 mos., 1862.
Martin, Benito, Co. H, 1st N. M. Inf., 6 mos., 1861-62.
Martin, Bernardo, Co. I, 2nd N. M. Inf., also 1st N. M. Vol. Cav.
Martin, Bibian, Co. C, K, 1st N. M. Inf., O. O.
Martin, Bicente, Co. B, D, 1st N. M. Inf., O. O.
Martin, Candelario, Co. B, 4th N. M. Inf.
Martin, Canuto, Co. E, D, 2nd N. M. Inf., also 1st N. M. Cav.; Graydon's Independent Co., N. M. Mtd. Vols.
Martin, Cristobal Calles y, Perea's Batt'n, N. M. Mil. Inf., 3 mos., 1861-62.
Martin, Concepcion, Co. A, 1st N. M. Cav. and 2nd N. M. Inf.
Martin, Cristobal, Hubbell's Independent Co., N. M. Mtd. Vols., 3 mos., 1861.

Martin, Cristobal Aragon y, Perea's Batt'n, N. M. Mil. Inf., 3 mos., 1861-62.
Martin, Desiderio, Co. D, 4th N. M. Inf., Corp.
Martin, Demetrio, Co. B, 1st N. M. Inf., and 1st N. M. Cav.
Martin, Diego Antonio, Co. K, 1st N. M. Inf., O. O.
Martin, Dolores, Del Balle's Co., Perea's Batt'n, N. M. Mil. Inf., 3 mos., 1861-62.
Martin, Domingo, Co. F, 1st N. M. Cav. and 4th N. M. Vols.
Martin, Enrigues P., Co. D, 1st N. M. Inf., O. O.
Martin, Eugenio, Co. C, 1st N. M. Cav.; Co. F, H, B, A, 2nd N. M. Inf.
Martin, Eulogio, Co. A, 1st N. M. Inf., O. O.
Martin, Eusebio, Co. A, 1st N. M. Inf.; Aragon's Co., Berea's Batt'n, N. M. Mil. Inf., 3 mos., 1861-62.
Martin, Felipe, Del Balle's Co., Perea's Batt'n, N. M. Mil. Inf., 3 mos., 1861-62.
Martin, Felipe, Jaramillo's Co., Perea's Batt'n, N. M. Mil. Inf., 3 mos., 1861-62.
Martin, Francisco, Vigil's Independent Co., N. M. Vols., 3 mos., 1861; 3rd N. M. Mtd. Inf.
Martin, Francisco Antonio, Co. I, 1st N. M. Inf., O. O., Corp.
Martin, George, Co. K, 1st N. M. Inf., N. O.
Martin, Geronimo, Co. C, Batt'n, N. M. Vols., 1866-67.
Martin, Gregorio, Co. C, Batt'n N. M. Mtd. Vols., 1866-67.
Martin, Guadalupe Alarid's Independent Co., N. M. Mil. Inf., 3 mos., 1861-62; Co. H, A, 1st N. M. Cav. and Co. 1, 1st N. M. Inf., O. O., Corp.
Martin, Hilario, Co. F, B, 2nd N. M. Inf., Sgt.
Martin, Ignacio Jose, Co. G, 1st N. M. Inf., O. O.
Martin, Jacinto, Co. K, 1st N. M. Inf., O. O.
Martin, Jesus, Vigil's Independent Co., N. M. Mtd. Vols., 3 mos., 1861; Co. C, 1st N. M. Cav. and Co. A, 1st N. M. Inf.
Martin, Jesus Maria, Co. A, 1st N. M. Inf., O. O., Corp.; Co. A, 3rd N. M. Mtd. Inf., 6 mos., 1861-62.
Martin, Jose, Co. K, 1st N. M. Cav. and Co. B, E, 4th N. M. Inf.
Martin, Jose Antonio, Co. F, Batt'n N. M. Vols., 1866-67.
Martin, Jose David, Co. K, 3rd N. M. Mtd. Inf., 3 mos., 1861-62, Corp.
Martin, Jose Gregorio, Co. H, E, 1st N. M. Inf., O. O., and 1st N. M. Cav.
Martin, Jose Guadalupe, Co. G, 1st N. M. Inf., N. O.
Martin, Jose Ignacio, Co. A, 1st N. M. Cav.
Martin, Jose Manuel, Vigil's Independent Co., N. M. Mtd. Vols., 1861-62, 3 mos.
Martin, Juan de Dios, Co. D, 1st N. M. Cav.; Co. C, N. M. Batt'n, 1866-67.
Martin, Juan de Jesus, Co. F, 1st N. M. Inf., O. O.
Martin, Juan Dolores, Co. B, 3rd N. M. Mtd. Inf., 6 mos., 1861-62; Co. D, 1st N. M. Inf.
Martin, Juan Domingo, Co. D, 1st N. M. Inf.
Martin, Juan Francisco, Co. K, 1st N. M. Inf., N. O.
Martin, Juan Ignacio, Co. C, 1st N. M. Cav.
Martin, Juan Jose, Co. K, 3rd N. M. Mtd. Inf.
Martin, Juan Lorenzo, Co. I, D, 1st N. M. Inf.
Martin, Juan Manuel, Co. C, 1st N. M. Cav. and 2nd N. M. Inf.
Martin, Julian, Co. A, 1st N. M. Inf.
Martin, Juan Ignacio, Co. E, 2nd N. M. Inf.
Martin, Genaro, Vigil's Independent Co., N. M. Mtd. Vols., 3 mos., 1861.
Martin, Leandro, Vigil's Independent Co., N. M. Mtd. Vols., 3 mos., 1861.
Martin, Lorenzo, Co. A, 1st N. M. Cav. and Co. D, 3rd N. M. Mtd. Inf., 3 mos., 1861-62.

Martin, Luis, Co. A, E, 2nd N. M. Inf., Sgt.
Martin, Manuel, Del Balle's Co., Perea's Batt'n, N. M. Mil. Inf., 3 mos., 1861-62; Co. F, 1st N. M. Cav.; Co. A, 1st N. M. Inf., O. O.; Co. D, 2nd N. M. Inf.; Co. D, 3rd N. M Mtd. Inf.
Martin, Manuel Gregorio, Co. B, 3rd N. M. Mtd. Inf., 6 mos., 1861-62, and Co. K, 1st N. M. Inf.
Martin, Marcelino, Co. D, 1st N. M. Cav.; Co. G, 1st N. M. Inf.; and Co. A, 2nd N. M. Inf.
Martin, Marcos, Co. A, 1st N. M. Inf.
Martin, Matias, Co. K, 3rd N. M. Mtd. Inf., Bugler.
Martin, Melchior, Co. L, G, 1st N. M. Cav.
Martin, Melquiades, Co. A, 1st N. M. Inf.
Martin, Meregredo, Co. M, D, 3rd N. M. Mtd. Inf.
Martin, Emereterio, Co. B, Batt'n, N. M. Vols., 1866-67.
Martin, Miguel, Co. D, 3rd N. M. Mtd. Inf.; Co. I, 1st N. M. Cav.
Martin, Narciso, Hubbell's Co., N. M. Mtd. Vols., 3 mos., 1861; Co. B, 1st N. M. Cav.
Martin, Nero, Vigil's Independent Co., N. M. Mtd. Vols., 3 mos., 1861-62.
Martin, Nazario, Vigil's Independent Co., N. M. Mtd. Vols, 3 mos., 1861.
Martin, Nestor, Co. D, 1st N. M. Inf., O. O.
Martin, Nicanor, Co. B, Batt'n N. M. Vols., 1866-67; Co. I, 1st N. M. Cav.
Martin, Nicanor Dolores, Mink's Independent Co., N. M. Mtd. Vols., 3 mos., 1861.
Martin, Norberto, Co. F, 3rd N. M. Inf., 6 mos., 1861-62.
Martin, Octaviano, Co. I, 1st N. M. Inf., O. O.
Martin, Pablo, Co. A, 1st N. M. Cav.
Martin, Patronillos, Co. H, 1st N. M. Cav.
Martin, Pedro, Co. B, 3rd N. M. Mtd. Inf.
Martin, Pedro Antonio, Co. H, 1st N. M. Cav. and Co. B, Batt'n N. M. Vols., 1866-67.
Martin, Pedro Jose, Co. D, F, 1st N. M. Inf.
Martin, Polonio, Co. C, D, 1st N. M. Vols., N. O.
Martin, Prudencio, Co. I, 1st N. M. Inf., N. O.
Martin, Quirino, Co. C, Batt'n N. M. Vols., 1866-67.
Martin, Quinto, Alarid's Independent Co., N. M. Mil. Inf.; Co. D, B, 1st N. M. Cav., O. O.
Martin, Quirino, Co. K, E, 1st N. M. Cav. and Co. C, 4th N. M. Inf.
Martin, Rafael, Sena's Co. A, 1st N. M. Mil., 3 mos., 1862, and Co. F, 1st N. M. Inf.
Martin, Ramon, Co. C, A, G, 1st N. M. Cav. and 2nd N. M. Inf.
Martin, Refugio, Co. F, 1st N. M. Inf., O. O.
Martin, Salvador, Co. A, B, 1st N. M. Inf., O. O.
Martin, Samuel, Co. K, 3rd N. M. Mtd. Inf., 3 mos., 1861-62.
Martin, Santiago, Co. B, 1st N. M. Cav. and Co. A, 1st N. M. Inf.
Martin, Santos, Co. K, 3rd N. M. Mtd. Inf., 3 mos., 1861-62.
Martin, Seferino, Co. K, 3rd N. M. Mtd. Inf., 6 mos., 1861-62, Sergt.
Martin, Teodoro, Co. I, 1st N. M. Inf.
Martin, Tiburcio, Del Balle's Co., Perea's Batt'n, N. M. Mil. Inf., 3 mos., 1861-62.
Martin, Tomas, Co. B, 1st N. M. Cav.
Martin, Venturo, Co. B, 3rd N. M. Mtd. Vols.
Martin, Vicente, Co. H, 1st N. M. Inf.
Martin, Vidal, Co. A, 3rd N. M. Mtd. Inf., 6 mos., 1861-62.
Martin, Victor M., Co. C, 3rd N. M. Mtd. Inf., 6 mos., 1861-62.
Martin, Viterbo, Co. B, 3rd N. M. Mtd. Vols., 6 mos., 1861-62.
Martin, Concepcion, Co. A, 1st N. M. Cav.
Martinez, Domingo, Co. F, 1st N. M. Cav.
Martinez, Geronimo, Co. I, 1st N. M. Inf.
Martinez, Gregorio, Co. L, G, 1st N. M. Cav.

(Note: In New Mexico, Martin and Martinez were interchangeable names, so that a descendant of a Martinez family should not fail to look under Martin should he fail to find the name he is interested in under Martinez.)

Martinez, Jesus, Co. I, C, 1st N. M. Cav.
Martinez, Jose David, Co. D, 1st N. M. Cav.
Martinez, Jose Felipe, Co. M, 1st N. M. Inf.
Martinez, Juan Jose, Co. C, 1st N. M. Inf., N. M.
Martinez, Jose Manuel, Co. I, 1st N. M. Inf., N. O.
Martinez, Lorenzo M., Co. A, 1st N. M. Cav.
Martinez, Manuel M., Co. F, 1st N. M. Cav.
Martinez, Matias, Co. A, 1st N. M. Cav.
Martinez, Melchior, Co. G, Batt'n N. M. Vols., 1866-67.
Martinez, Pablo M., Co. A, 1st N. M. Cav.
Martinez, Pedro, Co. A, H, 3rd N. M. Mtd. Inf., 3 mos., 1861-62.
Martinez, Prudencio, Co. I, 1st N. M. Inf., N. O.
Martinez, Vidal M., Co. A, 3rd N. M. Mtd. Inf., 6 mos., 1861-62.
Martinez, Acacio M., Duran's Co., N. M. Mil.
Martinez, Albino M., Co. H, 3rd N. M. Mtd. Inf., 6 mos., 1861-62.
Martinez, Alcario, Co. E, 1st N. M. Vols., O. O.
Martinez, Anastacio, Co. H, D, 1st N. M. Cav.
Martinez, Antonio, Vigil's Independent Co., N. M. Mtd. Vols., 3 mos., 1861.
Martinez, Antonio Domingues, Co. C, 3rd N. M. Mtd. Inf., 6 mos., 1861-62, Corp.
Martinez, Antonio Jose, 3rd N. M. Mtd. Inf., 6 mos., 1861-62.
Martinez, Antonio Jose, Duran's Co., N. M. Mil. Inf., and Co. B, 1st N. M. Inf.
Martinez, Benito, Co. H, 3rd N. M. Mtd. Inf., and Co. B, 4th N. M. Inf.
Martinez, Candelario, Co. A, 1st N. M. Inf.
Martinez, Desiderio, Co. C, 1st N. M. Mil. Inf., 3 mos., 1861-62; Co. E, 1st N. M. Cav.
Martinez, Donaciano, Co. D, 1st N. M. Inf., and 1st N. M. Cav., Bugler.
Martinez, Esteban, Co. B, 1st N. M. Mil. Inf., 3 mos., 1861-62.
Martinez, Felipe, Co. C, D, 1st N. M. Mil. Inf., 3 mos., 1861-62.
Martinez, Francisco, Co. D, 1st N. M. Cav.
Martinez, Guadalupe, Co. D, 1st N. M. Inf., O. O.
Martinez, Hermerejildo, Co. H, 1st N. M. Inf., Corp.
Martinez, Hilario, Co. D, 1st N. M. Cav.
Martinez, Jesus Maria, Co. B, 1st N. M. Mil. Inf., 3 mos., 1861-62.
Martinez, Jose Antonio, Co. K, 3rd N. M. Mtd. Inf., 6 mos., 1861-62.
Martinez, Jose de la Luz, Co. H, 1st N. M. Inf., O. O.
Martinez, Dionicio, Co. F, 1st N. M. Mil. Inf., 3 mos., 1861-62.
Martinez, Jose Guadalupe, Co. H, 1st N. M. Mtd. Vols.
Martinez, Jose Ignacio, Co. D, 1st N. M. Cav.
Martinez, Jose Isaias, Co. D, 4th N. M. Inf.
Martinez, Jose Manuel, Co. K, 1st N. M. Inf., N. O., 2nd Lieut.
Martinez, Jose Maria, Co. E, 1st N. M. Cav.
Martinez, Jose Maria, Co. D, 1st N. M. Inf., O. O., Musician.
Martinez, Jose Marcelino, Co. A, 3rd N. M. Mtd. Inf.
Martinez, Jose Nicanor, Co. M, 1st N. M. Cav.
Martinez, Jose Pedro, Co. D, 1st N. M. Cav.
Martinez, Juan de Jesus, Co. D, 1st N. M. Inf., O. O.
Martinez, Juan Dolores, Co. D, 1st N. M. Inf., O. O.
Martinez, Juan Jose, Co. A, 1st N. M. Inf., N. O.
Martinez, Juan Sena, Co. C, 1st N. M. Inf., N. O.
Martinez, Juan Pablo, Co. M, 3rd N. M. Mtd. Inf., Captain.
Martinez, Jesus Rafael, Co. F, 3rd N. M. Mil. Inf., 3 mos., 1861-62, Corp.
Martinez, Juan Inez, Perea's Batt'n, N. M. Mil. Inf., 3 mos., 1861-62.
Martinez, Lorenzo, Co. D, 1st N. M. Mil. Inf., 3 mos., 1861-62.

Martinez, Manuel Del Balle's Co., Perea's Batt'n, N. M. Mil. Inf., 3 mos., 1861-62.
Martinez, Manuel, Duran's Co., N. M. Mil.
Martinez, Manuel Gregorio, Co. B, 3rd N. M. Mtd. Inf., 6 mos., 1861-62, Sergt.
Martinez, Mariano, Co. F, 3rd N. M. Mtd. Inf.
Martinez, Marcelino, Co. I, 1st N. M. Vols., N. O.
Martinez, Matias, Co. D, E, 1st N. M. Inf., O. S.
Martinez, Melquiades, Co. G, E, 1st N. M. Inf.
Martinez, Miguel, Co. A, 3rd N. M. Mtd. Inf., 6 mos., 1861-62, O. O.
Martinez, Miterio, Co. D, 1st N. M. Inf., N. O.
Martinez, Narciso, Co. B, 3rd N. M. Mtd. Inf., 6 mos., 1861-62.
Martinez, Nestor, Co. D, 1st N. M. Inf., and 4th N. M. Inf.; Co. D, 3rd N. M. Mtd. Inf., 6 mos., 1861-62.
Martinez, Nicanor, Co. D, 3rd N. M. Mtd. Inf., 6 mos., 1861-62.
Martinez, Nicanor, Co. L, 3rd N. M. Mtd. Inf., 6 mos., 1861-62.
Martinez, Pablo, Co. I, 1st N. M. Cav., Sergt.
Martinez, Pedro, Co. A, 3rd N. M. Mtd. Inf., 6 mos., 1861-62.
Martinez, Jose Pedro, Co. F, D, 4th N. M. Inf.
Martinez, Polonio, Co. E, I, 1st N. M. Inf., O. O.
Martinez, Roman, Sena's Co. A, 2 mos., 1862.
Martinez, Salvador, Co. B, 3rd N. M. Mtd. Inf., 6 mos., 1861-62.
Martinez, Sixto, Co. B, 1st N. M. Inf., O. O.
Martinez, Teofilo, Co. I, 1st N. M. Cav., Bugler.
Martinez, Tomas, Co. D, 1st N. M. Cav.
Martinez, Tiburcio, Co. F, 1st N. M. Mil. Inf., 3 mos., 1861-62.
Martinez, Vicente, Co. A, 1st N. M. Mil. Inf., 3 mos., 1861-62.
Martinez, Agapito, Co. A, 1st N. M. Mil. Inf., 3 mos., 1861-62.
Martinez, Albino, Co. H, 3rd N. M. Mtd. Inf., 6 mos., 1861-62.
Martinez, Alcario, Co. E, 1st N. M. Inf., N. O.
Martinez, Alejandro, Co. D, 1st N. M. Inf., N. O.
Martinez, Anastacio, Co. B, 5th N. M. Inf. and Batt'n N. M. Vols., 1866-67.
Martinez, Antonio de Jesus, Co. G, H, 1st N. M. Inf., O. O.
Martinez, Camilo, Co. E, 1st N. M. Mil. Inf., 3 mos., 1861-62.
Martinez, Candelario, Co. A, B, K, 1st N. M. Inf., N. O.
Martinez, Carlos, Co. K, 1st N. M. Inf.
Martinez, Desiderio, Co. K, 3rd N. M. Mtd. Inf., 6 mos., 1861-62.
Martinez, Dolores, Co. H, 1st N. M. Cav.
Martinez, Donaciano, Co. E, I, 1st N. M. Cav., Wagoner, and 3rd N. M. Mtd. Inf., 6 mos., 1861-62.
Martinez, Eusebio, Co. D, 1st N. M. Inf.
Martinez, Francisco, Co. D, 1st N. M. Cav., Wagoner, O. O.
Martinez, Vicente, Co. C, 3rd N. M. Mtd. Inf., 6 mos., 1861-62.
Martinez, Jesus, Co. M, B, A, 2nd N. M. Inf.
Martinez, Jose Antonio, Co. A, E, 3rd N. M. Mtd. Vols., 6 mos., 1861-62.
Martinez, Juan Cristobal, Co. A, 1st N. M. Mil. Inf., 3 mos., 1861-62.
Martinez, Juan de Jesus, Co. G, H, 1st N. M. Inf.
Martinez, Jose Nicanor, Co. H, 1st N. M. Inf.
Martinez, Luciano, Gonzolez Independent Co., N. M. Mil., 3 mos., 1861.
Martinez, Santiago, Mink's Independent Co., N. M. Mtd. Vols., 3 mos., 1861.
Martinez, Juan Jose Sanchez y, Co. K, 3rd N. M. Mtd. Inf., 6 mos., 1861-62.
Madrigal, Natividad, Co. E, 1st N. M. Vols.
Mascarenas, Crecencio, Co. A, 1st N. M. Vols.
Mascarenas, Jose B., Co. B, 1st N. M. Inf.
Mascarenas, Antonio, Simpson's Independent Co., N. M. Mtd. Spies and Guides, 2nd Lieut.
Mascarenas, Demetrio, Co. K, 2nd N. M. Inf.
Mascarenas, Francisco, Co. D, 3rd N. M. Mtd. Inf., 3 mos., 1861-62.

Mascarenas, Jose D., Co. A, 1st N. M. Inf.
Mascarenas, Nicolas, Co. K, 2nd N. M. Inf., Corp.
Mascarenas, Jose Santiseban y, Co. K, 2nd N. M. Inf.
Mascarenas, Vicente, Mink's Independent Co., N. M. Mtd. Vols., 3 mos., 1861.
Mason, Epitacio, Co. G, 2nd N. M. Cav., Corp.
Maestas, Carmen, Co. D, 1st N. M. Cav.
Mata, Blas, Del Balle's Co., Perea's Batt'n, N. M. Mil. Inf., 2nd Lieut.
Mata, Bruno, Del Balle's Co., Perea's Batt'n, N. M. Mil. Inf., Sgt.
Mata, Gabriel, Co. I, 1st N. M. Inf., N. O.
Maurijo, Pablo, Co. F, 1st N. M. Inf., N. O.
Maurino, Antonio, Co. A, 1st N. M. Cav.
Maxwell, William, Co. B, H, 1st N. M. Inf., and Co. D, E, 1st N. M. Cav.
Matta, Juan Maria, Co. A, 1st N. M. Cav.
Mayer, Adolph H., Co. A, 1st N. M. Cav.
Mayer, William, Co. G, 1st N. M. Cav., and Co. I, 1st N. M. Inf.
Meyers, Henry, Co. B, 1st N. M. Inf.
Meyers, William, Co. G, 1st N. M. Cav.
Mayo, Casimiro, Co. C, 2nd N. M. Inf.
Mayo, Santerio, N. M. Mtd. Vols., 3 mos., 1861.
McAllister, David, Co. G, 1st N. M. Cav., 2nd Lieut.
McCabe, Francis, Co. K, L, 1st N. M. Cav.
McCarthy, Michael, Co. D, 1st N. M. Inf.
McDonald, Michael, Co. D, Batt'n N. M. Vols., 1866-67.
McDougall, William, Simpson's Independent Co., N. M. Mtd. Spies and Guides.
McEllroy, Michael, Co. G, 2nd N. M. Inf.
McGee, John, Co. F, 1st N. M. Inf., O. O.
McGlane, James, Co. D, 1st N. M. Inf., O. O.
McGuire, George, Graydon's Independent Co., N. M. Mtd. Vols., 3 mos., 1861-62, Corp.
McGuire, John, Co. C, 1st N. M. Cav.
McHugh, Pierce, Co. F, 1st N. M. Inf., Corp.
McKee, James, Co. B, 5th N. M. Inf., Sgt.
McKetrick, Cardwell, Co. F, I, 1st N. M. Inf., O. O.
McKenzie, Thomas, Co. F, 1st N. M. Inf., O. O.
McKeogh, Pierce, Co. F, 3rd N. M. Mtd. Inf., 3 mos., 1861-62.
McLaughlin, William, Co. F, 3rd N. M. Mtd. Inf., 6 mos., 1861-62, Sgt.-Major.
McMahon, James, Co. C, 4th N. M. Inf.
McNealis, Francis, Co. K, 1st N. M. Cav.
McNulty, Henry, Co. K, 1st N. M. Cav., Sgt.
McRae, Nathaniel M., Co. C, 1st N. M. Cav., 1st Lieut.
McSweeney, Eugene, Co. F, I, 4th N. M. Inf.
Meagher, Philip, Co. B, 1st N. M. Inf., N. O.
Malo, Bernabe, Co. B, 1st N. M. Cav.
Maes, Jesus, Co. B, Batt'n, N. M. Vols., 1866-67.
Maes, Barnabe, Co. C, 1st N. M. Cav.
Maestas, Casimiro, Co. D, 1st N. M. Cav.
Madero, Camilo, Co. B, Batt'n N. M. Vols., 1866-67.
Medina, Antonio, Co. H, 1st N. M. Inf., O. O.
Medina, Antonio Domingo, Mink's Independent Co., N. M. Mtd. Vols., 2 mos., 1861.
Medina, Antonio Jose, Co. D, 3rd N. M. Mtd. Inf., 6 mos., 1861-62.
Medina, Celso Cuellar y, Co. E, 2nd N. M. Inf., 2nd Lieut.
Medina, Deisderio, Co. I, 1st N. M. Inf., 3 mos., 1861-62.
Medina, Enriquez, Co. A, 1st N. M. Inf., O. O.
Medina, Florentin, Co. G, 1st N. M. Inf., N. O.
Medina, Ignacio, Co. A, 1st N. M. Inf., O. O.
Medina, Jose, Co. F, 1st N. M. Inf., N. O.
Medina, Jose de Jesus, Co. D, 1st N. M. Cav.

Medina, Jose Francisco, Co. F, 4th N. M. Inf.
Medina, Jose Mateo, Co. F, 1st N. M. Inf., N. O.
Medina, Jose Rafael, Co. G, 1st N. M. Inf., O. O.
Medina, Juan, Co. F, 1st N. M. Inf.
Medina, Juan Bautista, Co. H, 1st N. M. Inf.
Medina, Juan Ignacio, Co. G, 1st N. M. Inf., O. O.
Medina, Juan Jose, Co. D, E, 1st N. M. Inf., O. O.
Medina, Juan Ramon, Co. I, 1st N. M. Inf., O. O.
Medina, Marcelo, Co. C, 3rd N. M. Mil. Inf.
Medina, Ignacio, Mink's Independent Co., N. M. Mtd. Vols., 2 mos., 1861.
Medina, Merijildo, Co. D, 1st N. M. Inf., N. O.
Medina, Pablo, Co. K, F, N. M. Mil. Inf., 3 mos., 1861-62.
Medina, Pedro Jose, Co. C, 1st N. M. Inf., O. O.; and Mink's Co., 2 mos., 1861.
Medina, Ponciano, Co. D, E, 1st N. M. Inf., Sgt.
Medina, Santiago, Co. E, D, 4th N. M. Inf.
Medina, Venturo, Co. I, 1st N. M. Inf., O. O.
Medina, Victor, Co. D, 1st N. M. Inf., N. O.
Medina, Ignacio, Romero's Independent Co., N. M. Mil. Inf., 3 mos., 1861-62.
Medrano, Florentino, Co. I, 1st N. M. Inf., and Co. A, 2nd N. M. Inf.
Medrano, Juan, Co. C, 1st N. M. Inf., N. O.
Medrano, Jose Antonio, Co. A, 2nd N. M. Inf.
Medrano, Marcos, Co. C, Batt'n N. M. Vols., 1866-67.
Medrano, Quirino, Co. A, Batt'n N. M. Vols., 1866-67.
Manhold, Charles, Co. F, 5th N. M. Inf., Adgt.
Mier, Henry, Co. M, 1st N. M. Cav.
Meira, Pedro Jose, Co. E, 2nd N. M. Inf.
Meister, Antonio, Co. I, 1st N. M. Inf., N. O.
Meister, Jose, Co. I, 1st N. M. Inf.
Meister, Juan Isidro, Co. I, 1st N. M. Inf.
Mejicano, Antonio, Co. D, 2nd N. M. Inf.
Mejicano, Jose, Co. D, 2nd N. M. Inf.
Mejicano, Jose Chavez y, Co. D, 2nd N. M. Inf.
Mijillas, Arano, Graydon's Independent Co., N. M. Vols.
Melano, Desiderio, Co. G, 1st N. M. Cav.
Maldonado, Juan, Co. C, Batt'n N. M. Vols., 1866-67.
Maldonado, Pedro, Co. F, 3rd N. M. Mtd. Inf., 6 mos., 1861-62.
Melgares, Pascual, Co. C, 1st N. M. Inf., O. O.
Molina, Jose Trinidad, Co. D, 2nd N. M. Inf.
Melroff, John H., Co. A, Batt'n N. M. Vols., 1866-67.
Melchides, Sanchez y, Co. D, 1st N. M. Cav.
Mijares, Antonio, Co. H, 1st N. M. Cav.
Men, William, Co. K, 1st N. M. Cav.
Mendez, Juan, Co. B, C, 4th N. M. Inf.
Mendoza, Juan, Co. D, 2nd N. M. Inf.
Mendoza, Julian, Co. C, 1st N. M. Cav.
Mendoza, Miguel, Co. D, 2nd N. M. Inf.
Mendoza, Crecencio, Co. A, 1st N. M. Inf.
Mendoza, Filemon, Co. E, 1st N. M. Inf.
Mendoza, Jose, Co. B, Batt'n N. M. Vols., 1866-67.
Menett, Adolph, Mink's Independent Co., N. M. Mtd. Vols., 2 mos., 1861-62, Sgt.
Menoso, Francisco, Co. H, 1st N. M. Inf.
Montano, Norberto, Co. F, 3rd N. M. Mtd. Inf., 6 mos., 1861-62.
Montano, Jose Encarnacion, Co. D, 1st N. M. Inf., N. O.
Montano, Antonio, Co. D, 3rd N. M. Mtd. Inf., 6 mos., 1861-62.
Montano, Francisco, Co. F, 3rd N. M. Mtd. Inf., 6 mos., 1861-62.
Montano, Crecencio, Co. A, 1st N. M. Mil. Inf., 3 mos., 1861-62.
Menser, Francisco, Co. D, Batt'n N. M. Mtd. Vols., 1866-67, Sgt.
Menose, Francisco, Co. H, 1st N. M. Inf., N. O.

Meraval, Antonio, Graydon's Independent Co., N. M. Mtd. Vols., 3 mos., 1861-62.
Marcado, Dolores, Co. A, 5th N. M. Inf.
Mercer, William, Co. C, 4th N. M. Inf.
Mercure, George, Co. F, 1st N. M. Inf.
Mercia, Francisco, Hubbell's Independent Co., N. M. Mtd. Vols., 3 mos., 1861.
Merin, Martin, Co. A, 1st N. M. Inf.
Merritt, Edward, Co. A, Batt'n N. M. Vols., 1866-67, 1st Lieut.
Mes, Antonio, Co. B, 1st N. M. Mil. Inf., 3 mos., 1861-62.
Mes, Casimiro, Vigil's Independent Co., N. M. Mtd. Vols.
Mes, Jose Francisco, Tafoya's Independent Co., N. M. Mil., 3 mos., 1861-62.
Mes, Jose Rafael, Tafoya's Independent Co., N. M. Mil., 3 mos., 1861-62.
Mes, Juan Domingo, Co. C, 1st N. M. Mil. Inf., 3 mos., 1861-62.
Mes, Manuel, Co. F, 1st N. M. Inf., 3 mos., 1861-62.
Mes, Miguel, Vigil's Independent Co., N. M. Mtd. Vols., 2 mos., 1861.
Maes, Tomas, Tafoya's Independent Co., 3 mos., 1861-62.
Mascarenas, Jose E., Co. B, 1st N. M. Inf., N. O.
Mese, Jesus, Co. B, Batt'n N. M. Vols., 1866-67, Sgt.
Maes, Pedro, Co. F, 1st N. M. Cav.
Mesner, John, Co. I, 1st N. M. Inf., Corp.
Maestas, Jose Maria, Co. H, 1st N. M. Cav.
Maestas, Antonio, Co. B, 1st N. M. Mil. Inf., 3 mos., 1861-62.
Maestas, Antonio Domingo, Co. K, 1st N. M. Inf.
Maestas, Antonio Maria, Montoya's Co., Perea's Batt'n, N. M. Mil. Inf., 3 mos., 1861-62.
Maestas, Baltazar, Co. D, 3rd N. M. Mtd. Inf., 6 mos., 1861-62.
Maestas, Candido, Mink's Independent Co., N. M. Mtd. Vols., 3 mos., 1861.
Maestas, Cresencio, Co. A, 1st N. M. Cav.
Maestas, Casimiro, Co. C, 1st N. M. Inf.
Maestas, Ferrer, Co. K, 1st N. M. Inf.
Maestas, Francisco, Co. K, 1st N. M. Inf., O. O.
Maestas, Francisco Antonio, Co. D, 1st N. M. Mil. Inf., 3 mos., 1861-62.
Maestas, Jose Garcia y, Co. I, 1st N. M. Inf.
Maestas, Jose Francisco, Mink's Independent Co., N. M. Mtd. Vols., 3 mos., 1861.
Maestas, Jose Maria, Co. B, 2nd N. M. Inf.
Maestas, Jose Rafael, Co. A, 1st N. M. Inf.
Maestas, Jose Silverio, Co. G, 1st N. M. Inf.
Maestas, Juan, Co. A, 1st N. M. Mil. Inf., 3 mos., 1861-62.
Maestas, Juan Andres, Co. D, 1st N. M. Cav.
Maestas, Mariano, Co. F, 1st N. M. Mil. Inf.
Maestas, Pedro, Co. D, 1st N. M. Inf.
Maestas, Prudencio, Romero's Independent Co.
Maestas, Roman, Co. I, 1st N. M. Cav.
Maestas, Seferino, Co. B, 1st N. M. Inf.
Maestas, Vicente, Co. B, 1st N. M. Mil. Inf., 3 mos., 1861-62.
Maestas, Antonio, Co. D, 1st N. M. Inf.
Maestas, Estanislao, Mink's Independent Co., N. M. Mtd. Vols., 3 mos., 1861.
Maestas, Francisco Antonio, Co. A, 1st N. M. Mil. Inf.
Maestas, Guadalupe, Co. A, 1st N. M. Mil. Inf.
Maestas, Jose, Co. D, 1st N. M. Inf.
Maestas, Bautista, Co. D, 3rd N. M. Mtd. Inf., 6 mos., 1861-62, Corp.
Maestas, Manuel Antonio, Co. D, 3rd N. M. Inf.
Mexicano, Jose, Co. D, 2nd N. M. Inf.
Mexicano, Jose Antonio, 2nd N. M. Inf., 2nd Lieut.
Mexicano, Preciliano, Co. G, 2nd N. M. Inf.

Meyer, Henry, Co. M, 2nd N. M. Cav.
Meyers, William, Co. M, 1st N. M. Cav.
Meara, Pedro Jose, Co. A, 2nd N. M. Inf.
Michael, Ellen, Co. F, 1st N. M. Vols.
Mitchand, Alexander, Co. B, 1st N. M. Inf.
Miera, Jose Maria, Co. K, 2nd N. M. Inf.
Miera, Jose Ignacio, Vigil's Independent Co., N. M. Mtd. Vols.
Miera, Juan Maria, Co. D, 2nd N. M. Inf.
Miera, Pedro, Co. A, 2nd N. M. Inf.
Miller, C. B., Co. H, 1st N. M. Inf., 1st Lieut.
Miller, Edward, Alarid's Independent Co., N. M. Mil. Inf., 3 mos., 1861-62.
Miller, John, Co. F, 1st N. M. Inf.
Miller, Julian, 3rd N. M. Mtd. Inf., 6 mos., 1861-62.
Miller, Samuel, Graydon's Independent Co., 3 mos., 1861-62.
Miller, William H., Co. P, 5th N. M. Inf.
Mills, David, Co. B, Batt'n N. M. Vols., 1866-67.
Munez, Santiago, Co. E, 1st N. M. Inf.
Mink, John Henry, Mink's Independent Co., 3 mos., 1861.
Minton, William P., Co. K, 1st N. M. Inf., N. O.
Mirabal, Pedro, Perea's Batt'n N. M. Mil. Inf., 3 mos., 1861-62.
Mirabal, Jose, Perea's Batt'n, N. M. Mil. Inf., 3 mos., 1861-62.
Mirabal, Monico, Co. G, 1st N. M. Mil. Inf., 3 mos., 1861-62, Corp.
Morales, Juan, Co. A, 4th N. M. Inf.
Miranda, Jose, Co. E, 1st N. M. Cav. and Romero's Co., 3rd N. M. Mtd. Inf., 6 mos., 1861-62.
Morales, Antonio, Co. E, 1st N. M. Inf., N. O.
Morales, Miguel, Co. E, Batt'n N. M. Vols., Corp.
Morales, Jose Mariano, Co. K, 2nd N. M. Inf.
Medrano, Florentino, Co. G, 1st N. M. Inf.
Mohr, Francis, Co. H, 1st N. M. Cav. Sgt.
Molina, Damacio, Co. G, 1st N. M. Cav.
Molina, Eulogio, Baca's Co., Perea's Batt'n, N. M. Mil. Inf., 3 mos., 1861-62.
Molina, Catarino, Co. L, 1st N. M. Cav.
Molina, Conrado, Baca's Co., Perea's Batt'n, N. M. Mil. Inf., 3 mos., 1861-62.
Molina, Genoevo, Co. E, 1st N. M. Cav.
Molina, Jose Trinidad, Co. D, 2nd N. M. Inf., Drummer.
Molina, Juan, Co. D, 2nd N. M. Inf.
Molina, Miguel, Co. H, 1st N. M. Inf., O. O.
Molina, Francisco, Co. B, 1st N. M. Inf.
Molla (Moya?), Albino, Co. H, 3rd N. M. Mtd. Inf., 6 mos., 1861-62.
Molla, Antonio Maria, Co. B, 1st N. M. Cav., and Co. E, 3rd N. M. Mtd. Inf.
Molla, Jesus, Co. E, 3rd N. M. Mtd. Inf., 6 mos., 1861-62.
Molla, Juan, Co. H, 1st N. M. Inf., and Co. G, 2nd N. M. Inf.
Molla, Juan Maria, Co. K, 1st N. M. Inf., Musician.
Molla, Rafael, Co. B, 1st N. M. Inf.
Molla, Santiago, Co. A, 1st N. M. Inf.
Molla, Jose Francisco, Co. I, 1st N. M. Inf.
Molla, Marcelino, Hubbell's Co., Perea's Batt'n, N. M. Mil. Inf., 3 mos., 1861-62.
Monos, Reyes, Co. K, 1st N. M. Cav.
Manchaca, Juan, Co. D, 1st N. M. Inf., Corp., N. O.
Monclova, Marcelino, Co. G, 1st N. M. Inf.
Monclova, Marcos, Co. G, 1st N. M. Inf., Corp.
Mondragon, Antonio, Co. D, 3rd N. M. Mtd. Inf., 6 mos., 1861-62.
Mondragon, Bartolo, Co. F, 4th N. M. Inf.
Mondragon, Gregorio, Co. K, 1st N. M. Cav.
Mondragon, Jose, Co. A, 1st N. M. Cav.
Mondragon, Desiderio, Co. E, 1st N. M. Mil. Inf., 3 mos., 1861-62.

Mondragon, Juan D., Co. B, Batt'n, N. M. Vols., 1866-67.
Mondragon, Juan Lorenzo, Alarid's Independent Co., N. M. Mil. Inf., 3 mos., 1861-62.
Mondragon, Manuel, Co. B, 3rd N. M. Mtd. Inf., 6 mos., 1861-62, 2nd Lieut.
Mondragon, Vidal, Co. K, 3rd N. M. Mtd. Inf., 6 mos., 1861-62.
Montano, Pedro, Co. C, 1st N. M. Inf., O. O.
Monroe, Charles, Co. F, 4th N. M. Cav., Sgt., and Co. A, 4th N. M. Inf.
Montoya, Juan Francisco, Co. L, 1st N. M. Cav.
Montoya, Santiago, Co. K, 1st N. M. Cav.
Montoya, Domingo, Co. B, 3rd N. M. Mtd. Inf., 6 mos., 1861-62.
Montoya, Jesus Maria, Co. B, 3rd N. M. Mtd. Inf., 6 mos., 1861-62.
Montoya, Juan Jose, Co. A, 2nd N. M. Inf.
Montoya, Juan, Co. B, 3rd N. M. Mtd. Inf., 6 mos., 1861-62.
Montoya, Jose, Co. B, 3rd N. M. Mtd. Inf., 6 mos., 1861-62.
Montano, Toribio, Co. I, 2nd N. M. Inf., Corp.
Montano, Hilario, Hubbell's Co., Perea's Batt'n, N. M. Mil. Inf., 3 mos., 1861-62.
Montano, Jose G., Co. B, Batt'n N. M. Vols., 1866-67.
Montano, George, Co. I, 1st N. M. Inf.
Montano, Antonio, Co. B, 1st N. M. Cav.
Montano, Anastacio, Co. I, 2nd N. M. Inf.
Montano, Apolonio, Co. G, 3rd N. M. Mtd. Inf., 6 mos., 1861-62.
Montano, Camilo, Co. F, 1st N. M. Mil. Inf., 3 mos., 1861-62.
Montano, David, Co. A, Batt'n N. M. Vols., 1866-67.
Montano, I. M., Perea's Independent Co., N. M. Vols., 1862.
Montano, Geronimo, Romero's Independent Co. A, N. M. Mil. Inf., 3 mos., 1861-62.
Montano, Jesus Maria, Co. G, 2nd N. M. Inf.
Montano, Jose, Co. G, 3rd N. M. Mtd. Inf., 6 mos., 1861-62.
Montano, Jose Encarnacion, Co. D, 1st N. M. Inf.
Montano, Jose Ignacio, Graydon's Independent Co., N. M. Mtd. Vols., 3 mos., 1861-62.
Montano, Juan, Co. C, 1st N. M. Cav.
Montano, Juan Jose, Jaramillo's Co., Perea's Batt'n, N. M. Mil. Inf., 3 mos., 1861-62.
Montano, Juan Nepomoceno, Romero's Independent Co. A, N. M. Mil. Inf., 3 mos., 1861-62.
Montano, Luis, Co. A, 1st N. M. Mil. Inf., 3 mos., 1861-62.
Montano, Manuel, Vigil's Independent Co., N. M. Mtd. Vols., 3 mos., 1861, Corp.
Montano, Melquiades, Co. D, 1st N. M. Inf.
Montano, Norberto, Co. F, 3rd N. M. Mtd. Inf., 6 mos., 1861-62.
Montano, Pablo, Co. F, 1st N. M. Cav.
Montano, Pedro, Co. A, 1st N. M. Cav.
Montano, Pedro Jose, Hubbell's Independent Co., N. M. Mtd. Vols., 3 mos., 1861.
Montano, Quirino, Romero's Independent Co. A, N. M. Mil. Inf., 3 mos., 1861-62.
Montano, Rafael, Co. H, 2nd N. M. Inf.
Montano, Ramon, Co. K, 1st N. M. Cav.
Montano, Ramon, Co. H, 5th N. M. Inf.
Montano, Ruperto, Co. K, 2nd N. M. Inf.
Montano, Santiago, Co. K, L, 1st N. M. Cav., and 3rd N. M. Mtd. Inf., 6 mos., 1861-62.
Montoya, Ambrosio, Co. F, 1st N. M. Cav. and Gonzolez Independent Co., 3 mos., 1861.
Montoya, Rallos, Gonzolez Independent Co., N. M. Mil. Inf., 3 mos., 1861-62.
Montoya, Victor, Gonzolez Independent Co., N. M. Mil. Inf., 3 mos., 1861-62.

Montoya, Juan, Hubbell's Independent Co., N. M. Mtd. Vols., 3 mos., 1861.
Montez, Juan D., Co. D, 1st N. M. Cav., 1st Sgt.
Montez, Luis, Co. A, 1st N. M. Inf.
Monteith, Georgiana, 1st N. M. Inf., Matron, O. O.
Montieth, Leonora, 1st N. M. Inf., Matron.
Montoya, Benino, Co. D, 3rd N. M. Mtd. Inf., 6 mos., 1861-62.
Montoya, Perfecto, Co. A, 1st N. M. Cav.
Montoya, Ramon, Hubbell's Co., Perea's Batt'n, N. M. Mil. Inf., 3 mos., 1861-62.
Montez, Pedro, Co. G, 1st N. M. Inf.
Montez, Samuel, Co. M, 1st N. M. Cav.
Montez, Gregorio, Co. C, 4th N. M. Inf.
Montez, Luis, Co. A, 1st N. M. Inf.
Montez, Manuel, Co. M, 1st N. M. Cav.
Montoya, Candido, Co. I, 1st N. M. Inf.
Montoya, Agapito, Co. H, 3rd N. M. Mtd. Inf., 6 mos., 1861-62.
Montoya, Antonio Jose, Co. B, 1st N. M. Mil. Inf., 3 mos., 1861-62.
Montoya, Esquipula, Co. A, 2nd N. M. Mtd. Inf., Musician.
Montoya, Francisco, Baca's Co., Perea's Batt'n, N. M. Mil. Inf., 3 mos., 1861-62.
Montoya, Jesus, Del Balle's Co., Perea's Batt'n, N. M. Mil. Inf., 3 mos., 1861-62.
Montoya, Jose, Del Balle's Co., Perea's Batt'n, N. M. Mil. Inf., 3 mos., 1861-62.
Montoya, Jose Abran, Co. I, 1st N. M. Inf., O. O.
Montoya, Jose Anastacio, Co. E, 1st N. M. Cav.
Montoya, Jose Leandro, Graydon's Independent Co., N. M. Mtd. Vols., 3 mos., 1861, Sgt.
Montoya, Juan Jose, Co. H, 1st N. M. Cav., Corp.
Montoya, Juan Pablo, Co. I, 1st N. M. Inf.
Montoya, Manuel, Co. B, 1st N. M. Inf.
Montoya, Margarito, Co. A, 2nd N. M. Inf.
Montoya, Pedro Jose, Co. H, 3rd N. M. Mtd. Inf., 6 mos., 1861-62.
Montoya, Romualdo, Del Balle's Co., Perea's Batt'n, N. M. Mil. Inf., 3 mos., 1861-62.
Montoya, Ramon, Co. A, 1st N. M. Cav.
Montoya, Sacramento, Co. F, 3rd N. M. Mtd. Inf., 6 mos., 1861-62, 1st Lieut.
Montoya, Santos, Co. E, 1st N. M. Cav. Sgt.
Montoya, Severino, Co. G, A, 1st N. M. Inf.
Montoya, Tomas, Tafoya's Independent Co., N. M. Mil., 3 mos., 1861-62, Corp.
Montoya, Victorio, Tafoya's Independent Co., N. M. Mil., 3 mos., 1861-62.
Montoya, Sipriano, Co. G, 1st N. M. Inf.
Montoya, Alejandro, Alarid's Independent Co., N. M. Mil., 3 mos., 1861-62.
Montoya, Cruz, Co. E, 1st N. M. Inf.
Montoya, Demetrio, Duran's Co., N. M. Mil.
Montoya, Dionicio, Co. B, 1st N. M. Inf.
Montoya, Domingo, Co. B, 3rd N. M. Mtd. Inf., 6 mos., 1861-62.
Montoya, Donaciano, Co. I, 1st N. M. Cav., 2nd Lieut.
Montoya, Felipe, Co. D, 3rd N. M. Mtd. Inf., 6 mos., 1861-62.
Montoya, Francisco, Graydon's Independent Co., N. M. Mtd. Vols., 3 mos., 1861-62.
Montoya, Francisco, Vigil's Independent Co., N. M. Mtd. Vols., 3 mos., 1861, Corp.
Montoya, Francisco, Montoya's Co., Perea's Batt'n, N. M. Mil. Inf., 3 mos., 1861-62.
Montoya, Francisco, Sena's Co. A, N. M. Mil., 2 mos., 1862.
Montoya, Francisco, Co. D, 2nd N. M. Inf.

Montoya, Jesus, Gonzolez Independent Co., N. M. Mil., 3 mos., 1861.
Montoya, Jesus Maria, Co. B, 3rd N. M. Mtd. Inf., 6 mos., 1861-62.
Montoya, Jose, Graydon's Independent Co., N. M. Mtd. Vols., 3 mos., 1861-62.
Montoya, Jose, Co. G, 3rd N. M. Mtd. Inf., 6 mos., 1861-62.
Montoya, Jose, Duran's Co., N. M. Militia.
Montoya, Jose, Andres Co. A, 1st N. M. Mil. Inf., 3 mos., 1861-62.
Montoya, Jose Antonio, Co. D, 4th N. M. Inf.
Montoya, Jose Benito, Alarid's Independent Co., N. M. Mil. Inf., 3 mos., 1861-62.
Montoya, Jose de Jesus, Co. D, 1st N. M. Militia Inf., 3 mos., 1861-62.
Montoya, Jose Encarnacion, Co. E, 3rd N. M. Mtd. Inf., 6 mos., 1861-62.
Montoya, Jose Esquipula, Co. A, 2nd N. M. Inf., Musician.
Montoya, Jose Florentino, Co. H, 2nd N. M. Inf.
Montoya, Jose Prudencio, Co. C, 2nd N. M. Inf.
Montoya, Jose Ignacio, Co. C, 2nd N. M. Inf., and Perea's Independent Co., 60 days, 1861.
Melendez, Jose, Co. C, 3rd N. M. Mtd. Vols., 6 mos., 1861-62.
Melendez, Jose Meliton, Co. E, 3rd N. M. Mtd. Inf., 6 mos., 1861-62.
Melendez, Jose Pedro, Co. I, 1st N. M. Inf.
Melendez, Jose Victor, Co. D, 1st N. M. Mil. Inf., 3 mos., 1861-62.
Melendez, Juan, Alarid's Independent Co., N. M. Mil., 3 mos., 1861-62.
Melendez, ———, Aragon's Co., Perea's Batt'n, N. M. Mil. Inf., 3 mos., 1861-62.
Melendez, Juan, Co. G, 3rd N. M. Mtd. Inf., 6 mos., 1861-62.
Melendez, Juan, Co. D, 3rd N. M. Mtd. Inf., 6 mos., 1861-62.
Melendez, Juan, Abran Co. I, 1st N. M. Inf.
Melendez, Juan Anastacio, Co. K, 1st N. M. Inf.
Melendez, Juan Antonio, Co. E, 1st N. M. Inf.
Melendez, Juan Antonio, Co. F, 1st N. M. Mil. Inf., 3 mos., 1861-62.
Melendez, Juan de Jesus, Co. A, 4th N. M. Inf.
Melendez, Juan Domingo, Co. A, 1st N. M. Mil. Inf., 3 mos., 1861-62.
Melendez, Juan Francisco, Co. L, 1st N. M. Cav.
Melendez, Juan Jose, Co. B, 1st N. M. Cav., Corp.
Melendez, Juan Pablo, Co. F, 1st N. M. Inf.
Melendez, Margarito, Co. A, 2nd N. M. Inf.
Melendez, Pedro Jose, Co. H, 3rd N. M. Mtd. Inf., 6 mos., 1861-62.
Melendez, Perfecto, Co. C, 1st N. M. Inf.
Melendez, Romualdo, Del Balle's Co., Perea's Batt'n, N. M. Mil. Inf., 3 mos., 1861-62.
Melendez, Roman, Co. A, 1st N. M. Inf.
Melendez, Tomas, Tafoya's Independent Co., N. M. Mil., 3 mos., 1861-62, Corp.
Melendez, Diego, Graydon's Independent Co., N. M. Mtd. Vols., 3 mos., 1861-62.
Melendez, Juan Ramon, Co. F, 1st N. M. Mil. Inf., 3 mos., 1861-62.
Melendez, Lorenzo, Alarid's Independent Co., N. M. Mil. Inf.,, 3 mos., 1861-62.
Melendez, Lorenzo, Co. K, 3rd N. M. Mil. Inf., 6 mos., 1861-62, 2nd Lieut.
Melendez, Luciano, Co. E, 3rd N. M. Mtd. Inf., 6 mos., 1861-62.
Melendez, Luis, Co. C, 3rd N. M. Mtd. Inf., 6 mos., 1861-62.
Melendez, Manuel, Aragon's Co., Perea's Batt'n, N. M. Mil. Inf., 6 mos., 1861-62.
Melendez, Pedro, Co. I, Batt'n N. M. Vols., 1866-67.
Melendez, Pedro Jose, Co. C, 1st N. M. Cav., and Co. H, 3rd N. M. Mtd. Inf., 6 mos., 1861-62.
Melendez, Rafael, Co. G, 2nd N. M. Inf., and 3rd N. M. Mtd. Inf., 6 mos., 1861-62, Sgt.
Melendez, Ramos, Co. E, 1st N. M. Inf.

Melendez, Quirino, Co. C, Batt'n N. M. Vols., 1866-67.
Melendez, Santiago, Co. E, 2nd N. M. Inf.
Melendez, Santos, Co. D, 1st N. M. Inf., O. O.
Melendez, Seferino, Co. G, 1st N. M. Inf.
Melendez, Francisco Sisneros y, Vigil's Independent Co., N. M. Mtd. Vols., 3 mos., 1861.
Melendez, Tomas, Simpson's Independent Co., N. M. Mtd. Spies and Guides.
Melendez, Trinidad, Del Bale's Co., Perea's Batt'n, N. M. Mil. Inf., 3 mos., 1861-62.
Melendez, Victoriano, Co. B, 5th N. M. Inf.
Melendez, Trinidad, Alarid's Independent Co., N. M. Mtd. Inf., 3 mos., 1861-62.
Melendez, Alejandro, Alarid's Independent Co., N. M. Mtd. Inf., 3 mos., 1861-62.
Melendez, Ireneo, Alarid's Independent Co., N. M. Mtd. Inf., 3 mos., 1861-62.
Moore, Edward, Co. K, 1st N. M. Cav., Sgt.
Moore, Francis Graydon's Independent Co., N. M. Mtd. Vols., 3 mos., 1861-62.
Moore, James, Co. C, 1st N. M. Inf.
Moore, John, Co. C, 2nd N. M. Inf.
Moore, Joseph, Co. F, 1st N. M. Inf.
Moore, William, Co. D, 1st N. M. Cav., Corp.
Moorehead, Wiliam, Co. B, 5th N. M. Inf., Corp.
Mora, Abelino, Gonzolez Independent Co., N. M. Mil., 3 mos., 1861.
Mora, Alejo, Co. H, 1st N. M. Inf.
Mora, Antonio, Duran's Co., N. M. Mil.
Mora, Antonio, Simpson's Independent Co., N. M. Mtd. Spies and Guides.
Mora, Francisco, Alarid's Independent Co., N. M. Mil. Inf., 3 mos., 1861-62.
Mora, Jesus, Perea's Independent Co., N. M. Vols., 60 days, 1862.
Mora, Jose Leon, Co. K, 1st N. M. Cav.
Mora, Jose Maria, Aragon's Co., Perea's Batt'n, N. M. Mil. Inf., 3 mos., 1861-62.
Mora, Juan, Montoya's Co., Perea's Batt'n, N. M. Mil. Inf., 3 mos., 1861-62.
Mora, Matias, Graydon's Independent Co., N. M. Mtd. Vols., 3 mos., 1861-62.
Mora, Miguel, Co. A, 1st N. M. Inf.
Mora, Romaldo, Co. B, 1st N. M. Cav.
Morales, Antonio Abran, Hubbell's Independent Co., N. M. Mtd. Vols., 3 mos., 1861.
Morales, Bonifacio, Co. E, 1st N. M. Inf.
Morales, Juan, Co. E, 1st N. M. Cav.
Morales, Luciano, Co. E, 2nd N. M. Inf.
Morales, Teodoro, Co. C, 1st N. M. Inf.
Morales, Teodocio, Co. A, 1st N. M. Cav., Corp.
Morales, Antonio, Batt'n, N. M. Vols., 1866-67.
Moreno, Ambrocio, Co. C, 2nd N. M. Inf.
Moreno, Juan, Co. K, 1st N. M. Cav.
Moreno, Jose Basilio, Graydon's Independent Co., N. M. Mtd. Vols., 3 mos., 1861-62.
Moreno, Jose Lorenzo, Co. D, 1st N. M. Cav.
Moreno, Juan Jose, Co. C, Batt'n N. M. Vols., 1866-67.
Moreno, Meterio, Graydon's Indepentent Co., N. M. Mtd. Vols., 3 mos., 1861-62.
Mores, Simon, Co. D, 1st N. M. Inf.
Morfin, Jose Maria, Co. K, 3rd N. M. Mtd. Inf., 6 mos., 1861-62, Sgt.
Morgan, George, Co. D, 1st N. M. Inf.
Morgas, Juan de Jesus, Co. E, 4th N. M. Inf.

Morio, Pedro, Co. G, 2nd N. M. Inf.
Morris, Philip, Co. H, 1st N. M. Cav., 1st Lieut.
Morrison, Arthur, Co. F, 1st N. M. Cav., Major.
Morrison, James H., Co. C, 1st N. M. Inf., 1st Lieut.
Morrison, William, Co. K, 1st N. M. Cav., Sgt.
Mortimore, Wiliam, Co. M, 1st N. M. Cav., 2nd Lieut.; Co. A, 3rd N. M. Mtd. Inf., 6 mos., 1861-62, Captain.
Martinez, Salvador, Co. B, 3rd N. M. Mtd. Inf., 6 mos., 1861-62.
Moya, Albino, Co. K, 3rd N. M. Mtd. Inf., 6 mos., 1861-62.
Moya, Antonio Maria, Co. A, 1st N. M. Inf., O. O.
Moya, Jesus Maria, Co. I, 1st N. M. Inf.
Moya, Jose, Co. L, 1st N. M. Cav.
Moya, Jose, Romero's Co., 3rd N. M. Mtd. Inf., 6 mos., 1861-62.
Moya, Jose Francisco, Co. I, 1st N. M. Inf., O. O.
Moya, Jose Rafael, Co. E, 3rd N. M. Mtd. Inf., 6 mos., 1861-62.
Moya, Juan, Co. H, 1st N. M. Inf.
Moya, Juan Maria, Co. E, 1st N. M. Cav.
Moya, Santiago, Co. A, 3rd N. M. Mtd. Inf., 6 mos., 1861-62.
Moya, Valentin, Tafoya's Independent Co., N. M. Mil. Inf., 3 mos., 1861-62.
Moya, Jose, Co. L, 1st N. M. Cav.
Muanes, Jose Alijo, Graydon's Independent Co., N. M. Mtd. Vols., 3 mos., 1861-62.
Mucklegrew, John, Co. G, 1st N. M. Cav.
Miller, Julio, Co. K, 3rd N. M. Mtd. Inf., 6 mos., 1861-62, Bugler.
Mullens, John, Co. K, 1st N. M. Cav., Sgt.
Mumford, Harry, Co. F, 1st N. M. Inf.
Munez, Cristobal, Co. C, 2nd N. M. Inf.
Munez, Miguel, Co. L, 1st N. M. Cav.
Munez, Antonio, Mink's Independent Co., N. M. Mtd. Vols., 3 mos., 1861.
Munez, Antonio, Aragon's Co., Perea's Batt'n, N. M. Mil. Inf., 3 mos., 1861-62.
Munez, Antonio, Montoya's Co., Perea's Batt'n, N. M. Mil. Inf., 3 mos., 1861-62.
Munez, Faustin, Co. G, 1st N. M. Inf.
Munez, Jose, Aragon's Co., Perea's Batt'n, N. M. Mil. Inf., 3 mos., 1861-62.
Munez, Jose, Co. G, 3rd N. M. Mtd. Inf., 6 mos., 1861-62.
Munez, Juan, Aragon's Co., Perea's Batt'n, N. M. Mil. Inf., 3 mos., 1861-62.
Munez, Mariano, Co. H, 1st N. M. Inf.
Munez, Rellis, Vigil's Independent Co., N. M. Mtd. Vols., 3 mos., 1861-62.
Munez, Santos, Mink's Independent Co., N. M. Mtd. Vols., 3 mos., 1861, Corp.
Munez, Domingo, Co. A, 1st N. M. Mil. Inf., 3 mos., 1861-62.
Munez, Encarnacion, Co. A, 1st N. W. Inf.
Munez, Jesus, Del Balle's Co., Perea's Batt'n, N. M. Mil. Inf., 3 mos., 1861-62.
Munez, Juan, Co. A, 1st N. M. Mil. Inf., 3 mos., 1861-62.
Munez, Miguel, Co. L, 1st N. M. Cav.
Munez, Ignacio, Del Balle's Co., Perea's Batt'n, N. M. Mil. Inf., 3 mos., 1861-62.
Munez, Crespin, Co. H, 1st N. M. Inf., Corp.
Munez, Cristobal, Co. G, 1st N. M. Inf.
Munez, Francisco, Co. H, 1st N. M. Inf.
Munez, Reyes, Co. K, 1st N. M. Cav.
Murphy, John, Co. D, 1st N. M. Inf., Lieut.
Murphy, Lawrence G., Co. F, L, 1st N. M. Inf., Lieut. and Q. M.; and 1st N. M. Cav.

Murphy, Santiago, Del Balle's Co., Perea's Batt'n, N. M. Mil. Inf., 3 mos., 1861-62.
Murray, Charles, Co. K, 1st N. M. Cav., Farrier, Sgt.
Murray, John C., Co. B, 4th N. M. Inf.
Murray, Patrick, Co. K, 1st N. M. Cav.

Nabarretez, Tiburcio, Co. D, 2nd N. M. Inf.
Nabarretez, Bartolo, Co. C, 3rd N. M. Mtd. Inf., 6 mos., 1861-62, Wagoner.
Nabarretez, Secundino, Co. A, 1st N. M. Inf.
Need, William, Co. K, 1st N. M. Cav., Sgt. Major.
Naevo, Juan, Co. G, 1st N. M. Cav.
Nanez, Bicente, Co. B, 1st N. M. Cav., Bugler.
Naranjo, Jose de la Cruz, Co. C, 1st N. M. Inf.
Naranjo, Juan Luis, Co. I, 1st N. M. Inf., and Eaton's Co. D.
Naranjo, Jose de la Luz, Co. A, 1st N. M. Inf.
Naranjo, Julian, Co. D, 1st N. M. Mil. Inf., 3 mos., 1861-62.
Naranjo, Miguel, Co. G, 1st N. M. Inf.
Naranjo, Jose Manuel, Co. B, 1st N. M. Mil. Inf., 3 mos., 1861-62.
Naranjo, Antonio, Co. A, 1st N. M. Inf.
Nash, James, Co. M, 1st N. M. Cav.
Nation, Isaac W., Co. G, 2nd N. M. Cav., 1st Sgt.
Nava, Antonio, Co. C, 1st N. M. Cav., 1st Sgt.
Navarretto, Bartolo, Co. C, 3rd N. M. Mtd. Inf., 6 mos., 1861-62, Wagoner.
Navario, Francisco, Co. B, 1st N. M. Cav.
Naveo, Juan, Co. G, 1st N. M. Cav.
Naville, James, Co. K, 1st N. M. Cav.
Needhan, Hugh John, Co. M, 1st N. M. Cav.
Nieto, Rafael, Co. B, 1st N. M. Inf.
Nerio, Felipe, Co. B, 1st N. M. Inf.
Nerio, Jose, Co. B, 1st N. M. Inf.
Newman, Antonio, Co. D, 1st N. M. Cav.
Neurantes, Joseph, Co. K, 1st N. M. Inf.
Neville, James, Co. K, 1st N. M. Cav.
Nevins, John L., Co. D, 1st N. M. Cav., 1st Lieut.
Nichols, James H., Co. K, 1st N. M. Cav., Corp.
Nichols, William, Co. A, 1st N. M. Cav., Sgt.; Simpson's Independent Co., N. M. Spies and Guides.
Nieto, Jose Dolores, Jaramillo's Co., Perea's Batt'n, N. M. Mil. Inf., 3 mos., 1861-62.
Nieto, Juan Rafael, Aragon's Co., Perea's Batt'n, N. M. Mil. Inf., 3 mos., 1861-62.
Nolan, Daniel, Co. A, 1st N. M. Cav., Bugler.
Noeirga, Antonio Domingo, Co. D, 1st N. M. Cav.
Nuanes, Cristobal, Co. E, 2nd N. M. Inf.
Nuanes, Juan, Aragon's Co., Perea's Batt'n, N. M. Mil. Inf., 3 mos., 1861-62.
Nuanes, Juan, Graydon's Independent Co., N. M. Mtd. Vols., 3 mos., 1861.
Nuanes, Pedro Jose, Aragon's Co., Perea's Batt'n, N. M. Mil. Inf., 3 mos., 1861-62.
Nunley, Commodore P., Simpson's Independent Co., N. M. Mtd., Spies and Guides.
Nunoz, Santiago, Co. B, Batt'n N. M. Vols., 1866-67.
Naranjo, Crecencio, Co. A, N. M. Mil. Inf., 3 mos., 1861-62.

O'Brien, John Patrick, Co. E, 1st N. M. Inf.
Ocana, Antonio, Co. I, 2nd N. M. Inf.
Ocana, Juan Antonio, Co. D, 1st N. M. Inf.
Ocana, Luis, Co. D, 1st N. M. Inf.
Ocana, Meliton, Co. E, 1st N. M. Inf.

Ochoa, Jesus, Co. B, Batt'n, N. M. Vols., 1866-67.
Ochoa, Antonio, Co. K, 1st N. M. Cav.
Ochoa, Carlos, Co. L, 1st N. M. Cav.
O'Connell, Daniel Simpson's Independent Co., N. M. Mtd. Spies and Guides.
O, de La, Thomas, Co. A, 1st N. M. Cav.
O'Donald, William, Co. G, 1st N. M. Cav.
Olaga, Gabriel, Co. C, 2nd N. M. Inf.
Olona, Antonio Maria, Co. F, 1st N. M. Cav.
Olona, Jose, Co. F, 1st N. M. Cav.
O'Leary, Patrick, Co. B, 1st N. M. Cav.
Olguin, Geronimo, Co. H, 1st N. M. Cav.
Olguin, Apodaco, Co. B, Batt'n N. M. Vols., 1866-67.
Olguin, Diego, Co. D, 1st N. M. Mil. Inf., 3 mos., 1861-62.
Olguin, Jesus, Co. H, 1st N. M. Inf.
Olguin, Jose, Co. B, 1st N. M. Cav., and Tafoya's Independent Co., N. M. Mil. Inf., 3 mos., 1861-62.
Olguin, Jose Gregorio, Vigil's Independent Co., N. M. Mtd. Vols., 3 mos., 1861-62.
Olguin, Juan Reyes, Co. I, 1st N. M. Cav.
Olguin, Mateo, Co. K, 2nd N. M. Inf.
Olguin, Melquiades, Co. B, 1st N. M. Cav.
Olguin, Onofre, Co. H, 1st N. M. Inf.
Olguin, Paulino, Baca's Co., Perea's Batt'n, N. M. Mil. Inf., 3 mos., 1861-62.
Olguin, Sabino, Co. E, 1st N. M. Cav.
Olguin, Eulogio, Co. F, 1st N. M. Inf., Sgt.
Olguin, Felipe, Co. H, 3rd N. M. Mtd. Inf., 6 mos., 1861-62.
Olguin, Juan Pedro, Co. A, 1st N. M. Mil. Inf., 3 mos., 1861-62.
Olguin, Pedro, Co. K, 1st N. M. Inf., N. O.
Olguin, Rafael, Aragon's Co., Perea's Batt'n, N. M. Mil. Inf., 3 mos., 1861-62.
Olguin, Santos, Co. D, 1st N. M. Inf.
Olguin, Mateo, Co. K, 2nd N. M. Inf.
Olibarri (Ulibarri), Candelario, Romero's Independent Co. A, 3rd N. M. Mil. Inf.
Olivares, Sihon, Co. I, 3rd N. M. Mtd. Inf., 6 mos., 1861-62.
Olivares, Albino, Co. H, 1st N. M. Inf., Musician.
Olivares, Dolores, Co. F, 1st N. M. Mil. Inf., 3 mos., 1861-62.
Olivares, Pedro, Co. D, 1st N. M. Mil. Inf., 3 mos., 1861-62.
Olivares, Polito, Co. C, 1st N. M. Inf.
Olivares, Ricardo, Vigil's Independent Co., N. M. Mtd. Vols., 3 mos., 1861-62.
Olivares, Miguel, Gonzolez Independent Co., N. M. Mil., 3 mos., 1861.
Olivares, Jose Guadalupe, Co. C, 1st N. M. Cav.
Olivares, Aparisco, Co. E, 1st N. M. Inf.
Olivares, Dolores, Co. F, 1st N. M. Mil. Inf., 3 mos., 1861-62.
Olivares, Juan Guadalupe, Co. A, Batt'n N. M. Mtd. Vols., 1866-67.
Olivares, Antonio Maria, Co. F, 1st N. M. Cav.
Olona, Ignacio, Co. A, Batt'n N. M. Vols., 1866-67, and Co. E, 3rd N. M. Mtd. Inf., 1861-62.
Olona, Jose, Co. F, 1st N. M. Cav.
Olona, Manuel, Co. H, 1st N. M. Inf., 1st Lieut.
Olona, Isidro, Co. G, Romero's 3rd N. M. Mtd. Inf., 6 mos., 1861-62.
Olona, Isidoro, Co. A, 4th N. M. Inf.
Orantia, Candido, Co. H, 1st N. M. Inf.
Orias, Orcine, Co. E, 1st N. M. Inf.
Orgibes, Teodoro, Co. F, 1st N. M. Inf.
Olguin, Sabino, Co. E, 1st N. M. Cav.
Ortiz, Alejo, Duran's Co., N. M. Mil., Corp.
Ortiz, Eugenio, Duran's Co., N. M. Mil.

Ortega, Atanacio, Baca's Co., Perea's Batt'n, N. M. Mil. Inf., 3 mos., 1861-62.
Ortega, Manuel, Co. F, 3rd N. M. Mtd. Inf., 6 mos., 1861-62.
Orono, Francisco, Hubbell's Co., Perea's Batt'n, N. M. Mil. Inf., 3 mos., 1861-62.
Orr, Matthew, Co. A, 3rd N. M. Mtd. Inf., 6 mos., 1861-62.
Orona, Francisco, Hubbell's Co., Perea's Batt'n, N. M. Mil. Inf., 3 mos., 1861-62.
Ortega, Tomas, Co. K, 3rd N. M. Mtd. Inf., 6 mos., 1861-62.
Ortega, Antonio Jose, Co. O, 2nd N. M. Inf., Corp.
Ortega, Augustin, Co. E, 1st N. M. Cav.
Ortega, Antonio, Co. K, 1st N. M. Cav.
Ortega, Benito, Alarid's Independent Co., N. M. Mil. Inf., 3 mos., 1861-62.
Ortega, Blas, Co., A, 4th N. M. Inf.
Ortega, Caterino, Co. I, 1st N. M. Inf.
Ortega, Encarnacion, Co. A, 1st N. M. Inf.
Ortega, Juan Esquibel y, Co. K, 3rd N. M. Mtd. Inf., 6 mos., 1861-62.
Ortega, Esteban, Co. G, 1st N. M. Inf., Sgt.
Ortega, Eulogio, Co. G, 1st N. M. Inf., Musician.
Ortega, Faustin, Co. D, Batt'n N. M. Vols., 1866-67.
Ortega, Felipe, Co. K, 2nd N. M. Inf.
Ortega, Francisco, Co. D, 2nd N. M. Inf.
Ortega, Guadalupe, Co. A, 2nd N. M. Inf.
Ortega, Jesus Maria, Co. D, 3rd N. M. Mtd. Inf., 6 mos., 1861-62.
Ortega, Joaquin, Co. C, 1st N. M. Inf.
Ortega, Jose, Hubbell's Co., Perea's Batt'n, N. M. Mil. Inf., 3 mos., 1861-62.
Ortega, Jose Antonio, Co. K, 2nd N. M. Inf.
Ortega, Jose de Jesus, Co. H, 3rd N. M. Mtd. Inf., 6 mos., 1861-62.
Ortega, Guadalupe, Co. B, 1st N. M. Mtd. Inf., 3 mos., 1861-62.
Ortega, Jose Julian, Co. H, 1st N. M. Inf., N. O.
Ortega, Jose Manuel, Hubbell's Co., Perea's Batt'n, N. M. Mil. Inf., 3 mos., 1861-62.
Ortega, Jose Maria, Co. A, 2nd N. M. Inf.
Ortega, Jose Turnino, Co. A, 2nd N. M. Inf. (See: Court Martial File on case of Saturnino Ortega); Co. B, 3rd N. M. Mtd. Inf., 6 mos., 1861-62.
Ortega, Climaco, Alarid's Independent Co., N. M. Mil. Inf., 3 mos., 1861-62.
Ortega, Juan de Dios, Co. C, 3rd N. M. Mtd. Inf., 6 mos., 1861-62.
Ortega, Juan Pedro, Co. F, 1st N. M. Cav.
Ortega, Justo, Co. C, 1st N. M. Cav.
Ortega, Luciano, Co. C, 3rd N. M. Mtd. Inf., 6 mos., 1861-62.
Ortega, Manuel, Co. E, 1st N. M. Mil. Inf., 3 mos., 1861-62.
Ortega, Nepomoceno, Co. K, 1st N. M. Inf., Sgt.
Ortega, Co. K, 1st N. M. Inf.
Ortega, Pablo, Co. K, 3rd N. M. Inf., 3 mos., 1861-62, Corp.
Ortega, Pedro, Co. C, 1st N. M. Inf.
Ortega, Pilar, Co. D, 1st N. M. Cav.
Ortega, Roman, Romero's Independent Co. A, 3 mos., 1861-62.
Ortega, Tomas, Co. K, 3rd N. M. Mtd. Inf., 6 mos., 1861-62.
Ortega, Vicente, Alarid's Independent Co., 3 mos., 1861-62.
Otero, Antonio, Hubbell's Co., Perea's Batt'n, N. M. Mil. Inf., 3 mos., 1861-62.
Otero, Iturbirgen, Hubbell's Co., Perea's Batt'n, N. M. Mil. Inf., 3 mos., 1861-62.
Otero, Jose, Co. D, 1st N. M. Cav.
Otero, Jose Manuel, Hubbell's Co., Perea's Batt'n, N. M. Mil. Inf., 3 mos., 1861-62.
Ortiz, Clemente, Co. E, 1st N. M. Cav., 1st Lieut.
Ortiz, Jose, Co. D, 1st N. M. Cav.

Ortiz, Antonio Jose, Co. H, 3rd N. M. Mtd. Inf., 6 mos., 1861-62.
Ortiz, Jose Felipe, Co. H, 3rd N. M. Mtd. Inf., 6 mos., 1861-62.
Ortiz, Antonio, Co. E, 1st N. M. Cav., Corp.
Ortiz, Encarnacion, Co. B, 1st N. M. Cav.
Ortiz, Jose Felix, Co. E, 1st N. M. Cav.
Ortiz, Jose Maria, Co. C, 1st N. M. Cav., Sgt.
Ortiz, Juan Rafael, Co. C, Batt'n N. M. Vols., 1866-67.
Ortiz, Mateo, Co. D, Batt'n N. M. Vols., 1866-67.
Ortiz, Quirino, Co. L, 1st N. M. Cav.
Ortiz, Ramon, Co. I, 1st N. M. Inf.
Ortiaga, Anselmo, Co. H, 1st N. M. Inf., Bugler.
(Ortega?)
Ortiaga, Benino, Co. H, 1st N. M. Inf.
Ortiaga, Andres, Co. H, 1st N. M. Inf.
Ortiaga, Manuel, Co. F,, 3rd N. M. Mtd. Inf., 6 mos., 1861-62.
Ortiaga, Francisco, Co. H, 1st N. M. Cav.
Ortiz, Jose Benito, Co. I, 1st N. M. Inf., and Co. B, 3rd N. M. Mtd. Inf., 6 mos., 1861-62.
Ortiz, Jose Francisco, Co. B, 3rd N. M. Inf.
Ortiz, Lucas, 4th N. M. Inf.
Ortiz, Manuel, Co. C, 3rd N. M. Mtd. Inf., 6 mos., 1861-62.
Ortiz, Agapito, Co. C, 2nd N. M. Inf.
Ortiz, Aresteo, Del Balle's Co., Perea's Batt'n, N. M. Mil. Inf., 3 mos., 1861-62.
Ortiz, Anastacio, Alarid's Co., 3 mos., 1861-62.
Ortiz, Jesus, Romero's Independent Co., N. M. Mil. Inf., 3 mos., 1861-62.
Ortiz, Jose Benito, Co. I, 1st N. M. Inf., and Co. B, 3rd N. M. Mtd. Inf., 6 mos., 1861-62.
Ortiz, Jose Guadalupe, Co. H, 3rd N. M. Mtd. Inf., 6 mos., 1861-62.
Ortiz, Juan, Alarid's Co., N. M. Mil. Inf., 3 mos., 1861-62.
Ortiz, Juan Francisco, Co. I, 1st N. M. Cav.
Ortiz, Juan Rafael, Co. C, 1st N. M. Cav.
Ortiz, Luciano, Co. C, 4th N. M. Inf.
Ortiz, Marcelino, Co. I, 1st N. M. Cav.
Ortiz, Merced, Mink's Independent Co., N. M. Mtd. Vols., 1861-62.
Ortiz, Miguel, Co. D, 1st N. M. Mil. Inf., 3 mos., 1861-62.
Ortiz, Nicanor, Co. F, 1st N. M. Inf.
Ortiz, Pedro, Co. G, 1st N. M. Inf.
Ortiz, Quirino, Co. L, 1st N. M. Cav.
Ortiz, Ramon, Co. E, 2nd N. M. Inf.
Ortiz, Ricardo, Sena's Co. A, 1st N. M. Mil. Inf., 2 mos., 1862, Sgt.
Ortiz, Romualdo, Alarid's Independent Co., N. M. Mil. Inf., 3 mos., 1861-62.
Ortiz, Isidro, Alarid's Independent Co., N. M. Mil. Inf., 3 mos., 1861-62.
Ortiz, Aparacio, Co. B, 1st N. M. Inf.
Otero, Manuel, Co. H, 1st N. M. Cav.
Otero, Gregorio, Co. D, 2nd N. M. Inf., Captain.
Otero, Juan Jose, Co. G, 2nd N. M. Inf.
Overall, Albert, Co. H, 1st N. M. Cav.
Ortiz, Herculiano, Co. A, 2nd N. M. Inf.

Pablo, Pablo, Co. A, 5th N. M. Inf.
Pacheco, Eusebio, Co. E, 1st N. M. Inf.
Pacheco, Anselmo, Co. E, 1st N. M. Inf.
Pacheco, Antonio, Co. G, 1st N. M. Inf.
Pacheco, Jose Amado, Co. I, 3rd N. M. Mtd. Inf., 6 mos., 1861-62.
Pacheco, Jose Luciano, Co. G, 1st N. M. Inf., Corp.
Pacheco, Miguel, Co. B, 1st N. M. Cav.
Pacheco, Antonio Rafael, Co. E, 1st N. M. Inf., O. O.
Pacheco, Nepomoceno, Co. C, 1st N. M. Inf., O. O.

Pacheco, Anastacio, Vigil's Independent Co., N. M. Mtd. Vols., 3 mos., 1861.
Pacheco, Antonio Esteban, Co. I, 1st N. M. Inf., O. O.
Pacheco, Custarque, Co. C, Batt'n N. M. Vols., 1866-67.
Pacheco, Fernandez, Mink's Independent Co., N. M. Mtd. Vols., 3 mos., 1861.
Pacheco, Francisco, Co. E, 1st N. M. Cav.
Pacheco, Francisco, Graydon's Independent Co., N. M. Mtd. Vols., 3 mos., 1861-62, Corp.
Pacheco, Francisco, Co. D, 1st N. M. Mil. Inf., 3 mos., 1861-62.
Pacheco, Francisco, Co. H, 3rd N. M. Mtd. Inf., 3 mos., 1861-62.
Pacheco, Gregorio, Hubbell's Independent Co., N. M. Mtd. Vols., 3 mos., 1861.
Pacheco, Jesus, Co. K, 1st N. M. Inf.
Pacheco, Jose Amador, Co. D, 3rd N. M. Mtd. Inf., 6 mos., 1861-62.
Pacheco, Jose Antonio, Vigil's Independent Co., N. M. Mtd. Vols., 3 mos., 1861.
Pacheco, Esquipula, Mink's Independent Co., N. M. Mtd. Vols., 3 mos., 1861.
Pacheco, Jose Francisco, Co. G, 1st N. M. Inf.
Pacheco, Jose Ignacio, Co. D, 1st N. M. Inf.
Pacheco, Jose Manuel, Co. H, 1st N. M. Inf.
Pacheco, Jose Rafael, Co. H, 1st N. M. Inf.
Pacheco, Juan, Co. B, 3rd N. M. Mtd. Inf., 6 mos., 1861-62.
Pacheco, Juan Antonio, Co. B, Batt'n N. M. Vols., 1866-67, and Co. A, 3rd N. M. Mtd. Inf.
Pacheco, Juan, Cristobal, Co. E, 1st N. M. Cav.
Pacheco, Juan de Dios, Co. A, 3rd N. M.2 Mtd. Inf., 6 mos., 1861-62.
Pacheco, Juan Gregorio, Co. C, 1st N. M. Mil. Inf., 3 mos., 1861-62.
Pacheco, Leandro, Co. B, 1st N. M. Inf.
Pacheco, Miguel, Graydon's Independent Co., N. M. Mtd. Vols., 1861-62.
Pacheco, Norbeto, Vigil's Independent Co., N. M. Mtd. Vols., 3 mos., 1861.
Pacheco, Paulin, Co. D, 1st N. M. Mil. Inf., 3 mos., 1861-62.
Pacheco, Rafael, Co. H, 1st N. M. Inf.
Pacheco, Prudencio, Co. I, 1st N. M. Cav.
Pacheco, Ramon, Co. D, 1st N. M. Cav.
Pacheco, Santiago, Del Balle's Co., Perea's Batt'n, N. M. Mil. Inf., 3 mos., 1861-62.
Pacheco, Tomas, Co. I, 1st N. M. Inf., Corp.
Pacheco, Valentin, Co. C, 3rd N. M. Mtd. Inf., 6 mos., 1861-62.
Pacheco, Vicente, Mink's Independent Co., N. M. Mtd. Vols., 3 mos., 1861.
Pacheco, Francisco Ortiz y, Co. A, 1st N. M. Cav., Sgt.
Pacheco, Juan Antonio, Co. B, Batt'n N. M. Vols., 1866-67.
Pacheco, Romaceno, Co. L, 1st N. M. Cav.
Pacheco, Jose, Co. H, 1st N. M. Cav.
Padilla, Esteban, Co. D, 1st N. M. Cav.
Padilla, Jose Maria, Co. D, 1st N. M. Inf.
Padilla, Jose Leandro, Co. C, 1st N. M. Cav.
Padilla, Alejo, Co. H, 1st N. M. Cav.
Padilla, Bicente, Graydon's Independent Co., N. M. Mtd. Vols., 3 mos., 1861-62.
Padilla, Casimiro, Perea's Independent Co., N. M. Vols., 60 days, 1862.
Padilla, Desiderio, Co. F, 1st N. M. Cav., and Co. H, 3rd N. M. Mtd. Inf., 6 mos., 1861-62.
Padilla, Esteban, Co. D, 1st N. M. Cav.
Padilla, Bernardo, Alarid's Independent Co., N. M. Mil., 3 mos., 1861.
Padilla, Francisco, Co. G, 1st N. M. Cav.
Padilla, Jose, Co. G, 3rd N. M. Mtd. Inf., 6 mos., 1861-62.

Padilla, Jose de Jesus, Co. E, 2nd N. M. Inf.
Padilla, Jose Esteban, Co. E, 1st N. M. Inf.
Padilla, Jose Julio, Co. I, 1st N. M. Inf.
Padilla, Jose Leandro, Co. C, 1st N. M. Cav., Corp.
Padilla, Jose Manuel, Jaramillo's Co., Perea's Batt'n, N. M. Mil. Inf., 3 mos., 1861-62.
Padilla, Jose Maria, Co. F, 1st N. M. Inf.
Padilla, Jose Prudencio, Co. C, 1st N. M. Inf.
Padilla, Jose Seledon, Co. I, D, 3rd N. M. Mtd. Inf., 6 mos., 1861-62.
Padilla, Jose Venancio, Aragon's Co., Perea's Batt'n, N. M. Mil. Inf., 3 mos., 1861-62.
Padilla, Juan, Perea's Independent Co., 60 days, 1862.
Padilla, Juan, Co. G, 3rd N. M. Mtd. Inf., 6 mos., 1861-62.
Padilla, Juan de Dios, Aragon's Co., Perea's Batt'n, N. M. Mil. Inf., 3 mos., 1861-62.
Padilla, Juan de la Cruz, Co. H, 3rd N. M. Mtd. Inf., 6 mos., 1861-62.
Padilla, Juan Jose, Alarid's Independent Co., N. M. Mil. Inf., 3 mos., 1861-62.
Padilla, Leandro, Co. B, Batt'n N. M. Vols., 1866-67.
Padilla, Lorenzo, Co. B, 5th N. M. Inf.
Padilla, Lucas, Co. B, 1st N. M. Inf.
Padilla, Manuel, Aragon's Co., Perea's Batt'n, N. M. Mil. Inf., 3 mos., 1861-62.
Padilla, Mariano, Aragon's Co., Perea's Batt'n, N. M. Mil. Inf., 3 mos., 1861-62.
Padilla, Pablo, Co. E, 3rd N. M. Mtd. Inf., 6 mos., 1861-62.
Padilla, Pedro, Co. A, 1st N. M. Mil. Inf., 3 mos., 1861-62.
Padilla, Prudencio, Graydon's Independent Co., N. M. Mtd. Vols., 3 mos., 1861-62.
Padilla, Rafael, Co. G, 3rd N. M. Mtd. Inf., 6 mos., 1861-62.
Padilla, Salas, Co. F, 1st N. M. Inf.
Padilla, Salvador, Co. F, 1st N. M. Mil. Inf., 3 mos., 1861-62.
Padilla, Santiago, Co. H, 3rd N. M. Mtd. Inf., 6 mos., 1861-62, Sgt.
Padilla, Santos, Perea's Independent Co., N. M. Vols., 60 days, 1862.
Padilla, Vicente, Aragon's Co., Perea's Batt'n, N. M. Mil. Inf., 3 mos., 1861-62.
Padilla, Alejamdro, Co. D, 2nd N. M. Inf.
Padilla, Andres, Co. H, 1st N. M. Inf.
Padilla, Antonio, Co. A, E, 3rd N. M. Mtd. Inf., 3 mos., 1861-62.
Padilla, Desiderio, Baca's Co., Perea's Batt'n, N. M. Mil. Inf., 3 mos., 1861-62.
Padilla, Donaciano, Co. H, 3rd N. M. Mtd. Inf., 6 mos., 1861-62.
Padilla, Epitacio, Baca's Co., Perea's Batt'n, N. M. Mil. Inf., 3 mos., 1861-62.
Padilla, Casimiro, Montoya's Co., Perea's Batt'n, N. M. Mil. Inf., 3 mos., 1861-62.
Padilla, Felipe, Co. H, 1st N. M. Inf.
Padilla, Bernardo, Alarid's Independent Co., N. M. Mil. Inf., 3 mos., 1861-62.
Padilla, Jose Antonio, Co. F, 1st N. M. Inf.
Padilla, Juan de Jesus, Co. A, 2nd N. M. Inf.
Padilla, Juan de la Luz, Co. H, N. M. Mtd. Inf., 6 mos., 1861-62.
Padilla, Luz, Co. K, 3rd N. M. Mtd. Inf., 6 mos., 1861-62.
Padilla, Pascual, Duran's Co., N. M. Mil. Inf., 3 mos., 1861-62.
Padilla, Cristobal Jose, Baca's Co., Perea's Batt'n, N. M. Mil. Inf., 3 mos., 1861-62.
Padilla, Ignacio, Co. G, 3rd N. M. Mtd. Inf., 6 mos., 1861-62.
Padilla, Marcos Baca y, Co. K, 2nd N. M. Inf., Captain.
Padilla, Carlos, Graydon's Independent Co., N. M. Mtd. Vols., 1861-62, Bugler.
Paez, Arbano, Co. K, 1st N. M. Inf.

Pacardo (Fajardo?), Juan, Hubbell's Co., Perea's Batt'n, N. M. Mil. Inf.. 3 mos., 1861-62.
Pais, Juan, Hubbell's Co., Perea's Batt'n, N. M. Mil. Inf., 3 mos., 1861-62.
Pais, Lucario, Vigil's Independent Co., N. M. Mtd. Vols., 3 mos., 1861-62.
Pais, Santiago, Co. E, 1st N. M. Cav.
Paiz, Luciano, Co. C, 4th N. M. Inf.
Pais, Miguel, Co. K, 1st N. M. Inf.
Pais, Pedro, Co. L, 3rd N. M. Mtd. Inf., 6 mos., 1861-62, Corp.
Pais, Polonio, Co. E, 1st N. M. Cav.
Polonio, Poloniares, Co. F, 2nd N. M. Inf.
Polonio, Francisco, Co. L, 1st N. M. Cav.
Pena, Jose M., Co. B, 2nd N. M. Cav.
Pando, Juan Antonio, Co. D, 1st N. M. Mil. Inf., 3 mos., 1861-62.
Pando, Juan Cristobal, Co. K, 3rd N. M. Mtd. Inf., 6 mos., 1861-62.
Pando, Miguel, Co. C, 3rd N. M. Mtd. Inf., 6 mos., 1861-62.
Pando, Vicente, Co. C, 3rd N. M. Mtd. Inf., 6 mos., 1861-62.
Parada, Augustin, Co. A, 1st N. M. Cav.
(Prada?)
Parada, Basilio, Co. F, 1st N. M. Cav.
Parada, Braulio, Co. G, 1st N. M. Inf., Sgt.
Parada, Esteban, Co. H, 1st N. M. Cav., Corp.
Parada, Guilliermo, Co. H, 1st N. M. Inf., Bugler.
Parada, Jesus, Co. H, 2nd N. M. Inf.
Parada, Luz, Co. C, Batt'n N. M. Vols., 1866-67.
Parada, Mercedes, Co. G, 1st N. M. Inf., Corp.
Parada, Juan, Co. G, 1st N. M. Inf.
Perea, Catarino, Co. A, 1st N. M. Mil. Inf., 3 mos., 1861-62.
Perea, Domingo, Co. A, 1st N. M. Mil. Inf., 3 mos., 1861-62.
Perea, Juan, Co. D, 4th N. M. Inf.
Parker, John, Co. H, 1st N. M. Inf. See also Cal. Vols.
Parras, Dionicio, Co. H, 1st N. M. Cav.
Parras, Doroteo, Co. B, 1st N. M. Inf.
Parras, Jesus, Co. K, 1st N. M. Cav.
Parras, Manuel, Romero's Co. A, N. M. Mil. Inf., 3 mos., 1861-62.
Peck, Allen F., Co. F, 3rd N. M. Mtd. Inf., 6 mos., 1861-62, Surgeon. See: Colorado Vols.
Peterlen, Paul, Co. E, 4th N. M. Inf., Musician.
Pena, Eulogio, Co. B, 1st N. M. Inf.
Pena, Francisco, Co. A, 3rd N. M. Mtd. Inf., 6 mos., 1st Lieut.
Pena, Jose, Co. G, 2nd N. M. Inf., Sgt.
Pena, Jose Maria, Co. A, 2nd N. M. Inf.
Pena, Jose Ramon, Co. A, 1st N. M. Inf.
Pena, Juan Jose, 2nd N. M .Inf.
Pena, Miguel, Co. L, 1st N. M. Cav.
Pena, Paulino, Co. B, 1st N. M. Inf.
Pena, Pedro, Alarid's Independent Co., N. M. Mtd., Vols., 3 mos., 1861-62.
Pena, Co. B, 1st N. M. Cav.
Pena, Segurio, Co. F, 1st N. M. Mtd. Vols., 6 mos., 1861-62.
Pena, Rumualdo, Co. G, 2nd N. M. Inf.
Peneda, Jose M., Co. F, 1st N. M. Cav.
Penada, Pedro, Co. A, 1st N. M. Inf.
Penido, Pedro, Co. A, 1st N. M. Cav.
Peauet, Jose A., Co. D, 4th N. M. Inf.
Pequett, Francisco, Mink's Co., N. M. Mtd. Spies and Guides, 3 mos., 1861.
Perado, Luz, Co. F, 1st N. M. Inf., Corp.
Perales, Jose Miguel, Baca's Co., Perea's Batt'n, N. M. Mil. Inf., 3 mos., 1861-62.
Peralta, Jose Manuel, Co. D, 2nd N. M. Inf.

Peralta, Juan, Co. A, Baca's Co., Perea's Batt'n, N. M. Mil. Inf., 3 mos., 1861-62.
Peralta, Juan Jose, Tafoya's Co., Perea's Batt'n, N. M. Mil. Inf., 3 mos., 1861-62.
Peralta, Pedro, Co. D, 1st N. M. Inf.
Perales, Rumualdo, Tafoya's Co., Perea's Batt'n, N. M. Mil. Inf., 3 mos., 1861-62.
Perales, Tomas, Co. K, 2nd N. M. Inf.
Perales, Juan Augustin, Co. D, 2nd N. M. Inf.
Perales, Pedro, Co. I, 1st N. M. Inf.
Peran, John, Co. K, 1st N. M. Cav., Corp.
Perales, Merced, Co. I, 1st N. M. Inf., Corp.
Perales, Lorenzo, Co. E, 1st N. M. Mil. Inf., 3 mos., 1861-62.
Perales, Crispin, Co. K, 2nd N. M. Inf.
Perales, Cornelio, Tafoya's Co., Perea's Batt'n, N. M. Mil. Inf., 3 mos., 1861-62.
Perales, Felipe, Co. K, 2nd N. M. Inf., Sgt.
Perales, Fernandez, Gonzalez Independent Co., N. M. Mil., 3 mos., 1861.
Peralta, Jose, Co. A, 3rd N. M. Mtd. Inf., 6 mos., 1861-62.
Perea, Albino, Co. D, 1st N. M. Inf.
Perea, Anselmo, Co. B, 1st N. M. Cav.
Perea, Antonio, Del Balle's Co., Perea's Batt'n, N. M. Mil. Inf., 3 mos., 1861-62.
Perea, Domingo, Graydon's Independent Co., N. M. Mtd. Vols., 3 mos., 1861-62.
Perea, Felipe, Co. I, 2nd N. M. Inf.
Perea, Francisco, Co. B, 3rd N. M. Inf.
Perea, Jose, Co. H, 1st N. M. Inf.
Perea, Jose Angel, Del Balle's Co., Perea's Batt'n, N. M. Mtd. Vols., 3 mos., 1861-62.
Perea, Jose Cayetano, Del Balle's Co., Perea's Batt'n, N. M. Mil. Inf., 3 mos., 1861-62.
Perea, Jose Pedro, Perea's Independent Co., N. M. Vols., 60 days, 1862, Captain.
Perea, Jose Manuel, Aragon's Co., Perea's Batt'n, N. M. Mil. Inf., 3 mos., 1861-62.
Perea, Juan, Hubbell's Independent Co., N. M. Mtd. Vols., 3 mos., 1861.
Perea, Juan, Tafoya's Co., Perea's Batt'n, N. M. Mil. Inf., 3 mos., 1861-62.
Perea, Julian, Co. B, 4th N. M. Inf., Captain.
Perea, Loreto, Co. B, Batt'n N. M. Vols., 6 mos., 1861-62.
Perea, Luciano, Co. E, 1st N. M. Cav.
Perea, Meliton, Co. K, 1st N. M. Cav.
Perea, Manuel, Montoya's Co., Perea's Batt'n, N. M. Mil. Inf., 3 mos., 1861-62.
Perea, Marcelino, Co. B, 4th N. M. Inf.
Perea, Miguel, Co. L, 1st N. M. Cav.
Perea, Narciso, Co. A, 1st N. M. Cav.
Perea, Pedro, Co. K, 1st N. M. Cav., and Co. D, 3rd N. M. Mtd. Inf., 6 mos., 1861-62.
Perea, Jose Pedro, Co. C, 1st N. M. Cav.
Pompase, Jose, Romero's Co. A, 3rd N. M. Mtd. Inf., 6 mos., 1861-62.
Pena, Remijido, Co. E, 4th N. M. Inf.
Pena, Ignacio, Del Balle's Co., Perea's Batt'n, N. M. Mil. Inf., 3 mos., 1861-62.
Perez, Dionicio, Co. G, 2nd N. M. Inf.
Perez, Jesus, Co. A, 1st N. M. Cav.
Perez, Norberto, Co. A, 1st N. M. Inf.
Perez, Tomas, Co. F, 1st N. M. Inf.
Perez, Hilario, Co. B, 1st N. M. Inf.

Pineda, Jose, Co. A, 1st N. M. Cav.
Pellis, George, Co. F, 1st N. M. Inf., 1st Lieut.
Pfeiffer, Albert, Co. H, F, D, 1st N. M. Cav., Major.
Pfeiffer, Antonio, Co. B, 1st N. M. Inf.
Phepps, John W., Co. F, 1st N. M. Cav.
Phillips, George, Co. H, 1st N. M. Cav.
Phillips, John W., Co. F, 1st N. M. Cav., Corp.
Phol, Herman, Co. F, 1st N. M. Cav., Corp.
Pickering, James, Co. D, 2nd N. M. Inf., Sgt.
Piedad, Jose Maria, Co. F, 1st N. M. Cav.
Pineda, Jose Maria, Co. B, 1st N. M. Cav.
Pineda, Romualdo, Co. F, 1st N. M. Cav.
Ponida, Jose Ambrosio, Co. I, 1st N. M. Cav.
Pike, Henry Clay, Vigil's Independent Co., N. M. Mil., 3 mos., 1861.
Pino, Felipe, Co. B, 1st N. M. Cav., Sgt.
Pino, Francisco, Romero's Co., 3rd N. M. Mtd. Inf., 6 mos., 1861-62.
Pino, Guadalupe, Co. A, 2nd N. M. Inf.
Pino, Jose de la Luz, Co. P, 1st N. M. Cav.
Pino, Juan E., Co. A, 2nd N. M. Inf., Corp.
Pino, Juan R., Perea's N. M. Vols., 60 days, 1862.
Pino, Manuel, Co. F., 1st N. M. Cav.
Pino, Manuel Ambrosio, Co. A, 2nd N. M. Inf., Sgt.
Pino, Manuel D., Co. F, 2nd N. M. Inf., Major.
Pino, Mariano, Co. G, 1st N. M. Inf.
Pino, Miguel E., Co. F, 4th N. M. Inf.
Pinones, Leonides, Co. E, 1st N. M. Inf.
Pirand, John, Co. K, 1st N. M. Vols.
Portillos, Eugenio, Co. I, 1st N. M. Cav.
Portillos, Antonio, 1st N. M. Mil. Inf., 3 mos., 1861-62.
Portillos, Rafael, Co. 1, 1st N. M. Inf.
Portillos, Rafael, Co. B, 1st N. M. Inf.
Portillos, Dionicio, Co. H, 1st N. M. Cav.
Portillos, Narciso, Co. I, 1st N. M. Inf.
Postle, Robert, Co. L, 1st N. M. Cav.
Prada, Augustin, Co. C, 1st N. M. Inf.
Prada, Casildo, Mink's Independent Co., N. M. Mtd., Spies and Guides.
Prada, Santiago, Co. H, 3rd N. M. Mtd. Inf., 6 mos., 1861-62, Sgt.
Prendle, Charles Simpson's Independent Co., N. M. Mtd. Spies and Guides.
Prescott, Thomas, Co. M, 1st N. M. Cav., Corp.
Provencio, Antonio, Co. E, 1st N. M. Inf.
Provencio, Julian, Co., A, 3rd N. M. Mtd. Inf., 6 mos., 1861-62.
Provencio, Francisco, Co. G, 1st N. M. Inf.
Provencio, Severiano, Co. H, 1st N. M. Inf.
Prudencio, Gabriel, Co. H, 1st N. M. Cav.
Prudencio, Francisco, Co. E, 1st N. M. Cav.
Prudencio, Jose, Co. H, 1st N. M. Cav.
Puenta, Monico, Del Balle's Co., Perea's Batt'n, N. M. Mil. Inf., 3 mos., 1861-62.

Quarand, Jesus, Co. B, 1st N. M. Inf.
Quigley, James, Co. H, 1st N. M. Cav., Saddler.
Quilamaca, Miranda, Co. H, 1st N. M. Cav.
Quiromes, Tomas, Co. D, 1st N. M. Cav.
Quintana, Andres, Co. A, 2nd N. M. Inf.
Quintana, Anselmo, Co. I, 1st N. M. Cav.
Quintana, Antonio, Co. C, 1st N. M. Inf.
Quintana, Antonio, Co. F, 3rd N. M. Mtd. Inf., 6 mos., 1861-62.
Quintana, Baltazar, Co. I, 4th N. M. Inf., Sgt.
Quintana, Benino, Co. K, 1st N. M. Inf.
Quintana, Crisantos, Co. A, 1st N. M. Inf.

Quintana, Crestino, Duran's Co., Perea's Batt'n, N. M. Mil. Inf., 3 mos., 1861-62.
Quintana, Blas, Co. B, 1st N. M. Inf.
Quintana, Feliz, Co. A, 1st N. M. Mil. Inf., 3 mos., 1861-62.
Quintana, Gregorio, Co. H, 1st N. M. Inf.
Quintana, Isidro, Co. H, 3rd N. M. Mtd. Inf., 6 mos., 1861-62.
Quintana, Jesus, Co. A, 2nd N. M. Inf., Sgt.
Quintana, Jesus M Sena y, Co. A, 1st N. M. Cav., Blacksmith.
Quintana, Jose, Co. B, 1st N. M. Cav.
Quintana, Jose Bernadino, Co. B, 1st N. M. Cav.
Quintana, Jose Manuel, Sena's Co. A, 1st N. M. Militia, 2 mos., 1862.
Quintana, Jose Maria, Co. A, 1st N. M. Cav.
Quintana, Jose Ramos, Co. H, 1st N. M. Inf.
Quintana, Juan, Co. K, 3rd N. M. Mtd. Inf., 6 mos., 1861-62.
Quintana, Juan Antonio, Co. A, 3rd N. M. Mtd. Inf., 6 mos., 1861-62.
Quintana, Juan Francisco, Co. C, 3rd N. M. Mtd. Vols., 6 mos., 1861-62.
Quintana, Juan Pablo, Co. G, 1st N. M. Cav.
Quintana, Lucas, Co. C, 3rd N. M. Mtd. Inf., 6 mos., 1861-62.
Quintana, Marcelino, Co. B, 1st N. M. Inf.
Quintana, Martin, Co. E, 1st N. M. Cav., Lieut.
Quintana, Mateo, Co. A, Sena's Co., 1st N. M. Mil., 2 mos., 1862.
Quintana, Melquiades, Co. C, 3rd N. M. Mtd. Inf., 6 mos., 1861-62.
Quintana, Miguel, Co. H, 1st N. M. Cav.
Quintana, Miguel Antonio, Co. I, 1st N. M. Cav.
Quintana, Nestor, Co. E, 1st N. M. Inf.
Quintana, Nicanor, Co. E, 1st N. M. Mil. Inf., 3 mos., 1861-62, Sgt.
Quintana, Nicolas, Co. A, 1st N. M. Cav., Major.
Quintana, Polonio, Co. H, 1st N. M. Cav., Corp.
Quintana, Rafael, Co. G, 1st N. M. Inf.
Quintana, Seferino, Co. A, 3rd N. M. Mtd. Inf., 6 mos., 1861-62.
Quintana, Tomas, Co. K, 3rd N. M. Mtd. Inf., 6 mos., 1861-62.
Quintana, Rafael, Co. G, 1st N. M. Inf.
Quintana, Ramon, Co. I, 1st N. M. Cav.
Quintana, Vicente, Romero's Co., 3rd N. M. Mtd. Inf., 6 mos., 1861-62.
Quintana, Jesus, Co. B, 2nd N. M. Inf.
Quintana, Juan Domingo, Co. B, 3rd N. M. Mtd. Inf., 6 mos., 1861-62.

Ribera, Vidal, Co. L, 1st N. M. Cav.
Robles, Jesus, Co. B, 2nd N. M. Inf.
Rodriguez, Francisco, Co. H, 1st N. M. Inf.
Rodriguez, Gregorio, Co. H, 1st N. M. Cav.
Reagan, William, Co. D, 1st N. M. Inf.
Rael, Atanacio, Co. F, 1st N. M. Inf.
Rael, Andres, Co. H, 1st N. M. Cav., Corp., and Duran's Co., N. M. Militia.
Rael, Antonio, Jose, Co. K, 2nd N. M. Inf.
Rael, Francisco, Co. P, 1st N. M. Cav.
Rael, Ignacio, Co. H, 1st N. M. Cav.
Rael, Jose, Duran's Co., N. M. Mil.
Rael, Jose Antonio, Co. D, 1st N. M. Mil. Inf., 3 mos., 1861-62.
Rael, Jose de Jesus, Co. H, 1st N. M. Inf.
Rael, Jose Manuel, Co. G, 2nd N. M. Inf.
Rael, Juan, Co. E, 1st N. M. Cav., Corp.
Rael, Marcos, Co. A, 2nd N. M. Inf.
Rael, Pedro, Co. H, 1st N. M. Cav.
Rael, Rafael, Co. F, 3rd N. M. Mtd. Inf., 6 mos., 1861-62, 1st Sgt.
Rael, Ramon, Co. K, 1st N. M. Inf.
Roybal, Eutimio, Co. C, 4th N. M. Inf.
Roybal, Juan, Co. F, 4th N. M. Inf.
Rainer, Peter, Co. I, 3rd N. M. Mtd. Inf., 6 mos., 1861-62, Bugler.

Rains, Abraham, Simpson's Independent Co., N. M. Mtd. Spies and Guides.
Ruiz, Miguel, Co. K, 2nd N. M. Inf.
Ruiz, Inez, Co. G, 2nd N. M. Inf.
Roybal, Joaquin, Co. E, 1st N. M. Cav.
Roybal, Juan Domingo, Co. P, 1st N. M. Cav.
Ramirez, Dionicio, Co. A, Batt'n N. M. Vols., 1866-67.
Ramirez, Manuel, Co. B, 2nd N. M. Inf.
Ramirez, Andres, Co. C, 1st N. M. Cav.
Ramirez, Cristobal, Co. G, 2nd N. M. Inf.
Ramirez, Jesus, Co. I, 2nd N. M. Inf.
Ramirez, Ramon, Co. G, 1st N. M. Inf.
Ramirez, Candido, Co. P, 1st N. M. Cav.
Ramirez, Cruz, Co. E, 1st N. M. Cav.
Ramirez, Vicente, Co. D, 1st N. M. Cav.
Ramirez, Valentin, Co. F, 1st N. M. Cav.
Ramirez, Luciano, Co. D, 1st N. M. Mil. Inf., 3 mos., 1861-62.
Ramirez, Nepumoceno, Co. A, Batt'n, N. M. Vols., 1866-67.
Rankin, Sylvester, Co. F, 2nd N. M. Inf., Ass't Surg.
Roybal, Jose dela Cruz, Co. B, 1st N. M. Inf.
Roybal, Salvador, Co. M, 1st N. M. Cav.
Roybal, William, Co. F, 1st N. M. Cav.
Real, Andres, Co. H, 1st N. M. Cav.
Real, Candelario, Hubbell's Independent Co., 3 mos., 1861.
Real, Ignacio, Co. H, 1st N. M. Cav.
Real, Jose de Jesus, Co. I, 1st N. M. Cav.
Real, Pedro, Montoya's Co., Perea's Batt'n, N. M. Mil. Inf., 3 mos., 1861-62.
Roybal, Jose Mauricio, Co. B, 5th N. M. Cav.
Roybal, Juan, Co. I, 1st N. M. Inf.
Ribera, Roque, Co. B, Batt'n N. M. Vols., 1866-67, Sgt.
Ribera, Jose Maria, Co. B, Batt'n N. M. Vols., 1866-67.
Ribera, George, Co. A, 1st N. M. Inf.
Ribera, Jose Pablo, Co. G, 1st N. M. Inf.
Ribera, Pablo, Co. K, 3rd N. M. Mtd. Inf., 6 mos., 1861-62.
Rodriguez, Marcial, Co. I, 1st N. M. Inf.
Reed, Richard, Co. G, 1st N. M. Cav., Sgt.
Ridel, John M., Co. M, 1st N. M. Cav.
Reeder, David, Co. A, 1st N. M. Cav., Saddler.
Rael, Pedro, Montoya's Co., Perea's Batt'n, N. M. Mil. Inf., 3 mos., 1861-62.
Ragalado, Reducindo, Co. H, 1st N. M. Cav.
Rogers, John, Co. G, 1st N. M. Inf., Sgt. Major.
Riley, James, Co. K, 1st N. M. Cav., Corp.
Rael, Lazaro, Baca's Co., Perea's Batt'n, N. M. Mil. Inf., 3 mos., 1861-62.
Roybal, Jesus, Montoya's Co., Perea's Batt'n, N. M. Mil. Inf., 3 mos., 1861-62.
Rendon, Felipe, Co. M, 1st N. M. Cav., Corp.
Rendon, Antonio, Co. D, 1st N. M. Mil. Inf., 3 mos., 1861-62.
Rendon, Jesus Maria, Co. L, 1st N. M. Cav.
Rendon, Jose, Co. L, 1st N. M. Cav.
Rendon, Jose Antonio, Co. D, 1st N. M. Mil. Inf., 3 mos., 1861-62.
Rendon, Pedro, Co. B, 1st N. M. Mil. Inf., 3 mos., 1861-62.
Rendon, Rafael, Co. K, 1st N. M. Inf.
Ribera, Zenobio, Co. G, 1st N. M. Cav.
Revemthow, Ludwig, Co. H, 1st N. M. Cav. See: Cal. Vols.
Ribera, Gormecindo, Co. B, 5th N. M. Inf.
Reyes, Apolonio, Co. H, 1st N. M. Inf.
Rhodes, Henry C., Co. G, 1st N. M. Inf., 2nd Lieut.
Roybal, Desiderio, Co. L, 1st N. M. Cav.
Roybal, Domingo, Co. E, 3rd N. M. Inf.

Roybal, Esquipula, Co. K, 1st N. M. Inf.
Roybal, Pedro, Co. K, 1st N. M. Inf.
Roybal, Benito, Sena's Co. A, N. M. Mil., 2 mos., 1862, Sgt.
Roybal, Jose Maria, Vigil's Independent Co., N. M. Mil., 3 mos., 1861.
Roybal, Jose Ignacio, Vigil's Independent Co., N. M. Mil., 3 mos., 1861.
Roybal, Lauriano, Baca's Co., Perea's Batt'n, N. M. Mil. Inf., 3 mos., 1861-62.
Ribera, Jose Pablo, Co. G, 2nd N. M. Inf.
Ribera, Juan Eteban, Co. K, 3rd N. M. Mtd. Inf., 6 mos., 1861-62.
Ribera, Julian, Romero's Co., 3rd N. M. Mtd. Vols., 6 mos., 1861-62.
Ribera, Luis, Alarid's Independent Co., N. M. Mil., Corp.
Ribera, Marcos, Alarid's Independent Co., N. M. Mil.
Ribera, Matias, 1st N. M. Mil. Inf., Sena's Co. A, 2 mos., 1862, Sgt.
Ribera, Miguel, Romero's Co., 3rd N. M. Mtd. Inf., 6 mos., 1861-62.
Ribera, Nicolas, Co. G, 1st N. M. Inf.
Ribera, Juan, Co. C, 1st N. M. Cav.
Ribera, Juan Esteban, Co. B, 2nd N. M. Inf.
Rios, Francisco, Co. I, 1st N. M. Inf.
Rios, Carlos, Co. E, 1st N. M. Inf.
Rios, Luis, Co. A, 1st N. M. Cav.
Ritter, John, Co. M, 1st N. M. Cav., Sgt.
Ribera, Cecilio, Co. K, 3rd N. M. Mtd. Inf., 6 mos., 1861-62.
Ribera, Crestino, Romero's Co., 3rd N. M. Mtd. Vols., 6 mos., 1861-62.
Ribera, Gabriel, Co. I, 1st N. M. Inf., and Co. M, 1st N. M. Cav.
Nebel, James, Co. G, 2nd N. M. Inf.
Ribera, Atanacio, Co. D, 1st N. M. Inf., O. O.
Rivali, Desiderio, Co. I, 1st N. M. Inf.
Rivali, Juan Ignacio, Co. C, 3rd N. M. Mtd. Inf., 6 mos., 1861-62.
Rivali, Juan, Co. I, 1st N. M. Inf.
Ribera, Venceslao, Co. A, 2nd N. M. Inf.
Ribera, Camillo, Co. K, 3rd N. M. Mtd. Inf., 6 mos., 1861-62.
Ribera, Cecilio, Co. K, 3rd N. M. Mtd. Inf., 6 mos., 1861-62.
Ribera, Guadalupe, Co. K, 3rd N. M. Mtd. Inf., 6 mos., 1861-62.
Ribera, Roman, Co. A, 1st N. M. Cav.
Ribera, George, Alarid's Independent Co., N. M. Mil.
Ribera, Jose, Alarid's Independent Co., N. M. Mil.
Ribera, Jose Antonio, Montoya's Co., Perea's Batt'n, N. M. Mil. Inf., 3 mos., 1861-62.
Roybal, Antonio, Co. B, 1st N. M. Inf.
Roberts, Benjamin S., Co. F, 5th N. M. Inf., Colonel.
Robinson, Josiah, Co. H, 1st N. M. Cav.
Robinson, Oliver B., Co. D, 1st N. M. Cav., Blacksmith.
Robinson, George, Co. A, 3rd N. M. Mtd. Inf., 6 mos., 1861-62, Bugler.
Robero, Bernadine, Gonzolez Independent Co., N. M. Mil., 3 mos., 1861.
Robles, Antonio, Co. A, 5th N. M. Inf., 1st Lieut.
Robles, Cecilio, 1st N. M. Mil., Sena's Co. A, 2 mos., 1862, Lieut.
Robles, Jesus, Co. C, 1st N. M. Cav.
Rocha, Carmen, Co. F, 1st N. M. Cav.
Rocha, Miguel, Co. B, 1st N. M. Inf., Corp.
Rodarte, Santiago, Co. B, 1st N. M. Mil. Inf., 3 mos., 1861-62.
Rodarte, Juan Antonio, Jaramillo's Co., Perea's Batt'n, N. M. Mil. Inf., 3 mos., 1861-62, Corp.
Rodela, Pedro, Co. A, 1st N. M. Cav.
Rodriguez, Guadalupe, Co. A, 2nd N. M. Inf.
Rodriguez, Gorgonio, Co. H, 1st N. M. Cav.
Rodriguez, Pascual, Co. I, 1st N. M. Inf., O. O.
Rodriguez, Reyes, Co. K, 1st N. M. Inf.
Rodriguez, Pedro, Co. F, 2nd N. M. Inf.
Rodriguez, Jose Rafael, Co. C, 1st N. M. Inf.

Rodriguez, Anastacio, Co. I, 1st N. M. Inf.
Rodriguez, Rafael, Co. I, 1st N. M. Inf.
Rodriguez, Blas, Co. E, 1st N. M. Cav.
Rodriguez, Casimiro, Co. B, 1st N. M. Mil. Inf., 3 mos., 1861-62.
Rodriguez, Donaciano, Co. E, 1st N. M. Cav.
Rodriguez, Francisco, Co. A, 1st N. M. Cav.
Rodriguez, Manuel, Co. G, 3rd N. M. Mil. Inf., 6 mos., 1861-62.
Rodriguez, Marcos, Co. H, 2nd N. M. Inf.
Rodriguez, Silverio, Co. C, 2nd N. M. Inf., 1866-67.
Rodriguez, Concepcion, Co. A, 2nd N. M. Inf.
Rodriguez, Encarnacion, Co. E, 2nd N. M. Inf.
Rodriguez, Francisco, Co. A, 2nd N. M. Inf.
Rodriguez, Jesus M., Co. B, 1st N. M. Inf.
Rodriguez, Jose, Co. D, 1st N. M. Cav.
Rodriguez, Jose Rafael, Co. I, 1st N. M. Inf.
Rodriguez, Juan, Co. A, 1st N. M. Inf.
Rodriguez, Juan Esteban, Co. G, 1st N. M. Inf., Sgt.
Rodriguez, Juan Ignacio, Co. F, 1st N. M. Mil. Inf., 3 mos., 1861-62.
Rodriguez, Ramon, Co. H, 3rd N. M. Mil. Inf., 3 mos., 1861-62.
Rodriguez, Regel, Co. C, 1st N. M. Cav., Sgt.
Rodriguez, Ruperto, Co. D, 1st N. M. Cav.
Rodriguez, Reyes, Co. K, 1st N. M. Inf., O. O.
Rodriguez, Marcial, Co. A, 1st N. M. Cav.
Roybal, Joaquin, Co. A, 3rd N. M. Mtd. Inf., 6 mos., 1861-62.
Rogers, John, Co. F, 2nd N. M. Inf., Sgt. Major.
Roybal, Anastacio, Co. L, 1st N. M. Cav.
Roybal, Desiderio, Co. L, 1st N. M. Cav.
Roybal, Esquipula, Co. K, 1st N. M. Inf.
Roybal, Teodocio, Co. F, 3rd N. M. Mtd. Inf., 6 mos., 1861-62.
Roybal, Gregorio, Co. C, 1st N. M. Cav.
Roybal, Gorgonio, Co. B, 2nd N. M. Inf.
Roybal, Manuel Antonio, Co. F, 1st N. M. Cav.
Roybal, Pedro, Co. K, 1st N. M. Inf.
Roybal, Ignacio, Co. A, 1st N. M. Inf., Corp.
Roybal, Antonio, Mink's Independent Co., N. M. Mtd. Vols., 3 mos., 1861.
Roybal, Jose de la Cruz, Co. B, 1st N. M. Inf., O. O.
Roybal, Juan Domingo, Co. A, 1st N. M. Inf.
Roybal, Marcelino, Mink's Independent Co., N. M. Mtd. Vols., 3 mos., 1861.
Romero, Carmel, Co. A, 3rd N. M. Mtd. Inf., 6 mos., 1861-62.
Romero, Narciso, Co. C, 1st N. M. Inf.
Romero, Paul, Co. I, 1st N. M. Cav.
Romero, Jesus, Co. F, 1st N. M. Mtd. Inf., 6 mos., 1861-62.
Romero, Lorenzo, Co. A, 5th N. M. Inf.
Romero, Abad, Co. E, 1st N. M. Mil. Inf., 3 mos., 1861-62, 1st Lieut.
Romero, Agapito, Co. C, 1st N. M. Cav.
Romero, Albino, Vigil's Independent Co., N. M. Mtd. Vols., 3 mos., 1861.
Romero, Alejandro, Co. H, 1st N. M. Cav.
Romero, Andres, Romero's Independent Co. A, N. M. Mil. Inf., 3 mos., 1861-62, Sgt.
Romero, Antonio, Gonzolez Independent Co., N. M. Mil., 3 mos., 1861.
Romero, Antonio, Mink's Independent Co., N. M. Mtd. Inf., 3 mos., 1861.
Romero, Antonio, Hubbell's Independent Co., N. M. Mtd. Vols., 3 mos., 1861.
Romero, Antonio, Simpson's Independent Co., N. M. Mtd. Spies and Guides.
Romero, Antonio Domingo, Co. E, 1st N. M. Mil. Inf., 3 mos., 1861-62.
Romero, Antonio Maria, Co. E, 1st N .M. Mil. Inf., 3 mos., 1861-62.
Romero, Benicio, Co. E, 1st N. M. Mil. Inf., 3 mos., 1861-62.

Romero, Benito, Vigil's Independent Co., N. M. Mtd. Vols., 3 mos., 1861.
Romero, Bicente, Co. H, 1st N. M. Cav., Bugler.
Romero, Buenaventuro, Co. D, 4th N. M. Cav.
Romero, Candido, Co. D, Batt'n N. M. Vols., 1866-67.
Romero, Carmen, Alarid's Independent Co., N. M. Mil. Inf., 3 mos., 1861-62.
Romero, Carpio, Co. F, 1st N. M. Inf.
Romero, Casimiro, Co. A, 1st N. M. Mil. Inf., 3 mos., 1861-62.
Romero, Cristosto, Co. G, 3rd N. M. Mtd. Inf., 6 mos., 1861-62.
Romero, David, Co. K, 3rd N. M. Mtd. Inf., 6 mos., 1861-62.
Romero, Dilubino, Co. C, 1st N. M. Cav.
Romero, Dionicio, Co. F, 1st N. M. Inf.
Romero, Polonio, Co. D, Batt'n N. M. Vols., 1866-67.
Romero, Encarnacion, Gonzolez Independent Co., N. M. Mil., 3 mos., 1861.
Romero, Epimento, Co. D, Batt'n N. M. Vols., 1866-67.
Romero, Esteban, Co. B, 4th N. M. Cav.
Romero, Eugenio, Co. D, 3rd N. M. Mtd. Inf., 6 mos., 1861-62, Sgt.
Romero, Eugenio, Duran's Co., New Mexico Mil., 1861.
Romero, Felipe, Co. I, 1st N. M. Inf., Corp.
Romero, Felix, 1st N. M. Mil., Sena's Co. A, 2 mos., 1861-62.
Romero, Francisco, Tafoya's Co., N. M. Mil., 3 mos., 1861-62.
Romero, Francisco Antonio, Co. I, 1st N. M. Inf.
Romero, Francisco, Romero's 3rd N. M. Mtd. Inf., 6 mos., 1861-62, Sgt.
Romero, Gabriel, Vigil's Independent Co., N. M. Mtd. Vols., 3 mos., 1861.
Romero, Geronimo, Co. D, 2nd N. M. Inf.
Romero, Guadalupe, Co. F, 1st N. M. Inf.
Romero, Ignacio, Co. E, 1st N. M. Cav.
Romero, Isidro, Co. B, 1st N. M. Inf., Sgt.
Romero, Jesus, Hubbell's Co., Perea's Batt'n, N. M. Mil., 3 mos., 1861-62.
Romero, Jesus, Jaramillo's Co., Perea's Batt'n, N. M. Mil. Inf., 3 mos., 1861-62.
Romero, Jesus, Alarid's Independent Co., N. M. Mil., 3 mos., 1861-62.
Romero, Jesus, Co. D, 2nd N. M. Inf.
Romero, Jesus, Co. C, 3rd N. M. Mtd. Inf., 6 mos., 1861-62.
Romero, Jesus Maria, Co. I, 1st N. M. Cav.
Romero, Jose, Hubbell's Co., Perea's Batt'n, N. M. Mil. Inf., 3 mos., 1861-62.
Romero, Jose, Graydon's Independent Co., N. M. Mtd. Vols., 3 mos., 1861-62.
Romero, Jose, Co. C, 2nd N. M. Inf.
Romero, Jose A., Perea's Independent Co., N. M. Vols., 60 days, 1862.
Romero, Jose Bonifacio, Co. G, 1st N. M. Inf., Captain.
Romero, Jose de la Cruz, Co. C, 1st N. M. Mil. Inf., 3 mos., 1861-62.
Romero, Jose de Jesus, Co. H, 2nd N. M. Inf.
Romero, Jose de Jesus, Romero's Co., 3rd N. M. Mtd. Inf., 6 mos., 1861-62, Captain.
Romero, Juse Eugenio, Co. I, 1st N. M. Inf.
Romero, Jose Guadalupe, Romero's Independent Co. A, N. M. Mil., 3 mos., 1861-62, Captain.
Romero, Jose Inez, Co. B, 3rd N. M. Mtd. Inf., 6 mos., 1861-62.
Romero, Isidro, Co. I, 1st N. M. Cav.
Romero, Luis, Co. G, 2nd N. M. Inf.
Romero, Jose Luz, Co. B, 1st N. M. Inf.
Romero, Jose Ramon, Gonzolez Independent Co., N. M. Mil., 3 mos., 1861.
Romero, Jose Isidro, Co. H, 1st N. M. Inf.
Romero, Jose Saturnino, Co. I, 1st N. M. Inf.

Romero, Juan Tafoya's Independent Co., N. M. Mil., 3 mos., 1861-62, Sgt.
Romero, Juan, Gonzolez Independent Co., N. M. Mil., 3 mos., 1861.
Romero, Juan, Romero's Independent Co. A, N. M. Mil. Inf., 3 mos., 1861-62.
Romero, Juan Antonio, Co. F, 1st N. M. Cav.
Romero, Juan Catarino, Romero's Independent Co., N. M. Mil. Inf., 1861-62.
Romero, Juan Clemente, Co. B, 1st N. M. Inf.
Romero, Juan de Jesus, Co. C, 1st N. M. Inf.
Romero, Juan Felipe, Mink's Independent Co., N. M. Mtd. Vols., 3 mos., 1861.
Romero, Juan Jose, Graydon's Independent Co., N. M. Mtd. Vols., 3 mos., 1861-62.
Romero, Juan Pablo, Jaramillo's Co., Perea's Batt'n, N. M. Mil. Inf., 3 mos., 1861-62.
Romero, Juan Perfecto, Montoya's Co., Perea's Batt'n, N. M. Mil. Inf., 3 mos., 1861-62.
Romero, Julian, Co. D, 1st N. M. Cav.
Romero, Leandro, Co. A, 1st N. M. Cav.
Romero, Leon, Co. A, 1st N. M. Cav.
Romero, Lino, Co. D, 1st N. M. Cav.
Romero, Lorenzo, Co. A, 5th N. M. Inf., and Co. A, 1st N. M. Mil. Inf., 3 mos., 1861-62.
Romero, Luciano, Co. H, 3rd N. M. Mtd. Inf., 6 mos., 1861-62.
Romero, Luis, Romero's Independent Co. A, N. M. Mil. Inf., 3 mos., 1861-62.
Romero, Luis Maria, Co. H, 2nd N. M. Inf., Corp.
Romero, Manuel, Mink's Independent Co., N. M. Mtd. Vols., 3 mos., 1861.
Romero, Manuel, Co. I, 3rd N. M. Mtd. Inf., 6 mos., 1861-62.
Romero, Narciso, Co. C, 4th N. M. Inf.
Romero, Mauricio, Co. C, 1st N. M .Inf.
Romero, Melquiades, Co. A, 1st N. M. Inf., Sgt.
Romero, Miguel Antonio, Hubbell's Co., Musician.
Romero, Miguel, Alarid's Independent Co., N. M. Mil. Inf., 3 mos., 1861-62.
Romero, Nicanor, Co. D, 3rd N. M. Mtd. Inf., 6 mos., 1861-62.
Romero, Nicolas, Co D, 1st N. M. Mil. Inf., 3 mos., 1861-62.
Romero, Pablo, Simpson's Independent Co., N. M. Mtd. Spies and Guides.
Romero, Pablo, Co. A, 3rd N. M. Mtd. Inf., 6 mos., 1861-62.
Romero, Patricio, Co. D, 1st N. M. Inf.
Romero, Perfecto, Gonzolez Independent Co., N. M. Mil. Inf., 3 mos., 1861.
Romero, Pimenio, Co. A, 1st N. M. Inf.
Romero, Rafael, Alarid's Independent Co., N. M. Mil. Inf., 3 mos., 1861-62.
Romero, Rafael, Co. D, 1st N. M. Mil. Inf., 3 mos., 1861-62.
Romero, Ramon, Co. I, 1st N. M. Cav.
Romero, Salvador, Co. A, 1st N. M. Inf.
Romero, Silverio, Co. E, 1st N. M. Mil. Inf., 3 mos., 1861-62.
Romero, Simon, Co. F, 1st N. M. Cav.
Romero, Tomas, 1st N. M. Mil., Sena's Co. A, 3 mos., 1861.
Romero, Tomas Antonio, Co. G, 1st N. M. Inf.
Romero, Torencio, Perea's Independent Co., N. M. Vols., 60 days, 1862.
Romero, Vicente, 1st N. M. Mil., Sena's Co. A, 2 mos., 1862.
Romero, Victor, Co. F, 1st N. M. Cav.
Romero, Delfino, Co. I, 1st N. M. Cav.
Romero, Jose Leon, Romero's Independent Co. A, N. M. Mil. Inf., 3 mos., 1861-62.

Ronquillo, Timoteo, Co. K, 1st N. M. Cav.
Ronquillo, Pedro, Co. K, 3rd N. M. Mtd. Inf., 6 mos., 1861-62.
Ronquillo, Jose, Co. M, 1st N. M. Cav.
Rosali, Tiburcio, Co. D, 1st N. M. Inf.
Ross, John Joseph, Co. L, 1st N. M. Cav., Com. Sgt.
Ross, Rodney, Co. K, 1st N. M. Cav.
Rowe, John, Co. G, 1st N. M. Cav.
Rowe, Nathaniel, Co. M, 1st N. M. Cav.
Roybal, William, Co. G, 1st N. M. Cav., Farrier.
Roybal, Ignacio, Co. A, 1st N. M. Cav.
Roybal, Salvador, Co. F, 1st N. M. Cav.
Roybal, Antonio, Mink's Independent Co., N. M. Mtd. Vols., 3 mos., 1861.
Roybal, Eutemio, Co. C, 4th N. M. Inf.
Roybal, Cruz, Hubbell's Co., Perea's Batt'n, N. M. Mil. Inf., 3 mos., 1861-62.
Roybal, Faustin, Co. F, 2nd N. M. Inf.
Roybal, Juan Melchior, Co. M, 1st N. M. Cav.
Rudulph, Milnor, Co. F, 1st N. M. Inf., Sgt.
Ruiz, Ynez, Co. C, 1st N. M. Cav.
Ruiz, Francisco, Co. D, 1st N. M. Cav.
Ruiz, Pablo, Co. B, 1st N. M. Inf.
Ruiz, Ricardo, Co. F, 1st N. M. Inf.
Roybal, Bartolo, Co. B, 3rd N. M. Mtd. Inf., 6 mos., 1861-62.
Russell, Nathaniel, Co. M, 1st N. M. Cav., Blacksmith.
Russell, Richard, Co. H, E, 1st N. M. Inf., 2nd Lieut.
Russell, William B., Co. E, 3rd N. M. Mtd. Inf., 6 mos., 1861-62, 1st Lieut.
Ryan, James, Co. G, 1st N. M. Cav., Sgt.

Saavedra, Antonio, Co. D, 2nd N. M. Inf., Bugler.
Saavedra, Jose, Co. D, 2nd N. M. Inf.
Saavedra, Justo, Co. E, 2nd N. M. Inf., Corp.
Saavedra, Nestor, Co. D, 1st N. M. Inf.
Saavedra, Teodocio, Co. I, 2nd N. M. Inf., and Hubbell's Independent Co., 3 mos., 1861.
Saavedra, Santos, Co. A, 1st N. M. Cav., Corp.
Sainz, Jose Eulogio, Co. D, 1st N. M. Cav.
Saiz, Alejandro, Baca's Co., Perea's Batt'n, N. M. Mil. Inf., 3 mos., 1861-62.
Saiz, Andres, Co. E, 3rd N. M. Mtd. Inf., 6 mos., 1861-62.
Saiz, Bicente, Co. G, 3rd N. M. Mtd. Inf., 6 mos., 1861-62.
Saiz, Jose, Co H, 1st N. M. Cav., Corp.
Saiz, Jose Dolores, Jaramillo's Co., Perea's Batt'n, N. M. Mtd. Inf., 6 mos., 1861-62.
Saiz, Jose Dolores, Baca's Co., Perea's Batt'n, N. M. Mtd. Inf., 6 mos., 1861-62.
Saiz, Jose Maria, Romero's Independent Co. A, 3 mos., 1861-62, N. M. Mil.
Saiz, Juan, Co. D, 1st N. M. Inf.
Saiz, Juan Jose, Co. D, 1st N. M. Cav.
Saiz, Juan Andres, Co. K, 2nd N. M. Inf.
Saiz, Rafael, Capt. Romero's Co., 3rd N. M. Mtd. Inf., 6 mos., 1861-62.
Saiz, Eulogio, Co. B, 1st N. M. Cav.
Saiz, Jose Maria, Romero's Independent Co. A, N. M. Mil. Inf., 3 mos., 1861-62.
Salendez, Jesus, Co. H, 5th N. M. Inf.
Solano, Felipe, Co. F, 1st N. M. Inf.
Solano, Luciano, Co. E, 3rd N. M. Mtd. Inf., 6 mos., 1861-62, Wagoner.
Salas, Bicente, Montoya's Co., Perea's Batt'n, N. M. Mil. Inf., 3 mos., 1861-62.
Salas, Desiderio, Co. A, 1st N. M. Mil. Inf., 3 mos., 1861-62.

Salas, Felipe, Co. F, 1st N. M. Inf., Corp.
Salas, Gregorio, Co. H, 1st N. M. Inf.
Salas, Gomecindo, Co. A, 1st N. M. Cav.
Salas, Juan de Dios, Hubbell's Co., Perea's Batt'n, N. M. Mil. Inf., 3 mos., 1861-62.
Salas, Miguel, Jaramillo's Co., Perea's Batt'n, N. M. Mil. Inf., 3 mos., 1861-62.
Salas, Nerio, Co. G, 1st N. M. Inf.
Salas, Octaviano, Co. H, 2nd N. M. Inf., Corp.
Salas, Santos, Co. K, 1st N. M. Cav.
Salas, Seferino, Co. D, 3rd N. M. Mtd. Inf., 6 mos., 1861-62.
Salas, Severiano, Montoya's Co., Perea's Batt'n, N. M. Mil. Inf., 6 mos., 1861-62.
Salas, Teodoro, Co. D, 1st N. M. Cav.
Salas, Tomas, Co. B, 1st N. M. Inf., O. O., Corp.
Salas, Unescinco, Co. C, 1st N. M. Inf.
Salazar, Antonio, Co. B, 1st N. M. Cav.
Salazar, Bernardo, Co. A, 4th N. M. Inf., Lieut.
Salazar, Candelario, Co. E, 1st N. M. Inf.
Salazar, Cruz, Co. D, 1st N. M. Inf., Sgt.
Salazar, Desiderio, Co. A, 4th N. M. Inf., Sgt.
Salazar, Esteban, Co. M, 1st N. M. Cav.
Salazar, Francisco, Co. C, 3rd N. M. Mtd. Inf., 6 mos., 1861-62.
Salazar, Gervasio, Aragon's Co., Perea's Batt'n, N. M. Mil. Inf., 3 mos., 1861-62.
Salazar, Jesus, Capt. Romero's 3rd N. M. Mtd. Inf., 6 mos., 1861-62.
Salazar, Jose, Co. I, 1st N. M. Inf.
Salazar, Jose Antonio, Co. D, 1st N. M. Cav.
Salazar, Jose Cecilio, Co. I, 1st N. M. Cav.
Salazar, Jose Manuel, Co. G, 3rd N. M. Mtd. Vols., 6 mos., 1861-62.
Salazar, Jose Pablo, Co. A, 1st N. M. Inf.
Salazar, Juan, Co. K, 1st N. M. Cav.
Salazar, Juan de Jsus, Co. M, 1st N. M. Cav.
Salazar, Manuel, Co. B, 5th N. M. Cav.
Salazar, Marcelino, Alarid's Independent Co., N. M. Mil. Inf., 3 mos., 1861-62.
Salazar, Merejildo, Co. G, 3rd N. M. Mtd. Inf., 6 mos., 1861-62.
Salazar, Miguel, Co. C, 3rd N. M. Mtd. Inf., 6 mos., 1861-62.
Salazar, Miguel Antonio, Co. B, 3rd N. M. Mtd. Inf., 6 mos., 1861-62.
Salazar, Nasario, Co. H, 2nd N. M. Inf.
Salazar, Porfirio, Co. I, 2nd N. M. Inf., and Baca's Independent Co., Perea's Batt'n, 1861-62.
Salazar, Polonario, Alarid's Independent Co., N. M. Mil. Inf., 3 mos., 1861-62.
Salazar, Roman, Co. G, 3rd N. M. Mtd. Inf., 6 mos., 1861-62.
Salazar, Ruperto, Co. G, 1st N. M. Inf., Lieut.
Salazar, Vicente, Aragon's Co., Perea's Batt'n, N. M. Mil. Inf., 3 mos., 1861-62.
Salazar, Victor, Co. C, 3rd N. M. Mtd. Inf., 6 mos., 1861-62.
Salazar, Fidel, Co. B, 1st N. M. Inf.
Salazar, Diego, Co. H, 3rd N. M. Mtd. Inf., 6 mos., 1861-62.
Salazar, Esteban, Co. C, 4th N. M. Inf., Bugler.
Salazar, Francisco, Co. C, 3rd N. M. Mtd. Inf., 6 mos., 1861-62.
Salazar, Francisco Ortiz y, Duran's Co., N. M. Mil., 1st, Lieut.
Salazar, Guadalupe, Co. B, 1st N. M. Mil. Inf., 3 mos., 1861-62.
Salazar, Ignacio, Co. D, 1st N. M. Mil. Inf., 3 mos., 1861-62.
Salazar, Jesus Maria Baca y, Co. F, 2nd N. M. Inf., Major.
Salazar, Jose Benito, Co. A, 4th N. M. Inf.
Salazar, Jose Guadalupe, Co. A, 1st N. M. Mil. Inf., 3 mos., 1861-62.
Salazar, Juan, Perea's Independent Co., N. M. Vols., 60 days, 1862.
Salazar, Juan Candelaria, Co. L, 1st N. M. Cav.
Salazar, Juan de Jesus, Co. I, 1st N. M. Cav.

Salazar, Juan Jose, Co. A, 3rd N. M. Mtd. Inf., 6 mos., 1861-62.
Salazar, Juan Pascual, Co. M, 1st N. M. Cav.
Salazar, Juan Pomoceno, Co. G, 1st N. M. Mil. Inf., 3 mos., 1861-62.
Salazar, Lucas, Co. A, 1st N. M. Inf.
Salazar, Luciano, Co. K, 3rd N. M. Mtd. Inf., 6 mos., 1861-62.
Salazar, Matias, Co. A, 1st N. M. Inf.
Salazar, Miguel Ambrosio, Co. B, 3rd N. M. Mtd. Inf., 6 mos., 1861-62.
Salazar, Pablo, Co. K, 1st N. M. Cav.
Salazar, Placido, Co. F, 1st N. M. Inf., 2nd Lieut.
Salazar, Rafael Rael y, Co. B, 1st N. M. Inf., Sgt.
Salazar, Sencion, Co. B, 1st N. M. Inf.
Salazar, Telesfor, Co. A, 3rd N. M. Mtd. Inf., 6 mos., 1861-62.
Salazar, Tomas, Co. A, 4th N. M. Inf.
Salcedo, Bicemte, Co. I, 1st N. M. Inf., Sgt.
Salcedo, Lazaro, Co. E, 1st N. M. Inf.
Salcedo, Santa Rosa, Co. E, 1st N. M. Inf .
Sandoval, Felipe, Co. D, Batt'n N. M. Vols., 1866-67.
Solis, Teodoro, Co. D, 1st N. M. Cav.
Salas, Bicente, Co. G, 1st N. M. Inf.
Salas, Gregorio, Co. H, 1st N. M. Inf.
Salas, Teodoro, Co. I, 1st N. M. Cav.
Salas, Tomas, Co. B., 1st N. M. Inf.
Salmaron, Roque, Co. A, 1st N. M. Cav.
Salas, Hermecindo, Co. A, 1st N. M. Cav.
Sambrano, Jose, Co. H, 1st N. M. Inf.
Sambrano, Papillo, Co. H, 1st N. M. Inf.
Samora, Eleno, Co. B, Batt'n N. M. Vols., 1866-67.
Samora, Juan, Co. B, 2nd N. M. Inf.
Samora, Alejandro, Co. L, 3rd N. M. Mtd. Inf., 6 mos., 1861-62.
Samora, Amador, Co. C, 1st N. M. Inf.
Samora, Antonio, Hubbell's Co., Perea's Batt'n, N. M. Mil. Inf., 3 mos., 1861-62.
Samora, Benino, Romero's 3rd N. M. Mtd. Inf., Vols., 6 mos., 1861-62.
Samora, Cristobal, Co. F, 1st N. M. Cav.
Samora, Diego, Co. B, 1st N. M. Inf.
Samora, Desiderio, Hubbell's Co., Perea's Batt'n, N. M. Mtd. Inf., 3 mos., 1861-62.
Samora, Elanor, Co. E, 1st N. M. Cav.
Samora, Felipe, Jaramillo's Co., Perea's Batt'n, N. M. Mil. Inf., 3 mos., 1861-62.
Samora, Francisco, Co. A, 1st N. M. Inf.
Samora, Gabriel, Co. B, 1st N. M. Mil. Inf., 1861-62.
Samora, Jesus, Romero's Independent Co. R, 1st N. M. Mil. Inf., 3 mos., 1861-62.
Samora, Jose, Montoya's Co., Perea's Batt'n, N. M. Mil. Inf., 3 mos., 1861-62.
Samora, Jose Domingo, Co. A, 1st N. M. Mil. Inf., 3 mos., 1861-62.
Samora, Jose Manuel, Hubbell's Co., Perea's Batt'n., N. M. Mil. Inf., 3 mos., 1861-62.
Samora, Juan, Co. C, 1st N. M. Cav.
Samora, Julio, Co. A, Batt'n, N. M. Vols., 1866-67.
Samora, Eulario, Co. K, 2nd N. M. Cav.
Samora, Manuel, Hubbell's Co., Perea's Batt'n, N. M. Mil. Ind., 3 mos., 1861-62.
Samora, Pablo, Co. H, 1st N. M. Inf.
Samora, Policarpo, Co. B, 1st N. M. Inf.
Samora, Rafael, Co. G, 1st N. M. Inf.
Samora, Rufino, Hubbell's Co., Perea's Batt'n, N. M. Mil. Inf., 3 mos., 1861-62.
Samora, Vicente, Co. H, 1st N. M. Inf., and Hubbell's Co., Perea's Batt'n.

Samora, Victor, Vo. B, 1st N. M. Inf.
Sanchez, Agapito, Co. H, 1st N. M. Cav.
Sanchez, Anastacio, Co. K, 2nd N. M. Inf., Corp.
Sanchez, Andres, Co. E, 1st N. M. Inf.
Sanchez, Antonio Jose, Co. K, 2nd N. M. Inf., Corp.
Sanchez, Antonio, Co. K, 3rd N. M. Mtd. Vols., 3 mos., 1861-62.
Sanchez, Antonio Manuel, Co. G, 3rd N. M. Mtd. Vols., 3 mos., 1861-62.
Sanchez, Antonio Maria, Co. F, 1st N. M. Cav., Sgt.
Sanchez, Bartolo, Co. G, 2nd N. M. Inf., Corp.
Sanchez, Benino, Co. B, 5th N. M. Inf.
Sanchez, Bicente, Co. A, 5th N. M. Inf.
Sanchez, Bictorio, Co. G, 3rd N. M. Mtd. Inf., 6 mos., 1861-62.
Sanchez, Canuto, Co. K, 1st N. M. Inf.
Sanchez, Cecilio, 1st N. M. Mil., Sena's Co. A, 2 mos., 1862.
Sanchez, Clemente, Co. B, 5th N. M. Inf.
Sanchez, Concepcion, Vigil's Independent Co., N. M. Mtd. Vols., 3 mos., 1861.
Sanchez, Dario, Hubbell's Co., Perea's Batt'n, N. M. Mil. Inf., 3 mos., 1861-62.
Sanchez, Desiderio, Hubbell's Co., N. M. Mtd. Vols., 3 mos., 1861.
Sanchez, Diego, Co. E, 1st N. M. Cav.
Sanchez, Dolores, Co. F, 1st N. M. Cav.
Sanchez, Merejildes, Co. K, 2nd N. M. Cav., Corp.
Sanchez, Eugenio, Co. C, 3rd N. M. Mtd. Vols., 6 mos., 1861.
Sanchez, Encarnacion, Co. B, 1st N. M. Inf.
Sanchez, Eusebio, Co. A, 1st N. M. Cav.
Sanchez, Felipe, Mink's Independent Co., N. M. Mtd. Vols., 3 mos., 1861. Lieut.
Sanchez, Felipe, Co. L, 3rd N. M. Mtd. Inf., 6 mos., 1861-62.
Sanchez, Filomeno Peralta y, Co. E, 2nd N. M. Inf.
Sanchez, Francisco, Co. G, 3rd N. M. Mtd. Inf., 6 mos., 1861-62.
Sanchez, Francisco Antonio, Mink's Independent Co., N. M. Mtd. Vols., 3 mos., 1861.
Sanchez, Tranquilino, Co. I, 1st N. M. Inf., O. O.
Sanchez, Faustin, Co. K, 1st N. M. Inf.
Sanchez, Gabriel, Co. C, 4th N. M. Inf.
Sanchez, German, Co. C, 1st N. M. Inf.
Sanchez, Guadalupe, Co. B, 3rd N. M. Mtd. Inf., 6 mos., 1861-62, Corp.
Sanchez, Herman, Co. A, 1st N. M. Cav.
Sanchez, Jesus, Mink's Independent Co., N. M. Mtd. Vols., 3 mos., 1861.
Sanchez, Jesus Maria, Jaramillo's Co., Perea's Batt'n, N. M. Mil. Inf., 3 mos., 1861-62.
Sanchez, Jose Atanacio, Hubbell's Independent Co., N. M. Mtd. Vols., 3 mos., 1861.
Sanchez, Jose Antonio, Co. I, 2nd N. M. Inf., and 3rd N. M. Mtd. Inf., 6 mos., 1861-62.
Sanchez, Jose Antonio, Romero's Co, 3rd N. M. Mtd. Inf., 6 mos., 1861-62.
Sanchez, Jose Concepcion, Co. E, 4th N. M. Cav.
Sanchez, Jose Dolores, Co. F, 1st N. M. Cav.
Sanchez, Jose de Jesus, Co. B, 1st N. M. Inf.
Sanchez, Jose Celso, Co. K, 3rd N. M. Mtd. Inf., 6 mos., 1861-62.
Sanchez, Jose Gregorio, Co. D, 1st N. M. Inf.
Sanchez, Jose Maria, Co. C, 1st N. M. Inf., Lieut.
Sanchez, Jose Manuel, Co. E, 1st N. M. Inf.
Sanchez, Jose Santos, Co. I, 1st N. M. Inf., Musician.
Sanchez, Jose Sylvestro, Co. E, 1st N. M. Inf., Corp.
Sanchez, Juan, Co. I, 1st N. M. Cav., and Co. B, 3rd N. M. Mtd. Inf., 6 mos., 1861-62.

Sanchez, Juan Antonio, Vigil's Independent Co., N. M. Mtd. Vols., 3 mos., 1861.
Sanchez, Juan Jose, Hubbell's Co., Perea's Batt'n, N. M. Mil. Inf., 3 mos., 1861-62.
Sanchez, Juan Jose, Co. A, 3rd N. M. Mtd. Inf., 6 mos., 1861-62.
Sanchez, Juan Jose, Co. C., 3rd N. M. Mtd. Inf., 6 mos., 1861-62.
Sanchez, Justo, Co. C, 1st N. M. Inf.
Sanchez, Lino, Tafoya's Independent Co., N. M. Mil., 3 mos., 1861-62.
Sanchez, Lino, Co. L, 3rd N. M. Mtd. Inf., 6 mos., 1861-62.
Sanchez, Lupe, Co. D, 1st N. M. Inf., O. O.
Sanchez, Marcos, Hubbell's Independent Co., N. M. Mtd. Vols., 6 mos., 1861-62., Corp.
Sanchez, Mariano, Graydon's Independent Co., N. M. Mtd. Vols., 3 mos., 1861-62.
Sanchez, Maximo, Co. H, 1st N. M. Inf.
Sanchez, Melquiades, Co. E, 1st N. M. Cav.
Sanchez, Miguel, Co. D, 3rd N. M. Mtd. Inf., 6 mos., 1861-62.
Sanchez, Pedro, Co. B, 1st N. M. Inf., and Co. C, 3rd N. M. Mtd. Inf., 6 mos., 1861-62.
Sanchez, Pedro, Co. L, 3rd N. M. Mtd. Inf., 6 mos., 1861-62, Lieut.
Sanchez, Prudencio, Co. C, 1st N. M. Inf.
Sanchez, Rafael, Co. D, 1st N. M. Inf.
Sanchez, Ramon, Co. D, 1st N. M. Mil. Inf., 3 mos., 1861-62.
Sanchez, Romoceno, Co. D, 1st N. M. Inf.
Sanchez, Santiago, Jaramillo's Co., Perea's Batt'n, N. M. Mil. Inf., 3 mos., 1861-62.
Sanchez, Teodoro, Baca's Co., Perea's Batt'n, N. M. Mil. Inf., 3 mos., 1861-62.
Sanchez, Teodocio, Co. C, 3rd N. M. Mtd. Inf., 6 mos., 1861-62.
Sanchez, Isidoro, Hubbell's Independent Co., N. M. Mtd. Vols., 3 mos., 1861.
Sanchez, Ireneo, Sena's Co. A, 1st N. M. Mil., 2 mos., 1862.
Sanchez, Ysidro, Co. L, 3rd N. M. Mtd. Inf., 6 mos., 1861.
Sanchez, Venturo, Aragon's Co., Perea's Batt'n, N. M. Mtd. Vols., 3 mos., 1861-62.
Sanchez, Victoriano, Co. E, 3rd N. M. Mtd. Vols., 6 mos., 1861-62.
Sandoval, Albino, Co. F, 1st N. M. Cav.
Sandoval, Juan B., Co. B, Batt'n N. M. Vols., 1866-67.
Sandoval, Agapito, Co. H, 1st N. M. Inf., 3 mos., 1861-62.
Sandoval, Atanasio, Co. H, 2nd N. M. Inf.
Sandoval, Antonio, Mink's Independent Co., N. M. Mtd. Vols., 3 mos., 1861.
Sandoval, Antonio, Co. A, 3rd N. M. Mtd. Inf., Bugler.
Sandoval, Cecilio, Co. E, 1st N. M. Cav.
Sandoval, Cruz, Co. C, 1st N. M. Cav.
Sandoval, Daniel, Co. D, 1st N. M. Cav., Corp.
Sandoval, David, Co. F, 2nd N. M. Inf., Corp.
Sandoval, Domingo, Co. L, 1st N. M. Cav.
Sandoval, Felipe, Co. A, 1st N. M. Inf., 3 mos., 1861.
Sandoval, Francisco, Del Balle's Co., Perea's Batt'n, N. M. Mil. Inf., 3 mos., 1861-62.
Sandoval, Geronimo, Co. C, 1st N. M. Inf.
Sandoval, Jesus, 1st N. M. Mil., Sena's Co. A, 2 mos., 1862.
Sandoval, Jose, Del Balle's Co., Perea's Batt'n, N. M. Mil. Inf., 3 mos., 1861-62.
Sandoval, Jose Desiderio, Co. I, 1st N. M. Inf.
Sandoval, Jose Maria, Co. A, 1st N. M. Cav., Sgt.
Sandoval, Juan, Hubbell's Independent Co., N. M. Mtd. Vols., 3 mos., 1861.
Sandoval, Juan Jose, Hubbell's Independent Co., 3 mos., 1861.
Sandoval, Lazaro, Co. A, 3rd N. M. Mtd. Inf., 6 mos., 1861-62, Corp.
Sandoval, Matias, Co. F, 1st N. M. Inf.

Sandoval, Miguel, Co. B, 1st N. M. Inf.
Sandoval, Nicanor, Co. I, 3rd N. M. Mtd. Inf., 6 mos., 1861-62.
Sandoval, Pablo, Co. F, 1st N. M. Inf., Sena's Co. A, 2 mos., 1862.
Sandoval, Pablo, Co. A, 3rd N. M. Mtd. Inf., 3 mos., 1861-62.
Sandoval, Pedro, Co. D, 3rd N. M. Mtd. Inf., 6 mos., 1861-62.
Sandoval, Placido, Co. E, 1st N. M. Cav.
Sandoval, Quinto, Co. A, 1st N. M. Cav.
Sandoval, Rafael, Co. G, 1st N. M. Inf.
Sandoval, Remigio, Co. E, 1st N. M. Cav., Bugler.
Sandoval, Santos, Co. G, 1st N. M. Inf.
Sandoval, Doroteo, Co. E, 3rd N. M. Mtd. Inf., 6 mos., 1861-62, Corp.
Sandoval, Epitacio, Co. A, 1st N. M. Inf.
Sandoval, Matias, Co. F, 1st N. M. Inf.
Sandoval, Ranjel Trinidad, Alarid's Independent Co., N. M. Mil. Inf., 3 mos., 1861-62.
Santallanos, Domingo, Co. D, 1st N. M. Inf.
Santallanos, Gabriel, Mink's Independent Co., N. M. Mtd. Vols., 3 mos., 1861-62.
Santallanos, Antonio, Hubbell's Independent Co., N. M. Mtd. Vols., 3 mos., 1861-62.
Santallanos, Jose Domingo, Co. I, 1st N. M. Inf.
Santallanos, Jose Leon, Co. L, 3rd N. M. Mtd. Inf., 6 mos., 1861-62, Corp.
Santisteban, Jacinto, Co. D, 3rd N. M. Mtd. Inf., 6 mos., 1861-62.
Santisteban, Jose Antonio, Co. D, 3rd N. M. Mtd. Inf.
Santisteban, Jose Ignacio, Co. E, 1st N. M. Mil. Inf., 3 mos., 1861-62.
Santisteban, Julian, Co. D, 1st N. M. Mil. Inf., 3 mos., 1861-62.
Sapateta, Francisco, Vigil's Independent Co., N. M. Mtd. Vols., 3 mos., 1861.
Sarracino, Gregorio, Co. L, 1st N. M. Cav.
Sarracino, Jesus, Co. D, 1st N. M. Cav., Corp.
Sarracino, Juan Agaton, Co. C, 1st N. M. Inf.
Serrano, Pedro, Co. I, 1st N. M. Cav.
Sarbonte, Gabino, Co. C, 1st N. M. Inf.
Sierlla, Santos, Co. D, 1st N. M. Cav.
Sarracino, Juan Antonio, Co. A, 3rd N. M. Mtd. Inf., 6 mos., 1861-62, Captain.
Saylor, Carl Teodore, Co. I, 1st N. M. Inf.
Sacaeffer, John, Co. D, 1st N. M. Inf.
Schley, Francis, Co. D, 1st N. M. Inf.
Schoernor, Frederick, Co. F, 1st N. M. Mil. Inf., 3 mos., 1861-62.
Scott, Sammy R. Simpson's Independent Co., N. M. Mtd. Spies and Guides.
Scramp, George, Co. B, 1st N. M. Cav., Blacksmith.
Scaman, Samuel, Co. A, 1st N. M. Cav., Sgt.
Seballes, Juan Antonio, Co. B, 1st N. M. Inf., Bugler.
Servantes, Gabriel, Co. C, 1st N. M. Inf.
Seber, Carl F., Hubbel's Independent Co., N. M. Mtd. Vols., 3 mos., 1861, Farrier.
Sedillo, Domingo, Co. H, 1st N. M. Inf.
Sedillo, Francisco, Co. H, 1st N. M. Cav.
Sedillo, Bicente, Graydon's Independent Co., N. M. Mtd. Vols., 1861-62.
Sedillo, Jesus, Del Balle's Co., Perea's Batt'n, N. M. Mil. Inf., 3 mos., 1861-62.
Sedillo, Polonario, Co. B, 1st N. M. Inf.
Sedillo, Francisco, Co. H, 1st N. M. Cav.
Sedillo, Gregorio, Tafoya's Independent Co., N. M. Mil., 3 mos., 1861-62.
Sedillo, Francisco, Hubbell's Independent Co., N. M. Mtd. Vols., 3 mos., 1861.

Sedillo, Ignacio, Co. H, 2nd N. M. Inf.
Sedillo, Juan (1) and Juan (2), Tafoya's Co., Perea's Batt'n, N. M. Mil. Inf.
Sedillo, Juan de Dios, Tafoya's Co., Perea's Batt'n, N. M. Mil. Inf., 3 mos., 1861-62.
Sedillo, Pablo, Graydon's Independent Co., N. M. Mtd. Vols., 3 mos., 1861-62.
Segura, Guadalupe, Co. C, 4th N. M. Inf.
Segura, Pablo, Co. L, 1st N. M .Cav.
Segura, Anastacio, Co. E, 3rd N. M. Mtd. Vols., 3 mos., 1861-62.
Segura, Felipe, Co. H, 2nd N. M. Cav.
Segura, Francisco, Romero's Independent Co. A, 1st N. M. Mil. Inf., 3 mos., 1861-62.
Segura, Francisco, Co. F, 3rd N. M. Mtd. Inf., 6 mos., 1861-62, Bugler.
Segura, Guadalupe, Co. C, 4th N. M. Inf., Bugler.
Segura, Jose, Co. G, 1st N. M. Inf.
Segura, Jose Antonio, Co. C, 1st N. M. Mil. Inf., 3 mos., 1861.
Segura, Manuel, Co. F, 1st N. M. Cav.
Segura, Cencion, Alarid's Independent Co., 1st N. M. Mil. Inf., 3 mos., 1861-62.
Segura, Jose Antonio, Co. D, 1st N. M. Mil. Inf., 3 mos., 1861-62.
Segura, Jose Vicente, Co. A, 2nd N. M. Inf.
Segura, Julio, Romero's Independent Co. A, N .M. Mil. Inf., 3 mos., 1861-62.
Segura, Manuel, Co. F, 1st N. M. Cav.
Seiler, Carl Theodore, Hubbell's Co., and 1st N. M. Inf., Farrier-Blacksmith.
Salende, Jesus, Co. H, 1st N. M. Cav.
Selden, Henry R., Co. F and others, 1st N. M. Inf., Colonel—(Fort Selden named for him)
Serna, Trinidad, Co. H, 1st N. M. Cav.
Sembrano, Papias, Co. H, 1st N. M. Cav.
Sena, Antonio, 1st N. M. Mil., Sena's Co. A, 2 mos., 1862, Captain.
Sena, Antonio, Duran's Co., N. M. Mil.
Sena, Bibiano, Co. A, N. M. Mtd. Inf., 6 mos., 1861-62.
Sena, Catarino, Romero's Independent Co.
Sena, Clemente, Co. C, 1st N. M. Cav.
Sena, Felix, Co. F, 3rd N. M. Mtd. Inf., 6 mos., 1861-62.
Sena, Felipe, Romero's Independent Co. A.
Sena, Felipe, Co. F, 3rd N. M. Mtd. Inf., 6 mos., 1861-62, Sgt.
Sena, Francisco, Co. B, 2nd N. M. Inf., Corp., and Co. H, 3rd N. M. Mtd. Inf., 6 mos.
Sena, Ignacio, Sena's Co. H, 3rd N. M. Mtd. Inf., 6 mos., 1861-62, 2nd Lieut.
Sena, Jesus, Duran's Co., N. M. Mil.
Sena, Jesus Maria, Co. A, 1st N. M. Cav.
Sena, Jesus Maria Quintana y, Co. C, 1st N. M. Inf.
Sena, Jesus Sandoval y, Co. I, 1st N. M. Inf., O. O.
Sena, Jose, Co. B, 2nd N. M. Inf.
Sena, Jose D., Co. F, 1st N. M. Cav., Major.
Sena, Jose de Jesus, Co. A, 1st N. M. Cav.
Sena, Jose Dolores, Co. F, 1st N. M. Cav.
Sena, Jose Maria, Co. B, 1st N. M. Inf.
Sena, Juan, Co. E, 1st N. M. Cav.
Sena, Juan, Co. H, 1st N. M. Cav., Captain.
Sena, Juan Antonio, Co. F, 1st N. M. Cav.
Sena, Juan Cristobal, Co. B, 1st N. M. Inf.
Sena, Maria—Matron, 1st N. M. Inf.
Sena, Mariano, Co. A, 1st N. M. Inf., Sgt.
Sena, Mateo, Co. B, 4th N. M. Inf.
Sena, Pablo, Co. A, 1st N. M. Cav.
Sena, Patricio, Co. A, 2nd N. M. Inf., Corp.

Sena, Roque, Co. H, 3rd N. M. Mtd. Vols., 6 mos., 1861-62.
Sena, Santiago, Co. H, 3rd N. M. Inf., Corp.
Sena, Tiburcio, Duran's Co., N. M. Mil.
Sena, Tomas, 1st N. M. Mil., Sena's Co. A, 2 mos., 1862, Corp.
Sena, Isidro, Sena's Co. K, 1st N. M. Cav.
Sepuveda, Prudencio, Co. H, 1st N. M. Inf.
Serano, Julio, Co. L, 1st N. M. Cav. Corp.
Servena, Cosmo, Co. I, 1st N. M. Inf., Bugler.
Servantes, Pascual, Montoya's Co., Perea's Batt'n, N. M. Mil. Inf., 3 mos., 1861-62.
Servantes, Serviano, Co. B, 1st N. M. Cav.
Servantes, Gabino, Co. C, 4th N. M. Inf.
Serbin, Juan, Co. A, 3rd N. M. Mtd. Inf., 1861-62, 6 mos.
Serna, Isidro, Co. L, 1st N. M. Cav.
Sereservy, Louis, Co. B, Batt'n, N. M. Vols., 1866-67.
Serna, Francisco, Co. F, 1st N. M. Inf.
Serna, Bictor, Co. H, 5th N. M. Inf.
Serna, Dolores, Tafoya's Independent Co., N. M. Mil. Inf., 3 mos., 1861-62.
Serna, Domingo, Co. G, 2nd N. M. Inf.
Serna, Francisco Antonio, Co. B, 1st N. M. Mil. Inf., 3 mos., 1861-62.
Serna, Jose de la Luz, Co. C, 3rd N. M. Mtd. Inf., 6 mos., 1861-62.
Serna, Jose, Co. D, 2nd N. M. Inf
Serna, Jose Antonio, Co E, 1st N. M. Cav.
Serna, Jose Vicente, Co. B, 1st N. M. Mil. Inf., 3 mos., 1861-62.
Serna, Juan, Co. A, 5th N. M. Inf.
Serna, Manuel Toricio, Co. A, 1st N. M. Inf.
Serna, Trinidad, Co. H, 1st N. M. Inf.
Serna, Victor, Co. C, Batt'n N. M. Vols., 1866-67.
Serna, Isidro, Co. L, 1st N. M. Cav., Corp.
Serna, Geronimo, Co. F, 1st N. M. Inf.
Serna, Jose Victor, Co. B, Batt'n N. M. Vols., 1866-67.
Serna, Miguel, Hubbell's Co., New Mexico Mil., Sgt..
Serrano, Antonio, Co. A, 2nd N. M. Mil.
Serrano, Antonio, Albino, Co. L, 1st N. M. Cav.
Serrano, Benturo, Vigil's Independent Co., N. M. Mtd. Vols., 3 mos., 1861.
Serrano, Jesus, Co. D, 1st N. M. Inf.
Serrano, Jesus Maria, Mink's Independent Co., Mtd. Vols., 3 mos., 1861, 1st Sgt.
Serrano, Julio, Co. A, Batt'n, N. M. Vols., 1866-67, Corp.
Serrano, Pedro, Co. D, 1st N. M. Inf.
Servantes, Pascual, Montoya's Co., Perea's Batt'n, N. M. Mil. Inf., 1861, 3 mos.
Servantes, Margarito, Co. A, 2nd N. M. Inf.
Servantes, Severiano, Co. B, 1st N. M. Cav.
Sisneros, Manuel, Co. H, 1st N. M. Cav.
Sisneros, Juan, Jose, Co. F, 1st N. M. Cav.
Shairer, John, Co. L, 1st N. M. Cav.
Shannon, James B., Co. F, 1st N. M. Cav.
Shannon, Peter, Co. F, 1st N. M. Mil. Inf., 3 mos., 1861-62, Sgt.
Sharpe, William, Simpson's Independent Co., N. M. Mounted, Spies and Guides.
Shaw, Julius C., Co. F, 1st N. M. Cav., Captain.
Sheets, William B., Co. K, 1st N. M. Inf.
Sheffner, Wilson, Co. C, 1st N. M. Inf.
Sheinpflug, Joseph, Co. C, 1st N. M. Inf.
Sherrot, William, Co. C, 4th N. M. Inf., Farrier.
Shoemaker, Edward, Co. D, 4th N. M. Inf., Lieut.
Shout, J. H., Co. F, 1st N. M. Inf., Major Surgeon.
Silba, Carpio, Co. B, 1st N. M. Cav., Sgt.
Silba, Jose Dolores, Co. C, 1st N. M. Cav., Sgt.

Silba, Jose S., Co. A, 1st N. M. Inf.
Silba, Juan, Co. E, 2nd N. M. Inf.
Silba, Juan Cristobal, Mink's Independent Co., N. M. Mtd. Vols., 3 mos., 1861, Corp.
Silba, Mateo, Alarid's Independent Co., N. M. Mil. Inf., 3 mos., 1861-62.
Silba, Ramon, Co. H, 1st N. M. Cav.
Silba, Jose, Co. L, 1st N. M. Cav.
Silba, Diego, Co. K, 2nd N. M. Inf.
Silba, Jose Manuel, Co. D, 1st N. M. Cav.
Silba, Juan Nepumoceno, Co. I, 1st N. M. Cav.
Silba, Tomas, Co. A, 1st N. M. Cav.
Silba, Luis, Tafoya's Independent Co., N. M. Mil., 3 mos., 1861-62.
Silba, Mauricio, Co. A, 1st N. M. Cav.
Silba, Nieves, Romero's Co., 3rd N. M. Mtd. Inf., 6 mos., 1861-62, Bugler.
Silba, Surano, Co. C, 1st N. M. Inf., O. O.
Simms, William, Co. I, 1st N. M. Cav., Corp.
Sisneros, Juan de Dios, Co. B, 1st N. M. Inf.
Sisneros, Marcos, Co. E, 1st N. M. Cav.
Sisneros, Antonio, Co. K, 1st N. M. Cav.
Sisneros, Antonio Maria, Co. K, 1st N. M. Cav.
Sisneros, Felipe, Co. H, 1st N. M. Inf.
Sisneros, Augustin, Co. L, 3rd N. M. Mounted Inf., 6 mos., 1861-62.
Sisneros, Merced, Co. L, 3rd N. M. Mtd. Inf., 6 mos., 1861-62.
Simpson, Smith H., Co. I, 1st N. M. Inf., Captain.
Simpson, William, Simpson's Independent Co., N. M. Mtd. Spies and Guides, Captain.
Sisneros, Juan de Dios, Co. B, 1st N. M. Inf., Drummer.
Sisneros, Diego, Co. H, 2nd N. M. Inf., 2nd Lieut.
Sisneros, Felipe, Co. H, 1st N. M. Inf., O. O.
Sisneros, Francisco, Co. A, 1st N. M. Inf.
Sisneros, Jose, Co. H, 2nd N. M. Inf., Sgt.
Sisneros, Jose Victor, Co. B, 1st N. M. Inf.
Sisneros, Juan, Co. H, 2nd N. M. Inf., Corp.
Sisneros, Juan Andres, Co. C, 3rd N. M. Mtd. Inf., 6 mos., 1861-62.
Sisneros, Juan de Dios, Co. A, Batt'n N. M. Vols., 1866-67.
Sisneros, Juan Jose, Co. F, 1st N. M. Cav.
Sisneros, Julian, Co. K, 1st N. M. Cav., Corp.
Sisneros, Manuel, Co. H, 1st N. M. Cav.
Sisneros, Marcos, Co. E, 1st N. M. Inf.
Sisneros, Martin, Co. F, 1st N. M. Inf.
Sisneros, Matian, Co. F, 4th N. M. Inf.
Sisneros, Nestor, Co. F, 1st N. M. Cav.
Sisneros, Pedro, Mink's Independent Co., N. M. Mtd. Vols., 3 mos., 1861, Corp.
Sisneros, Rumualdo, Co. C, 4th N. M. Inf.
Sisneros, Victor, Co. B, 1st N. M. Cav.
Smith, Albert H., Co. L, 1st N. M. Cav., Sgt.
Smith, Benjamin F., Co. F, 1st N. M. Cav.
Smith, Fedreick, Co. G, 2nd N. M. Inf.
Smith, James K., Co. F, 1st N. M. Inf.
Smith, John Wilkes, Co. M, 1st N. M. Cav., Corp.
Smith, George F., Co. F, 1st N. M. Cav.
Smith, Samuel, Co. K, 1st N. M. Cav., Corp.
Smith, Simon H., Hubbell's Co., Perea's Batt'n, N. M. Mil. Inf., 3 mos., 1861-62.
Smith, Thomas W., Co. K, 1st N. M. Mil. Inf., 3 mos., 1861-62.
Smith, William M., Co. H, 1st N. M. Inf., 2nd Lieut.
Suaso, Jose Albino, Co. B, 1st N. M. Inf.
Snyder, Simon L., Co. A, 1st N. M. Cav.
Snyder, Frederick, Co. H, 1st N. M. Inf. (See: Cal. Vol. list.)

Snyder, Philip, Graydon's Independent Co., N. M. Mtd. Vols., 3 mos., 1861-62.
Soazo, Joaquin, Co. B, 3rd N. M. Mtd. Inf., 6 mos., 1861-62.
Solano, Francisco, Co. A, 3rd N. M. Mtd. Inf., 6 mos., 1861-62.
Solano, Santiago, Co. H, 1st N. M. Cav., Corp.
Solano, Luciano, Co. A, 3rd N. M. Mtd. Inf., 6 mos., 1861-62, Wagoner.
Solano, Pablo, Romero's Independent Co., N. M. Mil. Inf., 3 mos., 1861-62.
Solano, Bicente, Co. G, 1st N. M. Inf.
Solano, Julian, Co. K, 1st N. M. Inf.
Sosalla, Pedro, Co. F, 2nd N. M. Inf., 1st Lieut.
Sosalla, Sabino, Co. F, 2nd N. M. Inf., Corp.
Soto, Bibian, Co. E, 1st N. M. Cav., Corp.
Soto, Jose Dolores, Co. L, 1st N. M. Inf.
Soto, Ramon, Co. L, 1st N. M. Cav.
Sutherland, James, Co. G, 1st N. M. Cav.
Spicer, Elijah, Co. B, 1st N. M. Cav.
Spielman, David, Co. D, 1st N. M. Cav. (See Colorado Vol. list.)
Sprouse, William, Simpson's Independent Co., N. M. Mtd. Spies and Guides.
Spurr, John, Co. H, 1st N. M. Inf., N. O. (See Cal. Vol. list.)
Stahl, Francis, Co. G, 1st N. M. Cav., Corp.
Stanton, Charles, Co. B, 1st N. M. Cav.
Staton, John W., Co. F, 3rd N. M. Mtd. Inf., 6 mos., 1861-62, 1st Lieut.
St. Clair, William, Co. M, 1st N. M. Cav.
Stevens, Benjamin, Co. M, 1st N. M. Cav., 1st Lieut.
Stillwell, Jesse, Co. K, 1st N. M. Inf.
Stenger, Jacob, Co. A, 2nd N. M. Inf., 1st Lieut.
Stevens, Henry H., Co. D, 1st N. M. Inf., 2nd Lieut. (See Cal. Vol. list.)
Stewards, Isaiah, Co. F, 1st N. M. Cav.
Stewards, Joans, Co. K, 1st N. M. Inf., O. O.
Stover, W., Co. B, 1st N. M. Cav.
Strong, George, Co. F, 1st N. M. Cav.
St. Vrain, Juan, Co. F, 1st N. M. Inf.
St. Vrain, Papias, Co. K, 1st N. M. Cav.
St. Vrain, Sapellas, Co. G, 1st N. M. Inf.
Suaso, Desiderio, Co. B, 1st N. M. Cav.
Saurez, Miguel, Co. H, 1st N. M. Cav., Corp.
Suarez, Rafael, Co. I, 1st N. M. Cav.
Suaso, Abelino, Co. I, 1st N. M. Cav.
Suaso, Francisco, Co. K, 1st N. M. Cav.
Suaso, Jose Aquilino, Co. B, 1st N. M. Mil. Inf., 3 mos., 1861-62.
Suaso, Pedro Nolasco, Co. F, 3rd N. M. Mtd. Inf., 6 mos., 1861-62.
Subia, Antonio, Co. G, 2nd N. M. Inf.
Subia, Antonio, Co. G, 2nd N. M. Inf.
Subia, Luz, Co. C, 1st N. M. Cav., Sgt.
Sullivan, Timothy, Co. G, 1st N. M. Cav.
Sune, Nazario, Co. C, 3rd N. M. Mtd. Inf., 6 mos., 1861-62.
Surella, Santos, Co. D, 1st N. M. Cav., Bugler.

Tafoya, Francisco, Co. E, 2nd N. M. Inf.
Tafoya, Jose Francisco, Co. B, 3rd N. M. Mtd. Inf., 6 mos., 1861-62.
Tafoya, Juan, Co. B, 3rd N. M. Mtd. Inf., 6 mos., 1861-62.
Tafoya, Juan Antonio, Co. F, 1st N. M. Cav.
Tafoya, Jesus Maria, Co. B, 1st N. M. Inf.
Tafoya, Lorenzo, Co. C, 3rd N. M. Mtd. Inf., 3 mos., 1861-62.
Tafoya, Sabino, Co. I, 1st N. M. Cav.
Tafoya, Santiago, Co. F, 3rd N. M. Mtd. Inf., 6 mos., 1861-62.
Tafoya, Placido, Alarid's Co., N. M. Mil. Inf., 3 mos., 1861-62.
Tafoya, Juan, Co. A, 1st N. M. Mil. Inf., 3 mos., 1861-62.

Tafoya, Juan Jose, Tafoya's Independent Co., N. M. Mil., 3 mos., 1861-62, Sgt.
Tafoya, Leon, Tafoya's Independent Co., N. M. Mil., 3 mos., 1861-62.
Tafoya, Luis, Tafoya's Independent Co., N. M. Mil., 3 mos., 1861-62, Captain.
Tafoya, Nestor, Co. I, 1st N. M. Inf.
Tafoya, Agapito, Montoya's Co., Perea's Batt'n, N. M. Mil. Inf., 3 mos., 1861-62.
Tafoya, Candelaria, Co. H, 1st N. M. Inf., Sgt.
Tafoya, Damasio, Co. D, 2nd N. M. Inf.
Tafoya, Jesus, Co. K, 1st N. M. Inf.
Tafoya, Tomas, Co. F, 1st N. M. Mil. Inf., 3 mos., 1861-62.
Tafoya, Jesus Maria, Co. E, 1st N. M. Cav., 1st Sgt.
Tafoya, Damasio, Co. D, 2nd N. M. Inf.
Tafoya, Francisco, Co. F, 3rd N. M. Mtd. Inf., 6 mos., 1861-62, and Co. E, 2nd N. M. Inf.
Tafoya, Loranzo, Co. C, 3rd N. M. Mtd. Inf., 6 mos., 1861-62.
Tafoya, Miguel, Graydon's Independent Co., N. M. Mtd. Vols., 3 mos., 1861-62.
Tafoya, Ventura, Co. F, 2nd N. M. Mil.
Tafoya, Jose, Graydon's Independent Co., N. M. Mtd. Vols., 3 mos., 1861-62.
Tafoya, Jose Antonio, Co. A, 1st N. M. Inf.
Tafoya, Jose Antonio, Mink's Independent Co., N. M. Mtd. Vols., 3 mos., 1861.
Tafoya, Juan, Co. B, 1st N. M. Cav.
Tafoya, Juan Antonio, Co. F, 1st N. M. Cav.
Tafoya, Juan Isidro, Co. C, 3rd N. M. Mtd. Inf., 6 mos., 1861-62.
Tafoya, Nestor, Co. F, 1st N. M. Inf.
Tafoya, Isidro, Alarid's Independent Co. A, N. M. Mil. Inf., 3 mos., 1861-62.
Tafoya, Ramon, Co. I, 1st N. M. Cav., Corp.
Tafoya, Sabimo, Co. I, 1st N. M. Cav., Sgt.
Tafoya, Santiago, Co. A, 3rd N. M. Mtd. Inf., 6 mos., 1861-62.
Tafoya, Marcos, Co. F, 1st N. M. Cav.
Tajado, Epifanio, Co. B, 1st N. M. Cav.
Talabera, Jose Maria, Co. A, 1st N. M. Cav.
Talarid, Damacio, Co. F, 1st N. M. Cav. (Priest), Chaplain.
Talavera, Rafael, Co. F, 2nd N. M. Inf.
Talmadge, Joseph, Co. D, 1st N. M. Inf.
Tenorio, Andres, Co. A, 5th N. M. Inf.
Tanfield, James W., Co. D, 1st N. M. Cav., 1st Lieut.
Tapia, Andres, Co. B, 1st N. M. Cav., Captain.
Tapia, Antonio, Co. B, 3rd N. M. Mtd. Inf., 6 mos., 1861-62.
Tapia, Desiderio, Co. F, 1st N. M. Cav., Corp.
Tapia, Francisco, Co. B, 1st N. M. Cav.
Tapia, Isidro, Aragon's Co., Perea's Batt'n, N. M. Mil. Inf., 3 mos., 1861-62.
Tapia, Jesus, Aragon's Co., Perea's Batt'n, N. M. Mil. Inf., 3 mos., 1861-62.
Tapia, Jose de Jesus, Hubbell's Independent Co., N. M. Mtd. Vols., 3 mos., 1861.
Tapis, Jose Domingo, Co. K, 1st N. M. Cav.
Tapia, Jose Gregorio, Hubbell's Independent Co., N. M. Mtd. Vols., 3 mos., 1861.
Tapia, Jose Maria, Co. B, 1st N. M. Inf., O. O.
Tapia, Juan, Co. I, 2nd N. M. Inf.
Tapia, Juan Climaco, Co. A, 1st N. M. Inf.
Tapia, Manuel, Romero's Independent Co. A, N. M. Mil. Inf., 3 mos., 1861-62., Corp.
Tapia, Miguel, Co. F, 3rd N. M. Mtd. Inf., 6 mos., 1861-62.
Tapia, Prudencio, Co. E, 3rd N. M. Mtd. Inf., 6 mos., 1861-62.

Tapia, Tomas Antonio, Co. A, 3rd N. M. Mtd. Inf., 6 mos., 1861-62.
Tapia, Ysidro, Co. I, 2nd N. M. Inf.
Tarayta, Felipe, Co. L, 1st N. M. Cav.
Tarbor, Waldo, Simpson's Independent Co., N. M. Mtd. Spies and Guides, Corp.
Taren, Abel, Co. H, 1st N. M. Cav.
Tarin, Manuel, Co. I, 1st N. M. Cav.
Tarin, Lino, Co. K, 2nd N. M. Inf.
Tarin, Olallo, Co. H, 2nd N. M. Inf.
Tarin, Eugenio, Mink's Independent Co., N. M. Mtd. Vols., 3 mos., 1861-62.
Tarin, Antonio, Co. C, 1st N. M. Inf.
Tarin, Jose, Co. D, 1st N. M. Inf.
Tarin, Juan, Co. E, 1st N. M. Inf.
Tarin, Manuel, Co. I, 1st N. M. Cav.
Telles, Marcos, Co. F, 1st N. M. Cav.
Taylor, Charles W., Co. F, 1st N. M. Cav.
Taylor, Silas M., Co. K, 1st N. M. Cav.
Telles, Francisco, Co. C, 1st N. M. Inf.
Telles, Jose, Co. F, 3rd N. M. Mtd. Inf., 6 mos., 1861-62.
Tenorio, Carlos, Co. F, 1st N. M. Cav.
Tenorio, Jose Maria, Co. F, 1st N. M. Inf.
Tenorio, Miguel, Co. G, 1st N. M. Inf.
Tenorio, Juan, Co. I, 1st N. M. Inf.
Tenorio, Quirino, Co. I, 1st N. M. Inf., and Co. C, 3rd N. M. Mtd. Inf., 6 mos., 1861-62.
Tenorio, Jose, Co. I, 1st N. M. Inf.
Tenorio, Jose Ignacio, Co. B, 1st N. M. Cav.
Tenorio, Jose Maria, Co. E, 1st N. M. Cav.
Tenorio, Jose Rafael, Co. B, 1st N. M. Cav.
Tenorio, Manuel, Hubbell's Independent Co., N. M. Mtd. Vols., 3 mos., 1861.
Tenorio, Miguel, 1st N. M. Mil., Sena's Co, A. 2 mos., 1861.
Tenorio, Ramon, Aragon's Co., Perea's Batt'n, N. M. Mil., 3 mos., 1861-62.
Tenorio, Jesus, Co. F, 1st N. M. Inf.
Tenorio, Refugio, Co. H, 1st N. M. Inf.
Tenorio, Jose Lino, Co. F, 3rd N. M. Mtd. Inf., 6 mos., 1861-62.
Telles (could also be Velez) Juan, Tafoya's Independent Co., N. M. Mil., 3 mos., 1861-62.
Thomas, Daniel, Co. F, 1st N. M. Inf.
Thompson, John D, 1st N. M. Cav., Captain.
Thompson, Robert, Co. G, 1st N. M. Cav., Lieut.
Thompson, William, Co. G, 1st N. M. Cav.
Tierning, James, Co. B, 1st N. M. Cav., Sgt.
Tiffner, Anton, Co. C, 1st N. M. Inf.
Tirand (Pirand), John, Co. K, 1st N. M. Cav.
Tafoya, Venturo, Co. B, 3rd N. M. Mtd. Inf., 3 mos., 1861-62.
Tafoya, Jesus Maria, Co. E, F, 1st N. M. Cav., 1st Sgt.
Tafoya, Francisco, Co. F, 1st N. M. Cav.
Tafoya, Juan Antonio, Co. F, 1st N. M. Cav.
Tafoya, Ramon, Co. A, Batt'n N. M. Vols., 1866-67.
Tafoya, Jose Maria, Co. F, 1st N. M. Cav.
Tafoya, Leonardo, Simpson's Independent Co., N. M. Mtd. Spies and Guides.
Tafoya, Lorenzo, Co. B, 3rd N. M. Mtd. Inf., 3 mos., 1861-62.
Toledo, Pablo, Co. B, 1st N. M. Cav.
Tomies, Joseph, Co. B, 1st N. M. Inf.
Tenorio, Pedro, Co. B, 5th N. M. Inf.
Toomey, Cornelius, Co. C, 1st N. M. Inf.
Tonry, Patrick, Co. C, 1st N. M. Inf.
Tapia, Juan, Co. I, 1st N. M. Inf.

Torres, Anastacio, Co. D, 1st N. M. Inf.
Torres, Andres, Tafoya's Independent Co., N. M. Mil., 3 mos., 1861-62.
Torres, Cruz, Co. C, 1st N. M. Inf.
Torres, Felipe, Hubbell's Independent Co., N. M. Mtd. Vols., 3 mos., 1861-62.
Torres, Isidro, Co. F, 1st N. M. Cav. and Graydon's Independent Co., N. M. Mtd. Vols.
Torres, Jose, Graydon's Independent Co., N. M. Mtd. Vols., 3 mos., 1861-62.
Torres, Jose Eugenio, Co. D, 4th N. M. Inf.
Torres, Juan, Co. A, 1st N. M. Mil. Inf., 3 mos., 1861-62.
Torres, Julian, Tafoya's Independent Co., N. M. Mil., 3 mos., 1861-62.
Torres, Manuel, Co. F, 1st N. M. Cav., Sgt.
Torres, Monico, Co. C, Batt'n N. M. Vols., 1866-67.
Torres, Nicanor, Co. D, Batt'n N. M. Mtd. Vols., Bugler, and Co. A, 1st N. M. Cav.
Torres, Pablo, Co. C, Batt'n N. M. Mtd. Vols., 1866-67, Sgt.
Torres, Pedro, Co. G, 1st N. M. Cav.
Torres, Prudencio, Co. D, 3rd N. M. Mtd. Vols., 3 mos., 1861-62.
Torres, Teodocio, Co. G, 1st N. M. Inf.
Torrick, Joseph, Hubbell's Independent Co., N. M. Mtd. Vols., 3 mos., 1861, Bugler.
Torres, Canuto, Co. E, 2nd N. M. Inf., Sgt.
Torres, Casimiro, Co. D, 3rd N. M. Mtd. Inf., 6 mos., 1861-62.
Torres, Casimiro, Hubbell's Co., Perea's Batt'n, N. M. Mil. Inf., 3 mos., 1861-62.
Torres, Ignacio, Hubbell's Co., Perea's Batt'n, N. M. Mil. Inf., 3 mos., 1861-62.
Torres, Jesus, Hubbell's Co., Perea's Batt'n, N. M. Mil. Inf., 3 mos., 1861-62.
Torre, Jose, Gonzolez Independent Co., N. M. Mil., 2 mos., 1861.
Torres, Jose, Baca's Co., Perea's Batt'n, N. M. Mil. Inf., 3 mos., 1861-62.
Torres, Jose, Co. K, 3rd N. M. Mtd. Inf., 6 mos., 1861-62.
Torres, Jose Maria, Co. D, 1st N. M. Cav.
Torres, Juan, Co. I, 3rd N. M. Mtd. Inf., 6 mos., 1861-62.
Torres, Juan Andres, Hubbell's Co., Perea's Batt'n, N. M. Mil. Inf., 3 mos., 1861-62.
Torres, Juan Jose, Co. H, 2nd N. M. Inf.
Torres, Juan Chavez y, Co. F, 2nd N. M. Inf.
Torres, Juan Goremcindo, Co. D, 2nd N. M. Inf.
Torres, Juan Pedro, Co. H, 2nd N. M. Inf.
Torres, Justo, Co. C, 3rd N. M. Mtd. Inf., 6 mos., 1861-62.
Torres, Longino, Co. B, 1st N. M. Inf.
Torres, Incarnacion, Co. A, 1st N. M. Mil. Inf., 3 mos., 1861-62.
Torres, Marcial, Co. F, 1st N. M. Inf.
Torres, Marcos, Romero's Co., 3rd N. M. Mtd. Inf., 6 mos., 1861-62.
Torres, Matias, Hubbell's Independent Co., N. M. Mtd. Vols., 3 mos., 1861.
Torres, Monico, Co. A, 1st N. M. Cav.
Torres, Nicanor, Co. A, 1st N. M. Cav.
Torres, Pablo, Alarid's Independent Co., N. M. Mil. Inf., 3 mos., 1861-62, Sgt.
Torres, Paulino, Baca's Co., Perea's Batt'n, N. M. Mil. Inf., 3 mos., 1861-62.
Torres, Pedro, Co. G, 1st N. M. Cav.
Torres, Santiago, Co. A, 1st N. M. Cav.
Torres, Romualdo, Gonzolez Independent Co., N. M. Mil., 3 mos., 1861.
Torres, Romolo, Co. G, 2nd N. M. Inf.
Torres, Santiago, Co. G, 1st N. M. Inf.

Torres, Valentino, Tafoya's Independent Co., N. M. Mil., 3 mos., 1861-62.
Torres, Victor, Co. E, H, 2nd N. M. Inf.
Torres, William, Co. C, 4th N. M. Inf.
Torres, Ysidro, Co. C, 1st N. M. Inf., Sgt.
Tragillo (Trujillo?), Julian, Co. B, 1st N. M. Cav., Corp.
Trujillo, Miguel, Co. M, 1st N. M. Cav.
Transue, Levi, Co. F, 1st N. M. Cav.
Tarayta, Felipe, Co. L, 1st N. M. Cav.
Trevino, Manuel, Co. B, 3rd N. M. Mtd. Inf., 6 mos., 1861-62.
Trujillo, Crestin, Co. H, 1st N. M. Inf., O. O.
Trejo, Tercio, Co. G, 1st N. M. Inf., Wagoner.
Trexler, William A., Co. B, 1st N. M. Inf.
Trujillo, Mariano, Baca's Co., Perea's Batt'n, N. M. Mil. Inf., 3 mos., 1861-62.
Trujillo, Gabino, Co. A, 1st N. M. Mil. Inf., 3 mos., 1861-62.
Trujillo, Jose R., Co. C, 1st N. M. Cav.
Trujillo, Tranquera, Co. E, 1st N. M. Inf.
Trujillo, Antonio, Co. K, 2nd N. M. Inf.
Trujillo, Ricardo, Co. C, 2nd N. M. Inf.
Trujillo, Jesus Maria, Jaramillo's Co., Perea's Batt'n, N. M. Mil. Inf., 3 mos., 1861-62.
Trujillo, Juan Jose, Jaramillo's Co., Perea's Batt'n, N. M. Mil. Inf., 3 mos., 1861-62.
Trujillo, Cristobal, Co. K, 1st N. M. Inf.
Trujillo, Anastacio, Co. E, 2nd N. M. Inf.
Trujillo, Ignacio, Co. A, 3rd. N. M. Mtd. Inf., 3 mos., 1861-62.
Trujillo, Juan Domingo, Co. D, E, 1st N. M. Inf.
Trujillo, Albino, Co. B, 1st N. M. Cav.
Trujillo, Andres, Co. C, 3rd N. M. Mtd. Inf., 6 mos., 1861-62.
Trujillo, Antonio Abran, Co. H, 1st N. M. Mil. Inf., 3 mos., 1861-62.
Trujillo, Antonio Jose, Co. B, 1st N. M. Mil. Inf., 3 mos., 1861-62.
Trujillo, Antonio Maria, Co. C, 1st N. M. Inf.
Trujillo, Anthony Rafarl, Co. D, E, 1st N. M. Inf.
Trujillo, Augustin, Co. I, 1st N. M. Mil. Inf., 3 mos., 1861-62.
Trujillo, Benedito, Simpson's Independent Co., N. M. Mtd. Spies and Guides.
Trujillo, Gregorio, Co. I, 1st N. M. Cav.
Trujillo, Jesus, Co. G, 1st N. M. Inf.
Trujillo, Jesus Maria, Co. K, 1st N. M. Inf.
Trujillo, Julian, Co. A, 1st N. M. Cav.
Trujillo, Jose Dolores, Mink's Independent Co., N. M. Mtd. Vols., 3 mos., 1861.
Trujillo, Jose Dolores, Co. C, 1st N. M. Mil. Inf., 3 mos., 1861-62.
Trujillo, Benito, Simpson's Independent Co., N. M. Mtd. Spies and Guides.
Trujillo, Bibiano, Co. F, 3rd N. M. Mtd. Inf., 6 mos., 1861-62.
Trujillo, Carlos, Co. B, 1st N. M. Inf., Corp.
Trujillo, Esquipula, Co. A, 3rd N. M. Mtd. Inf., 6 mos., 1861-62.
Trujillo, Felipe, Co. E, 1st N. M. Mil. Inf., 3 mos., 1861-62.
Trujillo, Francisco, Co. D, 1st N. M. Mil. Inf., 3 mos., 1861-62.
Trujillo, Jose Eugenio, Co. I, 1st N. M. Cav.
Trujillo, Jose Encarnacion, Co. F, 1st N. M. Cav., Corp.
Trujillo, Jose Felipe, Co. B, 1st N. M. Cav.
Trujillo, Francisco, Co. E, 1st N. M. Mil. Inf., 3 mos., 1861-62.
Trujillo, Jose Francisco, Co. G, 1st N. M. Mil. Inf., 3 mos., 1861-62.
Trujillo, Jose Gregorio, Co. I, Mink's Independent Co., N. M. Mtd. Vols., 3 mos., 1861.
Trujillo, Jose Ignacio, Co. G, 3rd N. M. Mtd. Inf., 6 mos., 1861-62.
Trujillo, Jose Manuel, Co. B, 1st N. M. Mil. Inf., 3 mos., 1861-62.
Trujillo, Jose Miguel, Co. D, 1st N. M. Mil. Inf., 3 mos., 1861-62.
Trujillo, Jose Maria, Co. A, 1st N. M. Inf.

Trujillo, Jose Nestor, Co. A, 1st N. M. Cav.
Trujillo, Jose Pablo, Co. B, 1st N. M. Inf.
Trujillo, Jose Rafael, Co. B, 1sh N. M. Mil. Inf., 3 mos., 1861-62.
Trujillo, Jose Ramon, Co. D, 1st N. M. Inf.
Trujillo, Jose Seferino, Vigil's Independent Co., N. M. Mtd. Vols., 3 mos., 1861.
Trujillo, Juan, Co. D, 5th N. M. Inf.
Trujillo, Juan Andres, Vigil's Independent Co., N. M. Mtd. Vols., 3 mos., 1861, Sgt.
Trujillo, Juan de Jesus, Co. B, 1st N. M. Cav.
Trujillo, Juan Domingo, Co. D, E, 1st N. M. Inf.
Trujillo, Julian, Co. B, 1st N. M. Inf.
Trujillo, Lucan, Co. E, 3rd N. M. Mtd. Inf., 6 mos., 1861-62.
Trujillo, Luciano, Co. H, 1st N. M. Inf., Corp.
Trujillo, Manuel, Vigil's Independent Co., N. M. Mtd. Vols., 3 mos., 1861.
Trujillo, Manuel, Co. A, 1st N. M. Mil. Inf., 3 mos., 1861-62.
Trujillo, Manuel, Co. K, 3rd N. M. Mtd. Inf., 6 mos., 1861-62.
Trujillo, Manuel, Co. B, 5th N. M. Inf.
Trujillo, Manuel Antonio, Co. D, E, 1st N. M. Inf.
Trujillo, Matian, Co. B, 3rd N. M. Mtd. Inf., 6 mos., 1861-62.
Trujillo, Miguel, Co. D, 1st N. M. Inf., Corp.
Trujillo, Pablo, Co. D, E, 1st N. M. Inf., Musician.
Trujillo, Pedro, Mink's Independent Co., N. M. Mtd. Vols., 3 mos., 1861.
Trujillo, Jose, Co. B, 1st N. M. Cav.
Trujillo, Pedro, Ignacio, Co. A, 1st N. M. Cav.
Trujillo, Rafael, Co. E, 3rd N. M. Mtd. Inf., 6 mos., 1861-62.
Trujillo, Ramon, Co. B, 1st N. M. Mil. Inf., 3 mos., 1861-62.
Trujillo, Ricardo, Co. K, 1st N. M. Inf.
Trujillo, Saloma, Co. B, Batt'n N. M. Vols., 1866-67.
Trujillo, Santiago, Co. A, 3rd N. M. Mtd. Inf., 6 mos., 1861-62.
Trujillo, Seferino, Co. B, 3rd N. M. Mtd. Inf., 6 mos., 1861-62.
Trujillo, Vicente, Co. C, Batt'n N. M. Vols., 1866-67.
Trujillo, Ignacio, Co. A, 3rd N. M. Mtd. Inf., 6 mos., 1861-62, Corp.
Trujillo, Jose Ramon, Co. A, 1st N. M. Inf.
Trujillo, Jose Guadalupe, Co. E, 1st N. M. Inf.
Trujillo, Tomas, Co. B, 1st N. M. Inf., N. O.
Trujillo, Cristobal Cisto, Co. K, 1st N. M. Inf.
Trujillo, Romualdo, Co. G, 1st N. M. Inf., Sgt.
Trujillo, Bernardino, Co. G, 1st N. M. Inf., Sgt.
Trujillo, Victoriano, Co. F, 3rd N. M. Mtd. Inf., 6 mos., 1861-62, Bugler.
Trujillo, Blas, Co. H, 3rd N. M. Mtd. Inf.
Trujillo, Felix, Tafoya's Independent Co., N. M. Mil. Inf., 3 mos., 1861-62.
Trujillo, Felipe Jose, Co. B, 1st N. M. Inf.
Trujillo, Gaspar, Co. K, 2nd N. M. Inf.
Trujillo, George, Co. D, 3rd N. M. Mtd. Inf., 6 mos., 1861-62.
Trujillo, Julian Chavez y, Co. B, 3rd N. M. Mtd. Inf., 6 mos., 1861-62.
Trujillo, Juan de Jesus, Co. F, 3rd N. M. Mtd. Inf., 6 mos., 1861-62.
Trujillo, Juan Domingo, Co. E, 1st N. M. Inf.
Trujillo, Juan Jose, Co. H, 2nd N. M. Inf.
Trujillo, Juan Maria, Co. D, 1st N. M. Cav.
Trujillo, Juan Manuel, Co. F, 3rd N. M. Mtd. Inf., 6 mos., 1861-62.
Trujillo, Joaquin, Co. D, 3rd N. M. Mtd. Inf., 6 mos., 1861-62, 1st. Lieut.
Trujillo, Lazaro, Co. E, 1st N. M. Inf.
Trujillo, Leanor, Co. C, 3rd N. M. Mtd. Inf., 6 mos., 1861-62, Corp.
Trujillo, Luciano, Co. A, 3rd N. M. Mtd. Inf., Corp.
Trujillo, Manuel Antonio, Romero's Independent Co. A, N. M. Mtd. Inf., 3 mos., 1861-62.

Trujillo, Quirino, Co. H, 2nd N. M. Inf.
Trujillo, Pilar, Co. H, 1st N. M. Cav.
Trujillo, Ricardo, Co. D, 2nd N. M. Inf.
Trujillo, Tabessi, Co. D, 1st N. M. Cav.
Trujillo, Zelerono, Co. B, 3rd N. M. Mtd. Inf., 6 mos., 1861-62.
Tierney, James, Co. B, 1st N. M. Cav., Sgt.
Tarayta, Felipe, Co. L, 1st N. M. Inf.
Turrieta, Jose de la Cruz, Aragon's Co., Perea's Batt'n, N. M. Mil. Inf., 3 mos., 1861-62.
Turrieta, Leandro, Co. D, 1st N. M. Cav.

Ulibarri, Feliciano, Co. I, 3rd N. M. Mtd. Inf., 6 mos., 1861-62.
Ulibarri, Pedro Jose, Co. C, 1st N. M. Inf.
Ulibarri, Paulino, Co. H, 1st N. M. Cav.
Ulibarri, Faustin Baca y, Co. F, 3rd N. M. Mtd. Inf., 6 mos., 1861-62.
Ulibarri, Desiderio, Co. B, 1st N. M. Cav.
Ulibarri, Atanacio, Co. A, 3rd N. M. Mtd. Inf., 6 mos., 1861-62.
Ulibarri, Francisco, Co. E, 3rd N. M. Mtd. Inf., 6 mos., 1861-62.
Underhill, Robert S., Co. K, 1st N. M. Cav., 1st Lieut.
Unopa, Francisco, Co. I, 1st N. M. Inf.
Urban, Dionicio, Co. A, 2nd N. M. Cav.
Urban, Manuel, Co. B, 3rd N. M. Mtd. Inf., 6 mos., 1861-62.
Urioste, Juan, Co. G, 1st N. M. Inf.
Urieste, Acune, Co. E, 1st N. M. Inf.
Urieste, Ignacio, Co. K, 1st N. M. Cav.
Urieste, Cruz, Co. H, 3rd N. M. Mtd. Inf., 6 mos., 1861-62.
Urioste, Felix, Co. A, 2nd N. M. Inf., Sgt.
Urioste, Juan, Co. G, 1st N. M. Inf., and Co. B, 3rd N. M. Mtd. Inf., 6 mos., 1861-62. Corp.
Urioste, Matias, Duran's Co., N. M. Mil.
Urioste, Trinidad, Co. A, 2nd N. M. Inf.
Urioste, Ignacio, Co. K, 1st N. M. Cav.
Urioste, Francisco, Co. D, 1st N. M. Cav.
Urtado, Hurtado), Jose, Co. D, 1st N. M. Cav.
Urtado, Francisco, Co. D, 1st N. M. Cav., Herrera's Batt'n.
Urtado, Jose Antonio, Graydon's Independent Co., N. M. Mtd. Vols., 3 mos., 1861-62.
Urtado, Jose Maria, Co. H, 1st N. M. Cav., Bugler.
Urtado, Nicolas, Co. G, 1st N. M. Inf., Sgt.
Urtado, Balentino, Romero's Co., 3rd N. M. Mtd. Inf., 6 mos., 1861-62.
Utierez (Gutierrez), Roque, Co. C, 2nd N. M. Inf.

Vaca (Baca), Jose Maria, Vigil's Independent Co., N. M. Mtd. Vols., 3 mos., 1861, Sgt.
Vaca, Luis Maria, Co. F, 3rd N. M. Mtd. Inf., 6 mos., 1861-62, Major.
Velesquez, Jose Francisco, Co. I, 1st N. M .Inf.
Velesquez, Antonio Juan, Co. E, 1st N. M. Cav.
Valdez, Francisco, Co. F, 2nd N. M. Inf.
Valdez, Aniseto, Co. D, 3rd N. M. Mtd. Inf., 6 mos., 1861-62.
Valdez, Antonio, Co. B, 1st N. M. Mil. Inf., 3 mos., 1861-62.
Valdez, Francisco, Co. D, 1st N. M. Cav.
Valdez, Isidro, Co. B, 1st N. M. Mil. Inf., 3 mos., 1861-62.
Valdez, Jesus, Co. K, 3rd N. M. Mtd. Inf., 6 mos., 1861-62.
Valdez, Jesus Maria, Co. D, 1st N. M. Cav.
Valdez, Jose Antonio, Co. I, 1st N. M. Inf., O. O.
Valdez, Jose Francisco, Co. G, 1st N. M. Inf.
Valdez, Jose Ignacio, Co. G, 1st N. M. Mil. Inf., 3 mos., 1861-62.
Valdez, Seferino, Co. B, 1st N. M. Mil. Inf., 3 mos., 1861-62.
Valdez, Juan Antonio, Alarid's Independent Co., N. M. Mil. Inf., 3 mos., 1861-62.
Valdez, Juan Nepomuceno, Co. C, 3rd N. M. Mtd. Inf., 6 mos., 1861-62.
Valdez, Juan Nestor, Co. B, 1st N. M. Mil. Inf., 3 mos., 1861-62, Sgt.

Valdez, Manuel, Co. F, 1st N. M .Cav., Sgt.
Valdez, Marcelino, Co. B, 1st N. M. Inf.
Valdez, Marcelino, Co. B, 1st N. M. Inf.
Valdez, Marcos, Co. K, 3rd N. M. Mtd. Inf., 6 mos., 1861-62.
Valdez, Mariano, Co. K, 3rd N. M. Mtd. Inf., 6 mos., 1861-62.
Valdez, Meliton, Co. B, 3rd N. M. Mtd. Inf., 6 mos., 1861-62.
Valdez, Pablo, Vigil's Independent Co., N. M. Mtd. Vols., 3 mos., 1861, Musician.
Valdez, Pedro, Perea's Independent Co., N. M. Vols., 60 days, 1861.
Valdez, Rafael, Sena's Co. A, 1st N. M. Mil., 3 mos., 1862.
Valdez, Salino, Co. A, 1st N. M. Inf.
Valdez, Tomas, Co. B, 1st N. M. Inf.
Valdez, Brigido, Co. F, 3rd N. M. Mtd. Inf., 6 mos., 1861-62.
Valdez, Concepcion, Co. I, 1st N. M. Inf.
Valdez, Desiderio, Co. K, 1st N. M. Mil. Inf., 3 mos., 1861-62.
Valdez, Jesus Maria, Co. D, 1st N. M. Cav.
Valdez, Joaquin, Co. G, 1st N. M .Cav.
Valdez, Jose, Co. M, 1st N. M. Cav.
Valdez, Jose Antonio, Co. I, 1st N. M. Inf.
Valdez, Jose Baca y, Co. A, 3rd N. M. Mtd. Inf., 6 mos., 1861-62.
Valdez, Jose Florentino, Co. I, 1st N. M. Inf.
Valdez, Jose Francisco, Co. A, 1st N. M. Inf., Sgt.
Valdez, Jose Maria, Co. A, 1st N. M. Inf., and Co. F, 3rd N. M. Inf., Captain.
Valdez, Jose Matian, Mink's Independent Co., N. M. Mtd. Vols., 3 mos., 1861.
Valdez, Jose Miguel, Co. F, 3rd N. M. Mtd. Vols., 6 mos., 1861-62.
Valdez, Jose Serafin, Co. B, 1st N. M. Mil. Inf., 3 mos., 1861-62
Valdez, Jose Ygineo, Alarid's Independent Co., N. M. Mil. Inf., 3 mos., 1861-62.
Valdez, Juan Nepumoceno, Co. B, 3rd N. M. Mtd. Inf., 6 mos., 1861-62.
Valdez, Julian, Co. D, 1st N. M. Inf., Sgt.
Valdez, Manuel, Co. F, 1st N. M .Cav., Sgt.
Valdez, Manuel, Co. C, 1st N. M. Inf., and 1st N. M. Mtd. Inf., 3 mos., 1861-62.
Valdez, Manuel Lorenzo, Co. C, 3rd N. M. Mtd. Inf., 6 mos., 1861-62.
Valdez, Marcelino, Co. F, 1st N. M. Cav.
Valdez, Francisco, Co. I, 3rd N. M. Mtd. Inf., 6 mos., 1861-62.
Valdez, Francisco, Co. K, 3rd N. M. Mtd. Inf., 6 mos., 1861-62.
Valdez, Matias, Co. C, 1st N. M. Cav.
Valdez, Meliton, Co. F, 3rd N. M. Mtd. Inf., 1861-62.
Valdez, Rafael, Co. I, 1st N. M. Cav. and Sena's Co. A, 1st N. M. Mil., 3 mos., 1861-62.
Valdez, Sabino, Co. A, 1st N. M. Cav.
Valdez, Santiago, Co. H, 1st N. M. Inf., Captain.
Valdez, Seferino, Co. A, 1st N. M. Cav., Corp.
Valdez, Vences, Co. B, 1st N. M. Inf., Sgt.
Valdez, Vivian, Co. A, 1st N. M. Cav.
Valdez, Ygineo, Co. I, 1st N. M. Cav.
Valdez, Marcelino, Co. B, 1st N. M. Inf.
Valencia, Antonio, Co. F, 1st N. M. Inf.
Valencia, Catarino, Romero's Independent Co. A, N. M. Mil. Inf.
Valencia, Juan Maria, 3rd N M. Mtd. Inf., 6 mos., 1861-62.
Valencia, Jose, Co. G, 1st N. M. Inf., O. O.
Valencia, Jose Antonio, Co. F, 2nd N. M. Inf.
Valencia, Ignacio, Co. B, 3rd N. M. Mtd. Inf., 6 mos., 1861-62.
Valencia, Jose Atanacio, Co. F, 3rd N. M. Mtd. Inf., 6 mos., 1861-62.
Valencia, Juan, Co. F, 1st N. M. Cav.
Valencia, Juan Miguel, Alarid's Independent Co., N. M. Mil. Inf., 3 mos., 1861-62.
Valencia, Julian, Co. F, 1st N. M. Cav., Corp.
Valencia, Justo, Co. I, 3rd N. M. Mtd. Inf., 6 mos., 1861-62.

Valencia, Manuel, Co. F, 3rd N. M. Mtd. Inf., 6 mos., 1861-62.
Valencia, Matias, Co. D, 1st N. M. Cav., Sgt.
Valencia, Nemecio, Co. K, 1st N. M. Cav.
Valencia, Pedro, Co. K, 3rd N. M. Mil. Inf., 6 mos., 1861-62.
Valencia, Pablo, Co. B, 1st N. M. Inf.
Valencia, Ramos, Co. I, 3rd N. M. Mil. Inf., 6 mos., 1861-62.
Valencia, Locario, Co. H, 1st N. M. Cav.
Valencia, Marcos, Co. D, 1st N. M. Cav.
Valencia, Felipe, Co. D, Batt'n N. M. Vols., 1866-67.
Valerio, Antonio, Co. B, 3rd N. M. Mtd. Vols., 6 mos., 1861-62.
Valesquez, Tomas, Co. F, 1st N. M. Cav.
Valesquez, Jose Maria, Co. F, 1st N. M. Cav.
Valles, Manuel, Co. A, 2nd N. M. Inf., Corp.
Van Dorn, John, Co. B, 1st N. M. Cav.
Van Reen, William, Co. D, 1st N. M. Cav., Sgt.
Varda, Bernard, Co. B, 1st N. M. Cav.
Varela, Bernardo, Co. F, 1st N. M. Inf.
Varela, Desiderio, Co. B, 3rd N. M. Mtd. Inf., 6 mos., 1861-62.
Varela, Felipe, Co. I, 1st N. M. Cav.
Varela, Francisco, Co. G, 1st N. M. Cav.
Varela, Jesus, Co. A, 2nd N. M. Inf., Bugler.
Varela, Jose, Co. B, 1st N. M. Mil. Inf., 3 mos., 1861-62.
Varela, Jose Francisco, Co. G, 3rd N. M. Mtd. Inf., 6 mos., 1861-62.
Varela, Leandro, Co. A, 2nd N. M. Inf.
Varela, Librato, Co. F, 1st N. M. Inf.
Varela, Pancho, Co. E, 1st N. M. Cav.
Varela, Juan Nepumoceno, Co. B, 3rd N. M. Mtd. Inf., 6 mos., 1861-62.
Varela, Francisco, Co. K, 1st N. M. Cav.
Varela, Jesus, Co. E, 2nd N. M. Inf.
Varela, Damasio, Co. D, 4th N. M. Inf.
Varela, Jesus Maria, Vigil's Independent Co., N. M. Mtd. Vols., 3 mos., 1861.
Varela, Antonio Abran, Co. E, 4th N. M. Inf., and Co. F, 1st N. M. Mil. Inf., 3 mos., 1861-62.
Varela, Mariano, Co. B, 1st N. M. Mil. Inf., 3 mos., 1861-62.
Varela, Juan de Jesus, Co. B, 1st N. M. Cav.
Vasquez, Andres, Co. E, 1st N. M. Cav.
Vasquez, Felipe, Co. E, 1st N. M. Cav.
Vasquez, Francisco, Co. E, 1st N. M. Cav.
Vasquez, Miguel, Co. E, 1st N. M. Cav., Sgt.
Vasquez, Rafael, Co. B, 3rd N. M. Mtd. Inf., 6 mos., 1861-62.
Vianes, Eusebio, Co. H, 1st N. M. Inf.
Vega, Cruz, Co. H, 1st N. M. Cav. (Later killed in the Colfax County War), and Co. E, 3rd N. M. Mtd. Inf., 6 mos., 1861-62.
Vigil, Juan, Batt'n N. M. Mtd. Vols., 6 mos., 1866-67.
Vigil, Mariano, Co. M, 1st N. M. Cav.
Vigil, Pedro Antonio, Co. D, 1st N. M. Cav.
Vigil, Zacarias, Co. A, 1st N. M. Cav.
Velarde, Jesus, Co. B, 1st N. M. Cav.
Velarda, Antonio, Co. E, 1st N. M. Cav.
Velarde, Gregorio, Co. E, 1st N. M. Cav., Corp.
Velarde, Jose Francisco, Co. E, 3rd N. M. Mtd. Vols., 6 mos., 1861-62.
Velesquez, Antonio Isidro, Co. K, 3rd N. M. Mtd. Vols., 6 mos., 1861-62.
Vasquez, Cruz, Co. D, 1st N. M. Mil. Inf., 3 mos., 1861-62.
Vasquez, Jose Maria, Co. I, 1st N. M. Cav.
Velesquez, Jose Martin, Co. I, 1st N. M. Cav.
Velesquez, Jose Francisco, Co. I, 1st N. M. Cav.
Vasquez, Miguel, Co. A, 1st N. M. Inf.
Velarde, Esteban, Vigil's Independent Co., N. M. Mtd. Vols., 3 mos., 1861.

Velarde, Jose Domingo, Co. E, 3rd N. M. Mtd. Vols., 6 mos., 1861-62.
Venavides (Benavides), Juan, Co. E, 2nd N. M. Inf.
Venavides, Lorenzo, Co. C, 3rd N. M. Mtd. Inf., 6 mos., 1861-62.
Venavides, Miguel, Co. E, 1st N. M. Cav.
Vernal (Bernal), Jose, Co. E, 4th N. M. Inf.
Vernal, Juan Antonio, Co. E, 4th N. M. Inf.
Vernal, Luis, Co. D, 2nd N. M. Inf.
Vivian, Juan D., Co. D, 1st N. M. Cav.
Vivian, Jesus Maria, Co. K, 3rd N. M. Mtd. Inf., 6 mos., 1861-62.
Vivian, Agapito, Co. E, 3rd N. M. Mtd. Inf., 6 mos., 1861-62.
Vivian, Albino, Co. E, 1st N. M. Cav.
Vigil, Albino, Co. K, 1st N. M. Inf.
Vigil, Antonio, Sena's Co. A, N. M. Mil.
Vigil, Antonio, Co. C, 3rd N. M. Mtd. Inf., 6 mos., 1861-62.
Vigil, Antonio A., Co. A, 1st N. M. Mil. Inf., 3 mos., 1861-62.
Vigil, Antonio Jose, Co. E, 1st N. M. Cav.
Vigil, Antonio Maria, Vigil's Independent Co., N. M. Mtd. Vols., 3 mos., 1861-62, Captain.
Vigil, Apolonio, Co. I, 3rd N. M. Mtd. Inf., 6 mos. 1861-62 Captain.
Vigil, Bartolome, Co. D, E, 1st N. M. Inf.
Vigil, Cosme, Co. H, 1st N. M. Inf.
Vigil, Desiderio, Co. B, 1st N. M. Cav. (Son of Governor Donaciano Vigil.
Vigil, Diego, Co. C, 1st N. M. Mil. Inf., 3 mos., 1861-62.
Vigil, Francisco, Co. D, E, 1st N. M. Inf., Corp.
Vigil, Nasario, Co. A, 1st N. M. Mtd. Inf., 3rd N. M. Mtd. Inf., 6 mos., 1861-62.
Vigil, Jesus Maria, Co. I, 3rd N. M. Mtd. Inf., 6 mos., 1861-62.
Vigil, Jesus Maria, (1), Co. A, 3rd N. M. Mtd. Inf., 6 mos., 1861-62.
Vigil, Jesus Maria, (2), Co. A, 3rd N. M. Mtd. Inf., 6 mos., 1861-62.
Vigil, Jose, Co. B, 1st N. M. Cav.
Vigil, Jose Antonio, Co. H, 1st N. M. Inf.
Vigil, Jose Feliciano, Co. G, 1st N. M. Cav.
Vigil, Jose Francisco, Co. A, 4th N. M. Inf.
Vigil, Jose Julio, Mink's Independent Co., N. M. Mtd. Vols., 3 mos., 1861.
Vigil, Jose Lino, Co. D, E, 1st N. M. Inf., Musician.
Vigil, Jose Maria, Co. B, 1st N. M. Mil., 3 mos., 1861-62, Corp.
Vigil, Epitacio, Co. B, 2nd N. M. Inf., Son of Gov. Donaciano Vigil.
Vigil, Jose Miguel, Co. B, 1st N. M. Mil. Inf., 3 mos., 1861-62.
Vigil, Jose Zacarias, Co. D, E, 1st N. M. Inf.
Vigil, Jose Urban, Co. C, 3rd N. M. Mtd. Inf., 6 mos., 1861-62.
Vigil, Juan, Alarid's Independent Co., N. M. Mil. Inf., 3 mos., 1861-62.
Vigil, Juan, Co. I, 1st N. M. Cav., Sgt.
Vigil, Juan, Co. E, 1st N. M. Mil. Inf., 3 mos., 1861-62.
Vigil, Juan Antonio, Co. E, 1st N. M. Mil. Inf., 3 mos., 1861-62, Corp.
Vigil, Juan Antonio, Co. H, 3rd N. M. Mtd. Inf., 6 mos., 1861-62.
Vigil, Juan Bautista, Co. E, 1st N. M. Cav.
Vigil, Juan Bautista, Co. K, 1st N. M. Cav.
Vigil, Juan de Jesus, Simpson's Independent Co., N. M. Mtd. Spies and Guides.
Vigil, Juan de Jesus, Vigil's Independent Co., N. M. Mil. Vol., 3 mos., 1861.
Vigil, Juan de Jesus, Co. C, 1st N. M. Mil. Inf., 3 mos., 1861-62.
Vigil, Juan Jose, Co. A, 1st N. M. Cav.
Vigil, Juan Jose, Co. A, E, 1st N. M. Inf.
Vigil, Manuel, Co. H, 1st N. M. Inf.
Vigil, Marcos, Co. B, 1st N. M. Mil. Inf., 3 mos, 1861-62.
Vigil, Matias, Co. I, 2nd N. M. Inf.
Vigil, Miguel, Mink's Independent Co., N. M. Mtd. Vols., 3 mos., 1861.
Vigil, Miguel Antonio, Co. A, 1st N. M. Inf.

Vigil, Pedro Antonio, Co. D, 1st N. M. Cav.
Vigil, Pedro Ignacio, Co. B, 2nd N. M. Inf.
Vigil, Rafael, Co. D, E, 1st N. M. Inf.
Vigil, Ramon, Co. K, 3rd N. M. Mtd. Vols.
Vigil, Refugio, Co. K, 3rd N. M. Mtd. Inf., 6 mos., 1861-62.
Vigil, Simon, Co. A, E, 2nd N. M. Inf.
Vigil, Victor, Vigil's Independent Co., N. M. Mtd. Vols., 3 mos., 1861-62.
Vigil, Ysidro, Co. A, 1st N. M. Cav.
Vigil, Villa Miguel, Co. F, 2nd N. M. Inf.
Vigil, Ignacio, Co. A, 1st N. M. Inf.
Virgen, Prucenciano, Co. A, 2nd N. M. Inf., Sgt.

Wakeman, Edward (See Cal. Vol. Inf. list)
Walsh, James, Co. C, 4th N. M. Inf.
Walsh, Philip, Co. F, 2nd N. M. Inf., Hospital Steward.
Walters, Edward, Graydon's Independent Co., N. M. Mtd. Vols., 3 mos., 1861-62.
Watkins, Alonzo, (See Cal. Vol. list).
Watson, George, Co. E, 1st N. M. Inf.
Weber, George, Co. E, 1st N. M. Inf.
Welsh, Philip, Co. A, 1st N. M. Inf., Steward.
Whatley, Robert, Co. H, 1st N. M. Inf., Lieut.
White, Charles, Co. D, E, 1st N. M. Inf.
Whitehill, Harvey, Simpson's Independent Co., N. M. Mtd. Spies and Guides.
Whitelock, Jim, Co. G, 1st N. M. Inf.
Wiggins, William, Co. D, 1st N. M. Inf., Sgt.
Wilkins, John, Co. F, 1st N. M. Inf., Ordnance Sgt.
Williams, Stephen, Co. M, 1st N. M. Cav.
Williams, William, Co. A, Batt'n N. M. Vols., 1866-67.
Willis, Edward B., Co. F, 1st N. M. Inf., Lt. Col.
Wilson, John, Co. D, 1st N. M. Inf.
Willis, Charles, Co. A, 1st N. M. Cav.
Withers, H. C., Co. F, 1st N. M. Inf.
Wright, Joseph, Co. A, 1st N. M. Cav.

Yanez, Angel, Co. H, 1st N. M. Inf.
Yara (Jara), Francisco, Simpson's Independent Co., N. M. Mtd. Spies and Guides.
Ydalgo (Hidalgo), Jose Leon, Co. A, 1st N. M. Inf.
Young, Joseph, Co. H, 1st N. M. Inf.
Ysco, Jose Cristobal, Co. A, 1st N. M. Inf.
Yturbides, Jesus, Co. G, 2nd N. M. Inf.

Zalasar (Salazar), Jose Antonio, Co. E, 2nd N. M. Inf.
Zalasar, Jose Andres, Gonzolez Independent Co., N. M. Mil., 3 mos., 1861-62.
Zalasar, Jose Rafael, Co. E, 3rd N. M. Mtd. Inf., 6 mos., 1861-62.
Zalasar, Cencion, Co. D, 1st N. M. Inf. (See Cal. Vols.)
Zamora, Juan, Co. D, 1st N. M. Inf.
Zamora, Manuel, Co. D, 1st N. M. Inf.
Zamora, Francisco, Del Balle's Co., Perea's Batt'n, N. M. Mil. Inf., 3 mos., 1861-62.
Zamora, Juan, Co. D, 1st N. M. Inf.
Zamora, Amador, Co. C, 1st N. M. Inf.
York, Henry, Graydon's Independent Co., N. M. Mtd. Vols., 3 mos., 1861-62.
Zumwalts, Dalamon, Co. D, 1st N. M. Inf., Sgt.
Zunia, Pablo, Co. A, 1st N. M. Inf.

BIBLIOGRAPHY
(A) Primary Sources

Index to Compiled Service Records of Volunteer Union Soldiers Who Served in Organizations from the State of New Mexico, 1861-67, A to D. National Archives, Microcopy No. 242, Roll 1.

Ibid., E to L, Roll 2.

Ibid., M to Ri, Roll 3.

Ibid., Ro to Z, Roll 4, National Archives Building, Washington, D. C.

War of the Rebellion, Series 1—
  Volume L—1897.
  Volume IX—1883.
  Volume I—1880.
  Volume IV—1882.
  Volume XV—1886.
  Volume XXXIV—1888 (Part 2).
  Volume XXXIV—1889 (Part 3).

El Diario de la Camara de Representantes de la Asamblea Legislativa del Nuevo Mejico—O. P. Hovey Press, Santa Fe, New Mexico, 1860.

Acts of the Territorial Legislature—1851.

Acts of the Territorial Legislature—1853.

Acts of the Territorial Legislature—1857.

Acts of the Territorial Legislature—1859.

Laws of New Mexico—1854-55.

Laws of New Mexico—1855-56.

Laws of New Mexico—1856-57.

Laws of New Mexico—1857-58.

Laws of New Mexico—1858-59.

Laws of New Mexico—1859-60.

Laws of New Mexico—1860-61.

Laws of New Mexico—1861-62.

37th Cong., 2nd Sess., H. Ex. Doc. No. 11, Vol. 1, December, 1861, Serial 1127.

38th Cong., 1st Sess., Sen. Ex. Doc. No. 49, Vol. 1, 1864, Serial 1176.

38th Cong., 1st Sess., Sen. Misc. Doc., No. 127, Vol. 1, 1864, Serial 1177.

38th Cong., 1st Sess., Ho. Ex. Doc., Nos. 1, 41, 42, Vol. III, 1863, Serial 1182.

Cong. Globe, 33rd Cong., 1st Sess., App. 788.

Cong. Globe, 36th Cong., 1st Sess., 915—February 29, 1860.

31st Cong., 2nd Sess., Sen. Ex. Doc., No. 9.

32nd Cong., 2nd Sess., Sen. Ex. Doc., No. 13.

Cong. Globe, 32nd Cong., 2nd Sess., 139—December 23, 1852.

Cong. Globe, 32nd Cong., 2nd Sess., 314-316—January 17, 1853.

Cong. Globe, 33rd Cong., 1st Sess., 168-172—February 10, 1854.

The Reuter Collection of the Donaciano Vigil Papers, containing letters from Vigil, Manzanarez, C. Bent, J. Houghton, H. Connelly, etc., Archives Vault, American School of Research, Old Governor's Palace, Santa Fe, New Mexico.

32nd Cong., 2nd Sess., H. of Rep. 103 App. to Cong. Globe.

Letter of M. Fillmore to Gov. Bell of Texas, August 6, 1850.

Speech of Z. Taylor to the Senate and House of Representatives, January 4, 1850.

Letter of J. Bankhead Magruder to Gen. S. Cooper, February 26, 1863.

Messages and Papers of the Presidents, Vol. VII, 2754-3229—J. C. R., 1897.

Messages and Papers of the Presidents, Vol. VIII, 3230-3706—J. C. R. 1897.

Congressional Globe, 30th Cong., 2nd Sess., New Series No. 7.

Appleton's Encyclopedia of the Civil War, Vol. 1, 1862, An Account of Valverde.

(B) Secondary Sources

1. *Books*

Bancroft, Hubert Howe—History of Arizona and New Mexico, 1530-1888.

Bancroft, Hubert Howe—History of Nevada, Colorado and Wyoming, 1540-1888.

Barker, Wm. J.—The Forgotten War for the West—Rocky Mountain Empire Magazine, Denver, Colo., Nov. 6 and 13, 1949.

Blackmore, A. E.—The Southern Maiseillaise, New Orleans, La., 1861.

Bradford, Ned—Battles and Leaders of the Civil War—App. Cent. Crofts, 1956.

Bourke, John G.—On the Border with Crook—N. Y., 1892.

Conkling, R. P. and M. B.—The Butterfield Overland Mail—3 Vols., A. H. Clark Co., 1947.

Connelley, Wm. E.—Doniphan's Expedition—Topeka, Kansas, 1907.

Cremony, John C.—Life Among the Apaches—New York, 1868.

Dale, E. E.—The Indians of the Southwest—Norman, Okla., 1949.

Freeman, D. S.—Robert E. Lee—4 Vols., N. Y., 1934.

Freeman, D. S.—Lee's Lieutenants—3 Vols., N. Y., 1944.

Fagan, F.—Southern War Songs—Richardson Co., N. Y., 1890.

Ganaway, Loomis M.—New Mexico and the Sectional Controversy, 1846-1861—Alb., 1844.

Goodwin, John W.—Report to the First Legislature of Arizona, 1864.

Harris, Gertrude—Sibley's Brigade—A Tale of Men Who Knew No Fear—San Antonio, 1935.

Heightman, Francis B.—Historical Register and Dictionary of the U. S. Army, 1879-1903—Washington, D. C.

Hill, Joseph J.—A History of Warner's Ranch—Los Angeles, Calif., 1927.

Hollister, Ovando J.—Boldly They Rode—Lakewood, Colo., 1949.

Howles, Charles C.—This Place Called Kansas—Norman, Okla., 1952.

Hunt, Aurora—The Army of the Pacific—A. H. Clark, Calif., 1951.

Livermore, Abiel—The War with Mexico Reviewed—Boston, 1850.

Lockwood, Frank C.—The Apache Indians—MacMillan Co., New York, 1938.

Keleher, Wm. A.—Turmoil in New Mexico, 1846-1868—Santa Fe, 1952.

Nevins, Allan—Ordeal of the Union, 2 Vols.—N. Y. 1947.

Nevins, Allan—The Emergence of Lincoln, 2 Vols.—N. Y. 1950.

Noel, Theophilus—Autobiography and Reminiscences of Theo. Noel—Chicago, 1904.

Spring, Leverett—Kansas—Cambridge, Mass., 1885.

Stanley, F.—Fort Union, New Mexico—Denver, Colo., 1952.

Reeve and Brooks—Forts and Forays—Albany, New Mexico, 1948.

Williams, K. P.—Lincoln Finds a General, 3 Vols.—New York, 1949-51.

Williams, R. H.—With the Border Ruffians—Dutton Co., New York, 1907.

Webb, W. P.—The Texas Rangers—Cambridge, Mass., 1935.

Whitford—Colorado Volunteers in the Civil War—Denver, Colo., 1906.

Twitchell, R. E.—Leading Facts of New Mexico History—Cedar Rapids, Iowa, 1911.

Twitchell, R. E.—Spanish Archives of New Mexico, 2 Vols.—Cedar Rapids, Iowa, 1914.

2. *Magazine Articles and Miscellaneous*

The Texan Santa Fe Trail—H. B. Carroll, Panhandle P. H. R., Canyon, Texas, 1941.

Federal Indian Policy in New Mexico—F. D. Reeve, N.M.H.R., 1937-38.

Confederate Invasion of New Mexico—R. Twitchell, Sol., Santa Fe Mag., No. 9, 1916.

With the Confederates in New Mexico—Capt. H. Smith, Pan. Plains H. R., 1929.

Confederate Government in New Mexico—C. S. Walker, N. M. H. R., July, 1931.

Confederate Reminiscences—Halcomb and Wright, N. M. H. R., July, 1930.

The Battle of Glorieta Pass—J. F. Santee, N. M. H. R., Jan., 1931.

The Battle of Valverde—M. L. Crimmins, N. M. H. R., Oct., 1932.

Confederate Courts in New Mexico—E. D. Tittman, N. M. H. R., Oct., 1928.

When Las Vegas was Capital of New Mexico—F. S. Donnell, N .M. H. R., Oct., 1928.

New Mexico During the Civil War—W. I. Waldrip, N. M. H. R., July-Oct., 1953.

The Navajo Exile at Bosque Redondo—C. Amsden, N. M. H. R., Jan., 1933.

When Texas Owned New Mexico to the Rio Grande—F. S. Donnell, N. M. H. R., April, 1933.

Causes of the Confederate Invasion of New Mexico—Charles S. Walker, N. M. H. R., April, 1933.

The Confederate Territory of Arizona—F. S. Donnell, N. M. H. R., April, 1942.

An Unknown Chapter in Western History—History of the Column from California—Clarence C. Clendenen, N. Y. Posse Summer, 1954.

Doniphan of Missouri—Frank B. Latham, New York Brand Book, 1955.

Texas, C. S. A.—Jackson Co., 1947.

The Americana Encyclopedia.

The Handbook of Texas, 2 Vols.—Chicago, 1952.

World Almanac.

Texas Almanac.

Rand-McNally Atlas.

W. P. A. State Guide Books—All States West of the Mississippi.

All States West of the Mississippi—Historical Reviews and Quarterly Reviews.

3. *Newspapers*

The Santa Fe Gazette—All Issues from 1862 to 1869—some years incomplete.

The Santa Fe New Mexican—All Issues from 1859 to 1879.

Clippings Covering the Period 1861-1867 from New York papers, California papers, Texas papers, Kansas papers, Colorado.

The Niles Gazette—All Issues to 1869.

Glendale, California, 1958

Heyman, Max L., Jr.: Prudent Soldier, The Life of E. R. S. Canby, 1817-1873, Glendale, California.

New York Times Sunday Magazine Section, 1959.

New York Westerners Corral, 1958-59.

Los Angeles Westerners Corral, 1957-59.

The Saturday Review, 1959.

Life Magazine, 1959.

Time Magazine, 1959.

Newsweek, 1959.

Panhandle Plains Historical Review—All Issues.

Most newspapers and magazines for 1959 carry the story of John Brown and his raid as well as articles of forthcoming events for the celebration of the Civil War Centennial.

Williams, R. H.—With the Border Ruffians, 1852-1868—London, England, 1908.

Doolittle, M.—Report of the Condition of the Indian Tribes, 1867 —Washington, D. C., 1867.

Ladd, Horacio—The Story of New Mexico—D. Lathrop Co., Boston, 1891.

ADDITIONAL BOOKS CONSULTED SINCE THE FIRST DRAFT

Colton, Ray C.—The Civil War in the Western Territories—University of Oklahoma Press, Norman, Okla., 1959.

Nevins, Allan—The War for the Union, Vol. 1—Chas. Scribner's Sons, N. Y., 1959.

Chamberlain, Samuel E.—Notes Taken During the War With Mexico—Harper & Bros., N. Y., 1956.

Avey, John—Capture and Execution of John Brown—Brethren Publishing House, Elgin, Ill., 1906.

Carleton, J. H.—Letters to the Department of the Interior, 1863-1865.

Carleton, J. H.—Letters to the War Department, 1862-1865.

Kerby, Robert Lee—The Confederate Invasion of New Mexico and Arizona—Westernlore Press, Los Angeles, 1958.

La Farge, Oliver—Santa Fe—University of Oklahoma Press, Norman, Oklahoma, 1959.

Blakenship, Russell—American Literature—Henry Holt & Co., N. Y., 1931.

Williams, Kenneth P.—Lincoln Finds a General, Vol. IV—Macmillan Co., N. Y., 1956.

Williams, Kenneth P.—Lincoln Finds a General, Vol. V—Macmillan Co., N. Y., 1959.

Fitzhugh, Lester N.—Texas Batteries, Battalions, Regiments, Commanders and Field Officers, Confederate States Army, 1861-65—Mirror Press, Midlothian, Texas, 1959.

Jensen, Billie Barnes—Confederate Sentiment in Colorado—Denver Brand Book, Vol. XIII, Denver, Colo., 1957.

Peck, Stuart, Sturgis and Others—Relations with the Indians of the Plains—Edited by LeRoy and Ann Hafen, Arthur H. Clark Co., Glendale, Calif., 1959.

Hunt, Aurora—Major General James Henry Carleton, 1814-1873—Arthur H. Clark Co.

www.ingramcontent.com/pod-product-compliance
Lightning Source LLC
Chambersburg PA
CBHW030513230426
43665CB00010B/604